PRINC

Matt Thorne is the author of six novels, including *Eight Minutes Idle* and *Cherry*, which was longlisted for the MAN Booker Prize.

Further praise for *Prince*:

'Thorne is a good stylist and a deep thinker but primarily he's a fan . . . This ought to be a disaster but, when tackling Prince, that added layer of obsession carries a rare significance, because more than any other megastar of the 1980s, Prince's relationship with fans went beyond the call of duty . . . Thorne is a compelling, emotional narrator.' Kate Mossman, *New Statesman*

'Highly engaging.' Mark Ellen, *Observer*

'Everything I love in a book.' Nemone, BBC Radio 6 Music

'If you've ever craved the empurpled equivalent of Paul Williams' *Bob Dylan: Performing Artist* . . . you are well served.' Danny Eccleston, *Mojo*

'The final word on the mad genius known as Prince Rogers Nelson. There is now quite literally nothing more to say about Prince or his music. It's all here – dance, sex, romance, and above all, the music. Downright orgasmic.' *Current* magazine

'[Thorne] brings an enthusiasm, intelligence and maverick spirit to the 562 pages covering the 35-year career of Prince Rogers Nelson . . . It's to Thorne's credit that through painstaking research and interviews he manages to paint a picture of what the man, rather than the myth, is actually like. A must for the legions of Prince fans out there.' Doug Johnstone, *Big Issue*

PRINCE

MATT THORNE

FABER & FABER

First published in 2012
by Faber and Faber Limited
Bloomsbury House
74–77 Great Russell Street
London WC1B 3DA
This paperback edition first published in 2013

Typeset by Ian Bahrami
Printed in the UK by CPI Group (UK) Ltd, Croydon, CR0 4YY

A CIP record for this book
is available from the British Library

ISBN 978–0–571–23248–2

4 6 8 10 9 7 5

For Lee Brackstone,
who commissioned this book,
and for Luke and Tom,
who were patient while I wrote it.

CONTENTS

CONTENTS

ILLUSTRATIONS

Prince with his father and family.

Prince's fifth-grade yearbook picture from John Hay Elementary School.

André Cymone, Prince and Dez Dickerson performing at the Ritz club, New York, 22 March 1981.

Morris Day and Jesse Johnson of The Time performing at First Avenue, December 1985.

Vanity 6 publicity shot.

An early photo of Sheila E performing on stage.

Brown Mark, Prince and Dez Dickerson on the *1999* tour.

Prince and Dez Dickerson during the *Dirty Mind* tour.

Wendy Melvoin and Lisa Coleman in San Remo, 1988.

Wendy, Prince and Lisa accepting the Oscar for Best Original Song Score for *Purple Rain*, 25 March 1985.

Prince during a *Purple Rain* show at Nassau Coliseum, 18 March 1985.

Still from *Purple Rain*.

Apollonia Kotero performing in *Purple Rain*.

Under the Cherry Moon premiere in Sheridan, Wyoming, 2 July 1986.

Prince and Lisa Barber arrive at the *Under the Cherry Moon* premiere.

Prince on stage at Madison Square Garden during the *Lovesexy* tour, 1 October 1988.

Prince and Cat Glover on stage at Wembley Arena during the *Lovesexy* tour, 3 August 1988.

Prince on stage at Wembley Arena during the *Lovesexy* tour, 3 August 1988.

Still from *Graffiti Bridge*.

Prince and The New Power Generation during the *Diamonds and Pearls* tour, 1991.

Prince and Mayte Garcia opening a branch of the NPG store on Chalk Farm Road in Camden Lock, England.

Prince performing in 1995 with 'Slave' written on his face.

Prince (as Tora Tora) performing at the Virgin Megastore in London, 5 April 1995.

The Artist Formerly Known as Prince promoting his triple-CD set *Emancipation* at the San Jose Event Center, 19 April 1997.

Prince and Manuela Testolini watching an LA Lakers game, 25 December 2004.

Carmen Electra.

Prince performing at the El Rey Theatre in LA during the *Musicology* tour, 24 February 2004.

Prince announcing the 21 Nights tour at the Hospital Club in London.

Prince on stage at Hop Farm, Kent, 3 July 2011.

Prince with The Twinz at the O2, 24 August 2007.

Prince on stage at Hop Farm, Kent, 3 July 2011.

PROLOGUE: COME 2 MY HOUSE (PART 1)

In early 2006, I received an invitation to attend a party at Prince's home in Los Angeles, as part of the promotion of his then-current album, *3121*.

Since moving to LA in 2005, Prince had been re-establishing contact with Hollywood by inviting A-listers to exclusive parties. Parties had always been a central part of Prince's legend, but his Hollywood gatherings were different to those that had helped make his name in Minneapolis. These were invitation-only events and included annual post-Oscars celebrations to which aspiring gatecrashers, such as Karen O from the Yeah Yeah Yeahs, were refused entry. If the plan for these parties was to boost his profile among the rich and famous, he succeeded: over the next few years, American chat shows would often feature celebrities describing the experience. The actor Ryan Phillippe told Conan O'Brien he'd interrupted Prince in the middle of a song to ask him for directions to the bathroom; *30 Rock* star Tracy Morgan would later describe how he'd attended a party at the height of his alcoholism and had refused to leave until Prince came down and threw him out. American news anchor Anderson Cooper would tell daytime TV hosts Regis and Kelly about fighting comedian David Chappelle for one of Prince's discarded plectrums at a later party at the Hotel Gansevoort, a bash I also attended. Mortification seemed to be a common experience of celebrities who got to go to Prince's parties, usually cool stars thrown into a flap when encountering someone whose image and aura out-stripped their own.

On the night of the *3121* party, a limousine driver showed up at the Mondrian to drive me up to Prince's house for the eleven o'clock guest entry. As we slowly snaked through West Hollywood, the Russian chauffeur ranked his favourite Nabokov novels in order of preference and told me about the celebrities he'd taken to previous parties at Prince's place, and I realised that Prince was trying to transform Los Angeles into Uptown in the same way he'd managed with Minneapolis nearly thirty years earlier. When we reached the house, the numbers on the front gate had been rearranged to read '3121'. The title of Prince's album had prompted much speculation, with fans wondering if it was a year (making the title song a futuristic update of '1999'), a biblical line reference or something to do with numerology (the numbers added up to seven, a significant number for Prince). But they had read too much into it: it was merely the address of the Los Angeles property Prince had rented (and recorded in) before moving here.

Even for a private event like this, Prince was a stickler for detail. The security guards checking the guest lists had purple clipboards and collar pins in the shape of the ♀ symbol Prince adopted as a name in 1993. As I stood with the celebrities and wannabes by the front gates to Prince's house, a neighbour came by trying to wangle his way in. Prince had sent over a bottle of wine as an apology for any noise, but the neighbour wanted to come to the party instead, hopping from one foot to the other as the guards radioed the house. Whenever I've attended any of Prince's smaller shows, anxiety about getting in has given the evening an extra charge, and I wished the man luck as the rest of us clambered into the van for the ride up.

Prince's property was a bewitching example of that sinister

Walt Disney-meets-David Lynch architecture that appeals only
to the wealthiest celebrities, a surreal modern fantasy of feudal
living where you can remain in splendid isolation and yet con-
vince yourself the whole of Hollywood is at your command.
Prince captured the imagination of the '80s generation by con-
necting his music to a secret wonderland of exclusive shows:
for anyone other than the lucky denizens of Minneapolis, the
Paisley Park recording complex he started working in during 1987
seemed a distant utopia, as fans read about all-night sessions and
secret parties and wished they could somehow attend. With the
release of *3121*, Prince had (for the umpteenth time) returned and
reignited what remained a fantasy for most but was a daily reality
for him, as the whole album was designed as – and best under-
stood as – the aural equivalent of a private party.

From the duration of his shows to the access he allows his
fans, Prince has challenged all conventional notions of what an
audience might reasonably expect from an artist. Music critics
have often drawn parallels between the elaborate backstage envi-
ronments constructed by bands and a royal court – both places
where privilege and favour allow various members of the entou-
rage or esteemed guests to pass through a series of heavily pro-
tected barriers and get closer to the artist's inner sanctum. In this
world, drug dealers and groupies often have greater freedom of
movement than band members' wives and girlfriends, but from
an early stage in his career Prince has insisted he has no interest
in drugs[1] and only minimal interest in alcohol (wine, champagne
and, during an odd period in the mid-1990s, port). And while
his supposed sexual insatiability has always been a central part of
his persona, Alan Leeds – Prince's tour manager from 1983 until
1990 – has stated that Prince avoided all but the most interesting
female fans, such as Anna Garcia or Mayte, spending the major-
ity of his time with his female tour mates instead. So, rather than

offering freedoms to those who might offer him drugs or sex, Prince instead rewards them with money, fame or enthusiasm. The more tenacious the fan and, to a certain extent, the more money they can pay, the greater access they get (although the celebrity remains the most welcome visitor).

Even so, Princeland has to be delicately balanced. Because he's previously allowed his fans extraordinary access (such as his week-long Celebrations at Paisley Park), they complain whenever he plays shows for a celebrity audience or charges an extortionate ticket price.[2] But it's a mistake to expect consistency from Prince. Like almost all of the handful of household-name rock stars who have had careers that have lasted over several decades, he wants different things at different times, going through periods when he produces non-commercial albums and relies on the under-standing of his hard-core fan base, then attempting to win back the mainstream with greatest-hits tours and audience-friendly records like *Musicology* or *Planet Earth*. In recent years, money and power seem to have become increasingly important to him as, having predicted (and survived) the collapse of the record industry, he seeks out new ways of maintaining his success.

On the night I went to his house, he was in the middle of many campaigns. As well as impressing celebrities (the guests on this night included Bruce Willis, Sharon Stone, David Duchovny and Jessica Alba), Prince was throwing the party to promote his new album, blow a few fans' minds, encourage his record company to distribute an album he'd created with his then-current protégée Támar, and no doubt achieve half-a-dozen other aims as well. I'd been to Prince's after-shows and exclusive performances before, but nothing like this. I was about to experience the intimate Prince performance I'd been lusting for from the moment I first heard his music.

1

JUSTIFICATIONS FROM A
MAMMA-JAMMA

There are four main strands to Prince's music: first, the official releases, from his 1978 debut *For You* to 2010's *20 Ten*, including not only the studio albums and singles, but also myriad remixes and maxi-albums, often with as many as six or seven variations on the original track; second, the unreleased songs which have kept several bootleg labels afloat for decades, now so multitudinous that labels can put out collections that would take weeks to listen to and still not exhaust the material in circulation; third, the live recordings: two official releases – the *One Nite Alone . . .* box set and 2008's *Indigo Nights* – and literally thousands of bootleg recordings, including several versions of the same show in various fidelities; and fourth, the songs he has given to other artists and protégés, from Sue Ann Carwell in 1978 to Bria Valente's *Elixer* in 2009.

As far as Prince is concerned, the only person who knows anything about this music is Prince. He was done with critics as early as 1982, when he recorded the sardonic 'All the Critics Love U in New York', and he never misses an opportunity to remind the lowly writer that he has little regard for anyone who spends the majority of their time at a desk. To the Detroit DJ The Electrifying Mojo, Prince described writers as 'mamma-jamma(s) wearing glasses and an alligator shirt behind a typewriter'. And in a 1990 *Rolling Stone* interview with Neal Karlen, Prince maintained, 'There's nothing a critic can tell me that I can learn from,'

adding that he cares only what musicians think of him.[1] His atti-
tude towards journalists hardened still further in the early 1990s,
when he included a journalist character as part of the narrative
of his ♀ album who was ridiculed and, in the accompanying
stage show, stripped. Two albums later, on *The Gold Experience*,
he included a song, 'Billy Jack Bitch', that appeared deliberately
to address (and demean) one local journalist who had given him
a particularly hard ride (and there are rumours of an unreleased
track entitled 'Fuck D Press'[2]). Prince is far from the only musi-
cian who feels this way – check out any sophomore rap album
from an artist who got more than his fair share of press attention
first time round – but, with him, it goes deep.

He's equally dismissive of critical studies that include interviews
with people who've shared his studio, claiming that his engineers
and producers are not equipped to speak knowledgeably about his
work. Many of the most detailed accounts of Prince's unreleased
work have come from Susan Rogers – the engineer who worked
with him through five of the most successful years of his career –
but Prince maintains that she knows nothing about his music,[3]
and told respected rock writer Barney Hoskyns that he was play-
ing a role for his earliest biographer, Jon Bream, whose 1984 book
made much of his inner-circle access. 'If you look at it,' he told
Hoskyns, 'I've only really given you music.' In interview, he'd 'give
cryptic little answers . . . that made no sense'.[4]

Early band-mate Dez Dickerson confirms this was part of
Prince's interview strategy from near the beginning: 'If they
weren't going to print what he actually said, why not just make
things up? I don't believe there was any malice in this, but it was
just a precocious way of responding to what he felt was the press'
dishonesty.'[5] Looking at Prince's interviews over the years, this
is borne out. He can sound astonishingly strange in interviews,
even when appearing to be relaxed and normal. Television, in

particular, seems to bring out this side of him. Whether it's telling Oprah Winfrey in a 1996 interview he has a second person living inside him, an alternate personality created when he was five, or insisting to Tavis Smiley in 2010 that he was cured of childhood epilepsy by an angel, it often seems as if he's deliberately constructing myths for his own amusement.

Even when talking to journalists he's personally vetted, he tells them he considers their peers lazy. After playing the *LA Times* journalist Ann Powers a track that had lyrical references to Santana and Jimi Hendrix, he dismissed her suggestion that these guitarists were influences, claiming instead that he tries to make his guitar sound like vocalists he admires. This is Prince's way of emphasising how his musical abilities separate him from anyone who doesn't know how to play, the damned masses he describes as 'non-singing, non-dancing, wish-I-had-me-some-clothes fools'.[6]

When I started this book, I was prepared to take Prince's argument that the people he'd worked with didn't know that much about his music at face value. It's true he's worked with some extraordinarily accomplished people over the years, and some have experienced success without him, but it appeared the overwhelming majority did their best work while in his employ. Nevertheless, as I continued my research, talking to those closest to him during various periods, including former band members, such as Matt Fink, Wendy Melvoin and Lisa Coleman from The Revolution, it became clear to me just how important Prince's collaborators have been at various stages in his career, and that any proper critical overview also needs to address the various configurations of his band – to take a close look at, for example, the difference between The Revolution and the various permutations of The New Power Generation. It also seemed valuable to talk to some of those who helped, in various ways, Prince become one of the most famous and successful popular musicians ever.

Throughout his career, Prince has regarded his time in the studio and his time on the road as two different things. It wasn't until his third album that he invited a major collaboration from one of his band, and that was only on one song ('Dirty Mind'), and it wasn't until *Purple Rain* that he made a truly collaborative album, and even then he recorded four of the tracks largely solo. While The Revolution played a larger part on the two albums that followed, he has oscillated between drawing inspiration from those around him on stage or in the studio and producing work in near isolation. This means that for every album where it's possible to talk to some of the other people in the studio about what they contributed to a record, there's another where the only eye-witnesses are Prince and the engineer.

Prince is, most of the time, a lyricist whose work is unusually rewarding when studied closely, with most of his songs serving a larger narrative. Sometimes this is explicit – when he's sound-tracking a film, say, or writing a concept album; at other times, it's implicit. There are many interconnections between his thousands of songs, whether something basic, like his use of colours or numbers, or something more complicated, like his take on the concept of duality or the complex personal theology he has developed over decades of song-writing. The sense of continuity in his lyrics is also emphasised by his use of what Prince fans refer to as 'Princebonics'[7] ('2' for 'to'; an illustration of an eye for 'I'; 'U' for 'you', etc.[8]). Dez Dickerson, who played with Prince from 1978 onwards, takes credit for this style of shorthand in his autobiography,[9] claiming it was something he originated when writing set lists and stating, 'It may have been a subconscious "borrowing" on [Prince's] part, but no doubt it was "borrowed", nonetheless.'[10] There is also a larger psychological reason for this coherence. As Eric Leeds, who would become the saxophonist in The Revolution and remain one of Prince's most important collaborators for several years, told Paul Sexton: 'You have to remember that Prince looks at all of his music, in his whole life, as a movie, and everybody who's involved with him on whatever level is a character in his movie.'[11] If this book focuses more on the work than the life, it's because my interest is in Prince's movie, in all its forms, the giant super-narrative that he diligently adds to in a recording studio or onstage nearly every day, a work of art that remains narrowly focused on the same subjects and emotions that have driven him since day one – love, sex, rebirth, anger.

Prince's albums invariably improve with age, and while there are several astute Prince critics among music writers, those reviewing his albums at the time of release often find themselves at an unfortunate disadvantage. The records often come with their own myths, rumours and disclaimers, even on occasion with what seem like admissions that the work is substandard (both 1996's *Chaos and Disorder* and 1999's *The Vault* come with the warning that the enclosed material was originally intended '4 private use only'), and it's often only with the release of subsequent albums (or knowledge of how the records were put together, of what was lost in the creative process) that the depth of Prince's achievements becomes clear.

When I've attended playbacks of his recent albums, it's been immediately apparent that those present can't tell on one listen whether this new record is an important addition to his oeuvre or one that all but the most dedicated will wipe from their computers after a month. Prince's work is particularly hard to assess at speed, especially if you are focusing on the quality of the music in relation to the rest of his output rather than how a record will fare commercially.[12]

At times, this has led certain parts of the critical establishment to focus on the larger aspects of Prince's myth, something he's often encouraged. The most obvious example of this is the furore that followed Prince's decision to retire his name temporarily and record under an alias (taken as a sign of madness or egocentricity, it seems it was as much a business decision as a desire to erase his past). Also, Prince is so prolific that even when he's putting out substandard material he's often simultaneously stockpiling songs for alternative projects, and as he frequently returns to older recordings while constructing a new album, it can sometimes be hard to know exactly where an idea or song dates from.

In the meantime, alongside the official recordings and releases, there is an enormous body of unreleased work that has somehow reached the ears of collectors. Over the years there has been much finger-pointing about who is responsible. And while it's clear that Prince believes the true fan is the one who contents himself with what he's prepared to give him (at one point he even offered an amnesty for fans to return illegal bootleg recordings to him, in exchange, mainly, for goodwill), it's hard not to shake the worrying possibility that Prince may never make the majority of his vast body of work available, even after his death.

His attitude towards his back catalogue changes all the time, and though Prince has famously stashed tapes of his unreleased songs in his fabled 'Vault'[13] throughout his career and does often revisit old ideas or exhume lost songs, promised compilations such as *Roadhouse Garden* (a proposed collection of unreleased songs recorded with his most famous band, The Revolution) and *Crystal Ball II* (a sequel to his 1998 three-CD set of previously unreleased recordings) have, so far, failed to materialise, and some within the inner sanctum have expressed their anxiety about whether Prince is even protecting his physical recordings adequately.

Matt Fink told me that the Vault is humidity-controlled and that he believes Prince's masters were well preserved at the time of recording, but he doesn't know if the tapes have gone through the necessary baking procedure[14] to protect them since. Engineer Hans-Martin Buff, who worked with Prince during the late 1990s, echoed this, telling me, 'The Vault itself is A-OK,' but that he worried about some of the tapes because 'we would take things out of the Vault for various reasons, starting with the *Crystal Ball* box set, which were a lot of tapes from different periods, and then we wouldn't put them back in.

'There was a room in front of the Vault which held just paraphernalia – an Oscar, a picture of him as a kid and stuff – and I would just put the tapes on the floor,' Buff explains, 'and this continued for two years until the entire floor was covered with tapes. Not just the stuff that we'd taken out of the Vault, but also the stuff that we'd finished, which was a lot of tapes. And water got in and there was carpeting in there and it soaked the carpeting and went into some of those tapes, and I told him about it but it took a very long time until he let me put that stuff in the Vault.' Buff also wanted to digitise and bake the tapes, but it didn't happen while he was there.

What he witnessed instead was Prince making use of his old tapes to make new music, but without giving it the respect that a musical historian might hope for. For Prince, it seems, everything is raw material, and maybe it's wrong of us to wish to prevent him from painting over old canvases to produce new material. Prince has often emphasised the importance of the transitory, telling audiences that his shows should be for their memories only and resisting a full live album until late in his career. And though he has occasionally made alternative versions or old out-takes available, usually he seems to disregard the original sketches that led to the finished work. This is true of many musicians, of course, and leads to conflict between archivist and artist, but it presents a dilemma for anyone writing about him.

Prince has, on occasion, talked about music from the Vault getting a later release. In 2009, he gave a press conference in Paris during which he said that music from the Vault would come out eventually, but it was unclear whether he was referring to music he has recorded over the last few years – the Vault, it seems, is expanding all the time – or recordings from throughout his entire career.

Just as fans would love for some of these old songs to be released, so would the musicians who played on them, especially as in many cases they don't even have their own copies of the recordings. Dez Dickerson of The Revolution, for example, says that although Prince always had 'a major archival mindset', he himself has never broached the subject of releasing any old recordings and hasn't had a business conversation with Prince since 1984. Alan Leeds, Prince's road manager and a man who has done his bit to help bring sense to James Brown's similarly massive back catalogue in liner notes and through co-editing (with Nelson George) *The James Brown Reader*, notes: 'I suspect he'd have to do something with Warner Brothers. Theoretically, a normal recording contract would state anything he records while under that contract belongs to the label. But the majority, if not one hundred per cent, of the tapes are in his Vault.'

Brent Fischer, the son of the late Dr Clare Fischer – best known to Prince fans for his work on *Parade* – and a man who has his own shelf of scores written for unreleased Prince songs, says: 'It is going to be very interesting to see what happens in the next fifty years because Prince has recorded so much music, and so much of that music remains unreleased. It's just in the Vault, and it doesn't matter that he may have spent a lot of money to get a thirty-, forty-, fifty-piece orchestra, paid for the arrangement, added the orchestra on and put everything in place and then decided he doesn't want to release it. That's fine with him.

'This is not going to be like finding the one lost Beatles track. This is going to be an abundance of material, hundreds of songs. It's difficult to keep track of them all because [as well as] the ones the public know about, [there's another] seventy per cent that are unreleased that we've also dealt with, many of which are favourites of mine that I continue to play in my head, even though, for the time being at least, they'll never be heard in public.'

No one else will ever have a career like Prince. The main reason for this is, of course, his incredible range of ability across so many creative disciplines: we will not see his like again. But the age has also changed. Not only does the music industry no longer have the money or promotional power to help force a star of his magnitude into such a wide popular consciousness and give him or her the lift-off necessary to sustain such a long career, but Prince's career also took place over a period that saw changes and developments in the music industry that will never be repeated. Even something as simple as his fascination with maxi-singles and remixes reveals him exploiting formats that no longer really exist, and he seems to have largely given up producing (or, at least, releasing) extended versions of his hits now that there's little money to be made from them.[15]

This is not a book about the decline of the music industry, but it is, in part, about how Prince as an artist has managed to use the materials available to him to create a uniquely multifaceted body of work. As well as the music, his corpus also includes several hundred music videos for songs both released and unreleased, which differ from the music videos of most artists in that they often offer essential elucidation of the songs or work as short films of artistic merit in their own right; three narrative feature films (*Purple Rain*, *Under the Cherry Moon* and *Graffiti Bridge*); a theatrically released concert movie, *Sign o' the Times*;[16] three TV films; several officially released video recordings of (partial or complete) live shows; an 'orchestral-ballet'; a dance interpretation of Homer's *Odyssey*; two sanctioned comics; and four authorised book-length collaborations: *Neo Manifesto – Audentes Fortuna Juvat, Prince Presents the Sacrifice of Victor, Prince in Hawaii: An Intimate Portrait of an Artist* and *21 Nights*. Prince once stated to an interviewer that 'there are gems buried everywhere',[17] telling him that he didn't care that it might be only diehard fans who locate them.

This book is written from that perspective: it's an attempt to come to terms with the entirety of Prince's career, from the earliest demos to the latest radio-station sneak releases, by analysing the music, images and recorded performances that he's amassed, looking at influences, trends, thematic links and recurring preoccupations, all supported by interviews with his closest collaborators. It's a study of the surprisingly consistent conceits and ideas that have driven this workaholic to produce an extraordinary body of work that, for all the acclaim he has received for his most popular songs and albums, has yet to be truly appreciated and understood by the world at large.

2

THE BUSINESS OF MUSIC

Past biographers have attempted to build up a picture of Prince's childhood and family life from his songs ('Sister', 'Da, Da, Da', 'The Sacrifice of Victor' and 'Papa') that deal with childhood. And it is true that the content of some of these songs seems to chime with statements that Prince has made in interviews: his acknowledgement in a 2009 interview with Tavis Smiley that he had suffered from epilepsy as a child was treated as a major revelation by the media, but it was something he'd written about in 'The Sacrifice of Victor' seventeen years earlier.

It's important, of course, not to read all Prince's lyrics as autobiographical, and there is just as much myth-making in his work as there is personal revelation, but for all his reputation as an enigma, Prince is extraordinarily revealing in song and onstage, and often seems more truthful speaking to his audience than to any representative of a media he regards as hostile. The other problem with reading the work in order to understand the life is that there's a gothic quality to several of these songs that suggests a self-dramatising enjoyment of myth-making.

For anyone seeking a straight story rather than revelling in the obscurantism, it doesn't help that Prince's mythological approach to his past is shared by some of his family members. While attempting to launch a musical career in 1988, his one full sister, Tyka Nelson – Prince also has two half-sisters, Lorna and Sharon Nelson, and one half-brother, John, Jr, on his father's side, and one half-brother, Alfred, on his mother's – backed up Prince's early story (denied by his mother, Mattie Baker) in an interview with a British tabloid while promoting *Royal Blue*, a pleasant but lightweight collection of pop-funk that features a song about an imaginary friend, Marc Anthony, that the two of them would read her collection of pornographic novels, an autobiographical detail given by Prince that past commentators have occasionally questioned.

Much of Prince's early life has been turned into stories that seem to obscure as much as they reveal. Take, for example, his father's musicianship. John L. Nelson has been described as a jazz musician, but it seems that his music was not straightforward jazz but something far stranger, perhaps closer to outsider music.[1]

Whatever Prince's feelings towards his father (and they seem to have fluctuated over the years before his death), one thing that does emerge is his respect for his talent. He would make cassettes of his father's songs for members of The Revolution, and although it has been suggested that he was giving his father writing credits on songs like 'Around the World in a Day', 'The Ladder' and 'Scandalous' out of filial loyalty or kindness, it seems that he was genuinely inspired by memories of his father's piano-playing. Asked about his musical career by MTV VJ Martha Quinn during the premiere party for his son's second film, Nelson said: 'I was a piano-player for strippers down on Hampton Avenue in Minneapolis, having a lot of fun.' The son would grow up to share his father's interest in strip clubs as a source of creative inspiration, later sending a copy of the song he wrote for his protégée Carmen Electra to strip clubs across America.

Nancy Hynes, who was a contemporary of Prince at the John Hay Elementary School and lived in the same neighbourhood, gave me some background to the area and the school. Her parents, she told me, were 'white liberals who moved into the black inner city as a gesture of civil-rights activism and solidarity'. They moved in in 1967, 'just a month after the largest riot in West Minneapolis, which took out primarily the commercial area – between '65 and '67 that avenue lost thirty-two of its businesses. The house that we bought was being vacated by two elderly Jewish sisters [and] no one could understand why a white family was buying a house in that neighbourhood. The houses either side, one was sold to a mixed-race couple, which was legal in Minnesota at the time but not in many of the southern states, and [the other to] a black family. Prince at various times stayed across the street from us, [which was] where his aunt lived.'

Of the school, Hynes remembers an enthusiastic young staff, many of whom were choosing to teach in the inner cities. 'The kids were economically mixed, but the majority were black, which in US terms of the times included mixed-race kids. Classes were relatively small. There was a lot of music in the classroom, [but] formal music lessons were another matter. I remember peripatetic music-teaching. My friend remembers a music teacher who came once a week. There weren't any bands that I remember, but we listened to records and used to be asked, I think to settle us down, if we wanted to listen to the Osmonds or the Jackson Five, and the Jackson Five always won.'

What seems intriguing given the nature of Prince's later career and the ease with which he could move from music to film to art to live performance, is that a holistic approach was part of the school's ethos. Hynes remembers: 'You wouldn't have considered it odd to be asked to write a short story after watching a film or to make a painting. I don't remember painting being only something that happened in art class. In home room we'd talk about music, we'd talk about film.' Prince's sister Tyka told previous Prince biographer and sessionologist Per Nilsen about the privations she experienced at the school, noting that 'there weren't any school lunches'[2] and that students at the school had to go and find people prepared to feed them. Hynes, however, remembers things differently. 'I remember the school lunches vividly, and they were awful. Mash and gravy, and the mash would end up on the ceiling, where it deserved to be.'

Although she didn't share classes with Prince, she did share teachers, including a 'particularly good' teacher called Mrs Rader. Hynes's friend, Elizabeth Fuller, who went both to John Hay and later to the same high school, and who had more access to Prince than Hynes, recalls: 'OK, now just as a fan . . . what was Prince like in high school? Too cool for school? Absolutely. He spent most of his time in or around the music rooms on the fourth floor, often in a private practice room or sitting on one of the wide brick windowsills playing guitar to himself. The band directors never could convince him to actually join the band. I do seem to remember that his own band played at least one of our winter dances. The one song that sticks out in my mind consisted entirely of four-letter words.'

While not wanting to rehash old stories, there is one legend which shows up in most Prince biographies that it would be remiss not to include, and which Howard Bloom – who handled Prince's publicity from the early 1980s onward – says the musician told him was his most important formative memory: being five years old and seeing his father onstage in front of a screaming audience, surrounded by attractive women. Two years later, at seven, Prince completed his first song. In an early indication of the future direction of his lifetime's work, it was called 'FunkMachine'.[3]

When Prince was ten, his parents divorced. On several occasions, including a video interview in 1999,[4] Prince remarked that after this separation, his father left behind his upright piano. He had two years alone at this piano before leaving his mother and moving in with his father. Though Prince's early life is characterised by aloofness and isolation, he was also very interested in sports – a hobby that he retains to this day, as evidenced by his recently recording a song, 'Purple and Gold', for his home-town Minnesota Vikings – although Nancy Hynes has no memory of organised sports at John Hay. It seems he discovered this interest, at least according to early biographer Jon Bream, at his next school, Bryant Junior High, where, Bream suggests, he became 'a jock',[5] playing baseball, football and basketball (a photo exists of Prince as part of the school's basketball team).

This next period in Prince's life is usually presented as a time of turmoil. Alan Leeds, his road manager throughout the 1980s, told me: 'Prince's relationship with both his parents was somewhat strained. They had broken up in his formative years, and he ended up staying with his dad as opposed to his mum, which was unusual in those days.' While with his father, Prince befriended his father's stepson, Duane (who would eventually become part of Prince's road crew), before going back to his aunt's, opposite Nancy Hynes's house.

It was at his aunt's house that he encountered a man who would soon become an important presence in his life: Pepe Willie, who was dating Prince's cousin, Shantel Manderville. 'I was twenty-three, he must have been thirteen,' Willie told me, 'because he was just a little kid. I didn't pay him no mind.' But a few years later, when Prince was crashing at his friend André Anderson's house (Prince's warm feelings towards Anderson's mum Bernadette are expressed in the autobiographical song 'The Sacrifice of Victor') and had enrolled in an after-hours course on 'The Business of Music', he started having phone conversations with the older man.

According to Willie, Prince considered him an important

source of wisdom. Pepe Willie's uncle, Clarence Collins, was an original member of doo-wop band Little Anthony and the Imperials, and through this access, Willie had learnt about the music business. Part of his education had come from being around the band and becoming a runner, fetching cigarettes, hamburgers and cheesecake for artists such as Chubby Checker, the Coasters, Ike and Tina Turner and Dionne Warwick. But as well as this backstage access, he also attended lunches, dinners and business meetings with his uncle and the band, educating himself to the point where he was able to explain to the young Prince about copyright, publishing and performance rights organisations. 'He asked me, "What's this publishing all about?"' Willie told me. 'I said, "When I come to Minneapolis I'll sit down and talk to you about it."'

Willie was also a musician of some skill. 'When I was first started in the music business in Brooklyn, I was a drummer. And then by the time I left New York I played a little guitar.' When Willie came to Minneapolis, he witnessed Bernadette Anderson disciplining Prince. 'Bernadette reminded me of my own family. She was like his mom. I went to pick Prince up one time, and Prince had this girl downstairs that he was getting busy with, and he had done his business, and Bernadette walks in the door from work and asks Prince, "Did you go to school today?" And Prince goes, "No, I didn't." And immediately she started whipping his butt, right there in front of me, in front of the girl, everything. She busted him up. That was great, man.'

Though he often worked on music alone, from the beginning Prince also had a band. André Anderson (later to rename himself André Cymone), Prince and Prince's cousin Charles Smith formed a band called Grand Central and began rehearsing in André's basement. The story of the relative freedom Prince had in this basement to bring women home and enjoy himself has become an important part of Prince's self-mythology, but it has also been taken up by others. Indeed, Howard Bloom believes that much of the focus of Prince's career, and what drove him repeatedly to create imaginary Utopian societies like Paisley Park in his later work, was a conscious desire to replicate the happiness he found in André's basement.

Much has also been made – not least by Prince – of the radio stations he listened to in Minneapolis during this formative time, in particular a station named KQRS that played a variety of white and black music that may have helped shaped his sound. But Prince was also an active concert-attender, something he has maintained to the present day, though now he focuses almost exclusively on female musicians (a recent trip to see home-town band Gayngs at Minneapolis club First Avenue was a rare exception). One of Prince's favourite musicians and acknowledged influences, Joni Mitchell, has spoken of remembering Prince being in the audience when she toured her album *The Hissing of Summer Lawns,* which Prince later praised to *Rolling Stone.* 'I believe it was him. Front row to the left. Quite conspicuous because he's got those eyes like a puffin, those Egyptian eyes, those big, exotic eyes.'[6] And Todd Rundgren's former lover Bebe Buell has commented: 'I met Prince when he was sixteen, when Todd was playing Minneapolis in 1974 – this tiny little person with huge hair standing backstage who wanted to meet Todd. And Todd did his usual "Oh, hi, kid" number, and Prince was like, "I play everything and I'm real talented."'[7]

From the start Prince was promoting himself as a prodigy, focusing on his hard work, discipline and desire to become famous. In his first interview, to his high-school newspaper in 1976, he pointed out that he had already been recording with his band, now renamed Grand Central Corporation, for two years. Pepe Willie first saw the band at Shantel Manderville's father's ski party. 'I thought they were great,' Willie remembers. 'Prince was playing guitar, Morris [Day] was playing drums, André was playing bass, André's sister was playing keyboard and this other guy, we called him "Hollywood", William Daughty, was playing percussion.

'Prince's cousin Charles had really started the band but he was too busy playing football, so he had left the band two weeks before I got there. And he was the drummer. By the time I got there Morris Day was the drummer and his mom LaVonne was their manager, and she had bought him a seven-piece drum set. And she said, "I would love for you to work with them." They thought I was some big-time producer out of New York.'

Willie remembers the set being made up of covers, with the band playing songs by Earth, Wind and Fire and other acts who were big at the time. 'They didn't play any of their original music at that ski party. I went up to the attic where they used to prac-tise and asked them, "Do you guys have any original material?" Prince had this one song called "Sex Machine", André had this song "39th St Party" and this other song "You Remind Me of Me".

'They started playing "You Remind Me of Me", and I noticed that there was no introduction; they just started playing and all of a sudden they started singing. And I was trying to hear the words, but everyone was singing something different. And after they stopped singing they would just play music for another four or five minutes. So I stopped them and said, "OK, first of all, the construction is incorrect. You guys have got an intro, then a verse, then a chorus, and that's the hook, that's what people are going to remember."

'So we went on to Prince's song "Sex Machine". Prince had

gone over to Linda, André's sister, and he was telling her what to play. He put down his guitar and went over to the keyboards and showed her what to play. So then he put his guitar back on and started playing the song. Then he stopped and said, "André, let me hold your bass," and he started playing this amazing bass line. And André was just as talented. Before Prince had even finished playing the bass line he said, "I know what you want," and took the bass and played it exactly. Prince and André used to have contests – who could write the most songs in a day.'

Willie soon decided that he wanted Prince to come play with him in the studio. 'I was putting my band together, 94 East, with Wendall Thomas, who was dating my wife's cousin. Pierre Lewis was seventeen at the time. He was a keyboard player and he played like a lot of Herbie Hancock stuff, and then his brother Dale Alexander was a drummer. He was sixteen. Later on he played in [Prince's jazz band] Madhouse. Marcie and Kristie were two girlfriends, and we started hanging out together and I found out they could sing. And I was seeing Prince play all these instruments and I said to him, "I want you to come record with me," and he was thrilled because he had never been in a recording studio.'

They practised for two weeks and headed over to Cookhouse, which was, Willie remembers, 'a first-class recording studio. This was before Sound 80, which was the top studio in the Midwest. For me, just to get into that studio, I used to go and talk to the secretary every weekend, and then she would introduce me to the engineer. It took me three weeks. I was just some black kid from Brooklyn.

'When we went in with the band, we had to go pick everyone up, because none of them had driving licences. No one had cases on their instruments; things were put together with string and tape. And, of course, I had to pay these guys, but the union told me I could do a demo-recording contract and we could pay Prince a third, like twenty dollars, and that was great.'

94 East recorded five songs at Cookhouse – 'Games', 'I'll Always Love You', 'If We Don't', 'Better Than You Think' and 'If You See Me'. 'We did five songs in four hours,' recalls Willie. 'We just counted it off, bam-boom, and started playing.' But Prince wasn't entirely happy with the speedy experience. Willie remembers: 'The next day Prince called my house and said, "Pepe, I have to go back into the studio. I made a mistake."' Willie was already happy with the song but nevertheless persuaded the studio to let Prince back in to correct it while he went off to play golf.

This early example of Prince's perfectionism is, Willie says, audible on the recording. 'If you hear the part that he changed on "If You See Me", which is also titled "Do Yourself a Favor", you can hear what he did differently. The guitar part that he was playing, he did the same part when that part came up again, but the EQ was different because after our session they had another session, and for them to get it exactly the way they had his guitar set up was impossible.'[8] Willie would use the demos to get a deal for 94 East with Polydor, but they were dropped after recording a first single, and the songs didn't come out until almost a decade later.[9]

Looking at Prince's early musical career – by which I mean the period from when he first joined a band, at fifteen, in 1973, to the release of his second album, *Prince*, in 1979 – what's most striking is how hard he worked to be liked. There are plenty of provocative songs along the way, and it was in the period that followed this (1980–4) that he truly learnt how to capture mass public attention, but the overwhelming impression from these early years is of a young musician out to woo the world. From his very early childhood to the present day he has worked extremely hard, but still, he seems to have had a surprising number of people along the way who were not only prepared to help him with his ambitions, but also immediately recognised the enormous talent they were witnessing. There was no true striving in the wilderness to build up Prince's character. Part of this enthusiasm can be explained by the fact that so many of the musicians (and businessmen) of Minneapolis were looking for a break. And, unlike in Los Angeles or New York, where there was endless opportunity for the talented, this was not something easily achieved in Prince's home town. As Willie remembers: 'All these other musicians and band members had heard what we were doing. We were the talk of the town. Prince was in the studio, everyone knew who he was, and playing around town we had [legendary music producers] Jimmy Jam and Terry Lewis. They had this bus called Flyte Time that they used to drive around in and do gigs, and Prince and those guys played the same gigs sometimes. I was the only one who was telling them about the music industry, because people didn't know about it here. The only people that was doing anything was Bob Dylan and maybe Kenny Rogers and the First Edition, but no black acts were doing anything in Minneapolis.'

Pepe Willie wasn't the only person to pick up on Prince's talent. By the time Prince's band booked time at the recording studios of the English-born, Minneapolis-based producer and writer Chris Moon, they had changed their name from Grand Central to the more aspirational Champagne. Moon told me that he had set up his Moonsound studio by taking a trip at eighteen to Hong Kong to buy a reel-to-reel tape recorder, and built up a name for himself by offering free recording time to local bands, while also having a day job running the recording studio at ad agency Campbell Mithun. He also 'came up with this crafty plan to give myself credentials' by going down to the biggest radio station in town, KQRS, and persuading them to broadcast all the top concerts in Minneapolis, including The Rolling Stones, recorded in a studio he'd set up in his van. Given Prince's on-record admiration for the rock shows on KQRS, it seems likely he would have heard Moon's recordings before meeting him in person, and it's also an interesting antecedent for Prince's later use of mobile trucks to record live performances.

As well as establishing himself as a local producer, recorder and studio engineer, Moon had ambitions to write. 'I've always been a writer. Ever since I was really young I've written poetry. So I was sitting behind the console looking at all these bands and thinking, "Most of the lyrics these guys are singing are pretty dreadful. I know I can do better than that." But I didn't want to be the guy singing, so I came up with this idea: maybe what I'll do is find a band and write the material, and they'll produce the material and I'll promote the band out there doing my songs.

'So I started out on this process of figuring out who I'm going to pick. There's a steady stream of local bands coming through the studio all the time, and I started realising that one of the big problems with bands is that there's some chap in every band who can't get out of bed. Right around that time Champagne comes into the studio with this matronly lady [LaVonne Daugherty] who's the manager. She was a nice lady.' Moon remembers there being five members of Champagne, 'all about fifteen, sixteen years old', but previous accounts claim the band was a three-piece at this point, and these are the three members Moon referred to by name when recalling the session.

Moon remembers that during the recording 'It was a sunny day, and right across the street from me was a Baskin-Robbins 31 Flavors ice-cream shop, and we'd been recording for four or five hours and the manager for the band said, "OK, let's take a break before we come back and do the vocals." So everybody took a break, and she and all the members of the band went outside and over to the ice-cream shop. Well, all but one. Left behind in the studio, Mr Personality-I'd-Rather-Be-By-Myself, little five-foot-four Afro-headed kid, who was more Afro than kid. And so I'm sitting there drinking a can of pop with my feet up and I look through the window and there he is on the drums. I have another little sip and go to the window in the control room a few minutes later and there he is on piano. Another five minutes go by and there he is on the bass guitar. So I cranked up the mikes in the room to see if he's any good. He's not bad. He seems to be confident, better on some, not so good on others, but generally confident on all of these instruments. And I realise if I only have one artist, I don't have to worry about the drummer not showing up and screwing up the whole session.'

Moon waited until they were done with their material and then went over to Prince. 'He was painfully, painfully shy and extremely introverted. I went over to him and told him I had a proposition for him, and he gave me a grunt. And I said, "I'm a writer and producer and recording engineer and I don't want to be the artist, and I wondered if you'd like me to package you up and promote you and write your songs and teach you how the studio works and see if we can make something happen for you?"

'And he looked at me, and he was as surprised at the proposition as I was at making it because here was this kid from the north side of town I didn't know, I'd never spoken to him before, and I'm making this proposition to him. I don't think he said yes; he just nodded and I handed him the keys to my recording studio. That was everything I had in life. And that's probably not something a sane person or a rational person or a more prudent person would do.'

Moon says his deal with Prince was simple: he would pay for everything, and the only thing he wanted was to be given credit for the songs he wrote. Prince was pleased with the deal, but

Moon remembers the manager, Day's mother, 'was none too happy about it, and as I recall the band wasn't very thrilled either because Morris Day, he was a pretty flamboyant, outrageous, strong personality even back then, so I think it struck him as difficult that the quietest person in the band had been picked over him, the front man'. Day wasn't the only musician who would later join The Time that Moon passed over before deciding to work with Prince. 'We did a couple of sessions with [Jimmy] Jam and [Terry] Lewis with Prince. I brought Jimmy and Terry in to work on some other material I was working on. They came in and they had a very confident demeanour that they were bigtime. They played on a couple of tracks, and I always thought they left feeling I should have been a lot more impressed with them and pick them up in the way I picked Prince up. It wasn't that I wasn't impressed with them; just that, early on, they were so connected and such a team that it didn't feel there was room for a third person.' As far as Moon was concerned, Prince was the future.

WOULDN'T YOU LOVE TO LOVE ME?

For an artist who has appeared to shape-shift so many times in his career, Prince's influences have remained remarkably constant. On stage at Paisley Park in 2009, he reeled off the names: Larry Graham, James Brown, Stevie Wonder, George Clinton, Sly Stone, the Jacksons, Tower of Power, Miles Davis, Carlos Santana, Joni Mitchell, Rufus and Chaka Khan. Most of these influences can be found on Prince's earliest tape of home demos – recorded, it seems, after the Champagne sessions, and either before or around the time of the songs recorded with Chris Moon – which consist of four takes of 'For You', the title song from Prince's debut album; the first of several versions of a song called 'Wouldn't You Love to Love Me?'; five as yet unreleased songs; 'Don't You Wanna Ride?', an early run-through of the themes he'd later explore in 'Little Red Corvette', though bizarrely featuring a row-boat instead of a car; the straightforward love song 'I Spend My Time Loving You'; what almost sounds like a show tune about splitting from Minneapolis, 'Leaving for New York' (his half-sister Sharon lived there); the fragmentary 'Nightingale'; the primitive and self-explanatory 'Rock Me, Lover'; nine instrumentals; and a cover of Rufus's 'Sweet Thing'.[1]

While the songs have, for the most part, substantial lyrical content, they also feature Prince scat-singing in places, presumably as a way of filling lines for which he had yet to write lyrics.[2] Although sketchy, seemingly unfinished and primitively recorded, some of the songs on this tape have more complex lyrical content than Prince's first album, and a closer connection with his later recordings. It also gives us an insight, at this early stage at least, into Prince's method of composition: a man singing into a tape recorder with an acoustic guitar (and occasionally keyboard). But for all the primitiveness of the recording, it's already as sophisticated as any lo-fi record put out in the 1980s or '90s.

The most significant song on the tape, 'Wouldn't You Love to Love Me?' (the title being tease, boast and invitation), adumbrates the major theme behind Prince's early work: an explicit acknowledgement of both what he is offering and what he expects to receive. It is one of only two songs from that initial demo tape that would eventually be released, although not until 1987, and then by Taja Sevelle.[3] The delay doesn't seem to represent any anxiety on Prince's part about the song, and indeed, although he held it back from the first album, he recorded a (unreleased) version with his first protégée, Sue Ann Carwell, in 1978. But maybe he felt it better suited for a female vocalist, the request too needy even for his earliest persona.[4] As well as the Carwell and Sevelle versions, Prince has subsequently recorded the track three times, demoing it again in his home studio a year later and returning to it once more in 1987.

Of all the songs on the demo tape this presents the singer in his most seemingly powerful position, teasing his lover by refusing to settle down and dedicate himself to her (it will more usually be the male protagonist in this position in Prince's early songs). Although the song's lyrics are sung directly to a female lover, Prince is also addressing the listening audience, revelling in the attention he will get from female fans, while avoiding being imprisoned by their devotion. The only indication that the second version, recorded between the sessions for *For You* and *Prince*, is a demo is the return of the scat-singing (albeit here deliberately worked into the song's construction, and still there even in the Sevelle version). It's as good as anything on the first two albums, with a full arrangement and clear sound, and although some of the physical details refer directly to Prince, by the time of the third version – one of a number of early songs Prince returned to in 1987[5] – it's become clear that this is a song he wants someone else to sing.

The instrumentals are brief and fragmentary. Perhaps the most significant track on the tape, though, at least in the light it shines on Prince's creative future, is the cover of 'Sweet Thing', taken from a record whose arrangements were handled by Clare Fischer, who would go on to play such an important role in some of Prince's mid-1980s music. Prince went from loving this record on his home stereo to playing it to his band, later telling bandmate Lisa Coleman that one day they would have to get Fischer to do string arrangements for them. Coleman responded by feeling jealous because they were her responsibility, but she knew that one day Prince would feel compelled to work with him, and eventually he came to tell her that he had called Fischer and asked him to work on The Family's debut album, with Prince liking the result so much that Fischer was asked back to work on *Parade*.

For almost a year, Prince would come over from the north side of Minneapolis to the south on the bus after school, getting to Chris Moon's studio around lunchtime, with Moon joining him later in the afternoon. Moon remembers: 'The night before he would show up I would sit down and write three sets of lyrics for him to choose from and leave them on the piano. And his job when he showed up was to come in and if he liked one, work on it, and if not, tear it up and tell me, and I'd come up with another set. By the time I would show up, he would have worked out a guitar track or some kind of basic rhythm to one of the sets of lyrics that I had left with him.'

In time, Moon also taught Prince how to find his way round the studio so he could also record and produce himself while Moon was at the ad agency. Everything was working well, as far as Moon was concerned, until it came to the vocals, which Prince was singing so softly and so high that the microphone couldn't pick up his voice.

Worried about freaking him out or making him withdraw further, Moon went back into the studio and laid pillows on the floor. 'And I said, "Lie down and get really relaxed." And I take the microphone and I bring it down and stuff it in his mouth and turn all the lights off. So he's in there in the dark, on the floor, with the microphone halfway down his throat, pillows under his head, and over the course of the next few days I coaxed vocals out of him. A little, high, falsetto voice. Sweet, kind of reminiscent of Michael Jackson, and he had always said that Michael Jackson was his hero.'

Among the songs that Moon and Prince worked on together was 'Aces',[6] about which Moon remembers: 'I wrote that song because I wanted to really start playing with techniques, backward tracks, an experimental process, so I needed a song that would form the foundation for that. It was designed to be very experimental in nature, much longer too – seven minutes – not necessarily a really rounded set of words, but something that would give Prince an ability to step in many different directions – Mediterranean, Indian, all these different feels I envisioned him experimenting with.' This song was one of four on Prince's first demo tape, and the only one from that tape that wasn't reworked for his debut album. Though it has been suggested by past sessionologists that 'Diamond Eyes' was written by Moon, he told me that 'it was one of the first songs Prince wrote the lyric to', after he had started to worry that Moon would be writing all of his songs, and that more of the recording of this song was done in the control room than the studio as Moon taught Prince how to record. Ironically, Moon has forgotten about 'Don't Forget', a song they did 'that no one got that excited about'. Nor does he recall the details of 'Don't Hold Back'.

Moon recalls that in an early example of the recording process Prince has adopted for the whole of his professional career, most of the songs were worked on late into the night. Only one song, 'Fantasy', was recorded during the day and was, he remembers, accordingly much brighter than the rest of the tracks. He also says that 'Surprise', another song previously credited to him, was actually a Prince-penned lyric and that it came in response to thinking about Prince's potential career.

'I had told Prince, "We've got to think about how we're going to market you." What I had learned in the ad agency was that when you had a product, there had to be a theme to the product and a marketing direction, and so I was applying this to Prince. I said, "We've got to figure out our audience, and for you old teenagers are not going to be buying your stuff, this is going to be for young girls. You're cute-looking, you dance and jump around, so we need to have a marketing theme in the songs that speaks to them. Young girls, they're coming of age, they're becoming aware of their sexuality. I think that's probably the most powerful force that we can speak to, and if we can anchor the music to the strong new feelings they're having, we might really be able to gain some traction and connect with the audience."'

Moon says that while he was 'playing with songs that were of a general sexual nature, Prince was playing around with songs around the concept of getting pregnant'. 'Surprise' was one of these songs; 'Baby', also demoed during these sessions and later included on *For You*, was another. 'I don't know if this was something he was worried about or wary of, but I told him I think we want to stay away from babies because that's not something young girls are going to want to be thinking about.'

Instead, Moon suggested that Prince work with sexual sugges-tion. Past commentators have suggested that he gave Prince the concept of 'implied naughty sexuality' or 'naughty sexual innu-endo', but Moon says he now remembers very clearly that 'double entendre' was, in fact, 'the exact phrase I used with Prince. I'll never forget it. The way this all came about was I had Sundays off, and that particular Sunday I had a fortunate experience with more than one girl. It was a late-night party, and these girls had come back to my studio and it had been one of those pleasant, memorable experiences. And I think I'd drunk a little too much rum because the next morning I felt like hell and had to go to work. So I locked the door, and I'm lying there recovering from this wild night before and I'm replaying in my mind some of the highlights and this song comes to mind, "Soft and Wet". What I'd been trying to do was come up with the anchor tune that would summarise this marketing concept, that would deliver the positioning of this artist to the audience in just the right way. And so I wrote "Soft and Wet" sitting in ad agency Campbell Mithun after this wonderful evening, tired, a little bit hung-over, it was ten o'clock in the morning, and the original version was: "Angora fur, the Aegean sea, it's a soft, wet love that you have for me."'

With this song, which Prince liked and immediately started working on, Moon felt he'd hit on a template for their planned album. 'It was the first song where Prince introduced a break into the music. The words were so short and it was a lot more punctuated and a lot more staccato and abbreviated than any-thing we had done before.' There were a few more songs, penned by Prince, that were lost on the way to the debut album: 'Since We've Been Together', three instrumentals – one of which, 'Jelly Jam', became part of 'Just as Long as We're Together' – a revised version of 'Leaving for New York' and the Moon-penned 'Make It Through the Storm', which Prince later recorded with Sue Ann Carwell. But at the end of the session Prince produced a four-track demo tape containing 'Baby', 'Soft and Wet', 'Aces' and 'My Love Is Forever'. Before sending it out, Moon says he had a little more work to do with Prince, who, he claims, didn't want to release his records under his Christian name. 'He said, "It's gotta be Mr Nelson." I said, "Mr Nelson? Look, let me break it down to you this way. There's this white guy named Willie. Maybe you've heard of him, maybe you haven't, but we don't want to be getting confused with Willie Nelson."'

Moon was also involved in Prince's first concrete attempt to get a record contract. When Prince went to visit his sister Sharon in New York, he asked Moon to set some record-company meetings up for him. This proved harder than Moon expected, prompting him to pretend that he represented Stevie Wonder, only to switch and explain he had the *new* Stevie Wonder when he finally got someone on the phone. Prince got a meeting out of this but nothing came of it, and when he came back Moon remembers him being deflated. 'He thought the first person who heard him would sign him. And it didn't happen, and neither did the second guy or the third guy. So now what I got to do is get him into the record companies in the right way. Prince wanted me to be his manager. And I had no interest in being his manager. I didn't want to make sure he got on planes, I didn't want to book his hotel rooms, I didn't want to pay for his meals. I'm only interested in the music.

'[But] I realised it was all going to stop right then and there, unless I could find someone who could pick up where I left off, and build on what I'd done and take it to the next step. The only manager I could think of had come and booked some time in the studio for this folk group, two guys, a kind of Hall and Oates take-off.' This person was Owen Husney. 'And he owned a dinky ad agency, two or three people working for him in Minneapolis, and I thought, "There's a guy cut from the same cloth as me,"' Moon remembers. But it took a week of sitting in his office before Husney would see Moon. 'It started on a Monday, and by Friday I'd bugged the shit out of him enough that they finally said, "Look, this guy's not going away, you've got to sit down and listen to him."' Moon persuaded Husney to listen to the tape, and he remembers that when he came back a few days later, 'the lights had gone on for Owen'. Moon told Husney he wasn't looking for anything more from him or Prince than credit for the lyrics he had written.

Pepe Willie remembers being impressed with Husney because he found Prince an apartment and paid for it, allowing Prince to concentrate on his music. Prince spent much of the first half of 1977 recording at Minneapolis recording complex Sound 80, working on improving the songs he'd demoed with Moon, paying special attention to 'Baby', 'Just as Long as We're Together', 'My Love Is Forever' – which Moon says he had more involvement in than has been credited for, telling me that 'that song was about a girl that I slept with for a year, and we never had sex' – 'Soft and Wet', an instrumental, one song that would later be recorded and released by his first protégée, Sue Ann Carwell, 'Make It Through the Storm', and another, 'We Can Work It Out', that is Prince's first out-take to rival the quality of any official release.[7]

This song, which ends with Prince hoping for a harmonious relationship with Warner Brothers, must have been written after Husney had found him a deal with the label. Prince has spoken resentfully about biographers seeking out Husney for interview, and though I did contact him, when he didn't respond I didn't push it. Whatever Prince's feelings, Husney undoubtedly played an important role in bringing Prince's music to the public, creating deluxe press kits to accompany his demo tapes that eventually secured the deal with Warner Brothers. While at Sound 80, Prince is also believed to have contributed backing vocals and guitar to a song, 'Got to Be Something Here', on a self-titled album by The Lewis Connection, working with Sonny T, a musician who would later join Prince's New Power Generation and who Prince is on record as saying had an enormous influence on him as a young musician. He also ran into Pepe Willie and 94 East, who had come to the studio to record two songs for a single, 'Fortune Teller' (which had been written for the band by Hank Cosby, a member of Motown's studio band The Funk Brothers and co-writer of Stevie Wonder's 'My Cherie Amour', among several other hits) and '10.15'. 'We were going in and he was coming out,' Willie remembers, 'and he said, "What are you guys doing?" And we were like, "Hey, man, we're gonna go and record our single." And he says, "Can I play on it, man?" And we go, "Sure, you can play on our stuff." And he never even went home after his session, he just hung out with us in the studio and played guitar on "10.15" and "Fortune Teller".'

By now, Willie recalls, they had hired Bobby Rivkin as drummer. Soon after, Rivkin (later Bobby Z) would join Prince's first band. Also, on the first version of 'Fortune Teller', Colonel Abrams – who would eventually become famous as a house singer, best known for the hit 'Trapped' – was singing vocals. But when the tapes were taken back to New York, 'Hank Cosby didn't like the drums Bobby was playing, so he got this other drummer called Buddy Williams to play drums on "Fortune Teller", and Bobby was heartbroken.'[8]

It was tapes from the sessions at Sound 80 which led to early band-mate Matt Fink asking Bobby Rivkin for an introduction to Prince. Fink told me he was impressed by 'just the fact that he was my age, that he was eighteen at the time in 1977. Bobby Z hadn't been hired [by Prince] yet; he was working for Prince's manager Owen Husney. He brought in the demo and said, "Just listen to this stuff." When I discovered who he was, that he'd performed, written, played and engineered this stuff, I jumped out of my pants in excitement and asked if I could be involved. There was no one else around like him.'

Though it would be a while before Prince officially recruited a backing band, before he headed off, alone, to California to work on his first album, he recorded another dozen demos as part of a trio, eight of which were instrumentals. These 1977 instrumentals are of a much higher standard than those demoed the year before. Indeed, while occasionally lapsing into music-shop-demonstration-style vamping (and featuring one track – #4 – that tails off rather than finishes), these eight tracks are, in places, as interesting as Prince's first two albums with Madhouse. Though it would be a few years before playing with a band would become an important part of his creative process, hearing him here with bassist André Cymone and drummer Bobby Z gives a fascinating insight into his early musicianship. Lengthy jazz-funk with a tension and drama that quickly establish this is more than mere noodling, some of the tracks (#3, #6 and the first-melancholy-then-amusingly-upbeat #7 in particular) sound far more expansive than those on *For You*, revealing how in order to achieve commercial success, Prince would have to begin by narrowing his creative focus. There were other demos too, known only by their titles – 'Darling Marie', 'Hello, My Love', 'I Like What You're Doing' and 'Neurotic Lover's Baby Bedroom' – along with several other tracks lost or abandoned on the way to that first album.

For You, like Bob Dylan's and Neil Young's first albums, is both a perfectly realised masterpiece and something of a false start.

Prince admitted as much to Steve Sutherland in an interview tape that eventually got pressed up as a picture disc, in which he expressed his frustration that the executive producer Warner Brothers had forced on him didn't teach him how to use the studio as he had hoped. Prince claims he wanted to make a record 'bereft of mistakes'. His ambivalent attitude towards the record comes through in comments like 'it took a long time, it was pretty painstaking', that 'most of it was pretty old stuff', that 'it was a perfect record' but that it was 'too scientific', and that after he finished it he could no longer listen to it.

Prince spent longer working on it than he did on any of his three subsequent albums, not taking this much time crafting a record again until he made a successful bid for a substantial new audience with *1999* and *Purple Rain*. The time in the studio paid off: it has the smoothest, most complete sound of the first four records, although Prince's lyrical skills are still developing: it is the work of a nineteen-year-old, and as such has little in its head.

Only 'Soft and Wet', the collaboration with Chris Moon, made it onto 1993's hits compilation and remains in his live set, and while *For You* is, in places, stylistically similar to Prince's second, self-titled album, it has otherwise little connection with his later records.

All the songs on the first two albums are addressed to 'you'. On the multitracked title song, a chorus of Princes (in a visual version of this trick, there are three of him in the bed on the inner sleeve) make the listener an offering of Prince's life, and throughout the record we are forced to assume the role of his various girlfriends. 'In Love', which was the B-side of the album's second single, 'Just as Long as We're Together', is one of Prince's simplest songs, more basic than most of his early demos. Prince sings of restraint and chains, but not in the sadomasochistic context he'll soon explore on *1999* and *Purple Rain*, instead merely suggesting

35

that if his love is reciprocated, it will liberate the object of his affection. 'Soft and Wet' is the record's most memorable track, largely because it prefigures the sexual explicitness so important to Prince's later records.

One of the lyrical limitations of this record is that Prince has (for the most part) yet to work out how to introduce developed narratives into his songs. 'Crazy You' begins with the promising set-up of Prince falling in love with a crazy woman, but while the eccentricities of his female acquaintances and lovers – such as the well-built exhibitionists of 'Raspberry Beret' or 'Gett Off' – will provide him with much material in the future, here he quickly qualifies the woman's craziness by saying love makes him mad too, and the song is over in two short minutes. It is a mark of the album's 'perfection' that even a slight track like this has a fascinating (and unique) arrangement, utilising water drums and wind chimes for a complexity of sound that prefigures the later experimentation of *Around the World in a Day*.

Along with 'Soft and Wet', 'Just as Long as We're Together' is Prince's most important early song. He demoed it five times on the way to the studio – the song growing in musical ambition with each version – and as these various versions included a test pressing for both CBS and Warners to prove his ability to play multiple instruments and produce himself, it can, without exaggeration, be seen as the track that got him his deal and kick-started his career. Knowing this, it's easy to hear the 'look-ma-no-hands' ambition in the music. Lyrically, it seems oddly ambivalent for a song about devotion, with Prince oscillating between singing about how he will allow his lover her freedom and wanting her near by. One of the demo versions cuts off after three minutes, and this seems the natural end point of the song, the remaining three minutes in the released version being mainly a chance for Prince to showcase his musical skills.

The song about pregnancy that did make the record, 'Baby', is, whatever Moon's concerns, the album's most lyrically sophis-ticated track and is somehow more touching than any of the songs Prince wrote for 1996's *Emancipation*, when he was actually expecting a child. What's most impressive about the song is its economy and its lyrical sure-footedness. In relation to Prince's career as a whole, it also sees him touching on two themes that will reoccur several times throughout his body of work: money and contraception. Although the press and biographers have made much of the occasions when Prince appears to have had brief money difficulties, from his first deal onwards he has expe-rienced near constant financial freedom, and it is only in his relatively early songs that he sings about impoverishment,[9] here worrying about whether he will be able to support his child and if he should marry his girlfriend.[10]

'My Love Is Forever' and 'So Blue' are lyrically similar in that both songs are about lifetime devotion (although it's worth remembering that in the later 'Let's Go Crazy' there is something *beyond* for ever). Both are lyrically generic ('So Blue' being the second song on the album in which Prince observes that the sun shines, although given the weather in Minneapolis maybe this is excusable) but as musically appealing as the rest of the album, Prince's acoustic guitar on 'So Blue' already far more measured and sophisticated than it is on his home demos. Far better is 'I'm Yours'. There is only one recording from Prince's first tour in circulation – which doesn't feature the song – so it's possible he may have played it at some point during that run,[11] but the song didn't return until thirty-one years later, when Prince played it as part of his set at the Conga Room in Los Angeles. That the song slipped easily into the set seems somehow terrifying, indicating that no matter how long Prince lives, he'll never get to do full live justice to his recorded work (although it would help if he retired some concert chestnuts). But he did make a significant change to the lyrics, skipping the verses from the original version in which he claims to be a virgin. As with 'Do You Wanna Ride?', this is a song in which Prince approaches a more experienced woman, but this time there is a distinct absence of braggadocio, and it's among Prince's most submissive songs, though the musical bombast hides some of the sentiment.

The interviews Prince gave to promote his debut were unrevealing. Cynthia Horner's interview for *Right On!* is typical, Prince rebuffing each question with silly or contradictory answers, telling her he hates clothes, that his favourite foods are mashed yeast and Bubble Yum and that he doesn't want to get married until 2066. Curiously, he complains about the late hours rock musicians have to keep, and his late-night sessions, which seems odd given that for most his life he has seemed almost completely nocturnal.

After the release of *For You*, Prince bought his first house and set up a primitive studio in the basement, beginning the practice of private demoing and recording that he would maintain for ever afterwards. Six short instrumentals, five unreleased songs and another version of 'Wouldn't You Love to Love Me?' have emerged from this era. 'Down a Long Lonely Road' is a catchy chorus without a song, 'Baby, Baby, Baby' is little more than the title, a pretty-but-barely-there sketch, and 'Miss You' is even more minimalist than the songs on the debut. Two songs about girlfriends, real ('Nadera') or, I assume, idealised ('Donna') don't really tell us much about these women, other than that they're pretty and unobtainable ('Donna') or cool ('Nadera'). Either way, neither the women nor the songs stuck around long. He was moving on.

Still, for a while, at least, Prince didn't forget Pepe Willie or Chris Moon. As Willie remembers: 'We got dropped from

Polydor before our record even came out, and Prince and André and myself were hanging out in Minneapolis and he was so heartbroken that he said to André, "We got to go back into the studio with Pepe." So André says, "Sure, let's go," and I'm going, "Well, where's this money coming from?" I didn't know. [But] I booked the time at Sound 80 and me and Prince wrote this song called 'Just Another Sucker', and me and my other friend wrote 'Lovin' Cup', and then I wrote this other song called 'Dance to the Music of the World', and we went and recorded those three songs, and Prince played drums and keyboards and guitar and I played acoustic guitar and André played bass. I was feeling real good because I had support from Prince and André. For me, they were the two best musicians in Minneapolis.'[12]

Prince remained friends with Willie, letting him house-sit while he was away in Los Angeles in the summer of 1978. Willie found that being left alone in Prince's home studio was inspiring. 'He had this four-track recorder in his house. So I was house-sitting and I started writing. When I was in Minneapolis hanging out with Prince and all these guys, I'd started playing keyboard and a little bass. When I was at his house, he's got all these instruments here. I turned on the recorder and started playing guitar and keyboards and wrote these songs, 'Love, Love, Love' and 'You Can Be My Teacher'. And then Prince came in from LA and I played it for him, and he played bass and some other things on it. And that was at 5,215 France Avenue, here in Minneapolis. That was fun.'[13]

A short time after the success of the first album, Chris Moon remembers, 'I get a phone call from Prince. He's with Warner Brothers now. He says, "Being famous is kinda lonely. It's hard to know who your friends are. I'm calling to ask you for a favour. I want you to do for my dad what you did for me. Can you make him famous?" I said, "Prince, I've never even met your dad." A couple of days later, I get a phone call. "This is Prince's dad, my son says you can make me famous." So he came by, and he was an older guy, a little weathered. He came with a case, and he opened up the case and took out an accordion. I'm thinking, "Oh my god, there is a limit to my capabilities." He left unhappy and I never heard from him again.'

4

STILL WAITING

It wasn't long after the release of *For You* – which was respectfully reviewed and did well enough to establish Prince as a presence midway up *Billboard*'s Soul Chart, but didn't break out to a mass audience – that Prince stopped wanting to just be Stevie Wunderkind and set his sights on besting Sly and the Family Stone too. Dez Dickerson suggests that right from the very beginning Prince 'had a definite vision for the make-up of the group. He wanted a multiracial, rainbow-coalition kind of band'. Dickerson's book provides a touching account of the frustrations and joys of those early days, suggesting that for all his early success, and deliberate separation from the band, at this point at least Prince was looking for a gang, auditioning players in Los Angeles but eventually bringing together a band made up entirely of Minneapolis musicians: his close friend André Cymone, the man he'd been practising with from the beginning, Bobby Z, Dez Dickerson, Gayle Chapman and Matt Fink. In the process of assembling this team, he also came across four people who would later return to his orbit: Paul Peterson (of The Family)'s brother Ricky, Jimmy Jam, Morris Day and Sue Ann Carwell.

Gayle Chapman remembers that she met Charles Smith, Prince's cousin and the original drummer in Grand Central, through 'some friends of his, and those friends were into Prince's music, his first album at the time. Apparently they knew Prince, but they didn't tell me that Charles was his cousin. They introduced me to Charles, and Charles would come over and we would jam together. We spent many hours just playing together. One day I was alone in my home listening to *For You* as loud as I could, and it was late at night and the stereo was cranked and I couldn't have heard anything aside from the music, except I heard this voice, and it came through the ceiling and shot through my head and went out the other side. All it said was: "In order to tour he's gonna need a band." And I turned the music down and I went, "What?" I'd never had such a clear thought; it wasn't my head speaking. So I asked Charles if he knew anything about it, because I knew these other people that we knew also knew him. And he said, "Well, Prince is my cousin." And I said, "Why didn't you tell me?" And he said, "I thought you were already playing with someone." And I said, "I'm playing with you in my living room. Get me involved!"'

Of those auditions, Chapman remembers: 'I showed up at his house at Edina on France Avenue. I was wearing a blue Jean Shrimpton dress and I had wild, kinda crazy hair. I looked like the Granola Queen, a hippy chick. I showed up and sat on the couch with all these other girls and some guys, and they all looked dressed for the part. And I'm thinking, "Well, maybe not." And I went downstairs, and these guys all gave me the rude eye. I descended the stairs, and there was Bobby Rivkin, André Cymone – or Anderson, as his name was then – and Prince. They had a keyboard down there and said, "OK, we're gonna jam." And I thought, "I hate jamming. Can't we just play something?" But no, they had to jam and see if I could "hang". So I jammed and I didn't think that I did very well, so I said, "OK, so if you guys can do that, then you follow this." So I started one, and they were like, "So now we have to follow this? OK." I left and I didn't feel real good about it. I went home and I moved to another place further away from downtown Minneapolis and waited three months. By that time I wasn't even thinking about it. Then one day – it was the end of summer, in September – I was taking a nap, nice fall day, sunny out, I was depressed, I think, and the phone rang and this monotone voice said, "Hello, Gayle, this is Prince, what are you doing? Can you make it to rehearsal in an hour?" And I said, "Sure." I loaded up everything, stuck it in my VW and made it in forty-five minutes.'

The best account of these early years of development can be found in Dez Dickerson's 2003 autobiography, *My Time with Prince: Confessions of a Former Revolutionary*, the only book written by a member of Prince's band. I also interviewed Dickerson, but over the phone he displayed a caution that is not so apparent in his revealing, but respectful, autobiography. What's striking about the accounts of almost all the members of Prince's early band is how they were immediately struck by the quality of his work. Chapman wasn't the only one who'd been cranking up Prince's first album. Dickerson had, by his own admission, a little more adolescent arrogance than Matt Fink, but after borrowing his younger sister's copy of *For You* he was equally impressed.

Though Prince's band included Prince's childhood friend André Cymone and long-term associate Bobby Z, from the beginning Dickerson felt he in particular had a special creative affinity to Prince, believing that at this stage in his career Prince was still listening to those around him as he shaped his sound and persona. As Dickerson told me: 'In the early days I really was closest to Prince. We had a different relationship than he had with some of the others. He'd come over and we'd work through things.' It seems that what they worked through was not only music, but also burgeoning fame and the pressures of being in a band.

Dickerson's musical tastes were in some ways closer to Matt Fink's than Prince's. Fink says his were broad, but that he had a particular fondness for rock, including Fleetwood Mac, The Beatles, The Who and the Stones. Dickerson and Prince shared an interest in Grand Funk Railroad, but otherwise Dickerson was much like Fink, though his tastes ran to new wave and metal rather than classic rock, with particular favourites being The Cars and Van Halen (after Dickerson left Prince's employ, his next most high-profile gig was playing with Billy Idol). So it was unsurprising that when the band first played live, though the show was based around *For You*, they produced more of a rock sound than Warner Brothers – who, after all, had signed a sweet-voiced child protégé singing love songs – were expecting.

The rehearsals had been intense. At first the band practised in a building called Del's Tyre Mart, which Chapman says 'was an old tyre shop that was owned by Bonnie Raitt's brother Steve in Seven Corners. It was a kinda dark, dingy place, and all this stuff was in there already set up. Everybody was there and I was the last person to walk in.'

Pepe Willie, who had lent Prince his speakers, remembers the reason for abandoning this rehearsal space. 'Either he left the door open to Del's Tyre Mart or somebody broke in. I think he forgot to lock the door. Somebody went in there and took everything. The only thing they didn't take was my speakers. And so I said, "OK, that's it, move everything to my house in south Minneapolis."'

When they got there, Willie recalls the band rehearsing ten hours a day. During these rehearsals, Chapman remembers, improvisation was not particularly welcome. 'He would tell us what he wanted us to play. There was one part on "I Wanna Be Your Lover" where he was really specific about what he wanted, and I think he always has been. I knew I was working with some-body completely knowledgeable of what he wanted when he would come over repeatedly and stand there behind me, kinda like my mom did, and say, "Not that, this. Play it for me." And it would be just milliseconds different than what I was playing. But it was a feel he wanted it to have. I tolerated it from him much better than from my mother.'

Of Chapman, Willie says: 'Gayle was real cool for a white girl. She used to like to eat that Brie cheese, and I hated that because it made her breath smell.' For her part, Chapman remembers: 'Pepe was an asshole. As far as I'm concerned, he always will be. He thinks he's the reason I was in the band. I never met Pepe until we moved to his basement, which was several months later. Pepe wasn't at the original audition. I've heard all the stuff about he was persuasive in my getting into the band. I never met him until I was in the band and we were hiring Matt Fink. But Pepe seemed to be a misogynistic fella that had talent in his own right. Whatever he did for Prince, God bless him, but we didn't hit it off at all.'

Chapman says Bobby Z was very reserved. 'I never really got to know him. I think because I was the female in the band and got preferential treatment on hotel rooms none of the guys really liked me. They had a discussion once and said, "You always get this," and I said, "I wasn't asking for it." I was the chick in the band. "Look, I'll room with you guys, but you're gonna have to give up the bathroom for a little." Matt Fink and I have remained friends throughout the years. We're not close, but if I've ever wanted to talk to him about anyone or anything, I could call him. He talks to me. I don't know what Dez thought. Dez is a different character. These were my band-mates, we weren't friends. We were all young, egotistical and in it for ourselves, and we realised that once you're in Prince's band, you're in it for Prince, whether you wanted it for yourself or not.' Fink also remembers Chapman with fondness. 'Gayle is a wonderful person and an excellent keyboardist.'

It's clear from Dickerson's autobiography that he had no doubts about his own talent, something Willie also observed. 'Dez had come from this other group called Romeo, where he was the lead guy,' Willie says, 'and for him not to be the lead in Prince's band was crazy, and when they had a break in rehearsals, I told Dez, "Look, Dez, I'm gonna produce you." So me and Dez flew to New York and I produced three songs [with] Dez that I still have. And then Prince called me when I was in New York with Dez and goes, "Pepe, what are you doing? Dez is part of my band." And I said, "Look, Prince, I brought you to New York, I brought André to New York. It's no different. What's the big deal?"'

It was also during these rehearsals that Prince parted ways with his first manager, Owen Husney. Everyone seems to agree that it was over Husney's disinclination to drop everything and get Prince some space heaters, but in his autobiography Dickerson puts the blame for the split largely on Prince, commenting that '[Prince] was expecting more of a concierge than a manager'. Willie, however, says: 'Prince needed some heaters in the basement. He was already signed, and I told him, "Your manager's supposed to be doing this." Owen had this company called the Ad Company. I told him, "Owen is not supposed to be in the Ad Company right now. As far as I'm concerned he's supposed to be in New York or LA lobbying for you." So I go over to Owen's office and I says, "Owen, Prince is unhappy, he's cold, he don't have no space heaters." And these are Owen's exact words: he said to me, "So I'm supposed to leave my company and do all of this stuff for some artist that probably won't make it?" When I told that to Owen a while ago, he denied it. Later on, he said he quit or whatever, but I told him, "Owen, you're fired," because Prince told me to fire him. Owen had said, "Well, Pepe, you manage him then." And I said, "Owen, I am not a manager, but I am not going to let him get screwed up in this business.'"

So Willie temporarily took over Prince's management, organising his first two live shows, the second of which Warner Brothers representatives were attending to see if they felt it was time for Prince to go on the road. 'We set it up with the Capri theatre, we printed the tickets, we did the lighting. And when Warner Brothers came around we shuffled them into the theatre, and those were Prince's first performances after rehearsing at my house for five or six months. He thought they were ready, and I thought they were great. But Warner Brothers thought he wasn't quite ready. Now I felt they were flexing their muscle a little bit. Not wanting to give Prince a big ego. I've seen bands out there much worse. Maybe they saw something I didn't.'

Dez Dickerson says this disappointment played a crucial part in his bonding with Prince. 'There was a level of respect with Prince that came from our dynamic early on. That dry-dock experience when we didn't get to tour. I really helped Prince through that. I gave him the benefit of my experience and helped him to lead the band. It was a devastating experience, but it was really necessary, more so than they understood because it allowed Prince to live up to all the qualities of his character. It was one of the heads of Warners. Warners had the best artist development in the history of the business.'

I told Dickerson I was surprised he had come to this conclusion and asked him whether he *really* felt it was right to keep them off the road in their early days. 'I really did. I'd been doing it for so long, I was the point man, the drill sergeant who ensured the show had a flow, a beginning, middle and end. The show at the Capri theatre, we weren't ready yet. If you looked at the band, if it was possible to view the Capri footage and compare it to later bootleg footage – and there's a lot of it out there – it would be night and day. It's about chemistry. It can't be learnt and you can't teach it. It's an organism.' Perhaps because of Prince's feelings of disappointment, a new rock song he played that night, 'I Am You', has never been released, though Prince had warned the local *Minneapolis Star and Tribune*, 'We've got a few songs we'll do at the Capri that I'll probably never record on an album because they're too spicy.'[1] Chapman doesn't have strong memories of the show, but does remember the impact it had. 'It was a learning experience for everyone. It was the first gig with Prince, who was clearly becoming this very important little monster in the music business, and it was good to see what that would be like in his home town.'

Willie says Prince's reaction to being told he couldn't go on the road was to rehearse harder than ever. 'He had to rehearse more. One time I remember he was rehearsing at my house from ten o'clock in the morning. At ten at night we kicked everybody out and I wanted to get hold of Prince, so I called him on the phone and I couldn't get him on the phone. So I drove over to his house and I'm knocking on the door and nobody answers, and I hear this little tapping, so I walk around the house and look through the window, and it was Prince in the basement playing drums. This is after ten hours of practice.'

But he still needed new management. Willie got in touch with a friend of his named Don Taylor, telling him he had an artist already signed with Warner Brothers. 'Don Taylor did the same kind of job that I did with Little Anthony and the Imperials when they went to Jamaica. They found this poor Jamaican dude who wanted to valet for them and they hired him and brought him back to America. And Don Taylor had learned the business like I had, and later on started managing the Imperials and also Bob Marley and the Wailers.

'I called Don because I wanted Prince to have the best. Don

flew me and Prince to Miami and got us both hotel rooms, and he picked Prince up. And I just stayed at the hotel room because I didn't want to influence nobody.' Willie believes that Taylor made an immediate difference to Warners' attitude in regard to Prince going on the road. 'Prince did sign with Don for a year, and Don knew Mo Ostin at Warner Brothers and immediately he got Prince's tour budget raised from $80,000 to $180,000, just on a phone call.'

Taylor's comments about Prince in his autobiography are mostly negative. He tried to engineer a collaboration between Prince and Bob Marley, to which Marley responded, according to Taylor, 'Don Taylor a dem dah man yo want me fe work with? – mi hum in a dem day batty boy business, mi nuh even wan cum a yah office an meet dem or even sit inna same chair as im.'[2]

Taylor himself found Prince emotionless and was put out by Prince's lack of concern about going over budget on his first album. Prince's association with him came to an end, Taylor writes, after Prince made aggressive comments about his sister to Taylor's assistant, Karen Baxter, and this side of his career was soon taken over by the Warner Brothers-approved management duo of Bob Cavallo and Joe Ruffalo, though in future years it would be their employee Steve Fargnoli (who would eventually graduate to full partner) who truly had Prince's ear and worked as one of his main representatives throughout the most creatively and commercially successful period of his career.

Cavallo told me that it was Prince who sought them out rather than vice versa. 'Supposedly the story is Prince saw Earth, Wind and Fire play at the big arena in Minneapolis and thought the show was unbelievable. He called and asked someone at Warner records, "Who's the manager who helped them put that big show together?" And they said me. So he reached out to me and we set up a meeting.' Cavallo says he had known about Prince even before he signed to Warners and 'tried to sign him to ARC records, which was the label that me and Earth, Wind and Fire and my partner Joe Ruffalo owned. He was then very young, and somehow the head of A&R from Columbia got to him, knowing that I was trying to sign him, and told him that if he came with them, he'd have Columbia's marketing and of course it would be possible for Maurice White [of Earth, Wind and Fire] to produce him. And that meant you had no chance of signing him.'

Still, he wanted him to audition and went to see a show. 'It was kinda funny really. He was very respectful to me up through *Purple Rain*. He was a nice kid. Quiet. But I brought my eight-year-old daughter when they performed somewhere down in Orange County, not really the right kind of place. I didn't set up the gig. And under the raincoat he had stockings and a little G-string. When he'd spin around, the coat would fly open, and I was sitting there with my daughter, going, "Holy Christ." The story goes I go in and say, "Young man, you can't really perform in your underwear," and then he comes out in the second show without any underwear.' Nonetheless, Cavallo was impressed with Prince's musical talents. 'I thought he was incredible and his band was very cool, a well-thought-out placement of characters. And I was all for it.'

Though he had sold around a hundred and fifty thousand copies of his debut, Prince was still prepared to work as a musician for hire, and when Pepe Willie got in touch to ask if he and André would work with his friend Tony Silvester from soul and R&B group The Main Ingredient, demoing new songs intended for performance by a new incarnation of Willie's uncle's band the Imperials, he quickly agreed.

Willie remembers: 'Tony Silvester called me looking for musicians, and I told him, "Look, I got two musicians who can play *everything.*" Don had this record label and he had hired Tony to produce the Imperials and they were going to use some of the songs that we played at Sound 80. So Tony flew me, Prince and André to New York and put us up at the Hilton Hotel. And Prince had started writing 'I Feel for You', and he had just wrote it on piano, and André had written this one song, 'Do Me, Baby'. And I had written this song called 'If You Feel Like Dancin'', and the Imperials recorded it but it didn't go anywhere, so we came back to Minneapolis.'[3]

Though Prince would pursue the rock/new-wave sound beloved by Dickerson and Fink on his side project with The Rebels (see Chapter 6), for his second record (recorded without the band) he remained focused on funk, taking into the studio the song he'd recently demoed in New York, 'I Feel for You'.

Just as *Controversy* is a more commercial reworking of the themes, ideas and style of *Dirty Mind*, so Prince's eponymous second album is a more commercial sequel to his debut. Although more songs from this record have endured in his set and at least three of them are considered classics ('I Wanna Be Your Lover', 'I Feel for You' and 'Sexy Dancer'), it initially seems less satisfying than either his debut or the record that followed, *Dirty Mind* – Prince's first truly great album, and one that remains among his very best. The reason for the record's slightly second-rate feel is simple: it's too driven by sheer naked ambition – Prince's desire to finish the job he started with *For You*. He took less care over it too. Recording it in a fifth of the time he spent on the first album, and with a reduced budget, he seemed to have learnt not to indulge himself in the studio, and from then on would always move relatively fast when recording.

But while there is something mercenary about *Prince*, it's an important record in the artist's creative development. It starts brilliantly, and Prince would use the first two songs to launch himself to a wider audience in January 1980, lip-synching with the band to 'I Wanna Be Your Lover' and 'Why You Wanna Treat Me So Bad?' on the then-popular Saturday-night rock show *Midnight Special* and Dick Clark's *American Bandstand*.

The *American Bandstand* performance also included an early and important part in Prince's creation of his popular image: an interview with Dick Clark that the veteran host would later describe as the most difficult he'd ever done. Although Clark lay the blame on Prince, this was no Bill Grundy moment. Prince sounded polite and shy, as Clark interviewed him in the sort of tone avuncular hosts usually reserve for maths or chess prodigies. His questions were insulting, suggesting that Prince's music wasn't the sort of thing that usually came out of his home town, making fun of his youth (which visibly increased Prince's anxiety, as he had shaved two years off his age), joking about Matt Fink's outfit – 'The man who escaped on keyboards,' he joshed, as Fink had yet to start dressing up as a doctor and was instead wearing a striped shirt and dark glasses, which did, admittedly, make him look like a convict – and mocking his ability to play many instruments.

When Prince paused to recollect how many instruments he could play, Clark turned to the audience and made fun of him, and then questioned why he needed a band. The only moment when Prince truly appeared in any way provocative was when he answered how many years ago he recorded his demos by holding out four fingers in Clark's face. *Bandstand*'s producer Larry Klein later defended Prince, saying that the audiences who were offended by his perceived rudeness to Clark 'misinterpreted what [he thought] was basic shyness on Prince's part'.[4] Pepe Willie, however, says: 'I ripped him a new one on that one. I didn't understand that at all. He came back to Minnesota, and I said to him, "What the hell happened to you?" I was so pissed at him because the media was something we needed. I wanted him to call radio stations and thank them for playing his records. He wouldn't do that, not after Dick Clark. What happened, he got stage fright, and he told me, "That will never happen again, Pepe." From then on, in his interviews, he never talks about his family, always about music, he never talks about his friends. It's what he wants to talk about. He doesn't want anything to do with Owen Husney, which is terrible, or Chris Moon.' Though Klein suggests it was shyness, and Willie stage fright, Dickerson writes in his autobiography that it was deliberate and that Prince had instructed his band not to talk to Clark backstage before they went on. Gayle Chapman agrees that this was the real reason: 'Prince told us when he started the interview we were not to say anything. Dick Clark is a professional at his gig and he had this child on his show thinking he's being mysterious. No smiling and no talking. And I couldn't help it – Dick said my name and I smiled.'

Prince also recorded his first-ever video, for 'I Wanna Be Your Lover'.[5] The well-known footage includes Prince in a low-cut leopard-skin top, playing all the instruments and backing himself on drums as he sings in a visual recreation of the studio process. But there was also an alternative version which focused on Prince's interaction with his band. Stripped to the waist, he is dressed in baggy shorts, leg warmers and shiny boots, his hair long and glossy as he snuggles against Dez Dickerson and strokes Gayle Chapman's face as she steps out from behind her keyboards. Ultimately unreleased, it shows Prince creating an inclusive world that – while still punk and potentially shocking to Establishment adults like Clark – let the audience know that anyone was welcome to worship him. Though it stopped just outside the *Billboard* top ten, the record was Prince's first real hit.

Even more straightforward, 'Sexy Dancer' is not just about voyeurism, but sexual interaction: whether she's a stripper or a girl in a club, the lyric establishes that she's touching Prince as well as moving for him.[6] Along the same lines, but lyrically more gauche, 'When We're Dancing Close and Slow' has Prince admitting to a clinical-sounding 'sex-related fantasy', with none of the lover-man prowess he would later develop,[7] while 'With You' is Prince promising devotion for the first of a thousand times across his oeuvre.

Only one song hinted at the more complicated sexual scenarios he would explore on his next record. When appraised in the context of the era, 'Bambi' can be dismissed as a jejune sexual fantasy – a way of taking his obsession with cruel, unkind or uninterested lovers to the next level – but Prince's very simplistic lyric is more troubling when considered in the light of his later conservatism. It seems telling that he played the song a few times in the very early 1980s, dropped it during the Revolution years, then returned to it in 1990 as his act became more macho again, including it (albeit very sporadically) in his set ever since. It's always a mistake to associate the mental and emotional state of the singer delivering the song with the cool mind that's constructed the lyrics, but with its premise that heterosexual love is superior to lesbianism, and its reference to making Bambi 'bleed' in the final line, this remains a difficult song.

The rest of *Prince* is far less confrontational. 'Still Waiting', a track easily passed over on the album, became an unexpected highlight in live shows: an early example of Prince's ability, like Bob Dylan and The Grateful Dead, to completely transform a song in live performance, and it would become increasingly baroque and bizarre as he stretched it out with odd improvisations, eventually reaching a strange extreme in Monroe and Minneapolis on the 1982 *Controversy* tour. 'I Feel for You' also had an intriguing development, growing out of Prince's earliest rehearsals, when he was still influenced by his early heroes, and then being offered to and rejected by Patrice Rushen[8] before becoming a massive hit for Chaka Khan, so much so that until he reclaimed it, it was more usually associated with Khan than Prince – the first of several occasions when an artist who covered one of his songs seemed more able to wring emotion from it than Prince himself. Far less significant, 'It's Gonna Be Lonely' is a romantic ode to a Parisian woman, the start of an obsession with European sexual sophistication that prefigures similar Francophilia on Sheila E's debut and would reach full fruition in Prince's second movie, *Under the Cherry Moon*.

After the disappointment at the Capri theatre, Prince and his band had to wait nine months before being given a second chance to impress Warner Brothers. Dickerson describes these shows as an unalloyed success, noting that it was at these shows that Prince began the tradition of the 'post-show jam' that remains an essential part of his stagecraft to this day. But as successful as these shows were, Prince still struggled with live performance. Though his first tour began with two successful shows in Los Angeles, Dickerson notes that the next night they were playing to twenty people at a cowboy joint in Dallas, and the night after to an inappropriately old-school audience at an R&B club. After a few more shows Prince lost his voice and had to cancel the entire tour.

Pepe Willie says the reason why this rarely happened again was because Prince got tips in performance style from jazz singer Al Jarreau (it was also at a Jarreau gig that Prince first met Sheila E, who would later become such an important collaborator). 'Prince was asking Al how he built his vocals up, and Al said, "When you go out there on your first tour, you just turn your mike up and don't give it your all. You build everything up, then you can give it your all." But Prince was out there on the first gig giving everything he got. Then the second gig, he ain't got nothing left.'

Taking two months rest, Prince and the band returned to the road for a handful of club shows, before joining Rick James's tour as support for a fifty-date run. Chapman has particularly vivid memories of a date in Jacksonville, Florida, which she says was her 'first experience with racial inequality and racial tension. People were quite upset with me for doing some of the things I was doing with Prince onstage, although it was all choreographed and part of the show. They're screaming, "White bitch, get away from him." It's hard to ignore that when it's a few feet from the stage. At one point in the same show, the audience started to press forward and people were getting hurt, and Prince finally did the right thing and refused to play until they backed up.'

The shows were billed as a 'Battle of Funk' between Prince and Rick James. Dickerson believes that Prince easily got the best response, arguing, 'The freshness of Prince's sound, the fact that he was being touted by the black teen mags as the next matinee idol, the sheer energy and flamboyance of the band and the show . . . all just added up to us destroying the audience every night, while Rick would struggle.'[9] James, however, remembered things differently, writing in his autobiography: 'At the end of his set he'd take off his trench coat and he'd be wearing little girl's bloomers. I just died. The guys in the audience just booed the poor thing to death.'[10]

It seems odd that James would pick on Prince's dress sense to ridicule him, as his own stage wear wasn't that dissimilar: it's not as if leather chaps, a bullet belt and neckerchief is that much more sensible than Prince's trench coat and briefs. James was forced to admit that Prince's performance improved during the tour, but he argued that this was because the younger artist was cribbing from his act.

The importance of pleasing the audience – such an important part of Prince's early studio records – was even more prevalent onstage. Announcing the title of the second song, 'Why You Wanna Treat Me So Bad?', as a question before launching into it, he would change the song from a rebuke to a lover to an encouragement to an audience that was already screaming its approval. These were less rock shows than mass seductions. Before starting 'Just as Long as We're Together', in a voice noticeably softer than his singing voice (or his famously deep speaking voice), he'd sweetly enquire of the audience, 'Is everybody wet?' It was also during this tour that Matt Fink adopted his arresting onstage uniform of green scrubs, a white face mask, hat, shades and stethoscope. Although this was in 1979, the image is as indelibly 1980s as Max Headroom: this strange, jerking figure at the back of the stage, ready to take off on a synth solo whenever Prince shouts 'Doctor!' – an essential part of what makes this band so visually interesting.

The end of this particular phase in Prince's development was marked by the departure of Gayle Chapman from the band. Previous biographies have always stated that Chapman left for religious reasons and because she was troubled with a stage act that involved kissing Prince during 'Head' or by the provocative costumes with which he was presenting her, but Chapman told me, 'That's all hogwash. For years people would write that stuff in the books, and all I could say was, "They never asked me." It's not like, "I served God here, now I serve Prince." I worked for this guy, I didn't worship him. But maybe young egotistical males want that.'

Fink was shocked by Gayle's departure, but even in the midst of his increased success and fame, Prince already seemed to be thinking way beyond the current moment, with a game plan that those around him sometimes found strange. Pepe Willie remembers a perplexing meeting with Prince at First Avenue shortly after the release of his second album. 'I remember him telling me he wanted to get to a place where people couldn't find him, and I just said, "Why?"' But Willie had witnessed Prince's occasional discomfort with fans, and could see this was something that might grow stronger in future, and shape his later behaviour.

5

CREATING UPTOWN

Dez Dickerson believes that in spite of Lisa Coleman having much broader abilities as a musician than Gayle Chapman, Prince's decision to draft her into the band was also due to her being younger: 'This pattern of replacing folks with younger players would continue in the future, I believe, at least in part, due to the fact that younger folks were more pliable.'[1] Prince's interest in young collaborators has remained constant throughout his career: from 1981, when he recorded an unreleased song called 'She's Just a Baby', which *The Vault* suggests may have been inspired by his relationship with sixteen-year-old Susan Moonsie, to 2011, when he was out on the road with a new young female independent musician named Andy Allo.

It's easy to see the darker side of such relationships, but it seems that Prince is attracted to talent as much as beauty, and if the two are combined, so much the better. What must it have been like to have a woman with the incredible musical breadth and ability of nineteen-year-old Lisa Coleman come into your life at twenty-one? The Prince myth is such that we think of everyone who worked with him as being lucky to have that opportunity, and it's true that many of Prince's early records are one-man shows. But still, Coleman is arguably his most important collaborator, and clearly facilitated his musical growth from 1980 until 1986, most notably in the way she opened him up to classical music and piano-based jazz, giving him a breadth of sound that none of his competitors could rival.

When I met Coleman, a charming and self-effacing woman, in Los Angeles, she went out of her way to play down her influence on Prince, admitting that she 'kind of' introduced him to classical music but being wary of taking full credit for this, semi-seriously suggesting that it was her car that he truly coveted. 'He considered me a source for that [sort of music], and sometimes he would ask me to bring some records around. I had a great car, my pink Mercury, which had a really cool sound system in it. He'd take rides in my car and borrow it. I always had classical-music tapes, Dionne Warwick and stuff, and yeah, we turned each other on. To impress him I'd play some Mozart on the piano when he "wasn't listening". I turned him on to lots of different composers – Vaughan Williams, Mahler, Hindemith, Bill Evans and Claus Ogerman. *Symbiosis*. He was blown away.'

Soon after Coleman came into Prince's life, he wrote a song with her name. But Coleman doesn't believe that the unreleased (but much loved) song 'Lisa' is necessarily about her, saying that 'there are other girls named Lisa' and that 'it was just a girl's name that he used in a song'. She remembers the song as being recorded at a soundcheck. One song that she is certain is about her, however, is the unreleased 'Strange Way of Saying I Love U', written after the two of them had a serious argument. 'I left the house feeling kind of droopy, and when I came home later that night he was like, "I wanna play you something," and he was really sweet and cute and said, "I'm sorry I hurt your feelings." And the chorus goes, "I guess I have a strange way of saying I love you." And I was like, "Thank you," and we had a little hug and a kiss and everything was OK. That song I knew was for me for sure.'

Prince's creative processes have remained consistent throughout his career, although as his income has increased, so have his facilities. From the very beginning, Prince had gone between demoing songs at home and then working on them in the studio, but now that he had a new band, songs started to come from those sessions. Matt Fink contributed the keyboard part to 'Dirty Mind' and remembers the song coming out of a 1979 rehearsal at which Gayle Chapman was present. As would start to happen more frequently over the next few years, the song came out of a jam that was part of the band's usual warm-up and rehearsal process. Prince noticed the chords Fink was playing and told him to remember them for a later session. They rehearsed the song until midnight and then, after Fink had gone home, Prince continued working on it, showing up the next day with a finished song that would point to the direction for the rest of the album.

Fink was surprised but not concerned by the graphic content of the album that grew out of that first song, finding the finished record 'really brilliant'. Although *Dirty Mind*'s credits clearly state that the record was 'produced, arranged, composed and performed' by Prince, with Dr Fink contributing synth to 'Dirty Mind' (on which he gets a co-writing credit) and 'Head' – featuring Lisa's backing vocals – his full touring band is pictured on the inner sleeve, dressed in their stage outfits. It's surprising that he would bother to tell us their names, unless it was an ad for the upcoming tour, but this can be seen as the beginning of a period when he would move more towards collaboration.

Three other songs on the album allegedly also had outside input. Fink and Coleman contributed to 'Head', and Dez Dickerson writes in his autobiography that '"Uptown" was built on a bass groove that André wrote in rehearsal'. Dickerson also contends that 'the most clear-cut "borrowing", though, came in the form of the song "Partyup". That song was originally written by Prince's friend (ever present in the summer of '80 rehearsals) Morris Day.'[2] It seems from other accounts, however, that Dickerson slightly overstates Day's ownership of the song: if it was a collaboration, it seems likely that Prince considerably reworked the track, particularly the lyric.

For all the qualities of the first two albums, it was with *Dirty Mind* that Prince truly determined his future, producing a record that was so much more than the sum of its influences and which made a mainstream impact. Describing the record to Steve Sutherland of the *NME*, Prince seemed to hint that it was autobiographical, but that could be as much tease as truth: while Prince was grumpy in the same interview about being considered homosexual, this was a period where he preferred more to provoke than explain. Beginning in his 'daddy's car', the album's title song sets up the persona for this album, a man so fixated by sex that nothing – social taboos, conventional morality – can get in the way of his pursuit of it. And yet the record is so charming that this seems less like obsession than the ideal way to live. It helps that Prince is constantly being rejected or humiliated by women as sexually free-spirited as him. There are more synths than guitars on the album, but it's the sparse guitar that gives the most impact and makes *Dirty Mind* feel like Prince's first rock record – particularly on 'Partyup', 'Sister', and most obviously 'When You Were Mine', one of his greatest and most enduring singles, and which Prince says he wrote 'in a hotel room in Birmingham after listenin [*sic*] to John [Lennon] sing'.[3] (If this is true, it might have been on the Alabama date in April shortly before sessions for *Dirty Mind* began in earnest.) Invariably, 'Head' would be the highlight of all those early live performances, a song that relies heavily on the Oberheim – the synth that Prince would use on this album, *Controversy* and *1999*, and which Lisa played during sessions for *Purple Rain*. It's an album that moves between sulky boasts ('Do It All Night') and revelling in rejection ('Gotta Broken Heart Again'), but which is most notorious for 'Sister', a seemingly pro-incest song that is the most provocative track Prince ever recorded. Among the many ecstatic notices, Robert Christgau, the self-appointed 'dean of American rock critics', put it best, in a review that would still be being quoted when he left the *Village Voice* twenty-six years later: 'Mick Jagger should fold up his penis and go home.'

The *Dirty Mind* tour began with a month's worth of dates in December, before a three-month break and a downsizing of venues. During that break Prince performed 'Uptown' on *Saturday Night Live*. The band had grown in confidence, with Prince, Dez and André cocky punks in trench coats and Dr Fink in his scrubs. Prince ended the performance by knocking over his microphone and running from the stage, quickly followed by the rest of the band, looking more like a street gang than they ever had before.

After a rehearsal at the Shea theatre in Buffalo, New York, Prince met with Howard Bloom, who had taken over his publicity campaign and ran the most significant PR company of the late 1970s and '80s, the Howard Bloom Company. Recently, Bloom has become a prominent author dealing largely with metaphysics, and indeed, having come from a scientific background, considered working with musicians and helping them win over mass audiences as a form of field experiment in mass culture.

'Prince is normally afraid of men,' he told me. 'You can understand why. Imagine how he must have been treated in school – it must have been brutal. He's most comfortable around women. He let me into his life for three years and then he became afraid even of me, and for me that was a punishing loss.'

Prince's manager Bob Cavallo had come to Bloom because, Bloom says, at that time 'no one knew who Prince was. I had spent seven years fighting to bring down racial barriers within record companies. They were intense.' Cavallo assumed Bloom hadn't heard about Prince, but Bloom remembers that 'before Bob and I spoke about Prince I'd watched his album on the R&B charts. His record went platinum – something stunning was going on here. He was a goddamn fucking phenomenon.'

Alan Leeds, Prince's later road manager, shares with Bloom the belief that it was hard for a black artist to win a mainstream audience. 'Throughout the '80s one of his biggest challenges was to sidestep the categorisation that the media at that time would put on you as being a black artist. If you happened to be African-American, you were immediately cast into that African-American ghetto in the industry and somehow challenged to work your way out of it. Earth, Wind and Fire had managed to do so, but George Clinton, for example, had not. Prince was steadfastly determined from the beginning not to be typecast because of how restrictive the radio formats were. It wasn't the audience that was restrictive, it was the media.'

Howard Bloom had a tactic for getting an artist to a mass audience. He believed that in order to promote an artist he needed to see them in their own environment for between one and three days, interview them extremely intensely and discern their passion points. This is what he did with Prince after that rehearsal in Buffalo. 'At 2 a.m. in the morning we went backstage to a dressing room by ourselves and I interviewed Prince from two until nine in the morning and I found his imprinting points.' The first was seeing his father onstage, which Bloom says was a more personal version of what he encountered with most of the rock stars he interviewed, who were usually inspired by having watched Elvis Presley or The Beatles on *The Ed Sullivan Show*. The second was his time with André Cymone in Bernadette Anderson's basement. Bloom worked with Prince to come up with material he could use in interviews, and Prince began doing press again for the next two years, before beginning a long period of not speaking to the media.

Bloom believes that he and Bob Cavallo were an essential part of Prince's success. 'Prince had two fucking geniuses working for him. He didn't just have ordinary human beings. I was a scientist in disguise. I was as much a child prodigy as he was.' Cavallo, in turn, believes Bloom deserves more credit for having established Prince's profile. 'He would tell people, "Prince sees sex as salvation," and then you'd see that in the *Washington Post*, the *New York Times* . . . He comes up with that phrase and then ten writers use that phrase.'

Mick Jagger's interest must have been piqued by Robert Christgau's 'penis' comment – especially coming from a hard-core Stones fan who could even find something nice to say about *Dirty Work* – as he showed up to watch the young pretender when he played one of the Stones' favourite venues, New York's Ritz club, on 22 March 1981. But another of the old guard, fellow Minnesotan Bob Dylan, had already attended an earlier date on the tour – a home-town show at Sam's in Minneapolis.

Channelling Dorothy, Prince had opened the show by repeating, 'There's no place like home,' and there wasn't: his home-town shows were often the site of his most significant transformations, with a friendly audience that he would use to road-test new ideas and directions. That night Prince played two songs which still remain unreleased, 'Broken' (a sort of epilogue to 'Gotta Broken Heart Again', which he'd also do in New York) and, as an encore, 'Everybody Dance', a short version of the extended robotic improvisations he would later favour in rehearsal. When fans fantasise about which concert recording they'd most like Prince to release officially, the show at Sam's in 1981 always ranks near the top of the list.

Prince would later loosen up his stagecraft on the *Sign o' the Times* and *Lovesexy* tours, but with all the early line-ups, including The Revolution, the band would be carefully positioned on stage, the two keyboard players, Dr Fink and Lisa Coleman, on either side of the drummer, with Prince up front and centre stage, flanked by Dez Dickerson and André Cymone (soon to be replaced by Mark Brown). At this stage, the choreography was simple and 1950s-influenced, with funny routines like 'The Walk', a dance step that he'd later turn into a song for The Time.

Coleman suggested that Prince's habit of mixing up the set list, which would later become an essential part of his appeal, was partly due to them gauging the audience. 'We were wise about which shows would work. If there was too much funk music, they didn't like it, so we'd go more rock and roll. There was a good balance. Dez was such a fiery rock-guitar player. Wendy is a better funk player than Dez, but Dez could stamp on his distortion pedal and woo-eee! He'd do some of those solos and the kids would be like, "All right, rock and roll!" Prince was very good at being the mastermind. He'd say, "This is the set list for this city."'

In a fringed green vest, red neckerchief, black pants and stockings, Prince looked like one of the Village People. When Lisa recited her lines in 'Head', she did so in a sulky, lazy voice from beneath her fedora, very different from the descriptions of how Gayle Chapman performed them. Rather than being objectified, she seemed as much a hoodlum as the rest of the band.

Prince would go on to have a long relationship with Europe – he's unusual among American artists in that he generally alternates between US and European tours rather than embarking on massive world tours – and everyone who attended his first London show at the Lyceum talks about it with the same reverence that punks feel for The Sex Pistols at the 100 Club. Among the audience were Barney Hoskyns, Green Gartside, Geoff Travis,[4] Lenny Henry and the late Paula Yates. Chris Poole, who would later handle Prince's PR, went with Yates and remembers: 'Paula had seen the ads – well, everyone had seen the ads in *Billboard*, the jockstrap and the raincoat – and she insisted on going and insisted on going upstairs so she could see the jockstrap, because she couldn't see it downstairs, to see how well-filled it was.'

To coincide with Prince's arrival in the UK, 'Uptown' was released as a single, backed with an unreleased track, 'Gotta Stop (Messin' About)', a censorious song about a promiscuous woman that was more conservative than the louche, boundary-pushing material on *Dirty Mind*.

After catching Prince on the *Dirty Mind* tour, Mick Jagger invited Prince to support The Rolling Stones, the occasion of Prince's biggest-ever rejection by a mainstream rock audience, which must have been especially traumatic for brand-new member Mark Brown (soon to be renamed, in one of Prince's less inspired formations, Brown Mark). As Lisa Coleman remembers: 'It was horrible, we were booed off stage. We were so excited, we'd rehearsed our little booties off, our funky black asses. This is it, we're gonna make the big time. Yay, it's the Stones. We were booked for a few gigs, two here at the LA Coliseum. The first gig, we had high hopes. There was an incredible atmosphere, there were big stars backstage. And we lasted five minutes before being pummelled with chicken, bottles, a sea of corn, and there were all these fingers. "Fuck you, faggot," the n-word, everything horrible. Prince took off, and the rest of us thought, "What do we do now?" So we finished the song and walked off stage. This was on Friday. We were supposed to play again on Sunday and we went back to our dressing rooms and Prince bolted. He went to the airport, he flew to Minneapolis. I thought Mick Jagger talked him back, but it turned out Dez Dickerson talked to him for forty-five minutes. He told him, "We can't let them run us out of town. We've fought this stuff already – the racism, the sexism. Let's hit and quit it." The tension in the dressing room was horrible; we could've all been throwing up. I was so nervous. We hit the stage and it was like a blood sport. The second day they'd actually planned it – "Let's boo these people." They'd brought things. Shoes, apples, oranges. We stuck it out and played a short set. We played more rock and roll songs – didn't matter, it was a game for them. We did it our way and ran. But we really thought it was going to be a great opportunity for us.'

Her friend Wendy Melvoin wasn't yet a member of the band, but is very familiar with the story: 'The roster was a nightmare – J. Geils, George Thoroughgood. Just Prince and the Stones would've been different. But this was a serious rock-and-roll crowd. They didn't want to see a black guy in a bikini and a trench coat.'

The one new song Prince managed to perform in his aborted five-song set was 'Jack U Off', from *Controversy*, which was released three days after the Stones show. Of the first ten albums that most consider as the essential canon of Prince recordings, *Controversy* – while a fascinating record in its own right – initially seems the most disposable. Prince went back and forth between his home studio and two studios in Los Angeles – Hollywood Sound and Sunset Sound – while recording the album in 1981, but though it has a remarkably polished sound, it ultimately lacks the freedom of his best home recordings or the experimentation of his best studio work. Every track on the record has its charms, and several have remained an important part of Prince's live show to this day, but none feel truly essential. As with *Prince*, the intentions are clear and somewhat mercenary: the record seems designed to capitalise on the reputation he'd gained with *Dirty Mind*, while softening the lyrical content to appeal to a wider audience.

Once again, it is essentially a solo album, although Lisa Coleman has a strong presence on backing vocals, and given her contributions to The Time records, may have also provided occasional home-studio assistance here. It's the only time in the early part of his career where Prince seems to lack a coherent conceptual vision. He had already shown on *Dirty Mind* how easy it was for him to create controversial content, but now he seemed to be commenting on the phenomenon rather than pushing more boundaries. With its references to Ronald Reagan and the political climate of the early 1980s (in the brief, inconsequential vamp 'Ronnie, Talk to Russia'), it is one of his most lyrically dated records. But its sound has been plundered by several subsequent generations of electronic musicians. This is largely because so many who have followed have adopted Prince's one-man-studio approach, his vocals mainly supported by his Oberheim synth and the drum machine he started using on this record that would famously become the bedrock of his sound – the Linn LM-1.[5]

'Controversy' has become one of Prince's favourite songs to perform live. Among his first attempts to mythologise himself, it sees him spending seven minutes emphasising how hard he is to define. In the midst of all this egoism, however, he finds time to recite the Lord's Prayer (always popular with musicians, from Elvis Presley to David Bowie), answering the question he poses in the song as to whether he believes most in himself or God. While 'Controversy' is devout enough to remain in the now much more religious Prince's set, 'Sexuality' – a defiant proclamation of the importance of sex to existence – clearly troubles him, and he's tried to make amends twice, first by smuggling lines from this song into a later religious song, 'The Rainbow Children', then by changing the name of the song (and the lyrics) to suggest that 'Spirituality' is really all that you need.

As with some of the tracks on *Dirty Mind*, there have been

suggestions that 'Do Me, Baby' owed a little to André Cymone (indeed, Pepe Willie says Cymone wrote the song himself). The high point of the album, it is the template for – and best example of – all Prince's later ballads – 'International Lover', 'Scandalous', 'Insatiable', 'Shhh', and so on. The song also features two narrative elements that Prince will return to several times throughout his career: the idea of being in an empty room, and a voyeuristic focus on watching sexual acts – something that would take on extra resonance, of course, when he sung the lines to the audience, challenging the barrier between those watching and the performer.

I've always found 'Private Joy' a little creepy. There are many Prince songs about keeping his lovers away from others, and the lyrical preoccupation with confining women will prompt some of his best work, but it also disturbs. It's partly the infantilism of the lyrics, but also the reference to the love object in the song as a toy. It's not a song Prince has continued to play, and after 1982 it disappeared from the set for ever.

Throughout Prince's recordings there are frequent references to 'work' and 'play'. Initially both are synonymous with sex, and it's this that is referred to in 'Let's Work' (although there's an additional resonance of 'working' with the band being the same as playing in the band). In yet another instance of what was once largely sexual becoming religious in Prince's music, a much later song about work, 'The Work Pt. 1', refers to Christian work. It's surprising how one of Prince's most sexual records would later inspire so much of the spiritual in his music.[6] It's there in the title of 'Annie Christian' too, which includes a reference to John Lennon's shooting, only in the song he isn't killed by Mark Chapman but instead by this female personification of Satan. Prince was in New York the day Lennon was shot, and Dickerson writes about it in his autobiography, stating that the band (but not, it seems, Prince) went over to the Dakota building after it happened. Dickerson even draws an explicit connection between Prince's band and Lennon, writing: 'Here we were, these young Midwestern kids, in the Big City living our dream, when, just a few blocks away, one of the men instrumental in blazing the very trail we were on, had his dream snuffed out.'[7]

Although 'Jack U Off' was the first time a song performed by the band appeared on an album, it did not – like the later 'Computer Blue' or 'America' – emerge out of a jam. Instead, as Matt Fink remembers, it was presented to the band with Prince teaching each member how to play their parts live. For Fink, it was a significant moment in the development of the band, and he was delighted to be made more a part of the creative process, even if this rockabilly number bore little relation to most of the music Prince had recorded previously or would in the future (at least for his own records).

The strange combination of licentiousness and religious devotion that would later become Prince's signature blend was also pursued on the *Controversy* live tour, where he would begin shows with a song that has never received an official release entitled 'The Second Coming'. At the time, a film of the same name was also in the works – a combination of concert footage from a show at Bloomington's Met Center and dramatic scenes, including autobiographical material. But Prince wasn't suggesting that he is the Second Coming, instead invoking the Book of Revelation to warn of an impending apocalypse, a theme that would become even more dominant on his next album.

Focusing mainly on *Controversy* and *Dirty Mind*, the show revealed just how well those two albums complemented each other and worked together live. In later years, Prince, confident in his success and abilities, would bait and tease the audience, but for this run he was still winning them over. 'Was that all right?' he'd ask after stretching 'Do Me, Baby' to a sublime thirteen minutes, before launching into 'Controversy', a song which is all about Prince being what we want him to be. But he still had expectations. 'Don't y'all wanna play?' he'd demand minutes later, an invitation that he'd repeat at many early shows, often contrasting it with 'Let's Work'. During a charged performance of the song in Detroit, Prince would shout 'Motor city, let's work' at the audience, following it up with 'I'm not fucking around' when they failed to respond adequately.

One song from the past that still had resonance in the stage show was 'Still Waiting', which remained a regular highlight. Shortly after completing the tour, he'd duet with the woman he'd chosen as his first protégée, Sue Ann Carwell (see Chapter 6), at a home-town show at First Avenue, Prince countering the warmth of the song with the breathtakingly cold declaration, 'See, I gotta little cause to celebrate . . . my girlfriend died. She made me wait for that love too long.' Relishing the death of a teasing lover doesn't fit well with the Christian side of Prince's early music, but he was, after all, experimenting and enjoying improvisation as he precision-tooled his persona. There would be similarly dark new songs to follow too, as Prince tested boundaries and worked out exactly how much disturbance a mainstream audience could swallow. The *Controversy* album and show had featured Prince toning down his work, but for his commercial breakthrough he would balance the new softness with extremes, only in a candy-coated package that would take him to a much wider audience than ever before.

6

GIGOLOS GET LONELY TOO (PART 1)

As with Prince's own releases, the records that his protégés and friends (and, in Mayte's case, wife) have put out over the last thirty years have been of variable quality: some are considered classics of their kind (much of the output of The Time, Madhouse, The Family, Jill Jones and Sheila E), others have split opinion (Mayte's very 1990s *Child of the Sun* or Ingrid Chavez's poetic *May 19 1992*) and a few (such as Carmen Electra's debut) are regarded as less successful. But just as almost every Prince track, even the bad ones, has something of interest, so any album or song that he has major involvement with is worth seeking out. It also seems significant to a deeper understanding of Prince's creative nature that he's continued to pursue this side of his career even in the face of record-company doubts and mass public indifference.

This strand of Prince's music is driven by two major motivations: his delight in hiding from public view, something that he suggested in an early interview was proof of his modesty; and his workaholic nature – the fact that for all his interest in sports and movies, ballet and fashion, he enjoys being in a studio or onstage over anything else. But it's more than a straightforward desire to release as much as possible. It goes beyond the recording studio and into his life. In fact, it isn't stretching things too far to see Vanity, Apollonia and Sister Fate as Prince's characters, part of the novel he sings about trying (and failing) to write in the unreleased 'Moonbeam Levels'. Others have suggested it makes more sense to see them as Prince's alter egos, and indeed, Prince is believed to have renamed Denise Matthews Vanity due to her physical similarity to him. Not everyone admires Prince's work with his protégés, and several would argue that only a few of these projects are up to the quality of the main body of his output. As Alexis Taylor, the singer with Hot Chip, who initially found fame with their jokey 'Down with Prince' song, told me: 'As a producer of his own work, I rate him as one of my favourites of all time – incredibly imaginative and unique sounding. In terms of producing anyone else, he seems to mainly strive to make them sound like himself, which I guess is an inherent problem with the protégés. They are great tools for him to use but they rarely seem to have been allowed to let their own personalities to come through fully.'

Prince's first collaboration – with soul singer Sue Ann Carwell – wasn't released, but it was the start of several trends that would play an important part in his subsequent work with protégés: his 'Idolmaker' instinct, Prince's attraction to women who have proved their raw talent by winning contests;[1] his desire to write songs either from a female perspective or come up with ones that would work when sung by a woman; and his willingness to share out his stockpile of songs, never fearing he might dry up. It was also the first time he attempted to give a protégé a new identity, suggesting Carwell rename herself Suzy Stone, although unlike Denise Matthews (Vanity) or Patricia Kotero (Apollonia), Carwell refused, reluctant to have her career co-opted in this way. Pepe Willie remembers: 'He knew Sue Ann from over north. Everybody knew Sue Ann because she was really good. She was, like, seventeen. There was so much talent here in Minnesota.'

Prince and Carwell worked together on a small number of songs (conflicting reports suggest there were three, four or five), of which the most well-known are 'Make It Through the Storm', the lyrics of which were written not by Prince but by his early collaborator Chris Moon, and 'Wouldn't You Love to Love Me?'. Both songs would later be released, the former three years later as the B-side of Carwell's single 'Let Me Let You Rock Me' (without Prince's music), and the latter not until 1987, when Prince would give it to Taja Sevelle. Demo versions of the tracks (including one on Prince's very first home session) reveal them to be in the *For You* mode, reminding the listener that by nineteen Prince was a fully mature talent. It would take him a while to regress to the point where he could write a song like Vanity 6's 'Wet Dream'. Though it's not in circulation, Pepe Willie remembers Prince playing him another song he'd written for Sue Ann Carwell called 'Kiss Me Quick'.[2]

In the summer of 1979, Prince asked his management to organise studio time and took his band of the era – guitarist Dez Dickerson, bassist André Cymone, keyboardists Gayle Chapman and Matt Fink and drummer Bobby Z – to Boulder, Colorado, to work on his first planned side project, a new-wave band named The Rebels. Unlike later side projects such as Vanity 6 or The Time (or, indeed, Prince's own early albums, which he recorded mostly alone) this was a fully collaborative project. There are conflicting stories about whether the band was going to be involved in the promotion. Bobby Z has suggested that the band was intended to be like Milli Vanilli or The Monkees, but Dez Dickerson told me this was never clarified, and that they were still talking about the photo shoot when everyone got distracted by the swift progression of Prince's career.

Although the nine Rebels songs are cherished by collectors, the album was never released. But unlike many of Prince's abandoned or unreleased side projects, this is a finished project, and as such is essential to understanding Prince's early development. While the record was clearly an exploratory enterprise and produced in a relatively speedy eleven days, this doesn't mean Prince took it any less seriously, as he completed his own second album in a month. Dickerson remembers Prince taking painstaking effort over the project, with whole days given up to getting the tracking and overdubbing right. 'You', which Prince later renamed 'U' and revisited twice – recording an unreleased demo in 1987 before giving the song to Paula Abdul for her 1991 *Spellbound* album – is a simple track, with Prince telling a woman a list of things he likes about her. Even on the Rebels version you can hear the seeds of Prince's own later take on techno (although it's definitely rock), which he would display on tracks like 'Loose!', from the 1994 album *Come*, or 'The Human Body', from 1996's *Emancipation*, but by 1987 (one year *before* 'techno' was properly defined as a genre), it sounds like it's come straight outta Detroit. When Abdul does it in 1991, she retains Prince's spoken sections from the 1987 version, but the techno-stomp is toned down, and the central sense of unblinking devotion loses something of its manic quality.

Another Rebels song that refused to die is 'If I Love You Tonight'. As well as the Rebels version, there are two Prince demos of the song from 1987, and it was later covered by both Mica Paris and Mayte, who recorded two versions on her 1995 album *Child of the Sun*, one in English and the other in Spanish. The Rebels version is sung by Gayle Chapman and is a variation on Kris Kristofferson's 'Help Me Make It Through the Night' from a seemingly suicidal woman prepared to hand over her gun to a one-night stand. Chapman recalls: 'I remember being told to cry on that song. That's why my voice sounded like it did. I don't sound like that when I sing. I've never ever liked it, but I've had people to this day who've heard it and liked it, and I say, "What do you like about it? The music? The voice?" To me it grates my ears. I could do that song a million times better, but I had to choke up and try to sing.'

Prince's versions, unusually, are the weakest of the six recordings, a strange blend of the slightly syrupy style he'd adopt in the early 1990s on tracks like 'Graffiti Bridge' and the more pared-down 'Sign o' the Times' one-man bass, keyboard and drum-machine approach. Mica Paris injects a bit of sarf London grit into her version, but by the time Mayte covers it, the song's been transformed from a despondent suicidal blues into a full-on (and good) sunny house track.

'Hard to Get' is the most new-wave song, seemingly written under the inspiration of The Cars' *Candy-O* album, which was released a month before The Rebels went into the studio and no doubt was still on Prince's turntable at this time. (Dickerson, a huge fan of the band, remembers playing Cars riffs in rehearsal, and was surprised to hear that Prince has recently started covering 'Let's Go' in concert.) Although musically appealing, it's a generic rock song about a girl who won't put out. The Cars' influence is even stronger on a second version of the track, recorded in 1981 during the *Controversy* sessions. It recently emerged that Prince included a snippet of the song on a sampler tape of thirty tracks offered for other artists to record seemingly sometime in the late 1980s, so it clearly remained high in his estimation for several years.

It's disappointing the record wasn't released in 1979; just as his recordings as Madhouse reveal Prince the jazz musician, the rock underpinnings of his Rebels songs reveal Prince the new-waver and Prince the rockabilly, pre-dating the style of *Controversy* and the much later *Chaos and Disorder*, and displaying a side of his work that still remains under-represented in his main catalogue. It's also the only album Prince has been involved in where he really is just one of the band rather than merely trying to give this impression; although he'd draw inspiration from many collaborators in the future, from now on he'd always remain in command.

Some critics have seen Prince's protégés and side projects as outlets for different aspects of his music that won't fit his mainstream releases, but this seems inaccurate. Better instead to see them as spurs to further production or a laboratory for experiments likely to find their way into his own albums, and as likely to inspire worthwhile music as the record company's request for a new album. With The Rebels, Dickerson believes there may have been some concern from management about keeping the focus on Prince's burgeoning career, but later side projects and bands slotted in easily alongside Prince's own releases, and as Dickerson points out, Prince would look forward to moving from his own projects to albums where he remained incognito in the same way the average person might look forward to a holiday.

Instead of The Rebels, then, Prince's most significant early side project was the first, eponymous album by The Time, which included one song, 'Oh, Baby', that was recorded and put aside during Prince's sessions for his own second album. The six-track record features Prince in deep disguise, eschewing a song-writing credit and co-producing under the pseudonym Jamie Starr. Although The Time would evolve into a band with a very clear identity, the project initially grew, Lisa Coleman told me, out of jokes and silliness. She was living with Prince at the time, and her contribution to the album was seemingly greater than has previously been acknowledged. 'My room was upstairs,' she explains, 'so he would call me down. "Lisa, would you help me do this string part? What about these lyrics? Can you finish this verse?" He involved me. I punched him in while he was playing the drums, whatever it was.'

Coleman wasn't there on the night they decided to make

Morris Day the front man, but she remembers him as a cute freckle-faced boy with a big 'fro who would run and get them hamburgers, a left-handed drummer who loved to jam. One version of the story of The Time's genesis is that Day was offered the band as compensation for giving Prince the song 'Partyup', although Coleman says she wasn't there the night this decision was made, and Dickerson can neither confirm nor deny the rumour. Coleman says Prince never doubted that Day would rise to the challenge, although she felt 'The guy had had a huge responsibility thrust upon him and what seemed like fun and games at first became a big deal.' But he soon got into it, especially once he'd established his uniform: Stacy Adams shoes and a leopard-print jacket. Prince also made use of his live band at the time, and Matt Fink remembers playing the synthesizer solo on 'The Stick'.

As well as being an artistic success, this is one of Prince's most commercially successful side projects, initially outselling his own *Dirty Mind*. The latter is arguably the better of the two records, but *The Time* feels more sophisticated, the lengthy nine- and ten-minute songs reminiscent of the *1999* songs 'D.M.S.R.', 'Automatic' and 'Something in the Water (Does Not Compute)'. The pleasure of this album is the looseness of the jams. While a tighter song like 'Girl' pales when compared to 'Free' or 'Scandalous', long, lyrically simple tracks like 'Get It Up' (which would gain particular power when played live, Day's slinky vocals sounding wonderfully sleazy-smooth) or 'Cool' work well, encouraging the listener to settle into a groove before shocking them to attention with a weird synth squiggle.

Vanity 6, Prince's first female-fronted side project, was closer to Dirty Prince. The band, a three-piece girl group that originally consisted of Prince's girlfriend Susan Moonsie, his costume designer Brenda Bennett and Bob Cavallo's employee Jamie Shoop, who would soon be replaced by Denise Matthews, started out as The Hookers and very nearly had a lead singer named 'Vagina', but they were always a pop band, and the first song Prince wrote for the project, 'Make-Up', has an almost child-like innocence. For all his later play with male and female identities, nothing in his oeuvre seems quite as odd (or delicious) as the idea of Prince going into the studio and play-acting this song. A clear influence on Chicago house (it's a toss-up whether this track or 'Little Red Corvette' was behind Frankie Knuckles's 'Baby Wants to Ride'), the song describes a woman putting on make-up, smoking a cigarette and lounging in a camisole as she waits for her lover to call.

'Wet Dream', the other song that Prince demoed for The Hookers, has a salacious title, but aside from the labial double entendre in the first line of the second verse ('my lips start shaking') and a mild sexual analogy ('deliver the dam to the river'), it is a relatively innocuous lust song about a woman's interest in a seemingly unobtainable man, a theme Prince would return to obsessively when writing songs for his female protégées.

What gives Prince's earliest work much of its charm is his tireless subservience before unkind, promiscuous or uninterested women, and it seems surprising but sweet that when writing his first songs for women to sing, he didn't take on the persona of the unavailable lover but imagined instead a sister to his poor, sexually frustrated brothers. As the lyric describes the woman's jealousy when she sees the object of her affection taking another girl to the soda shop for ice cream, it doesn't sound much like a song for a 'hooker' to sing. And from the description in the song of money changing hands in return for fulfilment of a fantasy, it seems this 'hooker' may have fallen for a gigolo.

It took over a year for The Hookers to metamorphose into Vanity 6. During that period, Warner Brothers put out Prince's fourth album, *Controversy*, and the first record by The Time, and

Prince went back on the road (supported by The Time) for a five-month, forty-eight-date US tour. Meeting a new woman often seems to inspire new bursts of creativity or changes in direction for Prince, and in a break during the *Controversy* tour he met Denise Matthews at a backstage party (an event he'd later dramatise in *Purple Rain*), renaming her Vanity and deciding to make her the front woman for his girl-group project.

Howard Bloom remembers that on several occasions when Prince began working with a protégée, he would send her to him to go through the same process of locating the person's passion points as he'd used with Prince. 'Prince had sent me Vanity, and I went out to Minneapolis, got the whole story of her life, and then went back and trained Vanity on how to do interviews. And then in 1981 I got a call from [Prince's assistant] Jamie Shoop, and Jamie says, "I have another one of Prince's artists, and he wants you to do what you do." And I said, "I'm sick. I'm at home in bed, I'm naked." And Jamie said, "We're going to be there at eleven o'clock tomorrow, be ready." And the next morning this limousine pulls up outside my house and this guy gets out in an absolutely immaculate zoot suit, so well-pressed it looked like a stylist had been in the limo with him, and Morris walked in and one of my dogs attacked him from the front and one from the rear.'

Vanity 6's most famous song, 'Nasty Girl', may be less well-known than Prince's greatest hits, but it's among the most influential songs Prince has written. It's easy to trace a line from Madonna, who in her earliest incarnation could have been a fourth member of the band, on to Janet Jackson, whose 1986 song 'Nasty' (produced by two former members of The Time) reverses the gender from 'nasty girls' to 'nasty boys', to Britney Spears, who claimed that the track 'Boys', from her 2001 album *Britney*, had 'a kinda Prince feel to it', but actually lifts directly from 'Nasty Girl' (the song is produced by The Neptunes, and its remixed version, 'Boys (The Co-Ed Remix)', features vocals from Pharrell Williams, a producer and rapper and diehard Prince fanatic). Britney's 'Let's turn this dance floor into our own little nasty world', and repeated invocations to 'get nasty', are clear Xeroxes of Vanity's 'my own little nasty world' and 'dance nasty girls'.

The video for Vanity 6's 'Drive Me Wild' begins with Susan in bed, wearing striped pyjamas and clutching a teddy (a look later borrowed by Britney for a *Rolling Stone* cover), before Brenda and Vanity emerge from the dry ice, looking like zombie hookers, and drag her out of her bedroom and into a waiting Cadillac. The creepy 1980s porn feel of the video is emphasised by the strange guests they then meet at a party: a fat white-haired man in a cardboard crown, red cape and rude-boy T-shirt; a man in a Richard Nixon mask juggling cassettes; and various men who have mislaid their trousers or shirts. Brenda, in dog collar and chain, punches a greasy-haired dude in shades who's been coming on to her, before the whole video is revealed to be Susan's peculiar dream.

'Drive Me Wild' is another invocation to a lover, but sweet-yet-strange Susan is a less demanding sexual partner than Brenda or Vanity, closer to Prince in her willingness to please (although she lacks his sexual confidence or experience: in the lyric, she compares herself to a car, telephone, radio and baby doll, and implies she's still a virgin). What's most appealing about the song is its simplicity, and in the extended version at least, the possibility that Prince might spin out this basic track for ever. The moments of Prince's music that give me greatest pleasure are when he stretches these jams to almost ludicrous extremes (e.g. the over fifty-minute-long 'Billy', inspired by a character in *Purple Rain*, or the hour-long original version of 'Soul Psychodelicide'), where you get a sense of Prince proving his youth, energy and exuberance by matching himself against machines. It's this side of Prince that seemingly influenced the bedroom-bound musicians of Detroit, and he played as important a role in influencing techno as the more commonly name-checked Kraftwerk, Prince's greatest contribution to this style and sound being the way he combined sexuality with technology.

While working on the Vanity 6 album, Prince had also been preparing The Time's second album, released a fortnight later. While the first album cover showed the whole band, Morris Day stands alone on *What Time Is It?*, checking his watch in front of a wall covered with clocks. The record has more character than its predecessor, and although it is similarly structured, with three long dance tracks and three shorter songs, the lyrics are sharper and less generic, the concept now clearly in focus. It would be the hits from the third Time album that would fix the band in the public consciousness, but this is just as good. Prince's association with the band was now well-established, as they'd supported him on his *Controversy* tour, but once again he kept his involvement hidden, with only the co-production credit for 'The Starr Company' – the anonymous Jamie Starr's[3] new enterprise, also responsible for the Vanity 6 record – hinting at Prince's involvement.

Dickerson says that as with 'Cool' on the first album, Prince gave him the title for *What Time Is It?*'s opener, 'Wild and Loose', and he came up with the words, which Prince sexed up. The lyric has some superficial similarities with the later 'Hot Thing'. Both songs are about a man picking up a young, sexually free woman and taking her to a party. In 'Hot Thing', she's 'barely twenty-one'; in 'Wild and Loose', her 'body's saying twenty-one' but her face 'seventeen'. In 'Hot Thing', Prince tells the girl to give her folks a call because she's going to the Crystal Ball; in 'Wild and

Loose', Day gives his girl the porno-creepy instruction to tell her mother she won't be home because they have plans for her. The disturbing sense that this groupie is going to be roasted by all the members of The Time is intensified by a mid-section breakdown in which multiple male and female voices bring to life the kind of after-party an R&B thug would appreciate, but countered by the fact that the groupie is played by Vanity, who's surely more than a match for Day.

While Dickerson was shocked to hear how Prince had altered his lyric, he was even more surprised to hear the second track on the album, as its title – '777-9311' – was his phone number, recalling that he was called by 'every bozo with a telephone and a cheesy sense of humour'. Although the song's a throwaway about Day trying to get a woman's number, it was the album's biggest hit. 'Onedayi'mgonnabesomebody' is similarly disposable, a short, itchy funk song about making it big.

The nine-minute dance track 'The Walk' is a dry run for the more famous 'The Bird', introducing a new dance style to First Avenue and ending with a hilarious exchange between Day and Vanity, as he persuades her to take off her skin-tight jeans and change into the lingerie he keeps in his car's glove box (none of his girls wear gloves), only to be surprised by the size of the butt she reveals when acquiescing to his request.

The silly party mood of the first two-thirds of the album is abandoned for the last two ballads, 'Gigolos Get Lonely Too' and 'I Don't Wanna Leave You', which would have sat well on any of the first four Prince albums. 'Gigolos Get Lonely Too' is the better song, a lament from a ladykiller who wants to make love without taking off his clothes. The other ballad is another Prince song about an impossible woman, and another frustrated lover prepared to put up with anything to keep the relationship going.

Prince took Vanity 6 and The Time on tour as support when

promoting *1999*, seemingly happy now to reveal himself as puppet-master. The live versions of Vanity 6's songs didn't differ that significantly from the record, but the more shocking lyrics lost some of their power when thrown away onstage. It's unclear whether this is due to vocal weakness or whether it's a deliberate tactic, but it seems telling that when introducing 'Nasty Girl' live in Minneapolis, Vanity has to psyche herself up: 'Listen, Minneapolis, in order for me to keep up with my reputation, I want you to tell me, "Vanity is nasty . . ."'[4]

Although it's now common for Prince to play up to five hours a night, his *1999* performance was little more than an hour, just twenty minutes longer than The Time's average set, and it seems he was being genuine when describing his fear of being upstaged by his support act. Playing the best tracks from The Time's first two albums, Monte Moir's and Jimmy Jam's electro keyboards sound incredible, and there's a truly manic, unhinged energy to their audience-pleasing chicanery. 'Gigolo's Get Lonely Too' is a live highlight, spun out to twice its recorded length and with a Morris Day soliloquy about his diamonds, 'baggies' (baggy trousers) and aforementioned Stacy Adams shoes as he invites a woman onstage for a glass of wine. During this tour, a screen-writer was on the bus with them, noting down details for what would later become *Purple Rain* (although the project would see a change of writer before reaching the screen). There was also friction between the various camps, and Lisa Coleman remembers there being no doubt as to who was in charge. 'There were three buses. Vanity 6 had a bus, we had a bus and The Time had a bus. Our bus had a video machine on it, and we stopped at a truck stop and the video machine was gone. Me and Dez went onto Vanity 6's bus, and Prince was on the bus watching something with Vanity. And we said, "Hey, that's from our bus.' And he said, "They're all my buses." "Oh . . . right . . ." But that really hurt us, and we had to do the walk of shame back to our bus.'

Almost two years would pass between the second Time album and Prince's next full-length project with a protégée, Sheila E's *The Glamorous Life* (1984). In the meantime, Prince worked on tracks for the third album by The Time, *Ice Cream Castle*, released a month after Sheila E's record; reconfigured the line-up of both his backing band The Revolution and The Time, axeing Terry Lewis and Jimmy Jam; recorded (and abandoned) half a second Vanity 6 record; completed the *Purple Rain* movie and soundtrack, alongside several songs that wouldn't make it onto the released version of the album; recorded two songs for *Around the World in a Day*; recorded a number of B-sides as good as anything on his albums, including 'Erotic City', his first collaboration with Sheila E; recorded an early version of an album for a new girl band called Apollonia 6; and perhaps most significantly, had his biggest success to date with 'When Doves Cry', the first single from *Purple Rain*.

As with previous protégés, Prince presented Sheila E with songs that he'd already recorded, allowing her to replace his scratch vocal and then building up most songs around her percussion. 'The Belle of St. Mark' is another unrequited-lust song, describing Sheila's love for a teenage Parisian. 'Shortberry Strawcake' is an instrumental, with Prince's back-masked lyrics buried deep in the mix. 'Noon Rendezvous' has Sheila looking forward to a lunchtime assignation with a possibly older (or at least more experienced) lover. The crepuscular pace seems inappropriate for a song about a daytime sex session, and the lyrics are awkwardly phrased, but the biggest problem is that this is a 'Purple Rain'-style epic condensed into four minutes. Prince's own live version of the song, which took place at a rehearsal for his 1984 First Avenue birthday show, ran to fifteen minutes and transformed the track into one of his most awesomely desolate performances.

Alongside Prince's version of 'Noon Rendezvous', the only track on the album that seems worth considering as an important part of Prince's (as opposed to Sheila E's) oeuvre is the nine-minute title track, 'The Glamorous Life', which gives the album its overall concept and helped fix Sheila E's pop personality (as well as giving her a showcase for her percussion skills, particularly when played live). The album's conceit was that it was an aural movie rather than a mere record, and along with 'Oliver's House', this is the album's most obvious story-song. It has some interesting lyrical parallels with Madonna's 'Material Girl', released the following year, which takes the opposite perspective from Sheila's insistence that money only pays the rent and it's love which is for ever.

The Time's third album, *Ice Cream Castle*, released a month later, features the two songs for which the band are now best known, 'Jungle Love' and 'The Bird' (they perform both in *Purple Rain* (1984)), but the first single was 'Ice Cream Castles', in which Morris Day drops his usual 'bring me a mirror' shtick to sing about falling in love with a white woman. Prince has performed all three songs live in concert.

Nothing else on side one of *Ice Cream Castle* is as powerful. 'My Drawers' is another tedious Prince song about underwear (not his worst: that honour goes to the unreleased 'Drawers Burnin'', one of the few Prince songs I'd be happy never to hear again), while 'Chili Sauce', like The New Power Generation's much later 'Mashed Potato Girl', is a silly skit set in a restaurant (which Prince considers the funniest location in the world, although he usually makes the same joke: a man buying a restaurant just to sack the staff) and is hard to listen to now.

But it's the three songs on side two that make this The Time's most commercially and artistically successful album. 'Jungle

Love', a simple party song, remains in the band's set to this day. More evidence of Prince's love of muddling concepts comes with 'If the Kid Can't Make You Come', in which Day voices a character named 'The Kid' who seems to have no connection with Prince's character of the same name in *Purple Rain*. Among the most explicit of The Time's seduction songs, it has a long central passage in which Day removes his date's bra, admires her breasts and makes her promise never to breastfeed, before his date, played by Sharon Hughes – an actress best known for parading around in Vanity 6-style underwear in the 1983 'women-in-prison' exploitation movie *Chained Heat* – announces titty time. 'The Bird' is a celebration of yet another imaginary dance craze, and the best yet, where you can dance how you like as long as you flap your arms in the air. Prince isn't the only Minneapolis musician to write a song about a bird-based dance craze, as before his rise the city was best known for The Trashmen and their immortal 'Surfin' Bird', recently given a new lease of life by cartoon show *Family Guy*. But for all his love of party time, Prince's musical experimentation with his side projects was about to get more serious, and the events surrounding his next project, The Family, would ultimately change the direction of his music, and the course of his career, for ever.

7

ROYAL JEWELS

As if in acknowledgement that his band was starting to become more important to his studio processes, the cover of *1999* featured the partially obscured words 'anD thE rEVOLUtioN' written in mirror-writing in the 'i' of Prince's name (here produced as a 'ı'). Matt Fink has no memory of where the name for the band came from, but Dez Dickerson told me it was possibly the representation of a development in Prince's thought processes that had been going on for some time. 'It was always part of the rhetoric. He wanted a movement instead of just a band. He wanted to create that kind of mindset among the fans.' But Bobby Z has commented that at this time, Prince may have still felt some ambivalence about crediting a group, 'because there was discontent among some of the members. But he was setting the public up for something that was yet to come.'[1]

This reluctance might also have stemmed from the fact that *1999* was still essentially a solo effort, with the band (and assorted others) in the main merely providing backing vocals. *1999* is one of Prince's finest records, and perhaps closest in his oeuvre to *Sign o' the Times*, the two essentially solo records bookending a period in which The Revolution would begin to play a role in his composition process. Prince still plays much of the album live, and it showed him beginning to latch onto the more mainstream rock sound that would ensure his success throughout much of the 1980s and provide the bedrock for his legacy ever since. As

Howard Bloom remembers: 'Steve Fargnoli, Bob Cavallo and I mounted a crusade to get Prince out of the black ghetto at Warner Brothers and demonstrate that Prince was as much an FM artist – which was all-white radio – as he was a black artist.'

A double album, it has more breathing space than *Purple Rain*, and its more peculiar corners reportedly troubled Warner Brothers at first, and possibly even his management. Bloom remembers that Prince's management team were not always sure where his head was at, and would occasionally come to him for advice. 'Bob would call me and he would say, "Howard, you don't know that I have the lyrics to Prince's album. I never told you that, right? If somehow by some miracle these lyrics show up in your office tomorrow morning, can you tell me what Prince is thinking?" And the answer was, yes.'

The first song to be written (and introduced live) from *1999* was 'All the Critics Love U in New York', which Prince performed at his home-town club First Avenue, telling the audience that the song might not appear for another year (or, he threatened, six). This live version was much harder than the album version, with notable solos from Dr Fink ('Let him out of his cage!' Prince demanded), a doomy electro-funk enlivened by the sort of synth noise that bands like Black Dice would later turn into a career, coupled with a half sneer–half celebration of the blasé attitudes of New York critics that somehow sounded less like provincial anxiety than a rallying call for experimental futurism.

From the mid-1980s onwards, jazz would become an important part of Prince's sound, but in both the live and eventual studio version of this song, Prince makes it clear that his new direction follows the death of jazz, the style of music that, however profi-cient or not he might have been at it, meant most to his father. The line might also have been directed at his band. Matt Fink remembers: 'After I joined Prince, I went back to study more jazz piano. I played jazz piano between the ages of thirteen and a half and my senior year, and I decided to return to this after joining Prince's band. And he asked me what I was up to, and I told him I was having jazz lessons, and he said, "What are you doing that for?" He said he didn't want a jazz sound coming into the band. I told him I wasn't planning to do it for that reason, but because it would improve my technical chops. But later he got more into it.'

Prince's 'new direction' was not as drastic as some of the changes he would pursue later, but there was definitely an increased ambition evident on the album. While *Controversy* felt like Prince consolidating the success of *Dirty Mind* by producing a slightly watered-down sequel, this new album showed him making a definite creative progression, both in the sound of the music and the ambition of the lyrics. But as would be the case with almost every subsequent Prince album, the record would come together first through a gradual accumulation of songs, before the process picked up speed and turned into a coherent concept, with the title track written last. It's this song that hints at the precision-tooled tracks of *Purple Rain*; the rest of the album is much looser, jam-based, and though always poppy and easy on the ear, experimental.

Prince's desire to create other outlets for his creativity had almost begun to overwhelm the work he was writing for himself. The next two songs to emerge for this project – 'Let's Pretend We're Married' and 'International Lover' – were both recorded in the midst of the large amount of tracks he was preparing for Vanity 6 and The Time (see Chapter 6), with the latter originally intended for Morris Day. Both songs see Prince moving forward from the wronged or frustrated lover persona he adopted in his early lyrics – literally so in 'Let's Pretend We're Married', in which Prince tells his new lover Marsha he needs a killer blow job if it's going to help him forget the woman who just left. Although it's not clear whether Prince got as far as getting Day to sing 'International Lover', the lyric floats midway between the boasting and banter of the Time tracks and the wooziness of 'Do Me, Baby'.

Once Prince had begun to conceive of the record as a complete piece and started working on it in earnest at Los Angeles's Sunset Sound studio, he recorded his finest expression of vulnerability, 'Something in the Water (Does Not Compute)', protesting about his own uniqueness like a neglected child, and 'Automatic', the video for which features backing vocalist Jill Jones, her hair bleached blonde as she dances in her black underwear, lighting Lisa Coleman's cigarettes.[2] After five minutes Jones and Coleman join Prince on a bed. The two women strip Prince to his waist and tie him to it, whipping him as he twists and kicks. That it is Prince being tortured by Coleman and Jones rather than the other way round highlights how at this stage he was still toying with the more submissive persona found in the earlier records and witnessed rarely in his later releases.

But while Prince was publicly portraying himself as a masochist, unreleased tracks from this era reveal that he was simultaneously indulging his more sadistic side. 'Extra Loveable' and 'Lust U Always' might have caused controversy if they had made it onto the album, as both tracks feature Prince threatening rape. If we are troubled by the songs, then does the fact that having recorded them Prince has (so far) exercised self-censorship and withheld them from a wide audience excuse their content? The notion of Prince's home studio being like a laboratory has been overplayed in criticism, but it's true that he constantly refines his sexual persona throughout his career, and he does this through relentless experimentation. Part of his development was clearly a reflection of his changing status – especially the movement from sexual submissiveness to dominance that accompanies his increased power – but there's also a conscious artistic ambition and development, and in order to write later songs like 'Computer Blue', 'Darling Nikki' or 'When Doves Cry' (all brilliant explorations of sadomasochism), it's easy to argue convincingly that he needed to visit these artistic extremes.[3]

It's also true that both songs are demonstrations of disturbed mental states (indeed, with his references to a therapist and the acknowledgement that this is a dramatisation of sexual monomania, it seems clear that the singer of 'Lust U Always' is mad); and in both cases the music seems to comment on the lyrics. 'Extra Loveable' is the more troubling, mainly because, with his shout-outs to band members, it's impossible to take this song as being in character. But Prince's threat to rape the woman he's addressing (his use of the second person 'U' gains a new and unwelcome power here) is at odds with the bouncy music, although it does become more frenzied when Prince's mood turns.

As with The Doors' 'The End', 'Extra Loveable' also has an Oedipal theme, albeit reversed, with Prince suggesting that the object of his desire is so sexy and skilled that she will turn his mother lesbian and make his dead father (another clue that the song is fictional) return from the grave to have sex with her. The lyric also includes lines about bathing together which recall 'The Ballad of Dorothy Parker', but while the shared bath in that song sounded like the most fun date ever, here he's threatening to drag an unwilling partner into the tub to violate her.[4]

Bathtub-related trauma also occurs in the unreleased 'Purple Music'[5] – the lyrics of which suggest that it might have been designed to follow 'Lust U Always' on *1999* or some other proposed Prince album – in which Prince's valet (somewhat oddly) asks him what he wants to bathe in and (even more oddly) is severely distressed by Prince's (unheard) response, a surreal sadism worthy of De Sade (or American postmodernists Robert Coover and John Hawkes). Bath time will remain a preoccupation for Prince throughout his career, the most famous example being the video for *Purple Rain*'s 'When Doves Cry', which begins with Prince bathing, an interest that would continue in the live show, where he would ask the audience if they wanted to have a bath with him and climb into a tub onstage.[6]

Aside from 'Lady Cab Driver', another car-and-sex song which works as a much angrier version of 'Little Red Corvette' and in which Prince makes up for all the social, biological and economic injustices meted out on him through the power of a transformative fuck (performed as a playlet, with Jill Jones – as J.J. – playing the chauffer role), the remainder of the album was made up of lighter material: 'Delirious', a rockabilly song which had the closest musical connection to *Controversy* and worked as a perfect pop single; 'D.M.S.R.', which appeared on the soundtrack to *Risky Business*, the movie which broke fellow 1980s icon Tom Cruise; and 'Free', a more optimistic cousin to 'Nothing Compares 2 U'. And it should be noted that it wasn't just dark, sexual stuff that Prince was secretly demoing; other notable unreleased songs from the era include the aforementioned 'Moonbeam Levels', a very pretty song that combines creative inertia with anxiety about an impending apocalypse, and the simplistic but very appealing rockabilly tracks 'No Call U' and 'Turn It Up'. Playing 'D.M.S.R.' in rehearsal Prince would change the vocals – 'Everybody say Dance, Mark,[7] Sex, Hamburgers, Hot Dogs, Pizza, Root Beer, Pussy . . . that's a perfect weekend' – before working in lines from Talking Heads' 'Once in a Lifetime'[8] and talking about New York nightclubs, suggesting that he had the dance floor in mind for this song from the beginning.

But the real move forward into fully-fledged popular success and mass consciousness came thanks to the album's first two singles, '1999' and 'Little Red Corvette', the perfect culmination of the 'seduced by an older lover' strand of Prince's music that had been evident since his earliest demos in songs like 'Do You Wanna Ride?'. Both songs were recorded at the end of the sessions. Dez Dickerson remembers Prince introducing him to the new material via demos of the songs, both of which he would appear on. According to H. M. Buff, the engineer who was later given access to the original tapes of '1999', the song initially contained a Latin section similar to one in the later reworking that was edited from the original recording. Given Prince's later interest in Latin music and his long-term collaboration with Dr Clare Fischer, this is an intriguing strand of his development, suggesting for all Prince's focus on electro-funk and rock during this period, the seeds of his later sound could have been sown sooner.

'1999' is now so fully established as one of Prince's most celebrated hits that the fact that it failed to reach the top forty on its first release is almost forgotten. It wasn't until the song was re-released following the success of the album's second single, 'Little Red Corvette', that it gained the recognition it has retained to this day. 'Little Red Corvette' is and remains a signature song. Looking at how Prince managed the crossover from minor pop artist to household name, past commentators have pointed to how well his music and persona were suited to MTV. His use of explicit sexuality ensured the videos for these songs hit big on the music channel, and it remains relevant – given that Prince is an artist who works best when his music is considered not in isolation, but also by looking at the videos, live performances and myth-making that accompanied each release during his most highly regarded era – that it took the heavy rotation of his visual iconography to really push him to the masses. But these clips weren't appreciated by everyone. As 1980's video producer Sharon Oreck later commented: 'Prince's "1999" and "Little Red Corvette" were just smoke, then Prince's face, then smoke, then Prince's butt . . . they were, like, porn bad.'⁹

But it worked for the teenage viewers, and 'Little Red Corvette' was Prince's most successful song up to that point. Further propelling his journey towards mainstream ubiquity, it caught the attention of soft-rock goddess Stevie Nicks, who became determined to work with him. Throughout his career, Prince has enjoyed an affinity with eccentric female singers, from Joni Mitchell (whose 'A Case of You' he's covered) to Kate Bush (with whom he recorded on the tracks 'Why Should I Love You?', for her album *The Red Shoes*, and 'My Computer', for his *Emancipation*), collaborating with them in the studio or inviting them onto his stage. Sometimes the overture has come from Prince, but usually it's the other way round. In this case, Nicks was inspired by 'Little Red Corvette' to write 'Stand Back', which has something of the drama of 'Little Red Corvette' but is a far less lyrically interesting song, a curiously phrased lament from a lonely woman let down by her lover.¹⁰ Recently, Nicks has claimed that Prince also offered her 'Purple Rain', telling long-time Prince-watcher Jon Bream that he sent her a cassette of a long instrumental track and asked her to write lyrics for it. 'It was so overwhelming, that 10-minute track, that I listened to it and I just got scared,' Nicks explained. 'I called him back and said, "I can't do it. I wish I could. It's too much for me." I'm so glad that I didn't, because he wrote it, and it became "Purple Rain".'¹¹

Alan Leeds, who joined the *1999* tour midway through, remembers that even though it featured Prince's band, The Time and Vanity 6, Prince was already separating himself from not just the support acts, but also his own band. 'When I joined, they had already gone through two road managers, and basically they were just looking for a road manager for Prince and his band. The biggest responsibility was for the band because Prince with his

bodyguard Chick Huntsberry were actually fairly independent.'
Still, it's touching proof of the possessiveness of Prince's band
that two weeks after the release of Stevie Nicks's 'Stand Back',
they were mocking it at rehearsal, playing comic versions of it
alongside spoofs of Madness's 'Our House' and Suburban Lawns'
'Janitor'.

These rehearsals, which took place at one of several warehouses
Prince would hire as rehearsal spaces in the years before he built
his own Paisley Park complex, were for what would turn out to
be the most historically significant show of Prince's early career.
It's hard to imagine many pop stars breaking in a new mem-
ber by getting them to perform a show that would provide the
basic tracks for three songs on the next record (using a mobile
recording unit, as he'd done with The Time's 'The Bird'), but that
Prince would choose to do this with Wendy Melvoin at a home-
town benefit show reveals just how certain he was during this
era. It also reveals Prince thinking less like a musician than a film
director, confident that he could build on and change the per-
formances in the studio. From the moment she entered the band,
Melvoin would take up the role of foil to Prince previously played
by Dickerson, as essential to him in onstage closeness as Keith to
Mick or Ronson to Bowie. As she now describes it: 'We played
off each other. We wore the same suits, had the same hairdo.'
In his autobiography, Dickerson depicts this period as a time
of personal disillusionment: although *1999* had gone platinum
and their tour had been the highest grossing of the year, he had
started drinking onstage and was resentful of those he considered
bandwagon-jumpers.[12] But his departure would prompt Prince
to even greater heights[13] (as well as informing the plot of *Purple
Rain*), as he took a private home-town moment and turned it
into a story that would captivate the world.

NIKKI'S CASTLE

Bob Cavallo remembers: 'Eventually Prince became quite a handful. We had a young guy, Steve Fargnoli, who did booking for us. He worked for me, and we had to make him a partner because Prince needed twenty-four-hour coverage. And he wanted me to move to Minneapolis. He told me if I really appreciated how great he was, I'd move immediately to Minneapolis and stop beating that dead horse, and the dead horse was Earth, Wind and Fire. And I said, "I can't do it, my kids are in high school." But who would move to Minneapolis on purpose?'

Alan Leeds would, and did. At the end of the *1999* tour, he moved to Minneapolis to become what he describes as 'an offroad road manager'. 'There was a bit of a void between Prince and his management team,' Leeds explains. 'It wasn't intellectual, it was more geographical, because they were LA-based and Prince was steadfastly Minnesotan. There was a geographical separation. Prince required a full-time management presence, but the three partners in the LA firm [Cavallo, Ruffalo and Fargnoli] couldn't afford to move to Minneapolis. So they needed a liaison of sorts. The responsibilities increased tenfold because all of a sudden I was the company, because there wasn't a business structure. Prince didn't have the revenue streams to support a full-time staff, so they needed someone to be responsible for anything Prince wanted to see happen.'

These responsibilities extended not just to Prince, but also to

The Time and Vanity 6, and increased when they began working towards what would become *Purple Rain*. 'There were dance rehearsals going on, acting lessons going on. And the actual band rehearsals and recording sessions, all of which were going on in various parts of Minneapolis simultaneously.' Leeds didn't even have an office: 'Any business was conducted in the rehearsal space or my living room.'

To this day, Bob Cavallo remains impressed by the chutzpah Prince displayed when he told his management that he wanted to make a movie. 'We thought we'd done an amazing job, and the first contract was coming due. Steve was with him in Atlanta, and I said, "Tell Prince we're going to organise a contract with him for another five years." And Steve calls me and says, "You're not going to believe this. The kid says he'll sign with us, but only if you get him a major motion picture. It has to not be from some jeweller or drug dealer but has to be from a major studio, and he wants his name above the title." I can't tell you what an impossible task that was.'

Finding a director proved equally tricky. 'We got turned down by every director,' says Cavallo. 'I personally went out and talked to everybody. I was trying to sign Jamie Foley, the director of a movie called *Reckless*,[1] and Foley passed. I was in the screening room alone with one person in the back and I assumed he was a PA. And when it was over he said, "What do you think of the movie?" And I said, "It was OK. I liked it, I thought the editing was good." And he says, "Oh, I did that." And so the kid was the editor, Albert Magnoli. And he had also produced and directed this movie called *Jazz* for the USC film school. I offered it to Albert, and of course Albert passed. I said, "How can you pass? You don't have a pot to piss in. I'm going to give you the DGA minimum, which is seventy-five grand." But he said, "The script is too square, it's too TV." And I said, "No, I agree, we'll have to change it."'

Cavallo gave Magnoli a week to think about it, and they met again at a restaurant and 'he basically acted out the movie for me. He's very athletic and energetic. We were in Art's Deli, and he's jumping out the booth showing me what he's going to do. And I remember him saying to me, "Do you remember the closing scene in *The Godfather*, as Al Pacino is standing there with his son being baptised, they keep cutting to all of Pacino's enemies being killed by his guys?" He said that'll be our opening. "We'll have Prince performing that opening song and I'll introduce the characters – Apollonia, Morris, Jerome, the club owner, and Prince himself, making up and driving in his motorcycle." And I thought it was very clever.'

Much has been made of the importance of Minneapolis club First Avenue to Prince, and in a documentary to accompany the twentieth-anniversary DVD release of *Purple Rain*, various luminaries queue up to testify about Prince testing out tracks there – or sitting in on punk shows at the club's next door wing, 7th Street Entry – but while he would become forever associated with the club after using it as one of the primary settings for *Purple Rain*, the benefit for the Minnesota Dance Theatre was only the third time he'd played there. As well as giving him the tracks for 'I Would Die 4 U', 'Baby I'm a Star' and 'Purple Rain', it was first time he played 'Let's Go Crazy' and 'Computer Blue', and the only occasion that he ever played the sublime 'Electric Intercourse' in front of an audience.[2] But as far as Leeds is concerned, 'I don't think any of us had any sense, perhaps even he, that these recordings were going to become the basis of an album, much less a movie soundtrack.'

There are recordings of rehearsal versions of 'Let's Go Crazy', played in preparation for this show, which reveal both how much fun this new song was to play and also how loose it was before it sharpened into the version we know today. It seems to have started out close to a punk song – although without even the pantomime danger of something like The Damned's 'Smash It Up', a not that dissimilar song. Much of *Purple Rain* is in a slightly overwrought rock-metal register, and it's clear Prince had to drill the band to get this sound, losing a lightness of tone along the way.

Of all the songs on *Purple Rain*, 'Computer Blue' underwent the most changes in its progress from the rehearsal room to the album. Wendy Melvoin and Lisa Coleman both occasionally feel tormented about the way the song has followed them around, suggesting that it came into being in what seemed like a fairly improvisational way. What intrigues most listeners, of course, is the exchange between the two women at the start of the song. Wendy wishes 'there was something more interesting [behind it], but Prince just gave us a piece of paper and said, "Say this."' The song, she says, came together at rehearsal and was based around Lisa's lead line. 'I had a cool sound on my Oberheim that day,' Lisa tells me. 'It took us about five minutes and that was the end of it, and here we are five hundred years later. Miss Haversham . . . what does it mean?' 'We didn't even think it was this weird psychosexual lesbian thing. I had no idea,' Wendy explains.

The version of 'Computer Blue' played at the First Avenue show was twice the length of the album track, but even longer, more complicated versions of the song were also experimented with. Instead of merely containing extended guitar parts or jamming, the ideas in these longer versions are the seeds of themes and imagery that Prince would pursue more thoroughly in his later work. There is a description of a house filled with hallways associated with different emotions, including lust, insecurity, fear and hate. Prince would play with something similar on *The Gold Experience*, a record that also emphasised his interest in computers. The song features a battle of wills between Prince and Wendy, in which she suggests that the 'computer' of the song should stop thinking of women as 'butterflies' and recognise them as computers too. There are also anguished lyrics about going to church and wanting to see 'the Dawn', something that would preoccupy Prince until 1997, and which he would also make reference to in another song from this era, '17 Days'. 'Computer Blue' interconnects with another song from this period, 'Father's Song', which appeared in *Purple Rain* and which Prince frequently played during the subsequent tour. This song is co-credited to John L. Nelson, and could be an example of Prince using one of his father's piano tunes as inspiration for his own work, something that seemed particularly appropriate to this project, given Prince's fictionalisation of his family for dramatic purposes, though Matt Fink told me categorically that Prince's father wrote the bridge melody and presented it to Prince.

The song from that night's performance which didn't make *Purple Rain*, 'Electric Intercourse', is not just one of Prince's finest unreleased tracks, but is among the best songs he's ever recorded. Although he ditched the song after coming up with 'The Beautiful Ones', it's the equal of anything on the officially released album and if given a release might be as well remembered as any other track on the record aside from the title song. While the lyric feels slightly obvious – a less subtle bringing together of sexuality and machine than 'Computer Blue' – it has all the charm of 'Purple Rain' with none of the bombast.

'I Would Die 4 U' continues the 'Computer Blue' theme of women as butterflies. It's the weakest track on the album, but Prince's decision to construct the song from live performance pays off in its urgency. Oddly, Prince would later put out a ten-minute rehearsal version of the song, performed with The Revolution, Sheila E and members of her band (including Miko

Weaver, who would eventually join Prince's band) while on the *Purple Rain* tour. With its long percussion breaks, this version has a more Latin feel not entirely in keeping with the hard-rock song but providing a useful reminder that the all-conquering *Purple Rain* showcased only one side of Prince's musical style. The prominence given to Eddie Minnifield's sax solo is also notable, especially as it would be soon after this that Prince would begin working with Eric Leeds, who would move from being saxophonist in The Family into Prince's main band.

Prince's later engineer H. M. Buff told me that Prince's guitar is out of tune on 'Baby I'm a Star', presumably as a result of basing the song on the tracks recorded from live performance. An original demo version of this song exists with Prince addressing the audience, but it's not substantially different from the released version. It's the last time Prince could get away – even in character – with singing about having no money.

No matter what else he is remembered for, it seems Prince will forever be most associated with 'Purple Rain'. He has self-consciously tried to replicate it at least twice, once for the title song of his fourth movie, *Graffiti Bridge*, and later under an alias as 'Gold'. It's the first song a concert virgin wants to hear and about the last (along with 'Cream', 'Kiss' and 'Let's Go Crazy') a concert veteran wants him to play.[3] He's used it to start sets, to finish them, made it a centre point and smuggled it away a few songs in where he can't make a meal of it without derailing the show. He's said onstage that it's what people shout instead of his name at airports, and although he has played it nearly every time he's got up onstage, somehow it still retains some emotional power. It is not a song that exists as a demo, and the first time Prince played it at First Avenue it had an extra verse. He played an alternative version at a rehearsal for his twenty-sixth birthday concert known as 'Gotta Shake This Feeling', in which he sings different lyrics (some from 'Another Lonely Xmas', others which have never been used again) over the chords from the song. When he first played the song on the *Purple Rain* tour, it would often seem endless, stretched out longer and longer as he continued his vast tour of the US, a lengthy run that Prince has subsequently dismissed, telling an interviewer: '*Purple Rain* was 100 shows, and around the 75th, I went crazy . . . It was bloody back then. I won't say why but there was blood on me. They were the longest shows because you knew what was going to happen.'[4]

Albert Magnoli has commented that it was this benefit show at First Avenue that truly gave shape to the film, and that the movie's central drama grew out of his performance of this song that night. 'Months before pre-production began, I was in the First Ave, 7th St. Club in Minneapolis and heard Prince perform a rough version of "Purple Rain" on stage with The Revolution. After Prince finished his performance, I met him backstage and asked him what the song was titled. He said: "Purple Rain." I suggested that this was the song that should be used for the pivotal moment in the story, after he discovers his father shot in the basement. Prince agreed, and asked if the title of the song could also be the title of the picture. I said, "Yes," and the film from that moment on was called "Purple Rain."'[5]

Knowing that the film grew out of the song rather than vice versa ensures that we don't have to fit the meaning of the lyrics to the action of the movie, though it seems likely Prince cut the extra verse missing from the finished version of the song – in which he tells the object of his affections that he doesn't want her money or her love – in order to ensure that it could be both dedicated to his father in the movie and fit the narrative of the film. For a song that has come to define Prince, it's ironic that the song (however anthemic) is actually all about uncertainty, with Prince initially contemplating roles offered to him (a lover, a leader), before finally accepting them.

There is some confusion about how the screenplay for *Purple Rain* came to be written. One thing that does seem certain is that the initial idea for the plot of the film came from Prince – whom Barney Hoskyns observed scribbling scenarios for a film in a purple notebook while on the Triple Threat tour, when Prince took Vanity 6 and The Time with him – and that he called in screenwriter William Blinn to observe life on the road and turn it into a screenplay. But Dez Dickerson told me that an earlier screenwriter 'wrote the first version, a screenplay that was slashed and rewritten. The screenwriter was very, very observant. He was quiet and low-key, sort of innocuous. He didn't say much.'

Wendy Melvoin remembers it differently, suggesting that it was the director who shaped the story. 'It was a weird situation. *Purple Rain* was written while we were all there. The draft was written around Prince. Al Magnoli had met with everyone independently and said, "If this situation were to happen, what would you say?" And that was the script, that was how we experienced it. But it was three months. During this period we were writing and rehearsing for the *Purple Rain* tour. It happened all at once. By the time the movie was done we went out on the road for a year. There was six months of writing, rehearsing and playing and filming, but we didn't see anything. I remember having a reaction to Matt Fink because I would hear Matt saying, "God must've got Wendy's periods mixed up," and it was a dumb thing to say. I thought, "That's what you would say if you were given that scenario, Matt, *that*?"'

Dickerson was not part of this experience. 'No, I remember a handful of personal conversations. The movie was loosely based on semi-autobiographical details. Even with the dynamic in the band, the Wendy and Lisa subplot in the movie was related to the relationship between Prince and I. It was a real-life thing. I never met with William Blinn. Really it all came from Prince.'

At the same time as working on songs for *Purple Rain*, Prince was also writing and recording for a planned second Vanity 6 album, which would mutate into an Apollonia 6 record after Vanity left both *Purple Rain* and the girl band (see Chapter 21). There was some slippage between the two projects, with Prince taking 'Take Me with U' from the Apollonia record, and also writing a song called 'G-Spot', which was considered for both records. 'G-Spot' would eventually be included on Jill Jones's debut album (see Chapter 21), but works much better as a Prince demo, although it is closer to the loose sexual funk of the songs on *1999* than anything else on *Purple Rain*. The song that Prince wrote to replace 'G-Spot', 'Darling Nikki', is closer in sound to the rest of the album, but is still arrestingly different in content to the remainder of the record.

Why, for example, does Darling Nikki have a castle? Is Prince making deliberate reference to the gothic in this song of sadomasochism? (And maybe even De Sade?) Is it a goth song?[6] Has he been inspired by *Justine* or *Juliette*; is he trading on some remembered imagery found in that library of erotic literature he once claimed inspired him? Or is he simply, in this crossover rock album, parodying heavy-metal imagery? As Mark Edmundson notes in his *Nightmare on Main Street: Angels, Sadomasochism, and the Culture of the Gothic*, 'Gothic is one of the most common aesthetics for rock videos.'[7] (Although for Edmundson, it's Madonna[8] and the late Michael Jackson[9] rather than Prince who are the gothic figures.) Barney Hoskyns has pointed out that the song combines the themes of horror-inflected American sitcoms *The Munsters* and *The Addams Family*, which suggests that the gothic undercurrents are both deliberate and yet at the same time knowingly camp.[10]

We know that Prince listened to all his contemporaries on Warner Brothers; did that extend to Frank Zappa's *Zoot Allures*, put out on the label the year before Prince signed with them? And if so, did he give more than a cursory listen to 'The Torture Never Stops', which though not similar to 'Darling Nikki' in sound or lyrics, takes place in a dungeon that sounds like a hard-core version of Nikki's castle, and has a similar Sadean influence?

Or is the castle a less frightening place? Prince first started singing about castles via The Time, whose Prince-penned 'Ice Cream Castles' came from a Joni Mitchell lyric. Was this song born from the same inspiration? (Incidentally, Prince's sister Tyka also sings of wanting a castle for two in her song 'L.O.V.E.', recorded four years after 'Darling Nikki', so perhaps it was a shared childhood aspiration.) In the live version of the song Nikki goes further, leaving her panties on the stairs instead of her phone number.

One of the many wonderful things about 'Darling Nikki' is that while it ended up at number one on the Parental Music Resource Center's Filthy Fifteen (for more on this, see Chapter 21) due to its sexual content, Prince's use of back-masking – a technique they persuaded a doctor to testify against at the United States Congress – was designed not to urge his listeners to devote their souls to Satan but instead to secrete a Christian message as a coda to his salacious song. The 'mirror message' in 'Darling Nikki' actually features Prince announcing his happiness at the thought of Christ's future resurrection.[11] Whenever there is darkness in Prince's work, light is rarely far away.

*

Reading PMRC head Tipper Gore's *Raising PG Kids in an X-Rated Society* (1987) now is a genuinely baffling experience. This is partly because music has gone through so many transformations since the book was published, and also because with his forsaking of profanity and developing interest in soft jazz, Prince now seems a relatively innocuous figure. Mainly, though, it is because even at the time Prince made an odd bedfellow with Mötley Crüe and W.A.S.P. and the directors of slasher movies like *Friday the 13th* and *I Spit on Your Grave*. Indeed, Prince's own later attitudes towards the violence of Hollywood are far more extreme than those espoused by Tipper Gore.

Gore seemed to focus solely on the lyrics, missing the nature of Prince's performance, something defined brilliantly by Miles Davis in his autobiography, in which he notes, somewhat resentfully: '[Prince] gets over with everyone because he fills everyone's illusions. He's got that raunchy thing, almost like a pimp and a bitch all wrapped up in one image, that transvestite thing. But when he's singing that funky X-rated shit that he does about sex and women, he's doing it in a high-pitched voice, in almost a girl's voice. If I said "Fuck you" to somebody they would be ready to call the police. But if Prince says it in that girl-like voice he uses, then everyone says it's cute.'[12]

Following his decision to stop swearing on stage, Prince would drop 'Darling Nikki' from the set in 2001 (although he still occasionally teases the audience with the intro), but in its last live incarnation it would become more nihilistic, with dancer Geneva inhabiting the role as a porno-schoolgirl. It seems unlikely we'll ever hear Prince play this song again.

A couple of weeks after playing the benefit concert at First Avenue, Prince returned to Sunset Sound to work on the album, during which time he decided to replace 'Electric Intercourse' with a new song, 'The Beautiful Ones'. Much of his finest work appears to have been inspired by his relationship with Wendy Melvoin's sister Susannah. 'The Beautiful Ones' fits thematically with these later songs, with its references to painting and confusion about levels of commitment. An all-solo effort, it is not – as might be expected, and as would undoubtedly be the case if it were a later Prince song – a narcissistic celebration of the band or Prince's retinue but instead a faux-lament about how the important women in one's life are the least pliable – a pleasing move forward from the sexual politics of Prince's earlier work, albeit a strand that would not last beyond the late 1980s.

Purple Rain, Prince's most successful movie, is really a cinematic equivalent of the Triple Threat tour:[13] it's all about competition, and yet it's a fake competition – the only person Prince is up against is himself. When Prince and Apollonia pass a music shop, there are several mannequins, including one holding a white cloud guitar. The subtext is obvious: everyone in the film is Prince's puppet. He emphasises this again in an argument with Wendy Melvoin over a tape she wants to play him – containing the music to 'Purple Rain' – in which he communicates by holding up a monkey puppet and becoming a ventriloquist. The three competing bands in the film – The Time, The Revolution and Apollonia – are all Prince's creations, and there's a deliberate, sly tension in the film in the way he presents himself as the underdog at the mercy of Morris Day's machinations, yet maintains his superiority throughout. In the opening scene at First Avenue, Prince is second on the bill to The Time, but this means he comes first in the film, playing a full version of 'Let's Go Crazy' before the headliners do a truncated 'Jungle Love'. Although Prince has a scene where he meets Apollonia in First Avenue, deliberately echoing his first meeting with Vanity (who refused to do the film after an argument about her fee), it's Morris Day who recruits Apollonia and presides over their rehearsals. Still, although Prince has rigged the game, the subplot about Wendy's tape acknowledges that this album, unlike the ones that had preceded it, is not just a solo record but, on five of the album's nine songs at least, a group project.

Not 'When Doves Cry', though. The album's second-most memorable song (and first single) was recorded alone. Alan Leeds was present at the rehearsal when Prince first brought in a cassette of it to play to the band: 'Everyone was teasing him about the fact that there was no bass on the record, saying, "How are you going to have a hit record without a bass?" And he was boasting about how only he could do it. But all I remembered was that simple little piano hook, and I knew it was going to be a hit.' Though it had the support of his management, it wasn't the first choice for a single from some at his label. Howard Bloom remembers Bob Cavallo flying out to New York to play it to him. 'He played me a song that Russ Thyret [from Warner Brothers] wanted to put out as the first single. It was a piece of funk dreck. And then he played me "When Doves Cry", and I could feel the entire film in three and a half minutes. Bob was pushing for support to have "When Doves Cry" come out as the single.'

As well as being among Prince's most loved hits, this song has always attracted interest as being a particularly convincing portrayal of female desire, at odds with heavy rock's usually phallic trappings. But while 'When Doves Cry' was celebrated for turning its back on a certain type of male sexuality, the film of *Purple Rain* disturbed many, particularly scenes such as Morris Day's bodyguard Jerome tossing a woman into a dumpster, or Prince tricking Apollonia into jumping in a freezing lake. Asked to address this subject during an MTV interview, Prince responded: 'Wait, I didn't write *Purple Rain*, someone else did, and it was a story, a fictional story, and it should be perceived that way, and nothing else. Violence is something that happens in everyday life, and we were only telling a story. I'm not sure it was looked at that way. I don't think anything we did was unnecessary. Sometimes for the sake of humour we may have went overboard, and if that was the case, I'm sorry, but that was not the intention.'

Howard Bloom did everything he could to help the film reach a mass audience, his campaign beginning from the moment the film started shooting. 'Bob hired an LA film PR firm and hired a standard set publicist. But the set publicist wasn't doing anything, she wasn't writing anything, finding anecdotes or planting them anywhere. One of the things I did for Prince was I felt that my rivals in publicity felt they'd done a superior job if they got six stories a month; I felt I'd failed if we got less than a hundred and twenty stories a month. People don't recognise a name until they've seen it six times, they don't recognise a song until they've heard it fifteen times. So you need hundreds of repetitions to establish an artist. I found all the gossip columns I possibly could and I found all the items I possibly could and I planted a Prince item every single week. And by the time of the film Prince was gaining recognition and name value.'

In spite of this, Bloom says Prince's management was still nervous, which is unsurprising given that, as Cavallo says, he and Prince had financed the film for the entire shoot. Bloom remembers: 'I got a call from Bob Cavallo, and Bob said, "You've got to be out here by eleven o'clock tomorrow morning. We've been in the editing room, we've done everything we could to turn it into a film, and it's not a film. We're screening it for Warner Brothers tomorrow, and you have to be there."' Bloom got on a plane immediately, and his experience in the screening room was very different. 'This music pounded me in the fucking gut, and this film was one of the most amazing experiences I've ever had in my life. From the time I was a kid what I've been seeking from art is something that would do something to you utterly beyond your ability to articulate. And one of the reasons it hit at gut level was because the plot came through the music.'

In the conference room after the screening, Bloom says 'it felt like we were at a funeral. The people in the room had faces that telegraphed exactly how they felt about this film – it was a failure – and they were wondering how to tell that to Bob Cavallo. It was not something they were going to bet their careers on. They were going to roll the film out at six theatres in Arizona. The minute you hear that expression you know you've been buried alive. Then came my turn to speak, and I got up and told them, if you do anything to kill this film, you will be killing a part of history. This is going to do for film what The Beatles did for popular music in 1964, and they would sin in every conceivable way if they failed to recognise that.' Bloom concedes this wasn't the only thing that saved *Purple Rain* and that Bob Cavallo also did an enormous amount to get the movie to a mass audience, but from this meeting onwards there was a change in perception.

'Instead of rolling out in six theatres we rolled out with a hundred theatres; instead of doing a naked roll-out we did a roll-out in conjunction with MTV, which was as hot as anything. For MTV to do something with a black artist was crossing a boundary, but they did it and it worked.'

While *Purple Rain* seems to have been largely one of those rare occasions when Prince did not dig particularly deep into his archive and mostly wrote songs that did end up, in whatever form, on the album or in the film, there are a handful of other songs that weren't included on the record or in the movie, some of which received official release, such as '17 Days'[14] and 'Erotic City'.[15] Of '17 Days' Wendy remembers: 'It came out of a "Purple

Rain" rehearsal. Me and Lisa started playing a riff, and Prince started singing that melody.' Lisa adds: 'I think we were being really playful because we started doing like a reggae groove and we were twisting things around. It's like musicians, we used to bust each other's chops all the time doing polyrhythms, this feel against that feel, ended up being cool. He was like, "Hey, I kinda like this." It was written quickly. We went to his house for the final bits.'[16] But as good as '17 Days' is, it was 'Erotic City' that pointed to the direction Prince would pursue instead. A duet between him and Sheila E, it would later become the opening song (and frequent highlight) of the *Lovesexy* tour; in the middle of this heavy-rock period, he produced this dance track, one of his very best songs, notable not particularly for the lyrics but for the speeded-up vocals, a creative avenue he would take a while to explore fully. Another less well-known but equally wonderful *Purple Rain* out-take is the aforementioned 'Billy', an undeniably throwaway rock-funk jam/rehearsal that nonetheless ranks in my personal Prince top ten. Unlike other rehearsals of this nature, the song is structured and sustained, perhaps closest to the much later 'The Scandalous Sex Suite' (although, at over fifty minutes, more than twice its length) in the way Prince builds a long song around repeated themes and sequences. The simple lyrics refer to the ugly sunglasses worn by Billy in *Purple Rain*, but both Prince's vocal and his guitar-playing have rarely been finer.

Alan Leeds believes that part of Prince's motivation for making *Purple Rain* was to patch things up with his parents. 'I just saw it as a father and son trying to re-bond. The father was replicated in this film, albeit fictitiously, and Prince had a lot of respect for his father as a musician. As he got older he understood the pressures that had turned his father into who he was – very reclusive, and he wasn't a particularly happy guy. Clearly, a guy whose life hasn't turned out exactly the way he'd like it to be. But here comes his son, who is an entrée to such an extent that he gets his father dressed up in a special wardrobe to come to movie premieres and MTV specials with a *Playboy* model on each arm. It gave them a form in which to bond.'

Though *Purple Rain* featured Prince turning his past into drama, not everyone from Minneapolis appreciated it. Pepe Willie remembers: 'That's when I got pissed off at him, because Prince called me and said, "Pepe, I gotta part for you in *Purple Rain*." He said, "You're gonna be the owner of this club." I was supposed to be the club owner, but Prince never called me back. So what I did, because I do acting too, I went and auditioned on my own and got in.'

Willie also told me that the movie led to a falling out between Prince and Morris Day. 'They had an argument. I don't know what it was about. Prince was yelling at Morris "You owe me", and I'm sitting down, going, "Oh no, here we go." And then Morris starts yelling, "I owe you? If anybody owes anybody anything, you owe Pepe." And I'm going, "Oh no, why did he bring my name into it?" So Morris left the group at that time. He went to Los Angeles, and a week later he calls me up and says, "Pepe, you got to help me." So I said, "Don't sign anything, I'll be on the next plane." So I flew out to LA and started getting his affairs in order. His mother was living out there and I had to build his team, and I had to say, "OK, Morris, we got to get you management, an accountant, and I gotta talk to the record label." And that's what I did. I went up to Warner Brothers and I talked with Mo Ostin on Morris's behalf and I helped get him management.'

Surprisingly, Prince's most rock album was the first to be appropriated by rappers, with MC Hammer constructing the song 'Pray' around samples from 'When Doves Cry' and 2Pac borrowing

from 'Darling Nikki' for 'Heartz of Men'. But at the time, Prince
seemed to be aiming directly for the heartland, with a bombas-
tic live show that took in ninety-eight dates across the US and
Canada and was officially documented with *Double Live*, a video
release of a show in Syracuse broadcast live to a worldwide audi-
ence of 12 million. The recording, like the rest of the tour, con-
centrated almost exclusively on tracks from *1999* and *Purple Rain*.
A few songs into the show, there was a weird interlude where the
band played 'Yankee Doodle Dandy' and Prince teased the audi-
ence about taking them to his house and making them stay there
for ever. The show also featured a rather strange song entitled
'God' that Prince released in two versions on the US and British
editions of the 'Purple Rain' single. The vocal version, entitled
simply 'God', can also be found on the B-sides disc of 1993's *The
Hits* box set; an instrumental version entitled 'God (Love Theme
from *Purple Rain*)' is harder to track down. The song, which fea-
tures Prince debating with God, also sees him making reference
to 'The Dance Electric', a song he wrote for André Cymone. I
asked Wendy Melvoin how serious she thought Prince was in his
theological questioning. 'I felt it was showbiz for me,' she told
me. 'I did not relate personally. But part of the beauty of it back
then is that there were Jews, Mexicans, blacks, whites, gays and
straights in his band. Everyone had their own opinions and they
were tolerated and embraced.'

Lisa Coleman developed this thought. 'I felt when I first joined
the band he thought it was more important to pose questions
than to get answers, and somewhere along the line he looked at
it and now he doesn't pose the questions any more, he tells you
what the answers are. That counts a lot of people out.' Wendy
agreed: 'He always had a tendency to speak in parables. He's not
a clear talker. He can speak quickly and monosyllabically and
get to the point of what he wants, but when you get down to

really philosophical questions and get into a conversation it can become very difficult to follow. He has a different language that he's learned.'

It was this segment of the show that also concerned critics, such as Ken Tucker of the *Philadelphia Inquirer*, who noted: 'he . . . chatted with a hand-puppet and mused portentously about big issues like life, death and God'. Although in retrospect this seems like the moment when Prince conquered the world, it's worth noting that many reviews of the tour were negative, although critics were uncertain whether Prince had lost his bite (as Robert Hilburn of the *LA Times* suggested) or become too offensive (as Matt Beer of the *Detroit News*, Richard Harrington of the *Washington Post* and Martin Keller of the *Twin Cities Reader* believed).

Howard Bloom was also concerned and surprised by these segments, and remembers of this time: 'In 1984, Prince started to withdraw from us. The first time I read that struggle was when I went to see him at the Nassau Coliseum. It was another fucking brilliant performance. Prince had immaculate taste in light shows, but in the middle of that tour all of a sudden a voice came from five storeys above your head and it was the voice of God. That was the first time Prince was having an inner conversation. Prince was going through a transition from the rebel to the moralist. And as a moralist he was judging himself very harshly. He was becoming his father, but he was becoming something larger than his father – his own interpretation of his father. And calling it God. And unfortunately he left the Dionysian God behind. And Prince needed both. Otherwise he's inauthentic.'

From then on, says Bloom, 'Bob would rarely see him, I would rarely see him. The only time I would see him would be when I was backstage and I felt this tap on my right shoulder, and I looked around and a hundred feet away to my left was Prince, running and laughing. But I knew he still loved me because there was this little "Hi, Howard," but he was afraid of me.'

Towards the end of the tour, in Inglewood, Prince played a show in which he invited two of the other biggest rock stars of the era – Bruce Springsteen and Madonna – onstage to take part in a mammoth version of 'Baby, I'm a Star'. The guitar solo Springsteen played when Prince asked, 'Bruce, you wanna play something?' merely revealed how much less subtle a musician he is than the more flexible Prince. But Prince's respect for Springsteen is genuine, and he is a musician he's continued to appreciate (and go and watch live) to this day.

Prince concluded the tour in Miami, finishing the show with an announcement that seemed to indicate that he might be considering retirement. When I asked Wendy if she'd believed the talk about getting off the road for ever at the time, she laughed. 'No. Artists all say that. "I'm gonna to quit, I'm gonna retire, I'm gonna take a two-year break" – they all say it. I don't know one best-selling artist – and we fucking know them all – who doesn't say it. Just go have a sleep and a good meal.'

THERE AREN'T ANY RULES

'The earlier records sound like shit,' says Wendy Melvoin, 'but then around the time of *Around the World in a Day* the quality of the recording and mixing started stepping up.' Of course, Melvoin is a true audiophile with a straight-talking manner and she's being playful here, but it's definitely true that after *Purple Rain* Prince began to develop his studio sound further, and that *Around the World in a Day* and *Parade* are two of his richest (and most adventurous) productions, representing a break with the sound that had sustained him until this point.

Although Prince had always kept up with his peers in the charts, after the success of *Purple Rain* – to his enormous credit – he began a new process of creative growth. It seems that having conquered the world, rather than consolidate this success with another record in the same vein, he was eager to make creative progress, and part of this involved opening himself up to new influences that he had previously eschewed. Some critics, both at the time and since, have suggested that *Around the World in a Day* was a result of Prince drawing greater inspiration from white rock music, but he had been a fan of Todd Rundgren since his teenage years, and Dez Dickerson and Matt Fink had previously encouraged his interest in rock, so it wasn't quite the huge transformation it might have seemed. Alan Leeds, however, believes that 'It was both ways. A lot is written about the fact that Wendy and Lisa and to some degree Sheila E were exposing Prince to music, but I'm not so sure he didn't do it in return. They were really just increasing his vocabulary as a composer.'

And while acknowledging the incredible importance of Wendy, Lisa and Susannah Melvoin (and the other members of The Revolution) during this time, Prince remained in control throughout, and was as influenced by old favourites such as Joni Mitchell, one of Prince's most lasting influences. Talking to Morrissey in 1996, Mitchell claimed that Prince copped to this at the famous playback of the album, when the record was previewed for twenty Warner Brothers staff and Prince's father, telling her that a harmonic passage in one of the songs had been inspired by her and Larry Carlton.[1]

Nevertheless, Wendy and Lisa — of whom Howard Bloom notes, 'They were the only musicians you could walk into their hotel room and find books on their desk' — are justifiably proud of their influence on *Around the World in a Day*. I asked Wendy if the record was influenced by The Beatles, something Prince has always denied.[2] 'Prince hates The Beatles,' she said. 'My take on it is that he hated The Beatles not for the music, but for something else. Maybe because of the iconic look of them or there was something about them that didn't ring true for him and his rock stardom. But I always knew if he listened to "Dig a Pony" and "Let It Be", he'd change his mind. Period. I know the guy's taste. And "Polythene Pam", if he just sat down and listened to that stuff, he'd get it. But he thinks of "I Wanna Hold Your Hand" or "Strawberry Fields Forever" and sees them as too populist.'

But fellow Revolution member Matt Fink told me that Prince never voiced a dislike of The Beatles to him, and remembers him listening to The Beatles and the Stones and revisiting them when recording *Around the World in a Day*. So, I asked Wendy, given that many have heard echoes of *Sgt Pepper* in the record (an association seemingly encouraged by the cover art), would she still say that The Beatles were categorically not an influence on the record?

'Not for him,' she told me, before adding, in a jokey way, 'but, y'know, we did that record.' Lisa Coleman explained further: 'But even still, it wasn't really. I think we came to it honestly. It wasn't The Beatles we were referencing, it was probably the same things The Beatles were referencing. We were seeking what they sought, we weren't seeking them. Also, our brothers were a heavy influence. My brother was a world musician, he played the oud and cello and finger cymbals, darbuka hand drum. When Prince met those guys he was really blown away and impressed. It was our scene that we had going that Prince tuned into.'

I wondered if by 'our scene' Wendy and Lisa were referring to the Paisley Underground, the concurrent rock revival that threw up two bands Prince would later have associations with – Three O'Clock (whom Prince would sign to his Paisley Park label, and to whom he would give the song 'Neon Telephone') and The Bangles (to whom Prince would give 'Manic Monday') – but Wendy suggested that the connection wasn't that strong. 'Prince's ear was pricked up by The Bangles because he thought Susanna [Hoffs] was cute.'

It's important to note that while some members of The Revolution were facilitating Prince's creative growth, the three songs that he started with for the record – 'Paisley Park', 'Pop Life' and 'Temptation' – follow on naturally from the songs on *Purple Rain*. Lisa Coleman told me: '*Around the World in a Day* wasn't the title until that song came along, and that was really far into the project. He was thinking of it as "Paisley Park".'

As an album title, 'Paisley Park' sounds like a logical sequel to *Purple Rain*, encapsulating the sense of hard rock giving way to something more in tune with the Summer of Love (even if Prince would never quite get over his disdain for certain hippie indulgences). The sleeve notes claim that several of the songs were recorded at Paisley Park itself, but this was Prince bringing a fantasy to life as the actual Paisley Park complex wouldn't be completed until 1988. 'Paisley Park' is one of several Prince songs about locations that offer liberation ('Uptown', 'Roadhouse Garden', 'Graffiti Bridge', '3121', '77 Beverly Park'). In this instance, the destination was not necessarily a location but rather a state of enlightenment every listener could realise.

But even as he was heading in this direction, 'Pop Life' pulled away from the possibility of peace and love. It's a song that's continued to rub people up the wrong way – the music writer Garry Mulholland wrote recently that the track 'essentially tells the listener to shut up about not being as rich as the singer, and stop whingeing, and put up with your essentially shitty life'[3] – and is one that also marks out *Around the World in a Day* as a disguised version of the post-super-success album that often follows when an artist reaches the top and looks back down.

One of Prince's common techniques when introducing new songs is to let them emerge slowly, so that they seem to grow out of other tracks onstage. He did this with 'Temptation' on the *Purple Rain* tour, including it as part of the 'conversation with God' segment of the stage show. Whether this was merely, as Wendy Melvoin suggests, 'showbiz', or a dramatisation of Prince's genuine theological concerns of the time, it's clear that 'Temptation' (which Prince had partly written and recorded before going on tour) was his latest attempt to bring together the sacred and profane. While it's unclear how seriously he took the notion that his songs or persona might have been sinful at this stage of his career, it's clearly something he started to take more earnestly later in life.

Asked about it at the time, Prince sounded as if his religious beliefs were still fairly lightweight. To Neal Karlen he said: 'It's just so nice to know that there is someone and someplace else. And if we're wrong, and I'm wrong, and there is nothing, then big deal!' Though he did add: 'A while back, I had an experience that changed me . . . I'm going to make a film about it – not the next one, but the one after that. I think when one discovers himself, he discovers God. Or maybe it's the other way around. I'm not sure . . . It's hard to put into words. It's a feeling – someone knows when they get it. That's all I can really say.'[4] It's unclear whether this film was *Graffiti Bridge* or an unrealised project – possibly the long mooted but unmade *The Dawn* – but certainly the sequel to *Purple Rain* had a more spiritual dimension than either that film or *Under the Cherry Moon*.

Placed at the end of *Around the World in a Day* and offering the record's dramatic climax, the conversation with Christ in 'Temptation' ('Oh silly man . . .') is impossible to take seriously, and aside from trying it out during one rehearsal, Prince didn't return to it in live performance after the end of the *Purple Rain* tour. The monologue that the lyrics grew out of seems to confuse two separate impulses – a sexual threat to a woman, warning her that she needs to make up her mind whether she wants him, and a semi-penitent sinner talking to God and pleading that he is only bad because the audience enjoys it. (Later he makes reference to the Garden of Eden and original sin, which Prince would write about over and over again in the later period of his career.)

Onstage, God wouldn't speak, but Prince would make His presence known by playing (relatively) discordant piano. In 'Temptation', Prince seems to voice God himself, but with no degree of solemnity. He may threaten Prince with death, but it's not something that the listener seems expected to fret about, and after some piano and FX, he is pardoned. But some did hear genuine penitence in the song. For journalist Kyle Parks of Florida's *Evening Independent*,[5] writing in direct response to some of the negative press Prince was receiving at the time, 'Temptation' represented a new 'maturity' in Prince's music also evident in '4 the Tears in Your Eyes', a song that Prince put out two versions of, before and after the release of *Around the World in a Day*. The first version was written for the USA for Africa *We Are the World* project after Prince declined to participate in the group's 'We Are the World' single; the second was an acoustic version presented only as a video, in which he's recorded in black and white singing with Wendy and Lisa and which premiered during Live Aid (and was later chosen over the original for Prince's *The Hits/ The B-Sides* collection, and is now the only version of the song widely available). The 'maturity' Parks located in the song (and in 'Temptation') seems largely to have come from the directness of the lyrics and the straightforward Christian message.

In one of Prince's most self-referential moments, he wrote a second song, 'Hello', about the writing of the first. As Alan Leeds observed, 'somehow his decision to pass on the We Are The World session became convoluted by an ugly encounter with an overzealous paparazzo and gossip mongers had a field day'.[6] It wasn't just paparazzi and gossip-mongers who had a pop at Prince for this; the cartoonist Garry Trudeau also worked it into his ongoing *Doonesbury* series. Invited to witness the recording session, Trudeau depicts Prince calling Quincy Jones to tell him he'll contribute if he cuts out Michael Jackson's parts.[7] According to Leeds, the criticism stung Prince: 'Downright defiant about his sensitivity to world hunger, for once Prince fired back. "Hello" is one of those rare cases where he used his studio forum for personal commentary, directly answering all those who second-guessed the effort and sincerity that had gone into "4 the Tears in Your Eyes".[8] While 'Hello' is autobiographical and '4 the Tears in Your Eyes' is straightforward sermonising, both songs contrast with the cryptic qualities of *Around the World in a Day*. Trips to the Vault during this period of composition were, it seems, largely confined to B-sides, such as 'Girl', which he revamped and placed on the reverse of 'America'.

Whether it was something he was always planning or something that occurred to him during the writing, there is a deliberate narrative link between at least three songs in the album, 'Around the World in the Day' introducing the concept of a ladder to salvation, searched for in 'Temptation' and 'The Ladder'. There is also an obvious conceptual connection between this song and the hoary Led Zeppelin chestnut 'Stairway to Heaven', a band Prince mentioned to *Rolling Stone* but whom Susannah Melvoin remembers him initially hating, in the same way her sister remembers him disdaining The Beatles. 'I remember playing a Led Zeppelin record, and he was saying, "Oh, this is terrible, this is awful,"' Susannah told me, 'and I just kind of rolled my eyes and thought, "One day." He just couldn't stand it at the time. He thought it was crap.' Susannah didn't have to wait long for Prince to change his opinion, again to Neal Karlen, to whom he said that he liked psychedelia 'because that was the only period in recent history that delivered songs and colors. Led Zeppelin, for example, would make you feel differently on each song.'[9] Now, Prince regularly plays 'Whole Lotta Love' in concert.

In 'Temptation', Prince sings of 'mamas', 'papas' and a 'daughter of morality' (whoever she is). Given his recurrent use of the name 'Elektra',[10] it might seem as if the narrative of 'The Ladder', in which a sinful king is beloved by a subject of this name, is a coded return to the incest Prince sang about in 'Sister'. The song is co-credited to Prince's father, and although once again this might have been because it reminded him of something he heard in his father's music, it seems intriguing that Prince should think of his dad when singing about a king (he also addresses his father in the other song co-credited to John L. Nelson on the record, 'Around the World in a Day', telling him he wants to dance). Certainly, there is evidence of Prince trying to involve his father in his creative processes at this time, and in the *Rolling Stone* interview mentioned above, Karlen witnesses Prince taking his father a tape of music Wendy and Lisa have mixed for his father's comments.

Wendy and Lisa both remember Prince making a present to them of studio time, and he extended this kindness to Lisa's brother David in 1984, giving him two days at Sunset Sound as a birthday present. While there he recorded 'Around the World in a Day'. Later, Lisa got the cassette and played it to Prince, and in her words, 'his mind went whoosh, this is the record, and he sent for our brothers and worked on the rest of the album'. The songs recorded later in the process include 'America', 'Raspberry Beret', 'Tamborine' and 'Condition of the Heart'. David Coleman is credited as playing the cello on 'Raspberry Beret', while 'America' is a full-band performance, but 'Tamborine' and 'Condition of the Heart' are Prince playing solo.[11]

Prince recorded an alternative version of 'Around the World of the Day' which was never released and which, while still featuring much of the arrangement and instrumentation of the finished song, is a more obvious pop track. Had Prince released this version, the album might not have been considered quite such a break from his past. Having decided on his new direction, Prince trailed 'Around the World in a Day' in the *Purple Rain* tour programme, including a scribbled note with the first verse among its pages, once again leading the faithful forward with seemingly cryptic messages that later became clear.

The version of 'America' on *Around the World in a Day* is just over three minutes long, edited down from a nearly twenty-two-minute version released on the twelve-inch single. But even this 'extended version' was an edit of the original recording. '"America" came from a massive jam,' Wendy told me. 'We were playing and rehearsing for hours and hours and we hit on this one groove that we continued to play for five hours, and then subsequent days afterwards we kept referring back to it, and then Prince came in and did that "America" solo and started singing and it turned into the song we know. To this day, we can put that track on and feel that band's energy and feel what we were like at our best together – a fucking freight train. No one was like "psst . . . psst . . . psst", like those cats he plays with now. It was just a massive freight train, and no one moved from the tracks. I'm really proud of that song. It's a perfect representation of Prince and The Revolution.'

There would be many of these massive jams during this era, and indeed throughout Prince's career. 'They were like meditations, total meditations,' Wendy says. 'When the groove hit that one plateau, it was like . . . it was incredible. It would be one chord progression for hours on end. Prince would be practising a dance step or coming up with lyrics. He was grooving and playing and soloing. One chord and you'd find your place. It was like a mantra.' Lisa agrees: 'You never knew what it was. He'd say, "Groove in A. Everybody groove B flat." It was an exercise in finding the cogs, especially with funk music, where there's syncopation, so we weren't playing on top of each other. We were experts at getting in synch, two guitar players, two keyboard players. Prince would call for certain people to drop out or come back in. "Lisa, what have you got?" "Let's see, I got this." What chords, things like that. It was an exercise – band yoga, relay racing. It was great training. We became Olympic musicians. It was great.'

For the video to accompany the song, rather than lip-synch in the conventional fashion, Prince recorded a third version, this time an entirely new live performance lasting for nearly ten minutes shot in front of an audience in Nice during the filming of

Under the Cherry Moon. During the rehearsal for the performance at the Théâtre du Verdure, Prince played one of his only full performances of 'Temptation', as well as 'Pop Life', 'Paisley Park', a long version of the B-side 'Love or Money' and the *Parade* outtake 'An Honest Man'. As he did not tour *Around the World in a Day*, not returning to the road until the release of *Parade*, this gives us the best sense of what an *Around the World in a Day* show might have been like, and the fact that he was performing a full horn-driven version of 'Temptation' suggests a lost opportunity.

The records that Prince was talking about in interview around the time of recording were not by The Beatles but were records that showed artists experimenting beyond their normal styles – he also name-checked Stevie Wonder's *Journey Through the Secret Life of Plants*, Joni Mitchell's *The Hissing of Summer Lawns* and Miles Davis's later records – and it seemed that part of the purpose of this album was experimentation for experimentation's sake. If the album is ultimately slightly unsatisfying, it's less to do with the quality of the music (the album includes several of Prince's very best tracks) than the sense that Prince was both trying on other styles to see how they fit and also constructing a secret code that, once cracked, revealed very little.

Nowhere was this more apparent than in the video for 'Raspberry Beret', the first to be shot by Prince himself, which begins with him coughing, a deliberate act designed to encourage speculation about his (confessedly meaningless) motives. 'Raspberry Beret' would go on to become one of Prince's most beloved songs – though this didn't stop him reinterpreting it years later as 'Raspberry Sorbet' and singing it to Rizzo the Rat.[12] And suggesting that Susannah's tastes might have really got to him, there's that famous reference to a Led Zeppelin album title in the lyric.

Around the World in a Day may be an album about utopian

community, but the post-success isolation blues evident in 'Pop Life' also drive 'Condition of the Heart' and 'Tamborine', a pair of songs driven by a new kind of itchy approach to love and sex. Aside from its obvious qualities, 'Condition of the Heart' is significant for two reasons: with its reference to Clara Bow, it reveals the interest in Hollywood history that would in part inspire *Under the Cherry Moon*, but it was also, according to Susan Rogers,[13] written for Susannah Melvoin, Wendy's sister and a muse who would inspire much of Prince's best writing. I was present on the only occasion (to date) Prince has played 'Tamborine' live, at an after-show at the Marquee Club in London in 2002, a short, minute-long blast (he also did a barely recognisable version at rehearsal). It seemed a strange song to revive in the midst of his most spiritual tour, indicating that while explicitness was out, suggestion remained fine. On the album, in its original version, it's a silly squib about genitalia, masturbation, (pornographic, it seems) models and distaste for promiscuous women, and is the worst song on any Prince album up to this point.

Ultimately, much of *Around the World in a Day*'s importance lies in the fact that it allowed Prince to step away from the potential artistic sterility of the stadium circuit and re-emphasise his interest in experimentation. While never losing sight of his musicality and still essentially a warm, pop album, it was a worthwhile sideways step from the more histrionic rock elements of *Purple Rain*, though this wasn't necessarily what the management wanted. Bob Cavallo thinks: 'I thought *Around the World in a Day* was Prince scratching an itch. It was wonderful but it hurt *Purple Rain*. We kinda stepped on *Purple Rain*. It was too soon for the marketplace.' Prince was moving so fast during this era that the record's overall style was largely quickly abandoned. The best indication of where Prince's head was at (and how important his side projects were to his artistic development at this time) comes from a show he played at the Prom Center in St Paul with The Revolution and guests to an audience of eight hundred friends flown in from all over the US to celebrate his twenty-seventh birthday. Completely ignoring *Around the World in a Day*, which was just over a month old, he began instead with three unreleased songs from three separate projects – 'A Love Bizarre', from Sheila E's second album, 'Mutiny', a song from The Family's record, and 'Sometimes It Snows in April', which would be one of the highlights of *Parade* – before playing two non-album *Purple Rain* tour songs – 'Irresistible Bitch' and 'Possessed', a song that has appeared on video recordings but not as a studio version – The Time's 'The Bird', the aforementioned throwaway 'Drawers Burnin'' and another yet-to-be-released Sheila E song called 'Holly Rock'. While the performance of 'Mutiny' was the undoubted highlight of the evening, anyone paying attention would have noticed from the care with which Prince treated 'Sometimes It Snows in April', shouting out instructions to Wendy, Lisa, Bobby Z and Brown Mark as if he were still in rehearsal – having disguised his intentions by telling the audience to go to the bar – that it would be this song that would prove central to his next transformation.

NEW POSITION

Over the next few years of Prince's career, his work was determined as much by what he didn't release as what he did, as he moved on from discarding (or mothballing) individual tracks to jettisoning whole albums and concepts. Having received the green light from Warner Brothers for a second major movie, he employed the then-untested but later Oscar-winning screenwriter Becky Johnston to start on a script, and walked into Sunset Sound to start recording songs for a soundtrack.

It wouldn't be until two months after these initial sessions at Sunset Sound that Prince would receive the first draft of *Under the Cherry Moon*, but he'd been carrying ideas for the film around since – it seems – childhood. Susannah Melvoin told me she saw various sections from rough drafts of scenes, written by Prince, that would end up in the script, mainly 'dialogue between him and Jerome that he thought was very funny'. This dialogue included the film's most memorable scene, where Prince's character Christopher Tracy writes the nonsense words 'wrecka stow' on a napkin and asks Mary, played by Kristin Scott Thomas, what the words mean. Susannah says that Prince wrote this scene and was very proud of it. 'He couldn't wait to shoot it. I guess some of these things were jokes from when he'd been a kid.' (The 'wrecka stow' joke certainly seems to have been knocking around for a while: Paul Peterson of The Family told Dave Hill that Prince made him do the exchange the first time they met.[1]) Another exchange that may have originated with Prince (and which was cut from the finished film) is a complaint from Mary about a refined man who loves environmental tapes that 'are supposed to make you horny' but that just make her 'wanna go to the bathroom', a grumble all Prince fans will recognise from the later song 'Movie Star'.

Prince would change the title of one of the recorded songs to reflect the film, but only three of the Sunset Sound tracks (the title song 'Under the Cherry Moon', 'Do U Lie?' and 'Sometimes It Snows in April') are connected to the film's narrative in any significant way. It may even have been that he chose the songs for *Parade* precisely because they were largely so deliberately vague. He also appears to have made a conscious decision with *Parade* not to pursue the lyrical questioning that was a central part of *Around the World in a Day*, replacing the lyrical sophistication with a new focus on creating elaborate new musical arrangements. In doing so, he removed the three most ambitious songs he'd written during sessions for the album: 'All My Dreams', a song more commonly associated with the *Dream Factory*-era (see Chapter 11); 'Old Friends 4 Sale', which features Prince responding in an unusually direct way to events in his life and would, in a revised version, become the title track of a later album, but which appears so autobiographical that it could never have sound-tracked a film in which Prince was playing a fictional character; and 'Others Here with Us', one of the creepiest songs Prince has ever recorded. Utilising all the spookiest samples from the Fairlight synthesizer he started using in this period, it features the death of a baby and the suicide of a boy's uncle, and the ghosts of these two characters, whose presence is supposed to be reassuring rather than frightening.[2]

While the removal of these narrative songs seems to be a deliberate attempt to simplify the album lyrics, *Parade* is arguably

Prince's most sonically adventurous album. What really marks out its sound is the balance between the minimalism of the majority of Prince's contributions – aided on several tracks by Wendy Melvoin and Lisa Coleman (the rest of The Revolution appear as a full band only on 'Mountains', although Eric Leeds, Sheila E, Susannah Melvoin and Jonathan Coleman also contributed smaller parts to various cuts) – and the orchestral arrangements by Dr Clare Fischer.

Whether it's coincidence, deliberate design or something to which he is subconsciously drawn, Prince has often worked with musicians who are, like himself, part of a musical family. As well as the Melvoins and Colemans (not to mention Paul and Ricky Peterson or Josh and Cora Dunham, the married couple who have played with him a great deal in recent years), there is also Dr Clare Fischer and his son Brent, who have a very close working relationship. Indeed, in an echo of Prince's own relationship with his musician father and his piano, Brent's earliest memory is of being three years old and lying under the piano with the family dog while Clare was composing.

Prince first worked with Clare Fischer on his protégé project The Family's album. Several people suggested to me that they had played a role in encouraging Prince to use Fischer for this record, including Lisa Coleman and Susannah Melvoin, whose famous musician father, Mike Melvoin, knew Fischer well. Brent Fischer told me that either of these connections was possible, but that the version he heard through various engineers was that 'Paul Peterson's mother was a big Clare Fischer fan as a jazz keyboardist.'

Of his father's work with Prince, Brent notes: 'He [Prince] was very good at giving us music that was pretty much in its final state.' For the *Parade* project Prince sent a cassette of the whole album. 'Up to that point in my father's career,' Brent told me, 'for all the arrangements he'd done for The Jacksons, Switch, DeBarge, Atlantic Starr, because they didn't read or write music, they'd send him a cassette tape, and he'd have to listen to the tape and make a rough chart. And that became a lot of work for him to have to do that and also write the arrangement on a tight deadline.

'When the *Parade* project came along, it was such a long project that he decided to hire me to give him extremely detailed transcriptions. So I started transcribing those Prince songs one-by-one and giving him the kind of detail that he had been missing from his rough sketches, writing out the entire bass line, the drum fills, all the vocal parts, including background vocal parts. Everything he needed to wrap the music in a velvet cloth of a Clare Fischer arrangement.'

Prince was supposed to attend the first session they did for *Parade*. 'We figured we would get two songs recorded in the first recording session and then send them to him and continue on like that. So he was very enthusiastic and let us know that he would be there and was looking forward to meeting us and hearing the orchestra. For some reason, something in his schedule precluded him from actually being there when the date came up, so we recorded on our own and sent the tapes back to Chanhassen, where his compound was located. He called my father on the phone and said: 'If I'd been there, I might have interfered, and I like what you did so much that I will always stay away from the recording sessions.' And he has. And it's worked out really well.'

Having decided that meeting Clare Fischer might jinx the relationship, Prince took avoiding him to a surprising extreme. Brent told me: 'In 1986, my dad won a Grammy award for the best jazz vocal album, and Prince asked us to send him a copy. So we gave one of the albums to his assistant, and she told us when she handed it to him he turned his head away and said: "Just put it on. I want to hear it, but I don't want to see what Clare Fischer looks like. I have the image of Clare Fischer in my head, and I don't want to change it.'"

Prince's interest in classical music would later prompt him to write a ballet for his wedding and would inform much of his later music, but it is most easily identified in the records from this period. After Lisa Coleman had introduced Prince to Vaughan Williams and Paul Hindemith, Clare Fischer, with his own interest in a synthesis between jazz and classical (or rather, orchestral) music, represented the perfect new collaborator. 'Usually an orchestral arranger might have a symphonic background or they might have a pop or jazz background,' Brent explained, 'but my father has a fusion of both.'

Through his own private musical study, Clare Fischer discovered classical composers, including Bach, Bartók, Shostakovich, Stravinsky and Henri Dutilleux, jazz musicians like Duke Ellington and Billy Strayhorn, and 1930s boogie-woogie keyboardist Meade Lux Lewis, bringing all these influences together in his own music.

His son told me that when they first received the *Parade* tape, the song that eventually became 'Christopher Tracy's Parade' was known as 'Little Girl Wendy's Parade'.[3] Both versions of the song are intriguing in terms of Prince's theological development, in that the Devil is defeated by music, although the fact that he's driving an 'evil car' makes the conflict seem somewhat comical. This is something Prince would exaggerate on stage by doing an impersonation of the Devil driving off.[4] This is not a particularly spiritual album, but it seems Prince wanted it to take place in an atmosphere of light.

I spoke to Brent Fischer about 'I Wonder U' and Clare Fischer's contribution to the record. 'At the beginning it was so sparse,'

Brent explained, 'with little bass riffs, a little bit of percussion and just the voice, a few other very minimal sounds, and the first approach was to add a large orchestra on it. Right as we were finishing up recording that, we actually got a note from his assistant that he had decided that he'd rather not have full orchestra on this one, just a family of flutes, so my dad gave him the best family of flutes that he could ever have, and then we went in and recorded that about a week later, and the engineer said: "Just for fun, let's play both of them back at the same time." And we played it all back, and except for one or two bars it all just blended together beautifully. And that was all coincidental; it wasn't intended that the flutes would complement the string part. It's just another hallmark of good writing. We sent both of them to Prince, and he used bits and pieces of both arrangements.'

The increased influence of classical music on Prince can also be heard on the album's 'Venus De Milo', a piano instrumental to which Clare Fischer added his arrangement. For all its prettiness, it sounds like incidental music. But this strand of Prince's music would become increasingly important to his work, the piano interludes onstage eventually leading to the mostly solo-piano album *One Nite Alone* . . .

There has been some controversy about what exactly John L. Nelson contributed to the two songs for which he receives a co-writing credit on the album, 'Christopher Tracy's Parade' and 'Under the Cherry Moon', but it seems likely from what those close to Prince have said that this was in recognition of a progression in the song that echoed something he remembered from his father's piano-playing. For an album that's soundtracking a film about a gigolo – a persona Prince had previously flirted with mainly through songs for The Time – several of the songs seem overly concerned with extending an existing sexual relationship, among them 'New Position'. What Prince seems to be saying to his lover – and also his audience – is: 'Let's not get bored with each other.'

In fact, 'New Position' was an old song, a home demo from 1982, but there were plenty of harsher songs he could pull from the Vault. Which is not to say the song doesn't contain a certain degree of sexual threat: listen to Prince's porny giggle after saying 'spunk'. It's the Carribean steel drum he plays on the track that gives the song much of its lightness, underlining the new position offered by Prince the lover with a new sound offered by Prince the performer. The album also includes six songs that have continued to be an important part of Prince's live act to the present day: the aforementioned 'Venus De Milo', 'Girls & Boys', 'Mountains', 'Anotherloverholenyohead', 'Sometimes It Snows in April' and the song he's played most often in concert aside from 'Purple Rain', his number-one hit in the US, 'Kiss'.[5] Much has been made of the fact that Prince took a while to register what he'd achieved with the song, originally offering it to former Revolution member Brown Mark for his band Mazarati.[6] The arrangement of the song is credited to Mazarati's producer David Z and the band are credited for background vocals, so it seems David Z played a similar role in developing the song as members of The Revolution did with other songs from this era, although the most famous innovation of the song – the minimalist sound achieved by dropping the bass – was a later decision by Prince.[7]

'Girls & Boys', though fairly slight lyrically, is another pointer to Prince's future direction, and the first track to feature horn from Eric Leeds, evidence of the widening of his sound. It was one of the few older songs to stay in the set during the *Sign o' the Times* tour and would show up on two live Prince albums recorded many years later. On the album version, the horns are used almost like a sample, but it's a song that would long continue to evolve in performance.[8] Only two songs on the album seem to have any continuity with *Around the World in a Day*: 'Mountains' and 'Anotherloverholenyohead'. As with 'America', the similar full-band rock performance from the previous album, 'Mountains' was also released in an extended alternative, though this long-form version is far less essential than 'America'. The Revolution play this song over the end credits of *Under the Cherry Moon*, and the video for the song was a colour version of the same sequence. It shares the same symbolic, faux-fairy-tale language as 'Paisley Park', Prince filling out his imagined fantasy world. 'Anotherloverholenyohead' is lyrically an extension of 'New Position', but musically a clear return to the broader palette of *Around the World in a Day*, and it stands out even more on this record, where it's surrounded by songs that seem like little more than fragments.

Prince commentators often pick up on the difference between the reception this album received in his home country and everywhere else, Michaelangelo Matos stating: '*Parade* will always mean more in Europe than in America . . . in Europe . . . *Parade* announced Prince as a man of the world, getting his quirks across more fully, and with more nuance, than any of his previous albums.'[9] And it's true that the European critics were more welcoming of the record, with Steve Sutherland in *Melody Maker* claiming: '*Parade* eclipses anything else you'll hear this year.'[10] But there were significant exceptions, such as Prince biographer Barney Hoskyns, who in an *NME* review entitled 'Sometimes It Pisses Down in April' observed: 'I find this album laboured and trite and self-satisfied and won't be listening to it again.'[11]

The inconsequential nature of Prince's lyrics is undoubtedly part of *Parade*'s charm, but notwithstanding the fact that it's many Prince fans' favourite album, the record has a high content of essentially pretty filler. 'Under the Cherry Moon' really feels like a sketch (and Prince would cannibalise it for 'The Question of U'); 'Life Can Be So Nice' is so busy that it takes several listens to realise how little it truly contains, especially compared to all the far richer unreleased material Prince was recording at the time; and 'Do U Lie?', while musically charming, is an inconsequential nursery rhyme.

But the album does feature one of Prince's finest achievements. The phrase 'Sometimes it snows in April' was something he had been using for a while, offering it as an explanation for why he wasn't going to tour any more after concluding the *Purple Rain* run (a threat he soon rescinded) and giving it as dialogue to Tricky in the first draft of *Under the Cherry Moon*. Wendy Melvoin remembers the recording session as being one of her very favourite. 'It was Sunset Sound, Studio 3, just the three of us, one take. I think I had some of the words written. Lisa playing the piano in an isolation booth, the guitars. It was written on the spot and recorded in a couple of hours. A beautiful moment, hanging out for a while, recording at Sunset Sound.'

Although Dr Clare Fischer's arrangements are a significant part of the record, more of the orchestrations ended up in *Under the Cherry Moon* than on *Parade*. I asked Brent Fischer if they knew when Prince contacted them that much of the music they were working on was intended for a film soundtrack. 'We did know about that, but it didn't change the way my father approached it because he's never been a programmatic writer. He wasn't interested in subscribing to the idea that many film composers have that if you want something comical you use oboe, if you want something ominous you use low strings, it's how you do the writing. So in those particular instances Dad asked him to send a video of the rough take of the scene so that he could watch the scene and get a sense of what was going on in the story.' Fischer remembers secrecy being paramount. 'Prince was determined to make sure that nothing would leak out. One day the doorbell rang and there was a purple limousine out front, and he [the driver] said, "Is Clare Fischer here?" And I said, "Is that the video clip?" And the driver said, "Yeah." And I said, "That's OK, I'll take it." And he pulled it back and said, "I have specific instructions that this is to go into Clare Fischer's hands only." And so I yelled upstairs, "Dad, put your pants on, you've got to come downstairs and get this clip."'

Prince's innovative sampling of Fischer's orchestrations led to the introduction of a new criterion for how soundtrack musicians should be paid if their music was used in an incomplete fashion. 'After the movie was done, right before they released it, we got a call from Warner Brothers that he had actually taken snippets of orchestral parts and he'd chosen those little snippets to be part of the background music in the movie, and that was sort of a first in the American Federation of Musicians' history. They had to devise a formula to calculate how people should be remunerated for this new use of music.'

While he hardly wants for acclaim, Prince has yet to get full recognition for his ability to fuse (admittedly largely using Fischer's arrangements) classical and pop. In the epilogue to his study of twentieth-century classical music, *The Rest Is Noise*, *New Yorker* music critic Alex Ross argues that 'some of the liveliest reactions to twentieth-century and contemporary classical music have come from the pop arena, roughly defined,'[12] yet the artists he names are all white musicians on the artier side of rock (Sonic Youth, Radiohead, Sufjan Stevens, Joanna Newsom and Björk), with no consideration of the arguably more interesting question of how classical music has influenced black artists such as Stevie Wonder, Outkast or Prince, and this is the record on which the marriage between the two styles is most fully achieved.

*

Purple Rain (1984) will always be the definitive Prince film, but time has been kind to his second movie, *Under the Cherry Moon* (1986). Of its making, Bob Cavallo remembers: 'Because they had made this very stringent deal with *Purple Rain*, we owned everything. I made them pay us so they couldn't screw us on the back end of the film, and I made a three-picture deal where Prince had all the control. But unfortunately, then Prince became enamoured with being the next Fellini and he decided that he should co-write, even though there's no credit. He demanded that the movie not be a musical, that he die at the end and that it be in black and white.'

Alan Leeds thinks the decision to set the film in France 'might have something to do with the fact that shooting it in Europe in black and white gave him more of a licence to do that sort of theme, because it was something that was obviously unusual for a black-orientated film'. Leeds also claims the decision was influenced by Steve Fargnoli, who, he says, 'was Prince's closest confidant throughout the years. He totally understood the Prince vision.' Cavallo remembers the behind-the-scenes discussions. 'I said, "Why are we shooting in black and white?" And he told me that's what he wanted. So I say, "Why are we shooting in the South of France? We can do this in the west or the south-west or Florida." And he said, "No, I want the people in the community to see the south of France." And I said, "Then why the hell do you want to do it in black and white?"

'After *Purple Rain* and the tour of *Purple Rain*, where we played multiple dates everywhere in the country, now he was a true monster star and his creative chops were unbelievable, so he thought he could become a director, even though he had only acted in one film. So we got a great deal from Warner and forced them to do it in black and white so he got what he wanted. And some people liked it, but of course we knew it was going to be a stiff. We didn't have high hopes for the movie. We just had a good time making it. We were in the south of France, we had big-time movie-business stuff: a beautiful villa on the Cap d'Antibes and two multilingual drivers. I bought a yacht. Fargnoli found me a 93-foot Benetti and he said to me, "We'll have the yacht the whole time we're shooting the movie and then the captain can take it across to Fort Lauderdale, and between the lira and the dollar and the scarcity of that kind of boat in America you'll come away with a profit, and we'll have had a yacht and a crew of four for ten weeks. I called it 'Fiddling while Rome burned'.'"

The original director was Mary Lambert, who, though she would go on to direct several guilty-pleasure movies, including *Siesta, Pet Sematary* and *The In Crowd*, was at that time best known for her videos for Madonna. Cavallo remembers: 'I was tasked with firing her on the second day of shooting because Prince thought she wasn't good' – after which Prince himself took over direction.

Considered a turkey by most on release, and subsequently referred to in a disparaging manner even by cast members Kristin Scott Thomas and Steven Berkoff, Scott Thomas's villainous father in the film, it did find favour among some critics, especially those, like Joe Baltake of the *Philadelphia Daily News*, who could appreciate the film's Warholian qualities as deliberate (he suggested that the reason why everyone in the movie is behaving like 'a vampire in those once-trendy Warhol/Paul Morrissey horror collaborations' is because the film is a deliberate portrayal of 'the expatriate as a young zombie'[13]), and has long been a firm fan favourite.

The *Lakeland Ledger* reported that Prince approached Martin Scorsese to direct the film after the two of them met for breakfast in Paris, and that Scorsese demurred, allegedly claiming that it wasn't a good idea for 'two geniuses to work together'.[14] The quote doesn't sound quite right for Scorsese, even if made ironically, but Prince did use Scorsese's director of photography from the era, Michael Ballhaus (something Cavallo says he arranged), and the film is unusual among Prince's film and TV work in that it features him working largely with recognised talents rather than with his own retinue or untested discoveries.

Various drafts of Becky Johnston's *Under the Cherry Moon* screenplay reveal an ambition not always apparent in the final film, suggesting a similar downsizing during the film's development as occurred with the later *Graffiti Bridge*. The original draft opens with several pages of heavy-handed art-house/music-video symbolism, a note suggesting that 'we should feel as if we are moving through a dream' as the screen shows an elephant in fog, a grand piano on the edge of a cliff, the *Venus de Milo*[15] being dragged through the ocean, a full moon, a flamingo next to a canoe buried in sand, a miniature merry-go-round, a St Christopher medallion and a Ford Thunderbird car, which fits with Cavallo's suggestion that Fellini was the primary influence. The finished film ditches all this and opens in a piano bar, with Kristin Scott Thomas filling in the back story via voice-over. The set-up of the film is beguilingly simple, and it's the only one of the three full-scale Prince motion pictures to have a workable plot: Christopher Tracy and his sidekick Tricky are hustlers running out of money and decide the only way to fulfil their childhood dream of wealth is for Tracy to seduce heiress Mary Sharon.

As in *Graffiti Bridge*, handwriting plays an important role. In the opening scene, Christopher Tracy's partner, Tricky (Jerome Benton, fulfilling the sidekick/servant role he had previously played to Morris Day), sends Tracy a number of notes on napkins, advising him on how to make his piano-playing appealing to a possible conquest. Soon after, the camera lingers on facile notes that Tracy has written for his various women, and the aforementioned 'wrecka stow' scene also hinges on a written note.

Bathtubs, once again, are important, to an almost absurd extent; if Christopher Tracy is a vampire (and he does give his landlady a 'Bela Lugosi look'), then these are his coffins. Giving credence to this reading, Rebecca Blake, who directed the 'Kiss' video from the same period, remembers that 'I was on a heavy vampire kick . . . so that's where the black veil on the dancer's head [in that video] comes from.'[16]

The original plan was for Prince to cast Susannah Melvoin in Scott Thomas's role. That she didn't end up playing Mary Sharon is not something Susannah regrets. 'Thank God [Scott Thomas] did it,' Susannah told me. 'Look at where she is now. It's beautiful.' In 1997, Liz Jones wrote that Prince 'didn't seem to be aware that [Scott Thomas] was still in the acting business'.[17] If this is true (and given his cineaste leanings, it seems unlikely), he was definitely aware by 2009, when he wrote her the song 'Better with Time', which can be seen as a belated apology for the indignities of the role.

The biggest area of change during the film's editing was the ending. Howard Bloom remembers getting a call similar to the one he'd received at the time of *Purple Rain*, saying that Bob Cavallo told him: '"We're doing a screening of the film tomorrow at a theatre in Sunset Boulevard. It's one of those theatres with a little dial, and you dial the dial to your right if you like a scene and to your left if you don't. So you have constant audience feedback, and we're not really sure if this is a picture." I went to this theatre in Sunset Boulevard, and Warner Brothers had done something I would usually oppose with all my heart: they had made Prince change the ending to a happy ending. And I watched the movie and it was light but it was delightful. It wasn't a classic like *Purple Rain*, but it was damn good entertainment, and I told that to Bob outside the theatre. My chest swelled with pride in someone I loved – I really loved this movie. Then two weeks later I got another phone call: "You've got to come out here immediately. Prince has changed the ending of the film." I wasn't supposed to be able to see this, so they got me a VHS of the film, waited till the building was closed for the night and made me sit on a rug on the floor of a storage room, watching this thing on a tiny TV because they were afraid that Prince would know that I had seen it. And I thought it was a piece of shit. I knew exactly why Prince had done what he did and killed off the main character, because in his mind the main character was a scamp – dishonest, defying God and breaking the rules of morality. To become moral, to become faithful to God, he had to kill his previous self off. It was a huge mistake.'

But maybe Bloom is wrong in perceiving that Prince was focusing his criticism on his inner self. Chris Moon, Prince's earliest mentor, believes he was the real target. 'Do you remember how the movie starts?' he asked me. 'It starts out this movie is about Christopher. Christopher only cares about two things – girls and money. You know what Cherry Moon is, right? C. Moon. In the movie, he plays a guy called Christopher and he hands out his business card, and the only thing that's on the business card is a crescent moon, and the only jewellery I've ever worn is a gold crescent moon around my neck. I watched that movie a couple of times and I thought, "I'm not quite sure what the message is here, but I know who you're trying to communicate to."' Alan Leeds isn't so sure about this: 'That's like me taking credit for Leeds University.' And Bob Cavallo has an entirely different interpretation of the end of the film, believing that Prince wasn't turning his back on his fans but instead thought 'they would like the operatic emotionality of that kind of thing'.

Prince opened what became known as the Hit N Run tour with a surprise home-town show at First Avenue, a month before the release of *Parade*. As he did when playing there in 1982, and would again when premiering the *Sign o' the Times* show in 1987, he was eager to establish that this was a rehearsal. In the time between the last *Purple Rain* show at the Orange Bowl in Miami nearly a year earlier and this performance, Prince had played only three shows, and this was the first chance for a paying audience to witness the major changes he had undergone since the bombast of the *Purple Rain* tour. Just as *Parade* represented a change in his sound from the rock-orientated previous two albums, so the Hit N Run tour revealed a more playful Prince than the angst-ridden kid last seen onstage.

At the First Avenue show, Prince announced that they'd only been rehearsing a week – in reality, they'd been working on the show for a month – but he clearly felt they needed more work as he took the band back into rehearsal after the show and appeared anxious about how the show might be received, offering up further apologies throughout the performance. 'Paisley Park' sounded particularly ragged that evening, as Prince struggled and strained to make it fit, and it's a song that he performed only a handful of times on the tour, as it didn't really work in a show more focused on the *Parade* material. He turned on his band-mates too. When someone began the intro for a song not due until later in the set, he snapped: 'Man, that's what I said: you let somebody new in the band, they always want to solo.'

The mention of new people joining the band was an acknowledgement of a recent sore point. After the break-up of The Time, Prince had absorbed several new members into the band, including Jerome Benton, his right-hand man from *Under the Cherry Moon*, and would now interrupt 'Raspberry Beret' to banter with him about breast sizes, giving an early indication as to why some members of The Revolution would soon become frustrated with the new direction. Prince would use Jerome as a foil throughout the tour, seemingly in an attempt to absorb The Time into The Revolution, the childish interplay between the two of them an odd contrast to the sophisticated music Prince and his band were playing. About the change, Matt Fink says: 'I wasn't completely crazy about it, but I warmed up to it. It was a result of what happened with The Family. Paul Peterson couldn't come to an agreement for his terms of contract. Prince wanted to tie him down for seven years, or at least three years with an option, but he just wanted one year with an option. So he walked away, and Prince felt bad so he offered places in The Revolution to members of The Family.' But Fink accepts that it wasn't just kindness or guilt behind the restructuring. 'There was some creative element. The music started to need people playing horns and stuff like that.' Other additions to the band included Eric Leeds, Atlanta Bliss, and more contentiously, as dancers and on backing vocals, Wally Safford, Greg Brooks and Wendy's sister Susannah Melvoin.

The conflict that would soon emerge shouldn't, however, overshadow the brilliance of this tour, particularly the American leg. Among the hard core, there are three candidates for Prince's greatest tour: the Hit N Run/*Parade* tour of 1986, the *Lovesexy* tour, and to a lesser extent, the *One Nite Alone . . .* tour. But to a certain breed of fan, the Hit N Run/*Parade* tour easily ranks highest, largely because Prince was debuting an extraordinary amount of high-quality new material (the same would be true of the *Sign o' the Times* and The Ultimate Live Experience tours, of course, but those shows were without The Revolution). These were Prince's densest, most complicated shows. While still introducing a lot of *Parade* to an audience who would just be getting familiar with the new record, there were even more unexpected highlights to the evening: the band performing without him on the instrumental 'Alexa de Paris'; an ever-growing 'Mutiny'; and a compelling new version of the song he'd given to André Cymone the year before, 'The Dance Electric', which, performed with The Revolution and with Atlanta Bliss on Miles-like trumpet and Prince on guitar, sounded every bit as strong as any *Parade* song and in its confident demonstration of Prince's burgeoning interest in jazz-funk provided the show's highlight.

At the Warfield Theater in San Francisco, Prince made space for Eric Leeds to take control of 'Mutiny' as he asked the girls in the audience for their phone numbers, before going into the unreleased 'Dream Factory'. André Cymone appeared to sing 'The Dance Electric', but the song didn't have the power it had when he wasn't there, performed as a more straightforward rock song than it had been in Boston. The Revolution were most evident on 'Anotherloverholenyohead', Lisa's pretty piano solo working its way up through the complicated arrangement. The show was one of the longest and loosest Prince had performed to date, the tightness of the first half giving way to extended jams (including fifteen minutes of 'America') towards the end.

A week later, Prince brought the show to Los Angeles. Three of the best performances from this night – 'Automatic', 'D.M.S.R.' and 'The Dance Electric' – were released in soundboard quality by Prince's NPG Music Club as part of the seventh Ahdio (*sic*) show, and it's these recordings that should be sought out as one of two official documents of the tour, the other being Prince's birthday show in Detroit, which was recorded for a concert film, *Parade Live* – long overdue a reissue. Although only featuring an hour of the show, along with the Dortmund *Lovesexy* show it's the best video recording Prince has ever released. Only here can you get a full sense of the true power of a Prince and The Revolution show from this era. Prince on his checkerboard stage, dancing atop his piano, stripped to the waist, a show with none of the longueurs so familiar from Prince's main shows over the past decade – no stop–starts, no dead spots: when he goes to the piano, it's a dancing run to an upright organ, the whole band working as one of the most formidable machines popular music has ever seen. And while the set may be one of his more pared down, the show is still theatrical: there's as much drama in Prince's out-on-a-limb performance of 'Head'/'Electric Man' as in any of his movies.

The next two shows were an undocumented appearance in Louisville and one in Sheridan, chosen for the premiere of *Under the Cherry Moon* via a competition organised by Warner Brothers and MTV in which the winning Prince fan, who turned out to be Wyoming resident Lisa Barber, would get the premiere in their home town. Wendy Melvoin remembers: 'We had the worst flight ever from Denver to Sheridan. Everyone was praying.' 'The plane was like a VW van with wings,' Lisa Coleman adds. 'We thought we were gonna die,' says Wendy.

'We arrived at the Holiday Inn in this tiny little town,' Wendy explains. 'I got in trouble for drinking a beer, and Prince docked me a bazillion dollars.' For Lisa, 'It was so strange to go to this little town and then do a gig in the ballroom. I was up on a riser but the ceiling was so low it was right there. The keys on the synth were curved from the heat. It was so hot on that stage it fried your head. There was all this hoopla. It was a tiny hotel.'

I asked them how Prince responded to the unexpected location. 'You know what, he never let on,' says Wendy. As far as Lisa could tell, 'He didn't care. He was like, "We're gonna rock Sheridan."' (And clearly he gave it his all. He spent eight hours going round town, responding to the repeated question about how he found the place by saying 'Purple' over and over.)

The MTV special to celebrate the occasion, *Premiere Party for Prince's Under the Cherry Moon*, is priceless, playing up the contrast between the ranches and rodeos of 'Big Sky Country' and 'Prince and Hollywood' (in the form of Ray Parker Jr,

Rosanna Arquette and Joni Mitchell). The mayor of the town, Max Debolt, takes the stage to say how Prince coming to town is a natural progression from the Queen of England's recent visit (when he says that some people think nothing ever happens in this part of Wyoming, a heckler can clearly be heard shouting, 'It doesn't!'). The live performance was high-energy but clearly a struggle for the band, a six-song mini-set of which only four songs were broadcast, the stained ceiling of the town's Holiday Inn an impossible contrast to The Revolution's glamour.

After a show in Denver, the tour finished with two dates in New York. Andy Warhol attended the first and recorded in his diary: 'Prince jumped out naked, or almost, and it [was] the greatest concert I've ever seen there, just so much energy and excitement. We went into the Mike Todd Room and it was just almost empty, tables set up, reserved, and there, in a white coat and pink bellbottoms, like a Puerto Rican at a prom, *all by himself*, was Prince. He danced with each and every girl – all these weird girls in sixties dresses. Literally with *every girl*, and he wasn't even a good dancer.'[18] Among the performances Warhol would have witnessed that night was an even more intense nine-minute version of 'Mutiny' featuring the 'Ice Cream Castles' and 'the roof is on fire' chants and a brilliant autobiographical monologue about his first trip to New York, when he was taken out by his sister's boyfriend Bill and taken to Madison Square Garden and told that if he ever made it, this was where he'd play.

The next leg of the *Parade* run marked the first time Prince had toured in Europe since 1981, and it's unsurprising that these shows rate so highly with fans on this side of the Atlantic and are considered by those who saw them as Prince in his prime. The tour opened with three nights at Wembley Arena. While the set was similar to the American one, he dropped 'Mutiny' after the first two nights (admittedly the song had lost some of its charm now that it featured former backstage man and new dancer Wally 'doing the kangaroo'), replacing it with the far less compelling 'A Love Bizarre'. He had also, as at the New York shows, replaced 'The Dance Electric' with 'When Doves Cry', which also made it a far more conventional show (although the performance of this song was still one of the most bracing moments of each night).

Even after his terrible treatment at the hands of their fans, there remained an affinity between Prince and The Rolling Stones. Partly it was the friendship he had with Ron Wood, partly the moves he'd copped off Mick Jagger, but most of all, they had songs he admired, and on this tour Prince played 'Miss You' with Ron Wood and Sting at Wembley, and then again with Wood at an after-show at a club called Busby's. (He also jammed with Eric Clapton at Kensington Roof Gardens.) Prince still plays 'Miss You' to this day.

The tour continued with three nights in Rotterdam, then Copenhagen and Stockholm, the exuberance draining still further, before a show at the Zenith in Paris taped on a mobile recording unit (during a one-off performance of '17 Days', Prince announced that they were recording the show and making a record, and that night they recorded the basic track for 'It's Gonna Be a Beautiful Night'), followed by one night in Frankfurt, a night in Brussels and four more German dates. The core members of The Revolution had become increasingly unhappy, sensing that the size and importance of their roles were steadily being diminished. As Wendy Melvoin remembers: 'I was totally jealous and hurt. I was bummed by it and I ultimately knew . . . it made me realise it wasn't the band I thought it was. It wasn't a democracy; he could do whatever he wanted, crew expendable. That was the beginning of the end for us. We knew. "Wait, what is Wally doing?"' Lisa shared her astonishment: 'Those guys were carrying our luggage, and now they're onstage?' Says Wendy, 'What? Excuse me! We were making the same pay cheque too. Oh, man! This is icky. We weren't getting paid. Yeah, he was getting ready to let us go.'

I asked Matt Fink if he had any inkling of the trouble that lay ahead. 'No, it came as a surprise. His arguments with Wendy and Lisa led up to it. Wendy and Lisa didn't want to quit. It was a shock when he got rid of them and Bobby in one fell swoop. I was disappointed. He asked me if I wanted to stay or go, but he clearly stated he would understand if I left. I felt maybe he was checking to see my loyalty. But there was also a question of making a living and not wanting to depart. I tried to dissuade him. We were an established group with an identity that he was busting up. I stayed on and felt terrible. It really saddened me; it was rough. Of course, he would've been doing what he did no matter what. It didn't change him creatively, although things were definitely different after the departure of Wendy and Lisa.'

Lisa also believes that Prince's development at this time wasn't solely creative: 'I think he wanted more party time. We were too serious and into the music. We weren't wearing the sexy clothes. In the beginning I did because it was more punk and I dug that, it was cutting edge, but then it moved into . . . I didn't want to be a hoochie mama, I wasn't into it any more. It changed. I think he was trying to put the party back into it somehow.' For Wendy there was another problem: 'And there was this weird personal spilky because he was involved with my sister at the time.' Lisa agrees. 'That put a damper on things.'

The European tour was followed by four dates in Japan. The band flew out at the beginning of September. By the time they returned, The Revolution was over.

ROADHOUSE GARDEN AND
SONGS FOR SUSANNAH

For Wendy Melvoin, the end of The Revolution is easily identi-
fied: the last night of the *Parade* tour at the Yokohama stadium
in Tokyo, which climaxed with Prince smashing up his 'Purple
Rain' guitar: a symbolic act that she believed indicated his desire
to break with the band and his past.

Before this dramatic end, Prince paid tribute to the era and
everything he had gone through with his band-mates by playing
one of his most heartfelt renditions of 'Sometimes It Snows in
April', concluding the song by thanking Wendy and Lisa for their
performances. Then he actually smashed two guitars – not, it
should be noted, in Pete Townshend axe-trashing style, but for as
controlled a performer as Prince it was significant enough, drop-
ping each to the floor in anger as if it was the instrument's fault
for failing to convey the strength of his emotions on this charged
night. He also drew back his arm as if to cold-clock his band
members as he took the second guitar, a playful act that neverthe-
less prompted a flinch in response. Although he'd announced his
retirement at the end of the *Purple Rain* tour, this time the duo
realised it was serious. 'We knew, "Oh fuck, this is it,"' Wendy
told me. 'We got back to LA, and he took me and Lisa aside and
he said, "I've got to let you go." And we're like, "But we just fin-
ished five records of material." So we figured the reason he let us
go was that he'd lost control and needed to get it back.'

What was on these five records has long been the subject of

speculation. Dozens of largely unreleased songs recorded during this period circulate, along with complex theories about how the tracks might have been arranged on vinyl. Indeed, it is the period from the end of *Parade* to the release of *Sign o' the Times* on which a large part of the legend of Prince's Vault rests.

The most famous of Prince's suppressed records is *The Black Album*, an album which became one of the world's most popular bootlegs[1] because, unlike most 'lost' recordings, it was finished and relatively easily located, its dissemination spreading far beyond the usual narrow circle of tape traders. And the record did, of course, eventually get an official release. But even more venerated are the lost albums believed to have been recorded in the run-up to *Sign o' the Times* – among them *Dream Factory*, *Camille* and *Crystal Ball*.

Much of the mythology that has grown up around these lost albums can be traced back to the writings of Princeologist Per Nilsen, and seems to hinge largely on what Nilsen has described as 'assemblies' of songs that he argues were made at certain points.[2] While Nilsen has been described by Prince's former manager Alan Leeds as a 'fastidious historian' and his sessionology is the cornerstone of any serious Prince study, all the members of The Revolution that I interviewed for this book cautioned me against reading too much intent into these early configurations. 'Fans talk about *Dream Factory* and *Crystal Ball*,' Wendy Melvoin told me, 'but all of these songs weren't records. *Roadhouse Garden*, *Crystal Ball*, *Dream Factory* and all the songs from *Sign o' the Times* that we did after *Parade* was done and by the time we were let go, that's all the music that was accumulated. I don't know who's turned them into what, unless people have got hold of Prince's cassettes that he'd play in the car that he'd title for shits and giggles and it'd turn into the *Crystal Ball* record, *Dream Factory*. That's all myth.' Lisa Coleman confirms this, saying: 'It

was never that he'd come up with these as proper titles; he'd label
the cassettes after the title of the last song.' Leeds adds: 'I think
it was just a process of evolution as he continued to record and
amass this vast archive of new material. He had to wrestle with
how to shape it into an album. There were points along the way
where he thought he was there, he would sequence something.
One of those sequences was called *Crystal Ball*, and he decided
that wasn't it, and he starts again, and one of those sequences was
called *Dream Factory*, and another was *Camille*.' Leeds says as
well as tapes, there were also 'reference discs', hard shellac acetates
of an album that would be mastered for Prince to live with and
make decisions about what he wanted to change. But Leeds says
three discs of *Sign o' the Times* were presented to Warner Brothers,
who asked Prince to slim it down to a double.

Even if the 'assemblies' were put together without as much
thought as some fans would like to believe, there's no question
about the quality of the songs themselves, and the period also saw
Prince playing with different overarching concepts – like disguis-
ing himself as the hermaphrodite Camille. 'There are loads of
those [songs] sitting around, including "Go", "Teacher, Teacher",
all those songs,' Wendy told me. 'That was the busiest time for
the three of us, pounding away in the south of France. When
Sign o' the Times was almost done, that's when he fired everybody.
I don't have any specifics other than this was a really busy time
when we were constantly recording.' Matt Fink agrees. 'There
were a few things that were worked on.'

Fink doesn't remember all the stuff they recorded during this
period, but he does say that it was another rumoured album,
Roadhouse Garden, that they 'were three-quarters of the way
through. We were doing session work in the studios in his house.
Paisley Park wasn't built yet.' And it was *Roadhouse Garden* – rather
than *Dream Factory* – that Prince used as a title for a proposed

box set of unreleased Revolution songs considered at the end of the 1990s but which ultimately never saw the light of day.

This box set was eagerly anticipated by fans who wanted an official record of this period and who were eager to hear the songs in greater fidelity, but it abruptly disappeared from the schedule. Prince said anyone wanting to know what happened to the project should ask Wendy and Lisa. So I did, and they told me: 'Because we're gay. The Lord thinks we're evil, and we're damning The Revolution to hell.' Fink also says that as much as he'd love for people to hear that stuff, Prince never discussed this planned later release with him. H. M. Buff, who worked on this later *Roadhouse Garden* project, says he's glad it was never completed. 'I'm glad it didn't work out, to be honest with you. I was very excited about it, but he thought he could improve on things, so I would transfer the mix of what was there and he would add those keyboards he liked so much at the time. But we didn't work on many songs. I remember "Splash" was worked on, "Roadhouse Garden" and "Wonderful Ass" once again came out of the Vault. Maybe there were a couple more that I don't remember.'

Although there are no proposed track listings for the first version of *Roadhouse Garden* in circulation, there are a sizeable number of Revolution-connected songs that haven't been linked to *Dream Factory* or any other immediately subsequent projects. If the album did indeed exist as a possible project, it has intriguing links with the *Purple Rain* era, and it seems it might have represented a deliberate step backwards to safer commercial-rock territory after the more experimental (and less popular) *Around the World in a Day* and *Parade*, working as a rock-orientated sequel to his biggest-selling album.

Prince played 'Roadhouse Garden' at the live show at First Avenue on his twenty-sixth birthday, and twice in rehearsal for that performance. With its use of a mysterious location as the focus for its drama, it resembles 'Paisley Park', only with a harder and more cinematic focus than the latter song's Haight-Ashbury fantasy. Prince would go on to write many songs about houses, real and imagined, and the parties within, but with its sense of lost pleasure, this is his most beguiling.

Both during rehearsal and onstage, 'Roadhouse Garden' was linked with another song, 'Our Destiny'. The show was only Wendy Melvoin's second full performance with the band, and the song was her initiation: a duet about a couple unable to resist each other, featuring a spoken-word passage from Prince in which he offers a lighter variation on the erotic threat that he usually would make more blatant when recording songs alone. Given the apparent flirtation in this song, I asked Wendy if Prince knew about her sexuality. 'He knew I was gay. I'm not a butch, but I'm not a super-femmy. I'm more androgynous.'

Wendy and Lisa later worked on both of these songs – it was for 'Our Destiny' that they originally wrote the string section that opens 'The Ladder' – but these revised versions are not in circulation. Even if Fink is right and *Roadhouse Garden* was nearly finished, we can only guess what else might have been on the album, although the proposed track listing for the 1998 box set included several Revolution tracks usually associated with *Dream Factory* ('Witness 4 the Prosecution', 'All My Dreams', 'In a Large Room with No Light'), as well as two other well-known out-takes from this era ('Wonderful Ass' and 'Splash'), and perhaps most enticingly, the original version of 'Empty Room'.

While Prince has written plenty of songs inspired by the end of a relationship, he's never written an out-and-out break-up album in the manner of Bob Dylan's *Blood on the Tracks*, Marvin Gaye's *Here, My Dear* or Nick Cave's *The Boatman's Call*. Some fans consider *Rave Un2 the Joy Fantastic* the closest he came to this, but this relies largely on speculation. For me, it's the songs he wrote during his relationship with Susannah Melvoin that give the closest sense of what such a record might sound like.

I got to talk to Susannah Melvoin about these songs, and what they meant to her. Like her sister, Melvoin is an extremely intellectual and artistic woman, although she is slightly less direct and has a more abstract way of expressing herself. It was intriguing to discover that the subject of these songs felt the same way about them as the fans do. 'Some people say I was his muse, and I don't know if that's what it was, but I can say I did inspire a certain kind of writing. There was a part of him that wanted to express himself in a deeper way, and I think our relationship was an opportunity for him to do that at the time. So if that's what being a muse is, that's what it was. I think Wendy and Lisa had the same effect.'

The first thing I wanted to ask Susannah about was a song called 'Wally'. Prince's engineer during this period, Susan Rogers, has made great claims for the song, suggesting that it was one of the few times she witnessed Prince truly expressing his emotions, and it has often been suggested that this is the Holy Grail of unreleased Prince tracks. He supposedly recorded the song twice, the first time feeling so freaked out by what he'd committed to tape that he deliberately destroyed the track, only to come back and record a second version a day later.

It's easy to mythologise a track that hardly anyone has had a chance to hear, and I think there's more than a little fetishism to the way this song has been built up. I don't know if Susannah had heard the first version or the second, but she told me that the track held little emotional import for her, and that it wasn't really significant that the song was an imagined conversation with Wally Safford – a later arrival to The Revolution, whose presence in the band caused great friction with Wendy and Lisa. 'Prince just used that guy's name. I have no attachment to that song.' But she did have emotional attachment to almost every other song that Prince had written about her, among them one of his most beloved tracks, 'Empty Room'.

'Empty Room' has only grown in stature over the years, eventually receiving an official release, of a sort, in 2003.[3] It is now a firm after-show favourite, but it took a long time, even in altered form, to escape Prince's Vault, and the original take is still unreleased. 'He played that for me right before we went to Europe,' Susannah told me.[4] 'Bobby Z was going to Paris to get married at the weekend, and he made the band come in and record the night of Bobby's wedding reception, and he recorded that song and played it for me the next day and left. He was having a hard time, I think, in the relationship that he had with me, and I don't know how much of that relationship I should be talking about, but he was troubled, and I could hear he was troubled in the song and he was sad, and I was sad, and he left and I got a call to come out to France.'[5]

There is an obvious companion song to 'Empty Room' called 'Go', which Prince, Wendy and Lisa worked on both in the studio and later recorded on tape during a rehearsal at the Théâtre du Verdure in Nice. This must have represented a strange recording experience for all concerned. As brilliant and as broad-minded as the Melvoins undoubtedly are, it can't have been easy for Wendy to sing the chorus on a song powered by the frustrations of Prince's relationship with her twin sister, and it's a mark of Susannah's sophistication that her response upon hearing the song was merely to note its brilliance.

Of the many songs she inspired him to write, it is (along with 'If I Was Your Girlfriend') one of her very favourites, 'where he was digging deep and really coming up with the great turning of phrases, and the clarity of thought and subtext and subject. If you were to dissect those lyrics, and the song-writing [itself], he was working it, they came to him at that time.'[6]

If the 'Go' session was hard for Wendy, it no doubt paled in comparison to the time Prince, Wendy and Lisa spent working on a new version of 'Wonderful Ass'. The anatomy of the female body is a recurring theme of Prince's. Even if one doesn't accept the suggestion that the title of 'Little Red Corvette' is a sly reference to female genitalia, New Power Generation member Tommy Barbarella mentions Prince writing a song called 'Good Pussy' in 1998,[7] and there's also the more famous *Gold Experience* song, 'Pussy Control'.[8] But Prince usually gets away with it because it is done either with humour or, as in this case, with a sense of the singer being overwhelmed by the pulchritudinous nature of the body before which he submits himself.

It's tempting to dismiss this song as a simplistic sketch in comparison to the more sophisticated discussion of sexual politics on much of *Sign o' the Times*, but two of that album's most emotionally compelling songs, 'Strange Relationship' and 'I Could Never Take the Place of Your Man', were also rescued from early-1980s tapes.[9] As with those two songs, the cold and somewhat cruel sexual bite of the lyrics works in elegant contrast to the accessibility of the music, a prime example of 1980s rock-pop. It's a song about a woman who's jealous of Prince's female friends because she thinks they're his bed mates, whom he tolerates because of his admiration for her butt. But there's a difference between Prince amusing himself about this idea alone and forming a chorus with Wendy and Lisa: their versions stretch out beyond all control. The song's intricate mix and musical depth explain why Prince considered it for official release, but the presence of Wendy and Lisa alongside Prince singing in a taunting fashion about the physical qualities of a third woman may not quite fit with Prince's latest reinvention of himself. Given what would happen to The Revolution soon afterwards, 'Wonderful Ass' also works as a fascinating dramatisation of the conflict that followed. In both versions, Wendy and Lisa insist 'The Revolution will be heard'. Not for much longer.

There are a handful of other songs recorded in this era not connected to *Dream Factory*. 'Splash', which eventually received two separate releases on different versions of Prince's later online ventures, is one of Prince and The Revolution's finest recordings. The water imagery and light psychedelia link the track with Wendy and Lisa's own later work as a duo, and in many ways their first two albums indicate where The Revolution might have taken Prince had the band stayed together. Among other tracks about which not that much is known is 'Fun Love', for which Brent Fischer retains his father's score. He told me: 'Unfortunately, we don't retain every single score. It's standard operating procedure when you're done writing an arrangement to give the original to the person who paid for the arrangement. You might keep a copy for yourself, but you give the original to either the record company or the artist. So we usually relinquished all those things [and] my dad didn't always keep copies.' But he has 'Fun Love' and 'Cosmic Day', among many others, in an archive of sixty years of Clare Fischer compositions, and of the former he says, 'The lyrics were very sensually suggestive.'

I haven't heard the complete version of 'Everybody Want What They Don't Got',[10] but I have read the whole lyric in Prince's 1994 book *Neo Manifesto* (about which more later), and it's one of those songs, like 'Pop Life' or the later 'People Without' or much later 'F.U.N.K.' or 'Rich Friends', which reveal the crueller side of Prince's social commentary. It's much easier to mock material greed when you have achieved enormous wealth. The fact that the items the characters in this song desire are so stupid (a Jack Benny album!) or that Prince implicates himself at the end by admitting he's got his eye on a neighbour's sprinkler system only make the song's moralising more galling.

The highlight of this era for me is the session that produced four songs over two days in June 1986, which represents the last time the band sound untroubled. It has been suggested that the songs were recorded for a planned Broadway musical,[11] although details on this are vague, and it was a project that never came to fruition. Another idea in the air at the time, Lisa Coleman told me, was a concept record about an imaginary nightclub, on which at least two of these songs would fit, as well as several others from this period. This concept seems to have been folded into the *Graffiti Bridge* project, on which two of these songs (in considerably different versions) later appeared.

Three of the tracks Prince took into Minneapolis's Washington Avenue Warehouse for this midweek session were old: he'd first committed 'Can't Stop This Feeling I Got', 'Girl o' My Dreams' and 'We Can Funk' to tape in the early 1980s, during the period while he was working on *1999* and before he'd started on *Purple Rain*, and all of the songs would undergo further reinvention before they were released.

'Can't Stop This Feeling I Got' and 'Girl o' My Dreams' are short, funny, rockabilly freak-outs, and the released versions of the songs are both disposable. On *Graffiti Bridge*, 'Can't Stop This Feeling I Got' is Prince solo (although surrounded by crowd noise and encouragement), as it was when he first recorded it in 1982,[12] and despairing – the song is still in the same style, but drawn out and much more of a genuine lament. But in the Warehouse, playing with a line-up of The Revolution that had swollen to nine members,[13] Prince performed the song with infectious joy. 'Girl o' My Dreams' is a short throwaway with a funny cinephile lyric about how his favourite women are old-time movie stars like Marilyn Monroe and Lauren Bacall. Prince can't resist making a joke about Bacall being old and wrinkled (at the time he wrote the song she was sixty-two), but the song is redeemed by a member of The Revolution (or Prince himself putting on a funny voice[14]) taking him to task for his chauvinism. Prince would never release the song himself, instead giving it to Paisley Park-signed rapper T. C. Ellis. It can sometimes seem as if Prince is either genuinely perverse about deciding which unreleased song goes to which artist (or perhaps, in most instances, he simply doesn't care), but giving T. C. Ellis 'Girl o' My Dreams' was a truly baffling move. It's not that the song is a lost classic, and the Paisley Park album on which it appeared (*True Confessions*) is long forgotten, so it would be easy for him to put it out again, but I can't help wondering whether he was having a little joke or conducting deliberate sabotage by deciding that an aspiring rapper should be singing about Lena Horne.

But it's the other two songs recorded during this session that really show The Revolution as a live unit at their very best. 'We Can Funk' is one of those songs through which it's possible to trace ten years of Prince's development. Prince has recorded at least eight versions, and it resurfaces at various points in his career, leaking poison along the way. The song began as a track on a 1983 tape called 'We Can Fuck' and ended up as a somewhat tepid PG-rated George Clinton duet on *Graffiti Bridge*. When Prince finally decided to ready the song for release, he took as the basis his original tape rather than the Revolution recording,[15] which seems surprising given that Wendy and Lisa also played on this early 1983 version (as well as Susannah, Jonathan Melvoin and David Coleman). Wendy remembers the song with particular fondness, preferring its original title.

While it's hard to fathom why Prince gave 'Girl o' My Dreams' to T. C. Ellis, I wonder whether 'Data Bank' might always have been intended for its eventual recipients, The Time, and if The Time might always have been part of whatever project Prince was working on then, the musical or the nightclub record. In the lyrics he mentions 'the time', 'Movie Star' (the title of a song Prince wrote for Morris Day a couple of months earlier) and 'The Kid', and although there are shout-outs to Eric and Lisa, the song's subject – getting women's numbers – makes it an obvious sequel to '777-9311'.

While little of this music can be said to be truly lost, largely having survived in alternative versions, it resists being fitted together into an easily identifiable package and remains an overlooked period in Prince's career. The mythology around *Dream Factory* and *Crystal Ball* may be frustrating to the former members of The Revolution, but at least it means those songs continue to be written and thought about. When I talked to Matt Fink about this era, he struggled to recall some of the songs, and needed me to jog his memory with song titles. As far as official endings are concerned, the last recorded evidence of The Revolution as a band is 'It's Gonna Be a Beautiful Night', which began as an onstage jam at the Paris Zenith before being almost completely overdubbed. And there are at least two more Revolution-connected out-takes – 'Eggplant' and the ominously titled 'It Ain't Over 'Til the Fat Lady Sings' – known to exist but which have never reached a larger audience.[16] Maybe one day we'll know the full story, but for the moment let's remember them like this, jamming away in the Washington Avenue Warehouse, with no idea how little time they have left.

THE STORY OF A MAN I AM NOT

The romantic version of the story is that Prince abandoned the *Dream Factory* project when Wendy and Lisa left, and it's true that the majority of the tracks involved them. But the project also included more heavily Prince-focused songs that he could have easily carried over to *Sign o' the Times*, and it seems he had yet to land upon a unifying concept, unless, as several close to Prince maintain, *Sign o' the Times* was indeed always the big album all along.

'When people ask what was on *Dream Factory*,' Lisa Coleman says now, 'I tell them, "I've no idea what you're talking about. I know there was a *song* called 'Dream Factory'." But was there an album? I know it got as far as having a cover, drawn by Susannah Melvoin, who was sharing Prince's bed and studio at the time.' This cover, Melvoin told me, was 'kooky and cartoonish, [with] great imagery of the doors of the Dream Factory opening and [someone] walking into space'. And although it has never appeared in any official form, *Dream Factory* has been the subject of several magazine articles, with many critics arguing that it represents Prince's finest achievement. But none of the three versions of the album suggested by bootleggers and sessionologists work as cohesive records, something at which Prince (at least at this point in his career) always excelled.

If he was seriously considering *Dream Factory* as a proper release, it seems that much like *The Black Album*, it was a project born out of anger that if taken through to completion might have inspired second thoughts. Although Wendy and Lisa's skill with light and shade gives the songs they worked on a brightness and energy, the Prince songs related to the project represent some of the darkest music he had considered releasing under his own name.

'Dream Factory' is a straightforward revenge song, Prince's equivalent of Bob Dylan's 'Positively Fourth Street'. This is something Prince didn't try to hide at the time, although the sleeve note he offered to explain the song when it was eventually released is a half-hearted attempt at obfuscation. The track was written, he writes, '4 a turncoat, who after a quick brush with success, lost themselves in a haze of wine, women and pills . . . or so the fiction goes? This person is not Prince – "Listen 2 the story of a man Eye am not."'[1]

Per Nilsen and his associates identify this person as The Family's Paul Peterson, who had aroused Prince's anger by walking out on his project in search of a solo career. Peterson refuses to discuss this era – although onstage he will occasionally make jokes about the clothes Prince used to make him wear – so while I did talk to him off the record, I cannot confirm the rumour.[2] But given the state of Prince's film career at this time – although coming off the flop *Under the Cherry Moon,* it wouldn't be long before he began plans for a sequel to *Purple Rain* – the song could also have been a note-to-self about the importance of keeping Hollywood at a distance.

The song makes the Dream Factory of the title (which Susannah also described as a building rather than merely a description of Hollywood) sound like a nightclub – partly because on one assembly of these songs it is preceded by 'Nevaeh Ni Ecalp A'. This short track is a snippet of the song 'A Place in Heaven' played backwards, over which you can hear Wendy and

Lisa pretending to be brattish teens mocking a bouncer questioning whether they're underage. When the 'man-that-Prince-is-not' gets into the club, he's immediately offered what seems like Ecstasy, a drug that would allegedly inspire at least one major creative decision from Prince soon after this. (Whenever Prince sings of the dangers of drugs or a dissolute lifestyle – as on the later 'The Undertaker' – he always either makes it sound desirable or, and this is more common, strikes the pose of a callous observer. He is not quite a libertarian, but neither quite a judge: you can do this, he allows, but if you do, you're on your own.)

'Movie Star' is a lighter exploration of the same themes. Prince sings over an extremely sparse backing in his Jamie Starr voice of going to a nightclub with the two Time sidekicks, Jerome and Gilbert. It brings together many of Prince's concerns at the time, and hints at a narrative that didn't quite come to life in *Graffiti Bridge* but that could have worked as an alternative *Purple Rain* sequel. There's an ambiguity in the song about whether Jamie/Morris is actually a movie star or merely imagining himself as a hero of his own imaginary film: it's the ultimate culmination of the dialogue-driven songs on the first three Time albums, a deconstruction of Day's persona that ends with him unable to pay for a round of drinks, the poverty of the sound reflecting his empty wallet. He also calls himself The Kid, an alias shared by Prince (in *Purple Rain*) and Morris (on *Ice Cream Castle*), which increases the sense of dislocation.

I felt embarrassed about bringing up 'Big Tall Wall' in front of Susannah Melvoin. It was as if I'd dug out an intimate love letter Prince had written her, filled with private detail, and asked her what she'd done to inspire it. Talking to Wendy and Lisa previously, I'd discovered that they'd heard out-takes, but didn't necessarily have copies of them. And although I assumed that

Susannah would have wanted to hear every song Prince had alleg-edly written about her, I had no idea if he'd played them to her at the time, and if not, whether she would have tracked them down.

Susannah told me he hadn't played her 'Big Tall Wall' at the time – and she hadn't heard it in many years – but it was clear from her reaction that she still remembered the impact the lyr-ics had made on her. It's easy to understand why, and also to appreciate why Prince has – to date – kept it from official release. Stylistically, it's among his most important out-takes – you can hear in it the seeds of many of the songs on *Sign o' the Times*, *The Black Album*, *Lovesexy* and *Graffiti Bridge* – but lyrically it's unbelievably reactionary, a throwback to the lock-her-up-in-a-trunk misogynist crap of Cliff Richard's 'Living Doll'.[3] The song is from the perspective of a possessive lover overwhelmed by a girlfriend – with a sexy body and curly brown hair – who decides to respond to her challenges by imprisoning her inside a circular stone wall, while continuing, it seems, to see another girlfriend on the side. This, the singer maintains, is true love. It would be a mistake to take the song too seriously: it's a definite exercise in black humour, but by the end of the song he's fully inhabited the persona of a psychopath.

In spite of its heavy title, 'Sexual Suicide' – a song which, it has been argued, Prince initially considered to close the record – is a throwaway. The title was seemingly chosen for its alliteration, and the lyrics are hard to make out beneath the sax and percus-sion. Reading them reveals that the song is merely a repeated threat that anyone leaving the singer would be committing sexual suicide. This is a theme Prince had been expressing in song since his earliest demo tape.[4] Prince again contradicts the suggested configuration of *Dream Factory* with his sleeve note to accom-pany 'Last Heart', another dark and aggressive love song that Per Nilsen suggests was on the second and third version of this record. Prince claims here that the song was 'intended as a demo, which is unusually unheard of in Prince's mind'. For a demo, it's remarkably polished. The song features Susannah on backing vocals and Eric Leeds on saxophone, and works an incredible sleight-of-hand, making a lyric about a man threatening to murder a cheating lover seem almost AOR.

Far more sophisticated is 'In a Large Room with No Light'. The darkness of this song's lyric seems less personal than political or theological: it points backwards to 'Annie Christian' and 'Ronnie, Talk to Russia' and forwards to 'Sign o' the Times' and *Diamonds and Pearls'* 'Live 4 Love'. Prince always seems to be spooked by threats of war, and the song was inspired by the geopolitical situation at the time. Of all Prince's political songs, it's the most nihilistic. It is less an exploration of theodicy than a statement of the darkness of life, and for once the response is not to party but to despair.

The bleakness of the lyric is balanced by an upbeat and unusual jazz backing, which surprises as Prince usually does this sort of song alone with his synth and drum machines.[5] I never imagined I would get to see Prince perform this long-lost track, but he exhumed it in 2009 for the third of three shows in one night in Los Angeles. Performed in the middle of a heavily jazz-influenced set, it was clear that the anguish that had originally driven the song was long gone.[6]

It's easy to see why Prince eventually decided to give 'Train' to Mavis Staples, as it is, in essence, a bluesy lover-done-me-wrong track that suits the power of her voice. It seems likely, too, that he was remembering the importance of trains in gospel music, although the train here is offering salvation only from a doomed relationship. Prince's version has a spoken-word intro in which he encourages a friend to pack his bags and leave with him, but aside from that the lyric is the same, which makes me wonder if the song was always intended for a woman: gender is often fluid in Prince's work, but his original version (if intended for release) puts a male singer in an unusual position, staying behind while encouraging his lover to go play Jack Kerouac.

In spite of the closeness of their working relationship, it's easy to see how Wendy and Lisa might not have realised where Prince was heading. Wendy told me if they'd stayed around, Prince and the band would have gone in a different direction, one that she believes would have been for the good. During this period, Prince was often off recording alone, and those Wendy and Lisa songs are (mostly) of such high quality that it must have been hard to believe that they would be permanently discarded. At the time, everything (it seems) was up for grabs, a creative scenario that Wendy says was not that different from the way *Around the World in a Day* and *Parade* were put together.

The difficulty of trying to draw any firm conclusions about the *Dream Factory* track listing is emphasised by Lisa Coleman's revelation that just as some commentators see *Sign o' the Times* as a digest of several contemporaneous alternative projects, so *Dream Factory* might *itself* have been a digest of yet more so-far-unheard projects. For example, 'Visions', the song which, it has been suggested, would open *Dream Factory*, was, according to Coleman, one of a number of two-and-a-half minute pieces Prince asked her to record both as a way of testing his new piano set-up of the time and as the starting point for some future release.[7]

'It's a Wonderful Day' sounds like a development or variation on 'Wonderful Ass', Prince, Wendy and Lisa once again singing in harmony, but this time without the sexual charge. Prince's voice is not quite at the pitch he would use when disguising himself as Camille, but it's much lighter than it is on the songs he was recording alone at the time, and if the track is dated by a drum machine set to generic pop settings he would rarely use when recording alone, it's still worthy of release. And while lyrically 'Teacher, Teacher' – an old cast-off that Prince gave to Wendy and Lisa to transform – returns to overfamiliar territory for Prince (whenever Prince sings about education, it's almost always of a sexual kind), it is more sophisticated than any of his other treatments of this theme. The song has a harpsichord-style keyboard sound that (as with much of Wendy and Lisa's work) gives it a pleasingly retro 1960s sound and elevates it above protégé territory.

But while all these tracks are appealing and worthwhile, they pale next to the remaining Wendy and Lisa/Prince collaborations, which represent a career high point for all concerned, though only one, 'Power Fantastic', has been released in its original form, hidden away at the end of a bonus disc of B-sides. Lisa Coleman remembers writing the music for 'Power Fantastic' when Prince gave her and Wendy studio time (it was originally for a song of theirs called 'Carousel'). She told me that, as with 'Visions', the song was born out of instrument testing and experimentation: 'A lot of the songs were test studies, to hear how something sounds.' Having written the music, they recorded the song at Prince's house with The Revolution, with Lisa on the new piano upstairs and the rest of the band in the downstairs studio. Unlike 'Visions', which has an improvisational feel, this is one of Prince's most sophisticated out-takes, Atlanta Bliss's trumpet-playing of such quality that for many years those who heard it mistook it for a collaboration between Prince and Miles Davis.

With both 'Witness 4 the Prosecution' and 'A Place in Heaven', Prince handed over a degree of control to Wendy and Lisa (and his engineer Susan Rogers), although with the former, he reclaimed the song as his own by recording a new version six months later. The difference between the two versions is fascinating, a similar transformation to the one Prince made to 'Strange Relationship' between recording it with Wendy and Lisa and redoing it for *Sign o' the Times*. Prince also revisited the idea of a relationship being tried in a courtroom, which gives this song its shape, in the much later *Gold Experience* song 'Eye Hate U', which has a similar, albeit even darker, feel. It's an extremely erotic idea, combining a sanctioned sadomasochism with the wish-fulfilment fantasy of sexual arguments being resolved in public.

On the first version of 'Witness' the three women were also joined by Eric Leeds on saxophone and Susannah Melvoin, who Susan Rogers has suggested was, once again, the subject of the song,[8] although if so, this is heavily disguised, as the vocal describes the relationship beginning in school. But even if the song wasn't about her, it is an indication of the uniqueness of Prince's set-up at the time that he could present these four women with a lyric in which he defends his obsessive behaviour and ask them to finish it off for him while he went to France. The second version makes explicit the suggestion that it is a song about childhood love, with a spoken intro from Prince stating that it is a story of two childhood sweethearts, and even implying that he is taking on a character's perspective in the track. With Prince singing of wanting to be given the 'electric chair' for his sins, the track also pre-echoes the later *Batman* song of this title.

'A Place in Heaven' also exists in two versions. Both feature piano and the harpsichord-sounding keyboard also evident on 'Teacher, Teacher'. The 'place in heaven' is described as a suite with no room service, which feints towards the 'it is easier to pass through an eye of a needle' of the Synoptic Gospels, and Prince gives an example of a self-pitying woman frustrated by this, but then the song ends up suggesting instead that given the trickiness of finding comfort (or luxury) in heaven,[9] we should concentrate on life on Earth.

Per Nilsen suggests that 'All My Dreams' – which at one time was considered for *Parade* – was not on the first assembly of *Dream Factory*. If he was ever considering putting out a single-album version of this record, it seems surprising that he would have left the track out. It is the last song on the suggested second and third assemblies – both double albums – a suitable place for such an epic track, among the most ambitious never to receive release from the Vault. Wendy has said of the song, 'It reminded me of classic Kid Creole and the Coconuts,' explaining how Prince sang through a megaphone on one track and kept the other clean, before mixing the two while she and Lisa did crazy background vocals.

The instructions for these vocals, Lisa has explained, was to 'sing like you are Bette Davis'. Revealing once again how important films are to Prince in shaping and driving his creative development – and also demonstrating how Prince was going in one direction with Wendy and Lisa and another more darker direction while alone – she explains they were watching 1930s 'Puttin' on the Ritz'-era films while working.[10] The track is also a favourite of Matt Fink's, who considers it 'a great piece of work', while Brent Fischer, who also worked on the song, says it's his favourite unreleased track: 'It's a great, great tune and I hope it will be released one day, and it's got a great orchestral arrangement to it too, if I can pat my dad on the back.' But unless Prince returns to his *Roadhouse Garden* project and pulls together these Revolution-related tracks into some sort of coherent order – which seems unlikely – or writes more liner autobiography about this period – and given the cryptic nature of his publications to date, it's doubtful – it seems that this era will remain the least understood but most talked about of Prince's career, a time when he was producing material of incredible quality yet failed to find a satisfactory way of putting it out.

REBIRTH OF THE FLESH

It has long been known that Prince was inspired to write the song 'Shockadelica' after hearing an advance copy of former Time member Jesse Johnson's album of the same name. But Susannah Melvoin suggested that the record may have kick-started not just the song, but this entire period of recording, believing that it represents the true starting point for the post-Revolution era. Still, it's worth remembering that things are rarely so clear-cut with Prince, and also that he often finds ways of moving forward through returning to his past. It's true that the character of 'Camille' was given a name in the lyric to 'Shockadelica', and the concept of *Camille* seems to have followed that song, but Prince first used the speeded-up vocal style that characterised this project three years earlier on 'Erotic City'. The inspiration, Prince confessed,[1] was the nineteenth-century hermaphrodite Herculine Barbin, nicknamed Camille, whose journals were brought to wider attention in the 1980s by French philosopher Michel Foucault. If Prince was inspired by Johnson's record, it was to return to a previous style of his own.

Susannah also believes that the *Camille* album and *The Black Album* are perhaps more closely linked than has previously been acknowledged, which is borne out by the recording times: Prince worked on the first song to be completed for *The Black Album*, 'Superfunkycalifragisexy', the day after finishing the first *Camille* song, 'Shockadelica'. 'I think it was a cathartic thing for him,'

Susannah told me, before suggesting that it eventually took him somewhere he might not have wanted to go, hence his decision not to release either album.

Although *The Black Album* (which begins with a song identifying it under the alternative title 'The Funk Bible') includes Prince's most obvious (and contentious) response to hip hop ('2 Nigs United 4 West Compton'), there also seems something of his answer to this genre in the *Camille* record, especially his underlying suspicion of anyone he doesn't consider sufficiently musically skilled.[2] *Camille* is not a rap record as such, but it's informed by the genre.

Because all of the *Camille* tracks were eventually released,[3] it is a relatively uncelebrated project, remembered mainly for the three tracks that ended up on *Sign o' the Times*. Maybe the excitement for the listener of finding songs credited to Camille on that album – including one, 'U Got the Look', that was written after Prince had abandoned the *Camille* album – and being led into the world of Prince's alter egos in such a subtle way was worth the death of this alternative project. But it's also worth considering as an album rather than merely the first appearance of a set of some of Prince's most appealing songs. It's actually a better record than *The Black Album*, and although it lacks the breadth of *Sign o' the Times*, it might have been the braver release. Certainly, these tracks work brilliantly as a suite, and as good as most are separately, they undoubtedly gain added power from being heard together.

'Rebirth of the Flesh' is a slightly sinister, heavily symbolic title for one of Prince's brightest, poppiest songs, but perhaps as well as its obvious significance – opening a record that features Prince moving away from rock back towards funk (or, in this case, even dance), and therefore offering a more explicit connection with the body – it might also refer to Prince's at the time recently abandoned jazz-jam side project The Flesh. (If it's too much of a stretch to imagine that this might have been Prince's way of noting that he was carrying ideas from that mostly unheard endeavour into a new planned side project, then maybe it was merely a word he was toying with at the time, a semi-conscious way of forcing himself in a new direction, as well as having obvious theological resonance.) There is also, of course, a more obvious joke: had Camille come into full existence to promote the record, he/she would have likely existed as a concept without a body, *sans* flesh.

'Housequake' was the second *Camille* track to be recorded (after 'Shockadelica'), and you can really feel the competitiveness starting to set in, the sense of Prince rediscovering a side of himself that had largely lain dormant (aside from the occasional unreleased song or track for other artists) since he had set his sights on mass appeal with *Purple Rain*. It was a track Prince would remain proud of, and some of the tensions underlying this era would be made apparent when, after losing a Grammy to U2, he claimed that they would never be capable of writing a song like 'Housequake'. Making up imaginary dances was nothing new for Prince, of course, but various commentators have suggested that he may have had other targets in mind. Michaelangelo Matos gave credence to Greg Tate's theory — expressed in the *Village Voice* at the time of the record's release — that the song was 'a swipe at Chicago house',[4] adding that it might also be a dismissal of hip hop.[5]

As with many Prince projects, the album was not written entirely from scratch. 'Feel U Up' was originally demoed in 1981, and shares the erotomania of many songs from that time, having an obvious lyrical twin in 'Jack U Off'. It's easy to see why Prince would have remembered this song for the project, and if Susannah Melvoin is right about recording as Camille liberating

Prince, then maybe one of the main attractions was being able to find a context for the darker sex songs that had been festering in the Vault. The main musical change to make it a Camille song was re-recording it with a speeded-up vocal, but singing this track with a hermaphrodite persona completely changes the impact of the lyrics. When Prince sings that he doesn't want to be someone's man, it seems like he's avoiding attachment; when Camille sings (s)he doesn't want to be someone's man, it suggests that she is offering a different sort of pleasure, and feeling someone up changes from being sleazy to a joyous celebration of non-penetrative sex. Without any change to the lyrics, the song becomes an obvious companion to 'If I Was Your Girlfriend'.

There were also earlier performances of 'Strange Relationship', all of which demonstrate an ambivalence towards the lyrics. Prince played it alone at the piano sometime in 1983, singing in a very deep voice and pushing the track almost to the point of parody, and again at rehearsal in 1984, when he joked about Stanley Kubrick's *The Shining* and hammered it out in an extremely loose style, calling changes to the band but hiding the subtleties of the song. Wendy Melvoin told me that by 1985, the track had become significant to Prince and that it was the song everyone was focusing on. An alternative (and much-loved) version of the track, recorded with major input from Wendy and Lisa, has a much closer connection with *Around the World in a Day* than the finished song, with Wendy on tambourine and congas, Lisa on sitar and flute, and a more helpless, morose vocal from Prince. From this flux, 'Strange Relationship' would go on to become a regular part of Prince's live set, and now he plays it the same way almost every show, hardened to the point where it no longer contains any real emotion; but there was one more radical reinterpretation of the song before it was committed to vinyl. Prince had occasionally played one-off shows before, but it was during the *Parade* tour with The Revolution that the after-show phenomenon as fans know it today was truly born, with two shows in London and one in Paris at Le New Morning.[6] The latter performance was notable for both the special guest – Prince's father, who joined them on piano – and because Prince played a very unusual version of 'Strange Relationship', the drums slowed down to a crawl while Prince scat-sang. He was still teaching chords to the band, but when Prince's vocals came in, they had the weariness evident on the Wendy and Lisa version taken to an even further extreme. Prince seemed barely able to express himself, dropping out to let the band take over as they extended the song to twice its normal length. This version had Eric Leeds on saxophone, as the *Sign o' the Times* version was once going to, before Prince changed his mind and discarded his contribution.

While promoting the far more spiritual *Emancipation*, Prince had an amusing way of responding to a question from a fan about whether 'Shockadelica' was his best song, saying that while it wasn't for him to judge, *Emancipation*'s 'The Holy River' was about redemption, while 'Shockadelica' was about a witch.[7] Rather than convince me of the superiority of *Emancipation*, it makes me long for the time when Prince was singing about witches. Susan Rogers has (rather cruelly) suggested that the song was inspired by *Weekend at Bernies II* actress Troy Beyer, another of Prince's girlfriends of the time,[8] who would go on to appear in the videos for 'Gett Off', 'Sexy MF' and the *3 Chains o' Gold* movie. Later, he would rename one of the Erotic City dancers at the LA branch of his Glam Slam nightclub empire after the song, which, if nothing else, seems an unusual way of inspiring a girl to dance for you.

Susannah Melvoin remembers 'If I Was Your Girlfriend' as being specifically about her. It is one of Prince's most convoluted and complex lyrics (when Liz Jones told Prince that students studied this lyric in universities, he burst into tears[9]), but it has a straightforward history. It was the last track to be recorded for the *Camille* record, only to become a highlight of *Sign o' the Times*. That Camille/Prince offers to dance a ballet is telling: Susannah had classical ballet training, and in her words, 'a musical library that Prince had too [which] validated his musical tastes', something also evident in another *Camille* track, 'Good Love', in which Prince name-checks Mahler, one of several classical composers who had a strong influence on him during this period. Susannah's belief that working on *Camille* was a positive experience for Prince is confirmed by his sleeve note to the eventual release of this song, in which he writes: 'Prince was very happy during this time and very optimistic about his musical possibilities with a new line-up of musicians, which included Sheila E.'

I'd hoped that asking Susannah about her contribution to 'Rockhard in a Funky Place' might reveal something about the composition of this murky song, but she told me it was merely part of her work as a session singer taken on after the dissolution of The Family. 'I was hired by Prince as a staff singer.' Susannah says that she didn't always 'know where [her contributions would] go. I knew they were a series of songs he wanted to record. With his history I knew they would turn into something, a particular project of his, but I didn't know what. I didn't know what he had in mind. I sang on a lot of different projects. He would just call me and say, "We're in the studio, come on down." He would record me. He would say, "These are the backgrounds, go in and do it." There were a few occasions when he'd say, "You go in and do it, you go find the vocal arrangements," and then Susan Rogers would send me the mix and I would get a call and he would say, "It was great."' Nevertheless, she did remember something of the mood of the time when this track was recorded. 'It was a really good time for Prince and I. We had a strong relationship, and that was just a great track to do. It was one of those, I was just there recording with him and it was given that I'd get in there and do the vocals. The two of us would get in there and pull the microphones together and sing these backgrounds. I think it was in Minneapolis.'

Camille was a coherent, fully developed project, but it seems that shelving it caused Prince no anguish. He kept Camille around as a character for the *Sign o' the Times* album and even credited his alter ego with one last song, 'Scarlet Pussy' – recorded long after this album and included as the B-side to 'I Wish U Heaven'. The ease with which Prince reached this decision seems to be evidence that, at least at this stage in his career, he was continuing with the same open approach to writing, selecting and discarding material that he'd always had. *Camille* was a powerful collection of songs, but the three tracks he would carry forward to *Sign o' the Times* would represent only one facet of that extraordinary record, the greatest (at that point) he had recorded. But if Prince had had his way, his masterpiece might have been more complex still.

It's time to go to the Crystal Ball.

CRYSTAL BALL . . .

Matt Fink claims that 'Crystal Ball' was a song rather than an album, and that it may have been dropped from the project due to the technical difficulties that playing the song live presented. 'He gave it to the group at the time and told us, "Here, learn this," and we started rehearsing and realised just how technically challenging it was. It's a continuous piece, like a symphony. We were used to playing four-minute pop songs. I think I was rising to the challenge, as I could write my own charts, but some of the others were ear-players. There was so much going on, and Prince realised this and gave up on playing it live.'

But Susannah Melvoin told me that The Revolution didn't necessarily know everything about what was going on during this period, and that she is the only one who knows the full story. She says that while Prince usually recorded songs without making it clear on what project they might end up, 'Crystal Ball' was an exception, and was intended for a grand new project. 'He did tell me about *Crystal Ball*. *Crystal Ball* was going to be an epic. I knew what we were going in to do with *Crystal Ball*. He would talk about what he wanted.' What he wanted, Susannah believed, was to write what was 'basically an opera'. She says that during this time, 'The Revolution were on a break,' not yet disbanded, and for the first time in a long while 'Prince just had time. He was going through some personal transformations, and that's how he expressed it. They weren't going on the road, and when he has idle time, that's how he plays it out. He doesn't go to the park and hang out with himself.'

Prince's version of events is different. Rather than being the beginning of an exciting new project, he claims he wrote the track in 'deepbluefunk [*sic*] depression' about his future in the music business, during which time 'his only solace . . . was his continuing search 4 a soul mate'.[1] The vagueness of this wording is telling. Hinting at a theme that would be evident not just in this song, but also in 'Sign o' the Times', Prince writes that 'the notion of making love during the apocalypse was an interesting notion 2 us at the time'.[2] Is the 'us' here Prince and Susannah? Or Prince and the band? Or the citizens of the 1980s?

As well as the version released on the 1998 disc, which was heavily edited by engineer H. M. Buff, there were three alternative takes of 'Crystal Ball'. These feature Wendy and Lisa on vocals, as well as Susannah (the released version is just Prince and Susannah). On the Wendy and Lisa versions, the intensity is increased by a spoken-word section panned across the speakers that addresses 'sisters and brothers of the purple underground' and associates danger with blackness, a concept Prince would continue to pursue. This direct address recalls early band member Dez Dickerson's claim that Prince was always looking for more than just a band, wanting to shape his fans into a movement, something that would become of even greater importance to him during the 1990s and early twenty-first century before he would abruptly lose interest in the possibility of shaping mass opinion.

Brent Fischer remembers him and his father being sent the song in 1986. 'He was on a mission. When we first got that tape of "Crystal Ball", he said it was the most important thing he'd done in his life up to that point. It was a huge undertaking because it was just so involved, so it took a long time to transcribe, and then Dad and I sat and talked about what we wanted to do with the different ideas that Prince presented, how we were going to envelop them in an orchestra and which instruments we were going to use to emphasise different ideas that Prince had come up with. That was a long, very complicated process. Because it was so important to him, we took more time to put this together. He didn't give us a deadline, and that made it a lot easier. I remember we took our time in the studio. Normally, we would like to record two songs during a standard three-hour recording session. We can do that easily. We just set aside this whole one song, especially it being eight or nine minutes, to have its own session.

'It was recorded at Ocean Way Studio 1. It was a very large room. We had a huge orchestra, a lot of unusual instruments, a lot of interesting techniques that we incorporated in there. We had eight French horns, I remember that, because there is something where [Dr Clare Fischer] used different horns with different mutes. He paired them into groups of two, and he would have a melody line, a short phrase of Prince, and then he would have a French horn answer it. The second French horn would answer with a certain type of mute, and then the third French horn would answer with an even deeper mute, and then the final French horn would answer with a metal mute. It almost sounded like a different instrument at that point; you could barely tell it was a French horn. And the idea behind this was that we were echoing the melody notes of Prince's phrases and that the echoes were being produced naturally. There were no engineering techniques employed other than pressing "record" on a tape machine. The echo process was created through the different use of different mutes on the French horns.

'There was also a great deal of difficult woodwind and string parts. I did most of the percussion parts on there. It took three hours between all the different overdubs we had to do as well. There were some times when [Clare Fischer] had the orchestra leave the room and just have the French horns be by themselves. That way we would give absolute mixing control to Prince later on. There wouldn't be any bleed through the headphones of any of the other instruments. I was in the process of finishing a symphony-percussion degree, so we had a lot of fun with all the different orchestral instruments. There were a lot of percussion parts, and it was done with myself and another pretty well-known percussionist named Luis Conte. He did the Latin percussion stuff that I don't generally play, like congas and timpani, and I did all the symphony percussion, such as marimba, xylophone, vibraphone and crash cymbals.

'And then we sent it off, and we never heard a word back about "Crystal Ball".'

'Crystal Ball' is undoubtedly an extraordinary song, regarded by most Prince fans as one of his very best, and it seems extraordinary that Prince held it back for twelve years. When it did appear in 1998, although it was the title track of a box set, it came out without any real sense of its historical context or place in Prince's creative development – the three-CD set it kicked off contained three hours of randomly assembled tracks, seemingly deliberately sequenced to destroy any continuity or chronological or thematic links and instead reminding the casual listener of the quality of *all* his unreleased work. It's possible to understand Prince's thinking in 1998: recently freed from Warner Brothers and following up *Emancipation*, he was presenting another three hours of unreleased music (along with, depending which package you bought, another brand-new album and a ballet), releasing in fourteen months more new music than most bands deliver in a decade. Fans could hardly complain of being short-changed, but in the process he destroyed 'Crystal Ball''s mystique (as well as editing out the most interesting parts).

If, as Brent Fischer and Susannah suggest, the song did

represent a true new direction for Prince, it seems that he may have abandoned his highest ambitions for the new project mid-way through. Only four songs recorded in this era seem to have obvious connections with this larger concept, particularly if it was being considered as a rock opera: 'The Ball', 'Joy in Repetition', a sixty-minute track called 'Soul Psychodelicide' and the *Sign o' the Times* song 'Hot Thing'. None of these three tracks quite share the sophistication of 'Crystal Ball', and in fact indicate that if *Crystal Ball* was a concept record, it might have been similar to some of The Time's work, particularly their second album, *What Time Is It?*. As with 'Darling Nikki', there seems to be a combination of fairy tale and De Sadean narratives: the Crystal Ball is a place where innocents are exploited by libertines.

These innocents include the barely twenty-one-year-old 'Hot Thing' who Prince appears eager to corrupt in the song of the same title. The song includes the only reference to the Crystal Ball on the finished *Sign o' the Times*. Heard in that context, it's easy to pass over it as more of the nonsense talk that peppers the album – including quotations from Edward Lear's 'The Table and the Chair' in 'It's Gonna Be a Beautiful Night' – but placed alongside 'The Ball' it gains a more sinister quality. When Prince tells his date to inform her parents that she's going to the Crystal Ball, the fact she might never return becomes far more frightening. Is the song recorded as a cautionary tale? It sounds like lover-man preening, but Prince is not singing in his normal voice, shrieking and screaming and moving beyond language in the last verse, and maybe it's more threat than come-on. The extended version is even more of a blunt instrument, Prince's shuddering and animal calls sounding like a man about to ejaculate. 'The Ball' opens with distorted voices talking about this party and finishes with similar deliberate distortion masking Prince telling the girl he's talking to not to stop him from what he's doing to her and to hit him instead. In one of the takes of this song, horns lead the listener into the less disturbing, but still mysterious, 'Joy in Repetition', one of Prince's most beloved tracks. It would go on to become a centrepiece of *Graffiti Bridge*, and would always be of great importance in his live performances, and seems even here, in its earliest two versions, another narrative song that hints at a story Prince was still making up. During the track, Prince sings of a band playing a year-long song called 'Soul Psychodelicide'. A few days later, he had a crack at recording if not a year-long song, then certainly one of his longest jams.[3]

While 'Soul Psychodelicide' has length, there is nothing else on the planned triple that demonstrates the same range and ambition as the title song, and if 'Crystal Ball' was intended as the opening of an opera, I can only conclude that Prince didn't get round to writing any more of it. He would return to this ambition – if not the song – in the early 1990s (and some of the narrative seems to have been carried forward into the plot of his fourth feature film, *Graffiti Bridge*). But later that year, while rehearsing a song called 'The Sex of It', which he would later give to Kid Creole and the Coconuts, you can hear Prince being dismissive of what he calls 'stupid storytelling stuff' to his band.

While he was clearly disappointed to be forced to abandon his larger ambitions for this set – unless there are some vital missing pieces locked in his Vault – it's important to acknowledge that the *Crystal Ball* concept was largely inchoate. Would the triple set have been a greater artistic achievement than the double album? Undoubtedly. Look at all the songs dropped during the editing process – 'Rebirth of the Flesh', 'Crystal Ball', 'Rockhard in a Funky Place', 'The Ball', 'Joy in Repetition', 'Shockadelica' and 'Good Love'. And this battle could be seen as the beginning of the conflict between artist and record company that would continue for much of the next decade. But it also seems likely that

Crystal Ball or an extended *Sign o' the Times* might not have been as big a commercial or critical success: the four sides of *Sign o' the Times* took long enough to absorb, and an extra seven songs might have prompted listeners and critics to dismiss the record – as some did with the later *Emancipation* – as an overstuffed folly. Certainly, Alan Leeds believes there was no possibility that Warner Brothers were criticising the actual music on offer, only the feasibility of putting out a triple album. 'The argument wasn't about the music,' he says now, 'it was about doing three records. It was too high a retail price point, too cumbersome and difficult to market. It just wasn't wise. *Sign o' the Times* was an important record because *Purple Rain* had gone through the roof and *Around the World in a Day* did quite well but turned its back on some of his fan base, and there had been a backlash in the black media particularly. And *Under the Cherry Moon* didn't do what Prince wanted it to do. This was the record where we needed to get radio back on our side, quit being too cutting edge and too difficult and deliver a fastball down the middle.'

. . . OR *SIGN O' THE TIMES*?

Sign o' the Times' reputation has dipped slightly in recent years – it no longer tops the lists of various rock-heritage magazines' hundred best albums, and sometimes doesn't appear at all – but it remains not just among the high points of Prince's career, but a central reference point for contemporary musicians. Should it ever be remastered and reissued, it will undoubtedly have a new life, especially if Prince puts out everything from the period. Alan Leeds says: 'I often wish Prince were more interested in dealing with his archive, because first of all there's no properly remastered versions of his classic albums because he refuses to participate in the process or allow Warner Brothers to do anything, but if I was in charge of his archive I would do the deluxe edition of *Sign o' the Times* and recreate the three-disc version. Even perhaps a *Dream Factory* release.'

If Wendy Melvoin's contention that Prince was always thinking about *Sign o' the Times* as a self-contained album is true, it seems likely she was referring to the period between Prince recording the title song – during a week in Sunset Sound Studios in mid-July 1986 – and the disbanding of The Revolution. Although the song is Prince on his own, he did first introduce it during a performance with The Revolution in Osaka, singing the first two lines of the song before going into 'Pop Life' instead.

Prince often introduces new songs in this teasing way, but the connection between 'Sign o' the Times' and 'Pop Life' is significant: as always with Prince's political commentary, there's an apocalyptic fatalism that makes 'Sign o' the Times' something more[1] (or for some listeners, less[2]) than a straightforward protest song. While there are straightforward digs at Ronald Reagan and the American administration in the song – an attack on his Star Wars programme and a suggestion that the *Challenger* space shuttle disaster is an argument for halting space exploration – and a criticism of US economic policy, he's equally concerned with disease and natural disasters. Given the presence of a straightforwardly Christian song elsewhere on the record, 'The Cross', the absence of any mention of God in the track surprises, as does the suggestion that the best way to cope with the question of theodicy is to get married and have a baby. But focusing on whether the lyric hangs together misses the point. The reason why this song is so beloved is the way it sounds. After all the avenues that Prince didn't pursue, the song he finally settled on delighted because it sounded even more crisp and spare than *Parade*.

The way Prince controlled the slow release of information at the beginning of the record's promotion was a masterclass in creating anticipation. There were two months between the single coming out and the album appearing, the period of greatest excitement for Prince fans who bought the records as they were released. Millions of listeners had deserted Prince after *Around the World in a Day* and *Parade* – and *Sign o' the Times* would see only a small upswing in sales – but for those still paying attention, this was Prince's most mysterious statement of intent to date. The cover of the single appeared to show Prince in drag, holding a black heart in front of his face (it was actually Cat Glover, a dancer and choreographer and another new member of his band). The video for the song told the audience nothing about the new personnel, the new direction or indeed the new album, instead forcing the audience to focus on the lyrics and sound of the song, as it consisted mainly of the song's lyrics and the occasional heart or geometric graphic. Watching the video now, it doesn't seem that groundbreaking, the pastel pink and electric blues in the graphics and lettering immediately marking it out as a typical 1980s project. But compare it to the majority of rock videos from 1987 – a year dominated by the big hair and glam metal of Starship, Heart and Def Leppard – and its restraint seems revolutionary.[3]

Although not included on the actual album, the single's B-side, 'La, La, La, He, He, Hee', was as much a clue to the album's eventual contents as the main track. The nonsense talk so important to the album is most in evidence on this co-write with Sheena Easton. Per Nilsen has argued, without citing his source, that the song wasn't a true collaboration, and that the credit was handed out for inspiration alone after a conversation between Prince and Easton in which she argued that lyrics had to be meaningful, while he protested (during a time when he was becoming increasingly preoccupied with surrealism and deliberate use of nonsense imagery) this needn't be the case. If this is true – and it fits with his explanations of how he composed similarly lyrically lightweight songs such as 'Poom Poom' and 'Make Your Mama Happy' – it's easy to imagine Prince walking into the studio, programming the drum machine to start barking and improvising the song to prove his point. But if so, he makes up for the simplicity of the chorus – which is about a cat and a dog who pursue each other sexually – with one of his most beguiling vocals and verses that play against the simplicity with weird psychodrama. It seems to be a song about groupies, or one-night stands, power and control: a foreshadowing of the serious themes that would preoccupy him in the early 1990s.[4]

Cats, dogs and sex would also inspire a *Lovesexy*-era B-side too,

'Scarlet Pussy', credited to Camille. Whether these feline references were inspired by Cat Glover[5] – or merely the cat/pussy/vagina connection – is unclear, but there's something very beguiling about these songs. If this conversation about lyrical content did take place, maybe it was the lyrics to the duet Sheena Easton sings on the album, 'U Got the Look', which inspired it, as although it was the album's third (and most successful) single, it's the album's least lyrically sophisticated track.

Sheena Easton wasn't the only woman Prince was having these kinds of creative conversations with: 'Slow Love' is co-credited to actress, singer and writer Carole Davis. I called Davis and asked her how the collaboration had worked, wondering if it was a similar situation to Prince's work with Easton. But she said with her things were very different. 'It wasn't much of a collaboration. I wrote the song and he wanted to buy it from me. He had his lawyers call me, and they offered me $25,000 to own the song outright, and I refused, and they got back to me about a month later to give me 50 per cent of publishing and writers, which I accepted for the opportunity to appear on a Prince record.'

Davis is an accomplished actress, which is how she first came into Prince's orbit. 'I met him through auditioning for *Purple Rain*. They offered me the role, but at the time I'd just come off *The Flamingo Kid* and the script was only ten pages long and had page after page of what looked like porn. In the movie business, Prince was completely unknown.' Davis wasn't present when the song was recorded and found out about it through his attorneys. She knew it would appear on *Sign o' the Times*, and he had already recorded it before he had Davis's agreement. 'He's an emperor, you know.'

You can hear the additions Prince made to the song by playing it back-to-back with Davis's own recording of the song, released

on her 1989 album *Heart of Gold*. In Davis's version, it's the man
on the moon rather than the man *in* the moon who's smiling,
and the race-car driver bit is new. That Prince should choose
this song for the only appearance of Clare Fischer's orchestra-
tions on the album is further evidence of just how carefully this
seemingly scattershot record was put together, and Brent Fischer
remembers his father taking particular pleasure in playing on this
track. '"Slow Love" was very fun for my father to work on, simply
because he really likes those kinds of bluesy ballads, and he's done
a lot of work like that as a jazz musician, playing on somebody
else's record as a keyboard artist or playing on his own recordings.
So he got to put into play all of those great influences – Ellington,
Strayhorn, and also a little bit of Shostakovich in there too.'

Each of the four sides is linked just enough to work as coher-
ent parts of the whole, but not so much that the record becomes
an over-schematic concept album: where you expect fullness it is
sparse, and vice versa. It grows in emotional intensity with each
side (the opening track aside, it starts with party tracks, moves
into sex songs, has a third side mainly of psychosexual drama, fol-
lowed by a final side that combines religion and romantic devo-
tion). There is no filler. But while the album is given emotional
force by two of the *Camille* songs, 'Strange Relationship' and
'If I Was Your Girlfriend', there is also much in the lyric sheets
that remains mysterious, although never lacking in psychological
impact.

Later in the 1990s, Prince would start filling up his records
with all sorts of samples and references that seem to lead nowhere
deliberately, and there's some of that on *Sign o' the Times*, but for
the most part his nursery-rhyme imagery is deployed with delib-
erate intent. It's important not to play rock detective, though. I'd
often wondered whether the character of Cynthia Rose in 'Starfish
and Coffee' was a secret homage to Cynthia Robinson and Rose

Stone of Sly and the Family Stone. But Susannah Melvoin told me the song portrayed a girl they knew. 'We knew somebody named Cynthia Rose and [the song has] beautiful imagery, and we were at the house and he went downstairs and came upstairs a few hours later and there it was, "Starfish and Coffee". I said, "It's fantastic, it's so sweet. Cynthia, if she really knew, she would love this."'

Other songs never quite seem to reveal their secrets. 'Play in the Sunshine' seems like a straightforward party song, but there's a sadness to the lyric: Prince sings about wanting to have fun as if it was the last time, and the initial take was recorded during his final recording session with Susannah. It would be reading too much into the song to suggest that Susannah's encouragement to Prince to play and his refusal towards the end of the track might reveal something of the dynamic of their relationship in its final stages, but the song is undoubtedly more emotionally powerful than a light, bright pop track should be. It was also one of the few songs I asked Susannah about that she wouldn't discuss.[6]

The lyric of 'The Ballad of Dorothy Parker' is similarly beguiling. Prince's Dorothy Parker (a blonde waitress) has no relation to the great Algonquin Round Table wit (although it's certainly fun to imagine her in a bathtub with Prince), and the lines in the song about Dorothy being quick-witted and the fact that the real Dorothy Parker died on the day Prince was born are merely fodder for the conspiracy theorists. The song was inspired (once again) by an argument with Susannah, or a dream Prince had, or a combination of both. Although the Parker reference seems accidental, that Dorothy's favourite song is Joni Mitchell's 'Help Me' seems more than just a shout-out to one of his biggest influences,[7] as the song mentioned (from 1974's *Court and Spark*) is a female inversion of the situation in which Prince has placed her.

Not all the songs are lyrically ambiguous. Never performed

live in full, and recorded by Prince alone, 'It' is a straightforward statement of sexual obsession. Prince is back having sex on the stairs (he finally sounds like he's a perfect match for Darling Nikki), and the song is essentially a repeated insistence of how much he likes 'it'. But it's all about the delivery. In chorus with himself, taunting himself, whispering, standing up close to the microphone and sounding so far away he can barely be heard, this is one of his most complex performances. 'Forever in My Life', which he confessed he wrote for Susannah,[8] is delivered almost entirely without kink. Susannah believes the reason why this song (and the others he wrote for her) are so significant and lasting is that there was more 'on [the] line'. The song has remained potent: the late John Kennedy Jr played it at his wedding, and I saw Prince reinvent it on his 2010 tour, singing it with a power he hadn't brought to *Sign o' the Times* songs for years (he usually throws them away as part of his synth or piano medleys) while his new girlfriend, Bria Valente, stood at the side of the stage, smiling.

Alongside the three Camille songs on side three is 'I Could Never Take the Place of Your Man', another track rescued from his early-1980s home-studio tapes. It's another variation on a theme that preoccupied Prince during the early years: that he is such a good lover that no woman would be satisfied with having been with him for only one night. The complication here is that the woman he approaches is a single mother, and it's not just sex she wants, but a husband. The song is almost a short story – Prince the dirty realist – and a model of coherence compared to his sketchier later lyrics.

But it's not just love and sex that inspires straight-talking on the record. Prince's use of religious imagery is almost always cryptic – and his two most spiritual albums, *Lovesexy* and *The Rainbow Children*, are so dense they seem to be written in secret code – but 'The Cross'⁹ is unusually direct, a straightforward tale of the Second Coming that fits with the apocalyptic themes elsewhere on the record. Surprisingly, given Prince's frustration at losing out to U2 at the Grammys when *Sign o' the Times* came out, when Bono took the stage with Prince at The Pod in Dublin in 1995, Prince let him sing 'The Cross'. Halfway through, a source who was present confirmed for me, Bono forgot the words ('Eastertime?' he improvised hopefully at one point) and started ululating.¹⁰

'It's Gonna Be a Beautiful Night' is described in the sleeve notes as a straightforward live track, the last song to be credited to Prince and The Revolution until he briefly revived the name for *1999: The New Master*. In reality, it's a far more complicated creation. Beginning as an onstage jam at the Zenith in Paris recorded by a mobile truck in the same way he did with the original versions of 'I Would Die 4 U', 'Baby, I'm a Star' and 'Purple Rain', the song was subject to endless tinkering. Susannah says Prince told her the song needed backing vocals, and that he got her and Jill Jones to add these during a session with Susan Rogers at Sunset Sound. He then recorded Sheila E doing her rap interpretation of Edward Lear down a phone line from Mississippi over the song, and got Matt Bliss and Eric Leeds to add new instrumentation. It's hard to understand why Prince wanted to expend so much effort on the track, especially given the superiority of tracks like 'We Can Funk', but he'd talked onstage earlier that night about making a live album, so perhaps when that project was abandoned, this was a way of justifying the expense of recording the show. Although I doubt this was a deliberate intention, there's also something poignant in the fact that Prince was literally recording over his work with The Revolution with members of his new line-up.

*

More than any other Prince album, *Sign o' the Times* is structured as an experience that requires deep immersion. Any seeming sloppiness in the construction generally proves to be a case of second-guessing. If Prince was going to include a long live (or pseudo-live) track on the record, the obvious place for it is at the end of the final side. But he flipped the order of the last two tracks, so that once you've got through the looseness of 'Beautiful Night', there's one last beautifully constructed treat, 'Adore'. It's not a hidden track, but the reason for the positioning seems similar. Later, Prince would ruin the song when playing it live by turning it into a stand-up routine.[11] But in its original version it's a perfect encapsulation of the album's themes, and a precursor to the sound and the mixture of spirituality and sex that he would expand on in *Lovesexy*.

At the time, if splitting from The Revolution was the price necessary for Prince to produce records of the calibre of *Sign o' the Times*, *The Black Album* and *Lovesexy*, it seemed an acceptable one. As wonderful a band as The Revolution undoubtedly were, it was the right time for Prince to change his line-up and return to the studio alone. And it is clear that Prince did feel a great deal of responsibility towards all the musicians working for him – the problems with The Revolution, after all, started when he overloaded the band with new personnel and created what some dubbed 'The Counter-Revolution'. But from the long perspective, and after twenty years of hearing Prince play with various permutations of The New Power Generation, it seems like a far more serious sacrifice and it's hard not to regret that Prince didn't find some way of treating the group like Neil Young does his Crazy Horse or Bruce Springsteen his E Street band. Prince has, at various times, used members of The Revolution again, as well as reviving the band's name – briefly – for an entirely different line-up, but some fans still remain desperate for a full reunion.[12] It seems clear that the reason Prince avoids this is due to his distaste for nostalgia (and possibly, Wendy has suggested, religions concerns) – although it's possible he will change his mind on this if and when he reissues his old records – but rather than hear the band rehash the past, a new collaboration could still produce interesting work.

Certainly, Susannah believes that Prince lost something after this period. And while she and Wendy both acknowledge the quality of some of the songs on *Lovesexy*, they are less impressed by his subsequent records. As Susannah says: 'Now he's let himself off the proverbial hook, he doesn't have to go to those places any more, he just stays right where he's supposed to, to be safe with his heart. And I don't know if we broke it for him. Good Lord, this is a guy who'd sleep on the couch in our house. We knew him the way he wanted to be known and we saw that guy on plenty of occasions, and we were the people who said, "You could be that guy all the time," but it took a big leap of faith that he wouldn't get his heart broken.' Wendy goes further, and although she has worked with him on several occasions since the disbandment of The Revolution – and wanted to emphasise to me that though she was feeling down on him the day we talked, her feelings about him fluctuated (Lisa adding that if he walked into the room now, they'd both give him a hug) – sometimes she did feel annoyance. 'People wanna talk about him all the time, and I'm happy to, but sometimes it's hard. Yeah, he was great, he was better than most, but he's not now.'

By the time he had finished *Sign o' the Times* and all the associated songs, Prince did not want to be *that guy* any more. Who he wanted to be instead would soon be revealed, in now traditional Prince fashion, to the audience at First Avenue.

FOR THOSE OF U ON VALIUM . . .

As with the 1983 benefit concert for the Minnesota Dance Theatre, when Prince played First Avenue in 1987 he was showcasing a substantial amount of new material and introducing new band members, but this time he wasn't in the early stages of engagement with a worldwide audience, instead competing with his past. In the years between these two shows, he'd become one of the most famous celebrities in the world, made two major motion pictures and recorded three albums still regarded as among the greatest pop records ever pressed to vinyl. But he must have drawn some confidence from knowing he had his best record to date about to ship.

Prince introduced the performance as a rehearsal, as he often did with home-town shows – a regular stage in his creative process. The actual rehearsals had taken place in his usual space at the Washington Avenue Warehouse (it wouldn't be long before Prince's Paisley Park complex, the focal point of so much of the later part of his myth, would be complete, but for the moment he was continuing to rehearse in a space that held a strong connection to his past with The Revolution), but this was the first time he'd tested the new songs in front of a paying audience.

In the Warehouse, they had been preparing a show somewhat different to the one he'd eventually take on the road, consisting almost entirely of the new album, plus 'Kiss', the Madhouse song 'Four' as an outro to 'The Ballad of Dorothy Parker', and a cover of Charlie Parker's 'Now's the Time'. The most significant change with this new band was the presence of Sheila E on drums: for all her evident qualities as a solo artist, this was her finest hour (and one of the very few rock shows in history when the drummer embarking on a solo wouldn't be a cue to visit the bar), and she knew it, telling *MTV News* that playing drums in Prince's band was 'more exciting, more fulfilling than being a solo artist'.

In front of the Minneapolis audience, Prince played a whittled-down version of the rehearsal set, which still included one song ('Strange Relationship') he'd dump before the tour. On the way he'd also jettison 'Starfish and Coffee' – rehearsal recordings suggest he'd yet to work out how best to perform this song; by the *Lovesexy* tour it had become part of a piano medley, where it's mostly stayed till this day – as well as 'The Ballad of Dorothy Parker' (the rehearsal version brought out both the Latin and soft-jazz inspirations, but lacked the album version's dark urgency) and 'U Got the Look', which Prince attacked with fury in rehearsal, accusing the object of the song of taking a 'fucking hour' doing her make-up before replacing half the track with a Vegas vamp. That it would later become one of his favourite songs to play live seems extremely unlikely at this point.

Wearing thick-framed glasses and a dangly earring, Prince introduced the band that night as 'new friends' – Levi, Miko, Greg Brooks, Cat, Wally, Boni – an 'old friend', Dr Fink, another new friend, his new polka-dot suit, Atlanta Bliss, 'Mr Madhouse' Eric Leeds, Sheila E on the drums, and then cracked, 'For those of you on valium, my name is Prince.'

Opening with 'Housequake' on this night was a defiant gesture: no one in the audience would know about the quake, and when they pretended they did, he called 'bullshit'. By now, he had decided to integrate old songs into the show, and he played some tonight – 'Girls & Boys' and 'Kiss' – but the highlight was the song he'd ditch, 'Strange Relationship', during which Prince seemed to be channelling Stevie Wonder.

The inclusion of Charlie Parker's 'Now's the Time' (on the road it was occasionally replaced by Prince's own jazz song, Madhouse's 'Four') was significant in a period when Prince was opening himself up to a stronger jazz influence in his music (his jazz band Madhouse were support for this tour[1]), and with this cover, Sheila's drum solo and an extended 'It's Gonna Be a Beautiful Night', which featured the 'squirrel meat' section and raps of the *Black Album* song 'Superfunkycalifragisexy', it was clear this new band were far less rock-focused than The Revolution. Still, there remained some rock-show clichés: a plasma lamp represented the Crystal Ball, which made it far less exciting than the lyrics had suggested.

For the tour proper, which took in thirty-four shows in Europe but no performances in either the US or the UK (some planned dates for London and Birmingham were cancelled due to weather and licensing problems), Prince expanded the show to include most of *Sign o' the Times* plus a few hits – 'Little Red Corvette', 'Girls & Boys', 'Let's Go Crazy', 'When Doves Cry', 'Purple Rain', '1999' and 'Kiss'. Though lacking the incredible cohesion Prince would bring to his entire songbook on the *Lovesexy* tour, there was still juice in the hits and true pleasure to be found in the horn- and drum-heavy reworkings of 'Let's Go Crazy' and (especially) 'When Doves Cry'. During this period, 'Purple Rain' was generally kept under control, a reminder of the past instead of an excuse to jam, and the band seemed to get a lot more out of 'It's Gonna Be a Beautiful Night', which would see Prince trying to bring together Duke Ellington and James Brown, a combination which perhaps best defines his ambition for this particular band.

*

Nineteen eighty-seven also saw the completion of Prince's Paisley Park complex. One of the first releases to emerge from there was the film *Sign o' the Times*, a strange hybrid of live-concert recording, self-conscious re-enactment and dramatic movie that provides a somewhat unsatisfactory document of the era.

Prince had wanted to put out a live concert video of the European show as a way of avoiding an American tour. Alan Leeds says he was disappointed at this decision. 'I think we all were. In hindsight I think it was a mistake. Aside from those "Hit and Run" dates, which were only a handful of dates, he didn't tour to his American fan base. Particularly his black fan base. To anyone who was concerned about his new pop image, the fact that he was ignoring the traditional US touring routes only kinda fed that. I don't want to say there was a backlash, but there might have been some confusion among his fan base because he seemed so completely focused on embracing Europe.'

Prince employed a British camera crew to record the last three dates of the tour at the Ahoy in Rotterdam, but dissatisfied with the low-quality recordings, decided to overdub the sound and re-record the show on a soundstage, adding dramatic interludes between the songs to create a story about a love triangle between Prince and his dancers Greg Brooks and Cat. The film opens with Prince lurking in the shadows, while Cat and Greg argue. Early in the show, Cat rejects Prince, then later, after being upset by Brooks's refusal to communicate, approaches Prince, who rebuffs her in turn with 'I Could Never Take the Place of Your Man'. By 'Hot Thing', some sort of arrangement seems to have been worked out, with Brooks and Prince both admiring the 'sweet sticky thing' as Prince slides through her legs to bite off her skirt. Soon, Prince and Cat are mounting a mirrored heart together, before Prince puts his clothes back on for the more spiritual conclusion of the show.

If you ever want to see evidence of the strong and lasting friendship between Sheila E and Prince, track down the footage from an MTV documentary about the film in which she plays along with this scenario and suggests that the fictionalised relationship between Brooks and Cat was very much on her mind during the *Sign o' the Times* performances, as if this was really what she was worrying about instead of keeping the beat.

Shortly after the film's release, Prince would play a handful of shows in the US: a show at Minneapolis venue Rupert's – a club that would soon play an important role in Prince's myth – attended by his father and Susannah Melvoin, where he debuted 'The Sex of It'; a ten-minute performance at the *MTV Music Awards*, followed by an after-show where he performed with Huey Lewis; and two significant jazz-orientated shows. At the first, Prince and his band masqueraded as The Fine Liners and covered Miles Davis's 'Freddie Freeloader'; at the second, a New Year's performance at Paisley Park, he performed with the man himself on a version of 'It's Gonna Be a Beautiful Night' that stretched for over thirty-three minutes. For all its historical significance, Davis commentator George Cole suggests the collaboration was of less value than might have been hoped, observing that 'although Miles's chops are good, his presence is less than imposing, and his body language lacks the confident swagger one is accustomed to seeing when Miles is on-stage. The interaction between Miles and Prince consists of a short section where Prince copies Miles's trumpet phases with scat vocals. In less than four minutes, Miles has blown his horn and gone.'[2]

Nevertheless, it marked a moment. And if the brief period when Miles and Prince collaborate onstage is not that significant beyond the fact that it happened at all, this is only one part of a huge performance of this song, which later includes Prince telling Miles it's past his bedtime and (somewhat half-assedly) dissing Greg Brooks and (with far more assurance) his biographer Jon Bream, comparing him (among other things) to Grover from *Sesame Street*, before, chuckling at his own malevolence, wishing him 'Happy New Year', and then at the end of the song and the show promising it was all a joke.

To those Prince fans (or casual admirers) who believe that he lost his way with *The Black Album* and *Lovesexy*, this show might even be seen as marking the end of his significance. So it seems ironic that this period seems to have meant so little to Prince, who couldn't be bothered to tour the US and would soon be completely swept up in an entirely new creative direction. While his management might have been irritated with him, Prince made the right decision and was about to achieve his creative peak. But before he could find the light, he first needed to lose his way.

SPOOKY AND ALL THAT HE
CRAWLS FOR . . .

For all the mythology around *Dream Factory* and *Crystal Ball*, it seems at least some of the stories surrounding *The Black Album* are true. The album was slated for release, and according to Matt Fink, Prince gave copies of it to his band, encouraging them to learn the songs for a forthcoming tour (in the event, only three of them were performed, 'Bob George', 'Superfunkycalifragisexy' and 'When 2 R in Love', which was rescued from this project and placed on *Lovesexy*, the album eventually released instead).

In his *Possessed: The Rise and Fall of Prince*, Alex Hahn marshals several sources to suggest that Prince decided to hold back the album after an experience with Ecstasy, writing that Matt Fink was told this by Prince's bodyguard, Gilbert Davidson.[1] The theological crisis Prince experienced at this time seems to be a mid-point in his religious development. Unlike the conversation with God that took place onstage during performances on the *Purple Rain* tour, this seems to have been a genuine crisis, albeit one that provided the music press with a useful bit of mythology with which to promote the new album. But at the same time, it doesn't seem to have been as deep-rooted a change in attitude as would take place later in the 1990s. Prince would begin a period of reading and searching in 1991, but at this time it still seems that his religious questioning was part of the performance, something that would give a shape to the shows on the *Lovesexy* tour.

Whatever his motives, the decision to withhold the release of the completed album was a publicity masterstroke. The record's cultural impact was enormous, and lasting, as it became one of the world's best-known bootlegs. A year after the official release of *The Black Album*, British novelist Hanif Kureishi published a novel of the same name set in London in 1989 that uses knowledge of the bootleg as a cultural test (pp. 18–19) and features a character, Shahid, who is encouraged to write a paper on the singer by his supervisor (p. 25), while Keith Richards writes in his autobiography of the record's impact on Mick Jagger.[2] Still, *The Black Album*'s reputation suffered a serious hit when it received official release.

Perhaps the most surprising thing about the record is that (a large portion of it) was conceived as party music, with songs recorded for Sheila E's birthday. There are references to dancing and sex, but there is also an unmistakably harsher tone to the album, and it's easy to see how Prince spooked himself with the disturbing quality of some of his lyrics. In another of the apparently deliberate contradictions that turn regular fans into obsessives, while Prince sneaked a message into the 'Alphabet St.' video telling fans not to buy the record, there is a semi-hidden intro to the beginning of *The Black Album* during the first song, 'Le Grind', which suggests that by locating the record listeners have been initiated into a secret club. Addressing the listener directly (but in a slurred, distorted voice), Prince announces his presence and conveys his pleasure that we have found him. This introduction makes it seem that Prince always knew that finding the record would be a challenge, although presumably because he planned to release it in a plain black sleeve as 'Something' by 'Somebody' rather than because he always planned to suppress it. That said, during an MTV report on the *Sign o' the Times* film premiere, the announcer reveals that Prince has announced the forthcoming release of his *Black Album* (as well as a 1988 US tour that never materialised), so every music fan of the time would certainly have known about it.

'Le Grind' resembles the party music on *Sign o' the Times*, and the connection of dancing to sex is nothing new, but the lyrics seem more reductive than ever before. It's ironic that the album that features Prince explicitly dismissing hip hop (on the track 'Dead on It') should feature his own rapper of the time, Cat Glover, swiping lines from J. M. Silk's 'Music Is the Key' on 'Cindy C'.[3] The song is inspired by the supermodel Cindy Crawford (there he goes once again, falling in love with a face in a magazine), but it's a strange tribute, with Prince rhapsodising about her 'furry melting thing', which sounds more like a Womble in a heatwave than anything you'd be hoping to find in a supermodel's underwear.

The two most significant songs, opening the second side of the vinyl album, while not officially released at the time, made it into the live performance. 'We learned some of the songs,' Matt Fink told me, 'and performed "Bob George" live on the *Lovesexy* tour and "Superfunkycalifragisexy", but not every night.' 'Bob George', which would be performed almost as a mini-play, is among the most theatrical of Prince's songs, almost spoken-word in places. Prince sings the song in character (exactly who he's playing is open to debate: when he performed the song onstage he would explicitly refer to himself as 'Camille', but this isn't the case on the album) as a man who beats his unfaithful girlfriend and is capable of scaring off the police when they arrive to arrest him. Though we never hear from the girlfriend, it becomes clear that she's seeing the Bob George of the title (the name believed to be a combination of manager Bob Cavallo and music critic Nelson George), who manages Prince. This man refers to Prince as a skinny motherfucker with a high voice,[4] before having a phone conversation with his conscience (onstage, it would be with a man named Joey, perhaps a reference to past alter ego Joey Coco). I asked Cavallo what he made of a song believed to be about him. 'I don't understand it. Why do people say it's a reference to me? I certainly didn't go around with any hookers or buy furs for women or whatever he was insinuating.'

'Superfunkycalifragisexy', which was accompanied in the live show by Prince and Cat performing S&M games onstage, is one of the most intense songs Prince has ever written. Sharing some of the surrealism of 'Play in the Sunshine', it appears to be an account of drug-fuelled sex, but instead of referring to the Ecstasy or cocaine one might imagine playing a role in such a sex session, the lovers are feeding on 'squirrel meat', brought to them by Brother Maurice.[5] The song also shares a mood with some of the *1999*-era out-takes, suggesting Prince pushing himself beyond all the boundaries that normally confine his work.

'2 Nigs United 4 West Compton', by comparison, is a dull funk-jazz workout, reminiscent of the worst of Miles Davis's late recordings. I wrote in Chapter 13 about Susannah's experience of working on 'Rockhard in a Funky Place', and it was clear from her comments there that the song was a throwaway, of little interest beyond the title's pun.

Some previous biographers and critics have dismissed *Lovesexy*. And some of the musicians around Prince at the time have also expressed misgivings. Those who approach Prince's career as a narrative often see this as the start of his creative decline (although it's striking how many of Prince's erstwhile associates refer to the album's first single, 'Alphabet St.', as his career highlight). For me it rivals *Sign o' the Times* as Prince's finest album. It's the record that proves Prince could survive creatively without The Revolution, and if *Sign o' the Times* was not quite the solo endeavour it appeared, then *Lovesexy* represents a true leap forward in

Prince's work on his own. It is not entirely a solo pursuit: Cat raps on 'Alphabet St.', the late Boni Boyer occasionally provides backing vocals, Sheila E plays drums throughout, and 'Eye No' was recorded with his band of the time. But although he makes light of his work by noting in the sleeve notes that he plays 'whatever' on the album, it is the most satisfying example of Prince (nearly) alone in the studio, striking out into new territory. It would be a long time until he would record another album as complete and satisfying as *Lovesexy*, and only twice after would he so successfully change gear and present a record that came as a true surprise (*The Rainbow Children* and *3121*).

While *Lovesexy* does feature the band playing on some tracks, it's evident that these aren't straightforward band performances. Matt Fink has no memory of playing on 'Eye No' (largely, I think, because the song was built up from the original outtake 'The Ball'), and of 'Lovesexy' he said dismissively: 'I guess I did [play on it]. I'm just in the mix. Sometimes you're not sure when you're being used.' Constructed initially as a single suite of music – with no track breaks on the original release – *Lovesexy* is Prince's densest and most coherent album. Unlike almost every other Prince album, it was almost entirely the result of a single concentrated, sustained period of writing and recording, with little second-guessing or trips to the Vault. 'When 2 R in Love', the one 'positive' song from *The Black Album*, was rescued and given a new placement, and 'Eye No', as mentioned above, was created from the bones of 'The Ball', but aside from that, the record was created entirely from scratch. The only out-take from the sessions is a not very good house-influenced track called 'The Line', which features Prince, Sheila E and Boni Boyer dicking around to a background of churchy synths and clicks.

Lovesexy is also Prince's most spiritual album, although the religious message is conveyed in a cryptic private code. As (almost) always with Prince, his beliefs are Manichaeistic, and the record (and the subsequent tour) gets dramatic purpose from an ongoing battle between God (personified here as 'Lovesexy') and the Devil ('Spooky Electric').

'Eye No' works as an origin story for the new Prince (and this record begins with him welcoming us to the 'New Power Generation'), and contains a defiantly simplistic statement of the drama to follow: Prince knows there's a heaven and hell, and this album is going to be the story of how he avoided the latter and found the former. The song combines what sounds like Prince's personal redemption from a private hell with some vague sermon- ising (avoid drugs, don't drink every day). The track turns largely on a homophonic pun ('know' and 'no'), but it's a confusing one: the song is initially a rejection of Spooky Electric's negativity, but then Prince suggests that saying 'no' to temptation is the key to survival. The lyrics, though clearly important, are, however, far less arresting than the incredibly busy arrangement, which – in common with the rest of the album – feels as if every instrument, every motif, every sound is in competition. The horns, the vocals, the percussion: everything fights for supremacy, but as soon as a guitar lick or sampled vocal emerges from the mix, it's brutally cut off. Prince has never been better.

'Alphabet St.' is one of Prince's very greatest singles, and yet it's also the one to which he's done the greatest disservice, now always turning it into a country hoe-down (often accompanied by a throwaway line about how he can do country music too) when he plays it live.[6] Peter Doggett has argued that the phrase 'Wham bam thank you ma'am', used by David Bowie in his song 'Suffragette City', first appeared (in music at least) on Charlie Mingus's 1961 album *Oh Yeah*.[7] Of course, by the time Prince used a variation of the phrase in his 'Glam Slam', it had long since passed into common currency, but it would be pleasing to think that, even if only subconsciously, the echo of glam rock in the title was an acknowledgment of Bowie's previous use of the phrase.[8]

'Anna Stesia' is another song cherished by fans, one of the few to survive the *Lovesexy* tour in Prince's live set. I write elsewhere in this book about how the song has become a vehicle for Prince's sermonising – his message often surprisingly trivial (anti-smoking and anti-doughnuts in Lisbon in the late 1990s; imploring people to join his fan club in the live version of the song on 2002's *One Nite Alone . . . Live!*) – but he has never quite destroyed the magic of the original in the same way he has with 'Alphabet St.'. The song seems to fit with the *Black Album/Lovesexy* mythology, as well as Prince's habit of attending nightclubs in search of material. The back story is this: on the first day of December 1987, Prince had gone to Minneapolis club Rupert's to play his new album to club-goers. There he met local musician Ingrid Chavez, who supposedly contributed to his decision to abandon the release of *The Black Album* and work on a spiritually fulfilling album instead.

There's more than a whiff of self-mythologising here, but 'Anna Stesia' offers a fascinating dramatisation of a similar club scene. Prince, lonely and lost, in search of anyone, of either gender, to save him from a nocturnal world, goes dancing with 'Gregory' presumably his dancer Greg Brooks, serving the same valet service Jerome does for Morris or Wally did in 'Wally' – although rather than backing up his boss, tonight he looks like a 'ghost'. Prince encounters 'Anna Stesia' (renaming the women around him again), who transforms his life by leading him back towards God, and the light.

Lyrically, 'Dance On' is essentially a rewrite of 'Sign o' the Times' that ends with a variation on 'All the Critics Love U in New York'. It is even more cryptic and generalised than 'Sign o' the Times', and more resigned – here people are dancing on not in defiance of the apocalypse, but because they're past caring. The solution, Prince suggests, is a new power structure focused on production. But what makes this more than a funky economics lesson is the arrangement: the lyrics missing from the lyric sheet all relate to Prince's bass, which he is encouraged to pick up like a man in a Western being thrown a gun, and the song alternates between bass lines, synths and machine-gun noises. It's among Prince's most musically adventurous tracks, and it's a disappointment that he never returned to the song or the sound after the end of the *Lovesexy* tour.

All the contradictions of the album are in evidence on the title song, 'Lovesexy', in which it's deliberately unclear whether he's singing about God, a lover or the divine part of himself. He defines 'Lovesexy' as the feeling of falling in love with the heavens, but this seems linked to the cosmic oneness following ejaculation (in this song, in a chipmunk voice, he's caught dripping all over the floor) rather than going to church. Buried in the mix are some of his most explicit lyrics.

'When 2 R in Love' makes a lot more sense on this record than it did in the middle of *The Black Album*. It's Prince back in the bathtub, a standard ballad given an elegant arrangement that raises this above all the future Xeroxes. The shortest song on the album, 'I Wish U Heaven' is barely there, little more than the title repeated over and over, and yet it's still more moving and memorable than most of Prince's 1990s output. He extended the track for a twelve-inch release, adding Parts 2 and 3 to the song. The second part begins as a parody-reworking of 'Housequake', turning into essentially a gospel number before Prince announces that he's playing his 'blue angel' guitar, the blue cloud guitar he would famously favour during the *Lovesexy* tour. The final part of the song moves so far away from the original track that it's been suggested (by the authors of *The Vault*) that it's actually an alternative song called 'Take This Beat'.

'Positivity' sums up the album's message, but it has a curious querulous quality to it. Made up almost entirely of questions (this time to be answered 'Yes', the song keeps reminding us, instead of the 'No' that has pervaded the record so far), it's never quite clear whether the song is attacking money itself, immorality in making it, the educational system or those who drop out. Only at the end does any clear message emerge, and once again it's the rejection of Spooky Electric. But in spite of the relentless affirmation, as Prince sings with a mouth full of chewing gum, he's never sounded so demonic, and it would be this tension that would drive his subsequent tour and next album.

CROSS THE LINE

There are many Prince fans who regard the *Sign o' the Times* era as a live high point for Prince. But for all the obvious qualities of this period, I can't help but see it as a dry run for the tour that followed. While, ultimately, it's hard to call whether *Sign o' the Times* or *Lovesexy* is Prince's greatest album, the *Lovesexy* tour was clearly superior to the run that preceded it. All of the anxious energy that crackled during the *Sign* shows had clearly gone. Prince was relaxed at the *Lovesexy* rehearsals, chatting to his band about the acid-jazz/jazz-funk boom taking place in England at this time and telling them how much he enjoyed Weird Al Yankovic's Michael Jackson parody 'Fat'.

Among those present at these rehearsals was Steve Parke, a life-long Prince fan who would go on to become an important part of Prince's creative team during the 1990s. Parke, a visual artist, had grown up dreaming of working for Prince. '[I had] no idea [in] what capacity,' he told me, 'but as a kid I was always drawing and painting, so I thought, "I'll do paintings for him."' This ambition came true via a friendship with a musician in Sheila E's band, Levi Seacer, Jr. When Seacer was playing guitar in Sheila E's band, Parke had met him backstage, drawn his picture on a napkin and given him his number, and the two of them had stayed in touch as Seacer was drafted into Prince's band. Parke had taken to sending Seacer paintings of Prince through the post, and Seacer had been showing them to his boss. After a year of this, Parke received a call from Alan Leeds asking him if he'd be interested in working on the set for the 'Glam Slam' video.

When Parke got to Paisley Park, he says he 'literally looked at the stage in the round that was for the *Lovesexy* tour, all [made] out of plywood. And we sat down with a piece of board and drew out all these elements and went to the wardrobe department and looked at all the knick-knacks they had to see what he was into and came up with this design. He approved it and off he went. I had three days of him being out of town. I hired two people from the Minneapolis children's theatre and I said, "Let's get a third of this stage done before he gets back." I was twenty-five at the time, and I literally stayed up three days straight.' But he got the job done, and Prince was pleased with him. Parke remembers that Prince would generally start rehearsals at one o'clock, and that he was there to watch them every single day. 'Once I got in, my goal was to become as indispensable as possible,' he says. 'I told the merchandise woman I could design T-shirts for him. The first tour shirt I did for him, they were segmented into four pieces, they were different artistic styles, and I literally did that in my hotel room. I had to rent a compressor and an airbrush and just sit in my hotel room and paint. I remember at one point he thought the chin was a little too long, so I got him to sit down and drew him.'

At that point, Parke recalls, the previous art team had left and Prince wanted to bring everything in-house. Parke was asked if he wanted to be the art director and if he knew how to do graphics on a computer. 'I said, "Sure,"' Parke remembers, 'and I basically went out and bought a computer and taught myself.' He also remembers getting to hear the various parts of *Lovesexy* as separate tracks, which confirmed to him the quality of the album. 'I love *Lovesexy*. I thought it was a great step musically, but it was almost too much for people. My background is not as a musician but I like very complicated stuff. I grew up on fusion and was used to dissonant sounds and subtlety. I used to listen to an album thirty or forty times and wanted to be surprised every time. So getting to hear the separation of those tracks amazed me. It's that balance between being artistically satisfied and really wanting people to see what you did.'

The *Lovesexy* tour remains Prince's greatest achievement. It offered the best-ever setting for his songs, and it's the one show that truly integrated the best of his past with the music he had recently created. For seventy-eight shows across Europe, the US, Canada and Japan, Prince presented a show lasting between two and two and a half hours that dramatised the defining conflict in his art – a battle between the darker (occasionally violent, almost always sexual) side of his work, and his lighter, more spiritual music. Later in his career he would try to jettison almost all of the darker side, which meant that a reasonable amount of the first half of this show consists of songs that we will never hear live again. While Prince had had misgivings about releasing *The Black Album* as a whole, he was comfortable using 'Superfunkycalifragisexy' and 'Bob George' to take him deep into the darkness in the first half of the show.

After the failure to record usable footage of the *Sign o' the Times* show, this time Prince used a much bigger crew with a far greater number of cameras to record a show in Dortmund that is widely considered the best document of Prince's live performance in existence. Broadcast all over Europe, the performance was later released on two videos (inexplicably, the first half of the show was titled *Lovesexy Live 2* and the second half *Live 1*), but has never been re-released on DVD, a terrible oversight. The video recording is better than *Double Live, Sign o' the Times* or any other Prince film or video release, and for all the acclaim awarded *Sign o' the Times*, this truly deserves the accolade of the greatest concert film ever released.

The stage set was enormously expensive, costing a rumoured $2 million, but worth it. A car engine starts and Prince rides to the stage in a Ford Thunderbird. For the first half of the show he is involved in a series of sexual, romantic and occasionally violent negotiations with Cat, Sheila E (and less frequently Boni Boyer). On a circular stage, the band is mostly shunted to the edges, while the focus remains on Prince as he performs his best (and mostly darkest) material. 'Erotic City' becomes the soundtrack to a *ménage à trois*, 'Jack U Off' a promise at the end of a date (an offer Cat responds to by momentarily switching her attentions to Miko). 'Sister', his most controversial released song, was played live for the first time since 1981 (and after this tour, would never be played again). Prince and Cat successfully shoot basketball hoops on the court that is just one part of this enormous and versatile stage. During 'Head' (the highlight of all Prince's early shows), Cat would pretend to give Prince a blow job onstage, while he tried to silence the audience with a finger to his lips. In the mammoth show, with every song tightened to the bare minimum, he found room for an unreleased song too, and for many this version of 'Blues in C (If I Had a Harem)' was the highlight of the performance. (A studio version of this track does exist, but it is a pale sketch by comparison, and though Prince considered the song for a subsequent album, it was soon abandoned.)

The most psychosexual section of the show begins with Prince pressing Cat up against his daddy's car, before the two of them climb into a bed with a neon headboard. Suddenly, the mood changes, Cat escapes and Prince is left bouncing on the bed to 'Superfunkycalifragisexy'. Cat ties Prince to a chair with plastic hose before the lights go on for 'Bob George', less a song than a one-act play as the two of them act out the roles of a jealous gangster and his moll. Using his microphone as a gun, Prince pretends to shoot Cat as the band plays machine-gun FX. He mimes getting drunk, and then sirens sound and the police arrive. He pantomimes a shoot-out with cops, before making a phone call to his friend Joey and identifying himself as Camille. As the police close in, he recites the Lord's Prayer, as he once did during 'Controversy', only this time getting shot midway through.

After Prince's symbolic death, the darkness disappears and the show takes on a lighter, more spiritual quality, beginning with the stand-out track from *Lovesexy*, 'Anna Stesia'. Rather than re-enact the dramatic events of this song, Prince plays it alone at the keyboard as he's elevated upwards, sounding more serious about these lyrics than he's ever been about anything. After an intermission, he plays a recording of Ingrid Chavez reciting lines from *Romeo and Juliet* and her poem 'Cross the Line', before performing the entire *Lovesexy* album – barring 'Positivity', which was dropped from the set and reserved for after-shows after the first few performances in France – interspersed with the more uplifting or religious songs from past albums, such as 'The Cross' and 'Purple Rain', and a long piano set (performed this night in an embroidered frock coat) which would become a staple of later performances. The stagecraft for this half of the show is mostly much simpler, the songs presented without theatrics. They meant too much not to be delivered straight. But as sometimes happens when an artist bases a tour around an album, he clearly tired of the *Lovesexy* songs, and after this tour, he abandoned not just the darkness, but also the light: aside from 'Anna Stesia' and 'Alphabet St.', he would never play this music again.

Prince's show at the Het Paard van Troje in The Hague was the third of nine after-shows he would play on the *Lovesexy* tour, and has become the most legendary after-show he ever performed. That Prince had the mental and physical stamina to create such an overwhelming experience in the middle of the night for the

favoured few after what must have been an extraordinarily drain-
ing show in front of 30,000 people is a feat beyond any other
(pop) musician. Even his band couldn't keep up with him: Eric
Leeds went to bed and missed the chance to play a role in this
essential part of Prince's history, which for the band member
with the strongest memory and sense of occasion must have hurt
(I didn't ask him about this when I spoke to him – it seemed
tactless).

While the audience whistled, Prince began the show with a
long, downbeat but thrilling guitar-and-piano jazz instrumental
that expanded on the Madhouse-inspired jams he played at after-
shows on the *Sign o' the Times* tour and also resembled the Billy
Cobham song 'Stratus' that would much later become a staple
of Prince's after-show set. It is this show that most contributed
to fans' awareness of how his after-shows would differ from a
main concert, and this introduction immediately establishes the
musical and artistic difference between the two strands of his live
performances.

The show as a whole was given a narrative thread by the way
this instrumental (and 'D.M.S.R.', next in the set list) incor-
porated guitar elements from 'Rave Un2 the Joy Fantastic', the
song he would (coming full circle) end with. The show was also
defined by the heavy use of sci-fi synth throughout, most promi-
nently in the new song 'People Without'.

After thirteen minutes, Prince addressed the audience, prais-
ing them for their sobriety. Slowly, he put together 'D.M.S.R.',
a song that always gives Prince and the band room to improvise.
Having instructed Levi Seacer to 'just rumble, junior', he asked
Sheila E what beat she could put to his guitar. In subsequent
interviews, band members would talk about the joy and fear of
the after-show concerts, during which Prince would deliver direct
commands (although these can also be found on official albums,

such as the pseudo-live recording of 'It's Gonna Be a Beautiful Night' on *Sign o' the Times*) and correct mistakes in front of the audience. As the song continued, he pushed Levi and Miko, giving the audience a demonstration of 'chicken-grease' guitar[1] before playing a snatch from 'America'.

Although he's never recorded a studio version, Prince's cover of The Temptations' 'Just My Imagination' (via the Stones' version on *Some Girls*) is regarded by most as one of his live career high points.[2] He played the song a dozen times during 1987 and 1988, and footage of him doing so (with Mica Paris guesting) at an after-show in Camden Palace a month earlier is one of the highlights of the *Omnibus* documentary finally broadcast in 1991. Sour immediately followed sweet: 'People Without' makes me sad, and uncomfortable. It reminds me of the much later 'PFunk' (aka 'F.U.N.K.'), in which Prince's scattershot approach seems to equate disease, ugliness and poverty. It was around this time that he started to toy with the concept of the 'New Power Generation', which would, of course, become the name of his backing band, but which also, at times, referred to the audience, and it tied into the occasionally authoritarian side of Prince's message. Per Nilsen, who admires 'People Without', quotes Cat as claiming responsibility for inspiring it. She told Nilsen the attack is on people who 'take for granted what they have, while there are others who don't have anything', but this doesn't quite square with the lyric, which maybe isn't that surprising given that, as Cat elaborates, 'he was making all this up as we went along'.[3] He would play the song again at the next after-show, but by then the menace had gone; in this version he's almost paying penance for the cruelty of the first rendition.[4]

Attempting to lighten the mood, Prince made a bad knock-knock joke, and when the audience didn't get it, distanced himself from the gag with a jazzier, loose version of 'Housequake' with much less of the anger it used to have now that Holland did indeed know 'bout da quake. The next few songs were covers, the sort of blues and funk he'll often dig out for his band to work on: a version of 'Blues in C' including 'Down Home Blues' and Charlie Parker's 'Billy's Bounce', then 'Kansas City' and James Brown's 'Cold Sweat' for Boni. Often the covers section can be where an after-show loses its power, but there was something cold and precise about the performance that held the attention, plus the weird way that Boni sounds like she's Brown's sister and the return of Edward Lear the proto-rap lyricist as his 'The Table and Chair' is appropriated once more.

Tonight, 'Forever in My Life' began with the music from 'I Wish U Heaven (Part 3)', and Prince sang the song with no commitment whatsoever; it's a reminder that the song is sung to a lover and could easily be a closing-time lie. On vinyl 'Still Would Stand All Time' will sound like filler, but in front of the Dutch it became a lost slow-blues masterpiece (even if Prince sang in a slightly silly voice and the band cocked it up⁵) enlivened with peculiar imagery (who takes a black box of paraphernalia on a date?) and inappropriate anger. On this night, Boni did The Staple Singers' 'I'll Take U There' so well that it would forever afterwards be apparent that she was the best of the strong female voices Prince has surrounded himself with onstage ever since, and then he played the best version of 'Rave Un2 the Joy Fantastic' he'd ever do, a song so strong he'd twice try to create an album around it. His band were so emboldened by their performances that now when he gave them instructions, they answered back, so confident were they in what they'd achieved.

Alan Leeds was disappointed by Prince's last-minute decision to switch the US leg of the tour to after the European performances. 'It would have made a lot of sense to tour America first. His audience were clamouring for it. He hadn't really toured since *Purple Rain*, this was now the fourth record since then. And the record was being received a bit apprehensively: in retail because of the controversy over the cover, at radio because the record was programmed in one suite. So we had a lot of challenges. I don't understand why he was hesitant. I suspect that the success of *Purple Rain* had been so mammoth that he was just gun-shy about trying to compete with that. And feeling that anything he would do would pale in comparison. It just wasn't smart.' Bob Cavallo was no fan of this tour, telling me: 'I wanted him to do what he eventually did many years later. I said we shouldn't be doing all this production. He comes out in a car, he has a piano that goes two storeys high and he preaches during the intermission. I didn't like it. I thought he should have the best musicians he could have, whoever they may be, a clean stage, no production, and play music and show his unbelievable performance and songwriting ability.'

During the US leg, there were after-shows, all of which had their moments, but nothing to rival the Dutch Trojan Horse performance for quality or significance, before an eight-date tour of Japan to finish off the project. What Prince wants to do with his treasure trove of live recordings is up to him, of course, but if he put the Trojan Horse show out officially, it would lead to a reappraisal of his live work that might help the world at large move on from repeatedly calling him a 'genius' performer, without any real sense of what that 'genius' entails, to truly understanding how his work onstage and at after-shows is as vital a part of his art as anything manufactured in a recording studio.

This year, when Prince was truly at his peak, he also collaborated with his female equivalent in the pop world, Madonna, writing the track 'Love Song' with her. He also played guitar on two other tracks on her album *Like a Prayer*, 'Act of Contrition' and 'Keep It Together', as well as offering her the song 'By Alien Means'. But 'Love Song' is the only track that feels like a true meeting of their respective styles. In a 1989 interview, Madonna would tell Paul Zollo[6] how her collaboration with Prince worked, and also make critical comments about his relationship with the outside world. Assuming that everything she says is true,[7] she explained that in this instance it was more collaborative than Prince's usual process when writing songs for other artists. Prince played the drums, and Madonna played the synthesizer, and they came up with the melody line together. Then she improvised lyrics, and Prince overdubbed some guitars. Prince made a loop of this improvisation, and Madonna added sections and sang parts to it and sent it back, and the process continued in this way. As she explained, 'It was like this sentence that turned into a paragraph that turned into a little miniseries.'[8]

Madonna also made the pertinent observation that although Prince generally tended to dominate people, their collaboration was refreshing for him because they'd achieved the same level of success. Zollo encouraged Madonna to show off by suggesting that her two 1980s pop contemporaries, Prince and Michael Jackson, had experienced a weakening of their 'connection with the world', while hers had strengthened. Madonna took the bait, claiming that was because she'd stayed in touch with the world, while 'Michael Jackson and Prince have really isolated themselves.'[9] Still, in this interview she emphasises that she is a major fan of Prince's music, saying how incredible she found the tracks on his next album (presumably *Graffiti Bridge*, as Prince wanted Madonna to play the love interest in the movie, although she didn't consider the script worthy of her talents).

Zollo pointed out the similarities in Prince's and Madonna's early careers, and how they had both concentrated in their music on the separation between sexuality and religion. But there are also parallels between their later careers, particularly in the way that both artists have attempted to adapt or absorb subsequent musical trends: both faced the problem of having to follow up enormous world-conquering success; both suffered a stalled film career; both are ruthlessly upwardly mobile; and both ended up courting Hollywood anew with their Oscar parties. Prince critic Alex Hahn has suggested that Madonna proved a shrewder strategist than Prince, arguing that she fared better as an actor[10] and evolved more gracefully as an artist. This is debatable. It's true that Madonna didn't suffer the public ignominies that Prince did during the 1990s, that she tried to help him with his record label in 1997[11] and that he turned to her for assistance once more in 1999,[12] but although many of her records have been more enthusiastically received by music critics at the time of release, her body of work is ultimately far less interesting (and rewarding) than Prince's, and has already begun to feel dated.[13] While Madonna, who at the time of writing is well into a new career as a director, made the right decision in ducking *Graffiti Bridge*, the lack of further collaboration between the pair, as between Prince and Miles Davis (though Prince has boasted of treasures recorded with Davis still in the Vault), cannot but seem like a missed opportunity.

DANCE WITH THE DEVIL

It's easy to understand why Prince would be attracted to writing songs for the *Batman* film, and why its director, Tim Burton, would want to work with him. It must also have seemed like a good instance of creative synergy for Warner Brothers. Alongside the obvious money-generating benefits, it gave Prince a more commercial playground in which to explore the Manichaeism he had toyed with using invented personas such as Spooky Electric. The deal also came at a time of great behind-the-scenes turmoil for Prince, having recently made a business decision which from the outside looked extraordinary, replacing the management team that had served him so well with the director of *Purple Rain*. Alan Leeds remembers: 'Famously, at the end of 1988, he decided to clean house, and we came into work the day after New Year's and there were all these legal notifications that Fargnoli, Ruffalo and Cavallo were fired, Fred Moultrie, his business manager in accountancy, was fired. Even Lee Philips, his attorney, was fired. By this time, we had offices in Paisley Park, and by now we had clerical staff and engineers – twenty employees in the building every day. And I shared an office with Karen Krattinger, who helped run the building for Prince and took care of his personal stuff, and she said, "You're not going to believe the telegrams that have been floating around this morning. You'd better sit down." And the question became who in the world is he replacing them with and how come we didn't know this? This was all so clandestine. And all of a sudden the new manager is Al Magnoli. I thought it was insane. A music-business manager? He had absolutely no background or experience for that.'

But Prince had a history of forming close relationships with someone and then expecting them to take on roles beyond their normal capability, and the strange decision was not out of character. Leeds says: 'He was very frustrated with what he deemed the failure of the *Lovesexy* project. And the management stood up to him and wanted to hold him accountable for the decisions he had made and how they had contributed to that failure. And there were money issues at the time. *Purple Rain* was a cash cow, but he built Paisley Park from the ground up with cash. He had a sizeable staff on retainer year round. He had a wardrobe shop with seven or eight employees working five days a week. The overheads got completely out of hand. And he was frustrated with Warners. It was somebody waking up and thinking, "Let's start over."'

It wasn't just the appointment of Magnoli that Leeds questioned. 'The replacements for the business management and the legal team came recommended by Magnoli, so I saw it as a huge conflict of interest. That's not to suggest anybody in there had improper agendas, but there's going to be a point where decisions are made and there's differences between artists and management and you need somebody to be a tie-breaker, and you're putting them in a position where they can't do that.' Howard Bloom believes that this decision was fatal to Prince's career. 'When Prince withdrew, he withdrew not just from me, but also from Bob Cavallo, which was a big mistake because we were his contact with reality and his audience.'

Nonetheless, anyone who has experienced the difficulty of endeavouring with a creative project once you have lost the support of your closest confidants will understand the siege mentality that Prince appeared to adopt during this period – though it wouldn't be long before Albert Magnoli would also leave Prince's employ, and the repercussions of these decisions would continue to impact throughout much of the next decade. During the honeymoon period, however, there was *Batman*, and though this was always regarded as a shrewd business decision, it is rarely given its due as a work in itself. It should also be noted that this record wasn't the film's soundtrack – the score was by Danny Elfman and was released separately – and that only five of the album's nine songs ('The Future', 'Electric Chair', 'Partyman', 'Vicki Waiting' and 'Scandalous') appear in the movie, with 'The Future' heard only in the distance and 'Scandalous' buried in the end credits. It makes most sense, then, no matter how this sounds, to view it as a concept album about Batman, and it can be seen as the third of an unofficial trilogy following *The Black Album* and *Lovesexy*, the three Prince records that seem most concerned with a conflict between good and evil. Alan Leeds considers it a natural successor to *The Black Album*, but also sees in it the seeds of the hip-hop-influenced records that followed, pointing out that it's 'very dance- and funk-orientated'.

Weaker overall than most Prince albums, it's a significant work nonetheless,[1] and only *Purple Rain* sold more copies on initial release, although this seems more down to the publicity machine than the quality of the songs. But out-takes and alternative versions of songs intended for this record reveal that it could have been a much more adventurous project. The most substantial song not to be included on the finished album, and the one truly great track completed during this era, is 'Dance with the Devil', which resembles the later song (and video project) 'The Undertaker' in its personification of evil and the lure of wickedness. As with 'Batdance', the lead single released from the album, it was inspired (and built around) a line from Sam Hamm and Warren Skaaren's screenplay.

The *Batman* screenplay, rather like Prince's song-suite, has a curious surface-level to it, with many lines seeming to refer to themes or ideas that have been left out of the finished film. The line this song is built around also resurfaces in 'Batdance' (and is followed by terrible screams, sampled from the soundtrack but given an extra charge here) and is one of the most memorable from the film – The Joker's kiss-off to his victims, and in the movie, the line that unlocks Bruce Wayne's memory that it was The Joker who killed his father.[2] Prince even reworks the line in his acknowledgements, although in the twist he gives it here (and in the 'Dance with the Devil' lyric), it seems to take on an additional meaning not necessarily apparent in the original screenplay. Prince seems to blame the victim, suggesting that dancing with the Devil is something someone does out of curiosity, and in doing so the person dooms themselves. Although it has been suggested that Prince abandoned the song because it was too dark – if true, it seems like this was a period when there was a lot of self-censorship going on – it's also a song that doesn't fit with the drama. For Jack Nicholson's Joker, the Devil is someone to make jokes about, albeit of a sinister nature (for him, dancing with the Devil is just something of which he likes the sound). Prince, however, does not share this lightness: a song about the Devil is serious business. But in his interpretation, the victims deserve what's coming to them: it's a punishment for curiosity.

On the album as released, the sleeve notes suggest that each song is from the perspective of a *Batman* character or characters ('The Future' and 'Scandalous' by Batman;[3] 'Electric Chair' and 'Trust' by The Joker; 'The Arms of Orion' by Bruce Wayne and his girl-friend, Vicki Vale; 'Vicki Waiting' by Bruce Wayne; and 'Batdance' by Batman, Bruce Wayne, Vicki Vale, The Joker and a new character Prince had created for himself for the project, Gemini), but 'Dance with the Devil' doesn't appear in character (unless Prince

B9L BACK ROW:
    Geary Cain
    Stanley Sullivan
    Mrs. Rader
    William Pettis
    Paul Yanzer

Daniel Novack
Keith Waaraniemi
Danny Steinbach
Edward Braziel
SECOND ROW:
Danna Creighton

Kathy McDonough
Denise Smith
Esther Greer
Sharon Nunn
Lorna Livingston
Yvette Jackson
Dianna Sanders

FRONT ROW:
Prince Nelson
Roosevelt McDuffie
Candace Minton
Donald Hanson
Joe Tramel
John Nickens

Prince with his father and family. Prince remained a fan of his father's music and would play tapes of it to members of the Revolution in the mid eighties.

Prince and his sister Tyka attended John Hay Elementary School, which no longer exists.

Dez Dickerson (right) believes he was closest to Prince in the early days.

Morris Day and Jesse Johnson of The Time, which initially grew out of, Lisa Coleman believes, 'jokes and silliness'.

Vanity 6 brought together Prince's ex-girlfriend Susan Moonsie, Denise Katrina Matthews, whom Prince renamed 'Vanity' and his former 'wardrobe mistress', Brenda Bennett.

Sheila E has made regular appearances alongside Prince onstage from the mid eighties to the present day.

A planned concert video of the 1999 tour entitled The Second Coming was one of the first major projects to disappear into the Vault.

Lisa Coleman remembers that when Dez hit his distortion pedal the rock fans in the audience would go wild.

Wendy and Lisa were central to Prince's sound throughout the mid eighties.

Prince brought Wendy and Lisa up with him when accepting the Oscar for Best Original Song Score from Kathleen Turner and Michael Douglas, giving an incredibly dignified acceptance speech.

Prince's massive Purple Rain tour included a six-date stand at the Nassau Coliseum.

Some were troubled by the depiction of The Kid and Appollonia's relationship in Purple Rain. Prince answered criticism by pointing out he didn't write the movie.

Hollywood comes to Sheridan, Wyoming, Lisa Barber won the competition to get the film's premiere in her hometown, and Prince as her date for the evening.

planned for Batman to share his perspective). However, this system is further complicated by Prince's claim in an interview with a German journalist that The Joker wrote 'The Arms of Orion'. In the same interview, Prince also says that 'the album was supposed to be a duet between Michael Jackson and me . . . he as Batman, me as Joker'.[4] Liz Jones suggests this was a passing whim of *Batman* producer Jon Peters.[5]

The other songs that Prince demoed for the album but which didn't make the final record – '200 Balloons', 'Rave Un2 the Joy Fantastic', a revamp of the 'Batman Theme' and 'We Got the Power' – are far less compelling, with the first emerging as a B-side and lines from the third being rolled into 'Batdance'. As with much of the album, these are extremely minimalist, repetitive tracks that, while appealing, feel more like sketches than significant songs. Closer in sound to *The Black Album* than *Lovesexy*, they show Prince using this opportunity to explore dark and disturbing work (his lyrics in 'We Got the Power' are murky and violent) within a comic-book scenario.

Rather than shape the music to fit the film, Prince tried to shape the film to his music, creating a comic-book character for himself called Gemini[6] who appeared in videos for the album, including the 'Partyman' video that would later inspire a homage from electro band Hot Chip. As well as the unreleased songs themselves, there are also unreleased alternative versions of some of the tracks, including 'Electric Chair', which have a clear affinity with other late-1980s/early-1990s tracks built around old soul samples, like Chad Jackson's use of the sax intro from Marva Whitney's 'Unwind Yourself' in his 'Hear the Drummer (Get Wicked)'. Given Prince's lasting interest in James Brown, it was inevitable that this sort of thing would capture his attention.

Prince would dust off three recent songs for the project – 'Electric Chair', 'Anna Waiting' and 'Scandalous'. It seems from interviews that Tim Burton was aware of this recycling. The rest were written specifically for the album (though the wonderful *Camille*-era 'Feel U Up' also received official release during this period as the B-side to 'Partyman'). To support the album Prince performed 'Electric Chair' on *Saturday Night Live*, with a surprising line-up including Candy Dulfer and the protégé-who-never-quite-made-it, Margie Cox. While the stagecraft was overly regimented and slightly clumsy (you can understand why he hid the band as much as possible during *Lovesexy*), it was a surprisingly spirited performance, suggesting that no matter what motivated him to get involved with the project, Prince was capable of wringing some emotion out of work-for-hire material.

While 'Electric Chair' was a perfect fit for this comic-book retro-futuristic project, 'Anna Waiting', written for Anna Garcia (credited in the acknowledgements under the alias Prince gave her, 'Anna Fantastic'), didn't really work with the title changed to 'Vicki Waiting', especially not with the added penis and vagina jokes at odds with the gothic-but-stately mood of Burton's film. 'Scandalous' has not been explicitly linked to Garcia, but it seems that difference in age might well be the focus of the scandal in this song.[7] In the narrative context of the *Batman* album, the scandal instead is the relationship between Bruce Wayne and Vicki Vale. But by the time Prince put out an extended, nineteen-minute version of the song entitled 'The Scandalous Sex Suite', the source of the scandal had changed again, now seeming to refer to the real-life relationship between Prince and *Batman* actress Kim Basinger, who was already part of Prince's fantasy world due to her appearance in *9½ Weeks* (the sort of classy soft-core that Prince often uses for inspiration, such as his early-1990s interest in *Barbarella* and *Caligula*). Basinger contributes straight-faced, suggestive (and hilarious) dialogue to this extended version, which appeared on a maxi-disc that also contained the absurd

'Sex', an extended dance song sung by an alien called 'Endorphin' from the planet Venus, who has come to Earth in search of a sex partner so talented he'll be able to remain faithful to them.

By comparison to 'The Scandalous Sex Suite', 'The Arms of Orion', a duet with Sheena Easton, was one of Prince's blandest songs to date, and unsurprisingly, was not used in the actual film (the song's B-side, 'I Love U in Me', was far more impressive). But the most memorable instance of Prince's music in Burton's film is 'Partyman', used to convincing diegetic effect as The Joker's henchmen blast it from a 1980s boom box while the gang deface *Whistler's Mother* and other priceless artworks at Gotham City's Flugelheim museum. 'Trust', also used in the film, features Prince sneaking a Christian message into a Joker song, reminding us that we should trust God rather than a cartoon super-villain. 'Lemon Crush' (which didn't make the movie) features Prince rhyming 'jobba' with 'robba' and is so lackadaisical it seems the definition of filler, largely of interest for Prince's continued use of double entendre (at the risk of coming across like one of those awful English professors who see innuendo in everything, I'm assuming the 'lemon' here is a vagina and the crush both the sexual act and the secretions produced during it). Even 'Batdance', which was Prince's first US number one since 'Kiss', has a sketchy feel to it, built on samples of dialogue from the film and a multitude of other released and unreleased songs.

Brent Fischer, whose father's work is sampled on the album, remembers: 'We never knew about the whole *Batman* thing. We got a call from somebody at Warner Brothers saying that music that we had previously recorded for Prince for an unrelated song had been lifted from that song, the orchestra tracks had been lifted from that song and placed as sort of background noise behind a new song that Prince had recorded for *Batman*.' Although Fischer does not remember which song was sampled, he thinks it was one of the unreleased ones, and 'The Future' features string samples from the then yet to be released 'Crystal Ball'. 'I don't believe that the orchestra parts are in the same key or even in the same tempo as the new song in which they were used, but what they were used for was an effect.'

'I got a new band,' Prince announced onstage at the Civic Center in St Paul, previewing the Nude tour to a Minneapolis audience and acknowledging the reshuffle that had taken place since the *Lovesexy* run. His band had actually steadily diminished (in number, if not necessarily in quality) since the *Sign o' the Times* tour. Dancers Greg and Wally had gone before *Lovesexy*, while Boni Boyer, Eric Leeds, Sheila E, Atlanta Bliss and Cat Glover had departed afterwards, leaving only Miko Weaver, Levi Seacer, Jr and Dr Fink.

This was a tough period for Prince. Weaver and Fink would leave after this tour, and before it began the rest of the band witnessed Prince and Miko arguing after Prince kept asking him to turn his guitar down, prompting Prince to invite Miko to continue the conversation outside, something Miko refused to do because of Prince's bodyguards.[8] Nevertheless, for a while at least, both Weaver and Fink remained essential to Prince's band.

The new members for the Nude tour were Rosie Gaines, drummer Michael Bland and three new male dancers, The Game Boyz – Kirk Johnson, Damon Dickson and Tony Mosley – whose presence might initially have seemed risible but of whom at least two would go on to play a very important role in Prince's later direction. Indeed, playing in Prince's band was starting to resemble working for a company, with ample opportunity for promotion.

Given the showmanship and sheer ambition of the *Sign o' the Times* and *Lovesexy* concerts, the stripped-down, back-to-basics

Nude tour was inevitably going to be a let-down for those who came expecting to see Prince playing basketball while singing and riding around on top of a Thunderbird with Cat and Sheila E. It wasn't the first time that Prince had followed up a big, showy, theatrical tour with stripped-down concerts (such as the 1986 'Hit and Run' shows that followed *Purple Rain*), and he would do so again in the future, but the Nude tour was surprisingly long, with fifty-one dates in Europe before five in Japan. It was also frustrating to see Prince returning to so much of *Purple Rain* and sticking mostly to a relatively concise show, playing largely the same set night after night. But the set was given a unique dimension by the presence of *Batman* material, as well as songs from the as yet unreleased *Graffiti Bridge* (there would be no tour for that album, which came out during the Nude run). Every night he would open the show with 'The Future', but the song would undergo a fascinating development during the run, as Tony Mosley began to use it as the basis of a new rap song entitled 'The Flow', which would prove crucial to later changes in Prince's sound.

This tour would also be the only time Prince would play 'Batdance' live, and was also the only time he regularly played 'Partyman', until he inexplicably revived it in 2006. Fans who'd yet to hear *Graffiti Bridge* were astonished by the stunning blues of new song 'The Question of U', which occasionally saw him reviving his 'Electric Man' rap from 1985 to newly powerful effect. Blues was also present in the show with a hold-over of 'Blues in C (If I Had a Harem)', from the *Lovesexy* tour, and a cover of B. B. King's 'Don't Make Me Pay for His Mistakes'. And this was also the tour which saw Prince beginning his reclamation of 'Nothing Compares 2 U' from Sinead O'Connor, and I remember the one date I saw with great fondness. The disappearance of Fink and Miko after this tour didn't represent as dramatic a schism as the break-up of The Revolution, but it did accompany a significant change in Prince's sound, and for those who prefer the harder-edged Prince work, there is much to be found in this era, when Prince took one of the most commercially marketable intellectual properties in the world – *Batman* – and made it work for him.

20

WHAT'S WRONG WITH
GRAFFITI BRIDGE?

A recurring pattern in Prince's life is him inspiring, whether wittingly or unwittingly, other people to produce artistic work of their own which surpasses anything they do that is not connected to him. This is most obvious with musicians, but it's also true of artists and film-makers. And when he becomes aware of this, Prince can be enormously generous to other dedicated souls.

Steve Parke's female Baltimore neighbour told him that twenty years ago, she remembered walking past his house daily and noticing him working until three in the morning every day on a painting of Prince. It was this painting that helped inspire Prince's next album and new film. 'The *Graffiti Bridge* album cover', Parke says, 'was really a showpiece for my skills at the time. Basically, I said because I've got the contact with Prince, I might as well do something that he might like or might inspire an idea. A lot of it was channelling my inner fan. What has he done, what hasn't he done? What are elements that I hadn't seen him use? A lot of elements were just things I thought would be kinda cool, kinda trippy. It was a nod to the '70s *Bitches Brew* [-style] covers: not as dark, much poppier and more commercial.'

When he'd finished the painting, he got in touch with Levi Seacer, Jr, who said: '"Why don't you send the painting out here?" So I sent it out and one day he called me and said, "Hey, Prince has got that on his desk. He looks at it a lot." And then I get a call from Prince one day, and he says, "I think I want to make this the album cover." Oh, really? I thought it might inspire an idea but not become the cover. I did have to go back in and rework it a little bit. I had to put Morris Day in, I had to put in Ingrid and I had to take what was a picture of my wife and put Jill Jones's face on it.'

The dark-haired *Venus de Milo* among the imagery, which might have seemed either something Prince would have included for continuity with his past symbolism or something that Parke might have included in reference to Prince's previous work, was a subconscious inclusion, and not something Parke thought about. 'It's just like Shakespeare,' he says. 'Shakespeare's like, "Sure, you wanna think that?"'

While staring at the painting, Prince had been doing a lot of second-guessing. The process he went through to arrive at the eventual released configuration of *Graffiti Bridge* was almost as complicated as the writing, recording and revision that led to *Sign o' the Times* (and indeed, began around the same time). Once again he was working on several projects at once: an early version of what would become *Graffiti Bridge*, a record called *Rave Un2 the Joy Fantastic* (very different to the version eventually released in 1999), and a planned fourth album for The Time, *Corporate World* (which eventually emerged, in a different form, as 1990's *Pandemonium*), finally merging songs recorded for all three projects.

It's ironic that although so much of the music written for the various permutations of *Graffiti Bridge* seemed designed largely to explore or further a narrative, the released movie has hardly any story at all, and is often (and justifiably) dismissed as a collection of loosely interlinked music videos. By far the weakest of Prince's four theatrically released films, it is far closer to later TV movies or video releases like *The Beautiful Experience* or *3*

Chains o' Gold than *Purple Rain* or *Under the Cherry Moon*. Bob Cavallo remembers early on in the process, 'We were at odds with each other. Our contract was up; five years had gone by since *Purple Rain*. We met at the Four Seasons with his lawyer and his accountant, me and Steve Fargnoli to discuss some kind of rapprochement because he had fired us. Basically he said, "I'll work with you again but you've got to help me make this movie." I read the treatment and said, "This could be an interesting thing," and I said, "I'll try to put you together with some young hip writers and maybe we can come up with a script quickly, 'cause this is pretty detailed." And he went, "What are you talking about? That is the script." It was thirty pages. And he said, "I'm going to shoot it, I know exactly how to do it." So I said, "Maybe we could get this on Broadway for you. Would you be interested in that?" And he said, "No." Now he was pissed that I didn't think this was a good enough script, so we shook hands and that was the end of it. Then, about a year later, we were suing each other. But even when we sued each other, it was kinda funny. I said, "How could you not pay me?" He said, "How could you sue me?" He said, "You can't have my children, those songs. You're gonna give your involvement in those songs to your grandchildren?" And I said, "Yeah, I put ten years of my life into you, and you sucked all the air out of the room. I couldn't really manage anybody else except for your friends."'

Presented as a sequel to *Purple Rain*, it has some continuity with the earlier movie. Once again Prince plays a character called The Kid, who finds himself in competition with The Time – an imaginary rivalry which after nearly a decade was getting tiresome.[1] The Kid writes letters to his dead father (who committed suicide in the first film), and the various clubs in Seven Corners have been willed to their owners by Billy Sparks from *Purple Rain*. But instead of being rooted in the real Minneapolis venue of First Avenue, this movie takes place on an obvious sound-stage and features four rival clubs. And while the first film had originated from observations made by a scriptwriter who had observed the Triple Threat tour, this film, written and directed by Prince, is rooted in a far more uneasy blend of fantasy and reality.

Prince's famous response to the film's failure – 'It was non-violent, positive and had no blatant sex scenes . . . Maybe it will take people thirty years to get it. They trashed *The Wizard of Oz* too'[2] – was clearly an off-the-cuff defence, but he seemed genuinely unaware of the disturbing qualities of his third fiction movie. Although less hard-edged than *Purple Rain*, *Graffiti Bridge* has a dark undercurrent, with a recurrence of the troubling gender relations that for many feminists marred *Purple Rain*. The fact that much of this occurs on a pastel and neon set and there's lots of New Age talk seems only to heighten rather than smooth out these elements.

Still, much of the violence is directed inward. The Kid considers suicide throughout the film, wondering whether he will follow his father's example. And Prince's interest in sadomasochism returns – when he strips off his shirt he has the words 'Beat Me' written inside a heart on his chest. But the women get a tough time of it too. The relationship between Morris Day and his on–off girlfriend Robin Power is troubling: when Morris arrives at the club, his henchman, Jerome, wrestles her expensive coat from her to lay over a puddle to stop Morris dirtying his shoes; and once again pushing the gigolo lifestyle into the gothic, she is forced to dance in a cage at his nightclub and in her underwear at his home. And poor Jill Jones, who, according to Ronin Ro, was so incensed by changes in the script diminishing her role that she tore up the script and scattered it around the aeroplane taking her to Minneapolis,[3] had to make the most of a scene in which she responds to questions from The Kid by removing her panties and leaving them on the floor.

The Kid's main love interest, Aura, is treated less shabbily than Apollonia, but she's still threatened with a 'pimp sandwich', drugged and eventually run over. And there is a distasteful scene of homophobic panic when Morris and Jerome are provoked to retching after accidentally touching each other up in the dark. The film also feels airless in a way *Purple Rain* didn't, and makes the common mistake of low-budget films[4] in that it skimps on extras, with almost all the clubs seeming much emptier than First Avenue. (Significantly, Albert Magnoli noted of *Purple Rain*: 'We had over 900 extras who . . . gave the [film] a tremendous amount of realism.'[5]) Without this, *Graffiti Bridge* looks chilly. Certainly, it was something the film needed to explain away. 'Bit quiet tonight,' Aura comments to T.C. 'That don't ever stop The Kid,' T.C. replies.

While the film continues to be regarded as a turkey – the Fox TV film critic Shawn Edwards voting it top of a list of 'the worst black movies ever' in 2010 – revisionists seized upon the ten minutes or so of circulating out-takes when they leaked, arguing the more sophisticated elements of Prince's vision were lost in the edit suite. But these out-takes consist largely of three more scenes that are, like much of the film, essentially music videos, with only one additional dramatic scene. The music videos – for soundtrack songs 'Can't Stop This Feeling I Got', 'The Question of U', 'Round and Round' and 'The Latest Fashion' – while entertaining, don't really point towards any hidden extra layers.[6] Only 'The Question of U' expands the style of the film, with a troop of creepy black-and-white-clad mimes pretending to be spiders, while Aura scribbles in her diary. The additional scene shows Aura and The Kid on the soundstage playing a game of hangman that presumably precedes the scene in the released version where Aura and The Kid do this in bed. Aura fashions a noose, places this around The Kid's neck, draws a hangman game on the wall with a marker pen and encourages The Kid to choose a letter. The Kid proves no better than Aura at the game, offering as she did 'A', 'B', 'C' and 'D' (don't they know you're supposed to start with the vowels?) as she tightens the noose and threatens to kick his chair away. Fortunately, although he loses the game, she lets him live and we see the phrase she's written is the pleading request from 'Joy in Repetition' (and seen on the wall of the club in the finished film):

'LOVE ME.'

Which, of course, is all Prince has ever wanted.

There is sheet music visible in *Graffiti Bridge* for two songs – 'Rave Un2 the Joy Fantastic' and 'God Is Alive' – that didn't make it onto the final soundtrack, but it is unclear whether it is there as another demonstration of the fecundity of Prince's song-writing and as a tease to the fans, or if the songs were merely lost in an edit.[7] Certainly, at least one major plot-line was lost along the way, a quest narrative in which Prince is searching for 'The Grand Progression', a chord sequence that seems to have similarities with Pythagoras' harmonic scale. It's possible to see Prince's original conception of the story as being a more spiritual version of *Purple Rain*, and indeed a dramatisation of his own creative practice. In the script, Prince is seeking a song which will reveal the location of 'Graffiti Bridge', which is presented as a place of spiritual importance. In order for this to happen, he needs to come up with the right chord sequence. In reality, with each album Prince was trying to come up with the hit that would make the record, and he needed a song that would be even more epic and successful than 'Purple Rain' to make this sequel work a near impossible task, not because 'Purple Rain' was so good, but because it had been so successful and resonated with so many people. Though this narrative seems relatively clear, 'The Grand Progression', the unreleased song that deals with this part of the plot (and which is included in the original screenplay), is, as often with Prince, more cryptic, questioning the notion of time and the existence of God, and focusing on the importance of sex with the person he's with right at that moment. An overwrought, syrupy piano ballad backed with abrasive synth and FX, it has obvious echoes with the song that did appear on the album, 'Still Would Stand All Time', which shares some of the same ideas but lacks the theological questioning. Prince has clearly remained fond of 'The Grand Progression', implying that the song is one of his best in the lyrics to the much later track 'F.U.N.K.'. But 'Graffiti Bridge', his first attempt to replicate 'Purple Rain', is one of a handful of truly terrible Prince songs, up there with 'Poor Little Bastard' and 'Purple and Gold'. Though the song is awful, Brent Fischer remembers his father spending a great amount of time working on it. 'That was another fairly complicated song, not as involved as "Crystal Ball", but the level of complexities, the amount of hours it took to transcribe, then to sit and decide on an instrumentation.' The problem with the song is that the lyrics – a trite description, and reduction, of existential pain – don't justify the melodrama of the arrangement.

Perhaps realising this, the lead single was instead 'Thieves in the Temple', recorded at the end of the process, and it's one of only a few standouts on the album. I remember the excitement at the time of the release of the single, which did suggest that Prince may have found a way of moving on from 'Alphabet St.' and that this new album might be as significant a development from *Lovesexy* as *Lovesexy* was from *Sign o' the Times* (leaving aside

Batman for a moment). But it was a false lead. After the sustained writing period that had produced *Lovesexy*, Prince used the record as a clearing house for a lot of old material, dating back to the early 1980s, which made the double album seem thin. *Sign o' the Times* was an extraordinarily rich collection with no filler; *Graffiti Bridge* had plenty of substandard material, and represented the first weak moment after nearly a decade of constant innovation.

It's not just that the songs were old, but that the more time Prince had spent revisiting and reworking past tracks, the less compelling they'd become. The earliest track, 'Tick, Tick, Bang', had been around since *Controversy*, and the original power of the demo version had been completely neutralised by the time it appeared on *Graffiti Bridge*.[8] *The Vault* dates 'Can't Stop This Feeling I Got' back to some of Prince's earliest home sessions, suggesting it was recorded at home sometime between 1981 and 1982. As with 'We Can Funk', Prince had dug out the song in 1986, having two more shots at it with The Revolution. Both 'Can't Stop This Feeling I Got' and 'We Can Funk' are less compelling in their *Graffiti Bridge* versions, though the former does begin interestingly, with Prince speaking to his father, thus making one of the few explicit links between *Graffiti Bridge* and *Purple Rain*.[9]

Of greater significance are the *Crystal Ball*-connected song 'Joy in Repetition' and 'The Question of U', which though five years old by this time had not been considered for any previous projects.[10] Both match the standard of 'Thieves in the Temple'. In fact, one of the great frustrations of this album is that a third of it rates among Prince's finest work, while the worst of the record is among the weakest of his entire output.

There's too much of The Time on the album, four tracks – 'Release It', 'Love Machine', 'Shake!' and 'The Latest Fashion' – that seem incongruous here.[11] The guest spots from Tevin Campbell ('Round and Round') and Mavis Staples ('Melody

Cool') are substandard songs that don't belong on this album. And Prince's attempt to rename Staples Melody Cool in the way he did with past protégées is embarrassing. Staples gives the performance her all, but it is one of those songs that justifies criticisms that Prince didn't know how to work with this particular music legend.

The song that gave his new band their name, 'New Power Generation', is here in two parts, the watered-down Pepsi-punk a strange comedown for someone who once genuinely challenged the sensibilities of mass America but had long since found wide acceptance (although I admit to a fondness for T. C. Ellis's born-again anti-coke rap). Much of the rest of the record is equally substandard, though weirdly memorable, full of odd hooks that are hard to shake. 'Elephants and Flowers', for example, seems like a slight, silly song, but when Prince played the song live for the first time at his 'Xenophobia' celebration twelve years later, he became overwhelmed by the lyrics. It's clear in this version that in spite of the title's silly sexual analogies, it's as much a religious song in the vein of much of *Lovesexy* as it is smut. 'Still Would Stand All Time' sounded great live but is forgettable on vinyl, smothered and slowed down to within an inch of its life (it's easy to understand Prince's logic in getting gospel-singing siblings The Steeles to do backing vocals, but for all the qualities of the group, it's a polish too far).

Prince was coming off the road when *Graffiti Bridge* was released, and although he did a few dates in Japan after the album came out, it was the tail end of the Nude tour rather than a significant new run. The last batch of songs connected to *Graffiti Bridge* – but recorded after Prince had begun recording songs for *Diamonds and Pearls* – was a brace of tracks recorded for a 'New Power Generation'[12] maxi-single. The run of maxi-singles Prince recorded around this time, beginning with 'The Scandalous Sex Suite' and continuing for several subsequent years, demonstrate a peculiar new creative impulse of Prince's during this time – moving beyond straight remixes into large numbers of interconnected songs that all appear to grow out of the initial track. The repetitiveness is part of the songs' charm, although there's something about this process that doesn't seem entirely healthy. In his 1999 novel *Motherless Brooklyn*, Jonathan Lethem presents Lionel Essrog, a character with Tourette's who considers Prince a kindred spirit and is calmed by his remixes, which he considers 'the nearest thing to art in [his] condition'.[13]

It's easy (like Lionel Essrog) to get lost in this era, in the remixes and alternative versions and past takes, but for all the lost gems here, there is a lack of consistency, a sense of Prince putting out substandard work without truly contemplating how it worked as a whole. After the ruthless editing that had led to *Sign o' the Times* and the creative cohesion of *Lovesexy*, *Graffiti Bridge* is an end point to Prince's peerless run of pop achievement, to be followed by a period when the riches were sprinkled in far sparser amounts, a period when to be a Prince fan was no longer to marvel at the endless creativity but instead to focus hard on the records and try to convince yourself that this was still the same man, that what once was so easy to love had not been lost.

GIGOLOS GET LONELY TOO (PART 2)

Alongside the projects he's self-generated – the models, wannabe actresses or make-up girls pushed into the spotlight – Prince has always kept a keen eye on British (almost exclusively female) talent. The list of British women he has either spent time with in the UK or invited to his studios includes everyone from Lisa Stansfield to Spice Girl Mel B, Beverley Knight to the late Amy Winehouse. Now, no mooted collaboration would raise eyebrows, but in 1984 his work with Scottish starlet Sheena Easton startled some. Before Michael Hutchence boasted of corrupting Kylie, or the alumni of *The Mickey Mouse Club* (Britney/Justin/Christina) grew up and started taking an interest in adult pleasures, Prince set the template for the squeaky-clean-to-sex-machine transformation. Maybe driven by a sense of deliberate pop provocation, or perhaps merely wanting to see how far she would go, he wrote Easton – whose interest in and admiration for Prince had been relayed to him via an engineer who'd worked with both – a song ('Sugar Walls') so dirty it charted at number two on the Parental Music Resource Center's Filthy Fifteen.[1]

Vanity may have stopped working with Prince, but he hadn't given up on girl groups. The common perception of the Apollonia 6 project is that it is inferior to the work Prince produced with Vanity 6, and while it's true Prince strip-mined the eponymous album, taking 'Take Me with U' for *Purple Rain* and giving 'Manic Monday' to The Bangles, the record is by no means a failure, and is long overdue a reissue. Prince often seems uninterested in revisiting his past, but this CD deserves to be remastered. And it should be packaged with the nineteen minutes of footage from the unreleased Apollonia 6 video-album that surfaced on the Internet in 2008.

Directed by Brian Thomson, the production designer of *Shock Treatment* – a deeply peculiar 1981 follow-up to *The Rocky Horror Picture Show* – the incomplete Apollonia 6 movie feels like a collaboration between David Lynch, Kenny Everett and Greg Dark. Beginning at a funeral (the girls are attending in their underwear, and Susan has brought her teddy bear), the girls are informed that Mr Christian, the schoolteacher Apollonia sleeps with in the album's first song, has left everything to his beautiful blonde lawyer. 'Tough titty, girls,' he tells them. 'It's time you learned the value of hard, honest work.' 'But', protests Apollonia, 'we have nothing to wear.' 'Precisely,' announces the deceased Mr Christian from beyond the grave.

Nothing, that is, aside from French-maid outfits, which they don before heading off to a 1980s diner (soundtracked by 'Sex Shooter', the album's 'Nasty Girl' and the one song that had a life beyond the project). With scenes including Susan being groped through her lingerie by a succession of teddy bears and one prospective lover being teased and abandoned in a shopping trolley, looking as tormented as Winston Smith in Room 101, both the album and the video are guilty pleasures, all the more appealing for being so ephemeral.

Prince launched his Paisley Park label with a second record from Sheila E. As with her first, it is a concept album. This time Sheila even has a character, Sister Fate, while the rest of the band are saddled with aliases that make them sound like refugees from *Their Satanic Majesties Request*: Benintino the Wizard, Dame Kelly, Sir Dancelot, The Court Jester (on bongos, no less), The Nobleman, the Earl of Grey and Sir Stephen (had Prince been reading *Story of O?*). The album is called *Romance 1600*, and although Prince also works in references and ideas from the early-1980s New Romantic movement, which was largely inspired by the second half of the eighteenth century, there are several elements of the album that suggest Prince does know his history, such as the fact that court jesters died out with the Civil War, or that Prince also references the pre 1600 Renaissance artist Michelangelo in 'Dear Michaelangelo' (Prince clearly prefers Ruskin's spelling), or that the album's title song takes place at a masked ball. But as with all Prince conceits, this only goes so far, and trying to force all the songs to fit the overarching concept would be to misread (*mishear?*) the record. The album also has a hidden theme: an analysis of sexual difference and the importance of trusting individual desire. Forget Vanity and Apollonia: this is Prince's most sexually liberated album.

The first track, 'Sister Fate', introduces us to Sheila's new character and establishes the idea of the record being like a movie. It was also the first single, accompanied by a video that was a deliberate exercise in toying with Prince's loyal fan base and bringing them to the project. The most striking things about the video are that Sheila and her band are now dressed like Prince and The Revolution and that Prince himself makes a brief appearance. After a copy of the *Daily Tribune* (a disguised version of Minneapolis's *Star Tribune*) is flashed up on screen with the headline 'Who Is Sheila E's Mystery Love?', Prince appears in profile, grinning as he turns his head. Sheila plays two characters in the video, herself and 'Sister Fate', who shapes destiny by blessing lovers with a wand like a good fairy. The lyric refers to a 'nasty rumour' (the video suggests that this is that Prince and Sheila are in a relationship) that the singer doesn't deny but is leaving up to fate to resolve. The song's innuendo can be read in a different way, however, with several hints that it is really about a secret lesbian relationship, with references to 'goin' down' and the ensuing scandal if people discovered 'the real truth'. It's one of the most striking opening tracks on any protégé's album; Prince at his most playful. He gave extra encouragement to his fans to seek it out by putting the twelve-inch vinyl record of the song in Christopher Tracy's apartment in *Under the Cherry Moon*, along with a copy of Miles Davis's 1985 album *You're Under Arrest*.

'Dear Michaelangelo' is a peculiar song. On a literal level it's about a female peasant who is stopped from suicide only by her love for the artist. Aware that he is gay, she decides that nevertheless she will only sleep with him, or if she can't have him, other homosexual men. This leads conceptually to 'A Love Bizarre', an orgiastic celebration of 'bizarre love', 'outrageous sin' and getting rough in the back of the limousine, encouraging the listener to abandon the 'ivory tower' and join in the fun. But if you don't have a lover (or a limousine), there's always (for female listeners at least) the 'Toy Box'. Boxes are often sexual for Prince (who can forget the one in 'Gett Off'?), and here it's a metaphor for Sister Fate's vagina. It's the most perverse song on a perverse album, not because it celebrates masturbation, but because it does so in a childhood context. The first verse suggests that Sister Fate's brother is sad because he doesn't have a vagina, the second emphasises how easy it is to have an orgasm when you're young (one touch too much), and the third addresses how age brings sexual repression. Uh oh.[2] 'Yellow' sees Sheila E dropping her 'Sister Fate' guise for an autobiographical song in which she sings of her envy of her sister's breasts (using her sister's real name, Zina). For Prince, the playground is often a sexualised arena, and that's the case here, as Sheila describes cheerleaders being jealous of her ass-hugging yellow pants and boys envying her yellow Riviera star car. The song moves from the schoolyard to Sheila's frustration with relationships after a sexual encounter with an unworthy man. The album's title song, 'Romance 1600', describes a masked ball and a mysterious sexual encounter that fits with the orgiastic abandon of 'A Love Bizarre'.

'Bedtime Story', like 'Noon Rendezvous' on the first album, is a slight song when performed by Sheila E – a self-referential sketch about a Prince and a princess that recalls 'Temptation' from *Around the World in a Day* – but totally transformed in Prince's far longer demo version. Again unfinished (he shouts out key changes and identifies verses throughout), it nonetheless contains an emotional power absent from the released recording. Though Sheila E's third, self-titled album includes five songs co-written by Prince, it lacks the high concept of the first two records, with two tracks about partying, one straightforward, 'One Day (I'm Gonna Make You Mine)', the other, 'Koo Koo', including a darker discussion of abortion and war. Only 'Pride and the Passion' resembles previous Sheila E songs like 'The Belle of St. Mark' or 'Noon Rendezvous', another song about a woman who falls in love with a sophisticated, wealthy and seemingly older man, while 'Boys' Club' is a female version of the nightclub songs once sung by Morris Day, and 'Love on a Blue Train' a busy horn-and-percussion-driven celebration of inter-railing.

But while some fans rate the Sheila E or The Time or Jill Jones's albums as the best records by a Prince protégé, nothing compares to The Family, the first band to put out a debut on Paisley Park. The Family features some of the most talented musicians Prince has worked with on any side project, but as Eric Leeds – who plays sax on the album, the beginning of a creative relationship with Prince that initially lasted from 1986 to 1999, and which would be reignited between 2002 and 2003, when the focus of Prince's music shifted from funk to jazz – told me, 'The music of

The Family was primarily Prince,[3] and we were assigned roles.'[4] Lead roles went to Paul Peterson, a keyboardist with The Time who had featured with the band in *Purple Rain* (and who, like many Prince associates, took on a new name, St Paul, a play on the Minnesota state), and Susannah Melvoin. The two other members of The Family were also exiles from The Time: Jellybean Johnson and Jerome Benton.

For what seems to have been intended as a pop record, *The Family* is often driven by dark emotions. 'High Fashion' is one of many songs in Prince's oeuvre (see, for example, his two songs about models, 'Cindy C' on *The Black Album* and 'Chelsea Rodgers' on *Planet Earth*) in which he's caught between admiration and disdain for a woman with expensive tastes. Prince's demo version of 'Mutiny' is one of his angriest songs, a hint of the later darkness he'd pursue on parts of *The Black Album*. The metaphor he uses plays on the idea of a relation-'ship', with St Paul wanting to wrest control from his lover, but knowing that in doing so he'll destroy their love for ever. Towards the end, Prince has a hidden message, low in the mix, to the members of The Time who abandoned him. If you turn the stereo up loud enough you can hear what sounds like a pair of scissors and Prince asking, 'Morris, did you give? Miko, did you give?'[5]

The Family's first single, 'The Screams of Passion', is a duet between St Paul and Susannah. It's easy to see why it was chosen to lead – it's the most straightforwardly pop song on the album, accompanied as it was with a fun video showing the band performing over a video screen of crashing waves – but it's less immediately arresting than the two tracks that open the album. 'Yes', the first instrumental, is a dark jazz-funk song built around Prince's drums, Eric's sax and Prince's groans. 'River Run Dry' is the only song on the album not by Prince, written instead by The Revolution's drummer, Bobby Z (the brother of the album's producer, but not a member of The Family). It's a compelling depiction of the dog days of a doomed relationship, but it pales beside 'Nothing Compares 2 U', a song that got a second lease of life after it was covered by Sinead O'Connor, and which was subsequently reclaimed by Prince in performance and in duet with Rosie Gaines on his 1993 collection *The Hits*. Even before O'Connor added her tears, it was one of Prince's loneliest songs, and one of The Family's finest moments: a kind of answer record to *1999*'s 'Free', in which the liberation of breaking up collapses into despair.

The title of 'Susannah's Pyjamas' – the second, softer, instrumental – hints at the intimacy between Prince and The Family's singer, Susannah Melvoin, with whom he had a long, creatively inspiring relationship. On the record's final track, 'Desire', everything comes together: this is a poetic, mysterious song in which St Paul sings of unrequited love for a woman who's saving herself for a soldier who'd rather die than be with her.

Susannah told me that she and St Paul were in rehearsal for 'five months straight', preparing for a live tour. Unfortunately, the tour didn't happen, due, it seems, to Prince's other commitments during this period. A frustrated St Paul left the band in late 1985.[6]

Melvoin told me that even after St Paul left, a second Family album might still have appeared, built around the out-takes from the first album. 'After Paul went and did his own thing, Prince came to me and said, "Do you still want to do this?" And I was too young and dumb and I said, "If he doesn't want to do it, I don't want to do it." I should've said, "Sure."' Susannah told me that had this second album appeared, the starting point would have been two songs that didn't make the first album. While she didn't name these tracks, she said she was sure everyone had heard these out-takes, so I assume she was referring to 'Miss

Understood' and 'Feline', two unreleased Family tracks. While 'Miss Understood' is a far less lyrically sophisticated song than anything on The Family album, it's such a winning pop track that it seems extraordinary that Prince didn't use it in any of his subsequent female-fronted projects, especially as his engineer, Susan Rogers, is on record as saying that Susannah didn't like the song because she thought it didn't fit her character. The full version of 'Feline' is safely locked away,[7] but an instrumental version indicates that it is closer to the rest of The Family album, another sax-driven track that shares the strange dark power of 'Yes' and 'Susannah's Pyjamas' (Rogers has stated that it didn't make the album because St Paul objected to the lyrical content).[8]

Although both Prince's parents performed in a jazz group, his former manager, Alan Leeds, has argued Prince had little first-hand knowledge of jazz before Leeds's brother Eric (who would front Madhouse) joined The Revolution, suggesting that while Wendy and Lisa educated Prince in classic rock, Eric was introducing Prince to jazz. But Eric Leeds himself was very eager in conversation with me to emphasise how Prince's jazz projects were, at least at first, essentially 'Prince projects' he contributed to rather than collaborations.

Wendy Melvoin explains further: 'I still think that Prince isn't a be-bopper, he's not a cool jazz guy, he's not an avant-garde jazz guy, he's certainly not a Coltrane guy. He's like more of a contemporary-jazz guy, the kind of jazz that I always refer to as weather-channel music, the stuff you hear on the weather channel, really smooth, and he functions well in that environment, but I wouldn't put a fake book in front of Prince and say, "Can you go ahead and play 'Autumn Leaves' for me?"' Eric Leeds said something similar to George Cole: 'Prince is not a jazz musician in the traditional sense and certainly doesn't have the harmonic background that we would associate with straight-up jazz musicians, [but] he can apply a sense of spontancity, whether he's in the studio or in rehearsal or in a live situation that is more true to the jazz ethic than a lot of jazz musicians that I've played with.'⁹

One thing that everyone seems to agree on, though, is Prince's admiration for Miles Davis. Shortly after Davis signed to Warner Brothers, the two of them met at an airport in Los Angeles, and Davis asked Prince to submit a song for inclusion on what would eventually become *Tutu*. During this period, Davis had become increasingly interested in pop music, covering Michael Jackson's 'Human Nature' and Cyndi Lauper's 'Time After Time'. Like Prince, he also used new-wave elements in his music – collaborating with Scritti Politti's Green Gartside – and was eager for Prince to contribute a song for his new album.

For the past several years, Prince had merrily given away songs seemingly to anyone who asked, but this request evidently affected him more deeply than usual. He responded in his normal speedy way, going into the studio he'd booked over the Christmas period and recording a song called 'Can I Play with U' for Miles's consideration. The title, of course, has a double meaning, being an extra-diegetic invitation to Miles, but also referring in the narrative of the song to a woman Prince is trying to pick up in a club. Miles liked the song and added his trumpet.

At the same sessions Prince recorded a tribute to Davis called 'A Couple of Miles' (Davis would return the favour with 'Half Nelson'), and a few days later began two days of jazz-style jamming on a new project he called The Flesh with Eric Leeds. 'It was a lot of spontaneous, very improvisational, Madhouse-ish kinda stuff that included Sheila E and Levi Seacer, Jr. It was more of a quartet,' Alan Leeds remembers. When I asked Eric Leeds about these sessions, he explained that in spite of the mythology that has grown up around this record – it has been suggested that a potential album was assembled which would include on side one a twenty-minute version of 'Junk Music', an instrumental track that can be heard playing (for thirty seconds) on the soundtrack to *Under the Cherry Moon* – the project was nothing more than studio jams. 'Those sessions were in LA. Prince was finishing up the *Parade* album, working on tracks that would end up on *Sign o' the Times* and working on the incidental music for *Under the Cherry Moon*. Prince was happy with some of the stuff we produced, and there was a sense that something might come out of it that was worthy of release. But it was a very loose idea; there wasn't a plan there. Prince called out a key and we started playing.' Leeds also warns not to read too much significance into the fact that this project had a name. 'I suspect the name came up when we were sitting in the studio laughing and joking, and then it took on a life of its own. But the idea formed and then it disappeared for ever.'

Well, almost disappeared. We do still have the snippet of 'Junk Music' and the full 'U Gotta Shake Something', a fifteen-minute, very repetitive track which features the reappearance of what sounds suspiciously like Jamie Starr asking questions like 'You ever seen a black man play guitar with no clothes on?'[10] and a retaliation to the Parental Music Resource Center when Prince sings, 'Washington wives, you can't fuck with us.'

The meeting with Davis also inspired Prince to spend a day recording with his father, although it would be nearly a year before he began work on the Madhouse project. Between The Flesh and Madhouse, Prince had withdrawn 'Can I Play with U?' from *Tutu*, uncertain whether it would work alongside the rest of Davis's album. Although the song is easy to locate, and Prince would go on to work with Davis on a Chaka Khan song and later Davis would cover Prince tracks including 'Movie Star' in concert (as described in Chapter 16, Prince and Miles also played together live on New Year's Eve 1987), it's a shame this track wasn't included on *Tutu*, especially as it's better than anything else on that album. But even if the relationship with Davis didn't produce as much as might be hoped, Melvoin believes it was instrumental in giving Prince confidence in this style. 'He struck up a relationship with Miles after a while, and Miles was influential in convincing Prince, making him feel more confident in doing that thing you do when you're playing jazz, which is to stretch the scales, invert the chords, harmonically stretch something, screw with the rhythms and the polyrhythms. Miles gave him the confidence to do that because it really validated Prince. And then he got involved in working with Eric Leeds, and he was really instrumental in helping him mould a certain jazz philosophy, and Prince was learning quickly. I suppose you could say he was a quick learner.'

Recorded in September 1986 and released in January of the following year, the first Madhouse album, *8*, was, then, Prince's first proper jazz record. All Prince projects featuring Eric Leeds have jazz-influenced moments, but it would be fifteen years before Prince wholeheartedly engaged with the genre. With The Time and The Family, Prince disguised his involvement by sending forth a group of musicians to play his songs. When presenting Madhouse to the public, the group identity was initially less well-developed. Prince certainly had some ideas for the new project, approaching it once again as a complete conceit. He invented a new imaginary producer, Austra Chanel, paid a woman named Maneca Lightner to appear on the cover of both Madhouse albums but turn down all other modelling work, and handed over publicity to Eric Leeds, his main collaborator on the project, while denying any involvement himself. Alan Leeds believes his brother soon got bored with the pretence, though not the project, tiring of 'the whole idea of Madhouse being a fictitious band, and creating names and bios for the three musicians who were supposed to be on it with Eric and all of that silliness. Eventually, Eric got frustrated with it and said, "This is dumb. This is me and Prince making a record and my bio looks better if we say it's me and Prince."'

The album has eight numbered tracks, any of which would fit on Prince's later jazz records ('One', for example, could easily be a *Rainbow Children* B-side). Throughout the project Prince seems particularly interested in how to add drama to instrumental music, with little tricks like putting voices low in the mix throughout 'Two', or adding the sound of an overloaded telephone exchange to 'Five', as a squeaky female voice repeats 'How you doin', sexy?', or even recycling Vanity's orgasmic moans on 'Seven'. Several of these songs, such as 'Six', which was released as a single – and which worked particularly well in its heavy live version – sound more like break-downs or jams edited out of conventional Prince songs than jazz, but this doesn't weaken, or invalidate, the project. While Eric Leeds contributed and played a significant role, he says that it is a 'misconception' to see Madhouse as a band, even though the group did reform for a one-off show alongside The Family, Jill Jones and various other Prince associates in 2003, and when fDeluxe (which the group of musicians previously known as The Family called themselves when denied permission to perform under the original name) finally went on the road in 2012, there was a Madhouse medley ('Ten' and 'Six') as part of the show.

Jill Jones had to earn her solo album, working with Prince for a long time in a low-key and semi-secret capacity. He started working with her when she was very young, having first met her when she was providing backing vocals for Teena Marie. She's the J.J. who has a small role singing on '1999', 'Automatic' and 'Free', and who plays the Lady Cab Driver on the song of the same name. She provided backing vocals for both Vanity 6 and Prince on the Triple Threat tour, and has a perfectly judged cameo as a snotty but ultimately helpful waitress in *Purple Rain*. The album took a long time to come together, pieced together from sessions between 1982 and 1986 and including two of the best non-Family tracks from that era, 'G-Spot' and 'All Day, All Night'.

Maybe the reason why Jones is considered a more mature artist is that the album's first single, 'Mia Bocca', is sung from the perspective of a monogamous woman who's only had one lover since she was twelve. Prince uses this to intensify his favourite dramatic situation when writing from a female perspective: a woman who is devoted to her lover and yet tempted by another. But as good as 'G-Spot' undoubtedly is, particularly in its extended remix, I'm not entirely convinced it works when sung by a female vocalist. The original demo, recorded by Prince in 1983, feels slower and more insistent than the poppy released version, and the whole point of the song is that it's being sung by a frustrated lover failing to satisfy his girlfriend because he can't find her erogenous zone. The song's successful because it's Prince in lazy lover mode: he may not be able to locate his partner's G-spot yet, but he's going to keep going until he does. He's detached and icy: that man-machine again. When Jill Jones does the track, she has to sing from the perspective of a frustrated woman, either in the middle of making love or masturbating, but because she mirrors Prince's laid-back vocal approach, the song lacks erotic charge. Somehow the demo's sleaziness has ebbed away.

'Violet Blue' is yet another Prince song in which a woman objectifies the physical traits of a potential lover (here, his eyes), redeemed by Dr Clare Fischer's complex arrangement, which features nearly fifty musicians. Although regular gig-attenders had long since known about Prince's propensity for revisiting (and reinterpreting) past songs, the appearance of 'With You' on this album (bearing in mind Prince's huge stockpile of unreleased material) surprised. Given the stand-out tracks on *Prince* that Jones could have covered ('I Wanna Be Your Lover', 'Why You Wanna Treat Me So Bad?', even 'Bambi'), it's hard to understand why Prince decided to exhume this slight song, especially as his lyrical powers had developed so considerably since then. Maybe it's precisely because it was a forgotten song that he decided it needed a second chance. If so, it gains little from being revisited (although Jones's version is less queasy than the original), and has the unusual distinction of being the weakest track on two self-titled albums.

'All Day, All Night' is the other keeper. Built up from a live performance by The Revolution at First Avenue on Prince's twenty-sixth birthday, it features Jones singing of how excited she is by watching her lover having sex with other men.[11] One song later ('For Love'), she's offering to let a lover watch her make out with another man. After these two songs in which Jones boasts of her sexual liberation, 'My Man' comes as suddenly conservative. It's a musically and lyrically basic song about a woman who's annoyed with a cheating lover. There's a danger, once again, in reading this album as a narrative rather than a simple collection of unconnected songs. It's not a concept album, so there's no reason to look for themes or to see 'Jill Jones' as a created persona, but Prince always gives great thought to sequencing: maybe 'My Man' is there to counterbalance the licentious feel of so much of the record; to distinguish Jones from Apollonia and Vanity. The last track, 'Baby, You're a Trip', is a female take on 'Something in the Water (Does Not Compute)', even including similar lines. But while in the *1999* song Prince is constantly justifying himself and pointing out how other women can't understand why his lover treats him so bad, in this song Jones is resigned to the fact that her lover is so special that she should be grateful for whatever she can get from him.[12]

By the time of the second Madhouse album, Prince had put together a live band and taken them out as tour support. The touring band (introduced onstage as 'inmates') included three of the four musicians credited for the second album (Levi Seacer, Jr, Eric Leeds and Dr Fink), who would play four or five tracks each night. Prince must have had a high opinion of his audience to trust that they could deal with a jazz-funk opener, but Matt Fink says: 'They appreciated it. We would start out as Madhouse, and then there might be Madhouse tracks in the main show, and they'd also appear in the after-shows. Eric and Prince would come up with the set list. We knew all the songs for the first and second albums, and we could pick and choose, but some were more difficult to make fly live.'

The second Madhouse album, *16*, was the first thing Prince recorded after he finished the *Sign o' the Times* movie. Completed within a week, the album featured drums from an uncredited Sheila E on three tracks and came with another new concept: gangsters. Prince has often mentioned his fondness for the Francis Ford Coppola film *The Godfather*, and it has frequently shown up as a reference point in his music (it's where he got the name Apollonia), and on this album he samples dialogue from the first two instalments. While he'd featured gunfire on the live version of 'Six', *16* is given additional drama by this theme, and the cover shows Madhouse model Maneca Lightner toting a tommy gun. Maybe Prince deliberately used this image to contradict the belief that jazz-funk is soft. The album is not quite as consistent as the debut, with a couple of duff tracks ('Twelve' is a dull swing song, 'Fourteen' is elevator muzak), but it's also more varied and experimental. 'Ten' has truly brutal synths 'n' sax (even funkier on the twelve-inch's 'Perfect Mix'). 'Eleven' is sublime electro-jazz, Susannah Melvoin repeating the phrase 'Baby doll house' in an emotionless robot voice over Prince's squelchy keyboards. There was also an accompanying movie, *Hard Life*, and videos, both of which featured Matt Fink's parents. 'Prince knew my mom was an actress,' he told me, 'so he just thought of her for the piece, and put my father in one of the videos. It was meant to be a dark comedy, and it never saw the light of the day.'

16 was the final Madhouse album to see release, but Prince made several attempts in his later career to revive the band. His first attempt produced an entire album, *24*, that has never seen release in this form. Picking up where *16* ended, the tracks intended for this third album all have sexualised subtitles – Eric Leeds told George Cole that Prince was 'with' Maneca Lightner, the model who is pictured on the cover of the Madhouse albums with a puppy, and who may therefore be the subject of '20 (A Girl and Her Puppy)', though there are other candidates who may have inspired the titles of '17 (Penetration)', '18 (R U Legal Yet?)' or '19 (Jailbait)'. *24* began as a solo project, recorded during one of Prince's career high points, during and just after the *Lovesexy* tour, before he invited Eric Leeds to add his parts to the album. Leeds suggests that the third Madhouse album may have been a victim of Prince's continued conflict with Warner Brothers, though he himself 'wasn't that crazy about that album', objecting to the mix. The version in circulation is of such quality that it's hard to see why Leeds objected to it. '17 (Penetration)', which would go on to become a standard for Miles Davis, is one of Prince's finest and most forceful jazz tracks; '18 (R U Legal Yet?)' is even darker and repetitive, using lines from Leeds and engineer Heidi Hanschu to set up a dramatic scenario in which a man questions a possibly underage girl, while she talks about the threat of her father shooting him, with an aggressive saxophone and piano in harsh contrast, taking the dominant style of *The Black Album* one step further; '19 (Jailbait)' sounds like The Marketts, and indeed Prince would use this track as the basis for a proposed new version of the *Batman* theme for Tim Burton's soundtrack. '20 (A Girl and Her Puppy)' recalls the moments of full-band improvisation on the *Lovesexy* tour.[13]

After Leeds approached Prince about the possibility of remixing some of the songs, Prince responded by giving him around thirty-six tracks, encouraging him to sift through them and see if there was anything that might be the start of an alternative Madhouse album. But Leeds continued to focus on the 24 tracks, taking them and editing them down into the seven-minute 'The Dopamine Rush', which would become the stand-out track on Leeds's Paisley Park-released debut album *Times Squared*. A large part of Leeds's album (nine of the eleven tracks) was built around Prince's jazz work, and features a tremendous band made up of Atlanta Bliss, Levi Seacer, Jr, Sheila E and Larry Fratangelo. Among the finest Prince-related tracks on this largely forgotten album are 'Night Owl', with Prince on synthesizer; 'Overnight, Every Night', which sounds like a less threatening dry run for Prince's later 'Xenophobia'; 'Little Rock', based around a great tenor-sax Leeds line; and 'Times Squared', a very heavy number with room-shaking bass which, with lyrics, could have fitted perfectly with, and indeed elevated, the *Batman* soundtrack. Leeds's own songs are every bit the equal of Prince's on this project, and the weakest song is a solely Prince-penned composition humorously entitled 'Cape Horn'.[14] Alan Leeds observed the closeness of his brother's relationship with Prince. 'Eric and Prince were really a good team in the studio. With all respect to Wendy and Lisa, because they're pretty sharp too, Eric was the most sophisticated and advanced musician out of that gang. He had a more sophisticated sense of harmonics and structure than most of the people, so he brought something to Prince that Prince didn't already have. As a result, he became a confidant. He also has a personality that meshed pretty easily with Prince. He wasn't boisterous, he wasn't pushy, he wasn't territorial. He was just content to come in and experiment in the studio. I think he loved the process even more than the results.'

This was not the end of Prince's interest in either a third Madhouse album or indeed the songs he'd recorded for the project. While Leeds had made something out of tracks 21–24, in 1991 Prince sent tracks 17–20 to Miles Davis, but George Cole notes: 'Miles would not touch Prince's 24-track recordings. Instead, he opted to rehearse the tunes with his band live on-stage and then record them with the band'[15] in Germany,[16] but when they went into the studio, 'Miles was so weak and sick he just couldn't play.'[17] Nevertheless, he did manage to lay down guide tracks which he later considered of strong enough quality to ask Prince if he could include them on his 1992 album *Doo-Bop* (Prince refused). Prince was later approached to see if he would allow the songs to be included on a Miles Davis retrospective box, but again he withheld permission. (After Davis's death, Prince would honour him twice more, once with an unreleased instrumental called 'Letter 4 Miles' and much later co-crediting a silent segue on *Rave Un2 The Joy Fantastic* to him with the cryptic message '199?'.)

Now all these songs had found homes, when Prince returned to the possibility of a third Madhouse album in 1994, he composed a new set of songs with a band that have been referred to as 'New Power Madhouse', and for which Steve Parke remembers designing a cover that 'had a big bank vault, with the guys in front of the vault stealing money'. Though the album wasn't released, several of the songs have appeared officially. '17', which has no connection to '17 (Penetration)', was released on the *1-800-NEW-FUNK* sampler, and as with several of this era of Madhouse tracks, emerged from a five-hour rehearsal/improvisation session.

How you feel about this song and these tracks will depend largely on your feelings for this particular band (Michael B, Sonny T, Levi Seacer, Jr, Prince and Eric Leeds). It's among my favourite combinations of Prince's musicians, and for this reason I far prefer this second attempt at the third Madhouse record than the first. The enormously appealing 'Space' (Prince dropped the convention of naming all songs after numbers for this record) appeared in an alternative version on his *Come* album; 'Asswoop' (also known as 'Asswhuppin' in a Trunk') was later released as a download and given away – along with extracts from 'Parlor Games' and the whole of 'Ethereal', which consisted of half a minute of Prince on piano – on a sampler for attendees of The Ultimate Live Experience concert. But the album's five other tracks remain unreleased, although one is merely a short 'guitar segue', 'Michael B' a drum solo and 'Sonny T' a longer guitar flourish. This version of *24* would have been a far more eclectic record than either the first two officially released Madhouse records or the initial version of the album, including as it does an unfortunately somewhat anaemic cover of Marvin Gaye's 'Got to Give It Up' (with his daughter Nona on vocals) and far more emphasis on guitar than on the previous records. 'Rootie Kazootie' has a better saxophone performance from Leeds than almost anything on his solo album; Prince thought enough of 'Asswoop' to play it live (notably at a show at the London Emporium in 1995, where he also played '17' with Eric Leeds); and 'Parlor Games' is a beautiful instrumental that ranks with the best of Prince's soft-jazz songs, yet unlike most of the others, is completely lacking in schmaltz.[18]

A Madhouse album wasn't the only project to fail to see the light in what must have been an extremely frustrating period for Prince, some of his pain leaking out into the sleeve notes of the later *1-800-NEW-FUNK* compilation, in which he wrote of 'the pain endured by the "parents of these children"' (children here referring to songs) when their 'children' were left to die.[19] Among these 'parents' was Minneapolis musician Margie Cox, who had begun her career as the lead singer in Ta Mara and the Seen, a band whose first album had been produced by Time member Jesse Johnson. After her first band had disbanded, Cox had joined Dr Mambo's Combo, a Minneapolis bar band whose members would also include Michael Bland and Sonny T, both of whom would join The New Power Generation. With Cox, Prince was devising a band called MC Flash, a project that kept going for several years, during which Prince penned her numerous songs and also recorded covers with her.[20]

In 1989, road manager Alan Leeds took over as president of Paisley Park. He remembers: 'Paisley Park as an entity had really just been an orphan. No one was in charge of the label. It had no phone number, no office, no personnel. It was merely an imprint. Theoretically, Cavallo and Ruffalo were in charge of running the label, but they were more interested in running Prince's film career and his music career, and they had other artists. They only saw it as worthy for an act they thought was worth taking a crap shoot on. Like there was a couple of kids called Good Question who made a dance record. Tony LeMans was another Fargnoli thought was worth recording. So I said to Prince, "Let's start treating it as a real label."'

Prince's work with protégés had previously been largely separate from his main career, but as the 1990s approached, it began to bleed over into his main work. The prime example of this is *Graffiti Bridge*, which ended up becoming a showcase for Prince's entire stable. As well as the return of The Time, the project also involved Robin Power, Elisa Fiorillo,[21] George Clinton, T. C. Ellis, Tevin Campbell, The Steeles, Mavis Staples and Ingrid Chavez, but during and after the production of his own album Prince was also writing music for almost all of these artists. Prince had already produced (and written six songs for) Mavis Staples's first Paisley Park record, *Time Waits for No One*, and after her role on the soundtrack and in the film *Graffiti Bridge* he would also contribute nine songs to her second, *The Voice*.[22] But though turning her into 'Melody Cool' may have not been the most sympathetic use of this artist, and while the first album featured several songs from the Vault – including the standout 'Train' from the post-*Parade*, pre-*Sign* era and 'I Guess I'm Crazy', as well as 'Jaguar' and 'Come Home', songs originally written for other artists – he also made a real effort, especially on the second album, to draw from Staples's life and persona in his writing for her. Of the two songs specifically written for *Time Waits for No One*, the title track (a co-write with Staples), which echoes in theme and sound 'Still Would Stand All Time', works better than 'Interesting', but the latter, an account of a sleazy man approaching Staples in a bar, is still far more compelling than any of the non-Prince tracks on the record, such as the soporific nostalgia of 'The Old Songs'.

Prince pursued his interest in time as a subject for lyrics once more on *The Voice*, suggesting that 'Blood Is Thicker than Time' in a song that seems much more suited to Staples's personality, combining gospel, biblical references (Moses, Cain and Abel) and her biography, though still in the slightly sickly style of *Graffiti Bridge*. It's a far more thematically coherent record than their first collaboration, with the Prince tracks linked by content (in particular, a dismay for gang violence and a need for increased education, expressed in 'Blood Is Thicker than Time', 'House in Order',[23] 'You Will Be Moved' and 'The Voice'), but also featuring recurring imagery, with an 'Undertaker' figure, based on Staples's mortician ex-husband, showing up in two songs (Staples's wonderful version of 'The Undertaker', a song Prince would later try to make his own, and the misguided dance track 'House in Order'). There are also many connections with Prince's own music, not least with the covers of 'Positivity', which shares the subject matter of this album, and a revise of 'Melody Cool'. Alan Leeds says: 'The Mavis Staples record I thought was a really good record, a bit conservative, but it was the wrong time and the wrong place. The world wasn't ready for the renaissance that she's enjoying now.'

There had always been a degree of fluidity between which songs ended up on which project, but now tracks seemed multipurposed right from the start. One of the best (but disturbing) unreleased songs from this era, 'Nine Lives', was one of a number of feline-inspired songs ('Cat and Mouse', 'Cat Attack') considered for dancer Cat Glover's debut album. With Cat singing about her 'bad self', it also echoed the later tracks Prince would write for Carmen Electra. But when the Cat project folded, Prince kept her vocal and turned the song into a dialogue with Morris Day. As with many of his songs from this era, the focus of the Cat version of the song is psychological manipulation of a woman by her lover. Here, as elsewhere, it's what the woman (Cat in the original version, Margie Cox in the revised song) desires, at least if she did have nine lives, wanting a love who could 'kill' her again and again. The Morris Day lyrics, unusually, temper the song, suggesting that each death is nothing more than an orgasm. Most appealing about the revised version is Day singing about the 1990s, added when the song became the planned single for *Corporate World*, which was Prince's original title for the fourth Time album.

Unlike the record that was eventually released, the aptly named *Pandemonium, Corporate World* was a collaboration between Prince, Morris Day and Jerome Benton – though of course Prince's input was the most pronounced. The other songs written for *Corporate World* that didn't make it to *Pandemonium* were the title track, 'Corporate World', which perhaps surprisingly for a record (and a band) who have always boasted about their enjoyment of the high life has lyrics that could be recited at an 'Occupy Wall Street' demo, and 'Murph Drag', which did see eventual release (of a sort) credited to The Time when played on the third of Prince's NPG Ahdio (*sic*) shows. The latter song, another of The Time's finest tracks, about a new imaginary dance that only 'people with money' can do and which easily rivals 'The Bird', deserves a fuller release.

With the loss of these tracks – and the songs carried across to *Graffiti Bridge* – *Pandemonium* could only seem weak. Its ugly (and very 1990s) cover shows The Time cooking in a frying pan and surrounded by chicken drumsticks, cutlery and cooking oil – a reference, it seems, to the fact that three of the songs (or rather two songs, 'Chocolate' and 'Skillet', and one skit, 'Cooking Class') are about food. This tired conceit of cookin' up the funk is a much weaker idea to build an album around than Prince's original conceit.

Prince is responsible for a third of the record including another *Corporate World* standout – 'Donald Trump (Black Version)', which continues the theme of a black rewrite of *Wall Street* – and four tracks with rich histories. 'Jerk Out' was initially written in 1981, around the time that Prince was experimenting with more sexually aggressive lyrics such as 'Extra Lovable', and if released at this time would have seen him extending Day's gigolo persona into unwelcome new territory, forcing S&M on a white lover as a form of class and race war. Prince clearly wanted to maintain some of the nastiness in the released version, but here Day committed the more palatable sin of asking his lover to leave after sex.

'Data Bank', though perfect for Day, was also much weaker in this Time version than it was when Prince was backed by The Revolution (though musically rather than lyrically). 'Chocolate' also has Revolution connections: it began as a song recorded by Prince with Wendy and Lisa. There was no way a revised version of this would appeal as much as the well-loved out-take – with Prince in full Jamie Starr mode, teasing a brilliant performance from Wendy – but the longer Time reworking, which replaces Prince's vocal with Day's but keeps Wendy and Lisa in the background, is still among The Time's best tracks. Less worthwhile was 'My Summertime Thang', a song that having already provided the music for 'The Latest Fashion', had little fresh purpose.[24]

Prince's first collaboration with his Funkadelic hero George Clinton[25] was on a 1989 maxi-single entitled 'Tweakin'', from an album, *The Cinderella Theory*, put out by Paisley Park. Though it featured many of Prince's retinue, including Eric Leeds and Atlanta Bliss, Prince uncharacteristically avoided playing on the song. Alan Leeds remembers: 'I had known George Clinton for years. George was without a label at the time, and he'd sent me a tape of some of his most recent studio stuff. Prince walked into my office as I was playing the tape one day and heard it and liked it and wanted to put him out on Paisley.'

Though he was involved in several remixes of the fraught 'Tweakin'', it wasn't until after he had made Clinton a central part of *Graffiti Bridge* that he started writing songs for him, including the unreleased 'My Pony' (I wonder if it stayed in the Vault because someone alerted Prince to Bob Dylan's use of the same metaphor in 'New Pony'), which didn't make Clinton's charmingly titled second Paisley Park album, *Hey Man . . . Smell My Finger*, and the lascivious and very silly 'The Big Pump', which did.[26] Leeds believes that Clinton's music for Paisley Park 'was far from his best work. We inherited a lot of unfinished tracks. There were ideas about Prince and George doing some collaboration, which ended up being a hasty swapping of a couple of tapes.'

Fellow *Graffiti Bridge* star T. C. Ellis got two old songs (out-take 'Girl o' My Dreams' and 'Bambi', of which he did a ridiculous heavy-metal rap version that makes the listener feel guilty for excusing the original) and one new, vaguely misogynistic one ('Miss Thang'), which has a hilarious video in which a woman in a black lace teddy drapes bras over Ellis's shoulders, while his 1990s-style suited male dancers gyrate in the background. Tevin Campbell got to put a remix of 'Round and Round' on his *T.E.V.I.N.* record and got four Prince songs for *I'm Ready*, including the first release of what would become one of Prince's favourite tracks to play live, 'Shhh', and three others credited to Paisley Park: a deeply strange song, 'The Halls of Desire', in which Prince reworked the themes of the 'hallway corridor' version of 'Computer Blue'; the politically angry but musically weedy 'Uncle Sam'; and a linked song, 'Paris 1798430'. And when Jevetta Steele's album was released twice, Prince wrote two separate tracks for each version, co-writing (with David Rivkin and Levi Seacer, Jr) for the first release the idiosyncratically spiritual 'And How' and yet another creepy sexualised schooldays song, the awkwardly phrased 'Skip 2 My U Mya Darlin''. For the second version he wrote the generic ballad 'Hold Me' and collaborated with Martika on 'Open Book', an amusingly contradictory song which initially appears to be about the importance of openness between lovers but soon becomes an angry denial of its possibility; as well as another self-empowerment track, entitled 'Well Done', for an album recorded by The Steeles as a group.[27]

But the most significant protégé project with regard to his career as a whole is Prince's collaboration with Ingrid Chavez, which works as a (inferior but still worthwhile) companion piece to *Lovesexy*. Although it wouldn't be released until the autumn of 1991, by which time Prince's sound had changed considerably, Chavez's confusingly titled *May 19, 1992* also owes something to Enigma, who were in the *Billboard* charts while Prince was working on this album (he has also spoken of his interest in New

Age music in interviews, and it seems likely that the philosophy expressed on Enigma's *MCMXC a.D.*, with its references to the Marquis De Sade, may have caught his attention). While the project was slightly too esoteric to capture mass attention, Prince did put some energy into it, producing three maxi-singles by way of promotion. It is one of Alan Leeds's favourite records from his time at Paisley Park. 'It holds up. But it certainly wasn't the sort of thing Prince was known for or easy to promote.'

This wasn't the end, of course, of Prince launching projects in disguise, but the period surrounding *Graffiti Bridge* was definitely one of his busiest periods of composition, the process becoming increasingly fraught due to his ongoing struggles with Warner Brothers, and the paradoxical desire to hide in plain sight that had prompted so much of this work would soon grow so pressing that he'd even discard his own name, leaving 'Prince' to languish (temporarily at least) alongside Joey Coco, Alexander Nevermind and Jamie Starr as one more abandoned identity.

22

PLAYING STRIP POOL WITH VANESSA

The numbers lie. From a commercial perspective, the period 1991–3 seems to be a time of consolidation for Prince. *Diamonds and Pearls* was an extremely successful album, and while the ✤ album saw something of a drop-off, it still had two notable singles in 'My Name Is Prince' and 'Sexy MF'. The reviewers (mostly) lie too: *Diamonds and Pearls* received positive write-ups, and while some critics questioned whether Prince was losing his edge and originality, most seemed pleased by what they considered evidence of a newfound maturity. And there is no sense that Prince was holding back at this time: it's clear that he was giving it his all, and both albums suffer from being over-conceptualised rather than underdeveloped. But this is the second-least interesting period of Prince's career, behind only the nadir of 2004. While *Batman* and *Graffiti Bridge* had been disappointing in comparison to Prince's earlier work, neither album felt conservative. *Diamonds and Pearls* and, to a lesser extent, the ✤ album represent the beginning of what felt like a deliberate narrowing of Prince's world view, something that may have reflected the musical climate of the time but couldn't help but disappoint.

Throughout his career to date Prince had largely avoided what feminist musicologist Nancy J. Holland has referred to as 'the limited phallic sexuality' of rock, concentrating as much on a more free-flowing sexual discourse. Though he had often toyed with sadism, he was also quick to present himself as a victim, and while he liked to dress his muses in lingerie onstage, in the lyrics almost all of his many lovers were presented with respect. Holland believed that Prince might reshape 'our restricted sexual economy',[1] but she reckoned without the rise of hip hop and the influence some of its codes would play in moving Prince away from the more feminine side of his personality in the early to mid-1990s (and indeed, throughout his career from then on). But Holland and her ilk were projecting desires on Prince that he didn't want to fulfil. It's misleading to see Prince as some sort of sexual revolutionary, and he himself has expressed several times in interviews his unease at being seen as an individual celebrating libertarianism in rock music (when doing so, he has more than once used the phrase 'pushing the envelope', a prosaic way of belittling his artistic achievement during the first decade of his career).

It's not that *Diamonds and Pearls* doesn't contain songs about sex, but that the sex songs see a retreat from the polymorphous perversity of *Sign o' the Times* towards the normal, male-centred sexuality Holland believed was becoming outmoded in rock music, a development driven by the lyrical playfulness of Prince in his pre-New Power Generation guise. This new emphasis on sexual braggadocio is there right in the sleeve notes, which mention 'playing strip pool with Vanessa', and the return of patriarchal values is immediately apparent from the first new persona introduced on this record: 'Daddy Pop'.[2]

As with The Revolution – and indeed with most of Prince's concepts – The New Power Generation had a slow birth. When Prince sang of the 'New Power Generation' on *Lovesexy*'s 'Eye No', it seemed he was referring to his enlightened followers, echoing his intention, as Dez Dickerson suggested Prince wanted to do with The Revolution, of creating 'a mindset among the fans'. This concept seemed to be continued in the song of the same name from *Graffiti Bridge*, as if this was a generation-gap song, with Prince's contemporaries kicking against their elders. But now the NPG were an entity, and have remained so – in many different permutations – to this day.[3] The band would even go on to release three albums under their own name (although the third is hard to distinguish from a Prince album), along with the beginnings of a fourth that has yet to escape the Vault.

Personnel-wise The New Power Generation included two new members, Sonny T(hompson), who took over on bass as Levi Seacer, Jr graduated to lead guitar to replace the departing Miko Weaver, and new keyboard player Tommy Elm (whom Prince renamed Tommy Barbarella). Prince's induction of Sonny T into the group was particularly welcome, and generous, given that a couple of years earlier Sonny T's had been one of the more aggrieved voices in Dave Hill's Prince biography, *Prince: A Pop Life*, telling the author how he'd been an influence on Prince in the early days and was upset about being passed over.

While Prince seemed threatened by rap during the first half of hip hop's golden age, by 1990 he had started to see a way through. During rehearsals, Tony Mosley began to rap lines from Digital Underground's 'The Humpty Dance', and Prince noted the lyrical similarity between this song's chorus and that of his own song, 'Do Me, Baby'. Digital Underground's Shock G was one of the musicians Prince would later bring into the fold (Matt Fink confirmed to me Prince's lasting interest in the rapper), allowing him to remix his song 'Love Sign' for inclusion on *Crystal Ball*, and Prince and his band would subsequently often incorporate the rap from 'The Humpty Dance' into live versions of 'Partyman' and 'Do Me, Baby' on the Nude tour.[4] Public Enemy's Chuck D would later tell the BBC, after making the surprising confession that Prince's vocal delivery in 'Sign o' the Times' had inspired his own rapping, that he believed Prince's initial disdain for rap was a short-lived phase. '[Prince] started to get deeper and deeper into what was going on behind the scenes, that's when Prince's understanding of hip hop and rap started to be a little different . . . eventually he was able to absorb what was going on, the great aspects, and leave the bones to the side and use it in his music.'[5]

The hip-hop songs Prince had originally intended to include on *Diamonds and Pearls* were driven by braggadocio, but the boasting was inspired by the quality of the music or heterosexual desire rather than a need to glamourise violence. 'Something Funky (This House Comes)' served a similar purpose to 'The Flow' during the Nude tour concerts, with Tony M introducing the band during a frantic rap. (At one point, Prince considered including 'The Flow' on *Diamonds and Pearls*, as well as 'Call the Law', dropped from the album but released as the B-side to 'Money Don't Matter 2 Night' and later revised for the NPG's *Goldnigga* album.) Though not an official member of the NPG, rapper Robin Power performed on another hip-hop-influenced track, 'Horny Pony', also later relegated to a B-side after Prince wrote 'Gett Off'. 'Horny Pony' has a goofy charm and one of Prince's funniest raps, but by abandoning these four songs Prince undoubtedly softened the album. (Its engineer, David Friedlander, believes the original version of the album was better, both in the choice of songs and in that the songs had space to breathe before the keyboard overdubs were completed.[6]) The most highly regarded song abandoned during the development of *Diamonds and Pearls*, however, was not a rap song but 'Schoolyard', a sexually explicit autobiographical track[7] which moves from a graphic description of the experience of entering fourteen-year-old Carrie's vagina (compared to a glove filled with baby lotion) to a strange sermonising about how the listener might wish to protect their own children from similar experiences. Prince biographer Alex Hahn considers the song the brilliant conclusion to Prince's Linn drum-sound experimentation,[8] but this is one song that deserves to stay in the Vault.

Further evidence of Prince's unpursued creative direction can be found on recordings from one of the often overlooked treasures in his touring career: the short South American tour he undertook in January 1991, a year in which he played only a dozen shows. This three-date tour included two performances at the Rock in Rio II festival and one at the Rock and Pop festival in Argentina. Although short (75–90 minutes) and consisting largely of material from the Nude tour, the opening sections of the concerts were brilliant, including a stunning reworking of 'Let's Go Crazy' that made the track interesting again for the first time in years. Forty-five minutes of one show were broadcast, revealing that the quality of the music was not matched by the choreography and stagecraft. After the elegance of the *Lovesexy* dance-offs and the well-orchestrated sexual tension between Prince, Cat and Sheila E, it seemed strange that Prince had now decided that what he most wanted to do was a 'sex dance' with three men dressed as waiters.

'Live 4 Love' was also referred to at the shows, as it had been on the Nude tour (although by now Prince had written a first version of the complete song), with Prince reciting the title several times in the middle of a breakdown in 'Purple Rain' and telling the Rio audience that 'there's a war going on' – the shows took place the day after the aerial bombardment of Iraq by coalition forces – but not singing the song in full. An earlier take of the finished song is more affecting and easier to hear (the vocals are buried beneath FX on the released version), with Prince genuinely inhabiting the mind of a fighter pilot instead of playing it for effect and also providing clearer narrative detail.

*

While *Diamonds and Pearls* isn't the hip-hop album it could have been, there were four rap-influenced songs that did make the record: 'Daddy Pop', 'Willing and Able', 'Jughead' and 'Push'. Spaced throughout a long album, they have limited impact. 'Daddy Pop' is Prince celebrating himself, this time for his work ethic, comparing recording music to a regular job, as well as the first of eight songs he would write about playing cards in the next two years (maybe he was learning poker on the tour bus: the NPG can be seen playing cards in the *3 Chains o' Gold* movie). 'Willing and Able' also seems to have started out as a more jazz-influenced song, opening with a drum solo snipped from the released version, which features The Steeles on backing vocals. 'Jughead', taken personally by Prince's former manager Steve Fargnoli, was the first of several New Power Generation songs and skits (most of which appear on *Goldnigga* and *Exodus*) about management problems in the music business and getting paid. Lyrically, 'Push' (a co-write with Rosie Gaines) is an almost incomprehensible self-empowerment song, one of several that seem to be about fulfilling one's potential. No one could accuse The New Power Generation of being self-effacing. Tony, Prince and Rosie take it in turns to rap, with Prince, bizarrely, describing himself as a child-snatching clown who travels from Pakistan to Poland stealing people's children.

There is little on *Diamonds and Pearls* that rewards deep study. In an interview with the well-regarded Chris Heath, Prince was keen to point out that the extreme variety was deliberate: while all his recent records had been connected to films, this was an album with many perspectives rather than a single theme, showing the breadth of his abilities. But considered in relation to the rest of Prince's career, the only songs of lasting significance on the record are the first two singles, 'Gett Off' and 'Cream'.

'Gett Off' felt new at the time of release, but it's a strange, Frankenstein creation: Prince took the title from a song on the 'New Power Generation' maxi-disc, many of the lyrics from a previous song called 'Glam Slam '91' (a remix of the *Lovesexy* track, with lyrics from *Graffiti Bridge*'s 'Love Machine'), and introduced a selection of samples from various funk songs, including the famous James Brown line credited by Prince in the song. It exists in a bewildering number of alternative versions: at least twelve released remixes, as well as three songs with alternative names – 'Violet the Organ Grinder', 'Gangster Glam' and 'Clockin' the Jizz' – based on the original track.[9] Prince also released a video EP to accompany the single, thirty minutes of videos to accompany various versions of the song. Prince's cinephilia had always shaped his creativity but recently his taste had slipped: the inspiration for these latest promos was Tinto Brass's woeful Roman sex film *Caligula*. Beginning with Prince's new dancers Diamond and Pearl being let into a brothel-cum-factory guarded by two near-naked doormen, the film is nightmarish in its relentless procession of soft-core imagery: twins, blindfolds, candles, 'cage guests' and topless women in pristine white panties and face paint. 'Violet the Organ Grinder' takes Prince's phallocentric erotomania to a ludicrous extreme. Surprisingly, he connects the song back to the Crystal Ball, increasing the sense that this oft-mentioned occasion was a Sadean orgy.

The problem with 'Cream', if we're considering it as art instead of produce, is that much like 'Kiss', it seems precision-tooled for mass success, yet feels empty. I've heard Prince play it so often in concert that I've long grown to hate it – it's always a dead spot in shows and audience recordings – but just when I thought that this was the one song that Prince could never improve by changing the arrangement, last year he began playing it at after-shows, slowing it down, letting occasional New

Power Generation member Frédéric Yonnet gussy up the song with harmonica solos, changing it from its original Marc Bolan or Chuck Berry feel into loose jazz. Often when he plays it live Prince boasts about writing the song while looking in the mirror, saying it's all about self-celebration, but it's undoubtedly a love song too, and in its original form not merely masturbation. As with 'Gett Off', it prompted a whole album of remixes and spin-off songs.[10]

The tracks on *Diamonds and Pearls* that don't further build on Prince's myth are curiously lightweight. 'Thunder' is Christian heavy metal; 'Diamonds and Pearls' sickly sweet. 'Strollin'' expanded Prince's sound into light jazz, but couldn't compare to the jazz-influenced work he'd done with Dr Clare Fischer. I've never forgiven Prince for cannibalising one of his greatest ever songs, 'Rebirth of the Flesh', for one of his most forgettable, 'Walk Don't Walk', but at least now 'Rebirth' has received an official, albeit limited release. Prince didn't play 'Money Don't Matter 2 Night' live when it came out, but did exhume it eleven years later for the *One Nite Alone . . .* tour. The song feels similar to 'Pop Life' in its confusing mix of sneering at the less fortunate and its questioning of material values. What's unclear in the song – as it often is in Prince's work – is whether he's attacking the feckless, or the mercenary, or both. 'Insatiable' feels like an even sillier companion song to 'Scandalous', marred by that eternally embarrassing 'Carry On' moment when he uses sound FX to signify sexual organs. But the record's evident weaknesses didn't stop me (or millions of others, as it was Prince's most successful release since *Purple Rain*) playing the album to death at the time of release. Most Prince records only improve over the years. *Diamonds and Pearls* is one of the rare exceptions, and for all its period charm, there is little to bring the listener back to it.

*

With the release of the new record, Prince appointed a new European publicist, Chris Poole, whose company, Poole Edwards, had been doing the publicity for David Bowie's unfortunate Tin Machine project. Poole says that he didn't realise when he started working for Prince that this was 'the start of the war with Warners', which he believes was beginning even at this point. 'I think he grew superior,' says Poole. 'He didn't want to be told what to do any more.' Poole says by the end of his time working with Prince, he was 'the closest thing he had to a manager anywhere', and remembers of his boss: 'He has this kind of real mischievous, in some ways impish side to his character. At times he could be downright bloody nasty, but other times he could be very thoughtful and very generous.'

After the stripped-down Nude tour and the South American concerts, the *Diamonds and Pearls* tour, which went to Japan, Australia and crossed Europe but missed out the US, was a return to the grand showmanship and stagecraft of the *Lovesexy* shows. Poole believes Prince couldn't mount a successful tour of the US at this stage. 'I don't think he was big enough. His career had really slipped.'

The shows were well received by critics and audiences at the time, but it's not an era remembered especially fondly by most fans. The only official release that records live performances from this period is the *Diamonds and Pearls* video collection (since released on DVD), which contains concert footage of Prince performing 'Thunder', a cover of 'Dr Feelgood' with Rosie Gaines, 'Jughead' and 'Live 4 Love'. Some of these performances are taken from one of two professionally shot (but incomplete) videos of the eight Earl's Court shows Prince played on this tour, one of which was originally, it was rumoured at the time, intended for a Christmas release.

If this had come out, would the show be remembered in the

same way as the Syracuse 1985 performance or Dortmund 1988? No. Unlike almost all of the tours Prince undertook before this one, the *Diamonds and Pearls* tour has dated badly. The new songs sounded no more interesting onstage than they did on vinyl, and while the *Lovesexy* tour had offered a beautiful blend of the old and new, the hits he worked into the show ('Let's Go Crazy', 'Kiss' and 'Purple Rain') can be found in almost any era. This line-up of the NPG – Levi Seacer, Jr, Sonny T, Tommy Barbarella, Michael B and Rosie Gaines – are an underrated group who in some ways were as interesting a band as Prince has ever played with, but they were surrounded by too many people: eleven other dancers, rappers and musicians (Tony Mosley, Damon Dickson, Kirk Johnson, Michael B. Nelson, Brian Gallagher, Kathy Jensen, Dave Jensen, Steve Strand, Mayte, Diamond, Pearl and DJ William Graves). This group had none of the gang mentality of either The Revolution or the *Sign o' the Times/Lovesexy* bands, and the tour is only really worth seeking out by completists who want to hear live versions of the songs that didn't carry through to later eras.

The male and female members of Prince's band had never seemed as openly set in opposition as they were during this era. Every female onstage (with the exception of Rosie Gaines) was sexually objectified in a new way for Prince. And although Prince remained a sexually ambiguous figure throughout (when performing 'Insatiable' he was the one who was videoed and turned into a sex object, and he was lifted and tossed around by The Game Boyz), there was a new thuggery to some elements of his performance (a gun-shaped microphone, the way he introduced new song 'Sexy MF' by saying, 'This one's for all the whores'[11]) that didn't particularly suit him. When his rappers are telling women in the audience how to dress – even as a joke – it immediately makes the skimpy costumes of Diamond, Pearl and Mayte seem less playful and more of an enforced uniform than

Cat striding around in her underwear four years earlier. There were a few bright spots in the show, including Prince's best ever, lengthy performance of 'Thieves in the Temple' (occasionally mashed up with lyrics from 'It'). Sung in a peaked cap with chains over his face, he took this song to an even more emotional height than the already highly wrought studio version (the track, one of his very best, would disappear for ever after this tour). And he debuted several songs from his next album ('My Name Is Prince', 'Sexy MF' and 'Damn U') which, although driven by the same machismo and swagger as the show, were already irresistible.

The after-shows seemed uninspired too: for the most part, merely selections from the main show in a club setting. He didn't play any during the London part of the European tour, but Chris Poole remembers Prince holding an after-party at Tramp, where guest Mick Jagger 'had obviously had a couple of drinks and was in very merry mood, and grabbed hold of my leg and said, "Course, I knew her when she first started, y'know. I mean, she came on tour with us in stockings and suspenders, and I told her, "You'll never get away with that."'

Throughout this time, nightclubs and their denizens continued to be Prince's prime source of inspiration. Tramp had become Prince's favourite club during his London stay, and Poole remembers several occasions when he'd be getting ready to go to bed and his wife would hand him the phone and it would be Prince summoning him for a night out. 'All he'd do was sit there gazing at the women on the dance floor. He had this thing where he'd watch, taking everything in. And I'd be bored rigid. Tramp at that time was definitely not the place to be. He used to drink . . . was it . . . Drambuie and blackcurrant . . . something vile . . . I remember he said, "Eddie Murphy told me this is the drink to drink."' Poole's observation is echoed in Chris Heath's profile, which noted he'd do the same thing in Minneapolis clubs, occasionally causing resentment. As Heath notes: '[The waitress said], "You're always in clubs and you don't drink, you don't dance, you don't do anything, you just sit in the corner . . ." [to which] his bodyguard said, "He likes to people watch." [And she replied], "Why doesn't he go people watch on a park bench?"'[12]

23

THE CHAINS OF TURIN

Generally, engineers who have worked with Prince in the later parts of his career tend to make quite similar observations – that he keeps unpredictable hours, that he's impatient, that he's extraordinarily skilled on a wide variety of different instruments – but some observations from Kyle Bess,[1] who worked with Prince during this time, explain what seems like a drop-off in quality. The most significant change was Prince's decision to start working with a programmer, Airiq Anest. Most Prince fans admire Anest, whose work, they suggest, is more complicated and imaginative than that of his successor, Kirk(y) J(ohnson), but for the most part, the music he worked on has not endured. Bess's other pertinent observations suggest that Prince's process of composition had become even faster, but also more fractured. So much so that Bess is not even sure what records he was involved with. The reason for Bess's vagueness is partly because Prince would begin work in his Paisley Park studio and finish it with Bess at the Record Plant in Los Angeles, but also because he wouldn't even give Bess titles to the songs they were working on, with the engineer logging tracks as 'Thursday: groove' or 'New groove' or 'Sexy groove' (presumably Prince frowned on the engineer using more imaginative titles).

The problem with writing about a living musician is that even more so than authors or film-makers, the availability of their work is in constant flux, with records being deleted and reissued, songs for some film or theatre projects being easy to find, and others largely disappearing when the movie or play fails. This, of course, is more the case with Prince than any other musician, and the music he wrote for *I'll Do Anything* is another of the many frustrating gaps in the availability of Prince's work that make full assessment of his achievements difficult. At the time of writing, the director of the film, James L. Brooks, has been talking about the possibility of releasing the original version, prompted by the critical opinion of Jonathan Rosenbaum, one of America's most highly regarded film reviewers, who has said of that version (which contains nine Prince tracks) that 'it is far and away James L. Brooks' best movie, more than twice as good as what he finally released'.[2] At first, Brooks commented that he wanted to make a documentary where he could be 'honest about [his] own experience and tell the story of the first preview, where there were these massive walkouts, and then say, "and here's the picture they saw that night," and then show it . . . But we couldn't get the rights to Prince's songs – he had a caveat in his contract requiring his permission, and it was somewhere between not getting permission and not being able to get him on the phone.'[3]

The songs Prince wrote for the soundtrack of *I'll Do Anything* include some of the worst tracks he's ever recorded. The four songs that have been officially released from the project – 'The Rest of My Life', 'My Little Pill', 'There Is Lonely' and 'Don't Talk 2 Strangers' – are all worthwhile and will be discussed later, and at one stage Prince considered giving 'Empty Room' – one of his finest songs – to the project. But 'Poor Little Bastard', seemingly written in response to the screenplay, has the distinction of being the worst song Prince has ever recorded. In such a huge catalogue of work, it is inevitable that some of it will be throwaway, offensive or misguided, but nothing else quite rivals this song. Many hard-core fans keep it on standby as a corrective when they're getting too obsessed with Prince's music, and indeed I have used it to temper my own enthusiasm for Prince's music several times while writing this book.

Although the decision to change the film from a musical into a comedy was a result of a poor test screening rather than cold feet on director James L. Brooks's part, how must the poor man have felt when Prince walked into his office, lifted up the piano lid and started wailing the song's title? Nothing in the whole history of popular music can quite prepare you for the closing lines, in which Prince offers to be the poor little bastard's papa. It's beyond awful, beyond self-parody, a song so bizarre and misguided it makes 'Maxwell's Silver Hammer' seem sane. In an *LA Times* article from 1994, Chris Willman wrote about a camp cult that had grown up around the soundtrack, noting that one 'astonished professional songwriter' who played the album for friends observed: 'No matter how bad anybody thinks the music would've been – and I was expecting it to be horrible – it's worse. It's like "Springtime for Hitler" in *The Producers*.'[4]

Show tunes are not a genre that really suit Prince,[5] and these songs are both overwrought and smarmy, with an odd insincerity. Willman singled out not 'Poor Little Bastard' but 'Wow' for particular abuse, a song that exists in six versions, including one sung by a woman while giving birth, but although generic, it's an inoffensive upbeat squib. Far worse than 'Wow' is 'Be My Mirror', a song about fatherhood that could have only been written by a bachelor – what parent, no matter how virtuous, wants their child to mirror their behaviour? But the duet between Nick Nolte and Whittni Wright, whose performance even Rosenbaum describes as 'creepy', takes the song to new depths of horrendousness.

Rosenbaum has high praise for 'I Can't Love U Any More', writing of Julie Kavner's rendition that it's both 'the most beautiful and emotionally complex musical number' and also 'the most tormented, devoted to Hollywood hypocrisy at its worst'. Kavner is the voice of Marge Simpson, and it would be easy to mock her croaking, but there is something affecting about her delivery (the producers didn't think so, bringing in Melissa Etheridge to record another version), though it can't save what's essentially a listless fragment.

'I'll Do Anything', the lament of an artist desperate to please his audience, is the most compelling of the unreleased songs, particularly in Prince's original lo-fi demo version, which turns into a spoken-word rap midway through and which, given Brooks's butchering of his own film, seems deeply ironic. 'Make Believe' is lyrically less interesting, the title punning on the fantasy of films and TV and self-actualisation. Should Brooks get his wish and the film come out with the songs included, a reappraisal of the soundtrack might be necessary, but it seems unlikely that any of Prince's contributions will ever be regarded among his best work.

Having observed him in close quarters, Chris Poole thinks that Prince 'was going through a crisis throughout this period, because obviously rap had exploded and he had sort of been quoted saying he hated rap and didn't want to get involved with it . . .' Unlike Chuck D, Poole believes, 'I don't think Prince really understood rap. He was too far removed from the street at that point and it wasn't musical in the conventional sense . . . and when he did get into rap the guys he got involved with weren't very good, they were very second-rate.' Many fans, critics and musicians share this opinion. Arthur Baker, who worked with several musicians who have also worked with Prince and who has supported him with DJ sets in concert, says that had Prince come to him, he could have found far better rappers for him to work with. While Prince would continue to be influenced by hip hop to a lesser or greater degree throughout his subsequent albums, the ♀ record represents the last point when (notwithstanding all the alternative projects he was involved with at the time) Prince focused all his energies on one album. A record that has aged better than *Diamonds and Pearls* and is more consistent than *Graffiti Bridge* (although lacking its highlights), it was nonetheless irredeemably damaged by Prince's last-minute tinkering. It is not unusual for musicians to do damage to their albums by withdrawing the record's strongest songs at the last minute (this is a common complaint of critics when discussing Bob Dylan records,[6] and indeed Prince – in his ⚥ guise – would do something similar when he removed 'Days of Wild' from *The Gold Experience*), but with ⚥ the problem was that Prince added a song at the last minute, 'Eye Wanna Melt with U', which necessitated the removal of the spoken segues that he had originally included in what he referred to as a rock soap opera. The removed segues don't entirely resolve the album's complex storyline or explain its symbolism, but they do make the record possible to follow. Prince had often been interested in giving his albums a narrative, and the idea of a concept album was hardly new, but there's an intriguing parallel between this record and NWA's second album *Efil4zaggin* (1991) (Prince doffs his cap by sampling that record's 'Niggaz 4 Life' on the song 'Arrogance'), which also features imaginary TV news reporters. Chuck D famously referred to rap as 'the black CNN', and the journalistic nature of rap music was frequently emphasised as an important part of its appeal, which may have shaped Prince's initial approach to his construction of this record. But the record is far more surreal and convoluted than any rap album.

In its complete form, ⚥ is Prince's most conceptually ambitious album, an achievement to place alongside *Emancipation* and *The Rainbow Children* in its attempt to move beyond a suite of songs to make a unified grand statement, with a more intricate narrative than his past feature films, the story laid out in an accompanying video movie and comic, as well as on the album. It's also unusual in that, on one level at least, it seems a remarkably candid attempt to dramatise an ongoing love affair – although, as always with Prince, it's not quite that simple. For a record which addresses Prince's complex relationship with the press, it seems to give up an enormous amount of personal information. But it's also muddled and confusing, and untangling the record all these years on feels vaguely embarrassing, like adumbrating the plot of some long-forgotten children's programme.

On the original, unreleased version of the record, the opening segue sets up the action: it's Minneapolis, 1997, and a five-year-old boy named Michael is digging in the dirt when he finds three gold chains, for which he abandons his purple ball. Meanwhile, down the street at Paisley Park, Prince and the NPG are beginning a concert tour in which they are going to play 'an opera of entirely new music'.[7] Among the journalists covering the event is Vanessa Bartholomew, played – as on the few snatches of segues that did make it onto the record – by Kirstie Alley. Michael shows the chains to his mother, Princess Mayte, and it sparks a memory of five years earlier, although exactly what she's remembering is not clear. The *3 Chains o' Gold* film, directed by Parris Patton, Randee St. Nicholas[8] and Prince in his 'Paisley Park' guise, adds a more disturbing prologue: set in Cairo, shots of Princess Mayte swimming with four naked handmaidens is intercut with footage of her father being stabbed to death, before she takes the three chains of Turin and flees to Minneapolis. And the *Three Chains of Gold* (*sic*) comic book that Prince commissioned the late *Alter Ego* author Dwayne McDuffie[9] to write offers yet another variation on the central narrative (and on the significance of the chains), with a character named Tammuz explaining to his brother that the owner of the three chains of gold will be the ruler of 'Eridu, capital city of Erech, somewhere in the Middle East'. At the beginning of the comic, Tammuz, Mayte and Tammuz's brother all have one of the three chains. Tammuz's brother then kills him and goes in pursuit of Mayte to steal hers.

But on the album as released, there's a shout-out for Prince and The New Power Generation and it's straight into 'My Name Is Prince', another of Prince's narcissistic celebrations of his own talent. In the second verse, he talks about having a dual personality, something which seems to have developed from being merely part of his creative persona to something he believed (or pretended to believe) wholeheartedly during this era. As he later explained, seemingly straight-faced, to Oprah Winfrey while promoting *Emancipation*: 'Recent analysis has proved that there's probably two people inside of me, just like a Gemini, and we haven't determined what sex that other person is yet.'[10]

The artist may claim 'My Name Is Prince', but this song is quickly taken over by Tony M, in the first of the album's three collaborations, as if the henchman is offering to hold his boss's coat while he fights. The undercurrent of violence seems to come as much from Prince's desire to create cinematic drama in his concept album as a need to compete with gangsta rap. The 'Sexy MF' is not Prince but a woman, and in spite of the profanity in the title, this seems at first a heavily toned-down version of Prince's insatiable love tracks. Whereas the lust objects of 'Extra Loveable', 'Lust U Always' or 'Irresistible Bitch' would drive Prince into a frenzy, he is not only able to control himself in Mayte's company, but driven to control her too. This is a song about mind-fuckery (or, to use the Steely Dan term later borrowed by Prince's ex Susannah Melvoin for the title of the fDeluxe record, 'gaslighting'). In the song Prince imagines isolating his lover in a villa on the French Riviera (in the video this lover is not Mayte but past Prince associate Troy Beyer), tells her she has to learn how to avoid fighting with him, promises to cook for her and threatens to bind, gag and blindfold her in preparation for their future marriage. Throughout the song he belittles her and dismisses her imagined concerns. Prince sings in a much deeper register than he usually uses, and the jazzy track seems to owe something to Herbie Hancock (the album's final track, 'The Sacrifice of Victor', makes this connection more explicit by sampling The Headhunters' 'God Made Me Funky'[11]). Famously, this is also the video where Prince faux-humps his beloved yellow car, an automobile that he had been featuring in his movies since 'Gett Off'.

Of Mayte, Chris Poole remembers: 'She was a very young, very sweet young lady, a bit mesmerised like a rabbit in the headlights. She was quite a normal, down-to-earth person but she didn't know how to react to what was going on around her.' Prince's relationship with her seems, at least during the long period of courtship, to have had some similarities to his relationships with musical collaborators such as Dr Clare Fischer. Prince would send her songs, and she would send back videotapes of herself dancing to them. She also claimed that 'the kinkiest stuff we ever did was onstage – that was where I had the handcuffs'.[12] This back-and-forth in the early period of their courtship clearly inspired, on the unreleased version, a second segue, which relates to the back-and-forth of the tapes. Prince has sent NPG member Kirk Johnson to find Mayte, and he's returned with a gift of the three chains of Turin and a video message from her saying she's in Cairo. In the *3 Chains o' Gold* film, Mayte also gives Prince a tape containing (genuine) footage of her as an eight-year-old performing sword and belly dancing on the US reality stunt show *That's Incredible*.

As with 'Strange Relationship' and countless other Prince songs, there's an element of sadomasochism to 'Love 2 the 9's', which Prince begins but Tony again takes over, with Prince singing that he'd rather see Mayte crying than laughing, asking her to sleep on a bed of thorns and getting Tony to interrogate her. In an explicit reference to her age, she describes herself as 'jail-bait'.[13] 'The Morning Papers' explores this age difference further, and given one of the album's other major themes – the pursuit of Prince by the media – the press is presented in a surprisingly benign way. The truth is, Prince should have ditched 'The Max'[14] instead of the segues, a largely pointless rap track reminiscent of the worst of *Diamonds and Pearls*, accompanied, in *3 Chains o' Gold*, with footage of Tony M roller-skating and leading into one of the few segues that Prince kept on the record, with Alley-as-Vanessa-Bartholomew calling him for an interview. In the movie, he's wearing what look like pink pyjamas for 'Blue Light', a reggae-influenced love song about sexual difference built around an Eric Leeds sax line and the engineer's bass-playing which should be horrible but is actually one of the album's few highlights.

When Prince revised the album, he edited and moved back the next segue, further destroying the record's narrative. On the original version, this segue gathers up the record's themes and narrative so far with the return of Kirstie Alley, who, promising that she's not recording this time, interrogates Prince. The record's spoken-word section features Prince disguising his voice with a tone box ('Like in the movie *Barbarella*?' Alley asks, making this the second Prince record inspired by the Roger Vadim film, which also plays in Prince's private cinema while he makes out with Troy Beyer in *3 Chains o' Gold*).[15] Prince explains – as he also does on the released version – that he has chosen Alley to get his message across. She tells him the three chains are as old as the pyramids and contain magic powers, and then questions him about Mayte being sixteen.

*

Does it really matter that Prince got rid of a few segues in order to add a freshly written song he was enamoured with? The thing about music careers as long as Prince's – or the filmographies of directors on which studio's survival depends – is that aesthetic decisions invariably become tangled up with economics. It's possible to make a case that the ♀ album derailed his whole career. There were complicated record-company negotiations going on around this time, endless discussions that eventually resulted in Prince benefiting from a complexly structured but on the face of it extremely lucrative deal, and the relative failure of this album's singles in the US,[16] at least until the third single release – '7' – led to tension between Prince and the label. It's also possible to see the beginning of Prince's frustration with being Prince during this era from the way he had begun to cover his face continually with chains and masks. The gun microphone so prominently displayed on the cover of 'Sexy MF' also revealed that he was fantasising about swapping the life of a pop superstar for that of super-spy James Bond. Quite why this male fantasy should appeal to a man with no need for it is hard to discern.

But let's forget about the economics and look at what Prince gained by shoving 'Eye Wanna Melt with U' in the middle of the record.[17] Not until the faux-gangsterisms of the late 1990s would he again write anything quite so tacky, and those later songs are harder still to enjoy because of the puerile misogyny. The accompanying video continues from the same stock of bankrupt erotic imagery that Prince began using in the *Gett Off* mini-movie (as in Vanity 6's 'Drive Me Wild' video, it's a sexual nightmare: Prince is wearing a mask; there are menacing shots of the man who killed Princess Mayte's father holding a knife and frequent flashes of naked women at what looks like an orgy, while Mayte tosses and turns in bed. Prince likes his sweet women to be the victim of incubi[18]). If this was who he wanted to be now, it's difficult to comprehend why. To challenge gangsta rap? Fit in with his band members? Impress his fans? Impossible to tell.

Even songs that seemed saccharine hid new harshness. Presented as a love letter in *3 Chains*, 'Sweet Baby' seems at first to be another of the many throwaway self-empowerment songs that he wrote during this period. But as well as being one of the prettier (and relatively uncelebrated) deep cuts on any Prince album, it also sees him again (as in *The Undertaker* film and many other works from this era) taking on the perspective of a God-like observer, making the song an audaciously cruel piece of convoluted manipulation.[19] 'The Continental' is the first Prince song to be released featuring a guest appearance from dancer and rapper Carmen Electra, a trash-sex rap that reveals Prince revelling in strip-club glamour like he's planning an Abel Ferrara film. A reference in the song to a woman asking a man to marry her if she can flip coins with her belly echoes with comments Mayte made about Prince rushing people into the room to watch when she told him she could do this trick.[20]

Even his sex songs were now angry, as the title of 'Damn U' indicates.[21] A gentler variation on 'Tick, Tick, Bang', onstage Prince would take this song into even woozier territory, giving a remarkably convincing portrayal of a man approaching orgasm. It also features a prominent contribution from Dr Clare Fischer, who is credited with strings for the whole album.[22] That Prince would fill a song called 'Arrogance' with rap samples (from Eric B and Rakim, NWA) raises the possibility that this is less a justification of the perceptions of him than a more subtle version of the rapper-baiting 'Dead On It'. But its placing on the album suggests that Prince's attitude towards hip hop was increasingly ambivalent, followed as it is by 'The Flow'.[23]

In the next snipped segue, Mayte explains that seven men killed her father and are coming for her and the three chains of gold, setting up the next song. With Prince albums from around this period, it became much harder to predict which songs would stay in his set, and the survival of '7' through so many years is surprising. Prince clearly valued it enough to make it a single, and it proved the most successful from the album – puzzling for a record which also included 'Sexy MF' and 'My Name Is Prince' – which may explain why it's a track which has retained its value for Prince, undergoing a metamorphosis in recent years as Prince started to play it as part of a medley with The Beatles' 'Come Together'.[24] Perhaps the reason why the song has lasted is less down to its quality than its symbolic significance, being the track most closely linked with his decision to retire his name. In *3 Chains o' Gold*, the number seven refers to both the assassins and the seven alternative Princes, whom he kills off one by one in the video, foreshadowing the 'death' of Prince that would follow when he changed his name to ♀. This link is made explicit in a conversation between Mayte and Kirstie Alley that plays over the end credits of the film, in which Mayte hints at the change Prince is about to make, and which is followed by a literal explanation of the transformation written on screen.

The title of 'And God Created Woman' suggests that Prince's much-mentioned cinephilia remained limited – at this time – to soft-core classics. It's one of the many songs he has written about the Garden of Eden, a preoccupation that first appeared during the *Purple Rain* shows' stage conversations with God and which Prince would return to ad nauseam, constantly connecting the beginning of new relationships with a return to a prelapsarian state.

Having set up the narrative about the search for these three chains of gold, Prince now sings about having them but not caring any more about his lover (presumably Mayte), whom he considers evil and hopes will die before him.[25] A full-band performance,

'3 Chains o' Gold' is one of Prince's most OTT releases, resembling some ghastly Jim Steinman or Roy Baker production in its multipart faux-operatic silliness, complete with a chorus of multitracked Princes (maybe the seven personalities he killed in the movie), soft-metal guitars and drums. It also overlaps with imagery that Prince would go on to explore in more detail – an Undertaker figure that would later inspire an album and short film. Missing from the released album is a concluding segue with Prince and Mayte reunited, suggesting that this song is intended to represent some kind of dramatic conclusion.

The recorded version of 'The Sacrifice of Victor' is easy to mistake for another 'how great is the NPG' celebration, but Prince performed an exceptional live version at an after-show at the DNA Lounge in San Francisco, on a night when he had bronchitis but felt determined to perform nonetheless. This version brought out the chill of the lyrics and emphasised the harsh sentiment of the song previously buried by the NPG's wittering. Seemingly one of Prince's most autobiographical songs – although as with any track about his childhood, it's important to be aware of his myth-making (he notes the passage about his epilepsy is 'TRUE' in mirror-writing on his lyric sheet) – it features him singing about child abuse, the sense that the racial mix at his school was a social experiment, the death of Martin Luther King, the drug abuse his friends indulged in and the important influence in his early life of André Cymone's mother, Bernadette Anderson. Ditching the first verse, he intoned the second in a throaty murmur, before reworking the song into a slow-jazz Heron-esque grumble that cries out for official release.

The Act I show was paradoxically both Prince's most thuggish and his most romantic. One of the most appealing elements of almost all of his stage shows up to this point was the fact that the sexual energies were so free-floating: he was creating an adult playground where everyone was in costume and appealing to the audience. With Act I, the focus of the majority of the show was the relationship between Prince and Mayte, between musician and dancer. She spent most of it atop his piano, with Prince directing almost all of his lyrics to her (focusing mainly on the ⚥ album, this show featured Prince playing far more piano than guitar).

There are more disturbing moments in this show than those from any other era. Whether it was the aforementioned scene where a female reporter is stripped (admittedly only to her slip, which is still more than Cat got to wear during the *Lovesexy* shows) or Prince singing in front of a firing squad or Mayte's sword dance, the pantomime elements of the performance drained the typical fun of a Prince show. His outfits were more aggressive too: he had introduced the peaked cap with chains over his face for the last tour, but now he spent much of the show waving a cane as well, in his own take on hip-hop accessorising.

Using hip-hop language, Prince would refer to himself as a 'nigga' onstage during 'Peach', the first of five new songs that would show up in the set, all of which had an even heavier edge than the ⚥ material (the others were three NPG songs, 'Deuce and a Quarter', 'Johnny' and 'Goldnigga', and the frantic *Come* track, 'Loose!'). Usually, when Prince introduced unreleased songs in a set, they pointed at a future direction, but fun as 'Peach' and 'Johnny' both undoubtedly are, they represent dead ends. The only truly good-natured stretch of the show was the first of the mass stage invasions that would become a familiar part of Prince's stage show from this period onwards.

Prince would later look back at the time when he first started engaging with hip hop as his 'friction years', which I see as starting in earnest in 1993, telling Spike Lee in 1997: 'I've gotten some criticism for the rap I've chosen to put in my past work. But there again, it came during my friction years. If you notice, not a lot of that stuff is incorporated into my sets now . . . on the rap tip, though, it's an old style and I've always done it kind of differently – half sung, you know like "Irresistible Bitch" and some of the other things I used to do.'[26] But if the friction years did begin in the early 1990s, the conflict wouldn't truly flourish until it came to the last album Prince would put out before the most dramatic and important transformation of his entire career.

♀ PART I: INTRODUCING THE FRICTION YEARS

Rock history coagulates around shape-shifters. Dylan going electric, getting God, begging to join The Grateful Dead. Neil Young being sued by David Geffen for not being Neil Young enough. Bowie killing off Ziggy Stardust, fronting Tin Machine, becoming a junglist. But after electric Dylan, arguably the second-most famous rock transformation came from the self-styled Electric Man: the seven years Prince spent as ♀. He made the announcement on his thirty-fifth birthday, issuing a press release that caused such media confusion that he was continuing to clarify the matter two years later. In a statement on his website of the time, The Dawn, Prince explained that he felt his name had become commoditised by Warner Brothers, and that the only solution was to adopt as a moniker a symbol that could not be pronounced.

But why did he choose this particular symbol? According to his wedding programme, the decision came to him in a vision while visiting Mayte in Puerto Rico, where he saw the symbol, wondered what it meant and heard a voice telling him it was his new name. It was a nice attempt at a superhero-style origin story, but the symbol had been a developing part of his iconography for years, now gaining the extra horn from one of the alchemical symbols for soapstone (although some fans prefer the notion that the horn represents the fusion of man, woman and musical instrument).[1]

Prince's decision to change his name came two months after

he faxed a press release to the media saying he was retiring from studio recording. Earlier that same day, he had had a meeting with Warner Brothers in which he told them that he wouldn't be delivering any more studio albums, instead planning to fulfil his deal with old songs from his Vault. After releasing fifteen albums in fifteen years, Prince planned to concentrate instead on theatre, interactive media, nightclubs and movies. This has usually been reported as Prince being provocative, the opening salvo in a PR war that would cause untold damage to his career. And it's easy to understand why Warner Brothers executives would be upset by this after signing a reported $100 million deal with Prince barely a year before, but handled differently there might have been a different outcome to this situation.[2]

Alan Leeds believes that Prince's frustration was partly fuelled by the deal itself. 'His contract was coming up for renewal, and both Madonna and Janet Jackson had had contract renewals that had gained headlines, and he wanted a deal that would trump the Madonna deal. He was so desperate to get that headline that he was allowing his team to negotiate away certain royalties, certain publishing rights and all kinds of things in order to get bigger guarantees. It was one of those deals that was all on paper. It was all incentive-driven, so while it was technically accurate to say the deal was worth $100 million or whatever the number was, it was predicated on, "If you sell this many units, then you'll get this big advance, and if it all worked out, then you'll get this." It was a smoke-and-mirrors deal.'

Still, if Prince had allowed Warner Brothers to go through the Vault and select songs themselves rather than merely take what they were given, they could have compiled the best Prince release to date. And why even announce he was no longer going to record? Surely, with a bit of sneakiness, he could have presented (or reworked) old recordings as new albums without anyone (aside from obsessive fans with studio-production log reports) realising? After all, when he did finally escape from Warner Brothers, his second release under the ♀ alias was a three-CD set of old recordings.

When Prince stated that he would make no more studio recordings under his own name, he also explained that he would continue to write songs for other artists and tour. But almost every Prince interview had included talk of a side project – whether film, ballet or opera – and given the success of the Joffrey Ballet's *Billboards* the previous January, and the rock-opera nature of the ♀ album and accompanying tour, it may have seemed a logical way of developing his career.

Even before making this announcement, Prince had planned a change of direction, and for some time had been considering ways of releasing music without going through Warners. Alan Leeds remembers: 'We had a conversation where he said we had to start releasing records on our own because Warners couldn't absorb the product that he was putting out quickly enough, and this was a precursor to downloading music. He said the idea of going to record stores is old and it's not necessary. We should make a record, put it on our own label and buy advertising space on late-night television and sell it mail-order. And I said, "Prince, we can't do that, it's in violation of your deal with Warners." He wanted me to do it, and I told him, "I can't be the figurehead because I run a joint venture with them!" So he said, "Let's put in Gwen [Leeds's wife]'s name and she'll go on TV and advertise these records."'

Prince had also met with the Tony award-winning playwright David Henry Hwang to discuss collaborating on a musical. What Prince was interested in, Hwang explained in his introduction to 'From *Come*', the only extract of the libretto that survives (published in an anthology entitled *On a Bed of Rice: An Asian*

American Erotic Feast[3]), was 'sex between lovers who never meet'.[4] This concept would show up, in various ways, in most of Prince's work from the mid-1990s, across all media.

In all the later permutations – such as the TV movie *The Beautiful Experience* – the interaction would take place via the Internet, with a beautiful woman (occasionally played by Nona Gaye, who dated Prince for three years and may, just as much as Mayte, be the model for the character in the *Come* libretto) being drawn into Prince's world through a master computer. But in this first version of the story, their affair is conducted through letters, and the libretto focused on a particular relationship between a star and a fan. As Hwang would later explain: 'he [told] me this story based on his own experience. About his relationship with a fan. Which became obsessive and weird – in a sexual way (of course) [and he wanted] to do a show about it.'[5]

Prince's proposal to Hwang was that the intense erotic affair between the musician and fan should also spin off into 'exercises of fantasy and dominance', something that seemingly preoccupied Prince at this time. Nona Gaye would later complain that during this time, she 'was trying to be this woman I thought he wanted, very passive, just letting him lead',[6] describing the three years she said they dated as 'a whirlwind of head trips and mind screws'.[7]

The extract from *Come* combines retro and futuristic technology (Prince ever the *Barbarella* admirer), opening with Orlando[8] carrying a videosphere[9] and putting on virtual-reality equipment in order to talk to the fan, Marie-Anne. The cocky Orlando has much in common with previous Prince personas such as The Kid. The extract also features the use of twin identities, as Marie-Anne suggests she has 'another girl' deep inside her. The fantasy action[10] shifts first to the Garden of Eden,[11] then 'a mythical Babylon'. As on the ♀ album, the object of the rock star's longings is a princess, this time of the 'ancient empire of Babylon',[12] and as with Mayte's character on that record, she is sexualised while a young girl, stating that even at fifteen her mind was filled with 'the memories of a precious harlot'.[13]

This is troubling material, complicated further by the scene that follows, in which Marie-Anne as a fifteen-year-old spies on her father ravishing a slave girl, before she herself is ravished by strangers. The creative world of this piece is similar to that of the post-punk pornographic novelist Kathy Acker – although it is, of course, harder to accept this material when it comes from the imagination of two men, particularly when one has a history of relationships with younger women.

Prince's project with Hwang didn't come to fruition, although a smaller collaboration – the song 'Solo' – ended up on the *Come* album. This also came, Hwang said, from their first meeting. 'He [asked] me to write a poem for him. About loss. The way you feel when you've lost someone you love. And you know they're never coming back. And that, for the rest of your life, you're going to be alone. He [wanted] to do a song that suddenly breaks into a spoken word interlude. They're gonna say, "The boy's really lost it this time."'[14] It's intriguing Prince approached Hwang for this, as, along with the Garden of Eden, this scenario is the one that recurs most frequently in his later work. But after his failure to interest people in his and Hwang's *Come*, Prince turned his attentions instead to a dance interpretation of Homer's *Odyssey* entitled *Glam Slam Ulysses*.

This is an easy project to mock, with no clear connection between the various parts of the *Odyssey* being dramatised and the songs written for each section. The sappy 'Strays of the World' accompanied the arrival from a ship of a cast who looked like refugees from a fetish club. After a video insert of a woman being dragged around and roughed up, 'Interactive' soundtracked

Kenny Everett's idea of a Cyclops gurning in front of lightning on a video screen. 'Dolphin', a song that begs indulgence from the listener even on vinyl, gained nothing from being accompanied by synchronised swimming gestures. The sexuality of the piece is strip-club-influenced but fluid: 'Pheromone' had Circe (in a cat costume) and Carmen Electra cage-dancing (for more on Carmen and cages, see Chapter 34), while 'Dark', arguably the set's best song, was accompanied by footage of male dancers urinating, while Carmen (as Penelope) spied on them from a stall. 'Loose!' entered Kenneth Anger territory, while the sirens who undulated to 'Space' had skeleton bikinis, skulls protecting their breasts and finger bones curled over their genitals (an outfit Lady Gaga might consider plagiarising). 'Orgasm' provoked embarrassed laughter from the audience, and quite what the Scylla was doing during 'What's My Name' was almost impossible to determine. Another strong song, 'Endorphinmachine' – which Prince still performs to this day – was the most successfully choreographed, even managing to give some sense of the interaction between Calypso and Ulysses it was supposed to dramatise. 'Race', a serious song that intriguingly brings together a techno and jazz sound, was – although not obviously linked to the Ulysses story – another high point. A Trojan Horse would be dragged across the stage during another 'Come' reprise, before 'Pope' gave the cast something to dance to while they took their bows.

For all its silliness, Prince clearly brought the same intensity to this project as he did to his albums. And it was clear that whatever his relationship with Warner Brothers, Prince wasn't about to retreat from the media. His publicist, Chris Poole, remembers receiving the fax with the name-change press release and thinking: '"Well, [it's] barking but genius, this'll get them jumping . . ." And it did. And it was quite fun to be involved in something like that because no one had done anything like that before. There was this theory that if he wasn't Prince any more, he wouldn't be bound by his record contract with Warners. He had been reborn, Christ-like, with a new name, a new identity. But of course hot-shot American lawyers wouldn't have anything to do with that. Still, [it worked, as] the main point of publicity is to have people talking about you.' Among the many who were more doubtful about the strategy was his old collaborator Chris Moon, who, although he hadn't seen Prince since 1982, remembers 'screaming at the radio, "Do not change your name to a symbol, do not get rid of Prince, no, no no!"'

Prince's first creative project to be completed after he issued the name-change press release didn't appear until the end of the year, and wouldn't get a widespread release until two years later. *The Undertaker*, which began as another project for Nona Gaye,[15] was worked on with one of his favoured directors from this era, Parris Patton, and was eventually released in two versions,[16] starring a different actress, Vanessa Marcil. It's hard to tell whether the completed scenes are indicative of the uncompleted film, but they suggest that it would have been another Warholian home movie, with a surprisingly lysergic edge.

Prince is, much of the time, more moralistic than Warhol, but while the film does have an anti-drugs message (most explicitly defined in the title song, which Mavis Staples claimed Prince wrote for her after telling him that she was married to a mortician for eight years[17]), the way it is constructed presents Prince as, if not a passive force, then at least one without the ability (or interest) to save the overdosing addict in front of him (unless it's through the power of music).

Beginning in black and white, the longer edit opens with Marcil arriving at Paisley Park. Instructed not to disturb a rehearsal, she goes to a pay phone and tries to impress upon someone named Victor that she's changed and wants to be with him. Her pleas go ignored and Victor hangs up. Vanessa then repeatedly bashes the receiver against the pay phone, laughing hysterically, before going through her bag and finding some pills. She swallows them and takes out a small harlequin clown, spinning in circles with him. Eventually, she enters the rehearsal space, finds a seat for the doll and rolls on the floor staring at strobe lights as Prince plays. Halfway through the first song she finds somewhere to vomit, and her presence throughout makes an already sinister set of songs seem even more menacing. And while Marcil is not especially sexualised, in spite of her supposedly grungy look, there is definitely a darker edge in her submission to the music, even if it eventually fills her with the emotional strength to leave.

Prince's original intention was to release the film's soundtrack with the magazine *Guitar World*. Given that it caused so much drama when he did eventually release a CD with a newspaper in 2008, it's surprising no one noted he'd had the idea fourteen years earlier, and that it was one of the many points of conflict with Warner Brothers, although Prince's motivation for doing so seems to have been as much personal as financial. Rather than intending to establish a new business model half a decade or so before everyone began exploring alternative means of distribution, he was simply keen for readers of this guitar-tech magazine to appreciate his fretwork.

The Undertaker was substantially different from most of the music he was releasing via more conventional channels at the time. 'It starts off in a blues vein,' he told the magazine, 'but then quickly goes to funk. But because of that first song, people tend to want to put it in that [*blues*] glass of water.'[18] Who these people were is not clear: he was talking here about a record that had yet to leak out even unofficially and presumably at this stage had only been heard by record execs and his immediate circle.

It works better as a CD than a video. It has never been officially released: in a neat reversal of the legend of *The Black Album*, Prince is said to have privately pressed a thousand copies of the CD, which, it is claimed, Warner Brothers ordered him to destroy. 'The Ride' is one of Prince's most-loved blues-based songs, and this version is far superior to the one on the *Crystal Ball* set – a loose, long, near-eleven-minute jam that resembles guitar-driven tracks like 'Billy' that Prince had never previously officially released. 'Poorgoo', however, although it shares some of the same impressive blues-based guitar work, particularly when played live, is a throwaway about some unfortunate associate of Prince's[19] who has bad luck with women.

Prince often covers Rolling Stones songs in concert – notably 'Miss You' and '(I Can't Get No) Satisfaction' – but this version of 'Honky Tonk Women' is particularly spectacular, showing Prince abandoning most of the lyrics and indulging in the kind of Hendrix-style guitar-playing he'd return to in the *Lotusflow3r* era. For all his insistence that this is a blues and funk record, the new version of old song 'Bambi' is delivered in a similarly heavy-rock style, followed by a brief snippet of 'Zannalee' (a song that would later appear on this record's closest equivalent among Prince's officially released records, *Chaos and Disorder*) and another long ten-minute jam on 'The Undertaker'.

Nineteen ninety-three saw no new Prince album (although he did include six previously unavailable songs on *The Hits/The B-Sides* triple CD released in September), but he made good on his promise to record with other artists by releasing two substantial records: Carmen Electra's eponymous debut, and the first of the NPG albums, *Goldnigga* (although 'released' may be too grand a term for an album rejected for distribution by Warner Brothers and sold only at Act II shows in Europe and the NPG store).

There were several pleasing things about Prince's *Hits* compilations – the fact that he'd asked Alan Leeds to write the sleeve notes, which Leeds says Prince co-operated with, and which offer a fascinating close insight into his music; the inclusion of six unreleased songs, including the long-coveted 'Power Fantastic'; and the extra CD full of B-sides – but a greatest-hits record is no way to appreciate an artist whose best albums have no filler. The unreleased songs included 'Pink Cashmere', considered for the first version of *Rave Un2 the Joy Fantastic* and in the meantime sent to Dr Clare Fischer for his input; 'Pope', a slight rap inspired by Bernie Mac; and the only truly significant new song, 'Peach', a fun piece of comic smut with a questionable line about a gay preacher. The album also contained Prince's own version of 'Nothing Compares 2 U' (not the demo but a live version recorded at Paisley Park) and a 'video version' of '4 the Tears in Your Eyes'.

His first run of performances after changing his name from Prince to ♀, the Act II tour saw the newly anonymous Artist having great fun with the concept of identity. It appeared as if the show was beginning with Prince being lowered from the ceiling on a swing, dressed in his chained hat and brandishing a cane as he performed 'My Name Is Prince' in an even more aggressive way than he had on the Act I tour. But at the end of the song, the sleight of hand was revealed: the figure wasn't Prince but Mayte, who stripped out of her Prince outfit before gyrating around the stage in pink underwear and heavy boots. It was an audacious opening, another example of Prince having fun with this seemingly egocentric song. It also made clear that even in the most masculinist period of his career, Prince remained interested in gender roles and sexual identity.

The Act II shows were more audience-pleasing than the Act I tour, and not just because dancers The Game Boyz had gone. The set list ranged more widely through Prince's backlist, and this was the first of many occasions when a show would be hyped with the announcement that this would be the last time an audience would get to hear the hits (on his next tour he'd play almost entirely new music). Songs like 'The Beautiful Ones', 'The Cross' and 'Raspberry Beret' diluted the stodge of the ❦ album material, although the interaction between Prince and Mayte remained as central to the performance as it had been on the earlier tour.

Throughout the tour Prince gave clues to his future direction. Several shows saw him premiering songs that would end up on *Come* and *The Gold Experience* (as well as tracks from the just-released *Goldnigga*), and at Wembley Arena Prince made a nine-minute song-speech that incorporated lyrics from 'What's My Name', 'Come' and 'Race', and encouraged bootlegging of his concerts by telling audience members to bring tape recorders to his gigs if they wanted to keep up with him. Refusing to answer to the name Prince, he threatened to retire from recording, made cryptic remarks about having to sugar-coat his music and returned to one of his recurring bugbears in this era: his record company's concern that he was releasing too much.

The official documentation didn't arrive until two years later. *The Sacrifice of Victor* is a concert film again directed by Parris Patton that – along with the Terry Gydesen photo book published in 1994 – is the main record of the tour. At this stage, Prince had yet to put out a live album, but had always chosen wisely in the shows he officially released on videotape, which made it all the more disappointing that his first after-show recording seemed, in its heavily edited release, indigestibly eclectic, lurching from the soothing gospel of The Steeles to Tony M stripped to the waist and channelling House of Pain to Mayte stage-diving in the space of thirty minutes. Gospel, rap, blues and metal: Prince in the 1990s was proving impossible to pin down.

Of this night Chris Poole remembers: 'That was the after-show of all after-shows. He wanted a warehouse party, but for obvious reasons that wasn't going to happen. It was the nearest we could do to having a warehouse party and putting some boundaries around it so we wouldn't get into trouble. But it did get quite ugly.'

Poole was also involved in the next stage of Prince's slow emancipation from Warner Brothers, the independent release of a single entitled 'The Most Beautiful Girl in the World'. He believes Warners allowed this in the hope that it might make Prince more aware of how important they were to his continued career. 'I think what happened was that Warners thought, "Oh well, we'll show him. We'll let him release his own record and then he'll realise how difficult it is . . ."' But it backfired. 'Whoops, first number-one single he'd ever had [in the UK].' Poole says he played a large role in the record's campaign. 'I found the distributor, found the pluggers – I did everything.' The handmade nature of the project extended to every element, including the video. Steve Parke says of preparing Paisley for the accompanying shoot: 'I think everybody in the building was responsible for melting some of those candles. We had to get them melted very quickly and then film.'

But although Prince retained his extraordinary skill to surround himself with people who would fulfil their roles to the very best of their abilities, he was setting up an extremely large infrastructure, and could not oversee every element. Parke remembers of Prince's burgeoning nightclub empire: 'I ended up doing work down at the Glam Slam club in Miami. It was completely outside of the Paisley work ethic; it was the Miami-beach work ethic.

They were basically, "It's three o'clock (in the afternoon), we're done."'

Prince's interest in computers had been apparent from his earliest recordings, both in his delight in the way they allowed him to record without band-mates, and also as a lyrical preoccupation. It seemed inevitable, then, that as part of his move away from releasing albums in the conventional manner he would look to technology as a way of reaching a new audience, releasing a CD-Rom entitled *Interactive*. A year earlier, musicians had begun to explore 'multimedia', with Peter Gabriel releasing *Xplora 1: Peter Gabriel's Secret World* and Todd Rundgren an 'interactive' version of his album *No World Order* under the pseudonym TR-i which allowed the purchaser to alter the album's 'mix'. *Interactive* played once again on making Prince's private space public, beginning with the player crash-landing in a spaceship before getting out to explore the nearest building: Prince's mansion.

The game, which mainly consisted of putting puzzle pieces together in order to hear the then-unreleased 'Interactive', received warmer reviews than Bowie's contemporaneous *Jump: The David Bowie Interactive CD-Rom* but suffered from the same problem that would mar several of Prince/♀'s subsequent computer-based projects: the amount of effort required did not lead to sufficient reward. Howard Bloom believes that it was Prince's interest in computers, and subsequently the Internet, which helped make him relevant again. 'Prince began to live part of his life on the Internet. He established a beachhead in cyberspace. And cyberspace is a way of making contact with your audience without having the fearful presence of men's bodies. And Prince was able to get back in touch with his audience. And being back in touch brought Prince back.'

*

But he hadn't given up on old-fashioned ways of reaching fans. The publicity for *21 Nights* made much of the fact that this was Prince's first official book. Not so. In fact, it was his fourth. The first two, photo books entitled *Prince Presents the Sacrifice of Victor* and *Neo Manifesto – Audentes Fortuna Juvat*,[20] were published in July 1994. Though beautifully produced, the most interesting photograph from *Victor* is the one on the cover of *Come*, and while the pictures in *Neo Manifesto* are largely garish, the book is of more value in that it contains lyrics from then-unreleased songs. Other than as part of a multimedia blitz, it's hard to understand Prince's motivation for putting out these lyrics.[21] Was it his way of tipping off diehard fans (presumably the only people who would bother purchasing such a seemingly slight item from the NPG store) about songs available on bootlegs or soon to be officially released? Or a variation on his use of protégés to get more product out? Presumably, given that he was still under contract to Warner Brothers at this time, he wasn't yet able to produce CDs of unreleased material for the shops to sell, so maybe this was the next best thing. Or were these the lyrics that he felt proudest of, lines he felt stood up well enough to be analysed? The collection does include the lyrics to four of Prince's most highly regarded out-takes – 'Empty Room', 'God Is Alive', 'Old Friends 4 Sale' and 'Crystal Ball' – but also three far less distinguished songs – 'Color', 'And How' and 'Don't Talk 2 Strangers' – eventually given to The Steeles, Jevetta Steele and Chaka Khan.[22] Earlier that year, Prince had also attempted to launch a magazine, *10,000*, which had a provocative cover, included an interview with Vanessa Marcil from *The Undertaker* and included the lyrics to yet another (still) unreleased song, 'Adonis and Bathsheba'. But none of these projects truly took off and Prince would leave the print world behind, turning his attentions solely to the Internet for the next decade and a half, only returning to publications when he began to lose interest in the digital world.

25

♀ PART 2: 'IT WAS JUST ABOUT NEEDING TO GET IT DONE . . .'

Some (including many at Warner Brothers) believed Prince concluded his record deal with albums compiled out of spite. And *Come* is Prince's most confused and unappealing record. It appears to have a clear structure, beginning with cunnilingus and ending with an orgasm,[1] but anyone putting this record on for Barry White purposes will have a nasty shock when they get to the song about child abuse ('Papa'). Having decided to kill off 'Prince', it seems as if he wasn't going to include his best songs on the record, and it's really the soundtrack from *Glam Slam Ulysses* minus the five best tracks, but with the addition of two new, slightly more substantial songs – the appealingly smooth horn-driven 'Letitgo' and the aforementioned 'Papa', which some have read as autobiographical.

Evidently not an album Prince took particular care over, *Come* was nevertheless supported by two of his best maxi-discs, containing variations on 'Letitgo' and 'Space' respectively, and including one remix – the 'Universal Love Remix' of 'Space' – that many fans consider the best remix/alternative version of any Prince song. As with several Prince maxi-singles, these collections work as albums in their own right and in this instance rival their parent album.

Three months after *Come*, Prince continued the house-clearing with the official release of *The Black Album*. It would have been perfectly possible to turn this release into an event, but it seems that for whatever reason – Prince's continuing ambivalence about the record, the increasing sense of conflict between the artist and his label – it slipped out uncelebrated, and it seems destined to be remembered for its status as a 'once-legendary' bootleg rather than for the quality of the music itself.

While celebrating the death of Prince, the Artist was readying his debut album. Frustrated by delays (once he'd drawn a cross on his cheek; now he wrote 'SLAVE' there while attending recording-company meetings and making public appearances), Prince was road-testing new songs at small private shows at Paisley Park and embarking on a new period of spiritual growth brought on by adopting a new identity.

However personally rewarding he might have found this, my innate faith in Prince's intellect is seriously challenged by the fact that he was – for a few years at least – going round recommending the self-help book *Embraced by the Light*, by Betty J. Eadie. There is an obvious disconnect between the people who write about rock stars – unhealthy, obsessive types who have read, heard and seen (and in some cases, eaten) too much – and the superhumans they describe, and it's perhaps inevitable that pop stars are more likely to be impressed by New Age philosophy than anyone who has spent too much time inside a lecture theatre, concert hall or darkened screening room. But even so, *Embraced by the Light*? Come on! Still, as galling as it is to have to read this sort of dreck in search of what Prince found of value in it, it's easy to find in this book many sections that chime with Prince's occasion-ally mechanistic beliefs, such as Eadie's insistence that our bodies punish us for any sins of the flesh.

It is this sense of being 'responsible for our bodies' that lies behind 'P. Control', the opening track of *The Gold Experience*, the one album from this era that fans hold in high esteem. The next stage in Prince's development from sexual revolutionary to reactionary conservative, 'P. Control' brings together many of his long-running obsessions (the sexualisation of schooldays; the importance of money in sexual and romantic relationships; dominance and submission) in the most basic formation to date (can you imagine a male equivalent called 'Cock Control'?). The song is worth hearing for Prince's hip-hop inspired OTT delivery, but it's an offputting opening. If this is ♀, then bring back Prince.

The Gold Experience includes the two most immediate songs from *Glam Slam Ulysses* – 'Endorphinmachine' and 'Dolphin' – as well as 'The Most Beautiful Girl in the World', which has the silliest audio punctuation ever, not just the ticking clock but the plip of Prince's teardrops of joy, and more than the usual amount of filler: 'Shhh' is a fairly run-of-the-mill ballad – most notable for its drum solo – which Prince has played in concert more times than any song not from his classic era; 'We March' is another self-celebration song; 'Now' and '319' are almost instantly forgettable, though the former includes one of Prince's most suggestive lines and ends with him comparing the NPG to drugs. His claim that '319' – a song about a man photographing a woman masturbating in a hotel room – was inspired by the actress Elizabeth Berkley from *Showgirls* makes one want to see the pictures if nothing else.

The three best songs are stacked together towards the end of the record, each of them tinged with a darkness and violence more disturbing than anything since *The Black Album*. 'Shy' is Prince's psychosexual response to gangsta rap, featuring him meeting a woman who tells him about an initiation murder she's committed, while the narrator wonders if the story is true. 'Billy Jack Bitch' is Prince firing back after criticism from journalists, a pun in the lyrics suggesting the song's target is C.J., the gossip columnist from Minneapolis's *Star Tribune*, who would frequently mock Prince in her column and who gave him the insulting nickname 'Symbolina' (Prince denied the song was about her; she claimed Mayte confirmed it). But the album's most successful track is 'Eye Hate U', which was spun out with six versions on yet another maxi-disc, entitled 'The Hate Experience'. Beginning as a put-down of a woman who betrayed her lover, it continues with a comical courtroom scene reminiscent of 'Witness 4 the Prosecution' that ends with the singer tying up his lover and having sex with her in front of a jury. Funny, erotic and faintly ridiculous, the song's evident lack of sincerity only makes it more entertaining. A few more tracks like this and *The Gold Experience* might have truly represented a worthwhile new beginning.

A letter Mayte sent to the Prince fanzine *Controversy* (but believed to be written by Prince) suggested 'Gold' was Prince's latest attempt to write another 'Purple Rain'. Like 'Graffiti Bridge', the song is a failure, mainly because it relies on cliché and self-improvement mantras and is overblown instead of genuinely stirring. Of more lasting interest was 'Gold''s B-side, 'Rock N Roll Is Alive! (And It Lives in Minneapolis)', a witty answer song to Lenny Kravitz's sluggish lament 'Rock and Roll Is Dead'. This comedy comeback confirmed how good Prince's goof-offs can be, especially when he feels he has something to prove.

Steve Parke was brought in to help out on the album's design. Presented with an already-completed alternative concept, he tried to come up with a way of making it stand out on the stacks. 'I wanted to do gold-foil paper, and we had a company who could do it for us, but as you might imagine, it got real pricey. We did that one mock-up that he had on the David Letterman show. I even had a jewel case that had specks of gold inside the plastic. Then once Warner Brothers gotta hold of it, I'm sure they didn't want to put that extra bit of energy into it.'

*

Underappreciated at the time, receiving mixed reviews and even prompting audience members to request refunds, The Ultimate Live Experience was Prince's most audacious tour. It's not unusual for Prince to base a show primarily around music from a new album (indeed, he'd done so two years earlier with the Act I tour), but in this case not only had the record yet to be released, but it would be the first that Prince would release under his new ♀ identity. When you add in the fact that the Artist would open the show by announcing Prince's death, that the show's most compelling song, 'Days of Wild', wouldn't even appear on the new record, that during the show he promoted a different new album (the NPG's second record, *Exodus*) and that he was interspersing the new songs with covers of songs by his heroes Graham Central Station, James Brown and Sly and the Family Stone, it's easy to see why the audience (and critics) struggled to comprehend the change. But these shows really deserve to be documented with an official live release.

In this instance, however, a live album would suffice. The power of the music was not matched by the stage show, a *Spinal Tap*-style affair that featured an 'Endorphinmachine' stage so troublesome it led to the sacking of one member of staff[2] before it was abandoned in London. There was also a cumbersome conveyor-belt system, stagecraft which included Tommy Barbarella and Mayte being flown over the heads of the audience, and choreography that largely consisted of Mayte clomping around the stage in bikini and boots. Surrounded by this nonsense, Prince focused on his guitar and singing, giving his most powerful performance in years.

His dedication is all the more impressive given the technical and logistical problems they were facing. Poole remembers: 'He'd shipped over this huge big set that he'd had built, and he was at war with the band. He decided that he didn't want somebody in the audience mixing the sound. He didn't want a sound guy sitting in the middle of the audience mixing the sound where he couldn't communicate with him. So he had that sort of egg thing and the sound person was put in that egg thing. And suddenly I found myself as the only person who would speak to him.

'There was a revolt, and I had to say, "This can't work." What you want is to get the best possible sound, and to have your sound guy on the stage behind the speakers isn't going to achieve that. "Sorry, but the band don't want this. The sound is terrible out the front. It sounds awful." In the end he gave in.

'He was feeling very under siege on that tour because the accountants had made him strip down the whole set and he was entering crisis proportions with money. He borrowed a lot of money off Warner Music publishing, and of course his record sales were slipping, especially in America, and it was what happened to Michael Jackson a few years later. He's got this lavish lifestyle, and money was no object. "Are you sure you want me to rent a shop and fill it with stuff? Are you sure you want me to have a studio on standby twenty-four hours a day in case you fancy recording?" You'd have limos on standby, decoy limos . . . Vast amounts of money were being spent on these tours. And this accountant was the first guy who'd actually turned round and said, "Sorry, you haven't got the money to do this. It can't work." I was told by Gilbert Davidson that he'd made no money from the previous two tours; if anything, he'd lost money. But in a strange kind of way it wasn't about money with him. Money was a sign of success and enabled him to do what he wanted to do, but I don't know if money for money's sake was his motivation. But on that tour he went into this Chitlin Circuit mentality. He wanted to do after-shows every night and would say, "I won't go on for less than $10,000." I said, "Fine." I arranged a VIP area and I said, "Here's your VIP area, your personal waiter," worked out $10,000, bundled it into a Sainsbury's carrier bag, took it upstairs to where he was sitting with his feet on the table. I dumped it on the table and said, "There you go, $10,000. Right, what time do you want to go on?"'

Prince would conclude his deal with Warner Brothers (compilations aside) with two albums he dismissed on the sleeve notes as recorded '4 private use only', seemingly wanting to make the purchasers feel guilty for buying them. Warner Brothers held up the release of the second of these albums, *The Vault . . . Old Friends 4 Sale*, for over three years, finally putting it out between *Crystal Ball/The Truth* and *Rave Un2 the Joy Fantastic*.[3] Although Prince initially dismissed the first, *Chaos and Disorder*, as an album created in anger, he seems to have come to terms with it over the years, occasionally introducing songs from the record into his after-shows. And, of course, while it's no doubt true that he was eager to be shot of the label and that this was the most rapid way of doing it, at the same time the ambition to record a quick rock album had been there as far back as The Rebels. As he told Elysa Gardner of the *LA Times*: 'Someone told me that Van Halen did their first record in a week. That's what we were going for – spontaneity, seeing how fast and hard we could thrash it out.'

Only, as usual, this isn't the full story. It would have been perfectly possible for Prince to go into the studio with the NPG and thrash out a quick rock record, but as always, when he started thinking of a concept, old orphaned songs came to him. And while much of the record did come together in March and April while recording at South Beach Studios in Miami, he did also include older songs (such as the title track). It's obvious he wanted out of his contract, and he didn't appear bothered about the commercial success of the record, but this isn't a substandard collection. It's more a punk-rock equivalent to Marvin Gaye's

Here, My Dear, offered to a record company instead of a single woman. For the fan who appreciates ♀/Prince's rock songs, it's among his most exhilarating records, and for a pseudo-punk record, the arrangements are surprisingly complex, with an enormous amount of audio FX.

'Chaos and Disorder' and 'I Like It There' are defiant in their refusal to say anything. Prince takes on the guise of a 'no-name reporter' who doesn't want to say anything because Shakespeare has always got there first. For such a prolific lyricist, these songs are striking – Prince as ♀ boasting about how to write compelling songs without a single revelation. 'Dinner with Delores' is a pretty song with nasty lyrics, the reference to a woman stuck in 1984 suggesting a response to any wannabe Darling Nikkis who had yet to get the message. 'The Same December' is more cryptic pseudo-theology, but 'Right the Wrong' is an intriguing use of a Jagger-esque faux-country register to criticise the mistreatment of Native Americans.

The full version of 'Zannalee' reveals it to be a spectacularly silly song: policemen go out to investigate a disturbance, only to find Prince being double-teamed by two women (this is toned down in the accompanying promo). 'I Rock, Therefore I Am' shows Prince exploring rock-ragga, while boasting about his musical skill, alongside Minneapolis rappers Scrap D and Steppa Ranks, who encourage female listeners to reveal their breasts. 'Into the Light' is more Eadie-inspired spiritualism, and almost indistinguishable from 'I Will'. After this moment of brightness, the album ends in bitterness, with the techno-influenced and self-explanatory 'Dig U Better Dead' and the extraordinarily savage 'Had U', less a song than words you might find written on the mirror in lipstick at a crime scene.

The artwork is particularly primitive. Steve Parke says this was deliberate. 'It was trying to be, like, an angry look. It was thrown together very quickly. I shot a bunch of Polaroids around Paisley and just set up little scenes of things burning and stuff. I had a lot of worries about printing, because that was the point where colour calibration was not there yet. I remember asking the people at Warner Brothers, "Can you get back to me if there are colour issues?" I never heard anything from them, and then when I saw it come out there were some issues. My impression was at the time, the contentious nature with Warner Brothers . . . it wasn't about spending a whole lot of time on it, just about needing to get it done.'

♀ PART 3: 'ALL I GOTTA DO IS SELL A MILLION AND I CAN QUIT . . .'

Emancipation is an abandoned (white) mansion. At the time of release, Prince defined it as a happy album, in contrast to *The Black Album* or *Chaos and Disorder*, but there's something sad about these thirty-six almost entirely forgotten songs, many never played live, with those that did make it into a set unlikely to be exhumed again.[1] Nevertheless, it is also Prince as ♀'s finest achievement: his *Purple Rain*, his *Sign o' the Times*, championed by several critics at the time (it got his warmest reviews in years) and still highly regarded by those who have written full-length books about Prince,[2] if largely ignored by the listening public, regularly showing up in the discount bins at the world's last few remaining CD stores.

The three-CD set was largely a collaboration with Kirk Johnson, who had joined Prince as one of the Game Boyz dancers on the Nude tour before graduating to percussion and dancing, and who would eventually replace Michael Bland as the drummer in Prince's band (he was also Prince's best man when he married Mayte). Johnson is one of the many Prince associates his fans love to hate, blaming him for the 'plastic' production on this album and the later *New Power Soul* (he's also responsible for 'computer programming' on the final album Prince recorded as ♀, *Rave Un2 the Joy Fantastic*[3]), but this is unfair.

Johnson won favour with Prince thanks to his remixes of Prince's B-sides – one of which, a reinvention of the 'The

Continental' entitled 'Tell Me How U Wanna B Done', ended up on *Crystal Ball* – and now runs a gym in Minneapolis and plays with other Prince-associated artists, such as Candy Dulfer, offering advice on his website about the best food for a health-conscious person to eat on the road. I tried to interview him, but he didn't respond to my approaches, so the majority of this chapter relies on the testimony of the third person in the room during the second half of the production of this record – engineer H. M. Buff. I like Buff, an amusingly forthright German engineer who was initially very defensive, having read criticism of his work from fans over the years that has left him unable to truly relish his achievements. But during our conversations, as he realised I was a genuine fan of some of the albums he recorded for Prince, he became more expansive. Buff kept detailed notes of his time working with Prince which, coupled with his clear recall of sessions, helped fully explicate many of the mysteries of the next few years in Prince's recording history.

Before deciding to work with Johnson on *Emancipation*, Prince considered bringing in a producer from outside his immediate circle, largely, it seems, out of a desire to connect more fully with an R&B audience. During a show at Paisley Park in September 1995, he invited the Georgia-based producer and songwriter behind R&B girl group TLC, Dallas Austin – who had already worked for Prince, producing George Clinton's contribution to *1-800-NEW-FUNK*, 'Hollywood' – up to the stage and announced him as the producer of the forthcoming album, which at that point was planned to be even longer, a fifty-two-song set that would retail for $80, allowing Prince to estimate that if he could sell a million copies, he'd able to retire. Without wishing to dis Johnson, it's a shame this didn't happen, as it might have completely transformed the record – although it should be noted that 'Secret', the Austin-produced Madonna song that initially caught Prince's ear, now sounds far more dated than *Emancipation* – and one of the biggest missed opportunities of Prince/♀'s career to date is his reluctance to work with a well-known producer. Personally, I'd love to hear what Rick Rubin or Jim O'Rourke or even Steve Albini might get out of him.

Many 1960s artists struggled in the 1980s. It was the decade of Prince, Michael Jackson and Madonna, and they didn't know how to cope, ditching their styles and rushing into studios with equipment and producers that didn't suit their sound. Now, in the mid-1990s, Prince was the one who sounded out of synch. What must have been even more galling was that the popular sounds were so close to what Prince had once done. He was facing the same problem the hippies had in the plastic decade, when they abandoned their old style and tried to sound like the music that was charting. Prince *could* do the new R&B style, that mix of overly saccharine lover-man ballads and party tracks, and *Emancipation* even shares some of the eccentricities of these records – one track even credits sleeve artist Steve Parke's jeep as an instrument – but somehow this new style seemed to cheapen Prince's music.

The album *Emancipation* is closest to in style and spirit is not any other Prince or ♀ record, but R. Kelly's *R.*, recorded over the same period but released a year later. *R.* was far more successful commercially than *Emancipation*, selling eight million copies in America alone, and is almost as ambitious stylistically (and only fifty minutes shorter), but R. Kelly is a less interesting (though more amusing) lyricist than Prince (as well as a less versatile musician). Hans-Martin Buff told me that at one stage Prince even brought in R. Kelly's engineer, Peter Mokran, to see what he could do with 'Sleep Around'. 'He mixed "Sleep Around" for three days,' Buff told me, 'but Prince didn't like it.'

Buff became the main engineer on *Emancipation* through working his way up the ranks. 'Throughout the 1990s Paisley was a commercial studio where you could just book time and record, like you could at Abbey Road, for example,' he told me. 'It was fully staffed, and there was a group of engineers who were called internally "the Prince pool". They worked just for him directly because he's such an intense guy and likes to work many hours.

'It was usually three people, but then a situation arose where Prince only wanted one engineer and the whole studio to himself, so he closed Paisley as a commercial facility and let everybody go, with the exception of his direct engineer at the time, a man named Steve Durkee. I had a pager, which was the method of being summoned in those days, and it didn't go off for four months, until July of 1996, and then I dropped my current projects and came in.'

The situation Buff discovered when coming to work on the album was not a harmonious one. 'Steve Durkee had left not on friendly terms, which is not unusual in the Paisley world, and the whole place was a shambles. I arrived there at eight in the morning and found out that the guy I was supposed to assist didn't know about it and didn't have time that day, and so I put the studio together, and Prince came in and stood behind me and strummed his guitar and asked if I had time for him that week.'

This was the beginning of a working relationship that would last for the next four years.

It's tempting to see the process of stripping things back as Prince closing down everything to focus on this major project, but Buff suggests this is not how his creative process works. 'Unlike other musicians, Prince continuously works on whatever he works on and doesn't just listen to the one song he's working on but tries to always assemblage as a sequence right away. He always has segues of the current project, and usually at the end of the project he sees the direction and starts writing songs for the project rather than assembling the songs he was making into a project.' Buff also says that while Johnson was Prince's closest friend – 'at least until Larry Graham showed up' – the process of collaboration between the two 'would be on Prince's terms'. Johnson 'would do the rhythmic basis for every one of those songs. He would supervise a lot of the recordings.'

Prince, however, is on record claiming the project began with 'Right Back Here in My Arms'. This track was on the first projected assembly of *Emancipation*, along with the title song, two songs that eventually opened the third disc, a track later given to Chaka Khan ('Journey 2 the Center of Your Heart') and four as yet unreleased tracks.[4] The song doesn't represent any particular progression in Prince's work, though most of the songs on the set are in the same style: ill-fitting samples, fluctuations in Prince's voice, different vocal styles married – like much of the record – to a repetitive and straightforward lyric. And the other substantial song from this assembly, 'Emancipation', also relies strongly on Prince's past ideas rather than moving anywhere new – 'purple rain', the relationship between Adam and Eve (yet again!), chains, a character called Johnny, money problems, and the desire for freedom. Fortunately, when Prince expanded the CD from one disc to three, his ambition expanded, albeit gradually.

After all the years of him avoiding the press, to support this record Prince as ♀ talked to anyone who would listen, and there's more first-hand information about the recording of this album than any other. He told *Musician* that Johnson's production skills stemmed from him being a drum programmer. 'He's good at using the computer to put a rhythm track together. I don't like setting that kind of stuff up, because a lot of times the song will leave me while I'm doing it. But when Kirk and I are doing it together, we can keep each other excited.'

The joylessness of this comment reflects the worst aspects of this record: Prince sounds as if he's Brian Keenan describing how he passed time with John McCarthy while incarcerated in a Lebanese dungeon. Prince doesn't mean it this way; he goes on to disparage *1999* in comparison to *Emancipation*, arguing that the earlier record is less varied because he was doing all the programming himself. But the more he talks, the more he gives himself away: later in the same interview, he talks about constructing 'In This Bed I Scream' by putting a guitar on the ground and letting it feed back, which made him wonder whether instruments have a soul of their own and if they might start writing the songs without his input, a *Fantasia* fantasy revealing just how exhausted this sorcerer's apprentice was at the time. It's also revealing that he dedicated a song created in such a simple way to his former band-mates Wendy and Lisa (as well as his ex-lover Susannah Melvoin), who could do so much with even the simplest idea. When Wendy listened to *Emancipation* and heard this song, 'I was sad,' she says. Lisa, too, was troubled by it. 'It was surprising. He didn't make an effort to have a relationship. Whenever he's asked us to do something, we've done it. I understand how emotions come when you're writing a song. It's not "ripped from the headlines". I miss you sometimes too.'

When asked about how he decided whether a song was good enough to include on a record, Prince told *Musician* that he so hated criticising music that he couldn't even appraise his own. Pushed on this question, he responded with a non sequitur about how he and Mayte were 'into this thing now of wondering whether we're supposed to get out of bed when we get up', before concluding, 'each song writes itself. It's already perfect.' This might lead a reader to believe that *Emancipation* might be half-baked, or unfinished and scrappy. It's not, although it does feature the return of *Chaos and Disorder*'s Scrap D (on 'Mr. Happy' and 'Da, Da, Da'). Prince told the reporter that the pressure (both from himself and the record company) to produce hits cramped his writing process, and that on this album he wasn't trying to write great singles any more (indeed, the first single he'd release from *Emancipation* would be a cover), but was instead concentrating on expressing the truth, whether or not this was appropriate for the pop market.

Buff shed further light on the composition process. 'We would start something, then get Kirk in, and either Kirk would offer some of the beats he had created, or Prince would say, "I want something in a particular tempo." And it wouldn't be programmed like you usually would, where you'd programme the verse and then the chorus, it would be the same eight or ten sounds all the way through, and we'd record that to tape for about eight minutes, and then Prince would usually record some melodic instrument on top, usually a guitar or a keyboard, and pretty much straight away write a song around it, or if he'd already written it, do it just with vocals and embellish it with other arrangement bits and FX, and then he would take the ten rhythmic sounds that he did in the beginning and just erase them.'

When Buff started work on the album, he was presented with a song sequence that he put into ('dismal') sequencing software, as Prince started updating tracks he didn't like, taking songs out and working on the album's structure. Songs that Buff remembers being completed before his arrival included two of the record's four cover songs – The Stylistics' 'Betcha By Golly Wow!'[5] and Joan Osborne's 'One of Us' – as well as the Kate Bush collaboration, 'My Computer', and the second CD's 'Friend, Lover, Sister, Mother/Wife'. Even late in the recording, Prince was spontaneously producing an enormous amount of material. 'The first day

I worked for him we started five new songs,' Buff told me. These five were 'Emale', 'Sleep Around', 'Dreamin' about U',[6] 'The Love We Make' and a 'gospel-like ballad' that remains unreleased.

So what sort of music did Prince bring to the studio that first day? A revenge ballad that seems aimed at a writer, a song warning a man to satisfy his lover if he doesn't want her to stray, a fairly rote ballad enlivened by Prince singing again about the notion of having an imagined twin inside him, and the day's most substantial known achievement (assuming he didn't woodshed the session's best song), 'The Love We Make', one of very few *Emancipation* tracks that Prince has returned to subsequently in live performance. Towards the end of a long record, it's easy to miss, but it's one of the set's strongest moments. While it does rely on the occasional cliché and is essentially yet another self-empowerment song, it's heartfelt in a way much of the album isn't. Seemingly about a forthcoming Rapture, it echoes 'The Cross', a song Prince would soon rework – but with a more apocalyptic feel.

The other *Emancipation* songs Buff has strong memories of are 'Jam of the Year', which had been started but not finished when he arrived, 'We Gets Up', 'Mr. Happy', 'Sex in the Summer', 'Curious Child' and 'Joint 2 Joint', his favourite song, and the last track recorded for the album (Buff makes a guest vocal appearance on it, playing the role of Prince's driver). 'Jam of the Year' is the album in miniature: meandering low-key fun, in no hurry to go anywhere. This is one of several albums (*1999*, *Purple Rain*, *3121*) that starts with an invitation to dance, but this time it's not apocalyptic or cathartic or anything much really. Lyrically, it's utterly inconsequential: Prince is in a club, with a Puerto Rican woman (Mayte's parents are of Puerto Rican descent), when his favourite song comes on. Prince even acknowledges the limited

resources with which *Emancipation* was created, saying all he
needs is a drummer (or, it seems, a drum programmer) and a
funky bass line. 'We Gets Up' is one of countless songs praising
the musical skills of the NPG, an odd inclusion when the NPG
were in a state of flux and aren't that prevalent on the album. In
fact, the solitary nature of how Prince was working during this
period soon became apparent to Buff. 'Prince does a lot himself,
especially vocals. Of all the many, many times – I think it was
about two hundred songs I was involved in – he was present for
two lead vocals. Usually he has the microphone over the con-
sole and does it himself. When he's done recording it, and when
he wants to mix it or needs assistance, he calls people over the
intercom.'

Buff is dismissive of 'Mr. Happy', one of several rap-influenced
songs on the set, which features a sample from Ice Cube's 'What
Can I Do', the 1993 song that features a line about Cube moving
in next door to Prince,[7] considering it 'a waste of time', but hip
hop is an important part of this record. There are three sam-
pled appearances by the female rapper Poet 99, who first came
to attention on Canadian rappers Dream Warriors' 1994 record
Subliminal Stimulation (the sample on 'Face Down' is recycled
from this album), which was recorded around the same time that
Prince was working with her.[8]

'Sex in the Summer' is another of Prince's musical palimpsests,
an extremely mixed-up song built over an unreleased track called
'Conception' about exactly that which features the ultrasound
heartbeat of 'the 1st conceived 2 Prince', a process he would
describe in detail to Oprah Winfrey. How much of the original
song is left in this track is unclear, but the finished track see-saws
uneasily between the sacred and the profane. Particularly con-
fusing is Prince's choice of listening: Mahalia Jackson's famous
hymn, 'In the Upper Room'.[9] The reference is so incongruous

that it increases the sense that this album is just a series of present-tense snapshots, written without reflection.

Similarly, 'Curious Child' is little more than a melodramatic fragment, and, it seems, another Lolita song (unless Prince is the one who's underage). 'Joint 2 Joint' is more substantial. Buff remembers being more impressed by the way Prince recorded this song than any other, amazed by the way he built it up in the studio. This track is Prince goofing off, pulling everything down from the shelves and shoving it into the track, constructing a narrative beyond the lyrics in the way he did on 'Play in the Sunshine' or 'Crystal Ball', working in tap-dancing, distorted vocals and lines sung while munching cereal, all of which Buff remembers Prince doing live in the studio.

Buff told me that Prince's working processes during this time were so open-ended that when *Emancipation* was finally completed, Kirk Johnson – who'd started to fear it might never be finished – didn't even realise it was done. But Buff had noticed the songs written towards the end of the process – such as 'Joint 2 Joint' and 'The Plan' – seemed custom-fit to round out the album. Buff eventually told Johnson he knew they were done because he and Prince had spent a huge all-night session ensuring each disc lasted exactly sixty minutes. 'We edited it if it was over, we put some stuff in – like in "Saviour", we had guitar distortion and the sound of doors opening. We made segues and made little things here and there. It was a big deal.'

This might seem a fairly pointless pursuit, but the press liked it, a Spanish journalist suggesting to Prince that he was inspired by the pyramids of Egypt when he constructed *Emancipation* because it has three discs of the same duration. (Prince didn't disagree, merely observing that building the pyramids took a tremendous collective mental effort.[10]) *Emancipation* is also unusual in the extreme amount of audio punctuation it includes. Ticking clocks, thunderstorms, doors slamming – almost every track is tricked out with tiny details. 'We had a huge sound library called Sound Ideas,'[11] Buff told me. 'And I would get called in, and Prince would say, "I need a clock." And there was a huge index and we'd come up with some clocks.'

The album also features the first studio appearance of bassist Rhonda Smith, who would play an important role in the NPG over the next eight years, helping shape the group's heavier sound, and who would collaborate with Prince on songs for 1998's well-respected *The Truth*.[12] One song she appears on, 'Get Yo Groove On', also features a shout-out to D'Angelo,[13] the R&B singer who'd inherit Prince's road manager, Alan Leeds, although the line about playing D'Angelo's new CD has acquired a new irony now that it's taken him nearly twelve years to record the follow-up to *Voodoo*.[14] Prince's early work largely inhabited a closed universe, and although there were references to other musicians, they tended to be Prince side projects or protégés (Joni Mitchell or classical and jazz musicians aside), but from now on he would often record songs that would name-check musicians he admired.[15] (Live, he'd add in a reference to Boyz II Men.)

In concert, Prince would combine 'Get Yo Groove On' with Madhouse's 'Six' (played on his goldaxxe[16]), revealing the jazz underpinnings of this song. The importance of jazz as a renewed source of inspiration is also evident from 'Courtin' Time', written after Eric Leeds played Prince Paul Gonsalves's long sax solo from 'Diminuendo and Crescendo in Blue' – one of the most famous jazz recordings of all time. The 7 July 1956 performance at the Newport Jazz Festival is admired as a feat of endurance (Gonsalves playing consistently for twenty-seven choruses), but also as a moment of musical innovation, as Duke Ellington successfully introduced a blues beat to jazz. Prince was particularly impressed by the story behind the performance: as Leeds told him, 'the reason why this solo went as long as it did was that this lady jumped up on this table and started dancing to the rhythm, so nobody wanted to quit'. Prince claims that he initially played a twenty-minute version of 'Courtin' Time', with Leeds 'wailin' that whole time'. I've already confessed my weakness for Prince's longer tracks, and it seems a shame that he didn't put this version onto *Emancipation*, as it might have helped listeners realise the ambition of the set. I haven't heard this longer version (and don't know if it's in circulation), but to get a sense of how it might sound, listen to the live rendition played at a 1998 *New Power Soul* Festival Tour soundcheck officially released on the twelfth of the NPG Music Club downloads. This version isn't particularly long (the entire track is less than five minutes), but it's clear Prince is thinking of Gonsalves as he plays, making boasts about his guest horn player's physical ability.

Emancipation is a very busy record. 'White Mansion' is a potentially powerful, seemingly autobiographical song – perhaps even about that first trip Prince made to New York when he was looking for a record deal – with Prince singing about rags-to-riches success while being snubbed by a woman in the street,[17] a track that is pulled off course by an overly complicated arrangement, a confusing sample and the crass inclusion of brand names[18] at the end. The lyrics are crisp and witty, but the infuriating audio punctuation is there again (after Prince sings of needing a new guitar, you get a twang; when he talks of performing a song in a bar, there's the sound of an audience; when he talks about playing a game, it's underscored with the sound of a slot machine spitting out coins; when someone tells Prince to return to Minneapolis, you hear the sound of a plane taking off. Aarrggh!).

There's so much automatic writing on the album it's tempting to hear the whole thing as a diary. Is 'Damned If Eye Do' really about a conflict between Prince and Mayte, and the argument they have before deciding that they either have to get married or break up? Is it truth or dirty realist fiction when Prince describes Mayte drinking vermouth when he doesn't show up and getting cross when he doesn't give her enough time to get ready? (If true, it sounds like the son of the parents in 'When Doves Cry' struggling with his own personal life). The presence of Mayte's mother, Janelle, on the track, talking in Spanish with another man, increases the mystery, as does the strange line repeated in the lyric booklet ('I won't do it like Kevin'). Who's Kevin? Um, believe it or not, Kevin Costner. The line refers to Costner's character drinking his own urine in *Waterworld*: Prince is promising here that he won't serve his girlfriend piss, surely one of the oddest jokes he's made on record.

The Bonnie Raitt cover on *Emancipation* is a dig at Warner Brothers. The American country and blues singer-songwriter had her own vexed relationship with the label,[19] having an album shelved for three years when the label decided to drop her. Raitt nearly signed to Paisley Park,[20] although in his memoir former Warner exec Danny Goldberg notes of the sessions: 'Prince had simply plugged Bonnie into lyrics that easily could have been written for pop/R&B sex bombs like Vanity or Sheila E.'[21] It's clear in choosing 'I Can't Make You Love Me' (retitled, in the usual manner, 'Eye Can't Make U Love Me'), a hit song from one of Raitt's successful post-Warners albums, he was making a connection between her accomplishment after leaving the label and his own. The song has been covered many times, by everyone from George Michael to Bon Iver, and it's now become an *American Idol* standard. It's also worth remembering that it was Raitt's brother who had first rented Prince rehearsal space.

*

For all the tabloid or trash-biography criticism of Prince's attitude towards women, there remains something incredibly generous about the way he placed Mayte centre stage (literally: she would dance while he played) during this period of his creative life. Three years earlier, David Bowie had been inspired by his marriage to the model Iman Abdulmajid to compose his own wedding album (*Black Tie, White Noise*), but that record has nowhere near as much sincerity and passion as the most romantic tracks on *Emancipation*. It was during the *Emancipation* sessions that Prince married Mayte, and the final song from the second disc, 'Friend, Lover, Sister, Mother/Wife', was played during the wedding ceremony.[22] 'Let's Have a Baby' is hard to listen to now – on 16 October 1996, Mayte would give birth to a child with Pfeiffer syndrome who would die a week later – but it's a beautiful song, an adult response to all those 'I'm gonna get ya pregnant' R&B tracks.

There are songs on the album that don't seem connected to Prince and Mayte's relationship, like 'Somebody's Somebody', but which are worked into the narrative through the videos that accompanied the release.[23] Prince would release two alternative versions of this song, the 'Livestudio Mix' and an 'Ultrafantasy Edit'. Both improve on the original.

Perhaps inevitably given that the record is so long and Prince has never been concerned about recycling ideas or self-parody, some tracks feel like reworkings of his past successes. 'One Kiss at a Time', for example, is 'Slow Love' revisited for the R&B 1990s (which doesn't make it any less great). Other tracks fit together through shared lyrics and ideas, 'Soul Sanctuary' (another song that plays with by-now-surely-bankrupt Garden of Eden imagery) slotting together with 'The Love We Make'. The absence of Dr Clare Fischer's arrangements from the album – aside from on 'The Plan', a brief and uncredited extract from *Kamasutra* – is surprising, as Prince had always previously utilised his work on his most ambitious records. With the release of the *Crystal Ball* out-takes collection, Prince revealed that there had indeed originally been a track with Fischer orchestration on it, 'Goodbye' (included in this later box set), which was replaced with the similarly epic 'The Holy River'. Maybe Prince realised the perversity of saying farewell midway through a thirty-six-track record, and it's now the final track on *Crystal Ball*.

Aside from the covers ('La, La, La Means Eye Love U' and 'One of Us'), the third disc is mainly a compilation of more dance-floor-orientated material. The two songs from the original assembly – 'Slave' and 'New World' – are techno-influenced and resemble the worst of *Come*, providing further proof that Prince and rave really don't mix. Although he would soon use Buff exclusively, to begin with he brought in what Buff describes as 'trusted people he would use when he didn't want to think too much [about a song]', Cesar Sogbe and Joe Galdo, for two tracks on the final disc of the set, the ravey 'The Human Body' and the song that Prince also gave Peter Mokran, 'Sleep Around'. There's lots of this sort of stuff on the third CD, which, while it has its charms ('Style' is funny and sweet – it's nice to hear Prince take Jackie O as a style icon), is repetitive. The stand-out track on this disc, 'Face Down', would have something of an afterlife. Prince played it on *The Chris Rock Show*, the best of his *Emancipation* promo appearances: brought out in a brown raincoat and white fedora, he was placed face down on the studio floor, before springing up, plucking playing cards from his pocket, bashing at a piano, swearing at the audience and ending up back, with the rest of his band, prone on the floor.

A week before the album's release, Prince played an *Emancipation* gig at Paisley Park. Broadcast on the major American music TV channels, and around the world, the footage is worth revisiting. Prince would reuse the 'free at last' sample from Martin Luther King's 'I Have a Dream' speech on several occasions, but anyone troubled by his ongoing connection of a record contract with slavery would be most offended by its use here. If you compare the 'Freedom' concert with any of Prince's past transformations, it's underwhelming: 'Jam of the Year' and 'Get Yo Groove On' are not songs to hang your reputation on, and the many thousands who hated Joan Osborne's 'One of Us' were hardly going to be won over by Prince's rendition. But the two tours ('Love 4 One Another Charities' and 'Jam of the Year') that Prince embarked on while promoting this album, cherished only by hard-core fans, are less celebrated than they should be. The official releases from the tour are limited to a cassette release – 'NYC Live'[24] – but this is an era that deserves to be part of the official story. After introducing Prince songs to the previously all-⚥ set during the 1996 Japanese world tour, the 1997 Love 4 One Another Charities tour saw Prince bringing back hits like 'Purple Rain', 'The Cross' and 'Do Me, Baby', but integrating them into an ambitious set that presented a coherent new bass-driven sound, backed by an almost entirely new NPG.

During this time, Prince was starting to perform with Larry Graham, the former Sly and the Family Stone member who would go on to become his closest confidant and play an important role in changing Prince's creative process, but on another night on this tour, at San Francisco's Shoreline Amphitheatre, he would duet with another hero, Carlos Santana – the man Prince credits, far more than Jimi Hendrix, as being the inspiration for his guitar-playing style – on a long version of 'Soul Sacrifice' in which he paid full tribute to his idol, while matching him lick for lick. Across the two tours, Prince played over a hundred main shows, as well as more after-shows than he had ever played before. They would vary considerably in length (especially on the Jam tour), and this was one of those rare tours where the main shows are (for the most part) better than the after-shows, which tended to be short and often dominated by guests such as the rapper Doug E. Fresh, suggesting that Prince was now entirely comfortable with making hip hop part of his sound, as long as he had someone onstage to do it for him.

As with the Nude tour, Prince once more performed in front of a deliberately stripped-down stage set. After over half a decade of complicated, confusing, overly constructed live shows, it seemed stripping it back to the music once again suited Prince. This, it seemed, was his true emancipation.

WASTED KISSES . . .

Prince had begun the hype for *Crystal Ball* with the release of *Emancipation*, listing it among a set of forthcoming albums, including records from the NPG and Mayte. He seemed to have gone back and forth between intending this to be a limited-effort response to bootlegging and making it more of a statement, eventually loading the three-CD set with two extra discs, both of which contained material seemingly of greater significance to Prince than this selection from the Vault. H. M. Buff remembers of the process: 'That was nice and quick, two weeks. We really just took stuff out. One of the things I really like is to take the beef off, stuff that makes it long. There were two songs on that album that I edited until the cows came home – "Crystal Ball" itself and "Cloreen Bacon Skin". [The latter] was really long: there was another four minutes to it.' There were also, Buff told me, some songs considered for release that didn't make the cut, the most significant being 'Wonderful Ass'.

Designer Steve Parke remembers that the packaging of the record started out as something much more ambitious. 'Bootlegging was happening more and more online, and I was asking myself how could you do something that people would want. The original idea was to do an actual crystal ball . . . with the two halves separating and the CDs suspended in the middle. The reality became what we ended up with. It was this weird dichotomy because on the one hand we were making it look like a bootleg, and on the other we were doing this really cool production where this thing would sit on your shelf and look cool. And then they ended up doing a deal with *Best Buy* and we had to do a whole package for that, which shot the idea of it being underground and bootleggy. So the final version was the path of least resistance. It was less than I hoped for.'

The collection was also less than fans hoped for. While the set did feature some of Prince's best-loved out-takes – 'Crystal Ball', 'Dream Factory' and 'Movie Star' – and genuinely worthwhile songs from some of his most significant creative periods – 'Crucial' from the *Sign o' the Times* era, 'Sexual Suicide', 'Last Heart', 'Make Your Mama Happy', 'An Honest Man' and 'Good Love' from the fertile period that preceded it – the majority of the set was made up of less significant songs, including five remixes and five tracks that had already had some form of previous release. Of the four songs originally intended for *The Gold Experience* – 'Acknowledge Me', 'Ripopgodazippa', 'Interactive' and 'Days of Wild' – only the latter was as good as anything on the released album, and it was easy to understand why Prince had ditched the first three at the time. There were also two songs first played while promoting *Emancipation* – '2morrow', a sketchy song largely based around a sample from 'The Most Beautiful Girl in the World' which had already been released to radio, and the pretty but syrupy and inessential ballad 'She Gave Her Angels', which he'd performed on *Muppets Tonight* – plus another out-take from the record – 'Goodbye', worthwhile for Dr Clare Fischer's orchestration but in the same overly sweet register as the weakest tracks from *Emancipation*.

Worse still, of the five tracks most of us didn't know about – 'Hide the Bone', 'Da Bang', '18 & Over', 'Poom Poom' and 'Calhoun Square' – only the last was of any true lasting interest, the remaining four being a quartet of admittedly funky comedy songs largely consisting of Prince delivering euphemisms for genitalia and intercourse in a variety of funny voices that gave the worrying impression that what was left in the Vault was innuendo and silliness, recorded mainly as a way of letting off creative steam.

Of more lasting interest was *The Truth*, the bonus disc tucked into all versions of the set, which should be considered as a Prince album in its own right rather than an additional extra. Planned for release by EMI as a stand-alone album, the follow-up to *Emancipation*, it was shelved when the label folded. Prince subsequently considered releasing it as a limited-edition cassette, before including it with *Crystal Ball*. H. M. Buff has one of these cassettes, which, he says, Prince 'sent out to his buddies, and it was really cool to have it with that cover and stuff. It's a nice cover'.

Steve Parke, who designed this cover, was disappointed that this version of the record never saw the light of day. 'I would have liked to have seen that as a full CD with artwork and everything. I liked that because it was a different tone. And we actually did shoot a series of photos specific towards that. We even did a full layout where I was pretty happy with my typework on it. The cover got squeezed up for a CD single. The shot of Prince was pretty good even squeezed up, but I thought it looked great as a CD cover.'

Even if the record didn't get as wide a release as it might have, it was highly regarded by the few critics who heard it, with the *NME* describing it as 'a minor revelation' and suggesting it might represent the future for Prince's music. But it was a direction he chose not to pursue. Parke remembers: 'At the *The Truth* photo shoot he was playing all this great blues stuff [in the same vein], and I told him, "You need to put out an album like that." And he said, "When I'm old," because I think he thought you have to be old to play the blues.'

'The Truth' is one of the best openers on any Prince album, as startling and exciting as 'Sign o' the Times'. Prince's voice and guitar are clearer than on any other track, his bluesy keening given extra sparkle by cryptic sound FX (for once, a ticking clock adds rather than detracts from the arrangement). 'Don't Play Me' is even better, a highlight of Prince's output, in which – even if it is a bluff – he manages to make us feel he's singing from the heart for the first time – the truth indeed. Buff says both songs were recorded in one ten-minute session and seem to have prompted a change in Prince's creative direction, although he warns against thinking of the songs as a complete unit, noting that Prince had yet to think of *The Truth* as a cohesive album.

Which it isn't, really. 'Circle of Amour' is a very silly song. Yet another track that sexualises schooldays, it concerns four students who form a sex circle in high school. '3rd Eye' is also a repetition of a theme Prince has revisited obsessively – Adam and Eve in the Garden of Eden – combined with some woolly mysticism. 'Dionne' is a pleasing return of Prince in the role of rejected lover. Two of the songs are co-writes with NPG member Rhonda Smith: 'Man in a Uniform' is a depiction of a common female sexual fantasy (it's intriguing to note the change in Prince's lyrics around this era, when he becomes an observer or reteller of female sexual fantasy rather than the cause of it); and 'Animal Kingdom' is another celebration of the joys of veganism (I confess I preferred Prince when his perfect weekend required pizza and hot dogs). 'The Other Side of the Pillow' is another slight song that surprisingly made it onto Prince's live box set four years later, while 'Fascination' is most notorious for containing a bitchy aside which some fans have interpreted as a slap at Michael Jackson (who had a son known as Prince), although the date of the song's recording seems to disprove this, not to mention the fact that Jackson named his son after his grandfather. 'One of Your Tears' is perhaps Prince's all-time funniest song, written – the lyrics claim – in retaliation for being sent a used condom by a lover.

But 'Comeback' is the most important song on the record, dealing with Prince's interest in the afterlife and reincarnation, a subject that for obvious reasons still preoccupied him. Buff says the original version was even stronger. '"Comeback" had a little prelude – it was just a three-line a cappella singing that just touched me very much – that's not in there any more. That part he tried to develop into a song that sounded in an arrangement way, not a music way, like 'Man in a Uniform', little bits here and there, little vocal FX, and then he left it off.' The last song on the album is an acoustic version of a previously released song, 'Welcome 2 the Dawn'. After telling us for so many years how much he hoped we'd live to see The Dawn, it couldn't but come as a disappointment when we finally did.

The Truth was warmly received because it was released at a time when Prince's music was starting to seem samey and both the critics and the public were beginning to lose touch with his output. After the excess of *Emancipation*, *The Truth* seemed accessible (and no doubt would have done even better if released separately from *Crystal Ball*). As Parke says: 'When it came to the music, sometimes outside of Prince fans I don't know how many people were getting to hear what he was doing unless it was a single or a performance.'

Steve Parke also remembers hearing tracks intended for this album that never made the finished record. 'I heard a couple of things in *The Truth* vein that were really cool. I won't take credit for influencing him, but I did say one time that I didn't think his vocals ever get the credit that they're due. Later, he was working on *The Truth* and he said, "Come down, I want to play you something," and it was all vocals and it literally sent shivers down my spine. And I never heard that again. It never came out.'

Fans who ordered *Crystal Ball* direct from Prince received yet another bonus disc, containing the *Kamasutra* 'orchestral-ballet'. Brent Fischer remembers that Prince sent a note with this tape similar to the one they had received with 'Crystal Ball', emphasising just how important the project was to him. Transcribing the track presented an epic challenge. As Fischer remembers: 'In the early 1990s, we [got] one or another of the different movements of *Kamasutra*, I think one at a time. That was a difficult project because Prince had started experimenting around with his Synclavier, and one of the movements in particular he sent it to us right before I was going on tour with a band in Europe for about a month and it was very complicated music that I just recorded onto a forty-eight-track digital tape. I went into the studio and I transcribed track by track right there in the studio, but we couldn't finish up all forty-eight tracks, so I took those cassette tapes with me while I was on tour in Europe, didn't let any of the guys listen to it because of our confidentiality agreement with Prince, and I sat in the proverbial planes, trains, buses, everywhere I could, transcribing. I basically transcribed *Kamasutra* in ten different European countries.

'It took about three months to get everything done, and again we never heard anything until years later. And Prince didn't always send us CDs, but I think in that case he did because he was really proud of how it had turned out.' Prince generally wouldn't make any changes to the records after Fischer had sent the arrangements, but along with 'Crystal Ball', this was one case where he had completely changed everything and mixed and matched the orchestral parts.

The importance of *Kamasutra* seems largely down to the narrative charge it was supposed to carry – why Prince chose his new name, and how he and Mayte came together. But as is often the case with orchestral pieces by pop musicians, the work lacks the impact of his more commercial music, and in places, sounds almost muzak-y. That said, it is easy to see why Prince regarded it as a personal artistic breakthrough, as it sees him bringing together jazz, classical music and sound FXs in one of his most ambitious works. The most intriguing section of the suite is the track 'Cutz', in which the sound of scissors snipping contrasts menacingly with the orchestra. What's being severed is unclear, but it's the one track that would frighten you if you heard it in a lift.

Prince's next two releases, less than a month apart, would both be nominally NPG releases, but they are an essential part of his oeuvre. Although officially *New Power Soul* is an NPG album, during the process of composition it seems largely to have been thought of as a Prince record. Both *Goldnigga* and *Exodus* felt like New Power Generation albums, easily distinguishable from Prince's main body of work (and are discussed in Chapter 34), but *New Power Soul* has Prince front and centre, both in presentation – he's there on the front of the CD sleeve – and in the music.

The record features a song – 'The One' – that has showed up in the set list over a hundred times since he recorded it (often in a medley with 'The Question of U') and a hidden track –'Wasted Kisses', a noir playlet set in a hospital – that I consider to be the best Prince song of the 1990s. Buff says that 'The One' was actually the first song completed after finishing *Emancipation*, remaining in the Vault until this time, but that 'Wasted Kisses' was essentially a throwaway not considered significant by Prince (although the promo people couldn't understand why it wasn't the lead single). Buff also said that Prince was amused by the hidden track trick but didn't want to go as far as Buff's suggestion to identify every individual component of the song separately.

If the album is not quite as experimental as 'The War', the twenty-six-minute apocalyptic jam Prince and the NPG would release a month later, it is nonetheless well worth rediscovering. Buff has reservations: in spite of working on it, he believes it's the worst record Prince ever made. 'On *New Power Soul* they're all rough mixes,' he told me, 'and I think you can really hear that. "When U Love Somebody" could have been so much more. Mike Nelson [of The Hornheadz] offered to pay to have it mixed again, he wouldn't have any of it, and I know why, because he screwed up something for once. But you couldn't remix it. It's one of those mixes that just sounded like a rough mix.' While this is no doubt true, some of Prince's best work has vexed audiophiles, and though the record is slightly too reliant on get-on-the-dance-floor throwaways ('New Power Soul', 'Shoo-Bed-Ooh', 'Push It Up!' 'Freaks on This Side' and 'Funky Music'), the remainder of the album – 'Mad Sex', 'Until U're in My Arms Again', 'When U Love Somebody', 'Come On', 'The One' and 'Wasted Kisses' – has a dark energy and intent that makes these tracks stronger than most of *Emancipation*, and even the club songs are growers. It's also his most British record, with repeated references to London. Prince even shot a video for 'Come On' that featured him disguised as an old man – looking rather like Frank Zappa – making rude gestures at passers-by, busking, running around and eventually getting mugged in what looks like Regent's Park.

Buff has fond memories of some of the other songs recorded in this era that either came out later or remain unreleased. 'There was a period around *New Power Soul* that I thought was really good. Some of it ended up on *Rave*, like "So Far, So Pleased", "Baby Knows". It was all in that vein. It was Linn-y, it had guitars on it, and I thought it was really well done. And it had Marva King on it. And there were a couple that came out later, like "Sadomasochistic Groove", "Welcome 2 the Slaughterhouse", "Madrid 2 Chicago", "Beautiful Strange" I thought was a great song, "Silicon", "Y Should Eye Do That When Eye Can Do This?" is a really funky song. "Pretty Man" was great. Michael Bland played on "Y Should I Do That . . ." and "Baby Knows".' Other songs from this period that Buff recalls recording (and liking) include 'Golden Parachute', 'When I Lay My Hands on U' and 'If I Was the Man in Ur Life' (which Prince would leave in the Vault until *Musicology*). '"Vavoom",' he says, 'was a little later, afterwards.'

Steve Parke also has fond memories of this period. '*New Power Soul* . . . he was playing a bunch of stuff around the studio at that time . . . and he had some stuff that showed up on the online compilations [*The Slaughterhouse* and *The Chocolate Invasion*] with crunchy vocals . . . almost as if he was rapping through a megaphone . . . super-funky . . . and those songs never got the push they deserved.'

Buff says: 'At some point "Madrid 2 Chicago" and "Breathe" were one suite. There was something else I forget and "Man o' War". And that would be the start of the album for a while, and then we'd take some from the previous batch into it and then he would reconsider and make new sequences.' Steve Parke remembers: 'I did a type treatment on "Madrid 2 Chicago" which included using dashed lines almost like a map, and a big Madrid and Chicago with a bottom line swinging through it. That had a very old jazz-record look to it too, with just funky typefaces and colours. It was like a "Tiki Bar" kinda font. A swinging jazz font. I'd heard the record had a jazz element to it, so that's the direction I went.'

Parke remembers other unreleased projects. 'We did a collection of Prince's love songs that took some of the art from . . . it had a mood to it like an old Quincy Jones record . . . a lot of almost jazz in the early 1970s, African art quality. It would have been cool and something you wouldn't expect.' He also recalls: 'There was an "NPG2000" thing I didn't do but I remember seeing the artwork for. It was a picture of a model of a building in the shape of the symbol.' It is unclear whether this was a fourth NPG album or, as has been rumoured on fan boards, another anthology of songs by Prince-associated artists in the style of the previous compilation, *1-800-NEW-FUNK* (see Chapter 34).

The next project to receive official release – albeit only as a cassette and download – made the darkness bubbling beneath the tracks on *New Power Soul* explicit. In 'The War', Prince gives full voice to his most paranoid (or, depending on your perspective, prescient) science-fiction fantasies, reworking Gil Scott-Heron's 'The Revolution Will Not Be Televised' as 'the evolution will be colourised' and warning about the increasing hold technology companies have on Earth's citizens by suggesting it's a matter of time before we all have microchips in our necks. Originally part of a forty-five-minute jam recorded at one of the many late-night concerts Prince played at Paisley Park that year, it shows one side of his live band at this time, which included Larry Graham (on whom much more later), churning out an aggressive theological-political funk that made his shows during this era unique. Some of Prince's most challenging – and brilliant – performances took place around this time: a version of 'Anna Stesia' in Lisbon where he spent eight minutes trying to persuade the audience that their hands were out to kill them; a twenty-minute-plus version of 'Days of Wild' in Cologne that ended with him berating the audience for smoking marijuana; and perhaps best of all, a performance at the Hippodrome in London in which he gave full rein once again to the apocalyptic side of his imagination. Midway through the show, Prince played a jam[1] which was heavily reliant on Richard Strauss's *Also Sprach Zarathustra*[2] (the jam had been played during several shows on this tour: at an after-show in Tivoli he would sing over this music about needing to get back to the US because of his fear of a bomb attack from Osama bin Laden), before performing not just an eleven-minute version of 'The War', but also a new extension of the song confirming he was singing about a third world war. The audience immediately launched into the 'evolution will be colourised' chant as if it was the most natural thing in the world. Prince asked the audience how many of them owned a Bible and how many owned a gun (when this was greeted by silence, Prince was satisfied and drew attention to the recent bombing of Sudan, suggesting that Great Britain may have played a role in this attack). When 'The War' ended, he altered his 'Dearly beloved . . .' opening to 'Let's Go Crazy' to say tonight they were there to get through World War III. This one-off song is even more peculiar than 'The War' in that it feels jaunty and light, as if Prince is revelling in the NPG's musical ability throughout an apocalyptic period (admittedly, the idea of partying through a world-ending crisis was nothing new to Prince).

I am extremely fond of this period in Prince's live performances, and wish there was an official document of the era (there was a variety of brief TV appearances across the US and Europe, as well as thirty minutes of a performance recorded the night after the Hippodrome show at the Café de Paris, which was later extended into an eighty-minute video *Beautiful Strange*, but the focus of these broadcasts was on the non-apocalyptic side of Prince's performance). Others, however, consider 1998–99 the nadir of his live career. Certainly, his band at the time was an unusual combination of talents, his basic line-up of Mike Scott, Rhonda Smith, Morris Hayes, Kirk Johnson and Marva King frequently joined by Larry Graham and Chaka Khan, as well as continued appearances from the rapper Doug E. Fresh.[3]

The *Beautiful Strange* video is also notable for a segment in which Prince is interviewed by Melanie Brown of The Spice Girls. Given Prince's interest in female vocalists and girl groups, it was inevitable that the British band, riding high at the time, would catch his attention, and he brought the Scary One to Paisley Park to interview him before attending their show at the Target Center in Minneapolis. Telling her to call him 'Spud', he described *New Power Soul* as 'spiritually political' and said the album was one of the 'maddest' he'd recorded.

Prince's seeming determination to perform himself into obscurity was not halted by the release of his next album, the second of the two kiss-off records delivered to Warner Brothers. At the time of release, *The Vault . . . Old Friends 4 Sale* seemed a very curious collection. Given a low-key release in August 1999, it had little apparent connection with ♀'s work, but even though it was put out under Prince's name, it wasn't obviously linked to his past records either. As with *Chaos and Disorder*, the sense of antagonism driving the album was clear: if it is not as obviously a record created in anger, it was at least delivered with resentment. On the back cover Prince appears to be looking down in despair, and the title – with its multiple sense of betrayal – revealed that this was not a happy release.

As with *Chaos and Disorder*, the record came with a warning that seemed designed to make listeners feel guilty for playing it. Made up of material that was largely unfamiliar to all but the most hard-core of fans, it's actually one of his most varied and enjoyable later records (particularly for those interested in Prince's more jazz-influenced music), weakened only by the inclusion of slightly too much material rejected from *I'll Do Anything* (although, thankfully, no 'Poor Little Bastard'). Nevertheless, many listeners were bitterly disappointed when they heard how

Prince had altered 'Old Friends 4 Sale', removing the autobiographical details from the original version of the song – although there's still a small cocaine reference and a line about Prince losing a lover to his brother, which add a little spice to this otherwise sanitised reworking.

If it had come out when Prince first presented it to Warner Brothers, it would have been an interesting stylistic opposite to *Chaos and Disorder*, indicating the true breadth of Prince's stylistic range, and no doubt released together the two albums would have got more attention than they did. 'The Rest of My Life', cherry-picked from *I'll Do Anything*, gains an additional significance from being placed at the start of a record serving as a kiss-off to Warner Brothers; again, if it had come out at the time, it would have worked as an introduction to the forthcoming *Emancipation*. The other *I'll Do Anything* tracks include one bizarre skit, 'My Little Pill', similar to the later 'Wedding Feast' in its brevity and oddness, and which makes little sense outside of its original context; and a second, 'There Is Lonely', originally intended to be sung by Albert Brooks. Prince fans should be grateful the Brooks rendition never achieved release, as he sounds like a drunken muppet in comparison to Prince's version of the track, an expression of isolation not dissimilar to 'Empty Room'.

The arrangement of the horn-driven 'It's About That Walk' is so pretty that it takes a while for the lyrical unpleasantness to sink in. Written and recorded during the Act II tour, it's a song about a woman's ass (presumably, given her habit of shaking it onstage during this period, Mayte's). The recording has deliberate call-outs to the band and 'fellas' that make it sound like a live improvisation or rehearsal: as on 'It's Gonna Be a Beautiful Night', Prince calls out band instructions, here asking for a Vegas ending and the familiar 'on the one', but there's something about these shout-outs that makes them feel staged, as with the original version of 'Extra Loveable'. I can't decide if the snickering at the end which acknowledges the song as something of a joke justifies it or makes it worse. Certainly, the snippet of what sounds like a boxing match in the middle only increases the thuggishness.

'5 Women +' is the album's high point, a song that Prince had originally given to Joe Cocker. It's a kind of sister song to 'Blues in C (If I Had a Harem)', which Prince was still playing live on the Nude tour when he wrote this. Now, Prince does have a harem (of sorts), but working through them doesn't help erase the memory of the woman he's lost.

Among the most mysterious of his officially released tracks, with neither the personnel nor the date of recording known, 'When the Lights Go Down' is one of Prince's most accomplished pieces of light jazz, and hints at a darker subject matter. Lyrically, it's a song about a woman resisting a pick-up, but there seems to be something far more disturbing at work. Is the man after her merely a sleaze or a more obviously evil figure? And what's at stake when the lights go down? There's a line where Prince just repeats something like 'duh, dun' instead of using actual words, famously the sort of thing Bob Dylan does often, but unusual for Prince. One might imagine it marks out the song as a botched take or a work-in-progress, but I'm not so sure. Prince didn't perform the track live until 2002, when he performed it at his 'Xenophobia' celebration in a version that improves on the released recording: on this night, Prince made the missing line seem deliberate with his scat-singing. He played a more faithful rendition at a soundcheck in Australia later that year, then forgot about it for another seven years. It's a song I've always connected with the celebrated out-take 'In a Large Room with No Light', and on one of the few occasions Prince has performed the track at Club Nokia in Los Angeles (one of the best after-shows, sound problems notwithstanding, I've ever seen), he played it in a set with this song. This live version was darker still than the studio recording, with Renato Neto's keyboards at their most sci-fi and wiggly, but although the rendition lasted a good eleven minutes, he stopped before the mystery line and returned to the chorus. He played the song one last time (to date) at the Montreux Jazz Festival in 2009 (a suitable home for the song), a more awkward stop–start rendition which did include an approximation of the complete lyric.

'Sarah' is Prince at his most mischievous, a kiss-off to an unwanted woman in which he jokes about domestic violence, but then carefully makes it clear that this isn't to be taken seriously. The song is so ebullient it feels that the target of the song has to be invented. If any more proof were needed that no Prince song is truly throwaway to him, the last track of *The Vault . . .*, 'Extraordinary', became a concert staple in 2002 – and frequently the finest performance of the night – eventually being included on his *One Nite Alone . . . Live!* album of the same year, a song which, much like *The Vault . . . Old Friends 4 Sale* itself, reminds the listener why even Prince's most obscure or least valued records are worth tracking down.

. . . AND MISSED OPPORTUNITIES

With the millennium approaching, Prince was still trying to work out how to reclaim one of his greatest songs, and most significant albums, from Warner Brothers. 'The plan at the time was to redo the whole *1999* album,' says H. M. Buff. 'He even announced he was going to re-record the original album, but it never went anywhere other than my taking the original tapes and transferring them to digital tapes.' He does, however, remember Morris Hayes programming a quick-tempo drum-and-bass version of 'Let's Pretend We're Married' that, perhaps fortunately, never saw release. What did come out, though, was a new version of the title track. The title – '1999: The New Master' – is an ironic indication of the futility of the EP, and the fact that he had revived 'Prince and The Revolution' for a project that had nothing to do with his original band added to the insult. A maxi-single consisting of seven remixes, the record featured a fairly unfortunate combination of Prince/♀ associates (Larry Graham, Rosie Gaines, Doug E. Fresh), as well as the actress Rosario Dawson. Buff says: 'A lot of people complained about the Latin part in "1999: The New Master", [but] funnily enough, there was a Latin part on the original, [and that] was edited out at the time.' While 'The New Master' and the other mixes are horrible, Dawson does contribute to one worthwhile track, 'Rosario 1999', which resembles *Emancipation* out-take '2020' and features the chords of 'Little Red Corvette' behind her vocal, a fragment from this larger proposed project.

Even if this went nowhere, the mood at Paisley was optimistic. 'We all thought, "1999, that's Prince's year,"' says Buff. 'We did that stupid version late November of 1998, and it should have been ready to rock. [But] like I said, it's all on his terms, and we went with the flow.'

Rave Un2 the Joy Fantastic is among Prince as ♀'s least-loved albums, but Buff believes that it could have been as (commercially) successful as *Musicology* if Prince had done as much promotion as he did for that album, including high-profile moves like playing at the Grammys. Buff remembers the album's title track wasn't brought out from the Vault until well into the process. Well over a decade old, Prince told Steve Jones of *USA Today* that the reason for the delay was that it sounded too much like 'Kiss', so he 'put it in the vault and let it marinate for a while'.[1] It is one of a number of songs believed to be influenced by former muse Anna Garcia (such as 'Pink Cashmere', 'Vicki Waiting', 'Lemon Crush' and the Carmen Electra song 'Fantasia Erotica'), Joy Fantastic being the stage name Prince originally proposed for her. Although the track hasn't dated, and no doubt sounded fresh to those unfamiliar with it, the song was already well-known by most Prince fans.

His first release for Arista, the album prompted a lot of thought from Prince, who even put out an alternative version entitled *Rave In2 the Joy Fantastic* soon after the original record's release. Still, in such a big catalogue, it's an easy album to pass over. Certainly, it didn't move from its space on my shelf for a decade until I saw Prince perform 'The Sun, the Moon and Stars' and 'Eye Love U, But Eye Don't Trust U Anymore' at the Club Nokia after-show mentioned in the previous chapter, and while the rest of the Prince-loving world was getting into *Lotusflow3r* and *MPLSound*, I found myself giving *Rave* a second chance.

Brent Fischer says his memories of him and his father working on 'The Sun, the Moon and Stars' are vague, but that by 1999 there had been a couple of changes in their working process. 'I was at the point where I was making suggestions, because I had such an intimate knowledge of the tune after transcribing it. I would suggest, "How about putting French horns around this guitar line here?" for example. It was the beginning of our collaborative period.' Also, by now Prince was sending them Pro Tools files rather than tapes, something Buff – who remembers teaching Prince about the technology – helped facilitate.

In the summer before the November release of *Rave*, Prince gave an unusually revealing interview to Beth Coleman, of *Paper*, in which he compared his relationship with Mayte to the one he had with record companies (intriguingly, he put himself in the role of the evil record-company overlord and suggested Mayte was the victim in this scenario). Once again, he returned to the Bible as a reference point, tracing, Coleman claimed, 'the origin of the marriage contract to Pontius Pilate organizing the consensus to crucify Jesus'. He referred again to the Garden of Eden, saying of his marriage: 'we pretend it didn't even happen. Like a lot of things in life I don't like, I pretend it isn't there and it goes away. We decided to go back to the Garden.'[2] The desire to obliterate everything that came before is explicit on the record, with the lovers of 'The Sun, the Moon and Stars' throwing their past onto a fire.

Some have interpreted this record as a break-up album, but Buff says the very last song to be recorded for the album was 'The Greatest Romance Ever Sold', which Steve Parke remembers as coming from a time when Prince and Mayte were still together. 'I got to go to Spain to shoot Prince and Mayte at their house. A lot of the stuff for "The Greatest Romance Ever Sold" came from that.' So if it isn't a break-up record, why are the lyrics so angry and sad? The couple were still together at the time of *Rave*'s release, and wouldn't officially divorce until the following year, but it is clear the record appeared at the tail end of the relationship. As always with Prince/♀, it's dangerous to make too close a connection between his biographical situation and the content of the songs, as ideas and songs can 'marinate' for long periods, but the references to drinking in three consecutive tracks – 'Tangerine', 'So Far, So Pleased' and 'The Sun, the Moon and Stars' – particularly coming from this usually abstemious singer, increase the record's maudlin feel.

Rave sounds different to the other records Prince made at this time. 'The difference with this [album]', Buff told me, 'is that he brought out the old Linn drum machine. I took it out of the basement and it just didn't work. There was a really cool store in Minneapolis that fixed old stuff but they took their sweet time, the usual nerds with long beards, and Prince wanted to put MIDI into it, which I duly asked, but you couldn't. Once it was fixed I hooked it up and he started going at it, and it was really interesting to see how he worked with that because that was very creative. You know, he would do fills on the fly, he would just do that and record it at the same time, he wouldn't programme the drum machine per se, or he would take a tom-tom sound and run it through a flanger – really cool stuff.'

While *Emancipation* had featured several covers, following the template of Santana's *Supernatural*,[3] *Rave Un2 the Joy Fantastic* has a large number of guest appearances, including Chuck D, Eve, Sheryl Crow (whose song 'Everyday Is a Winding Road' is also covered on the album), Gwen Stefani and Ani DiFranco. In Chuck D and Eve, Prince was finally working with two of hip hop's finest, although it's worth pointing out that he was lagging way behind the times: white indie rockers Sonic Youth had recorded with Chuck D way back in 1990. And while 'Undisputed' was a little disappointing (the NPG getting rowdy

The late eighties would see a refinement of the spiritual side of Prince's performance. His stage shows would also grow ever more expensive, to the discontent of some members of his management.

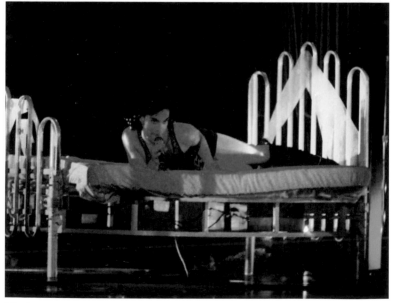

The Lovesexy shows would begin with a descent into darkness, including this bizarre S&M sequence.

Graffiti Bridge was more a sequence of music videos than a coherent movie.

In its earliest incarnations, the New Power Generation was not always the happiest of bands. With Rosie Gaines and his trio of male dancers, the Game Boyz, Prince's stage show changed dramatically.

Prince remained in the headlines, but for the average listener, it was hard to work out what on earth was going on. Opening shops that sold little of interest, painting 'Slave' on his face, appearing with his face covered and in increasingly bizarre outfits, Prince continued to hide in plain sight.

Prince's *The Rainbow Children* album seemed to have been influenced by his relationship with second wife, Manuela Testolini.

Prince was determined to make Carmen Electra a star, pouring an enormous amount of time, energy and promotion into her debut album.

In recent years, Prince has become an increasingly conservative figure. From the Musicology tour onwards, his main shows would grow more predictable.

The announcement of the 21 Nights in London tour delighted European fans, and was celebrated with a last minute show at the London nightclub Koko.

Prince, seen here with his dancers The Twinz, was understandably proud of his twenty-one night stand at the O2.

He returned to England in 2011 with his confusingly titled Welcome 2 America Euro Tour.

Now Prince has turned his back on the internet and distanced himself from record companies, fans await the next development in Prince's career with strong curiosity. But they still queue up for festival shows across Europe, such as this Hop Farm appearance.

yet again), Prince and Chuck D did make for a surprisingly seamless pairing, and 'Hot wit U' is a true guilty pleasure, and arguably the best song on the original version of the record, with Eve's response to Prince's sexual demands bringing a dynamic to the song completely missing from the mid-1990s strip-club songs. If Prince had given Carmen Electra comebacks of this quality, her musical career would have been assured.

Buff says: 'There's a song on there that wouldn't be on there if it wasn't for me, "Strange but True". I begged and pleaded for him to put that on there because I thought it was awesome, and then he had to add those scratches. Before it was just straight Prince 1980s stuff, which I loved.' He adds that he and Manuela Testolini, who would become Prince's second wife when the two of them married on New Year's Eve 2001, and who is thanked alongside Mayte in the album's sleeve notes, also fought hard for Prince to include 'Tangerine' – a savage song about a man trying to forget the colour of a lover's negligee – on the record. 'I tried to get "The Sun, the Moon and Stars" off. I thought it was terrible. And then he goes, "Hans, how's your sex life?" He thought he needed that to get laid.'

Buff says that as with *Emancipation*, there were a few songs that were written or recorded after the sequence had been set to round out and finish off the album: 'Silly Game', 'Eye Love U, but Eye Don't Trust U Anymore', the cover of 'Everyday Is a Winding Road' and 'The Greatest Romance Ever Sold'. But on the final assembly the album's final track is 'Wherever U Go, Whatever U Do', yet another positive affirmation song in the manner of much of *Diamonds and Pearls* and ♀'s 'Sweet Baby'. If the album is read as a divorce record, this can be seen as having a stronger sense of finality than the other 'he's gone, get over it' tracks.

Buff had to filter some of the flak coming from the record label about the album. 'I remember *Rave* was with Arista, so for a while I was part of this halo around him [and] put in a weird position of talking to Clive Davis before he could talk to Prince. And Clive, of course, took it as some underling standing in the way. I tried to explain to him, "You don't have to argue with me, Clive. I pass everything on that you tell me, but if he just says no, I work for him." And there was one thing where he wanted to do something for "Man o' War", this great guitar solo, and Clive said something to the effect of, "[If you do that,] they won't play it on urban radio." And Prince said, "Well, I'm a guitar player." There were two remixes of "The Greatest Romance Ever Sold", and Clive wanted to combine them to make something new, and I had passed that on and Prince didn't want to talk to him. And finally he was in the same room looking at me, and I gave him the puppy eyes, and he said, "Oh, that's what you want. I'd rather be dragged through nails."'

The album came with a poster. Steve Parke remembers: 'Those shots we took in Spain. I really liked the ones in the pool because I liked being out of the studio with him. I like the idea: he's in the water, at the time he was talking about bringing things to the Internet, making things virtual. I was thinking of the Kraftwerk album with the models for heads. I liked the idea with the hands: you think of connection, the organic with the digital.'

Less than six months after the release of the album, Prince put out a new version of the record, *Rave In2 the Joy Fantastic*, this time distributed to members of his Internet-based NPG Music Club. While fans debated earnestly over which version of the record was best, and all kinds of motives were ascribed to Prince for what seemed to be either a deliberate act of career sabotage or an angry response to the promotion of the original album, Buff is quick to note: 'It's not that different. There were a couple of steps taken making *Rave Un2 the Joy Fantastic*, they were just undone [from the original].' What Buff's referring to here, I believe, is the four songs that are slightly extended – 'The Sun, the Moon and Stars', 'Tangerine', 'Baby Knows' and the hidden track, 'Prettyman'. While Buff had managed to get Prince to include 'Strange but True' on the parent album, he couldn't stop him removing it from the remix, along with the Sheryl Crow cover. This new version opened with a truly dreadful 'rave' version of the title track, finally destroying all the magic of the original song. The three guest tracks got remixes, 'Undisputed' coming in a 'Moneyappolis Mix' with more space for Prince's complaining and boasting, and 'Hot wit U' mashed up with his old Vanity 6 hit, 'Nasty Girl'. In places, Eve's vocal is splintered into fragments, almost as if Prince is trying to get revenge on the song. Strangely, given his ambivalence to combining remixes of 'The Greatest Romance Ever Sold' on the album proper, the version on *Rave In2 the Joy Fantastic* is exactly that, spinning out to eight minutes. Maybe he included it out of spite.

But the second version of this album is most notable for the inclusion of 'Beautiful Strange', a song that ranks among Prince's finest. Prince clearly thought enough of it to make it the title track of the filmed Café de Paris concert, including a full video for the song in the package. It's also one of those videos that spells out the lyrics, which usually indicates Prince wants us to pay special attention to the words. It's a combination of a self-affirmation song (albeit more subtle and winning than most in this vein) and a celebration of God (I think), but as much as he wanted us to pay attention to the lyrics, it's a track most vital for Prince's guitar-playing, something he emphasises whenever he plays it in concert.

Of the unreleased tracks rumoured to have been recorded during these sessions, Buff doesn't remember 'Don't Say No', and although he does remember working on 'I Ain't Gonna Run', he can't recall details of it. Of 'This Is Your Life' he says: 'It's not quite as dramatic or as preachy as "We March", but it was a "Listen up, I'll give you some good advice" song.' It's always hard to say with any certainty that we've heard the best of Prince's work from any period, but this does seem to be a time when, thanks to him making use of the Internet to distribute more songs than ever before, the majority of his new music was officially released.

Warner Brothers also put out a spoiler of their own around this time, a single-disc greatest-hits compilation entitled *The Very Best of Prince* that was of little worth to anyone who already owned Prince's albums. Far inferior to the *Hits* collection, it was also of less interest than the third best-of, 2006's *Ultimate Prince*, which at least included a CD of remixes.

Prince made one further attempt to claim back '1999' from Warner Brothers, making it a feature of his seventh video of live-concert footage, *Rave Un2 the Year 2000*, with the anonymous author of the sleeve notes claiming that this would be the last time Prince would play the song in concert (in reality, he retired it for four years, before bringing it back without fanfare). Perhaps he was just nervous about how the song would work once it became nostalgic instead of futuristic, and then relieved when the tune carried it through.

This video, presented as if it was a New Year show (and broadcast on pay-per-view in America that night), was actually cobbled together from two shows recorded at Paisley Park earlier in December, one featuring The Time and the other with Prince and a large number of guests, including Lenny Kravitz, George Clinton, Rosie Gaines and Maceo Parker. After making Larry Graham such a central part of his previous few tours, here he also brought in Graham's former Family Stone band-mates Cynthia Robinson and Jerry Martini, who'd been joining Prince at shows around this time to play on 'Everyday People'. To fend off any criticism of the incredibly dull set list, the notes promise that the songs 'r plated [*sic*] with respect 2 the original versions, but with a new and xciting interpretation, often besting their studio counterparts'.

But with the best will in the world, I can't imagine anyone choosing any of these versions as their favourite renditions of any of Prince's hits, played as they are by the weakest assembly of the NPG (Morris Hayes, Kirk Johnson, Mike Scott and Kip Blackshire) and accompanied by lacklustre interpretative dance. As with *The Sacrifice of Victor* video, Prince gives over a generous portion of the recording to his guests – two songs from The Time's show; two Lenny Kravitz tracks where Prince (mostly) cedes the microphone to his guest and joins him on guitar; a Sly and the Family Stone section; various blues medleys – and while this desire to share the stage with heroes and epigones is a touching indication of his mindset during this era, this is a recording that will leave all but the most generous-minded Prince fan feeling short-changed. When the highlight of a concert video is a nondescript jam in which Prince puts aside his keytar for a splits competition, you know it's not one for the ages. (There's also a weird moment when Prince calls up blues singer Jonny Lang in the middle of a blues medley and he fails to appear on stage.) It's hard to shake the impression that Prince has mainly agreed to do a New Year's telecast merely to question the concept of celebrating dates, sermonising during 'Purple Rain' about how acknowledging birthdays causes one's body to deteriorate.

Continuing with the broken promises, also contained on the DVD is a robotic voice offering Prince's seven-CD sampling set (retail price: $700): seven hundred samples from Prince's catalogue for licence-free use, with no further royalties. Prince's motivation for this collection is made clear on two short tracts included on the DVD's menu under the heading 'Freedom News', in which he claims that the release of the sampler is intended as a political statement as well as an artistic one, a way of Prince claiming back what he believed was his rightful ownership of songs to which Warner Brothers owned the masters. But when it came down to it, he backed down and didn't release the collection.

I asked Buff why he stopped working for Prince. 'That was the hardest thing. I have a great wife who I've been with for eighteen years, since before I fell into the Purple trap, and one day she said she was down about the bad manners of the place sometimes and said, "The day you quit Paisley will be the happiest day of my life." And it wasn't a fight thing, but it really took a load off my shoulders in a big way. It made for a good lifestyle, especially as I hadn't been working with the Madonnas of this world before and it was certainly the tip of my mountain at that point. And one of the bad things was I didn't know I had a day off till it was over. Sometimes he would say, "We'll see each other again at two tomorrow," and I'd show up at two. But most of the time I'd get paged, not by him directly but either by the accountant or one of the bodyguards, "He wants you to come in." I'd come in. That would be round the clock. There was some type of rhythm in regular times. I'd show up around two in the afternoon and go home around four in the morning. I got called past midnight once in all those years. There was usually a cut-off time where if he hadn't called by nine or eight in the evening, I wouldn't get called in. But that was hard.'

Steve Parke left around the same time, for similar reasons. 'It was the birth of my son. The reality of working with Prince is that you need to be available. It's a full-time commitment. And my son was born, I went out a couple more times, and I came back and saw my son and he'd grown in a week, and I didn't want to be that guy who leaves for a week. And it's not just the week out there; you have a week of preparing yourself because you know you're gonna go out there, put in a huge number of hours, and when you come back you're kinda wrecked. He asked me to come back and do a few things here and there, but I didn't trust that three days wouldn't turn into a week. I would still love to do stuff with him, but he seems to have his bases covered.'

JOIN MY CLUB

Author interview with Stephin Merritt, of The Magnetic Fields, April 2006

MT: *What's your opinion of Prince?*
SM: I don't look fondly on Christianity. I went to see him two or three years ago, and that Christianity stuff is just unbearable. And not just for people who don't like Christianity. He is the worst evangelist I have ever heard. Totally counterproductive to his own cause. And for Prince to concentrate on *not swearing* as a major ethical principle? I think it's charmingly eccentric, maybe. I have a lot of problems with fifteen-minute jazz-funk jams as well. I don't care about instrumental prowess. I don't care about quick-thinking improvisational skill. At all. I'm a songwriter and I'm familiar with Cage and I couldn't really care about what notes people can think of quickly. It doesn't interest me and I'm astounded that it interests other people still. Improvisation is what you do in the process of making something better.

MT: *So he's not someone you admire as a songwriter?*
SM: Oh, definitely. The two-note melody of 'When Doves Cry' is famously brilliant. And as an arranger he made one-drum snare into an entire style, unheard of apart from Kraftwerk making the output of their keyboard an entire style. And he's my height or shorter, which counts for a whole lot, and he's impeccably tailored, which is difficult if you're a very short man.

MT: *I was thinking that you and he are the only popular musicians to release consistent three-hour albums.*
SM: Which consistent three-hour album do you mean?

MT: *Well,* Emancipation . . .
SM: Uh . . . is that the one with the cover of 'One of Us'?

MT: *Yeah.*
SM: Oh . . . ohhh . . . consistent in what way? Hmmm. That's the one with the acoustic album as the third disc?

MT: *No, that's the fourth disc of* Crystal Ball, *the* four-*hour album.*
SM: OK. 'Cause I loved that. I didn't like the electric part, but the acoustic disc was beautifully produced. It made it obvious what direction he ought to be going in instead of fifteen-minute jazz-funk jams. And the fact that he's still obviously capable of making beautiful music, he just doesn't want to, I respect that . . . but I don't want to listen to it.[1]

It's always depressing when a musician or group turns inward and starts asking fans for more of a commitment than just purchasing their albums or the occasional concert ticket. No one wants to wake up and find themselves part of some odd cult, paying for prog bands to host their own festivals or taking out a time share in the Santa Monica condo owned by Wedding Present front man David Gedge. But when Prince started going down this route, it seemed different. He wasn't asking fans to facilitate his continued existence, but was instead attempting a new model, one that seemed better suited to his manner of producing music than working with a record company ever had been. And I'm not trying to be controversial or facetious when I say that between 2001 and 2004, Prince became, once again, the most exciting musician in the US. His work may have been aimed at a smaller audience, and there was undoubtedly something insular about his new approach to disseminating his work, but the run of records from 2001's *The Rainbow Children* to 2004's *The Slaughterhouse* – albeit with greater and lesser success – reveal Prince indulging in a new stream of experimentation that prompted three of the most exciting years for Prince fans since his career began. And not only was the music interesting again, but so were the shows, the *One Nite Alone . . .* tour Prince's greatest since *Lovesexy*. It was also the period of his heaviest Internet activity, allowing him to build up a new relationship with fans that reminded them of why they had fallen in love with the artist in the first place.

His divorce from Mayte recently completed, Prince's first two shows after abandoning his ♀ alias[2] were low-key, late-night performances at Paisley Park. Three weeks later, however, he performed at a much higher-profile event: the first of his week-long annual Celebrations, when Prince would get fans to gather in Minneapolis to watch shows by old protégés (Taja Sevelle) and his band-mates' new projects (Kirk Johnson's Fonky Bald Heads). The week would also include parties where Prince would talk to fans and nights at Paisley where he would DJ. He was also continuing his resolution not to swear onstage, rebuking the audience for indulging in the now-familiar chant of 'play that motherfucking bass' during 'Days of Wild'.

Introducing Larry Graham, he went on to talk about how Graham told him that Sly and the Family Stone had a rule that they weren't allowed to play with other bands and that he had to turn down playing with Hendrix.[3] Prince extolled the virtues of Graham and Maceo Parker, before explaining how his New York lawyer, L. Londell McMillan, had been encouraging him to give the audience what they want – old hits – something he resisted, invoking the title of a song he'd released an excerpt from on his website that week, 'Y Should Eye Do That When Eye Can Do This?'. The question of whether to comfort his fans with songs from the past or offer them something new would become a constant dilemma for Prince over the next few years, before he largely gave in and focused on the hits that made his name. The last-ever Celebration show was significant for seeing a partial reunion of The Revolution, with Bobby Z, Brown Mark and Matt Fink coming onstage to play 'America', though the occasion also prompted Prince to joke about his former band-mates onstage, seeming to emphasise his distance from his old self.

For most of 2000, Prince limited himself to private performances at Paisley Park, before embarking on a short Hit N Run tour at the end of the year. These were hit-heavy shows, and the only truly interesting thing about the set lists for these performances was the return of 'Mutiny' as if it was a lost hit, and the debuting of a new song entitled 'The Work Pt 1' that was the first indication of the dramatic change in direction Prince would soon make. But his addresses to the audience also seemed at odds with a show designed to win back the masses. At a 'Hit N Run' show in Oakland, in the midst of one of his anti-record-company and pro-website rants Prince told his audience that if they weren't self-employed, they were slaves, which came across more as a criticism of his audience than encouragement to free themselves from their chains. At the same show he played an eleven-minute version of 'U Make My Sun Shine', talking to his dancer Geneva and criticising the length of her skirt, making her change her clothes and telling her to dress like a lady, saying he needed to be able to respect her before he could spend money on her.

During this period, Prince's website was becoming increasingly significant to him, although this new method of music distribution wasn't without its teething troubles. Given the fans' nostalgia for the NPG Music Club when Lotusflow3r went online, it's worth pointing out that criticism of his Internet ventures was nothing new. Indeed, eight years before *Rolling Stone* attacked Lotusflow3r's 'bandwidth problems . . . inability to recognise underscores in user name(s) and passwords, downloading issues, choppy videos and inaccessibility to Europe',[4] David Kushner wrote an article for the same outlet, in which he suggested that Prince's NPG Online Ltd 'just shows Prince's utter cluelessness'.[5] Just as music writers (and fans) would later be annoyed by the fact that you had to work out a riddle before being able to join Lotusflow3r.com, so Kushner was irritated that you had to follow cryptic messages to find two songs, 'U Make My Sun Shine' and his cover of 'When Will We B Paid?'. But this was only the beginning of what turned out to be a torrent (no pun intended) of new material during the site's first year.

The NPG Music Club seemed to offer fans exactly what they'd always wanted. By putting up single songs rather than waiting until he had compiled an album, it was possible to see his creative process at work, in the manner Buff described in the last chapter. The two albums that eventually brought together the best of the NPG Music Club downloads, *The Chocolate Invasion* and *The Slaughterhouse*, were different from the majority of Prince albums in that they were explicitly presented as compilations, but essentially this was a public version of the private process that had led to the creation of past albums like *Sign o' the Times* or *Graffiti Bridge*. There were even, in the usual manner, three albums – two Prince records called *Madrid 2 Chicago* and *High*, and a planned fourth NPG album, *Peace* – abandoned along the way (not to mention a promised seven-CD box set that would bring together all the NPG's full-length album releases).

The new songs that Prince released via this distribution method, along with many previously unreleased live recordings that didn't make it onto the eventual compilations (or the *One Nite Alone . . .* album), were 'Funky Design', 'Mad', the old unreleased Revolution song 'Splash', 'My Medallion', a cover of The Staple Singers' 'When Will We Be Paid?', an instrumental jam including elements of Jimi Hendrix's 'Machine Gun' (later removed) renamed 'Habibi' after one of Prince's guitars, an original version of 'Van Gogh', the song he co-wrote with Sandra St. Victor and gave to the band of the same name, 'I Like to Play', an instrumental song offered as a competition for fans to complete, a rehearsal version of 'Rebirth of the Flesh', 'Jukebox with a Heartbeat', 'Breathe' and 'Madrid 2 Chicago' (the two *Madrid 2 Chicago* songs Buff and Parke mentioned in Chapter 27), and a video-only release of 'One Song'.

'Funky Design' and 'Mad' both started out as songs for the NPG, and there are versions of both with Sonny T rapping that make more sense than Prince's renditions, as they are fairly basic, aggressive raps that suit T more than P. 'My Medallion' and 'When Will We B Paid?' were originally intended for *High*, an album that got lost in the shuffle but which actually seems to have got further than most of Prince's aborted projects, with a complete track listing. Neither song reveals Prince at his most graceful, and it's easy to see why he didn't include either in the later compilations of work from this era.

Prince's interest in country music is clear from his songs written for country stars under his Joey Coco alias, but 'I Like to Play' is closer to Jagger's pseudo-country songs, a piss-take sung in a croaky voice accompanied with booing from a roadhouse audience. It's good, though, and evidence of the new creative opportunities Prince explored while programming his Ahdio shows, a series of broadcasts from an imaginary radio station that were made available for download. 'Jukebox with a Heartbeat' is a downbeat grumble about the limitations of 'the people' as listeners and the methods of getting songs to them. More important than either of these squibs is 'One Song', one of a handful of Prince songs that genuinely frighten me. It begins as an update of 'Sign o' the Times', but with the funky music now gone as Prince intones a list of disasters as the words appear on the screen in the same way they did on his 1987 hit. After this catalogue of natural mayhem, he turns his attentions to artists who create violent films and TV programmes, suggesting that in doing so they are destroying people's minds, before using a variation of the story of the Tower of Babel to suggest that some languages take people away from God and that democracy is utterly without value.

These newly hard-line thoughts are pursued not just in the songs and videos, but in the radio programmes themselves. The second Ahdio show, for example, begins with a spoken-word intro from a female-voiced 'Salome' (but clearly written by Prince) that name-checks Bob Dylan, alongside his more usual heroes, and displays the evident ferocity of Prince's religious perspective at this time. In this intro, Salome suggests that art became a commodity when Satan became a lawyer and turned everything artistic into property. Salome imagines a future where lawyers want to carry music into the twenty-seventh century and 'replant the seed' of Curtis Mayfield, Mavis Staples, Aretha Franklin and The Jackson Five (carried as 'uploaded files') on 'the future planets'. She suggests that 'the top lawyers in Babylon' say that without them, artists wouldn't be famous, and yet this is a fallacy because Hendrix was Hendrix before he recorded a note and that irrespective of whether he became a recording artist, Bob Dylan (who, bizarrely, seems to be described here as a 'black musician') would have spoken out against injustice. The logic of the piece is torturous, as Prince tries to bring together science fiction, religious fervour and anger against the music business. But it would be these concerns that would define much of

Prince's work over the next decade, from *The Rainbow Children* to *Lotusflow3r*.

H. M. Buff told me he was 'personally pissed off that the greatest album [Prince] had recorded in ten years was the one he did after I left'. Buff's being hard on himself, but it's undoubtedly true that *The Rainbow Children* was Prince's most important album since *Lovesexy*. There had been many significant records in the time between these two albums, but *The Rainbow Children* was the first to truly expand on Prince's sound and see him returning to the experimentation that had driven his work throughout the 1980s. Initially broadcast as the ninth of the NPG Music Club shows, it was given a full release a few months later.

The Rainbow Children is a concept album, but as usual with Prince, the record's narrative is incredibly muddled and obscure. But at least, unlike the ♀ album, Prince took risks to ensure the record worked as a complete piece. Each song is a different chapter, and Prince narrates over the songs in a distorted, sinister voice (the most offputting feature for some listeners). The opening title track – which Prince would also use to open shows – features Prince elucidating a biblical narrative over light jazz, explaining how 'the Rainbow Children' built 'a new nation' based upon the teachings of the Jehovah Witness-favoured New Translation of the Bible. This is yet another Eden story, featuring a 'Wise One', 'his woman' and 'the Resistor'. The song goes on to describe the birth of Christ and the uprising of the Rainbow Children. To this day, Prince talks about becoming a Jehovah's Witness as giving him a necessary rebirth that allowed him to slough off his past once more, telling the *Vancouver Sun*: 'The rear-view mirror got broken a long time ago. Being baptized as 1 of Jehovah's Witnesses gave me a center & a release from a past way of life.'[6]

'Muse 2 the Pharoah' is a song about the 'Wise One' finding

a perfect wife, inspired by Proverbs 31:10 and featuring a controversial line that seems to dismiss the Holocaust. Both these songs initially seem, with their hard-core theology and oppressive sound, very different to anything Prince has released before, but though the devoutness is new, lyrically 'The Rainbow Children' and 'Muse 2 the Pharoah' can be seen as rewrites of 'The Beautiful Ones' and 'Sexy MF', and perhaps the most impressive element of Prince's new music was how he managed to map his old obsessions onto his newfound belief.

The complaints expressed in the world-music-influenced 'Digital Garden' are also familiar. The song introduces the Rainbow Children's enemies, the Banished Ones, who appear to work in the media (the 'Digital Garden' consists of 'whosepapers, hellavisions and scagazines') and are linked to the serpent in the Garden of Eden. 'The Work Pt 1' features the Rainbow Children deciding to destroy the Digital Garden, before discovering Paradise on Earth in 'Everywhere'. The 'Wise One' and his muse are united in 'The Sensual Everafter', before Prince sneaks in a nightclub song and a bit of name-checking (Macy Gray and Common) in 'Mellow', a song that also features the 'Wise One' seeming to bring 'the Muse' to orgasm through song alone, before hypnotising her by stroking her hair. The cryptic but funky '1+1+1=3' seems to refer to the importance of including God (and James Brown) in a marriage. 'Deconstruction' is not Prince's take on Derrida, but a continued attack on the Banished Ones' media empire. (In the light of 2011's hacking scandal, the album feels more contemporary than ever.)

The Rainbow Children feels more obviously related to what was going on in Prince's life at that moment than usual: a few months after releasing a record focused so strongly on the relationship between a 'Wise One' and his 'Muse', Prince married his second wife, Manuela Testolini, having recently purchased a new home to live with her in Toronto. Yes, *The Rainbow Children* is primarily funky theology, but it's also a sort of sequel to ♀, only with a new subject of devotion.

The last time Prince got married he produced a ballet; this time he composed a bizarre piece of comic opera entitled 'Wedding Feast'. The feast is vegan (as Prince now was) – something also true of the woman in 'She Loves Me 4 Me', the more substantial song which follows on the album. While it is not especially distinguished among Prince's many ballads, it does appear richly autobiographical, with Prince (or the 'Wise One') celebrating the fact that his new lover appreciates him for who he is rather than the fantasy Prince many of us like to imagine.

Those listeners concerned by the Holocaust line in 'Muse' were even more troubled by what they perceived as anti-Semitism in the song 'Family Name', which addresses the subject of African slaves who were forceably renamed. Because the family names of the people in the song ('Rosenbloom', 'Pearlman' and 'Goldstruck') were considered to be either Jewish surnames or corruptions thereof, the assumption was that Prince was attacking Jewish people. But the origins of the song can be traced back to an intro to the version of 'When Will We B Paid?' that Prince played at an early show on the 2000 Hit N Run tour, in which he makes a comparison between the unimaginative names given to African slaves, such as 'Lynch' and 'Payne' and 'Blackburn', and what he sees as poetic, nice names, such as 'Rosenbloom'. In this intro, Prince is keen to point out that terrible things have happened to Indians, white people and black people, and notes how pleased he is to see a mixture of races at his concert. He talks of Martin Luther King and Aretha Franklin, and there is nothing in his depiction of race relations that could cause offence. 'Family Name' also gave birth to a character, Violet Brown, who would later provide journalistic reports on his website – insider stories about what went down at private parties. The album's closing chapters, 'The Everlasting Now' and 'Last December', are more straightforward gospel, addressing the eternity of Christ's love granted to worshippers and the day of Revelation.

Prince seemed very keen that his new direction was understood by his fans, and when he previewed the record at the second of his annual Celebrations in 2001, he followed up the listening sessions with group discussions. In order to get this message to a wide audience, he invited director Kevin Smith (whose movie, *Dogma*, had impressed Prince) to make a film of these sessions. It was an unfortunate choice. Many directors might have experienced some misgivings about some of the messages put forward in this music, but only Smith would make their clash one of the main routines in two separate stand-up shows (admittedly prompted by questions from the audience). I approached the director to give a more considered description of his experience with Prince, but he was too busy podcasting and making terrible films for dwindling audiences and declined (politely), so I am left with the way he presents Prince in front of fans for laughs. In the first recording, released on DVD as *An Evening with Kevin Smith* (2002), Smith spends over thirty minutes explaining how Prince invited him to document people's reaction to the album at his second Celebration for a film intended to be taken to the Cannes film festival, something he struggled with (after accepting the invitation) because he didn't believe himself a documentary-maker and had concerns about some of Prince's more hard-line beliefs. In the second film, *An Evening with Kevin Smith 2: Evening Harder* (2006), he criticises *Musicology*, *Crystal Ball* and *Under the Cherry Moon* and suggests that Prince wanted to turn the footage into a recruitment film for Jehovah's Witnesses. It is easy to see why Smith's ego was bruised by the experience, but the loss to Prince fans is greater: if only Prince had approached someone who could have respected his intentions but still made the project their own.

Prince's *One Nite Alone* . . . tour is among the high points of his entire career, the most musically accomplished and sophisticated series of shows he's ever performed. And for once, there is a satisfactory audio document of the tour. While the *Lovesexy* tour was only officially documented on videotape, this time Prince finally released an official box set which, for all its flaws, is a good souvenir of the US leg of the tour (he would follow this with stints in Europe and Japan, during which the show would change). The *One Nite Alone* . . . *Live!* box set features two CDs covering the main show and a third intended to represent the after-shows. The first two are compiled from eight different performances from the US leg of the tour, edited together to represent a typical night. It's easy to see why such an approach would appeal to Prince and yet alienate purists who might have preferred a recording of a whole show rather than this stitched-together patchwork. I realise this is a regular complaint, and that musicians like to point to the fact that some of the most acclaimed live albums of all time are the product of multiple nights of recording and serious overdubbing, but no matter how much work was done to the recording after the performance, the first CD of the set at least is among Prince's finest releases. Although the show, like the tour, focuses largely on *The Rainbow Children*, it is more than just a live representation of this material. As with Prince's best live performances, the set sees him revisiting his back catalogue in an almost wholly original way. Beginning with sci-fi noises and drums, the opening – the first two tracks of *The Rainbow Children* – is even more disorientating than the *Rainbow Children* album itself, as the audience cheers while Prince intones in his new Darth Vader manner. His spoken addresses to the audience indicate just how hard he was working to make this new sound work. During 'The Rainbow Children' there is a much clearer division between Prince-through-tone-box and Prince singing normally – yet another representation of Prince's belief that there is more than one person inside him. 'Muse 2 the Pharoah' is much heavier and harder live, with a lyric change that makes clearer the importance to Prince of 'monotheism'.

But it's the third track that really makes this recording essential. This is the only official release of 'Xenophobia', Prince's best jazz-influenced track. Originally intended as the title track of an album, but removed from that recording after its appearance here, it's worth buying the set for this alone. Accompanied live by footage of people being searched at an airport, part of the song (and the title) is clearly Prince's response to increased security following the events of 9/11. This is only part of the twelve-minute track, which unlike the unreleased instrumental studio version, begins with Prince encouraging his audience to surrender to him, avoid 'dead blood' and rise up. Encouraging the audience to chant as Greg, Candy, Maceo, Renato and drummer John Blackwell take turns to solo, it's a wonderful example of how to bring jazz to a pop audience, a far greater achievement than any of his later jazz records. After five minutes he threatens to search his audience; after nearly eight the song becomes much softer as Prince conducts a combination sermon and trust exercise, encouraging audience members at the front of the stage to give up their seats to those at the back and pulling a fan up onstage before directing his performance to this lucky individual. This kind of stagecraft was not completely new, but it had a fresh purpose.

The intensity of this opening is broken with a surprising choice: 'Extraordinary', from *The Vault . . . Old Friends 4 Sale*, here used as a springboard for continued jazz improvisation, a three-way between Renato Neto, Candy Dulfer and Prince. It's one of the best examples of Prince taking a throwaway song and turning it inside out. It also flows perfectly into 'Mellow', making it clear that *The Rainbow Children* was less of a departure than it first seemed. Prince worked harder in these shows (and on this recording) than he ever did before (or has done since), and the version of '1+1+1=3' on this record features a continuation of this era's extraordinary showmanship. It's one thing to inspire an audience to get funky; quite another to get them up on their feet and dancing to celebrate 'the theocratic order'.

The first two 'hits' appear towards the end of the first side, although both – 'Strange Relationship' and 'When U Were Mine' – are fan-favourite deep(ish) cuts, Prince pretending this music is playing on his WNPG radio station. Of all the old songs on this album, 'Strange Relationship' is one of the few that has the impact of the original. The heat has definitely gone, but Prince makes up for it with a passionate delivery and scat-singing that hides this, rhapsodising over Rhonda's bass line. 'When U Were Mine' is less successful, Prince treating the track as if it is a cover of someone else's new-wave song (he even instructs Renato to play an 'old-time solo'). As if punishing the audience for their enjoyment of the oldies, he follows this with the furious 'Avalanche', delivered soft and smooth, another wonderful example of Prince voicing harsh sentiment in a gentle register.

The only truly brilliant performance on the second disc is the opener, 'Family Name', another song brought to life through interaction with the audience, Prince giving new names to the Portland people sitting up front. Given how much Prince has enjoyed renaming his protégés over the years, it seems ironic that he now finds this practice so outrageous.

Aside from 'Everlasting Now' and a very brief version of new song 'One Nite Alone . . .', the rest of the second disc is given over to oldies, including a seven-track piano medley and two attempts to reclaim songs from the artists who'd covered them ('Nothing Compares 2 U' and 'How Come U Don't Call Me Anymore'). The closing rendition of 'Anna Stesia' starts brilliantly: Prince inhabits the song so completely he could have written it yesterday, before he ruins everything by sermonising and berating the audience for not joining his music club.

While this box set is a good representation of the tour, there was one show that was dramatically different. When Prince arrived in Louisville, he did so without the NPG horns, which meant a certain amount of improvisation and rejigging of the set was necessary in order for the show to work, with Prince concentrating largely on piano instead. It's the sort of magic night that if Prince was a different sort of artist would be a perfect archive release, but instead it passed largely unnoticed, another inspired moment forgotten by everyone aside from those who were there.

After the US, Prince took the show overseas, first to Europe and then to Japan. I only saw two shows (and one rehearsal and aftershow) of the European leg of this tour, both in London, and wish I'd attended more. On the second of three nights at the Hammersmith Apollo, I went as a regular punter: the seats were bad and we were openly mocked by Prince for not being members of his club. The next night I went back with a friend who was a member of the NPG Music Club and enjoyed the best Prince experience I'd had to date (there would be better to follow). The rehearsals he was letting fans into were less rehearsals than mini-performances in themselves, with Prince joking and bantering with the crowd (a couple entering late were shocked to nearly bump into him in the aisle). From the back on the first night, surrounded by audience members intolerant of Prince's latest sound, it felt as if the new material was falling flat; up front the next day, it felt as if he only really cared about the dedicated fans in the first few rows, who'd been prepared for what to expect by the rehearsals. The after-show that night wasn't epic; the best after-show in Europe was an extraordinary night in Copenhagen when Prince and his band ranged freely through styles, going from an extraordinarily heavy version of 'Whole Lotta Love' to a cover of 'Take 5'.

The fact that the after-shows on this tour were largely less interesting than the main shows is also borne out by the third CD of his live set, *One Nite Alone . . . The Aftershow: It Ain't Over*. Consisting mainly of the highlights of two US after-shows (one from New York, the other from Los Angeles), plus one track from a Portland show, it does give an indication of the after-show experience, but suffers from the edits and unrecognisable versions of much-loved hits. The best Prince after-shows – such as the famous Trojan Horse performance – have a sense of purpose; the worst are given over to guests and formless jamming. This live album falls somewhere in the middle. The CD opens with a long version of 'Joy in Repetition' that Prince used to open the New York after-show, which took place in front of an audience who'd already watched a George Clinton show that night. It's a worthwhile performance, opening up the song into a jam without losing the lyric's mystique, but I've seen him do much better versions of the track live.

George Clinton is one of a number of high-profile guests on the CD, performing an unreleased original of his entitled 'We Do This'. Prince kept this cover but clipped the two that preceded it – James Brown favourites 'Talkin' Loud and Sayin' Nothing' and 'Pass the Peas' – robbing the show of the building funk jams that would have been a true representation of an after-show experience (he'd later do something similar with the *Indigo Nights* live album). The only other track from this particular two-hour performance to make it onto the CD is a medley from much later that morning, Musiq Soulchild performing his 'Just Friends (Sunny)' combined with Sly Stone's 'If You Want Me to Stay'. Aside from a vamp from 'The Everlasting Now', the remaining tracks on the album are all old songs, all in versions that don't compete with their originals. Frankly, '2 Nigs United 4 West Compton' could be anything, the only evidence that Prince is playing this song coming when he shouts out the title. 'Alphabet St.' is delivered in the country-and-western style he's unfortunately adopted whenever he's played the song in recent years. 'Peach', too, is barely recognisable, at least when compared to the recorded version. Sometimes when Prince extends or deconstructs a song it's the most exhilarating part of his performance; other times (as here), the jamming becomes excruciatingly dull. Chanting 'It Ain't Over' live is great fun; hearing it at home merely makes me want to scroll to the end of the track and shout, 'There. Now it's over.'

The hits are dull on this CD too. All the psychodrama of 'Dorothy Parker' has been removed in favour of Latin stylings – with a Sheila E percussion solo – and 'Girls & Boys' quickly turns into yet another jam that bears scant resemblance to the original song. It's almost as if Prince was using the CD to blow the mystique of his after-shows.

The DVD release covering the tour is an even greater disappointment. Billed as the '1st official NPG Music Club Concert DVD' – and, to date, the last – it's not that it's light on *Rainbow Children* tracks, as it does include 'The Work', '1+1+1=3', 'Family Name' and 'The Everlasting Now' (as well as The JBs cover 'Pass the Peas' that was an important part of many of these shows), but rather that a three-hour show in Las Vegas has been edited down to less than half its length, losing much of its structure and character along the way. The problem is not just that Prince has dumped half the show, but that he's edited out the most interesting bits:[7] by removing 'The Rainbow Children' and 'Xenophobia', the show immediately becomes a much lighter, more generic experience.

As on the *Lovesexy* tour, most nights during the *One Nite Alone* . . . shows Prince had sat down at the piano for an extended medley. His next major release was a fan club-only CD with the same title as the tour. The *One Nite Alone* . . . album works best when considered as a companion piece to *The Truth*, only this time focusing on piano and vocals instead of vocals and acoustic guitar. His decision to record an entire album in this manner, accompanied only by the occasional synth and John Blackwell on drums, seemed a fan's dream come true. 'One Nite Alone . . .' is almost as arresting as 'The Truth': it's unclear whether the 'undulating acrobat' is Prince, his lover or a servant, but it's certainly a surreal one-night stand. But much of the rest of the record consists of scrappy and lyrically peculiar fragments. 'U're Gonna C Me' is a dated account of Prince and a lover paging each other in the same way he once did his engineers. 'Here on Earth' is a bizarre dream of a woman in a building site covered in vomit, the lyric utterly at odds with the syrupy arrangement. An elegant cover of (part of) Joni Mitchell's 'A Case of You', which he'd performed live for decades and had revived for the *One Nite Alone* . . . tour, is more arresting, but might have been stronger if he'd recorded the entire song.

'Have a Heart' is an angry song in which Prince justifies his behaviour towards an ex. 'Objects in the Mirror' (surely one of his least inspired song titles) is an unofficial sequel to 'Insatiable', describing Prince and his lover brushing their teeth together after filming a sex tape, notable mainly for the synths accompanying the piano. The collection's most significant song, 'Avalanche', focuses Prince's fury on figures of larger historical import than the occasionally anonymous girlfriends, drawing a surprising parallel between Abraham Lincoln and the CBS producer John Hammond as figures who have exploited black Americans. 'Pearls B4 the Swine' (another uninspired title and song) features Prince comparing his ex-lovers to pigs. 'Young and Beautiful' is a gentler, but still slightly creepy, variation on 'P. Control'. The final song, 'Arboretum', is an instrumental seemingly inspired by the arboretum at Paisley Park. Steve Parke remembers that Prince liked to take photos in and around this garden, although it was never clarified whether they were for an actual project or for Prince's personal use. 'It was outdoors in the woods and it was really casual. We'd shoot at five in the morning with static lighting that would cast bad shadows.' It would be hard to come up with a more telling example of the more fruitless side of Prince's generally worthwhile workaholism than this.

30

NEW DIRECTIONS IN MUSIC

In 2003, Prince also put out three original jazz albums: the download-only *Xpectation* and *C-NOTE*, followed by the full-scale CD release of an album, *N.E.W.S.*, that served as the follow-up to *The Rainbow Children*. For jazz saxophonist Frank Griffith, an enormous admirer of the work of Dr Clare Fischer, Prince's jazz-influenced records are solid and worthwhile, the main influences, he believes, coming from the 1970s. For him, the first release, *Xpectation* (recorded in 2001, but held back until 2003), is well-played 1970s-influenced fusion – with Candy Dulfer the strongest soloist – although he considers the language and improvisational vocabulary not particularly deep or well-researched. The presence of the classical violinist Vanessa-Mae on the record works particularly well, indicating a continued desire to blend jazz and classical influences in the manner achieved by Clare Fischer. It's a shame that Prince removed the best song from the album, the aforementioned 'Xenophobia', which was also the original title of this record, as it might have given it some much-needed bite.

Only a couple of days after this record, Prince released his second jazz CD, *C-NOTE*, which owes something, Griffith believes, to 1970s CTI label influences. Recorded at soundchecks by the *One Nite Alone . . .* touring band, the album contains four songs named after the location where they were recorded (Copenhagen, Nagoya, Osaka, Toyko), and curiously, an official release of a live version of the long-lost song 'Empty Room', also recorded that year in Copenhagen. 'Copenhagen' feels less well thought through than the *Xpectation* tracks, the record-scratching from Dudley D giving the track an ersatz feel, more 'Cantaloop (Flip Fantasia)' than 'Cantaloupe Island'. 'Nagoya' has a similar problem, only this time it's what sounds like a whistle that disrupts the sound.

There's an anxiety in the *C-NOTE* tracks that betrays the circumstances in which they were recorded: even though the music was performed in front of a sympathetic, fan club-only audience, their presence seems to stop the players going as far as they might. 'Osaka' is far better: along with 'Xenophobia', it's one of the highlights of Prince's jazz recordings, an atmospheric piece with a sense of dread that feels much more significant than the band just warming up. A relatively under-celebrated feature of Prince's post-2002 shows is the interplay between Prince and Renato Neto, and this is at the forefront here, as the two of them dual on piano and guitar. 'Tokyo' has vocals, after a fashion, Prince singing the name of the city in a way that suggests less a shout-out to the audience than an attempt to get the spirit of the city into his music.

Clare Fischer gets a credit on *N.E.W.S.*, the only jazz record of Prince's to get a full-scale official release, but his son Brent believes: 'I would just guess that he again took snippets of string recordings that we've made for him over the years, stuff that my father had written, just lifted it and placed it on an entirely different track. So I would say this is a case of Prince sampling Clare Fischer's orchestral track, and it may not even be the entire orchestra; it may just be part of the orchestra.' This sampling of Fischer's work indicated how much of an influence he remained on Prince's jazz, and a source who wishes to remain anonymous told me that a couple of people who were close to Prince and worked with him in the 1980s and 1990s observed him listening to every single individual track of a Fischer arrangement, as if trying to crack the code of the composition and unlock the Clare Fischer secret.

Recorded, the sleeve notes claim, on 6 February 2003, *N.E.W.S.* is by no means a bad album, but it has fewer of the dynamics of *Xpectation* and is less distinguished light jazz, representing something of a dead end instead of a fresh start. Now that Prince has returned to making conventional albums, it's possible to see this era as a self-contained period of experimentation, but at the time it seemed perfectly possible that Prince had turned his back on a wider audience and might go on recording jazz albums for ever. If all the Prince albums from *Lovesexy* onwards force the listener to make a mental readjustment – this is what Prince sounds like now – *N.E.W.S.* was, for all its smoothness of sound, his most radical gesture yet.

While Prince would remain more open to jazz influences in all of his subsequent bands, perhaps the most lasting evidence of his continued interest in making jazz part of his sound is his regular performance of jazz drummer Billy Cobham's 'Stratus' (famously also sampled by Bristol's Massive Attack) in his live shows. Cobham covered 'Sign o' the Times' in the year of its release, and Prince has repaid the compliment by covering 'Stratus' live over thirty times. Indeed, in recent years, hearing what Prince decides to do with this song on any given night is usually a concert highlight.

The NPG Music Club era came to an end – at least as far as releases were concerned – with two compilations. For all his protestations of innocence, Prince would never fully abandon sexual innuendo in his songs, later even evoking 'Song of Solomon' as evidence that devoutness and desire need not be incompatible, but *The Chocolate Invasion* is his last truly sexually explicit record, even featuring a song about a sex toy that recalls the unreleased

'Vibrator'. In a month's time, the release of *Musicology* would see the emergence of the newly mature Prince with a largely inoffensive (and bland) record; *The Chocolate Invasion* and *The Slaughterhouse* represent Prince at the opposite extreme, two collections that, while not particularly challenging musically (although *The Slaughterhouse* has its moments), feature some of Prince's darkest and most claustrophobic lyrics.

Aside from one angry anti-industry song ('Judas Smile'), which would have made more thematic sense on *The Slaughterhouse*, one party song ('High') and an instrumental ('Gamillah') which shares its name – 'beautiful' in Arabic – with his then-wife Manuela's company (which now sells candles and other paraphernalia), *The Chocolate Invasion* is entirely about love, lust and sex. It begins with one of Prince's greatest tracks, 'When Eye Lay My Hands on U' (a song he's frequently revisited in concert since). He released a strange video for it which features a close-up of his Bible (with 'The Truth' emblazoned on it), before Prince appears to force a dancer to fellate him, the promo cutting out barely a minute into the song. I don't know whether this was to tease the fan club or if a complete version of the video exists, but fortunately we have the song (and several live performances) to display how even in the midst of his most secretive period, Prince could casually access the best of his abilities and produce a love song as cryptic and yet affecting as his most well-known releases.

The other love and sex songs are mostly good, but more prosaic. 'Supercute' is one of several songs Prince has written about lovers arriving home on aeroplanes. 'Underneath the Cream' begins with studio chatter and turns into a track about cunnilingus and a somewhat oppressive-sounding 'eternal wet dream'. 'Sexme? Sexmenot' is Prince doing R. Kelly again, with lyrics about after-parties and an inexplicable line in which Prince threatens to wet someone's pants. 'Vavoom' is a pale Xerox of a hundred other

Prince songs, a vague lyric enlivened only by what seems like a request to be allowed to orgasm inside his lover. 'U Make My Sun Shine' is a duet between Prince and Angie Stone that was released as a single. Nothing to do with the standard of the same name, it is an attempt at an old-fashioned soul song that falls flat due to the familiar-feeling lyrics.

The Slaughterhouse brings together the darker, more aggressive NPG Music Club songs. Even in its earlier version, 'Silicon' – as in 'rope of', as in movies – began with Prince welcoming the listener to 'The Slaughterhouse', suggesting that he had always perceived the song as part of this planned larger project, and although some songs stem from different eras, there's a uniformity of vision to this collection. As with 'One Song', 'Silicon' has Prince once more turning his back on popular culture, seeming in this song to attack Hollywood. Appropriately for a dark album only released over the Internet, Prince makes a comparison between computer and human viruses, apparently suggesting that a poor diet is comparable to not having a firewall, only more fatal. In the final two verses, he seems to address someone else, either the listener or a woman who has approached him in a club. He seems to find his audience wanting, believing that they (or we) are getting bored by his sermonising as he invokes Armageddon and indicates that he has gained thicker skin since taking on (and now abandoning) a pseudonym. He also gives a second, punning interpretation of the song's title, suggesting that film (or life, or the recording industry) is just a 'silly con'.

'S&M Groove' is less serious than it sounds, less a continuation of his interest in dominance and submission than Prince celebrating his sound, this time even resorting to reading out newspaper reviews of his concerts: the only freaks here are the ones on the dance floor. 'Y Should Eye Do That When Eye Can

Do This?', the aforementioned riposte to his lawyer (named in the song), doesn't really make a great case for what Prince wants to do instead of playing his hits: as much as I'm bored of hearing him play 'Cream', I don't really want him to become Doug E. Fresh either. 'Golden Parachute' is an update of 'Avalanche' concerning Prince's ire at the retirement package given to a music executive and the concept of intellectual property not belonging to the artist who created the music.

Prince's attitude towards contraception has changed drastically over the years. Describing himself as a 'very careful man' when he accidentally impregnates someone in 'Baby', but intimidated by Trojans when he finds them in the pocket of his lover in 'Little Red Corvette', he later sold his own condoms (Purple Raincoats, packaged in an imitation CD sleeve, with Prince, Mayte and the rest of the NPG staring out at the purchaser) through the NPG Store and advised his male listeners to practice monogamy on the 1989 B-side 'Sex', as well as singing of 'safe sex, New Power Generation style' on 'Eye Wanna Melt with U' and recommending condom use in the *Emancipation* sleeve notes to 'Joint 2 Joint'.[1] But Prince clearly had had a complete change of attitude by the time of 2004's 'Props N' Pounds'. (This may have been prompted by the scenario in *The Truth*'s 'One of Your Tears', where the girl he's addressing sends the singer a used prophylactic as punishment.) As he is occasionally prone to doing during this period, he breaks the word down into its 'prefix' and 'suffix', Gil Scott-Heron style, suggesting that alert people should have picked up on the fact that safe sex is a 'con' to 'dominate' people. Prince seems to suggest that we should be more concerned about what's in Trojan Horse lubrication than the possibility of sexual disease, although, in a sneaky piece of doublespeak, he presents this as a chivalrous intention to control what goes into 'his woman'. There is also, of course, the possibly religious and certainly moralistic additional concern that contraception may lead to promiscuity. Sheesh, where did the fun go?

'Hypnoparadise' is completely disposable, a dance track with speeding-car sounds that resembles the migraine-inducing worst of *Come*. 'Northside', though just as slight lyrically, is more appealing, a more approachable song reminiscent of the best of *New Power Soul*. While 'Peace' and '2045: Radical Man' were originally intended for a fourth NPG album, and originally released as a single under the NPG name, 'Peace' opens and closes with jokes about Prince's alternative identities, the song itself sounding like an extension of *Rave*'s 'Man o' War'. '2045: Radical Man', the song he gave to Spike Lee's *Bamboozled*, has a good rebuke to anyone discussing (writing about?) music without musical ability of their own, suggesting that such a practice can only be done from a consumerist point of view (Prince has so little respect for the critic he doesn't exist), and imagining a future dystopia where any 'radical men' get destroyed by the year 2045. Prince recorded a video for the last of *The Slaughterhouse* songs, 'The Daisy Chain', filled with clues and visual puns (a guitarist clutching a can of 'chicken grease'), as well as featuring Prince in one of his weirdest looks, with braided hair.

As variable as the music released during this period could be, it remains a golden era for Prince fans, the Internet years as fertile a period as Dylan and The Band's recording of *The Basement Tapes*. It would be a while before the NPG Club was completely phased out, and Prince would continue to think of ways to increase his accessibility to his audience, but it's undoubtedly the case that his next move was away from the hard core and back towards mainstream significance.

TRUE FUNK SOLDIER

After all the years of experimentation and reconnection with his fan base, Prince seemed to decide that what he wanted, most of all, was to be a big star again. So how did he do it? Promotion, mainly, with a new publicist and a new record label (Columbia) as part of a canny and well-orchestrated return to the top, which he achieved with, astonishingly, one of his weakest albums, a record that, seven years later, even his most diehard fans struggle to say anything positive about.

In the year before the release of *Musicology* – the same year that he put out the largely jazz-influenced and experimental albums described in the previous chapter – Prince embarked on a short tour of Hong Kong, Australia, Honolulu and Kahului. The set list he played on these dates was, after the well-thought-out and experimental *One Nite Alone . . .* tour, a return to a mainstream, hits-heavy, crowd-pleasing show structured largely around songs from *Purple Rain.* Though never explicitly acknowledged as such, the shows can be seen as a warm-up for the marathon ninety-six-date tour he would embark on to push his new record, and was commemorated with a book of photographs taken by Afshin Shahidi, *Prince in Hawaii: An Intimate Portrait of an Artist.* These simple but high-gloss pictures are accompanied – as in Prince's other books – with a text made up of lyrics from throughout Prince's career and maxims emphasising the newfound simplicity in his stage show (something Bob Cavallo would certainly have appreciated) and the change in his sartorial demands, as Prince notes that all he needs now is a well-cut suit: indeed, in one of these pictures he's wearing one of his own tour T-shirts.

In 2004, Prince would do everything he needed to do to promote an album and make it a hit, including old-fashioned strategies like playing his hits at the Grammys and duetting with the then-superhot Beyoncé; performing 'While My Guitar Gently Weeps' with Tom Petty, Dave Grohl, Steve Winwood and Jeff Lynne at the Rock and Roll Hall of Fame (Prince's performance of the Eric Clapton solo is an astonishing display, although there was something a little dismaying about Prince's triumphant end to this George Harrison tribute, as he clearly relished kicking the asses of the rest of rock's elder statesmen); contributing a cover of Jimi Hendrix's 'Red House', retitled 'Purple House', to a Hendrix tribute album, *Power of Soul*; and new approaches such as doing a deal with Sony to distribute the album in shops, while also producing an NPG version (containing the same songs) to build into the ticket price at shows. He would appear on TV shows including *The Today Show* and *The Ellen DeGeneres Show*, and blitz radio shows, doing twelve phone-in shows in one morning. He wanted back.

While some (including former manager Alan Leeds) were critical of this new approach, Brent Fischer has particularly fond, yet also slightly bittersweet, memories of the 2004 Grammys, where he had personal involvement in the proceedings, and which represented a rare opportunity to see Prince performing with a live string orchestra (as well as Beyoncé and the NPG). 'It was great', Brent says, 'to be able to put strings to "Purple Rain",' something that had never been done before. But making the deadline for this arrangement involved Brent having to use a new collaborative process that allowed he and his father to work to the same extreme creative schedule that Prince often uses.

'Dad would write an arrangement during the day, and when

he was finally exhausted at the end of the day, he would set down his pencil, even if it was in the middle of a phrase, and I would come over after I'd eaten dinner and stay there then for the rest of the night and I would pick up right where he left off. And I would also lay down my pencil around four or five in the morning, when I finally couldn't stay up any more, and even if that was in the middle of a phrase, he would just pick it up the next thing the next morning . . .'

When the piece was finished, Brent got an extra treat. 'They decided to have percussion in there, so I actually got to perform onstage with Prince as part of the orchestra, playing some of the percussion parts.' After the performance, he met Prince for the first time. 'I did meet him and talk to him and I found him very easy to work with, and we just talked for a few minutes but we got that whole thing done, we had rehearsal and soundcheck completed in under thirty minutes. But even though they were together in the Staples Center, he didn't meet Dad . . . And I guess now I understand why some of the other artists who performed that night who had orchestras backing them up also had conductors, and we had fully planned that my father – or I, if he weren't feeling well that day – would be conducting the orchestra. And they didn't have a conductor's podium set up on the stage. And I guess we found out later, or we surmised later, that it's because Prince still didn't really want to have any contact with Dad, not wanting to jinx the relationship because it was still working so well all these years later. I understand his reasoning, but just thought it was perhaps sad that Prince did not get to meet Clare Fischer.'

As with *Rave Un2 the Joy Fantastic*, *Musicology* was a self-conscious attempt at a hit, albeit with a new strategy. Instead of filling the record with fashionable guests and aping the sound of other successful artists, Prince resorted to self-parody, turning in what mostly sounded like pale Xeroxes of his past hits,[1] often with troublingly conservative lyrics. I've grown to love title song 'Musicology'[2] through its appearance on concert recordings or hearing it in live sets, particularly when it's part of an extended funk section of a show and linked with 'Prince and the Band' (which when he first played it would include a repeated line about Warner Brothers being a monumental waste of time), 'Play that Funky Music' or 'Pass the Peas', but on CD it sounds thin and dated, and that's the best track on an otherwise largely dull record.

For the first time in his career, Prince sounded mostly uninterested in competing in the charts (his desire to match others would return with *3121*), instead wanting to remind listeners of the sound he had once perfected. The title of the hip-hop-influenced 'Illusion, Coma, Pimp and Circumstance' is a meaningless play on a Shakespeare-coined phrase that seemingly unconsciously recalls the fear Prince expressed on 'I Like It There' – that he has nothing to say that Shakespeare hasn't said first. It's a lyric about money, thematically most similar to the songs he wrote for The Time in its depiction of the relationship between a gigolo and an older woman. The song also shows Prince still taking care to appropriate fresh ghetto vernacular, with the reference to 'whips and chips', which means cars and cash, and not – as a northern friend of mine surmised – Johnny Vegas trying to finish his fish supper while being flagellated.

Those fans who weren't too disappointed by *Musicology* to care speculated whether songs such as 'A Million Days' were addressed to his second wife or his first, a question raised by the song's focus on lovers separated by physical distance and Prince singing about packing a suitcase, recalling Mayte songs like 'Madrid 2 Chicago', to which I can add that H. M. Buff told me the song was recorded when he was working with Prince, which dates it to before *The Rainbow Children*. The sense of creative bankruptcy that hangs over this album is increased by 'Life o' the Party,' the second party song in four tracks, and for once a Prince party I'd be glad to leave.

'Call My Name', one of two songs (along with the title track) for which Prince won a Grammy that year, features samples from Clare Fischer's strings and is littered with clues that seem to suggest it is a song written for his new wife, although the reference to a Bridal Path door was actually inspired by the address of his new home in Canada (making reference to his various homes would become regular practice for Prince on his subsequent albums).[3] The video for 'Cinnamon Girl' (directed by Phil Harder, a daring choice for Prince as the director is best known for his work with alternative musicians like Big Black and Sonic Youth) connected the song to the footage Prince would play live during performances of 'Xenophobia' on the *One Nite Alone . . .* tour, again responding to increased security (and racial profiling) following 9/11. Attacked as 'the most tasteless video ever' by the *New York Post*, it mixes live action (shot on green screen at Paisley Park) and animation and features an Arab-American schoolgirl (making this the first Prince song about schooldays and schoolgirls not to be obviously sexualised) whose family is suffering attacks describing them as 'terrorist scum' following 9/11 and who fantasises about blowing up an airport in retaliation. Included with the 'NPG Enhanced Version' of the single was a documentary about the making of the video, in which Harder describes wanting to respond to what he described as the 'vigilante' atmosphere in the US following 9/11.[4]

The love songs on the record have no clear narrative. While 'Call My Name' may have seemed a representation of marital bliss (albeit challenged by, in a prescient touch, hackers trying to bug his phone), two songs later on 'What Do U Want Me 2

Do?' Prince was singing of his marriage being threatened by a new admirer. If we had any doubt that the old Prince was gone, the threat in this song that if they were living in 'other lands' and she slept with him she would be beheaded is breathtakingly cruel. There was a similar darkness to 'The Marrying Kind' and 'If Eye Was the Man in Ur Life', which seem linked both musically and thematically, both being an inversion of 'I Could Never Take the Place of Your Man', but H. M. Buff told me he was involved in the recording of the latter. Assuming this is true, it seems that Prince might have kept back the song until he found a project that suited it, and written the first with the second in mind. It also suggests that both songs are not autobiographical but instead Prince inhabiting the character of the kind of man who would move in on another's girlfriend (after warning him first, or rather, telling the woman that he warned her boyfriend, which is a different thing, of course). After threatening the aspiring lover with decapitation in 'What Do U Want Me 2 Do?', it's jarring to hear him here doing the same thing. The reference to marriage in 'On the Couch' encourages the listener to read this song as autobiographical, but it's a fairly generic representation of a domestic dispute that could just as easily be fiction.

'Dear Mr. Man' is the best of the album's political songs, and Prince would release a later version of the song that features him duetting with Dr Cornel West,[5] who seemed to become something of a mentor to Prince in a similar manner to his relationship with Larry Graham. 'Reflection' looks forward and back. The first half suggests that Prince believes he will survive long enough to import his essence into another body; the second half has him singing about his early life. A Prince-loving friend of mine believes this is bogus nostalgia, Prince not recalling his past but instead burnishing his myth.[6]

*

The shows which followed the album were Prince's most success-
ful greatest-hits tours, mainly because he finally seemed at peace
with his back catalogue and structured a set that showed the true
breadth of his life's work.

It was hard not to feel disappointed to see something so con-
servative after *One Nite Alone . . .*, but if you look at it from the
other direction, the shows seem better than much that followed,
and they did have a unique sound. I have a particular fondness for
Rhonda Smith's bass, and was sorry when she left the band. This
tour set a template that Prince has stuck to now for nearly eight
years, and while there have been many innovations and changes
during this period, there hasn't been a major move away from this
set of songs (at least at his stadium shows; I'm not counting the
after-shows, the guest appearances or the tour when he played as
a member of Támar's band), the important tracks – 'Musicology',
'Shhh', 'Purple Rain', among several others – still likely to be in
the set list if you go see him tomorrow. It was also a good year for
after-shows, with eighteen appearances alongside the enormous
number of main shows. At a series of concerts at Paisley Park (his
last performances there for five years), he'd play a wider selection
of songs and covers, but still work in tracks from the new album,
like 'Illusion, Coma, Pimp and Circumstance', with Mike Philips
squelching vocoder all over the music.

Evidence that Prince was moving on creatively came mainly
through the acoustic section of the tour, where he introduced
two songs that have never been released – '12.01' and 'The Rules'
– and a rougher version of 'Black Sweat', which would eventually
show up on *3121*. Both '12.01' and 'The Rules' are slight, comic,
bluesy, semi-spoken songs dealing with domestic triviality, simi-
lar to 'Telemarketers Blues' from the *One Nite Alone . . .* tour,[7]
included, it seems, mainly to get laughs, something which would
become increasingly important to Prince's live act. '12.01' is little

more than a few jokes strung together; 'The Rules' a more elaborate talking blues in which Prince depicts the difference between men and women in the broadest comic strokes (men's habit of not putting the toilet seat up when they urinate; men wanting to watch sport on Sunday; men not wanting to go shopping; men not wanting to hear their girlfriends complain or ask for directions; men's frustration that women always have headaches when they want to have sex).

The song, which would resurface again on the *Planet Earth* tour, would develop into a light-hearted (if sexist and predictable) comedy routine, but in its earliest performances, it has a more sinister structure, the whole song a conversation between Prince and a policeman who has come to his house. The singer's repeated insistence that his girlfriend has threatened to 'cut him in the middle of the night', and the sense that he may have been violent towards her (not to mention the singer's repeated imploring to the policeman to help him), gives the song a blackly comic edge similar to 'Bob George'. The lyrics in this version are crueller, too, with the singer mocking his girlfriend's weight. (Not that this seems to disturb the audience, who whoop with laughter throughout.) Later versions of the track (particularly during the *Planet Earth* tour) lose this structure, with Prince instead lecturing the audience like a hack comic, making it a much easier song to enjoy.

The NPG Music Club remained Prince's outlet for the less commercial side of his work: alongside the releases of *The Chocolate Invasion* and *The Slaughterhouse* there was also a handful of live releases, and tracks including 'Glass Cutter', a deeply weird song that sees Prince singing about baths again, appraising the beauty of a woman by suggesting that she looks so good she deserves to be shot, and free-styling about cheese. The final two songs to be released via the NPG Music Club before Prince's move to Universal were lighter: quiet-storm jazz songs 'Brand New Orleans' and 'S.S.T.' (which were later released as a charity single by Columbia). Inspired by Hurricane Katrina, it's a calm, altruistic end to an era when Prince was reaching out to a wider audience, and the two songs are among his most appealing recordings of this period. Both songs are inspired by Sade (who would also be an influence on Prince protégée Bria Valente's 2009 album *Elixer*[8]), the kind of AOR singer Prince was in danger of becoming. But he couldn't keep up the mainstream act for ever, and it wouldn't be long before he started to make curveball business and creative decisions once again, including taking a position in new protégée Támar's backing band and recording an album that represented his most significant creative leap forward since *The Rainbow Children*. Soon the hard core would have *their* Prince back, and the mainstream would just have to accept what they were given.

COME 2 MY HOUSE (PART 2)

So I'm standing in Prince's living room with the sweet, spiky-haired publicist from his then-current record label Universal, talking about how the one thing you know about any late-night Prince show is that you always have to wait, when I see Prince enter the empty room (the celebrity guests are still out on the balcony, drinking Prince's booze and enjoying the warm LA night) and stride purposefully towards the stage. The PR and I run to the front with some other British guests that she's shepherding, as the room quickly fills behind us. I am as close to Prince and the band – who are performing on the floor – as it's possible to be without actually joining them, and when The Twinz do their dancing or Támar sings I can feel the body heat coming from them. The PR whispers to me: 'I'd rather piss down my leg than miss a second of this.' I take a surreptitious step away from her.

As delighted as I am to be here, it's undoubtedly a strange point in Prince's career (although this only makes the connoisseur in me even happier) – his most recent tour has seen him playing as one of the band for his protégée Támar – and when he starts playing tonight, the first set is primarily a Támar show, made up mainly of songs from the as-yet-unreleased album that Universal execs have been listening to before I arrived. The only song Prince takes vocals for in this first set is a cover of Ani DiFranco's 'To the Teeth'. It's the only time Prince has ever played this song live – he and Maceo Parker play on the album this song is from, but not on this track – and it's an extraordinary number to play in front of Bruce Willis, David Duchovny and Sharon Stone, ending with the suggestion that the best way to improve the world is to open fire on Hollywood. Prince smirks as he plays the song. I wish you could hear this performance; I know the show was recorded, as the cameraman came over to tell me my head (I'm a good foot taller than most of the celebrities present) was blocking his shot.

When Prince returns after the interval, he plays a set that includes five songs from the new album. Maybe it's the experience of hearing the songs this night that makes me like this record more than most people. It seems to me that the reason why Prince's work over the last half decade has not seemed to capture the public imagination in the way his songs once did so effortlessly is not so much that the quality has dipped, but that the songs no longer have all the accompanying support that fix them in the listeners' imagination. Universal worked hard (for a while) with *3121* but ultimately seemed defeated by Prince's apparent unwillingness to truly push the record. Although he had seemed pleased to join the new label, announcing that he didn't consider Universal 'a slave ship', it was clear that this time round he didn't want to adopt the approach he'd used for *Musicology*, instead going for a more unusual publicity campaign, where rather than going out to woo the world once more, he would encourage the world (or at least the world's press) to come to him.

Though well-reviewed, the album undoubtedly didn't get as much attention as it deserved. It's Prince's last masterpiece to date. '3121' is a truly great song, Prince's best album opener since 'Sign o' the Times', and he's played it over a hundred times (occasionally in a longer version referred to as '3121 Jam', and it's now come to serve the purpose that 'Head' once had in his shows – the song that the band use to stretch out and experiment). The band also frequently work in old ragtime songs into the track, as

Prince encourages us to realise the connections between dance music from the beginning of twentieth century and dance music from the beginning of the twenty-first.

The studio version features a reunion of Prince's New Power Trio, the stripped-down line-up of Prince, Sonny T and Michael B that had previously recorded 'The Undertaker'. They recorded the song as part of a session that also resulted in tracks for subsequent albums. As well as re-engaging with his past, *3121* is the only time in the whole of the twenty-first century's first decade when Prince has really tried to record a mainstream album, a record that could be played alongside Outkast and The Neptunes and Kanye West's 'Gold Digger' (which Prince's DJ Rashida spun this evening).

As quixotic as promoting a record with private parties seemed (hell, I wasn't complaining), this theme is apparent throughout at least half the album. 'Lolita' begins with Prince telling the object of the song she's a VIP to him, then in the same breath demanding to see ID (presumably to determine age rather than credentials). But it's a scary party. You can never leave, the first song warns, and by the fourth song ('Black Sweat') his love-making is making his partner scream. While lyrically these songs are nothing new for Prince, there was a new, minimalist sound to them that seemed to update the sound of his earliest records without becoming a pale imitation of his past. 'Black Sweat' had originally been introduced as an acoustic blues song on the *Musicology* tour, but this electro version was the first track since 'Gett Off' to truly take a contemporary club sound and move it forward. Outside the party gates are angry, scorned women ('Fury', an old-fashioned Prince rocker with clichéd lyrics but a suitably hard guitar which he performed on *Saturday Night Live* and at the Brit Awards) and the 'Wicked One' ('The Word'), who even has his own evil spiders. Falling in love here ('The Dance') can lead to you losing your mind. Before playing 'Fury' at his house, Prince equivocated about it, saying he wasn't sure if he wanted to play this angry song when he was in such a good mood.

The other half of *3121* consists mainly of love songs, including one that Prince played in his house that night, an old-fashioned soul belter called 'Satisfied', which would remain a highlight of his shows for years afterwards, eventually birthing a comic sequel of sorts ('Beggin' Woman Blues') on *Indigo Nights*. These love songs are largely collaborations with Támar. Considering his own interest in Latin jazz, I asked Brent Fischer if his father was surprised to hear Prince going in this direction on 'Te Amo Corazón' when he sent the song to them for their input. But Fischer insisted: 'We had heard him do funky things like "Te Amo Corazón" before. Even wilder things. I would venture to guess that some of the very unusual things that we've heard Prince come up with recently are due to the influence that Clare Fischer's writing has had on him. We were sort of supposing that Prince would eventually get more involved with [Latin jazz], that's just a whole part of the process of the Latinisation of northern America as more Hispanics move here, and Latin music in general is higher up on the radar in mainstream culture. And I believe also at that time he had a Latin girlfriend, so that may have been part of it.'

The record has only one weak track, 'Incense and Candles', though I dislike it for personal reasons: it gives me a jolt when Prince sings to Támar that he's grateful to her parents for feeding her healthy dinners; there seems something creepy about the suggestion that Támar's mother is to be congratulated for keeping her daughter well fed for Prince (or maybe it's just my own anxiety that my parents raised me on burgers and fish and chips), and the sniggering reference to Prince's candle kills the mood. 'Beautiful, Loved and Blessed' (a co-write with Támar) is a variation on Prince's Eden stories, with Prince this time being a piece of clay, which seems non-Christian until he quickly follows it up with the 'blood on Calvary'. But by far the best of these ballads is the simply titled 'Love', a song which, to date, Prince has never played live. It shouldn't work at all – it's actually Prince listing a series of complaints about his partner – but it's the best track on the album, almost entirely down to the minimalistic electro-funk synths and drums in the arrangement (although an acoustic version of the song he later released on his website is equally good). The significance of the *3121* party is made clear in the final song, 'Get on the Boat', which explains why this party (once again) should feel so apocalyptic: the people with Prince are the chosen ones, the only ones who will achieve salvation.

On this night at Prince's house, the world doesn't end, and as often happens at private and not-so-private Prince parties, the show ends with covers and Prince and Larry Graham jamming. Later, outside on the balcony, I am introduced to Támar by an American record exec who tells me I violated what was supposed to be a strict hierarchy by standing in front of the celebs. It's a stressful night for Támar. Inserts in the *3121* CD sleeve said her record would be released the week before this party, but this hadn't come to pass. Someone has started a slightly tactless conversation about Prince's other protégés, and we talk about this for a while. I'm surprised to discover that she seems fully aware of everyone who's come before her, and am touched by her warm, open nature. 'Write nice things,' she whispers to me as she clutches my hands briefly before disappearing into the darkness.

Later, eating breakfast burgers in a diner as dawn approaches, as all Prince fans always do, we dissect the show. The Universal people ask me about the Brits performance I'd witnessed earlier that year, where Prince reunited with Wendy and Lisa. They consider this the perfect Prince performance and want him to do it again on all the important American TV shows. I can understand why: as good as it looked on screen, it was even better live, evidence of what happens when Prince pours all his energy into a four-song medley (Prince must have valued it too, releasing both video and audio recordings of the performance as B-sides and a download) rather than a two- or three-hour show. Though just over ten minutes long, it was one of the best Prince performances I've ever witnessed. A couple of years on, I would ask Wendy and Lisa about it, and Lisa would tell me that while they 'had a really good time rehearsing for it . . . at his house', and Wendy thought, 'The three of us are going to announce this, do that,' when they got there Prince didn't speak one word to the two of them. Lisa says: 'It was like he went, "Psyche!"' Wendy added: 'When we performed "Purple Rain", he had Támar up to sing, and then The Twinz, and me and Lisa, and we had no screen time, it meant nothing. He wouldn't let us talk to the press to announce that we were going to be there.'

As the sun comes up, we get a cab back to the hotel and leave Prince's fantasy land. The PR tells me I'll never experience a Prince show like that again. She's wrong. Two years later, in a hotel room in New York, I'll witness an even better private(ish) performance. But I'm getting ahead of myself.

Largely forgotten today, merely six years later, *3121* was a success, of sorts. It returned Prince to the top of the US charts – without the giveaway gimmick utilised for *Musicology* – for the first time since *Batman*, and the songs stuck around in his set for years afterwards, usually prompting the liveliest performances each night. But it could have done better, and with more promotion I believe Prince could have pushed this record further into the popular consciousness. The most significant missing project from this era is a film also called *3121*, shot around the same time the album was recorded. A trailer from it was leaked in early 2011, the footage suggesting it was more like *The Beautiful Experience* than a new narrative movie. Prince blogger Dr Funkenberry described having seen the full film, which, he explained, was mostly shot by Sanaa Hamri and later renamed *Lotus Flower* and was due to be featured on the website Lotusflow3r.com back in April 2009, before Prince decided not to add this content. Pressed by his followers, Funkenberry explained that the film was a collection of videos for '3121', 'The Word', the acoustic version of 'Love', 'Incense and Candles', 'The Morning After' and 'The Dance'. The later Lotusflow3r.com version of the film also included a video for the song 'Guitar' and a different version of the '3121' video, but it's yet another lost project, albeit, it seems, something with the home-movie calibre of *3 Chains o' Gold* than a significant missing work.

On Independence Day 2006, Prince shut down the NPG Music Club, declaring all the lifetime memberships void. The timing of this was peculiar as just a month before he had received a Lifetime Achievement Award from the 'Webby' organisation. There would be a *3121* website to promote the album and subsequent shows, but it was a far less successful enterprise and the 'Jams of the Week' offered via the site tended to be live versions of tracks he'd made available several times before (like 'Splash'). And while the *Lotusflow3r* had the potential to eclipse any online effort Prince had created before, the reality would turn out to be far less inspiring. For much of the previous two years, since the enormous *Musicology* tour, Prince had retreated from the larger world and concentrated instead on small private at-home concerts, as well as the tour during which he had performed as merely a member of Támar's band. But towards the end of 2006, Prince headed to Las Vegas for the first of the many residencies that would become a central part of his new touring policy. In retrospect, it's easy to see why this was a sound business decision, as well as being creatively liberating for Prince. But at the time, the fact that he was heading to Vegas worried me. It wasn't just the location, but the set lists too. Commentators were quick to point out the irony of this now deeply religious man setting up in Sin City. As if to answer them, on the first night Prince opened with a post-Jehovah's Witness version of his *Controversy* song 'Sexuality', now rewritten as 'Spirituality', and later argued that the old spiritual song 'He's Got the Whole World in His Hands' is really about Satan. This was one of only a dozen times that Prince played 'Fury', a song that seems to have spooked him. As the run went on, the shows appeared to grow more varied, with more compelling after-shows, especially the night he played 'Wasted Kisses' at the show following his well-received Super Bowl performance, and one of the new songs that Prince introduced at Vegas, 'Somewhere Here on Earth', was excitedly seized upon by fans as evidence of a fresh burst of inspiration, although in truth it was no advance on the piano ballads on *One Nite Alone . . .*, and with its reference to paging lovers as on that record's 'U're Gonna C Me' and a title one word away from the same album's 'Here on Earth', it seemed almost like flagrant recycling (unsurprising in one so prolific, but another factor that made these records feel like diminishing returns).

The central question about the last handful of Prince releases to date – *Planet Earth, Lotusflow3r, MPLSound* and *20 Ten* – relates to his intent. We know from past interviews that for a long time Prince put an enormous amount of care into constructing an album. At first, he thought about writing hits and then constructed albums around these songs; and later, when this became restrictive, he started thinking about his full-length releases (as musicians with a desire to tell grander stories and operate on a wider canvas often do) as grand statements. But from *Musicology* onwards, his main focus seems to have been on how to come up with innovative ways of getting his albums to as many listeners as he did before the collapse of the record industry. From a business perspective, giving away *Planet Earth* in the UK with the *Mail on Sunday* (it got a conventional release in the US) was a wonderful way to generate publicity, just like the name change a decade before.

But what I find hard to discern is whether he values his new songs as much as he did his previous recordings. Wendy Melvoin, who (with Lisa) contributed to two songs on *Planet Earth* – 'The One U Wanna C' (a pleasingly early-1980s retro song with playful lyrics that seem to owe a little to The Cars, whose 'Let's Go' Prince now plays in concert) and 'Resolution' – thinks that Prince doesn't care about recording any more, concentrating instead on the deal. And *Planet Earth* is a collection of mainly good songs that somehow don't quite cohere into a good album, suggesting that it was assembled without Prince's usual close attention. The title song, though pretty and musically a close cousin of 'Empty Room' – so much so it was easy to confuse them at the London O2 shows – has a lyric consisting of dull environmentalism, while the album's single, 'Guitar', is the *reductio ad absurdum* of Prince's music.[1]

The UK playback for *Planet Earth* was much the same as that for *3121*. It took place at the O2 rather than in a club in Mayfair's Air Street, but the same thing happened: a representative came out and told the assembled rock critics that this was the best Prince album since the 1980s and that we'd all be knocked out when we heard the return to form. They played the record a couple of times, and though people weren't knocked out, they enjoyed it and went home and generally wrote respectful reviews.² But I do think that ultimately Prince's heart wasn't in *Planet Earth* in the same way. Without a record company on his back, he seemed to toy with the idea of promoting the record properly, but soon gave up on doing anything substantial. He did shoot videos for two of the songs during his time in London, flying to Prague midway through the shows (as recorded in the *21 Nights* book) to record a video for 'Somewhere Here on Earth', and basing the video for 'Chelsea Rodgers' – the album's only standout song, more for Sheila E on percussion than the sexist lyrics – around his performance at London Fashion Week. The former is as desolate, sad and lonely as you would imagine from the circumstances in which it was shot.³ 'Future Baby Mama' is an astonishingly ungallant smooth-jazz song in which Prince says that all his past lovers looked alike because he was searching for a platonic ideal he briefly thinks he's found in a new partner. 'All the Midnights in the World' is another angry love song, populated this time not by sticky spiders but 'prickly fingered scallywags'. There's a link between 'Mr. Goodnight' and *MPLSound*'s '(There'll Never B) Another Like Me', with the same lyric repeated in both songs, but whereas such connections had previously hinted at a hidden world behind the released records, here it seemed to suggest merely that Prince wasn't keeping track of what he was releasing. The song is funny, though, with Prince revealing that his dating technique involves private planes, a little Spanish man, the Johnny Depp film *Chocolat* and, bafflingly, a mouth full of chocolate-covered raisins, which presumably he's using more imaginatively than the toddlers who usually consume such treats. 'Lion of Judah' features Prince wondering if he's passed his expiration date and issuing threats, while the other Wendy and Lisa collaboration, 'Resolution', ends a somewhat bitter and angry album by wondering why people don't want peace. (Well, maybe it's because there's too many people out there following Prince's example in 'Lion of Judah' and striking their enemies down and believing they have a theological right to do so?)

But in the US, where the album received a full release from Sony, the reviews were warm. This may have been because magazine editors seemed to have reached the point where they simply handed the record over to long-time supporters and true believers, like Alan Light of *Spin*, who suggested that it was no longer useful to compare new Prince records to past ones, but that the album still deserved four and a half stars when compared to everything else out there. As an example of a major artist challenging the means of distribution, *Planet Earth* is important; as a Prince album, it's negligible. But that doesn't matter. With *Musicology*, Prince had used his live audiences to get his album into the charts; now, he was reversing the trick, using a free(ish) album – it was given away at the 21 Nights shows as well as with the paper – to get audiences back into his shows. And it worked.

21 NIGHTS IN LONDON: A FAN'S NOTES

Hearing that Prince was going to play twenty-one nights at a venue a short distance from my house presented an irresistible opportunity to get a deeper understanding of Prince's abilities as a live musician. Normally, the only way to see an artist for that many shows is to follow them across the US or round Europe on tour; the fact that this was happening a short taxi ride from my home meant that even after-shows that ended at 4.30 a.m. would be easy to get back from. It also helped that Prince was pitching this as a stint that everyone would get more from if they attended multiple shows, suggesting he wouldn't be playing the same stadium set every night, even if it was unlikely to be as varied as the most dedicated fans might desire. I hadn't gone to Nevada to watch the Las Vegas residency, but I had felt a pang every time I read a report of a new song. Here was the opportunity to make up for it.

I went to nineteen of the main shows, deeply regretting missing the two I couldn't attend, and thirteen of the fourteen after-shows. I also attended the preview show Prince played the day the run was announced, at the smaller Koko club in Camden, north London. This sold out in five minutes, and was the first time I'd seen Prince live since the performance at his house in 2006. In the meantime, he'd done the dispiriting run in Las Vegas, and the excitement of seeing a small club show was tempered by anxiety that this might be where I finally fell out of love with Prince's music.

The last time I'd seen Prince play in London was the four-song set at the Brit Awards, but the last time he'd played a full set to a British audience was the *One Nite Alone . . .* tour in 2002. So much had happened to his career and reputation in the meantime, but most of it had taken place in the US. London had missed out on the audience-pleasing *Musicology* tour and the year he'd spent pretending he just wanted to be a session musician playing guitar in Támar's band. Did the fact that he was coming straight from his Las Vegas residency mean he would just be exporting this greatest-hits show, or did the length of the run suggest a return to his old ambition?

When Prince first came out on stage, the show could have followed straight on from the Jehovah jazz of the last British performance five years earlier, going directly into The JBs' jazz-funk song 'Pass the Peas', a cover he'd been doing live since 2002. The rest of the show was essentially a preview of tracks that would become very familiar over the twenty-one-night stand, the main surprise this night being two covers of recent hits – Amy Winehouse's 'Love Is a Losing Game' and Gnarls Barkley's 'Crazy'. But the Koko performance was most memorable for the moment when an overexcited female audience member tried to hump Prince and was hauled offstage.

Between the Koko show and the 21 Nights run, Prince returned to the US for a brief series of shows – inviting Wendy Melvoin to play with him at the Roosevelt Hotel and playing three shows on his birthday in Minneapolis – before returning to attempt to make good on his onstage promise at Koko that this series of shows would be his best yet. The length of the London run had ensured maximum hype, both for Prince and the relatively new O2 arena. The Koko show had reminded critics of the quality of Prince's live performances, and the *Planet Earth* newspaper giveaway had boosted his media profile in the UK to its highest point in years. Although Prince remained reluctant to give interviews, most music magazines and newspapers ran profiles or reassessments of his 'lost' years, the critical consensus being that he'd begun his return to prominence with the *Musicology* album. Promoters AEG staggered the release of tickets and ensured maximum coverage at every stage, while Prince's publicity department claimed once again that this would be the last time he'd play the hits, although this, of course, was something he'd later deny.

It had been announced that Prince had rehearsed a hundred and fifty songs and would be mixing up the set every night, an encouragement for long-term fans who might have been disappointed that the tour was neither going to introduce a large amount of new material (as with 1995's The Ultimate Live Experience tour) nor include a radical reinterpretation of his back catalogue (like the *Lovesexy* or *One Nite Alone . . .* tours) to buy tickets for several shows. As long as Prince's interpretation of 'hits' was loose enough to include beloved album tracks, it boded well. And this time he got in an announcement about his possible imminent retirement, amusing the pre-show press conference by telling people he'd be off to travel and study the Bible as soon as the shows were done.

Wednesday 1 August 2007
It wasn't the first time Prince had opened with 'Purple Rain' (indeed, he'd done so at the Target Center in Minneapolis a few weeks earlier), but it still seemed a clear statement of intent. British tabloid the *Sun* reported that Prince changed the entire set hours before going onstage after the original running order was leaked, a claim supported by the appearance of an alternative set list on Internet fan sites the day of the show. Whether this was true, there was undoubtedly something schizophrenic about this first night, a seeming tension between Prince's desire to impress

the critics and the show he really wanted to do. Among Prince's many onstage comments – he was chatty this first evening, the ad libs still fresh, joking about how he had more hits than Madonna had kids – the one that seemed most pertinent was that he was in a slow-jam mood, the ballads – 'Satisfied', 'Shhh', 'Somewhere Here on Earth', 'Pink Cashmere' (which he combined with the lyrics of the more recent song 'The One U Wanna C') and 'Planet Earth', none of them strictly speaking hits – easily the best part of the show.

Later, it would be possible to look back and see how this performance shared the basic structure of the concerts that immediately followed: how the show was divided into two parts by an instrumental cover of 'What a Wonderful World', played by Mike Philips and Renato Neto, or the way that just before this break there would be a two- or three-song jam session – this night including 'Musicology', 'Controversy' and 'I Feel for You' – where Prince would invite audience members to dance on stage in his traditional manner, but at the time there was simply too much new information to take in. Prince's new symbol stage[1] – 'I just got it, it's sexy, right?' The way he turned this stage into a playground that the whole band could roam around. Prince's shows always have incredible constant motion, and while any performance in the round would always struggle to match the *Lovesexy* tour, this current version of the NPG had a whole troop of people traversing the symbol. Although the core of Prince's band (Renato Neto, Josh and Cora Dunham, Morris Hayes) stayed in the centre of the symbol, the dancers and horn players were always moving, at least on this first night, making sure that every side of the audience had someone to watch. Támar had long since gone from the band, but Marva King, Shelby J and The Twinz were this show's cheerleaders. And when he left the stage after the second encore, many in the audience (including me) assumed it was the end and went to find their cars or queue for the after-show. But after the house lights had been up for several minutes, Prince returned again for a third encore – 'Little Red Corvette', 'Raspberry Beret' and 'Sometimes It Snows in April' – before concluding with Sheila E's 'A Love Bizarre' and Chic's 'Le Freak'.

Thursday 2 August (a.m. after-show)
No one knew yet what to expect from the after-shows. Prince's *3121* website posted a message that encouraged fans to take a risk on the twenty-five-pound entry, without making any explicit promises. It seemed unlikely that Prince would play every night, but did that mean a live show from Prince's band, a Prince-sanctioned guest, or DJ Rashida doing a Prince disco? Two hours after the end of the main show, the curtains in the Indigo opened to reveal Prince's band, jamming on A Tribe Called Quest's 'Can I Kick It?' After introducing everyone and playing another jam, they were joined by Maceo Parker and Candy Dulfer, who, according to her website, had been told by Prince that there wasn't room for her in the main show after getting her to come to London. With Candy in the band, the sound was closer to the *One Nite Alone . . .* tour, and it seemed as if these shows might be perfectly balanced (a more mainstream, but still horn-driven hits show, followed by a loose jazz-driven after-show). All that was missing was Prince.

And here I can't avoid a moment of hagiography.

If I had to define what makes Prince the perfect pop star, what puts him above David Bowie and Madonna or any of his lesser rivals, it's the fact that his desire to impress, his showboating, show-off sense of style, never stops. Just as his fans were beginning to flag, just as everyone (most of whom had now been here for seven hours) was reaching their physical limitation, our hero strolled out in a strawberry-coloured suit and matching boots and launched into a guitar solo more exciting than anything else he'd played all evening.

This first after-show included songs by Maceo ('Shake Everything You've Got'), The JBs (the now-familiar 'Pass the Peas'), Prince himself ('Anotherloverholenyohead' and the new horn-driven version of '3121' that he played at the Montreux after-show), The B-52s ('Rock Lobster'), two jazz standards familiar to fans with access to past show recordings (Billy Cobham's 'Stratus' and Wayne Shorter's 'Footprints') and a long jazz song by Cora, Prince's drummer. By this point, even the most critical fan had no choice but to submit.

Friday 3 August
The first show had received rave reviews from every newspaper. Simon Price claimed in the *Independent on Sunday* that it was 'the single greatest concert' he'd been to in his life. OK, this is a man with a ♀ tattoo, and until this point, as he explained later in the review, his previous favourite concert was a date at Wembley on Prince's 1988 *Lovesexy* tour, but still, that a commentator who has followed Prince throughout his career should be so impressed indicates the high quality of the opening show. Concluding the review, Price echoed comments regularly made about Bob Dylan, suggesting that anyone present at the concert should feel lucky to be alive at the same time as Prince.

But this tour wasn't about one night. If Prince was going to get through a twenty-one-night stint without fans getting restless, he needed to prove his claim that he would be making each show individual. And on Friday, it seemed as if this might have been mere hype. I had good seats, close enough not just to see that Prince's preferred form of transport to the stage is still an upright black equipment box, but to catch a glimpse of his eyes through the ventilation hole, but I couldn't help feeling disappointed. The first half of the show was a cut-down version of Wednesday night, and the only extra song in the first half of the set was a cover of Wild Cherry's 'Play that Funky Music', extending the jam section and giving the audience more time to dance on stage, but hardly raising the quality of the show.

Then, after the 'What a Wonderful World' interlude, a moment of magic: 'Joy in Repetition'. Not a particular rarity, but a fan favourite: the highlight of an otherwise lacklustre show. Like many of Prince's songs, it's a track that's undergone reinvention over the years, but tonight it was delivered with quiet authority, a moment of truth in an otherwise over-rehearsed set.

As the box containing Prince was wheeled out for a final time, there was a scuffle in the audience as someone tried to go to the gents at the wrong moment. The audience booed but refused to leave, having heard about Wednesday's extra encore and wanting more. But that was it. The sense of disappointment was compounded at the Indigo club, when the curtains opened to reveal not Prince, but Dr John, who'd being playing a set there earlier that evening and had presumably been asked to do another show in place of Prince.

[There were rumours that Cora, the drummer, had been ill. But what was Prince doing while we were waiting for him to come on stage? Well, if you consult *21 Nights*, the photo book Prince put out to commemorate the run, and look at 'Night 2', we see that by 12.21 a.m. Prince was back at the Dorchester Hotel, where he posed for some photos as he climbed out of his car and got into a lift.]

Saturday 4 August
Prince's first night with a support act (Nikki Costa). The show was the shortest yet, but length was irrelevant: tonight was the

best show of the run so far. Everything extraneous had been cut –
there was now room for only one ballad in the first half – and it
had become apparent what these shows were really about: pleas-
ing the audience. It was clear that this was a hits show he could
deliver without feeling bored or being cynical. Maybe there was
also a pleasure in the acceptance he was finding from the British
media, who were revising their opinion of him. Ben Thompson,
the *Sunday Telegraph*'s music critic, was so moved by the show he
was prepared to forgive Prince for everything:

> The melodramatic feuding with his record company, the end-
> less name-changes, the systematic devaluation of his own criti-
> cal currency via a series of ridiculously boring albums: these
> were not, it now transpires, the death-throes of a once-great
> talent. They were actually a kind of diversionary excrescence
> – like Linus's dust-cloud in *Peanuts*, or the flesh of an oyster
> within which a pearl might be discovered – buying this erst-
> while 1980s leftover the time to reconfigure himself for the
> new century in a more Princely fashion than ever before.[2]

Sunday 5 August (a.m. after-show)
Not that the perversity wasn't still there, of course. It was just
the diehard fans he wanted to suffer. The good news was that he
showed up for the after-show; the bad news was that he played
less than ten minutes, appearing briefly in the middle of Nikki
Costa's otherwise dull set before returning to the hotel to pose
sitting on his bed holding the telephone.

Tuesday 7 August
And then, just as Prince's shows were falling into a predictable
pattern, he mixes things up. The first sign that tonight was going
to be different was a new intro video, a short recording of a
recent show from Houston. The clip showed the band playing

'D.M.S.R.', but felt like a risky opening as the footage looked more interesting than anything we'd seen at the O2. Maybe it was the absence of backing singer Shelby J that prompted Prince to make changes to the set, or simply that he was getting bored, but on Tuesday night he made two changes that lifted the whole night. Prince's first change was an alteration in the show's order, opening with the acoustic section he'd previously used for a third encore. As well as the three songs he'd played then ('Little Red Corvette', 'Raspberry Beret' and 'Sometimes It Snows in April'), he played two songs for the first time, 'Alphabet St.' and 'I Could Never Take the Place of Your Man'. As good as this opening was, the true highlight of the night was a piano medley that started the second half (after the now-familiar 'What a Wonderful World' interlude), as Prince played snatches of *Planet Earth*'s 'Somewhere Here on Earth', then 'Diamonds and Pearls', 'The Beautiful Ones', 'How Come You Don't Call Me Any More?', 'Condition of the Heart', 'Do Me, Baby' and 'I Wanna Be Your Lover'. Although the truncated songs frustrate fans, these piano medleys have been the highlight of many of Prince's best tours, and while it wasn't yet clear whether it was a one-off bonus to compensate for the absence of Shelby J or proof that the set would develop in intriguing ways, it was a necessary reminder that no matter how choreographed the main show was starting to seem, just by stepping behind a keyboard Prince could change the entire mood of an evening.

Not everyone was impressed. The *Telegraph*, which was sending someone different to review each night of the run, had given British pop singer Sophie Ellis-Bextor the task of critiquing this evening's show. Ellis-Bextor complained: 'When I go to gigs I want to hear the hits, the songs I know, so on that level I thought it was disappointing. He plays lots of songs you don't know, and even worse he does these little medleys where he sits at the piano for twenty minutes and plays a few bars of a hit before switching to another.' These comments were placed on all the Prince fan sites, provoking a predictable response. The *Mail on Sunday* picked up on the story, describing how fans had responded to Ellis-Bextor's complaint about the lack of hits by pointing out that he'd played 'Little Red Corvette', 'Raspberry Beret', 'Alphabet St.', 'Cream', 'U Got the Look', 'I Feel for You' and 'Controversy'. Ellis-Bextor held firm. 'He just did bits of songs and a couple of hits, then all the jamming stuff.'

Wednesday 8 August (a.m. after-show)

Prince's support at the main show this night had been Grupo Fantasmo, an eleven-piece Latin band from Austin, Texas, who'd established a relationship with Prince over the previous year, playing a number of gigs with him (including the Alma awards and a Golden Globes after-party), as well as having a residency at the 3121 club at the Rio in Vegas. Prince had brought the band back onstage to join him in the final encore of the main show, 'Get on the Boat', so it seemed likely he'd jam with them at the after-show. The question was how long would he stay.

As with every after-show performance so far, Prince waited a few songs before joining the band. When he came on with Grupo Fantasmo, he performed with the same loose energy he had at the first after-show, his composed attire (white suit, red shirt and Versace sunglasses) at odds with his manic mood. He stayed for the full performance tonight, covering Stevie Wonder ('Superstition', 'Tell Me Something Good', 'Higher Ground'), Billy Cobham ('Stratus'), Sly and the Family Stone ('Thank You (Falettinme Be Mice Elf Agin)'), and for any fan disappointed at the lack of rarities in the main set, a long instrumental version of 'I Like It There' from *Chaos and Disorder*.

Friday 10 August

On almost every night of the run so far, Prince had followed Cora's drum solo at the end of 'Shhh' by quipping, 'Not bad for a girl,' a quip he'd been making back since Sheila E was in the band. Tonight Prince made her the focus of attention. Almost all of his onstage comments ('Give the drummer some,' etc.) seemed directed at her, and he kept catching her attention throughout the show, as he seemed to give her challenges that she invariably met.

The show began with a song they'd yet to play on the main stage ('3121'), went straight into 'Girls & Boys', and then Prince abruptly changed moods with his cover of 'Down by the Riverside' and lost the audience. Even following this with 'Purple Rain' didn't entirely get them back, and the only other innovation in the set was replacing 'What a Wonderful World' with an instrumental version of 'The Dance'. It was starting to seem that the Friday-night shows were the ones to miss.

Saturday 11 August (a.m. after-show)

The 'xpect the unexpected' message from the *3121* message board was now posted outside the Indigo, so I suppose I only have myself to blame for what follows, but it did say 'unexpected', not downright perverse. On the afternoon before Friday's after-show, there was a message on the official *3121* website, stating that he would not be at Friday's after-party, but would likely be at Saturday's.

Standing in the long queue waiting for the after-show, I heard people all around me excitedly talking about the songs Prince might play that night. I considered telling them about the message on the website, but didn't want to be responsible for spoiling their evening. It was clear that many people had decided not to come, and the club was half as full as it had been on previous evenings. Still, 'xpect the unexpected', right? On the other nights when Prince had appeared, his guitar tech had set up his guitar on the left-hand side of the stage, and there it was again tonight.

Around 1 a.m., Beverley Knight took the stage. She was vocal in her praise of him during the first forty-five minutes of her after-show performance. But when Prince's guitar tech came out and took his guitar away, I assumed the message on the website was true and he wouldn't be joining Knight tonight. Even if he did show, I told myself, he'd probably only play one solo and leave, as he'd done at the Nikki Costa show. So I left.

The moment I got on the Thames Clipper, the boat service that operated until 4.30 a.m. on after-show nights, I knew I'd made a mistake. Normally there were at least thirty people on the boat; tonight there were only two American women. Everyone else had stayed in the Indigo to witness Prince, Beverley Knight and the NPG playing a two-hour after-show including covers like the Stones' 'Miss You' and Blackstreet's 'No Diggity', along-side 'Controversy', '3121', 'A Love Bizarre' and 'Alphabet St.'.

Saturday 11 August
The best thing about this twenty-one-night stand was that there was no time to get upset about missing Prince's after-show the night before, because as soon as I got up it was just a few hours before I could see him again. Of course, the whole reason for going to so many shows was because of the fear that I might miss the one time he played a favourite song, or did an interpretation of a track that gave away some secret about its composition (and I mean a real secret, not the pretend confession Prince made every time he played 'Cream' on the main stage that he wrote the song while looking in the mirror). I felt bad that I'd failed as a Prince fan (and the worst thing was, failed by believing his website), but I'd shored up enough previous unique Prince experiences to cope

with missing this one show.³ But it didn't mean that I wasn't praying he'd turn up at tonight's after-show.

First, though, there was the main show to get through. The worst thing about the Prince experience is that the constant possibility of a more exciting after-show meant it was easy to take the main performance for granted. He opened with 'Purple Rain' again, and although it was probably the best show in the run so far (I realise I keep writing this, but he was getting better and better), it was a reshuffled version of most of the previous shows, opening with 'Purple Rain', with the funk section of 'Musicology', 'Pass the Peas' and 'Play that Funky Music (I was heartily sick of being asked to chant 'Hey, funky London' throughout these songs), and it wasn't until the synth encore that the show came alive for me. In a manner that no doubt would have enraged Sophie Ellis-Bextor, Prince had pre-sets for several of his most beloved songs ('Alphabet St.', 'D.M.S.R.', 'When Doves Cry', 'Erotic City', 'I Wanna Be Your Lover', 'Nasty Girl', 'Sign o' the Times' and 'Pop Life'), and played a few moments of each before stopping, enraging the crowd (he seemed to love the boos more than the cheers) but also pointing out once again just how one show could never truly represent the true breadth of his back catalogue.

The Indigo's bouncers came down the line for the after-show, telling everyone that Prince wouldn't be performing tonight. The crowd turned angry, with drunken women fighting the bouncers and being dragged away. After the website message, I thought this might just be an even bigger bluff, a way of ensuring that no one apart from the most ardent believers were in the front row. But as soon as we were inside and I saw the DJ set up in front of the stage curtains, it was obvious that the website message was totally wrong. Prince had tricked us again.

Tuesday 14 August

Although it felt perverse, part of me didn't want a good show tonight. I could cope with missing the next two shows after this if they were going to be the same basic set as the five I'd already seen; if he was about to change the set drastically it would be much more of a sacrifice. But once again, it was the best show so far. It had started to occur to me that maybe each show (aside from the ones that had obvious flaws) just seemed better than the ones before because there was still that fresh excitement of seeing Prince every time. And, of course, I'd now seen the show so many times that what made a good show for me was probably the opposite of what a first-timer would want from the concert. The main reason this show seemed so good was that he'd broken up the structure. A few nights earlier, the jam section where the audience dance on stage was my favourite part of the show; now, I was delighted that had gone. 'Musicology' was now the second song, and 'Controversy' had been moved towards the end of the show. Two *Planet Earth* songs ('Guitar' and 'Somewhere Here on Earth') had crept back into the set, and he played 'Forever in My Life' for the first time on the tour. But it was what was not there that made the show so different: no 'What a Wonderful World' interlude to slow things down. Without this, the show took on a new life.

Wednesday 15 August (a.m. after-show)

The Indigo bartenders had started taking bets on which nights Prince would appear. 'You guys all get so upset when he doesn't show up,' one woman said, explaining why she didn't like working the shift, 'but I think he'll play tonight.' In fact, the British fans had got so upset that the twenty-five pounds you paid for an after-show was really like buying a lottery ticket that their grievances had started to reach the national press and the BBC consumer-complaints programme *Watchdog*. But the fan sites also thought he'd show tonight, citing the importance of the number seven in Prince's numerology [it was the seventh show] and the fact that Beverley Knight was supporting again. I was sceptical, wondering if he'd find it too predictable to repeat the same experience that he'd had on Friday. Beverley was teasing the audience, referring to the previous after-show and singing 'Raspberry Beret', but giving no specific indication that he might come on. But there was no way I was leaving early tonight.

Knight kept referring to the fact that they were 'making history', a claim that seemed unnecessarily exaggerated.

Until Prince came on and played 'Empty Room'.

Prince is completely aware of the difference between his casual and hard-core fans. Sometimes it seems as if he wants to punish both groups equally. But when he decides to please them, he knows exactly how to do it. He understands that the majority of the audience who go to the main show are desperate to hear him play 'Purple Rain', and he knows that while the after-show crowd would probably prefer never to hear him play that again, a well-chosen rarity like 'Empty Room' can create exactly the same excitement in the hard core. He later admitted as much to the *Vancouver Sun*, anatomising his hard-core fans with unnerving accuracy: 'A smaller crowd of old school heads like to hear unreleased jams because they already own a lot of stuff on bootleg.'[4]

If I had to resort to hagiography to describe my feelings during the first night's after-show, then it's almost impossible to explain how hearing this version of this song on this night made me feel without sounding like a lunatic with no sense of proportion. It is, after all, just a man playing a song in front of a couple of thousand people. Followers of Bob Dylan might understand how it feels when you hear the perfect version of a song in the right context at the right time, but with Prince it's even more complicated. Aside from the fact that this was the best single performance of the tour so far, there was the generosity of the moment, the reminder that even beyond the albums, the B-sides, the hits for other artists, there are hundreds of further jewels; songs that have never quite reached the mass public. And the excitement of hearing this song was intensified by hearing Prince perform a Hendrix-style guitar solo that made it truly unique, one of the first times on this tour where, as far as such a thing is possible, he had nailed a definitive version of a track for ever.

Making history, indeed.

The rest of the two-hour after-show (which lasted longer than the main show) was completely different to Friday's. On Friday, he had covered several Stevie Wonder songs; now, he played two James Brown songs ('I Can't Stand It' and 'Cold Sweat'), as well as 'What Is Hip?', the Tower of Power song he loves so much. When he played at Koko, Prince had offered 'mad props' to Amy Winehouse and later told newspapers he wanted her to perform with him on the tour. But as Winehouse had recently taken an overdose of heroin, ketamine and ecstasy, it had seemed likely that clean-living Prince would have revised this idea.[5] If so, he was still in love with her music, letting Shelby J cover 'Love Is a Losing Game' once more. He showed off his influences again as he covered B. B. King, The Staple Singers, Sly and the Family Stone, Aretha Franklin and Mary J. Blige. The now regular Billy Cobham song 'Stratus' was still in the set, and among the half-dozen of his own songs we got 'Partyman', in the version he'd played when he was backing Támar, and even a brief snatch of 'Head', Prince's smile revealing that even if he had foresworn his most sexually explicit material for religious reasons, he still knew exactly how much people liked it, and that one day it might even reappear again.

Friday 17 August

The first of the two main shows I missed. It would have been easy for me to go – by this stage tickets were easy to get – but I'd been invited to read at the Green Man festival. As much as it pained me to miss these shows, I'd thought that at this stage in the run a short break might do me good. It seemed that going away to watch a different sort of music, albeit played by musicians – like Bill Callahan – who were themselves mostly Prince fans, would give me perspective when I returned to the O2. It was also good to be on a stage rather than watching one for a couple of nights – albeit only in the literary tent – and to remind myself that as good as being a spectator can be, particularly when you're watching Prince, performing is equally important.

Still, this didn't stop me from sitting with my wife's Blackberry in the middle of the night, trying to work out whether the main show might have been good from the set list posted on fan sites, and desperately hoping I hadn't missed out on a spectacular after-show. Fortunately, it seemed the set list was much the same as usual, and the only real event of the night was that the audience member pulled up to sing 'Play that Funky Music' wasn't the usual anonymous punter but the Hollywood actress Julia Stiles. [As a historical document, *21 Nights* also fails me here, as according to this book, the big events of 'Night 8' were a maid making Prince's bed and Prince posing with a guitar in what looks like a deserted stadium.]

Saturday 18 August

By now I was sitting with the Blackberry looking as each song was added to the set list, and was delighted to see that this was the shortest show to date – just eighty-five minutes, and nothing he hadn't played already. But then I started to worry: did a short main show mean he was saving his strength for a marathon after-show?

Sunday 19 August (a.m. after-show)
How can one tell the quality of an after-show one doesn't get to attend? The message boards are useless: according to those present, the best thing about this night's show was that Prince was wearing a funny hat, and the set list never tells the complete story. Throughout this time Prince was employing someone to write gushing '3121 spy' reports about his live performances ('The NPG were kickin' it,' etc.) that were equally useless. I gleaned that it was a short show, full of covers (Rufus, Stevie Wonder, Cobham's 'Stratus', Bill Withers, Sly, etc., two songs from Shelby) and light on Prince numbers.

Looking at the run in search of a narrative, the most significant inclusion this night was 'The Rules'. Playing it in connection with 'Satisfied', it was the beginning of Prince introducing a new dimension to his performance: stand-up comedy. This comic song about the differences between women and 'brothers', first introduced on the *Musicology* tour and never recorded, would crop up in his main show, and would soon be followed by an increasing number of comic monologues.

Friday 24 August
During Prince's week off from the O2, The Rolling Stones had played two gigs at the venue, and as he opened Friday's show, this was clearly on his mind. Prince has a long history with the Stones – from his ill-fated support of them at the LA Coliseum in October 1981 to his performance with Ronnie Wood at the Camden Palace after-show on the *Lovesexy* tour in July 1988. More recently, Wood's daughter had claimed that Prince had asked her father to appear with him at the Koko show – and he

was clearly enjoying reclaiming the stage from them at the start of this evening's show. 'Someone's been sleeping in my bed . . .' he growled, Goldilocks style, as he prowled the symbol stage, working three snippets of Stones songs ('Honky Tonk Women', 'Brown Sugar' and 'Miss You') into the set. After 'Miss You' he concluded 'Satisfied' with the 'Rules' song he'd played at the previous Saturday's after-show, beginning his list of instructions with the taunt, 'The Rolling Stones may have let you do what you want, but you're in my house now, and there are rules.'

The Chicago-based rapper Common had supported, and Prince got him up on stage to sing 'Play that Funky Music'. He proved as hopeless at the song as the dancers Prince usually hauled from the audience, but he made up for it with an anglophile rap ('I just saw a movie called *The Queen*,' etc.) that became increasingly absurd as it went on.

Saturday 25 August (a.m. after-show)
It had become clear that the best sign that we'd be getting a worthwhile after-show was when Prince was supported by either someone he liked or wanted to impress. With Common in the house, it seemed inevitable that Prince would show up, and he was out much sooner than usual, a few minutes after one, playing guitar while Common rapped several tracks. But the highlight for me was when Prince shouted at the poor bartender to jump up and down to 'Housequake'.

Saturday 25 August
Earlier, I was worried that I would conclude every account by saying it was the best night of the tour; now, my concern was that every subsequent night would be the worst night. There was a sharp decline in quality on this evening, not just from the night before but from the rest of the tour. Friday night's show

had dipped after the opening few songs; this show nose-dived straight after the opener, 'Planet Earth', played for the first time this tour, delivered as if it was as important to the audience as 'Purple Rain'.

The Rolling Stones were clearly still on his mind, as we got a fuller version of 'Honky Tonk Women', but he also played a truly horrible easy-listening version of 'The Long and Winding Road' that was even more saccharine than Phil Spector's treatment. The solo piano section seemed to have lost all its energy and it was clear that tonight Prince was going through the motions.

It was no surprise that tonight's after-show was the NPG only.

Tuesday 28 August

The least interesting show so far. The second half had both the piano and the synth set, plus the 'Lolita', 'Black Sweat', 'Kiss' segment that was still a low point, in spite of The Twinz's choreography. The encores were familiar too: 'I Feel 4 U', 'Controversy' and 'Nothing Compares 2 U'. He'd even brought back 'What a Wonderful World'. I was beginning to worry about how I'd get through the rest of the run.

Wednesday 29 August (a.m. after-show)

And then, two and a half hours later, Prince is transformed. What elevated this show above most after-shows (and the ones that had impressed me earlier in the run, before I properly realised exactly what he was still capable of) was the concentration and focus of the performance. Music fans often talk about Prince after-shows as if they're always legendary, but that isn't true. At their worst, they're a formless jam of cover versions, chanting and cameo appearances from far less talented guests. Even the best after-shows, no matter how great they seem at the time to the audience who witnessed them, often suffer if you hear a recording, as it's not always that interesting to listen to unfocused noodling. It's usually a bad sign, for example, if the band is having too much fun.

For this after-show, Prince had stripped the band down to a three-piece, a new variation on The New Power Trio, accompanied only by Josh and Cora Dunham, and concentrated on the blues-influenced, almost heavy-metal side of his oeuvre. This was what fans had hoped for from multiple after-shows: that instead of repeating a similar set each night, he would use the opportunity to display different sides of his work, or as tonight, to remind us of the highlights of long-forgotten albums like *Chaos and Disorder*.

Prince used his *3121* website to tease the fans, with his scribe writing that he had upset local residents by playing a CD recording of the show in his car stereo while taking photographs [either these photos didn't end up in the *21 Nights* book, or were moved to another night, as Prince posed in his car on the second, fifteenth and twentieth nights, but not the twelfth].

Friday 31 August

I enjoyed this show, mainly because it was the least crowd-pleasing of the run, beginning with a minor hit ('Musicology'), followed by an unreleased song ('Prince and the Band') and three covers (one new to the set – INXS's 'What You Need' – the other two now very familiar – Wild Cherry's 'Play that Funky Music' and The JBs' 'Pass the Peas'), so that it wasn't until six songs in that we got a bona fide Prince hit ('Cream'). In the piano set, Prince roamed way into the back catalogue for the unreleased 'A 1,000 Hugs and Kisses', which Prince's *3121* website described as a new song, but was originally recorded in 1992. Shorn of the overelaborate instrumentation of the out-take version, it seemed a strange choice for the main show, but I would have paid the entrance fee just to hear this song alone.

Saturday 1 September

Towards the end of a first half stuffed mainly with now-overfamiliar songs and enlivened only by a funny performance of 'The Rules', Prince followed the usual 'Cream' and 'U Got the Look' double bill with a medley of the intro of 'A Question of U', 'The One' and Alicia Keys's 'Fallin''. 'The One' section of the medley was the longest, almost the whole song, and this stand-out track from the underrated *New Power Soul* has always inspired some of Prince's best live performances. The nearly two-hour show had most of the high points from previous performances, including the two solo-synth and keyboard sets, and something else new: 'Strange Relationship' for the first time. OK, it was only one verse, but it made the evening.

Sunday 2 September (a.m. after-show)

After Wednesday's after-show, it was inevitable that this next one would seem slightly disappointing, but it was probably the most representative sample of everything Prince does at an after-show performance, with covers of songs by The Cars, the Stones, Janet Jackson, Graham Central Station, INXS, Billy Cobham, Amy Winehouse, Sly and the Family Stone and Beyoncé. I don't mind the covers – in fact, I enjoy Prince's version of 'Let's Go' more than almost anything else he plays – but it's the Prince rarities that make a show special, and there were few of these tonight, although Shelby J sang the Támar song 'Redheaded Stepchild' as a second encore, raising hopes that this excellent song may not yet be lost.

Thursday 6 September

Maceo Parker outta the band, off to Japan for his own tour, and much to the horror of his fans, Prince in trainers (the LA Gear kind that light up when you walk), but aside from that, showing no sign of flagging. In the middle of the show, Prince announced that he didn't think twenty-one shows was enough and that he should do fifty-two in London. I have to confess by this point I hoped he was joking.

Friday 7 September (a.m. after-show)
Tonight started out as a Shelby J show, with her taking vocals for the first eight songs. Only after a long cover of 'Stratus' did Prince take the microphone for the first four songs of *Planet Earth* (for one glorious moment it seemed like he might be playing the whole album in order). 'Alright, it's karaoke time,' he declared before 'When U Were Mine', 'Anotherloverholeinyohead', '3121' and 'Chelsea Rodgers'. It seemed Prince's latest album had been banished from the main show to the after-show. Maybe he thought it would get more appreciation there.

Sunday 9 September
It was time to mix things up. Prince livened up this show by starting off with a virtual reprise of his Super Bowl performance, a welcome burst of new energy. While there was something unsatisfying about the way he segues from 'All Along the Watchtower' to The Foo Fighters' 'Best of You' rather than having a real stab at a Hendrix-like version of Dylan's song, it does work as one of his many musical history lessons, showing us how one song leads to another in the same way he did when layering 'One Nation Under a Groove' over Gnarls Barkley's 'Crazy'. For the first time on the whole tour he dropped 'Cream' from the set, and 'Prince and the Band' was continuing to grow from a throwaway epilogue to 'Musicology' into one of the more entertaining songs in the set. *Planet Earth* song 'Somewhere Here on Earth' was back in the keyboard set, and he played 'Adore' for the first time this tour.

Monday 10 September (a.m. after-show)

At just under two and a half hours, this was the longest after-show of the run, and one of the best. This was Prince and his band at their most versatile (so versatile, in fact, that tonight's version of '3121' included 'The Entertainer', 'The Sailor's Hornpipe', and conjuring up horrible visions of what might be in Prince's DVD collection, the Benny Hill theme tune, 'Yakety Sax'), and oddly, ended with the same two songs with which he'd concluded the main show. The highlights of this show were a heavy 'All the Critics Love U in London', an extremely extended 'Joy in Repetition' which began with Prince wandering offstage and Renato looking nervously to the wings to see if they should continue playing and included an elaborate dance routine from one of The Twinz, and best of all, a bluesy improvisation based around 'Peach' in which Prince talked to us about his problems with the record industry, based on a conversation he'd had with 'a cat backstage'. He asked us if he should release 'The One U Wanna C' or 'Chelsea Rodgers' as a single, then joked that when people said he didn't sell records any more, he told them he never sold 'em in the first place, just made them.

Wednesday 12 September

Tonight I finally worked out what Prince meant when he said, 'You've got your twins, we've got ours,' during 'Kiss'. As he'd changed the 'You don't have to watch *Dynasty*' line to 'don't have to watch *Big Brother*', it seemed the rumours were true and he was a fan of the show and was referring to *BB*'s runners-up.[6] Although the order of the show was altered, this show was similar to Sunday's, with the Super Bowl segment shifted towards the end of the performance. The highlights of the show were three songs from *1999* in the piano set: 'Something in the Water (Does Not Compute)', 'Delirious' and 'Free'.

Thursday 13 September

Even up close, when tonight's special guest Elton John first got up, I mistook him for Ozzy Osbourne. His version of 'The Long and Winding Road' was horrible karaoke. After he'd gone, Prince added a snatch of 'Benny and the Jets' to his synth-set encore. He also teased with a sample of 'Darling Nikki', a song he no longer plays. I prayed John would go home before Prince got to the Indigo.

Friday 14 September (a.m. after-show)

Psychedelia night, a style of music he's only really explored in any depth on one album, *Around the World in a Day*. And it was the title song from this album that he opened with. Really using his rack of guitar pedals, and yelling at his sound man, Dollar Bill, to turn up the keyboards, he followed this with 'Beautiful Strange', Led Zeppelin's 'Whole Lotta Love' and an instrumental version of 'Paisley Park'. 'Partyup', from *Dirty Mind*, signalled the transition into a more conventional after-show, focusing on covers and ending with two songs he'd played in the main show, 'Musicology' and 'Prince and the Band' – in their best-ever live renditions – with Prince once again outlining his tax-evading land scam.

[After his song at the Indigo about which single to release from *Planet Earth*, we can see from *21 Nights* that Prince relaxed after this show by flying to Prague, where he shot a video for a different song altogether, 'Somewhere Here on Earth'.]

Sunday 16 September

Undoubtedly the most curious show of the run. The band played three songs before Prince even appeared, much to the bafflement of the audience, with Shelby J desperately trying to get the arena to respond to 'Chelsea Rodgers' and covers of 'Misty Blue' and 'Baby Love'. When Prince did appear for '1999', there was a sense that he was going through the motions this evening, with songs cut short or performed speedily. Maybe Prince was in a hurry to get to the Indigo.

Monday 17 September (a.m. after-show)
This was my least-favourite after-show, but it was certainly unique. More of a stand-up comedy night than a musical performance, it featured Prince improvising a song ('Just Like U')about how his life had changed since the days when he used to be able to go to the store to buy his mother tampons and cigarettes, and a very silly new song made out of old blues tracks that imagined a scenario where Prince was going out with a cock-eyed, three-handed woman. He also covered the Katie Melua song 'Nine Million Bicycles' and 'Somewhere Over the Rainbow' (why, Prince, why?). [Following the unwritten law that musicians never know which of their own shows to put out as live albums, half of this show is on the *Indigo Nights/Live Sessions* CD that accompanied the *21 Nights* book, which includes a track, 'Indigo Nights', consisting of band jamming and the chant 'London knows how to party.']

Thursday 20 September
For the first time, I started wondering if the main shows ever just seem like a job to Prince – if going out and chanting 'Hey, funky London' or 'Ladies and gentlemen, this is a trombone' ever grew old. But then he started playing 'Chelsea Rodgers', and I realised that by throwing in a new song he could always wake himself up. On a night like this, the only songs that work are the more recent ones, or the surprises, like a piano segment where he played 'When Will We B Paid?' and 'Money Don't Matter 2Nite', which admittedly was enough to make the whole night worthwhile. But it's still painful to hear 'If I Was Your Girlfriend' played as if he never cared about it, a cabaret parody of everything it used to

mean. And yet, if this was the only show you saw, you wouldn't feel short-changed. The performance was two hours long, the set list ranged freely over his career, and Prince was focused on giving the audience a good time from the moment he walked out. It just felt, tonight at least, a little bit like a grind.

Friday 21 September

Some shows are special largely because of the sense of occasion. A fully packed auditorium, TV in attendance (every show had been recorded by Prince's team, but the opening of the set tonight was being broadcast by Sky) and an audience who had taken it upon themselves to equip themselves with purple glow-sticks. Prince acknowledged the event almost as soon as he came on stage – 'Twenty-one nights, yeah' – but the main marker of the accomplishment came when The Twinz presented Prince with a jacket onto which had been spray-painted '21'. This show started out as Prince in celebration mode, playing familiar songs (he likes to play 'I Feel 4 U' and 'Controversy' when the cameras are present), before a brief move away from the now familiar set list for 'Somewhere Here on Earth'. After that, it was back to the hits, 'Pass the Peas' the only cover and 'Chelsea Rodgers' the only new song. But along with the opening night, it was the best of the run. We even got a brief snatch of one of his seemingly now-forbidden songs, 'Irresistible Bitch'.

Saturday 22 September (a.m. after-show)

[In writing this account of the 21 Nights shows I attended, I've missed out most of the personal details – the friends who accompanied me to the shows, the strangers I met in the queues – partly because this is primarily a critical study, but also because talk about all the beautiful people you met in the audience is strictly for the fan boards, but indulge me for a moment when I say that part of what made the last night so special was that everyone in London I knew who was regularly attending after-shows made it in for this last night, including my editor, Lee Brackstone, here celebrating his birthday. I had some friends who'd been lucky and almost always attended an after-show that Prince had actually played at; I had others who kept showing up for the wash-out nights when he didn't appear. And there was still a fear that he might yet leave us without a final after-show. But then Lee saw the sax and vocoder man Mike Philips come into the venue, strolled up and asked him if Prince was going to play that night. Mike laughed and showed him a brief glimpse of the marathon set list.]

The show started before the curtains opened, Renato stirring up suspense with his patented weird mix of new-age and sci-fi-sounding keyboards, and Prince letting us know he was there with a '1–2, 1–2' before going into the familiar 'Love Is a Losing Game'. The curtains opened, and there, at long last, as long promised, was the song's author, Amy Winehouse. Moved by the duet, Prince hammed it up. 'I got tears, I'm gonna have to put my shades on.' During a long version of 'Come Together', he bit the hand that feeds in his usual manner, making a dismissive remark about Sky News.

[You can hear some of the show on *Indigo Nights/Live Sessions*, including a long 'All the Critics Love U in London', which was a highlight. But most of the tracks he chose for the CD were the least interesting – the Beverley Knight duet instead of the one with Winehouse; two Shelby J covers – making it an unsatisfactory document of his final night. It was a long and unruly show, filled with crowd-pleasing covers of rock dinosaurs (The Beatles, The Rolling Stones, Led Zeppelin, Jimi Hendrix); not the best after-show, but a perfect way of saying goodbye to London.]

GIGOLOS GET LONELY TOO (PART 3)

As before, Prince's collaborations through the 1990s, 2000s and 2010s continued to fit into four categories: there were the protégés and side projects into which he put as much effort (sometimes, it seemed, even more) as he did his own work; the older artists he admired and whose careers he wanted to help relaunch (Chaka Khan, Larry Graham, etc.); the band members and associates he rewarded by collaborating with them and putting out their albums; and the occasional song he would give to established or up-and-coming bands who requested a track.

A handful of tracks he parcelled out to more established female singers, such as Mica Paris (to whom he gave the old Rebels song 'If I Love U 2Night'), who, rather like Beverley Knight, has continued to act as a cheerleader for Prince, fronting a well-received radio documentary about him in 2003; Paula Abdul (who got another Rebels song 'U'); Celine Dion (the suitably lachrymose 'With This Tear', which, admittedly, she delivered with such enthusiasm that it transcends its clichés); and Patti Labelle, whose 'I Hear Your Voice' exists in a demo version with Prince singing. Versions of Prince singing the songs he gave to rapper Louie Louie ('Get Blue') and Shalamar singer Howard Hewett ('Allegiance') are also in circulation.

The latter seems a surprising choice for Prince to have given away, as the language he uses in this song echoes how he writes about his past in the *Crystal Ball* sleeve notes, and though Hewett turns it into bland soul, the original version suggests that with a little more work, Prince could have transformed it into a much stronger track than most of the music he released under his own name in the early 1990s.

For El DeBarge (who had previously worked with Clare Fischer), Prince collaborated with Kirk Johnson – who would play an essential role in Prince's music in the late 1990s – on an undistinguished song called 'Tip o' My Tongue'. Prince and Johnson also wrote the similarly forgettable 'Qualified' for Nude tour support band Lois Lane (he also allowed them to re-record 'Sex'), but Joe Cocker got one of Prince's very best songs, 'Five Women', and though his version is nowhere near as good as Prince's own recording of the song, it's better than one might imagine, especially given that Prince had no involvement in the arrangement or playing: in a reversal of his usual approach, whether out of respect or lack of interest, he seems to have allowed Cocker to make the song his own.

His collaboration with Martika is more substantial, and seems evidence of a shared outlook. Already an established artist, it was *Graffiti Bridge* that drew her to Prince (there is a physical similarity between Martika and Ingrid Chavez, and it is easy to see how she could have imagined herself into a new Spirit Child role. The two collaborated on four songs for her second record. 'Martika's Kitchen', the album's title song, has dated, and though pleasant pop, has a troubling association for any feminist listener. 'Spirit' casts Prince as an angel, his presence clear from yet another lyric about playing cards, while 'Don't Say U Love Me' is about an unworthy man who steals Martika's credit card. But 'Love . . . Thy Will Be Done', a gospel song, is on a whole different level, with an entirely different sound and seriousness to the rest of the record: it became an important part of Prince's shows in 1995 and he was still performing it in 2012.

Although Prince's Paisley Park label would release two more records after Carmen Electra's[1] (Mavis Staples's *The Voice* and George Clinton's *Hey Man . . . Smell My Finger*), hers was the last album to receive a full promotional push from Warner Brothers, with $2 million spent on the campaign. Prince took Electra on the *Diamonds and Pearls* tour as opening support, with a huge band including Morris Hayes, who would later go on to play such an important role in the NPG, but dropped her from the show midway through the tour, and her record is among Prince's least appreciated projects. Prince had been hyping his audience for Electra's debut for three years, beginning with a pre-concert spoken intro at the *Diamonds and Pearls* shows in which, speaking of herself in the third person, she boasted that she was the scariest female on the planet, inevitable, addictive and habit-forming (promises eventually repeated on the CD's inner sleeve), and that 'to listen to her music on a loud system is to cum a thousand times'. But it would take three years before the record eventually appeared, and it would go through several permutations, with five major tracks being discarded from the running order during the process.[2] In *Prince: A Thief in the Temple*, Brian Morton even suggests there is some kind of cosmic justice in the fact that 'posterity has effectively "disappeared" Electra's lame effort',[3] but the same is true of many of Prince's most significant side projects or collaborations. I'm not suggesting that it's a lost classic, but whatever Prince's motivations in recording the album, he spent an enormous amount of time working on it, and it is an important and revealing part of his mid-1990s output, essential listening for anyone interested in the development of Prince's writing for protégés over the course of his career, and although the frenetic house-influenced style has dated badly, it remains a startling record.

Electra can be seen as a 1990s version of Vanity, although she seems more comfortable with the persona she's created, currently alternating between promoting aerobic striptease videos and spoofing her ultra-erotic image in films like *I Want Candy* and the *Scary Movie* series and TV programmes like *House* (she even played a character called Darling Nikki in the comedy show *Stacked*). That the album lacks the charm of the Vanity 6 and Apollonia 6 records is partly because the sexual and pornographic 1990s imagery that Prince played with on this record is somehow less charming than 1980s erotic iconography, the hard-body gym culture (for the most part) less appealing than lethargic lounging in camisoles.

Both the album itself and the out-takes are based around consistent concepts that hold through the whole project, such as the idea that Electra's rapping is in 'Carmenese', a playful idea that isn't consciously designed to undercut the singer but which nonetheless infantilises her. The completed album begins with a song that Prince wrote the music for, with lyrics credited to Electra and Tony M. But even if he didn't write the song, it seems likely to have begun from his suggestions about how Electra's persona might be established, as it fits so neatly with his usual thematic preoccupations. 'Go Go Dancer' takes the topic of confinement to an absurd extreme, with Electra singing from the perspective of a caged dancer, making comparisons between her own situation and that of an animal.[4] Although it was later rumoured that while playing his Las Vegas residency in 2006–7, Prince would counsel strippers about their career choice, his music had been connected with strip clubs as far back as Vanity 6's 'Nasty Girl', and it was a connection he seemed to encourage in the mid-1990s, giving '319' and 'Ripopgodezippa' to the *Showgirls* soundtrack and having a group of Erotic City dancers at his Glam Slam nightclub in Los Angeles.

As part of the promotional campaign for Electra's album, copies of 'Go Go Dancer', the album's first single, a kind of '9 to 5' for strippers, were sent to three hundred and sixty-nine strip clubs in America. The song's video also plays intriguingly on Prince's preoccupations. Picking up on the song's intro, which suggests that the lyric may be Electra's fantasy, it also echoes Sheila E's 'Yellow' in the way it begins with Electra at high school, doing gymnastics and being ostracised from a clique for being different from the other girls. Proving that it wasn't just the strip-club dollar Prince was after with this project, the maxi-single includes a radio edit and five remixes (including one by Junior Vasquez for his then-at-its-peak nightclub Sound Factory). Alan Leeds remembers that making this record a success was of great importance to Prince. 'I was really putting effort into the Ingrid Chavez record because we had a few nibbles, particularly in Europe. In Paris and parts of Italy there was real interest in the record. I decided to dedicate myself to exploiting that. And he came in one day and he had been working on the Carmen Electra record, which I couldn't give a shit about. It wasn't his best work as a writer and producer. I didn't see her as a real artist. It was completely about "Can she make a sexy video?" He was convinced that she could and that this would sell records. I didn't say anything because she was his girlfriend at the time. And he said, "I bet I'll sell more Carmen Electra records than you will Ingrid Chavez records." And I'm like, "What, we're competing now? It's your label!"'

Although Prince is not credited as having lyrical involvement in 'Good Judy Girlfriend' or 'Go On (Witcha Bad Self)', both tracks bear more than a trace of his fingerprints, not least in the way the chorus of the latter is partially borrowed from 'Nine Lives' and the way both songs emphasise the same point: that Electra, like Prince, has a dual personality, although in her case this is also yet another dramatisation of the Madonna/whore battle that Prince has explored many times before in his music for female artists. 'Step Up to the Mic' is further evidence against the accepted wisdom that Prince struggled with rap, featuring Electra rapping lines credited to British rapper Monie Love (to whom Prince gave two songs for her second album, *In a Word or 2*). 'S.T.', built around the Ohio Players' 'Skin Tight', is Electra and Tony M swapping lasciviousness and once again insisting on the uniqueness of the 1990s as a decade.

The album's next two songs, 'Fantasia Erotica' and 'Everyone Get on Up', came out as the third and second, respectively, of three maxi-singles (further evidence of just how important this record was to Prince). Originally recorded in 1989, *The Vault* suggests the former was originally intended as a song for Anna Fantastic, but I think it shares qualities similar to Prince's work with Madonna – and not just because it shares half a title with the album she would release in 1992, the same year this album and maxi-single would emerge. A great lost pop song of the early 1990s, it is perhaps the most pertinent argument for a reissue of this record. 'Everyone Get on Up' is almost as good, a prime piece of early-1990s hip hop in which Prince retooled a song he'd long had a fondness for – Chicago R&B band The Esquires' 'Get on Up' – and had even once performed with The Revolution (this version, recorded live, could sit easily on *Graffiti Bridge*), commissioning another rap from Monie Love and adding horns and scratches.

From this period on, Prince's use of samples in his own music and in songs for other artists becomes increasingly eccentric: no longer does he just sample loops and beats, but also extracts from sitcoms and comedians, although these are often lines and routines that either refer directly to him or have some pertinent connection. 'Everybody Get on Up' features a sample from a routine by his old friend Eddie Murphy, in which Murphy jokes about how easy it is for musicians from Mick Jagger to Michael Jackson to 'get pussy'. Although Murphy doesn't mention him, there is a long riff about Stevie Wonder taking too long to pick up awards that must have amused Prince.[5] In the 'Segue' which follows, Prince sneaks in brief snippets of a number of songs he'd written around this period, from the Celine Dion track 'With This Tear' to the then-unreleased 'Hit U in the Socket' to 'Goldnigga', as he pretends to tune a radio.[6] The second of two tracks to feature Eric Leeds, 'Fun' is credited to Prince and Electra, and features a lot of Prince's favourite imagery (the number seventeen, polka dots), but amounts to little. 'Just a Little Lovin'' is weak too, exposing the limitations of Electra's rap style. The next segue is baffling – Leeds on sax over some wave FX – but nowhere near as confounding as 'All That', which is Prince's most overt case of recycling (or self-plagiarism, as the academics would have it), consisting of a very slightly altered version of 'Adore' with new lyrics.

A segue about an oil spill sets up the environmental message for Electra's last rap, 'This Is My House'. The music is credited to Levi Seacer, Jr, but it's clear that Prince had some involvement in the composition as it features a sample from his unreleased song, 'The P', recorded while he was working on Electra's album and offered to Tevin Campbell.

The album was originally intended to be titled *On Top* and had the title track 'Carmen on Top', which is Electra's origin song, tracking quickly through a pseudo-autobiography in the manner of 'The Sacrifice of Victor'. Though unreleased, it's as good as anything on the album, and it's unclear why Prince decided to shelve it. The other tracks binned along the way include 'Power from Above', which exists in two versions and features an amusing back and forth between Electra and Prince, who's playing a farmer, and a couple of stupid-cop characters. Again, it's more fun than at least half the album. 'Go Carmen Go' is a hard-rock track, with Electra boasting about bringing rock to hip hop (predating tracks like Rihanna's 'Rockstar 101'), and with lyrical links to another less impressive unreleased song, 'The Juice', built – like so many hip-hop tracks – around a James Brown sample; as is 'Powerline', which appears to be about line-dancing ('Achy Breaky Heart' was about to hit big), although the 'chicken dance' is also mentioned. It's easy to see why this song was shelved.

By the time Alan Leeds resigned as president of Paisley Park records, he believes that 'Prince was frustrated with our lack of success. I was frustrated with our lack of success. Warners were frustrated with the fact that Prince really wasn't supplying his best work to the label. The calibre of the productions he was wanting to release really wasn't at the same level of the stuff he had produced early on. This all corresponded with Prince deciding he was their slave and becoming frustrated with Warners and their inability to release records when and how he chose. It was a conflict that had begun with *Lovesexy*, and it never really stopped. It got worse with every project.' Leeds also told me that Prince's deal of the time stipulated that he cross-collateralise Paisley Park's output with his own records, the result being that he decided to stop making records for the label.

After the demise of Paisley Park, the first band Prince tried to launch on his new NPG label was his backing band, The New Power Generation, whose album he had originally offered to Warner Brothers, who declined to release it. While it is perfectly possible Warners might have rejected the album as part of their ongoing conflict with Prince, it's also easy to see why they might have felt reluctant to put a big promotional push behind one of the most challenging Prince side projects, especially one which includes a segue that features Tony M bullying a couple of clueless record execs into giving him $6.5 million. Unlike the later *Exodus* and *New Power Soul*, both of which are appealing, commercial records, *Goldnigga* is an uncompromising, difficult album, albeit featuring two of Prince's most enjoyable songs from the era, '2gether' and the song introduced on the Act I tour, 'Johnny'. Although he'll become an increasingly prominent presence on NPG records, eventually taking over completely, on this album Prince remains largely in the shadows, handing over vocal duties to Tony M. How you feel about Tony M will shape your impression of this record, but it's definitely his finest hour. Still, for the first few listens, it sounds like an angry man shouting while a TV plays in the background. Only after spending time with the CD do the complexities (and qualities) of the record become clear. Unlike most rap albums of the time, it didn't rely too much on samples, instead utilising an enormous band with a big horn section and a large number of background vocalists.

The title song, 'Goldnigga', is split into three parts which come at the beginning, middle and end of the record, a Bob Marley-sampling mix of reggae and rap. 'Guess Who's Knockin'' was removed from the track listing when the album was reissued because it used portions of the Wings song 'Let 'em In'. Much of the early part of the record – including sketchy songs like 'Oilcan' and 'Deuce and a Quarter' – is sludgy and nondescript, the album not really sparking into life until Prince makes his presence known on 'Black MF in the House'. After a succession of segues and non-songs ('Goldie's Parade'), '2gether' is Tony M and Prince's most convincing hip-hop song, almost – but not quite – of the same calibre as Ice Cube's song of the same year, 'It Was a Good Day'. 'Call the Law' is weaker, but 'Johnny' is so much fun, Prince making the sillier side of rap that had always amused him his own. He would carry on playing this song live until 2002, and it always slayed.

*

As he'd previously done with Madhouse, Prince made the NPG his support band on the Act II tour, although they only played a few shows and not the whole run. A recording from a show in Madrid suggests it was a peculiar set, ignoring all the best songs from the album (which Prince would play in the main show and after-shows) and even including a cover of Madhouse's 'Six'. After selling *Goldnigga* at shows and at his newly established shops, Prince's next attempt at marketing his protégés to a wider audience came with the release of a new label sampler, *1-800-NEW-FUNK*. There was undoubtedly some strong material on this album – already released tracks from George Clinton and Mavis Staples; '2gether' from *Goldnigga*; 'Love Sign', a wonderful duet between Prince as ♀ and Nona Gaye, for which Prince would record a video in which Nona dons a red leather cat suit to play a hit woman employed to take out the local NPG DJ, played by Prince; a cover of Bobby Womack's 'Woman's Gotta Have It' by Gaye alone; and the Madhouse track '17' – but it didn't feel as if Prince was introducing greatness to the world with the remaining tracks: a song called 'Minneapolis' by MPLS, some formation of Prince associates who were never heard from in this form again (although they did also perform 'The Ryde Divine' on Prince's TV film of the same name); an undeniably funky but somewhat bland Prince-penned anti-racism song, 'Color', by the Steeles; and 'Standing at the Altar' by Margie Cox.

Far more worthwhile was the much higher quality second New Power Generation album, *Exodus*. The first was largely a show-case for Tony M, but he had left Prince's employ by the time of the second record, with Sonny T and Prince (using the alias Tora Tora) handling most of the vocals. Not quite a Prince album in disguise – like *New Power Soul* – but less obviously separate from his work than *Goldnigga*, the album has a number of first-rate tracks: live favourite 'Get Wild';[7] 'New Power Soul', which in spite of its title is actually an excellent slice of jazz; old-school funk 'Count the Days' (he'd perform this song on British TV's *The White Room*, his face completely covered with a red scarf) and 'The Good Life'; the creepy minimal funk of 'Big Fun' that antic-ipates the even better third album and some of *Emancipation*; and best of all, 'Cherry, Cherry' (my favourite side project song of the 1990s, featuring an exhibitionistic girl at a basketball game, it's the closest Prince has ever come to capturing the feel and flavour of his first three albums, combined with a wonderful pastiche of early-1970s soul and a new, darker social realism). The album is as significant a record in Prince's oeuvre as any Time or Madhouse record (and is arguably better than much of what Prince was pro-ducing under his own name at the time). There are some less accessible tracks on the album: 'Return of the Bump Squad' is over seven minutes of cut-price Funkadelic; 'Hallucination Rain' is Prince's most peculiar song, which plays like a soul version of Jefferson Airplane's 'White Rabbit' or a properly psychedelic ver-sion of 'Purple Rain' or 'Graffiti Bridge'; while 'The Exodus Has Begun' is over ten minutes of Prince sermonising over funk using a tone box, in the manner he would on *The Rainbow Children*, before ending with a dedication to 'His Royal Badness'.

The only similarity with *Goldnigga* is the fact that it works as a concept album, with lots of segues, sketches and chatter that swells the record to twenty-one tracks, over half of which could easily be removed (there were even more that were edited out). Still, some of the tomfoolery is amusing and revealing: the record opens with Prince playing a naive musician trying to get through to Paisley Park ('No, this is not that record company'), before being informed by Mayte that if he wants to join NPG's talent search, he must be free of contractual obligations so his music can be downloaded directly to fans' computers. In 'DJ Gets Jumped', Prince reveals his attitude to his old music by having a DJ who was playing 'Dream Factory' beaten up and the track replaced with 'New Power Soul' (no relation to the later album of the same name). Most of the remaining segues largely involve Sonny T (and occasionally Prince as Tora Tora), who is presented as a highly strung man with a serious aversion to TV (referred to here as on the later religious album *The Rainbow Children* as 'hellavision'). A full three minutes is given over to a typically unfunny (but unusually profane) Prince skit about assaulting a greedy girl in a restaurant, and another four to Prince (in a 'Bob George' voice) mugging himself and sneaking into a messy girl called Janelle's house, before heading to the Glam Slam nightclub and urinating in an alley. This is followed by a weird sequence (including some segues removed from the final version) in which Sonny is poisoned and starts hallucinating. He later imagines he's in space for a full-on intergalactic battle, before he wakes up and realises it was a dream, although there was an alternative, unreleased ending that suggested the narrative would be completed on *New Power Soul*.

The final New Power Generation releases, *New Power Soul* and *The War*, were Prince records in all but name, but the band did also make three significant contributions to film soundtracks, providing an alternative version of boring socio-funk track 'Super Hero', a song Prince had originally given to his childhood heroes Earth, Wind and Fire, to the soundtrack of the Damon Wayans 1994 superhero comedy *Blankman*; 'Get Wild' to Robert Altman's underrated fashion satire *Prêt-à-Porter*; and original song 'Girl 6' to the soundtrack of Spike Lee's turkey of the same name, which was made up entirely of Prince-penned songs. The latter, a horn-driven track featuring Nona Gaye full of samples from old songs like 'Housequake', is a surprisingly sympathetic and non-salacious song about sex-line operators that was far more impressive than Lee's film.

*

Rosie Gaines is one of Prince's more unfortunate associates, in that her talents have not been truly appreciated aside from the time that she spent in his employ. I approached her for interview for this book, but she ignored my request. She did, however, make her frustrations known to Liz Jones when she interviewed her for her 1997 book *Slave to the Rhythm*, telling her Prince 'wouldn't let me out of a three-year contract, which meant I couldn't sign to Motown'.[8] But she did later sign with the label, which released *Closer Than Close* in 1995. That album only includes two Prince songs – 'I Want U (Purple Version)' (there was also a single release with many mixes, in an attempt to launch Gaines as a Candi Staton-style club diva) and an autumnal love ballad with a twist, 'My Tender Heart' – but in 2010, Gaines released a version of an album that she and Prince had been working on beforehand entitled *Concrete Jungle*, which contains alternative versions of the two songs on *Closer Than Close* and one more, the trite 'Hit U in the Socket', that had been released in the meantime via Prince's NPG Music Club.

Prince's relationship with (and marriage) to Mayte transformed his performance style and prompted him to write a ballet, *Kamasutra*, which Brent Fischer suggests Prince believed was one of his most important works, but it must have been challenging for an artist who almost always treated the women he worked with as sex objects to compose a record, *Child of the Sun*, that managed to be both uxorious yet suggestive enough to ensnare a new audience of Mayte fans. The criticism I've read about the weakness of Mayte's voice strikes me as beside the point: what's most significant about this record is how Prince approached it and what he wanted from Mayte, not how well she fulfilled the role asked of her.

The album was released a few months before they were married, and it's significant that it was a much less strip-club-friendly album than Carmen Electra's, opening with a heavily rave-influenced party track, 'Children of the Sun', followed by the most spiritual song Prince had released since *Lovesexy*, 'In Your Gracious Name'.

Neither are particularly strong, and are immediately eclipsed by a much older song, The Rebels' 'If I Love U 2Night' (the record's strongest track, which Prince must have realised, as he had Mayte sing it twice on the album; it has since been renamed 'If Eye Love U 2Night'). Asked about the song's previous life by Prince's in-house *NPG* magazine, Mayte referred to the Mica Paris version of the track but not the Rebels version, telling Raven Worrell: 'I knew about it. I was sort of curious, but I didn't want to hear about it and get any ideas . . . I translated it into Spanish and it's totally different.'⁹

'The Rhythm of Your ♥' is another techno house track, with Prince (not for the first time) building a song around a sampled heartbeat. Tagged in the sleeve as an 'industrial love' song, 'Ain't No Place Like U' is a peculiarly downbeat song of devotion built around heavy guitars and featuring Mayte willingly singing of separating herself from the world to be with a man. A dreadful cover of The Commodores' 'Brick House', which Prince renamed 'House of Brick (Brick House)', seems to be on the record only because Prince noticed the 'mighty' in the chorus sounded like 'Mayte', and for some inexplicable reason it samples *Back to the Future*.

Maybe going after the Mariah Carey dollar, much of the record is twee, lacking the bite of Prince's best work either for his protégés or for himself. 'Love's No Fun' and 'Baby Don't Care' are both bland songs about losing a man, while 'However Much U Want', a self-empowerment song about extending life and the one track that credits Prince as ♀ as singer, opens with him using back-masked lyrics for the first time since 'Darling Nikki'. 'Mo' Better' is a grim song about sexual secretions which rhymes 'wetter' with 'better' and, more worryingly, 'rush' with 'gush', and after the Spanish version of 'If I Love U 2Night', the record ends with a switched-gender version of Prince's first UK number one, recorded here as 'The Most Beautiful Boy in the World'. The album was not a success, and Liz Jones suggests the record 'largely remained in boxes in record warehouses'.[10]

Just as he had done with Paisley Park, Prince also used the NPG label to attempt to relaunch the careers of two old musical heroes (and close friends), Chaka Khan and Larry Graham. As with Mavis Staples, there are some who consider Prince's work for Chaka Khan a case of her adapting to his style, but theirs is a closer fit, perhaps because the two were linked from early in Prince's career. They had a long history, from Prince covering 'Sweet Thing' on his early demo tape, to Chaka doing 'I Feel for You', and then the two of them collaborating with Miles Davis on 'Sticky Wicked'. In the sleeve notes to *Come 2 My House*, Pepsi Charles makes much of Khan's role in the record, quoting her as saying that it is unusual in her oeuvre because she wrote the majority of the songs, but it's not the lyrics that mark this out as a Prince production but the sound.

Khan gets a co-production credit, but this sounds less like any of her previous albums and more like the other records Prince was working on at this time, *New Power Soul* and the Graham Central Station album. Engineer H. M. Buff says there weren't many songs carried forward to this album from other projects – only 'Journey 2 the Center of Your Heart' (originally considered for *Emancipation*) and 'Don't Talk 2 Strangers' (carried over from the ill-fated *I'll Do Anything* soundtrack) – and that there weren't many out-takes from this project, the most significant being a cover of Etta James's song 'At Last'. But it is perhaps less appealing to Khan fans than to those who enjoy this particular era of Prince's music. The sound he created with Kirk Johnson and H. M. Buff has been much dismissed, yet when considered as part of Prince's long career, it is well worth reappraisal.

'Come 2 My House',[11] for example, is entirely dependent on the strange playing of The Hornheadz, transforming what could be a straightforward funk song into extremely off-kilter jazz. 'This Crazy Life of Mine' is, the notes suggest, 'Chaka's summation of her life as she's lived it thus far,' but the Clare Fischer strings and sound FX rob the story of any drama. 'Betcha Eye' is far more dependent on Larry Graham's bass than Khan's simple, repetitive vocal. 'Pop My Clutch' is a terrible song, Prince returning to the car = vagina link that once served him well, another example (like 'Hit U in the Socket') of the strange tendency he has of wanting older women to sing songs based around embarrassingly inappropriate R&B-style sexual metaphors, though it does at least feature a cameo from Queen Latifah.

H. M. Buff says that 'demo' is not the right word for the original songs produced by Prince and later covered by other artists, saying instead that they were always initially fully produced songs by Prince. Hence odd out-takes such as Prince's version of 'I'll Never B Another Fool', where he inhabits a female persona and sings about not opening his legs for insecure men and tattooing himself to get over another new heartbreak.

As it's a co-write with Chaka Khan, it's not entirely clear whether Prince is constructing it from her beliefs or his own, but 'Democrazy' is a somewhat disturbing song in which they explain why they don't believe in the democratic system.

'Eye Remember U', a snoozy light-jazz song, is a co-write not just between Khan and Prince, but Larry Graham too, though he doesn't appear on the track, the bass being played by Rhonda Smith, who played such an important role in Prince's sound during this era. 'Reconsider (U Betta)', meanwhile, could easily have fitted on *Emancipation*. The new creative relationship between Graham, Khan and Prince is also demonstrated in Khan's wonderful cover of Graham's 'Hair', which doesn't feature Prince but does have Mayte on finger cymbals. As Buff remembers: '"Hair" was great. I worked in two studios at once in that session. It was one of the highlights. I did [another non-Prince track] "Spoon" and "Hair" at the same time. It was really fun.'

The Graham Central Station album *GCS2000* was less reliant on Prince as a lyricist, and though he plays throughout the album, he co-wrote only one song for it, 'Utopia', in which Larry Graham declines fame and being a spiritual leader in favour of slapping his bass. Though many Prince fans resent Graham for getting Prince to give up swearing and for their shared religious beliefs, the record, which has a similar arrangement and cast of musicians as the Chaka Khan album, works as much as the third in a trilogy including *Come 2 My House* and *New Power Soul* as it does a Larry Graham album.

Prince's gifts to other bands have slowed in recent years. He helped try to launch former producer Kirk Johnson's Fonky Bald Heads project, and gave songs to two female singers renowned for their strength and independence – Gwen Stefani of No Doubt and Ani DiFranco, both of whom would appear on Prince's own *Rave Un2 the Joy Fantastic* (he would also allow Maceo Parker to cover three songs from this album on his own record) – but his most substantial next act of collaboration would initially take place onstage instead of in the studio.

As frustrating as it must have been for fans expecting a conventional Prince show, I think his decision to become a side-man for new protégée Támar on a 2006 tour was among the most interesting experiments he's attempted throughout his entire career, and while the eventual (still unreleased) album was, like much of his later work with protégés, not quite up to the standard of his own output, the Támar Featuring Prince tour was largely thrilling. The best shows were the ones where Prince mixed up the set list and dropped in unusual covers – such as one at the Butter restaurant in New York, where he played a lengthy version of 'The Ride' and covered Fleetwood Mac's 'The Chain' – but though seeing Prince as a side-man for a young R&B singer was a shock for most, the process clearly helped him realise that he wanted to be a front man again, and since then he has spoken onstage about the value of this period for him.

The Támar-era shows are underrated and her still-unreleased album, *Beautiful, Loved and Blessed*, while not quite as good as *3121*, is superior to many released protégé records. Támar is a talented singer, with a rapping voice similar to Eve's, and songs like 'Closer 2 My Heart', 'Milk and Honey' and 'Holla and Shout' are appealing R&B, with Prince producing perfect future-funk, while she alternates between singing and raps. The ballads ('Can't Keep Living Alone', 'All Eye Want Is U', 'First Love', 'Sunday in the Park') are more generic, and one song ('Holy Ground') is a true mish-mash that features Prince yet again constructing a song around the Lord's Prayer, this time combining it with *The Wizard of Oz* (he would soon begin covering 'Somewhere Over the Rainbow' in concert) and a little of 'These Boots Are Made for Walking'. But there are a few true standouts worthy of consideration as a significant part of Prince's oeuvre. 'Kept Woman' shows him stretching into new territory (for him, if not music in general; the situation is clichéd, a mistress singing about her plight), and it's more mature than anything he wrote for Sheila E, Vanity or Carmen Electra (and most of the songs he wrote for

Mavis Staples or Chaka Khan). 'Beautiful, Loved and Blessed' (also on *3121*) is one of Prince's most explicit acknowledgements of the process he goes through with a protégé, combined with yet another Edenic rebirth.

'Redheaded Stepchild' is a strange hybrid of R&B and metal and is among Prince's best tracks, the one point on the album when he seemed not to be imitating chart music but reminding the listener what he could bring to this sort of song that no other producer could. It remained in his set list after the departure of Támar. While the songs on which Michael B and Sonny T appear have not been identified, there seem some significant similarities between this song and the best of *Exodus*. While Prince kept 'Redheaded Stepchild' in his set, the one song he re-recorded for official release was 'Kept Woman', with Prince carrying it forward to the album he wrote for his next protégée, Bria Valente's *Elixer* (the punning title causing more than one Prince fan I know to shudder). Though Prince has remained quiet about the relationship, it would appear from interviews he gave to support *20 Ten* (most specifically with Peter Willis of the *Mirror*) that he was romantically involved with Valente, and that the relationship began during the recording of the record, offering a worthwhile point of comparison with the album he recorded with Mayte.

Of all the Prince protégé albums, this is the most musically somniferous. The worst of the record sounds like something you'd hear in a Greek disco, but the lyrics have surprising bite. There's a shout-out to his former girlfriend Kim Basinger in 'Here Eye Come' (the song that Prince used to introduce Valente to his fans via his *3121* website), in which Valente sings of fantasising about being the 'dirty blonde girl' in *9½ Weeks* while showering. Prince began by comparing the record to Sade (the smooth-jazz artist rather than the marquis), then backtracked in a later interview when he felt this comparison had blinded critics to the quality of the record. 'All This Love' is about obsession, while 'Home' has Prince using Egyptology once again, with a much more dramatic arrangement than anything else on the album. 'Something U Already Know' is as saccharine in its lyrics as the music, disrupted only by the image of making love on a rocking horse. Though it's distinguished by Clare Fischer strings, 'Everytime' is even less appealing schmaltz. '2Nite' has a house beat and a 'disco, disco' chant; with Valente celebrating sexy people dancing, it's embarrassing and awful. 'Another Boy', the album's single, is the strongest track, though it wasn't enough to make Valente's name. 'Kept Woman' is marginally less good (though better arranged) than Támar's unreleased version, but it's an undeniably impressive song, although there's something ruthless about the way Prince gave Valente a co-writing credit on a song first performed by a former protégée, especially one which seems designed to create the illusion of autobiographical truth and which features yet another controlling male. 'Immersion' continues the light sci-fi feel of much of Prince's music of this time, imagining an alternative universe beyond time and space, married to light jazz; it's a strange and not very good track that shares the weaknesses of *Lotusflow3r*. The album concludes with its title track, one Prince liked so much he would perform it live (as he also would with 'All This Love'). His vocal presence is more prominent here than anywhere else on the record, but it's an unpleasant song, the cunnilingus punchline somehow lacking all the charm Prince used to have when using such innuendo.

Bria Valente's record is the last of Prince's recordings with protégés to get an official release, but he hasn't stopped wanting to work with other female singers. He wrote a song for a new album by Sheila E and has occasionally made reference to a Shelby J record, which has yet to appear, as well as collaborating with a variety of new female singers in live performance, including Janelle Monáe, whom he took as support on his Welcome 2 America tour, jazz singer Esperanza Spalding and Portuguese fado singer Ana Moura, with whom he performed a fado during a Portuguese date on the *20 Ten* tour and about which she told the *Guardian*, '. . . it was magical. All the Portuguese went crazy, and then when he started to play everyone went quiet – people had the sensation that they went to another level.'[12]

In the time between the first publication of this book and this updated edition, Prince has worked on a variety of projects with other artists, but – prior to the arrival of 3rdEyeGirl – his most significant contributions appeared on protégée Andy Allo's 2012 album *Superconductor* and a new Larry Graham and Graham Central Station album entitled *Raise Up*.

Prince plays on three tracks on Graham's album – 'Raise Up', 'Shoulda Coulda Woulda' and 'Movin''. No author is credited for these lyrics, though 'Graham-O-Tunes' is listed as having copyright for all three. Prince and Larry Graham are often talking about how much time they spend together, and in the title song, inspired by apocalyptic lines from the Book of Luke (21:28), Graham runs through frustrations Prince has also regularly sung about – electronic surveillance, the inconvenience of having to take one's shoes off at airport security, the price of oil – in another of the pair's curious attempts to get funky about the world's ills. Prince also provides incomprehensible squeaky backing vocals, which add an extra dash of sci-fi surrealism to the sermonising.

'Shoulda Coulda Woulda' has less evidence of any Prince influence on the lyrics. Graham sings from the perspective of a man who regrets not having got his lover barefoot and pregnant before she had chance to escape. Prince plays everything but bass on the song, the arrangement immediately transforming what could have been a pedestrian lament into the most dramatic song on the album. On 'Movin",[13] however, he appears to be just one more guitarist in a busy arrangement. The song is yet another celebration of Graham the bass man, and is of little import – though it's worth noting the presence of Támar Davis among the chorus of backing voices, suggesting that this song might have been sitting around for a while before release, and also marking the final occasion this former protégée appears on a Prince-related project (though, of course, there might be more songs in the Vault, and I still hold out no doubt forlorn hope that her *Milk and Honey* might see full release).

Graham still regularly appears on tour with Prince, having been summoned to play at an Arizona date on the Live Out Loud tour in May 2013, and earlier in the year Prince told *Billboard* that he had been working on a documentary about Graham's life. According to the magazine, the project had 'hit an impasse' due to the prohibitive cost – $500,000 – of clearing the rights to the Graham songs used in the film,[14] something that appeared to be causing Prince considerable annoyance. Still neighbours in Minneapolis, it seems likely the pair will continue to collaborate for some time to come.

Andy Allo was introduced to Prince's audience in a similar way to Támar Davis. While Prince didn't assume quite as subservient a role as he did when he hid in Támar's backing band, he did once again show a surprising generosity in the way he promoted the artist to his own audience, frequently allowing her to effectively open his shows, frontloading his performances with her songs and their collaborations.

Nonetheless, the album they recorded together was little more successful than any of his other recent protégé albums, and though his persistence with these projects would seem to indicate that the commercial success of the records is irrelevant, he did reveal some frustration about the project to *Billboard*, asking them, 'What does it take to get a record played these days?'[15] (Earlier, he had suggested to Barry Egan of the *Irish Independent* that there was 'no reason why her record shouldn't sell 20 million copies',[16] suggesting that everyone on Facebook might buy a copy, perhaps overestimating the power of the social networks Allo was then utilising.)

In an interview with DirecTV's *Guitar Center Sessions*, Allo explained that she started out covering Grateful Dead songs before devising a genre of her own that she described as 'alterna-hip-soul' (her first album, *Unfresh*, recorded before she started working with Prince, sees her changing styles on virtually every song, which isn't, in itself, a problem – the concern is that on much of the album the styles come across as borrowed from better-known neo-soul singers). She told interviewer Nic Harcourt she'd focused from the very start on self-funding and social networking, beginning with MySpace, inspired by Prince-approved artist Ani DiFranco. Allo explained that she met Prince via the Africa Channel, which had broadcast specials on both artists, prompting Prince to invite her to jam with him.[17]

Prince wrote or co-wrote three tracks on Allo's second record, but the whole album features a full retinue of purple associates – among them John Blackwell, Michael Bland, Morris Hayes, Shelby J, Maceo Parker and Liv Warfield, plus the Hornheadz on four tracks, who give it an identifiably Paisley Park sound (Allo also told Harcourt that Prince was responsible for arrangements on the whole album). In fact, given that at the time of writing Prince has yet to produce a new solo album since *20 Ten*, and without wanting to belittle Allo's obvious talent (it's clear that the album is a genuine collaboration), for those who prefer albums to one-off downloads at least half of this record might be considered the only sustained example of the direction Prince was pursuing before the beginning of the 3rdEyeGirl era[18] – notwithstanding the songs in a similar style later released as downloads.

Superconductor is not a concept album as such, but the songs are linked by repeated imagery and themes, many of which are Prince's own regular concerns (regality, the importance of peace, the cosmos and how to avoid the demands of others). Is it too obvious to see Prince as the 'Superconductor' of the title? Described as possessing the ability to produce a 'perfect symphony' every night, he certainly shares Prince's prolificacy. A co-write with Prince, the title song has obvious similarities with 'Rock and Roll Love Affair', the single he put out under his own name that also features vocals from Allo. She sings the song directly to the 'Superconductor', addressing him as 'you' throughout. The listener is placed in the role of Prince as she turns the pair of them into Bonnie and Clyde. The lyric goes back and forth between focusing on the spiritual value of both their musical and romantic harmony and the demands of touring life – a line about sleeping till noon highlights how being a musician removes the singer from a nine to five lifestyle, but also plays off Prince's well-documented nocturnal existence.

Prince made the album's second song, 'People Pleaser', a regular part of his live show for a while and even played the song on TV as part of a tremendous performance on the French show *Le Grand Journal*, where he also debuted another yet-to-be-released song in a similar style, 'We Live (2 Get Funky)'. 'People Pleaser' is billed solely to Allo, and assuming this is true, it's easy to see why it caught Prince's attention (he told Egan it was the song he most wished he'd written), as it's a brilliantly belligerent expression of defiance that lends itself perfectly to Prince's horn-filled arrangement, as good as anything on the previous dozen Prince albums.

'Long Gone' is less compelling, a dreary ballad co-written by

Prince and Allo inspired by Allo's interest in soft-rockers James Taylor and Carole King, and sounding like those two at their sleepiest (it's certainly no 'You're So Vain', the King song Allo might have played with when writing with Prince). The one interesting image in the lyric is Allo singing about thinking she would be someone's 'king' as opposed to their 'queen' (something she also addresses in the song 'If I Was King',[19] which doesn't have any lyrical involvement from Prince). In a coy interview with Dr Funkenberry, Allo told the blogger that 'a friend' (for which read Prince) wanted to add strings to the song, but she resisted, wanting to keep it 'raw',[20] which encapsulates the problems with this record – there is a conflict between Prince's desire to smooth the record into blandness and Allo's desire to prove herself as a singer-songwriter, without quite having the song-writing ability to do so. Allo does appear to have a compelling personality and a good voice, but her lyrics can't sustain an album, and the quality tails further on the fourth track: 'The Calm' is a depiction of a troubled love affair based around the cliché of 'calm after a storm', though it's a muddled lyric that's hard to follow.

Though Prince had no involvement in the lyrics on the long remainder of the record, he plays on the other five – 'Yellow Gold', 'Nothing More', 'If I Was King', 'Story of You and I' and 'When Stars Collide'.[21] I'm not sure why this half of the album should be even less compelling than, say, the Carmen Electra album, on which he uses similar tricks ('Nothing More', for example, is built upon the bones of Prince's 'The Love We Make', just as 'All That' was built upon 'Adore'). It's partly because his arrangements seem designed to be timeless, but also because as much as I enjoy the Hornheadz, who play on four of the remaining tracks, they seem to be set to polite mode, as Prince and Allo are torn between their professed desire to replicate the style and sounds of the original 'nasty gal', Betty Davis,[22] and Prince's misguided desire to record yet another 'quiet storm' album. There are nice moments – the bass on 'Yellow Gold' (Prince doing his best Larry Graham impression); the band having fun and threatening to bust loose into a jam at the end of 'If I Was King'; and even Allo's vocals on 'When Stars Collide' – but unless Allo goes through some astonishing future transformation, it doesn't feel like a record I'm going to be regularly revisiting (the title track and 'People Pleaser' aside).

Alongside Allo's album, several more important tracks with Prince have appeared as downloads only or streamed via Allo's Facebook page. The majority of these are live versions of already-released Prince songs taken from performances with Allo ('Little Red Corvette', 'Alphabet St.', 'Hot Thing') or live covers ('Stratus', 'Come Together', 'Stand!' and 'Angel'), but a few merit closer attention, among them an acoustic version of the *Planet Earth* song 'Guitar'; the aforementioned 'Oui Can Luv' and 'Extraloveable'; a rehearsal version of 'Dark'; a cover of Cat Stevens's 'Wild Wood' with Prince on guitar; and, most excitingly of all, a demo of 'U Will B' – a song also discussed in Chapter 36 and Prince's most emotionally vicious creation since 1995's 'Eye Hate U'.

While Andy Allo's album received less attention – even from the hardcore than Prince believed it merited, the first song from a longer-awaited project,[23] Shelby J's mooted debut album *Just Shelby*, remained even further off the fan radar. 'North Carolina' is a download-only release brought to public attention solely through a broadcast on a North Carolina University radio station. Featuring backing vocals from renowned R&B singer Antony Hamilton, the almost eight-minute-long single is an extended, strange blend of reggae and talking blues in which Shelby J details darkness from her city's past and tells autobiographical stories about her singing career. More interesting than the majority of the soul covers she's been doing in Prince's show for years now, it isn't quite strong enough to make the listener count the days until the full record gets released, although it does work as an interesting curio, another intriguing footnote for the faithful to explore.

Should we consider Prince's new band 3rdEyeGirl another protégé project? I'd assumed not, believing that the rumoured album they are (at the time of writing) working on together would be largely his project, with his new trio serving mainly as backing band. But then an interview with Jon Bream appeared in the *Star Tribune* in which Prince suggested that the album – due to appear via the independent Kobalt Music Group – might be a 3rdEyeGirl project rather than a Prince one. Though Bream[24] reveals that Prince has written all but one of the songs on the record[25] (the exception being 'Plectrum Electrum'), he quotes Prince as suggesting that the band's legacy might be independent from his own. It seems another variation on the hiding-in-plain-sight tactic that also motivated him to pretend to be just another member of Támar's band. I get the impression that this humility might be religiously motivated, or part of a personal growth programme. I wonder which of his impulses is most prominent here: live the ambition seems to be to startle the hardcore (hence his onstage boasts about how people discussing which of his bands is the best are missing the point, as it is always his new band – a sentiment he shares with The Fall's Mark E. Smith); but when the recording starts, it seems to be yet another attempt at star-making. There is more about Prince and 3rdEyeGirl in the Epilogue, but it does make for a nice conclusion that Prince finally seems to have realised that the only way to make an audience care about the new musicians he's sought out is to remain front and centre. He keeps pushing 3rdEyeGirl into the limelight, but as talented as they are, it's the man behind the camera (literally so in one promo) that holds our interest.

AN ENTIRELY NEW GALAXY AWAITS . . .

[My father] used to say things like, 'Don't ever get a girl pregnant, don't ever get married,' don't this, don't that. When he'd say these things, I didn't know what to take from it, so I would create my own universe . . . and my sister's like that, a lot of my friends are like that, the ones that I still have, early musicians and things like that. Creating your own universe is the key to it, I believe . . . and letting all the people that you need occupy that universe.

Prince, interview on *The Tavis Smiley Show*, 27 April 2009

Imaginary universes, like the one Prince describes above, have been defined by psychologists as 'paracosms'. But this term is usually used to describe whole imaginary fictional worlds, like the one created by the Brontë sisters. Prince's have a more complicated relationship with reality than most. It is also worth noting that while fictional worlds are often created by isolated individuals who can't cope with reality, Prince's universe is not a solitary one, but one he's tried to fill first with talented fellow artists, then his fans.

The story of Lotusflow3r.com is a sad one. Prince's last attempt to date to create an alternative universe for his followers, it was, it seems, doomed to failure almost from the start. It could be seen as the final schism between Prince and the true believers, or at least the end of the super-close relationship between him and his fans, which has now been replaced with a much more distant one.[1]

As usual, news of Prince's new direction leaked out slowly. He went through a relatively quiet period following the 21 Nights in London run, with barely a handful of live shows in 2008, the majority taking place at Prince's own private residence. The main release that year was the *21 Nights* book and the accompanying *Indigo Nights* live album.

I reviewed this publication for a British newspaper and was rewarded with an invitation to both the British and the American launches. The British one, *sans* Prince, was a sedate affair at the Dorchester, the hotel Prince had stayed at during his O2 run and which featured in the *21 Nights* book. But the American launch, at the Hotel Gansevoort in New York's Meatpacking District, was the best book launch I've ever been to (and I've been to over a thousand) because it featured over four and a half hours of live performance from Prince and a stand-up set from Dave Chappelle. Only Prince could separate his book launch into a main show and after-show, especially as this performance took place in a hotel room in front of around two hundred people (midway through the party, overzealous staff threw out anyone with the wrong colour wristband, and they were just about to march me out when I produced the correct accreditation). It's further evidence of how brilliant Prince is at hiding the original composition time of songs, as when he introduced 'Colonized Mind' and made it seem as if he'd written it that afternoon in response to the stock-market meltdown that had taken place that day, it seemed perfectly plausible.

That night he also played 'Crimson and Clover' and '(There'll Never B) Another Like Me', the first indication of the new record(s) Prince had been putting together during his time off the road. In 2008, he released 'Colonized Mind' and 'Crimson and Clover' to Indie 103, a Los Angeles radio station, along with two other tracks, '4Ever' and 'Wall of Berlin'. Both '4Ever' and 'Wall of Berlin' featured musicians Prince had worked with on *3121*, but not since. From the perspective of 2011, these latter two songs are largely forgotten and seem like the sort of out-takes that might have been left in the Vault in earlier eras, but at the time Prince's choice of release method seemed chosen to make a point: these heavier tracks did seem more suited to an indie station than a dance one, and given the indie covers that began to appear in Prince's live set around this time (most notably Radiohead's 'Creep', which he'd played at that year's Coachella festival), it seemed that he might have had a new audience in mind.

Once again, after the innovative release strategies for *Musicology* and *Planet Earth*, Prince sought out the best way of getting money and hype for the records he possibly could, doing a deal with Target superstores in the US and setting up a website through which listeners elsewhere in the world would be able to download the albums. The only unique song people who had paid $77 to join the site received as an initial download was 'The Morning After', a brief and lightweight power-pop song (believed to be an out-take from an original version of *3121*)[2] in which Prince sings about wanting more commitment from a casual lover, which replaced 'Crimson and Clover' on the download version of the record. (Later, Prince would post the truly terrible 'Cause and Effect' on the site, although it wasn't an exclusive as he also released it to a radio station, one of many signs that he was not treating the site's users with any particular respect.) Site users did, however, get the album five days before Target shoppers, and for many of the world's Prince fans, the site was the only legal way of getting the CDs at all.

My experiences with Prince's previous Internet sites had been minimal; before I started writing this book I was far less interested in the computer side of his business. I'd got in at the tail end of the NPG Music Club experience, just in time to download the music and get a few decent tickets, but not long enough to feel like the site's closure was any great loss. But I confess to falling for the Lotusflow3r.com hype. While wiser (and already burnt) Prince fans moaned about the disappointment they felt when their 'lifetime' memberships to the NPG Music Club turned out to refer only to the lifetime of the website, I sat in front of my computer in the early hours of the morning, watching the timer click down on the purple dynamite on Lotusflow3r.com's home page, waiting for it to go live. Prince and the website designers had appeared to make many promises about what the site would contain, but in language so cryptic that it was hard to know with any certainty what we would get for our money. I contacted Lotusflow3r.com designer Scott Addison Clay about his experiences of working with Prince, but he told me he had to decline to comment. He did talk to the *Wall Street Journal* a year earlier, however, expressing his disillusionment with the process of creating the website. 'We only got stuff in dribs and drabs,' he told the paper, speculating that the number of fans who joined was a disappointment to Prince.[3]

The main inducement to join the site at the very beginning – aside from the albums – was the opportunity to buy advance tickets for three shows in Los Angeles in three different venues with three different bands (oh, and a T-shirt). New users' patience was tested by a secret code you had to crack before getting access to tickets, the sort of thing that might entertain a web designer but which irritated anyone expecting a reward for their investment. In spite of getting onto the site seconds after it went live, I could only get tickets to the first of the three shows Prince was playing: a main show in front of an enormous audience.

I flew to Los Angeles anyway, using secondary sites to get tickets for the second and third shows. On the way over, I considered the new album(s), hoping that my initial disappointment might be tempered by hearing the songs in performance. The best of *Lotusflow3r* appears to have come from the *3121* sessions, but there's too little stretched out over the album – indicating that *3121* could have been a truly phenomenal double-CD set. There are lyrical connections between several songs on both albums, as well as the presence of Támar, Sonny T and Michael B. The songs that appear to have come from this session (or sessions) are the instrumentals 'From the Lotus . . .' and '. . . Back 2 the Lotus'. There is also a third instrumental on the record named '77 Beverly Park' after one of Prince's homes, as well as the syrupy ballads '4Ever' (this only features Támar, not Sonny or Michael), 'Love Like Jazz' and 'Wall of Berlin'.

The most explicit statement of the 'new galaxies' theme in the record comes in 'Boom', which also indicates that the idea of creating a new galaxy is really a restatement of Prince's long-cherished concept of each new love returning him to the Garden of Eden (which he also sings about on 'Love Like Jazz'), only in this instance given a sci-fi twist, something also investigated in 'Wall of Berlin'. 'Feel Better, Feel Good, Feel Wonderful' is an intriguing example of Prince making his working processes public, as he'd placed an unfinished version of the song on his previous website for visitors to comment on. It is also his last released collaboration with the late Dr Clare Fischer, and when they heard it Brent Fischer noticed that 'none of the orchestra got used, and it was a lot different from what he sent us. There was a lot more organ on it. I can see with the organ on there why he would not feel the need for strings at that point.'

As with much of Prince's later work, the record features a couple of bitter, angry songs. '$' is another money song, criticising the pursuit of cash as meaningless and suggesting that rich folks rarely know where the action is. 'Dreamer' has similarities with 'The Sacrifice of Victor', another pseudo-autobiography that flashes through Prince's life from birth until now, but this time focusing on his ethnicity. Suggesting that he was born into 'a slave plantation', he implies he only became aware of his race with the assassination of Martin Luther King (which happened when he was nine), talks of fear of being harassed by policemen while out in his car, and perhaps most controversially, sings about how chemicals are being sprayed over the city while he sleeps. Prince expanded on his belief in the 'chemtrails' conspiracy – that the US Air Force is clandestinely spraying cities with chemicals for nefarious controlling purposes – on *The Tavis Smiley Show*, talking about being inspired by the activist and comedian Dick Gregory and the annual black-interest gathering the State of the Black Union.

MPLSound is a solo record, with everything recorded by Prince aside from a rap by Q-Tip (a rapper Prince had been friends with for some time). There are four true standouts on the album – ('There'll Never B) Another Like Me', 'Chocolate Box', 'Ol' Skool Company' and 'No More Candy 4 U' – and five less distinguished (but mostly still worthwhile) ballads – 'Dance 4 Me', 'U're Gonna C Me', 'Here', 'Valentina' and 'Better with Time'.

All four standouts owe something to hip hop, with Prince hitting on a more confident form of sing-rapping and a defiantly past-caring directness of keyboard accompaniment that is his true achievement of this era. 'Ol' Skool Company' and 'No More Candy 4 U' are just as bitter as anything on *Lotusflow3r*, but somehow they're funnier and more appealing when sung in a squeaky voice with squelches in the background. Prince suggested to Tavis Smiley that 'Ol' Skool Company' was an exercise in nostalgia, celebrating his home town and the music that came from Minneapolis. When playing it live, Prince would often begin by playing a few bars of 'Purple Rain' as a tease before switching into the song, and occasionally also work in sections from his classical fave, Strauss's *Also Sprach Zarathustra*. 'No More Candy 4 U' is among Prince's funniest songs, his occasional pettiness and petulance in full effect as he attacks Internet trolls.

The ballads are largely notable in that Prince sounds (lyrically, if not vocally) middle-aged for the first time, addressing ageing and love later in life with a new explicitness. 'Dance 4 Me' is a watered-down version of his earlier voyeuristic tracks, like 'Alphabet St.' and '319', but feels impotent compared to past expressions of this theme. It was subject to a number of remixes, including several that wouldn't officially emerge until after Prince had released a subsequent album. 'U're Gonna C Me', a dated song about Prince paging his lover, had already appeared in an alternative version on *One Nite Alone . . .* 'Here' has lyrics about wine not tasting as good when you're older and Prince using Donny Hathaway songs to seduce, but the two most significant songs in this vein both feature him singing about Hollywood actresses. 'Valentina' is addressed to Salma Hayek's daughter (Hayek had directed the video for 'Te Amo Corazón') and is an extraordinary song, in which Prince sings about the possibility of love (or partying at least) in a time of 'late-night feedings'; probably not one to play within earshot of any woman raising young children. 'Better with Time', which was inspired by Kristin Scott Thomas, is sweeter, an act of homage to his former screen co-star.

While the albums were disappointing, three shows with three different bands seemed exactly what Prince needed to do next. He promoted them with three consecutive appearances on *The Tonight Show*. At the time I assumed that this was the next stage in Prince's career – a stage show that complemented the album and website. Standing in the pit in front of 7,100 fans at the Nokia Theatre, I couldn't help being struck by the amateurishness of the set design, which looked like kids at an infant school had been handed the covers of *Lotusflow3r* and *MPLSound* and instructed to do their worst, the disco-ball jellyfish especially unconvincing. Suddenly the Jumbotrons flickered into life and Prince played us a new video that was a more sure-footed attempt to throw us into a new galaxy. The director of the 'Chocolate Box' video, P. R. Brown, claimed he was bringing Prince's vision to the screen in presenting him, according to the promo's press release, as 'an all-seeing Orwellian figure' with an 'omnipotent visage' projected onto the sides of skyscrapers and a 'psychedelic airship'. Given Prince's criticism of violent Hollywood product in songs like 'One Song' and 'Silicon', it seems surprising that among the credited inspirations for the video was Frank Miller's violent retro-noir *Sin City*. The video also indicated Prince's lasting interest in sci-fi film *The Matrix*.[4] And when the show started with 'Ol' Skool Company' and 'Dreamer', I thought that this might be the beginning of a run that would stand with his best tours. Soon, though, the show was beset by sound problems, and Prince began playing a listless mix of covers and old chestnuts.

The sound remained off all night, the problems so irritating to Prince and his audience that he halted the third set to complain at length, but the other two shows (in smaller, more exclusive venues) had many highlights. The Conga Room show (where Prince was backed with original New Power Trio members Sonny T and Michael B) featured several songs he had played with his New Power Trio in London, but began with a complete surprise – 'I'm Yours', from his first album *For You*, a song he had never played live before. For the third show Prince revisited songs from *Rave Un2 the Joy Fantastic* and played the much-loved unreleased track 'In a Large Room with No Light', with Renato Neto and John Blackwell. It was a wonderful show, but it had little to do with the new albums.

*

And there was no *Lotusflow3r* tour. Prince performed two well-received shows at the Montreux Jazz Festival, three in Monaco, four in Paris and a show at Paisley Park, and that was almost it for the album. A few songs from a performance for France's RTL radio channel were made available on the site – 'Feel Better, Feel Good, Feel Wonderful', 'Mountains' and 'Shake Your Body' – plus a rehearsal version of 'Why You Wanna Treat Me So Bad?' and some live performances from recent shows. But it never became the conduit for fans that they so desired. At some point during the process, whether it was because he fell out with the web masters or because he just grew tired of the Internet, he gave up on the experiment. In some respects, it's hard to blame him: the Internet brings out the worst in his fans, and with the mass move away from websites to Facebook and Twitter, the site had become irrelevant. But at the same time, it's hard not to see this as a fatal schism between Prince and his audience. Hundreds of thousands still attend his shows around the world, but a lot of the excitement associated with following Prince seems to have dissipated in the last few years.

The end of the *Lotusflow3r* era arguably came with the ignominy surrounding the demise of the website and some fans' outrage at being charged for a second year's subscription without warning (although they were quickly refunded). As always with Prince, it's hard to say when one period ended and the next began, but the most obvious conclusion to this period is a short performance at the Village Underground in New York in May 2010 when Prince performed with his back to the audience. Many suggested this was a move inspired by Miles Davis, but it seems more likely that he was making a protest at the fact that the show was being recorded. Either way, it seemed proof of something fans had known for a while: Prince was moving into a position where he no longer needed us.

ENDING ENDLESSLY

Speaking to an interviewer from the *Daily Mirror* in an interview to promote the *20Ten* giveaway, Prince confirmed that he had lost interest in the Internet, stating that it was 'completely over' and comparing it to a form of promotion – MTV – that had helped him earlier in his career. 'The internet's like MTV. At one time MTV was hip and suddenly it became outdated. Anyway, all these computers and digital gadgets are no good. They just fill your head with numbers and that can't be good for you.'[1] There may be something to Prince's argument, particularly for a musician who has always prided himself on being ahead of the game, but elsewhere in the interview he reveals that his concerns about the Internet are largely mercenary. 'I don't see why I should give my new music to iTunes or anyone else. They won't pay me an advance for it and then they get angry when they can't get it.'

Predictably, Prince's dissing of the Internet prompted much media comment, especially on Internet news sites. Milo Yiannopoulos of the *Daily Telegraph* had a more in-depth response, arguing that his album giveaway was a huge commercial blunder, but also analysing Prince's relationship with the Internet, detailing the Lotusflow3r.com debacle and describing it as 'a complicated relationship that began with utopian enthusiasm' and ended with 'contemptuous dismissal'. While the latter seems accurate, the argument that it was a commercial blunder, one that occurred because Prince 'doesn't understand the internet', suggested the author didn't fully understand Prince's motivations.[2] It seems that there is a very clear business decision behind this form of distribution, but there is also an artistically inspired one. On a business level, Prince presumably gets paid as much from the distribution deal as he could expect from a record label, and gets the album to a much wider audience than he would if it wasn't a giveaway. The release also promotes the shows (although in this instance, as he wasn't playing in the UK, it was no doubt less of a consideration). But it also takes Prince out of the review pages and into the rest of the newspaper, an effective way of cutting down the power of reviewers. By distributing his album in this way he ensured the first reviews (by *Mirror*-employed writers and sanctioned celebrities) were positive, and freed himself from the promotion cycle. It also fitted with his ongoing desire to hide in plain sight: his album got to a bigger audience than he'd had for years, although only hard-core fans had the passion to keep playing it.

Nonetheless, former confidant and publicist Howard Bloom believes this schism with his digital past is another terrible career mistake. 'Oh my god, not another extremist move. You cannot expunge pieces of life. You have to learn from every one of them. Even if they are adventures that you would never repeat again.'

I attended the third show of what fans were calling the *20Ten* festival tour at Arras in northern France. It was the first time I'd seen Prince live since the three shows in Los Angeles the year before, and I went there with low expectations. It was important to make allowances for the fact that this was a festival tour, and consequently would be hits-heavy, but it still seemed that Prince had retreated from the potentially interesting directions that he'd failed to explore fully when promoting the *Lotusflow3r* set and had headed back to Europe with a brutally stripped-down band to pick up some easy money. And for the first half hour or so of the set, there was nothing to suggest this wasn't the case. But then 'Guitar' lifted the performance, and a feint at 'Hot Summer' suggested that this throwaway song might develop into something purposeful live. The rest of the set returned to tedium, enlivened only by the mixed pleasure of watching Prince and Larry Graham jam together, two great musicians who in spite of their close friendship never really gel onstage.

But then, having dispatched the hits, he returned with more unexpected material that made up for everything that had come before. In recent years, Prince seems to have become increasingly open about his influences, but nevertheless, his decision to add Sylvester's 'Dance (Disco Heat)' to his set for this tour was still a surprise. Watching him tear into it at Arras reminded me of how Barney Hoskyns suggested Prince's croon was distilled from Sylvester, Michael Jackson (who Prince referred to in his set frequently now, calling him 'a friend') and Philip Bailey from Earth, Wind and Fire. Covering a song by a gay drag performer known as the Queen of Disco also seemed a neat riposte to anyone who suggested Prince had become more judgemental since becoming a Jehovah's Witness. It also seemed fun that he should (almost) end a rock show with a disco song, and I enjoyed hearing him debut lines from 'Everybody Loves Me' in this jam, a song from the new album I'd yet to obtain.

Before he returned for a third encore, the intro for 'Forever in My Life' started up with such sound and clarity that I assumed someone was DJing with the studio version. But Prince came back out to deliver a more heartfelt version of this track than I'd heard in years, inviting speculation that the lyric about settling down with someone had become pertinent to his personal situation again (Bria Valente was sitting at the side of the stage). Then, he played just a short burst of '7', before leading the audience in a chant of the phrase 'Let go, let God' as he played his guitar, Prince's most unobtrusive onstage sermonising in years.

Back in England, I absorbed the album. *20 Ten*, the third (or fourth, if you count *Lotusflow3r* and *MPLSound* as separate albums) of Prince's post-record-label releases, is the most coherent. Any worries created by the seeming low quality of the songs (and the terrible cover art) he'd already made public in 2010 – the dire 'Purple and Gold' and 'Cause and Effect', and the lightweight 'Hot Summer' – were quickly put to rest by the confidence of the album, a record given its own sonic identity by the number of songs (seven out of ten) in which Prince relies on his trio of female backing vocalists – Liv Warfield, Shelby J and Elisa Dease.

After an abrasively robotic opening track, 'Compassion', where he's backed by a horn section of Maceo Parker, Greg Boyer and Ray Monteiro, the majority of the record features Prince playing everything again. It's typical of him that what he currently claims will be his last album sounds more like a debut. 'Beginning Endlessly' is Prince returning to one of his favourite themes – his desire to start again (in a new relationship or in a new creative direction), and his desire to erase his lover's past (with a symbolic change of name). H. M. Buff told me that 'Future Soul Song' was a Vault item from when he worked with Prince. If this is true, then presumably it was reworked for the record, as it has vocals from the female backing vocalists, who weren't working with Prince at the time. Certainly it seems more accomplished than anything else on the record.

The rest of the album seems comically minimalist, both in lyrical content and style. 'Sticky Like Glue' doesn't make much of the obvious innuendo, instead focusing once again on Prince being separated from his lover by air travel. The record's one political song – 'Act of God' – continues the outrage of the previous album's 'Ol' Skool Company', attacking bankers and once again suggesting the answer to everything is monotheism. 'Lavaux', 'Walk in Sand' and 'Sea of Everything' all seem responses to global travel, suggesting that Prince had finally taken criticism that his songs had become too insular on board. Of the three, only 'Sea of Everything' has real resonance, a sort of fan letter, it seems, to an equally successful female musician. 'Everybody Loves Me' is a hilarious song for Prince to put out after such a tempestuous few years, even more of a rebuke to his fans than 'F.U.N.K.'. But the most enjoyable track is hidden at the end: 'Laydown', most notable for Prince referring to himself as the 'purple Yoda'.

Out-takes have yet to emerge, but there is an unreleased (sort of) song connected to the album, 'Rich Friends', which Prince allowed a radio station to broadcast at the end of 2010, with the announcement that it would appear on *20 Ten Deluxe*, an expanded version of the album (presumably for the US market, as the record has yet to appear there, an extraordinary situation for an artist of Prince's stature) which has failed to materialise, and seems likely to have been lost for ever. The song is dull musically, but the lyric, a straightforward rant against those who live off others, intrigues, reminiscent of 'Everybody Want What They Don't Got'. It fits well with a suite of songs that feature Prince seeming to separate himself off from the rest of the world: even the private parties are over now, as Prince sings of his global citizenship and fumes equally at bankers and freeloaders.

When Prince returned to performing live in the autumn, the shows had grown significantly more varied. In Bergen, he began the main show as if it were an after-show, opening with 'Empty Room' and 'Stratus'. At the next main show he opened with 'Future Soul Song', and at that night's after-show played a fifteen-minute version of 'Sticky Like Glue' from *20 Ten*. This handful of European shows were up to nearly three hours in length, but he soon fell back on the hits, with no indication that the *20 Ten* songs were going to stay around long in his set list.

Prince had intimated that the European shows were a warm-up for a major US tour, and he ended 2010 and spent much of the first half of 2011 playing the Welcome 2 America tour on home shores, including what was billed as a 21 Night Stand in Los Angeles, replicating his long run in London. The promotion for this tour was similar to the way he'd pushed the London dates, with a press conference (this time at the Apollo theatre) that was as much of an event as the tour itself and grand promises. It was suggested that this would be as much about Prince showcasing other artists as playing himself, but most of the guests (Larry Graham, Maceo Parker, Mint Condition) were the same people he'd had as support for years, and the others were artists he'd either already covered or been championing for a while (Janelle Monáe, Cee Lo Green, Esperanza Spalding). One of the greatest disappointments regarding Prince's work in recent years is his lack of engagement with the younger electronic artists for whom he remains a constant inspiration, and the bill for this tour reflected that. As an album, *20 Ten* is as innovative and peculiar as anything by Joker, Hudson Mohawke, SBTRKT or Odd Future, but live, post-*Musicology*, Prince seems to insist on presenting himself as a heritage act. Also, I understand that he has reservations about artists he considers musically inferior, and having guests on his records hasn't worked in the past, but it seems to me that one of the great advantages of music over writing is that you can bring fresh blood into your projects, and I can't understand why Prince doesn't invite, for example, Larry Graham's superstar nephew Drake into the studio for a collaboration.

Though there was no new album to promote, Prince did introduce a few new songs, including one it seemed the tour was named after – 'Welcome 2 America' – initially sung offstage but featuring lyrics about the way the US had yet to change under the new administration (his complaints remained the same as they were way back on 'Xenophobia', Prince still fuming about airport searches), which suggested the Gil Scott-Heron influence on his work had not disappeared entirely. There was also another example of him introducing new lyrics through an old song, 'Gingerbread Man', which he sang over the music of 'The Question of U', a surreal song about Prince's sexual skills that sounded like a fairy-tale rewrite of 'Electric Man'.

The opening four songs of the eleventh night of the tour were broadcast on 102.3 KJLH in Los Angeles. Listening to this broadcast, it's clear that no matter how pedestrian the set list seemed, Prince was on amusing form, adding musical jokes (a burst of jazz and a tribute to Stevie Wonder in 'Pop Life') and cryptic lines about phone numbers to 'Musicology/Prince and the Band'. If his voice didn't sound quite as strong as usual, this was understandable for the mid-point in a long run, and he covered this up well with the combination sing–rap vocals he has sometimes turned to in recent years, making it sound as if he was unstitching a song from the inside. He also sang a brilliant new song, 'U Will Be', over music from 'Shhh' (he'd first introduced the song three nights before, singing it over 'The Question of U'), a savage lyric about winning a woman from another man due to the fact that the size of his income dwarfed his love rival's.

In the summer, Prince played the idiosyncratically named Welcome 2 America European tour. To promote the shows, he conducted a joint interview with a French journalist from *Le Parisien* and Dorian Lynskey of the *Guardian*. Once again he talked about time being a trick, shutting off the possibility of addressing the subject of ageing in his music, territory other musicians not much older than him have found fertile. He's a long way off recording his *Time Out of Mind*, of course, but he should be wary of the example of Cliff Richard and even Mick Jagger. Pop's Peter Pans tend not to write the best lyrics in later life. Prince's comments about not recording any more music and the order found in countries with only one religion caused such a stir among the fan community that Prince-favoured blogger Dr Funkenberry ran a piece on his blog about the set up of the interview, suggesting that Lynskey (who, like most journalists who interview Prince now, wasn't allowed to record the exchange) had not delivered Prince's comments entirely without spin, an accusation to which Lynskey's editor responded robustly.

The last time I saw Prince to date was at Hop Farm in Kent, on this run, and although all the reviews were five-star raves, the show was, for a long-time supporter, boring. This is the experience of the Prince fan, for the time being at least: taking a gamble on when and where to see him, hoping that you get the magic instead of the hits. Later in the year, Prince told the *Toronto Star*: 'Each audience is different. What they respond 2 most favourably usually dictates the flow of the concert and the choice of material,'[3] suggesting that the quality of his performance is not in his hands but ours.

Perhaps this explains the frustrations of some shows and the delights of others. Whereas once Prince was one of the very few artists who could square the circle and perform a dense and fascinating show to a combined audience of hundreds of thousands, now most hard-core fans focus solely on the after-shows or special performances. As with other musicians in their fifties or older, after a lifetime onstage, Prince has to decide on a performance strategy. Some musicians in his position choose to perform their songs in new ways (Bob Dylan); others mix new songs in with classic hits (Neil Young); some even decide their set lists via a revolving wheel (Elvis Costello) or by grabbing song requests written on cardboard from the front rows (Bruce Springsteen). The ultimate way to move on is perhaps that offered by The Fall's Mark E. Smith, whose shows usually consist of the album in progress and the couple which came before, with only occasionally a couple of old songs. At the moment, Prince performs mainly predictable main shows, but his after-shows remain as good as ever.

What do I want from Prince now? Leaving aside his need to make money, and focusing solely on the art, I'd like him to either give up on the main shows or come up with a concept that allows him to give his old songs a worthwhile new setting, as he did with *Lovesexy* or *One Nite Alone . . ..* I'd like him to stop playing 'the hits', as has been promised at so many tours before. I'd like every performance to be as exciting or unexpected as seeing him in a small club always is. I'd like him to find a way of putting out his unreleased songs, either via the Internet or CD or whatever new way of disseminating the music he's currently considering. I'd like him to make public everything from his Vault. I'd like it if when he reworks an old song, as he's just done with 'Extra Loveable' (at the time of writing the latest 'new' Prince song to be released), he could make the original version available, even if only for comparison. I get that he feels protective about his old work, but why not make it public? Why do sales matter now? If collectors-edition sets only sell a few hundred thousand or less, it'll make no difference to the number of people queuing up at stadiums to watch him play. I'd like him to put out vast sets of out-takes and alternative versions, like The Beach Boys' *Smile Sessions* or the manifold Miles Davis releases. I'd like him to carry on releasing CDs, but either to put out a huge number of songs as they're composed, in the way he did in the late 1990s, or to release a CD that features enough songs he truly cares about for him to devote himself to promoting it and for him to find a way to get an audience, of whatever size, to care about it as much as they care about *Purple Rain*. I'd like to carry on seeing him live whenever he performs and find something new to love every time.

As most of the people I've interviewed during the writing of this book have maintained, Prince's story won't be over until long after he's dead and all the music he's recorded is in the public domain. But maybe that will never happen. During the time I've been writing, Prince's output has slowed to a trickle, though he has at least contradicted the claim that he made to Dorian Lynskey of the *Guardian* that he had no plans to record another album, even though he has hundreds of songs ready for release, subsequently telling the *Toronto Star* shortly before his Welcome 2 Canada tour that he would break the deliberate self-restriction because he has 'a writing addiction', and that although 'this break from recording is an attempt 2 curb the creative craving', his current band was 'way 2 talented' not to be recorded.[4]

As I write this, Prince has just concluded a tour of Canada; from the set lists the shows sound predictable, but set lists never tell the whole story and every night there's always at least one surprise. There are rumours that next year will bring more tours, shows in Australia and maybe a return to Europe. Reaching the end of this book, I find myself reflecting on the comment Pepe Willie made about Prince wanting to get to a place where no one can find him. Once, it was possible to see this as a geographical place, perhaps the fortress of Paisley Park. But he opened the doors of that location to fans and invited visitors in. So perhaps that place he's looking for is a position in popular culture, one that he exists in now. Aside from a hard core of devoted fans, few people have a very clear sense of where Prince is now, musically at least. There's no guarantee that new albums will be found in record stores, and many of his old ones are rapidly slipping out of print. His band is made up of largely anonymous figures who though charming onstage lack much of a media presence, and who rarely do interviews and are seemingly interchangeable at a moment's notice. Prince's relationship status is largely unknown, his lyrics are more cryptic than ever, and when he gives interviews his proclamations seem (deliberately, I believe) harder to follow than ever. He has been more successful at disengaging with the world than any major artist I can think of, and yet he can't make that final break, can't go into an extended hiatus like the one David Bowie is on now. This isn't what I wish for him, but the now-you-see-me-now-you-don't of the last decade has proved exhausting (at least for those of us still paying attention).

By the time this book is published, he might have gone back on his recent proclamations and delivered an album or two. Maybe a reissue programme might even have begun. Records and songs by Neil Young and Bob Dylan that most believed might never see release are now freely available, and perhaps Prince's recent revisiting of songs like 'In a Large Room with No Light' and 'Extra Loveable' might indicate that he's finally ready to come to terms with his past. One thing seems certain: he will be out there performing, somewhere, onstage or in the studio, every year for the rest of his life. Who knows how long this will continue? Endlessly, we can hope. Prince once said Wendy wants to live for ever. So does Prince. Maybe he will.

EPILOGUE: LIVING OUT LOUD

Right up until the moment this book was published in October 2012, I was anxiously waiting for Prince to do something that would mean I'd have to rewrite the whole volume. A reissue programme was my greatest fear – though as a listener it was also what I wanted most. Instead, Prince seemed to have gone into creative hibernation. He was touring, of course, as he always does: an eight-date tour of Australia (plus four 'after-jams' in the latest of his 'Welcome 2' stints), followed by some more shows in Chicago and LA designed, at least in part, to launch Andy Allo's *Superconductor*. But by his standards, he was unusually quiet. Behind closed doors, it would later emerge, recording had been going on as usual, but there seemed to be more uncertainty than ever about how (or even if) his new songs might see release.

It wasn't until after the book appeared that the publicity machine started up, beginning with the November release of a new single entitled 'Rock and Roll Love Affair'. Back when Prince was following conventional record-industry practice, this might have been the lead-off single for a new album, and listening to the track, it was easy to imagine what said album might sound like: a 1980s rock record, perhaps, returning to the new-wave sounds that had inspired the Rebels project. The next song to appear – 'Screwdriver' – also wouldn't have sounded out of place alongside his cover of The Cars' 'Let's Go' in some future set list – and indeed he did revive the latter when he next went out on the road.

'Screwdriver' seems inspired by touring with the female members of a young band, sharing clothes and sneakers (something he mentioned when being interviewed in France on *Le Grand Journal* in 2009). But what would prove ultimately more significant than the song itself was the way it was introduced to listeners.

Since starting to work with Andy Allo, there had been a notable softening from Prince on the (controlled) distribution of his work via social networking. After allowing Allo to make various live performances and songs available via her Facebook page, he now permitted new NPG drummer Hannah Ford to stream a rehearsal version of the *Chaos and Disorder* song 'I Like It There'. For those paying attention, the choice of song was another clue to Prince's new direction. 'I Like It There' was swiftly followed by an extract from 'Screwdriver', along with the message '2 C the rest of Donna's audition holla at ya girl! We've got bootlegs 4 daazzzzzze every good thing in the vault . . . Coming 2013.' The sloppy syntax gave enough wiggle-room for fans to remember past broken promises, but the energy in the new song (later released in full) excited the faithful. On New Year's Eve 2012, Prince (in disguise) launched a new YouTube channel, over which he streamed another song taken from the same rehearsal during which the extract from 'Screwdriver' was recorded: a version of 'Bambi' featuring new guitarist Donna Grantis, Hannah Ford and Ida Nielsen, NPG bassist and now, it seemed, the third member of Prince's new girl group 3rdEyeGirl.[1] Though 'Bambi' appeared on Prince's second album, it's a song he's only previously played with the most macho permutations of his band. That he decided to revive it with an all-girl line-up is another example of the psychosexual playfulness that defines Prince at his best.

At the start of 2013, Prince gifted his listeners another brace of songs via this new YouTube channel. If it was the start of a deliberate Internet campaign, the timing of the first salvo in the 3rdEyeGirl promotional blitz was somewhat unfortunate, at least if Prince was hoping to generate headlines, in that the four songs he put out – an 'Xtended' remix of the *20 Ten* song 'Laydown', a remix of 'Rock and Roll Love Affair' far superior to the Jamie Lewis remixes of the song that had come with the single; a studio-rehearsal version of old song 'Bambi'; and new track 'Same Page Different Book' (a bland piece of sermonising in which Prince once again wonders about the causes of conflict) – appeared on the same day that David Bowie decided to return after a decade of silence. Prince continued to insist that 3rdEyeGirl was a bootlegger, some sort of supposed 'international art thief', and even threatened to sue her. (He told *Billboard* that he employs 'a team of black female lawyers who keep an eye on such transgressions'.[2]) If this was a joke, it fell flat.

Fake or not, the conflict was soon resolved – with Prince's band members posting jokey clips about which of them was 3rdEyeGirl – and new tracks started to appear as links on the Twitter feed: first a live, 'slowed-down' rendition of 'I Could Never Take the Place of Your Man' from a show in Chicago the previous September; then Prince's remix of a song by Ana Moura entitled 'Dream of Fire (Purple Fire Mix)' and another extract from 'Screwdriver'. This was the beginning of a series of releases that would trickle out through the first part of 2013, accompanied by Prince's later assertion to *Billboard* that he was no longer interested in releasing albums, which must have come as a surprise to bass player Andrew Gouche, who had previously informed *Bass Musician* magazine he was on 'two or three songs' on Prince's new record.[3]

In time-honoured fashion, Prince debuted his new band and material in his home town first. It initially seemed as if he would be using the shows to introduce his new all-female group. A Fox 9 news report intended to promote the local shows featured interviews with 3rdEyeGirl, who explained how Prince had discovered them via YouTube and MySpace (so much for 'the Internet is over'). But it turned out Prince wasn't just introducing a new band and a new set of songs, but showing three sides of his interests and abilities, with six shows, split into pairs, billed as a 'soundcheck', a 'jam' and a 'surprise'. Each of the two sets of performances showcased a different genre, beginning with jazz, followed by funk and finishing with rock.

At the Dakota, Prince showed up on time, played eighty-minute sets and embraced the jazz and experimental side of his work, with songs like 'Muse 2 the Pharoah' and 'Xpectation' returning to the set for the first time since his jazz era. The first four shows were designed to break in new drummer Ronald Bruner, Jr, who performed with Prince alongside Andrew Gouche and Cassandra O'Neal, followed by the two-show debut of 3rdEyeGirl.

Prince soon made public a new song improvised at the fourth of the shows entitled 'Chapters & Verse'. The song is in the vein of 'Prince and the Band', 'Welcome 2 America' or the various talking-blues improvisations he's done at after-shows. He's never sounded as much like Frank Zappa as he does on this one, especially when he swallows a chuckle while amusing himself with a freshly coined joke. Once again the subject of getting paid seems at the heart of it, as he discovers sacks of 'purple money' in the yard. It's delightful to hear him singing about burgers again, even if he's concerned someone might have been putting fluoride in the patties. It sounded like the sort of thing he used to do privately at rehearsal, bonding exercises with the band now made public. (Later, he would also release a version of 'Stratus' from these performances.)

The six shows were followed by a subsequent night's DJ set

(where Prince appeared on sampler). During this evening, Prince's long-term DJ, Rashida, played a number of his songs – 'Angel Wish', 'Check the Record', 'Keep Begging', 'The Breakdown' and '2 Young 2 Dare' (aka '2Y2D') – that were yet to be released in any form. (Still another new song, 'Pulla Wagon', was shown to a Fox 9 employee during the interview with Prince's three new bandmates.)

And then appeared a new website, 20prInc3.com, with every sign he'd learnt from the problems of the past. No timer, no password, three new gifts: a trailer for a three-hour Montreux show; the 'Screwdriver' video, with the lyrics spelt out on screen in the style of 'Sign o' the Times' and 'One Song'; and a trailer showing 'what the critics are saying about "Superconductor"'. It couldn't last, and it didn't. The website still exists but all it offers now is the 'Screwdriver' video.

Instead, Prince introduced a different website, 3rdEyeGirl. com, through which – at the time of writing – he's offered for sale seven songs ('Screwdriver' again, plus a remix; another remix of 'Rock and Roll Love Affair' – number seven, we're told; 'Breakfast Can Wait'; 'Boyfriend'; 'That Girl Thang'; and 'Live Out Loud'), plus five videos (a 'film' and a 'music video' for 'Screwdriver'; a 'rough cut master 2' video for 'Live Out Loud'; a live recording of old song 'Bambi'; and a video for the *Planet Earth* song 'Guitar').

My favourite of all the songs and videos Prince has released as downloads is 'Breakfast Can Wait', the only track that simultaneously reaches back deep into the 1980s for inspiration and features Prince doing something he hasn't done before. It starts out like a standard example of morning-after lover-man R&B, with Prince telling a partner how much he prefers making love to her than having breakfast (while simultaneously seeming more lascivious in the way he describes his hot cakes and coffee than the love-making); then, just after he introduces a touch of menace into the imploring, he pitch-shifts his vocals way past Camille, past even the vocals on 'F.U.N.K.', until he sounds like a sex-crazed smurf.

Yes, I know it's only studio trickery, but it's one of those bizarre creative decisions only Prince would make (it's certainly more inventive than anything on Justin Timberlake's *The 20/20 Experience*). Is this a character, a new alter ego? No: in the squeaky voice he refers to himself as Prince, upending the song and mocking everything he set up in the first three verses. It's the sort of song that makes an album, and yet at present it is nothing more than a download, perhaps already forgotten by Prince.

I realise I'm old-fashioned but I'd love a twelve-inch of this track.

I was in Norway appearing as part of a panel of people who'd written books about musicians (among the panellists was a very distinguished music writer who early in his career had also written a book about Prince), when one of the audience asked us what we thought of Prince's latest song. I told the Norwegian I couldn't speak with any authority on Prince's 'latest song' as I was certain that by the time I'd returned to my hotel room and checked, another would have appeared.

And sure enough, when I did, there was 'Boyfriend', which upon hearing it first over a phone I dismissed as one of those songs in which Prince goes 'ooh', someone sets the keyboards off and three minutes later there's a song – of as little lasting interest as most of the filler tracks on the previous three albums. Listening to it again later, through a proper stereo, I realised that while the lyric offers little (other than the fact that as with the superior 'U Will B', Prince is singing about a man at the very least thinking about stealing another man's girlfriend, the latest in his continuing change of perspective from the oft-cuckolded lover of his earliest songs), having the Hornheadz on the track immediately elevates it above less polished tracks where it's just Prince, his synths and an effects library. It does feel slight, though. Perhaps it is merely (as blogger Dr Funkenberry suggested) a demo, one of three versions said to exist, and maybe the least interesting.

Even less substantial, the next track to appear, 'That Girl Thang', though featuring some of the prettiest acoustic guitar Prince has put out in a while, seems the sort of preliminary sketch that would have disappeared had he not been road-testing this new manner of quickly disseminating music. But even in a piece so slight Prince manages to sneak in a strange piece of sci-fi thinking in which he refers to himself as a 'fifth-dimension prisoner', which presumably is a reference to the multiverse and the fact that he cannot escape his time or circumstances.

Though 'Live Out Loud' appears to be a 3rdEyeGirl song, it was written not by the band but by another of Prince's female band members – Liv Warfield of the NPG. The dated rock-reggae self-empowerment number, which features Prince on backing vocals, is by far the least interesting of the download-only offerings to date.

So far, at least, the videos released on the site have been similarly uninspiring. The full-length video for 'Screwdriver' is a return to the amateurishness that marred some of the mid-1990s video releases – a combination of the chilliness of a soundstage not filled with enough extras *Graffiti Bridge*-style and an anachronistic attempt to revive the 'The Twist' as 'The Screw'. The 'rough cut master 2' video accompanying 'Live Out Loud' is equally uninspiring, with singing drummer Hannah Ford miming the lyrics while dancing among a bunch of hipsters-for-hire. And while it's nice to see The Twinz again, the only possible explanation for Prince putting the 'Guitar' video up five years after recording it must have been a nagging sense that he hadn't quite got as much out of *Planet Earth* as he might. It's hard to understand why he teases us with this sort of thing when there's so much we'd prefer to see made available. Is he testing the water? Afraid of not getting enough money for a clip he might be able to profit from in a different way later? Or simply having fun by continuing to frustrate expectation?

As I write this it has been several months since Prince has made anything available for download via his website (but then again, he has been out on tour), and the last few releases to date have come through other channels. As well as live versions of a combination of 'Boom' and 'Stratus' played in rehearsal (accompanied with a video of the girls going record shopping)[4] and a live version of 'She's Always in My Hair' – another track totally transformed in performance with 3rdEyeGirl[5] – there have been two more substantial semi-releases. He played on an instrumental by Donna Grantis entitled 'Plectrum Electrum', and 'Fixurlifeup' was given to a Canadian radio station as part of the promotion for the live show before being released via iTunes.

'Fixurlifeup' is a confusing song. In part it seems to be a feminist celebration of women in music. In a short item in the *Guardian*, an anonymous journalist approved of this, asserting on behalf of the paper's employees that '"Tryin' a be a star when you're just another brick in the misogynist wall of noise," is our favourite line from the new Prince song "Fixurlifeup".'[6] But it's also a political track. Prince performed the song at the *Billboard* Awards[7] and later released a video that played off the cryptic reference to London in the lyrics with footage of the protest march against the Iraq war. The video was, in places, mindboggling in its literalness (a reference to someone being 'toast' is accompanied with footage of toast being buttered). Musically, the track is pedestrian, and quite why Prince wants to sound like 4 Non Blondes in 2013 is a mystery only he can answer. *Spin* magazine suggested he had gone 'perplexingly grunge',[8] an assertion given some credence by his subsequent decision to cover Pearl Jam's 'Even Flow', a snippet of which he released via Dr Funkenberry. A few days later they made another connection – one which had previously occurred to me but which I'd dismissed given Prince's antipathy to male singers and 'untrained' musicians – linking the 'Fixurlifeup' video with Chelsea Light Moving's 'Lip' promo.[9] Prince and Thurston Moore, who split with his wife Kim Gordon and put his band Sonic Youth on hiatus while launching Chelsea Light Moving, are worlds apart – though they have more musical common ground than either man might realise – but they were born within a few months of each other, with the two fifty-somethings both fending off their pasts by embracing the music they listened to when they were starting out (funk-rock in Prince's case; hardcore in Thurston's) and embarking on long tours with a new band. I'd love to see the pair improvise together.

Still, it does seem as if Prince has not merely imposed his own sound onto 3rdEyeGirl but allowed the music to be shaped by the talents of the three women he's working with. The fact that Donna Grantis would frequently cover Billy Cobham's 'Stratus' must have been part of what drew Prince to the young guitarist, but it's easy to hear what else he might have appreciated in her album *Suites*, which seems inspired by the same 1970s funk-jazz-rock that has always been a part of Prince's sound. Though this has not been confirmed, it seems her 'Elektra (Elektra Suite)', now retooled into the new instrumental 'Plectrum Electrum', will be the title track of the 3rdEyeGirl album. Given Prince's previous uses of the name 'Elektra' – as the inspiration for both Carmen Electra's surname and the song 'Come Elektra Tuesday' – I wonder if there was any conversation in the rehearsal room about transforming a song about a daughter's grief and revenge into a song about a gold guitar pick. There are moments on this album that bring to mind Sonny T ('Gold Dust Vixen' makes you wish Donna had been around to add her guitar alongside his on 'Papa'), and it's clear why the record helped inspire Prince to launch a female version of the New Power Trio.

Though I have not seen a show on the 3rdEyeGirl tour and do not know whether Prince will bring the group overseas when he comes to Europe in the second half of 2013 or whether he will revert to his bigger band set-up, it strikes me from looking at the set lists and from what I have heard about the shows that they are perhaps closest to the Nude tour in their stripped-down nature or the Támar run in the way they have allowed Prince to focus on certain elements of his performance that he sometimes neglects in the big shows.

Ostensibly a rock show, as an opener Prince reworked 'Let's Go Crazy' for the first time since the South American tour in 1990, including elements of the Edgar Winter Group's 'Frankenstein' in the performance (previously, he had sometimes woven this tune into his version of 'Stratus') and turning the track into a slow funk song he shared with his fans via photographer Madison Dubé's Vimeo account. (Dubé was also responsible for the 'BoomStratus' video, the 'Plectrum Electrum' short film and a 'tour promo' for the Live Out Loud run in which the three women forcibly state their desire to rock.) A surprising mainstay of the set list was *The Gold Experience* track 'Endorphinmachine', which had accompanied a previous, similarly dramatic transformation back in 1995 when it was part of an all-new set on The Ultimate Live Experience tour (some nights he'd play 'Dolphin' from this era too). He'd play a recording of 'Screwdriver' and pretend he was about to lip-synch before performing the song live. 'Guitar' found its perfect setting at last, but he didn't neglect the piano, with room some nights for the *Emancipation* song 'The Love We Make', although he'd play 'Sometimes It Snows in April' on guitar. Not quite having enough tried-and-tested *Plectrum Electrum* material yet (or maybe fearing the audience reaction if he constructed a whole show out of it), the new tracks were limited to 'Plectrum Electrum', 'The Breakdown', 'Fixurlifeup' and '2Y2D', though he also played an older song yet to appear on any album, 'Cause and Effect'.

Just as he ended the Támar shows by returning to his own repertoire and reminding the audience of his true talents, so he followed the rock set most nights with a version of the sampler set he's been using as a way of rushing through a handful of hits on most recent tours. The Live Out Loud show appears to have been similarly structured most nights, but he also dug out rarities: 'When We're Dancing Close and Slow'; a surprisingly toothless version of 'The Ride'; the *Rave Un2 the Joy Fantastic* song 'So Far, So Pleased' (only performed once before); and, played to great effect and with unlikely respect to the original, 'The Max'. During the tour he also performed several tracks from *Sign o' the Times*, in a sincere way rather than fooling around with them in the way he's mainly done when performing them live in recent years. Fans who have seen the show rave about the new (but as yet unreleased) song 'The Breakdown', which some consider one of his most heartfelt lyrics in years. Reviews of the shows have been mixed, with the usual raves (Jon Bream claimed it was 'the most exciting Prince show I've seen since probably the Sign o' the Times Tour in 1987'[10]) tempered by less flattering accounts, including journalists in Vancouver suggesting the show was 'uneven'[11] (a strange criticism to make, as the variety of music on offer has been part of even Prince's very best shows) and suffering from 'the bloated excess'[12] of the 1970s.

But by the end of the run he was feeling confident enough to fly in journalists – Amy Nelson of the *Pioneer Press* and long-time supporter Jon Bream – to witness a 3rdEyeGirl performance, with Nelson noting how Prince's anxiety at unveiling a new band had gone now they'd played thirty-four shows together.[13]

In order for this revised edition to appear in late 2013, I have to stop here, at the end of May 2013. The Live Out Loud tour has recently concluded with two home-town shows at a club called Myth Live in Maplewood, Minnesota, where former Revolution member Bobby Z joined the band on drums for 'Purple Rain'.[14] There are a handful of European shows booked, with rumours of more to come. It is too early to know if the LOL tour was a one-off experiment or part of something more lasting.

At the time of writing, the latest news is that he has just signed a deal with Kobalt Music Group, who will provide distribution and marketing for future releases, whether under his own name or produced with protégés. The publicity is emphasising that, once again, it's an exciting new beginning for Prince. It's hard to imagine he'll turn all that's past into prologue, but that remains the ambition, as important as it's ever been.

ACKNOWLEDGEMENTS

It quickly became clear to me while writing this book that throughout his career Prince has surrounded himself with the most diligent, intelligent and charming people, and among his many accomplishments is his ability to seek out the most dedicated collaborators, and in this book I have endeavoured to tell their stories alongside my commentary on Prince's work. While he has not endorsed this book (or read it), I am grateful to Prince Rogers Nelson for allowing me to come to his house and to attend the launch of *21 Nights*, both unforgettable evenings.

Thanks to Shane O'Neill and Sarah Boorman for their part in getting me to Prince's house, and Hannah Corbett for helping arrange the trip to the Hotel Gansevoort.

For agreeing to be interviewed, thanks to Arthur Baker, Howard Bloom, Hans-Martin Buff, Bob Cavallo, Gayle Chapman, Lisa Coleman, Carole Davis, Dez Dickerson, Brent Fischer, Dr Clare Fischer, Frank Griffiths, Nancy Hynes, Alan Leeds, Eric Leeds, Susannah Melvoin, Wendy Melvoin, Stephin Merritt, Chris Moon, Steve Parke, Chris Poole, Alexis Taylor and Pepe Willie.

The deal for the book was completed by my wife, and at that time, agent Lesley Thorne, who has also put up with the seven years of research it has taken me to complete it.

Thanks to Thomas Patterson for introducing me to Renata Kanderz, who set up the interview with Lisa Coleman and Wendy Melvoin; Rachel Lichtman, aka DJ Rotary Rachel, for accompanying me to that interview, and to her and Tom for putting me up in Los Angeles; Wendy and Lisa for putting me in contact with Matt Fink and Dez Dickerson; Matt Fink for putting me in touch with Gayle Chapman and Alan Leeds; Julie Masi for setting up the interview with Susannah Melvoin in Los Angeles; Paul Peterson for helping me contact and interview Eric Leeds; and Gaby Green for getting me backstage at an fDeluxe show. I am grateful to Frank Griffith and Donna Fischer for putting me in contact with Brent and Dr Clare Fischer; Steve Johnson and Sarah Cheyne for introducing me to Chris Poole; and Anwen Rees at the BBC for putting me in contact with Kristie Lazenberry, who arranged the interview with Pepe Willie. Bernardine Evaristo helped me get in touch with Nancy Hynes. Barney Hoskyns let me try out some ideas on him, for which I am grateful.

Thanks to Brunel University for a sabbatical to complete this work, and in particular to Celia Brayfield, Professor Steve Dixon, Max Kinnings, Dr William Leahy, Sarah Penny, Professor Fay Weldon, Tony White and Tim Lott. I am also grateful to fellow Prince observer Professor Sarah Niblock and her partner-in-Paisley-crime Professor Stan Hawkins. Thanks to Stuart Batford, Nicholas Blincoe and Matthew De Abaitua (whenever there's a mention of 'a Prince fan of my acquaintance' in the text, it's usually him).

Thanks to Max Decharne for advice; Suzi Feay for commissioning a review of 21 Nights; Mark Lawson and the team at Front Row for allowing me to review 'Planet Earth' and the 21 Nights in London shows; Bernadette McNulty for commissioning a piece about Prince for the Telegraph and Jeb Loy Nichols for the illustrations for the extract from this that appeared in Loops; and Nick Stone for the many Prince-related conversations and for getting me into the New Marquee.

Thanks also to Daniel Blumberg, Carrie-Anne Brackstone, Richard Brazier, James Butler, Robert Clough, Fleur Darkin, Johnny Davis, Matt Dornan, Geoff Dyer, Amanda Emmett, Tibor Fischer, Alice Fisher, Nicholas Guyatt, Philip and Zoe Hood, Sarah Hornsey, Liz Jensen, David Jones, Toby Litt, Dee McGrudy, Stephen Merchant, Chris Metzler, Hannah Ross, Jim, Jamie and Catherine Shaw, Stav Sherez, Mark, Louise, Charlotte and Annabel Sinclair, Peter Straus, Michael Tant, Richard Thomas, Ben Thompson, David Thorne, Kaye Thorne, Theodore Vlassopulos, Willy Vlautin, Leigh Wilson, Rebecca Wilson and the members of the Board.

Richard King (along with Lee Brackstone) had the idea of getting me to write a long piece on Prince's protégés, which formed the basis of the 'Gigolos Get Lonely Too' chapters here and extracts of which appeared in Faber's *Loops* periodical. I would also like to thank Lisa Baker, Luke Bird, Richard T. Kelly and Stephen Page at Faber.

BIBLIOGRAPHY

OFFICIAL PRINCE BOOKS

Prince, *Neo Manifesto – Audentes Fortuna Juvat* (Minneapolis: Paisley Park, 1994).

Prince with David Henry Hwang, 'From *Come*', in *On a Bed of Rice: An Asian-American Erotic Feast*, Ed. Geraldine Kudaka (New York: Bantam, 1998).

Prince and Terry Gydesen, *Prince Presents the Sacrifice of Victor* (Minneapolis: Paisley Park, 1994).

Prince with Randee St. Nicholas, *21 Nights* (New York: Atria, 2008).

Shahadi, Afshin, *Prince in Hawaii: An Intimate Portrait of an Artist* (NPG Music Club, 2004).

SELECTED BOOKS ABOUT PRINCE

Bream, Jon, *Prince: Inside the Purple Reign* (New York: Macmillan, 1984).

Brown, Geoff, *The Complete Guide to the Music of Prince* (London: Omnibus, 1995).

Dickerson, Dez, *My Time with Prince: Confessions of a Former Revolutionary* (Tulsa, OK: Pavilion Press, 2003).

Draper, Jason, *Prince: Life and Times* (London: Jawbone, 2008).

—————— *Prince: Chaos, Disorder and Revolution* (New York: Backbeat, 2011).

Edrei, Mary J. (Ed.) *The Year of the Prince* (London: Sphere, 1984).

Hahn, Alex, *Possessed: The Rise and Fall of Prince* (New York: Billboard, 2003).

Hawkins, Stan and Sarah Niblock, *Prince: The Making of a Pop Music Phenomenon* (Surrey: Ashgate, 2011).

Hill, Dave, *Prince: A Pop Life* (London: Faber, 1989).

Hoskyns, Barney, *Prince: Imp of the Perverse* (London: Virgin, 1988).

Ivory, Steven, *Prince* (New York: Putnam, 1984).

Jones, Liz, *Slave to the Rhythm* (London: Little Brown, 1997).

Matos, Michaelangelo, *Sign o' the Times* (London: Continuum, 2004).

Morton, Brian, *Prince: Thief in the Temple* (Edinburgh: Canongate, 2007).

Muir, John Kenneth, *Music on Film: Purple Rain* (Milwaukee: Limelight Editions, 2012).

Nilsen, Per, *Prince: A Documentary* (London: Omnibus, 1990).

——— *DanceMusicSexRomance – Prince: The First Decade* (London: Firefly, 1999).

——— et al., *The Vault* (Europe: Uptown, 2004). (Although this is privately printed and, to the best of my knowledge, out of print, much of the information has been transferred to the website www.princevault.com.)

Ro, Ronin, *Prince: Inside the Man and the Masks* (New York: St Martin's, 2011).

Rosen, Steven, *The Artist Formerly Known as Prince* (London: Castle, 1995).

Till, Rupert, *Pop Cult: Religion and Popular Music* (London/New York: Continuum, 2010).

SELECTED OTHER BOOKS REFERRED TO IN THE TEXT

Ariosto, Ludovico, *Orlando Furioso* (1532; edition consulted, London: Oxford Classics, 2008).

Barbin, Herculine, *Being the Recently Discovered Memoirs of a Nineteenth Century French Hermaphrodite* (Great Britain: Harvester, 1980).

Bloom, Howard, *The Genius of the Beast: A Radical Re-Vision of Capitalism* (New York: Prometheus, 2010).

——— *The God Problem: The Five Heresies or the Big Bang Tango* (USA: Prometheus, 2012).

Cole, George, *The Last Miles* (London: Equinox, 2005).

Davis, Miles with Quincy Troupe, *Miles: The Autobiography* (London: Simon and Schuster, 1989).

Doggett, Peter, *The Man Who Sold the World: David Bowie and the 1970s* (London: Bodley Head, 2011).

Eadie, Betty J., *Embraced by the Light* (Detroit: Gold Leaf Press, 1992).

Edmundson, Mark, *Nightmare on Main Street: Angels, Sadomasochism, and the Culture of the Gothic* (Cambridge, MA: Harvard, 1997).

Goldberg, Danny, *Bumping into Geniuses: My Life Inside the Rock and Roll Business* (New York: Gotham, 2009).

Gore, Tipper, *Raising PG Kids in an X-Rated Society* (Nashville, TN: Abingdon Press, 1987).

Hackett, Pat (Ed.), *The Andy Warhol Diaries* (New York: Warner Books, 1989).

Heylin, Clinton, *Bootleg! The Rise & Fall of the Secret Recording Industry* (London: Omnibus, 2003).

Homer, *The Odyssey*, translated by Richard Lattimore (New York: Harper & Row, 1967).

Hoskyns, Barney, *Ragged Glories: City Lights, Country Funk, American Music* (London: Pimlico, 2003).

James, Rick, *The Confessions of Rick James: Memoirs of a Super Freak* (New York: Colossus Books, 2007).

Kureishi, Hanif, *The Black Album* (London: Faber, 1995).

Lethem, Jonathan, *Motherless Brooklyn* (London: Faber, 1999).

Lynskey, Dorian, *33 Revolutions per Minute: A History of Protest Songs* (London: Faber, 2011).

Marks, Craig and Rob Tannenbaum, *I Want My MTV: The Uncensored Story of the Music Video Revolution* (New York: Dutton, 2011).

New World Translation Committee, *New World Translation of the Holy Scriptures* (New York: Watch Tower Tract and Bible Society, 1984).

Richards, Keith (with James Fox), *Life* (London: Orion, 2010).

Ross, Alex, *The Rest Is Noise: Listening to the Twentieth Century* (New York: Farar, Straus and Giroux, 2007).

Shore, Michael with Dick Clark, *The History of American Bandstand* (New York: Ballantine, 1985).

Sixx, Nikki, *The Heroin Diaries: A Year in the Life of a Shattered Rock Star* (New York: MTV Books, 2008).

Taylor, Don with Mike Henry, *So Much Things to Say: My Life as Bob Marley's Manager* (London: Blake, 1995).

Zollo, Paul, *Songwriters on Songwriting* (expanded fourth edn) (New York: Da Capo, 2003).

NOTES

PROLOGUE

1 Although he does occasionally reference them in his lyrics, albeit usually in a negative light, as in his early unreleased song 'Cold Coffee and Cocaine'. 'Rock Me, Lover' has Prince as a 'junkie' for love (or sex); 'Purple Music' and 'Now' suggest that Prince's music is as powerful as any narcotic. Other anti-drug references include the opening lines of 'Eye Know' and Prince refusing X in the *Batman* track 'The Future'. And, while performing 'Automatic' on stage in the early 1980s, he would mime shooting up.

2 The excitement (or addiction) of attending ever more exclusive Prince shows was brilliantly satirised by the American novelist Bruce Wagner in *The New Yorker* (6 August 2007). In the article Wagner describes himself paying $325,000 to watch a concert in the company of 'Simon Cowell, the body of Christopher Isherwood, Shia LeBeouf, Michael Moore, Emma Watson and Stephen Hawking', only to later discover that at a concert at the Cedars-Sinai Medical Center, the audience paid $15 million to 'be so close to Prince that, for seven hours, the singer was technically inside their bodies'.

CHAPTER 1

1 He returned to this theme in a 2009 interview with Tavis Smiley in which he said: 'I've asked writers this before and a lot of the time they tell me that they write for each other, they're not really writing for . . . well, I really got him that time, didn't I!'

2 Prince has occasionally enjoyed friendlier relations with journalists, both local and international, such as Jim Walsh of the *St. Paul Pioneer-Press*. Walsh wrote the liner notes for *The Gold Experience* album, and after he published an open letter in the paper on 2 June 2000 challenging Prince to make 'a great record' again, the singer responded by inviting Walsh to Paisley Park for a two-hour chat. Prince also takes on the role of a

'no-name reporter' in the song 'Chaos and Disorder', and by 2004 he was singing about the review he got in the *Oakland Tribune* on the strange song 'S&M Groove', from *The Slaughterhouse*.

3 Susan Rogers had a very interesting response to this, telling now-defunct Prince fan site Housequake: 'Prince fans know how his music makes them feel, regardless of whether or not he intended the music to move them that way. Only he knows what inspired a song or what he wanted his music to say but there is a gap between how it felt to make it and how it feels to listen to it. Like a lot of things, it is a two-sided experience. Science isn't science until it is published; food isn't food until it is eaten; and art isn't art until it is interpreted. As for knowing him as a person, I have said for the record that I am only qualified to speak on his studio life from 1983 to 1988. His life beyond the studio doors, outside of that time-period, is not known to me. Since he has had a rich life, I don't entirely know him' (retrieved 1 Feb 2010 from http://www.psych.mcgill.ca/labs/levitin/media/interview_susan.html).

4 Barney Hoskyns, *Ragged Glory* (Pimlico, 2003), pp. 94–5.

5 Dez Dickerson, *My Time with Prince: Confessions of a Former Revolutionary* (Tulsa, OK: Pavilion Press, 2003), p. 31.

6 Ibid, p. 96.

7 Which makes a connection between Prince's invented abbreviations and ebonics, a term used since 1996 to refer to African American Vernacular English.

8 In recent years, many of Prince's abbreviations have gained popular currency through the practice of text-messaging and no longer seem as original or as startling as when he first started using them. However, they have been highlighted as part of the difficulty of analysing Prince's lyrics in a literary-criticism context. As Nancy J. Holland notes in her essay, 'Purple Passion: Images of Female Desire in "When Doves Cry"': '. . . the lyrics of "When Doves Cry" do not constitute a unitary text in any strict sense. The textuality of Prince's lyrics is ruptured by the use of numbers and single letters for their common homonyms (complicated by a very limited use of punctuation . . .)' (*Cultural Critique Number 10: Popular Narratives, Popular Images*, autumn 1988).

9 In the nineteenth century, this style of writing was known as Emblematic Poetry and practised by authors such as Charles C. Bombaugh, whose 'Essay to Miss Catherine Jay' collected in the 1867 book *Gleanings from the Harvest of Literature* contains the very Prince-like line, 'I 1der if U got that I wrote 2U B 4'.

10 Dickerson, *My Time with Prince*, p. 160.

11 Paul Sexton, 'It's a Family Affair', *The Times*, 13 November 2011.

12 Although given Prince's more recent interest in new forms of distribution for his records, this is a point that has become largely moot.

13 A secure storage space in the basement of Prince's recording complex, Paisley Park.

14 The process by which old magnetic tapes are restored in order to avoid chemical breakdown due to age.

15 That said, after many years of not releasing remix maxi-singles, in December 2011 he put out an extended release containing several remixes of *MPLSound*'s 'Dance 4 Me'.

16 Although *Sign o' the Times* regularly appears in lists of the top-ten concert movies, it is not a straightforward concert recording but actually an odd hybrid, consisting of music from one of the final shows of the *Sign o' the Times* European tour and footage of Prince and the band lip-synching on a Paisley Park soundstage.

17 Interview with Greg Kot, *Details*, 27 April 1998.

CHAPTER 2

1 Aside from the Prince songs for which he receives a credit, the main surviving recordings by John L. Nelson are from an album he released in 1994 called *Father's Song*. Recently, Prince's sister Sharon put out a compilation entitled *57th Street Sound* that makes further use of some of these tracks. While these recordings took place after Prince's success and are therefore hard to appreciate properly, it is easy to get a sense of Nelson's playing style – spectral, untutored, but with the odd moment that echoes his son's musical thinking and innovation. As strange as Nelson's piano-playing sounds on this recording, he did have some celebrity admirers, such as the soul and R&B singer Terence Trent D'Arby, who described meeting him in Germany and hearing him play Franz Liszt and Duke Ellington (the jazz musician who had the greatest influence on Prince before he was really opened up to jazz music by associates such as Lisa Coleman and Eric Leeds and by a late-1980s friendship with Miles Davis) and called him an 'unsung master'.

2 Per Nilsen, *DanceMusicSexRomance – Prince: The First Decade* (London: Firefly, 1999), p. 17.

3 AOL Live interview with Prince, 22 July 1997.

4 *Rave Un2 the Year 2000* (Geoff Wonfor, 1999).

5 Jon Bream, *Prince: Inside the Purple Reign* (New York: Macmillan, 1984), p. 21.

6 *Words and Music*, radio programme, interview with Joni Mitchell by

Morrissey, 18 October 1996, transcribed by Lindsay Moon.

7 Barney Hoskyns, *Ragged Glories* (London: Pimlico, 1993), p. 307.

8 Perhaps because he had taken so much time over the song – or perhaps in an early indication of his ability to recognise potential hits – this track would retain Prince's interest. He would record his own version – as 'Do Yourself a Favor' – in the early 1980s, and Jesse Johnson would later record it for his 1986 album *Shockadelica*, an album which would have a considerable impact on Prince.

9 Willie released one track – 'Games', in an updated form – from these sessions on a 1986 album entitled *Minneapolis Genius – The Historic 1977 Recordings*. Then, on a 1995 double CD entitled *Symbolic Beginning* and credited to '94 East featuring Prince', he released the original versions of the five tracks, as well as instrumental versions of 'Games', 'If You See Me' (retitled 'If You See Me First') and 'Better Than You Think'. The songs appeared again on 2008's *One Man Jam*. In 2011, Willie released the original demos again (in digital form, and remixed by later Revolution member Matt Fink) on a download entitled *The Cookhouse Five*.

CHAPTER 3

1 One of the many pleasing things about Prince as an artist is how frequently he'll return to his past, or just how deep an influence will run. An example of this is that this song not only appears on his earliest solo demo tape, but also in one of his most recent set lists, as he played the song with Chaka Khan at an after-show at Club Nokia in Los Angeles on Saturday 28 March 2009.

2 A habit he would retain for several years and which can be heard on subsequent rehearsal/demo tapes.

3 Sevelle is one of Prince's least well-remembered associates, having released one self-titled album on Prince's Paisley Park label, but is also the most industrious. She is currently writing self-published novels, managing rappers, inventing new kitchen appliances sold on home shopping channel QVC (seriously) and running Urban Farming, a Detroit-based charity that plants food on unused land and gives it to the homeless and which is supported by Atlantic Records and Prince to this day.

4 Although before giving it to Sevelle, he did offer it to Michael Jackson, after declining to duet with him on 'Bad'. Prince's motivations here are obscure: it's perfectly possible that he was doing so in good faith – after all, it's an excellent song that clearly remained high in his estimation for several years – but at the same time, maybe he recognised a similar desperation in Jackson's persona that he had since outgrown. Jackson himself

certainly felt some rivalry with Prince: in an *Entertainment Weekly* article (23 October 2009) about the posthumously released Jackson movie *This Is It*, Randy Phillips reported that Jackson said to his choreographer Kenny Ortega that he couldn't go to sleep or take a vacation because 'if I'm not there to receive these ideas, God might give them to Prince'.

5 See also The Rebels' songs 'You' and 'If I Love You Tonight', discussed later in the book.

6 Dave Hill contends in his 1989 book *Prince: A Pop Life* that Moon sold the rights to these songs to Prince's publishing company, Controversy Music. I did not raise this with Moon.

7 *The Vault* also lists two more non-circulating songs, 'Love in the Morning' and 'You Really Get to Me'.

8 These two songs – though not the last Prince worked on with 94 East – were the last to be released, emerging on a 2002 download entitled *94 East Featuring 10.15 and Fortune Teller Remix with Prince on Guitar*.

9 Getting paid will continue to be a subject that exercises him, however, as will the wider American economy, as in the 2009 song about that period's financial crisis, 'Ol' Skool Company'.

10 Contraception will be something Prince will have many different thoughts about throughout his career, as I'll discuss later in the book, but it's revealing that in this song he sings about being a very careful man, without indicating how this caution is maintained.

11 *The Vault* suggests that he played it at his first-ever show.

12 These three tracks first appeared on 1986's *Minneapolis Genius*, and were also included on 1995's *Symbolic Beginning* (as well as an alternate 'practice session' of 'Dance to the Music of the World') and 2008's *One Man Jam*.

13 These two songs are also included on 94 East's *Symbolic Beginning*.

CHAPTER 4

1 The interview is reprinted in Jon Bream's *Prince: Inside the Purple Reign*, pp. 38–9.

2 Don Taylor, *So Much Things to Say* (London: Blake, 1995), pp. 232–3.

3 Willie later released 'If You Feel Like Dancin'', along with another song from the sessions, 'One Man Jam', on *Minneapolis Genius*, *Symbolic Beginning* and *One Man Jam*.

4 Michael Shore with Dick Clark, *The History of American Bandstand* (New York: Ballentine, 1985), p. 185.

5 A song which, according to Alan Leeds's sleeve notes to *The Hits*, Prince originally wrote for R&B/jazz star Patrice Rushen. (Rushen also claimed in an interview that she wrote an unused string arrangement for *For You*'s

'Baby': http://www.smartalecmusic.com/patriceinner-viewII.htm.)

6 It was also Prince's first twelve-inch, and as well as an extended 'long version' there is also an extremely rare 'mad mix' credited to 'Prince Introducing Bobby Z', suggesting that Prince might have wanted to push Z forward as a DJ. The 'long version' is an early indication of how it would often be Prince's seemingly more slight tracks that would be the most significantly transformed when remixed, something that later caught the attention of dance artists in Detroit.

7 He only performed it once in 1982, but it's one of those older songs that he has suddenly dusted off decades later, playing it in 2010 and '11, turning it into a duet that he's performed first with Cassandra Wilson, and in 2011 in a beautiful long jazz version in Rotterdam with his most recent protégée Andy Allo.

8 Alan Leeds, liner notes, *The Hits/The B-Sides*, Paisley Park/Warner Brothers, 1993.

9 Ibid., p. 90.

10 Rick James, *The Confessions of Rick James: Memoirs of a Super Freak* (New York: Colossus Books, 2007), p. 166.

CHAPTER 5

1 Dickerson, *My Time with Prince*, p. 107.

2 Ibid, p. 108.

3 *AOL Live Interview with Prince*, 22 July 97. Prince's thoughts about The Beatles are discussed at length elsewhere in this book, but it seems whatever his thoughts about the band as a whole, his antipathy seems not to have extended to John Lennon and his solo work. Of particular relevance, perhaps, is the fact that Lennon's name is there alongside Billie Holiday and Martin Luther King on the side of the Graffiti Bridge.

4 Robert Fitzpatrick, 'Facetime: Green Gartside', *The Word*, April 2011.

5 For more on the Linn LM-1, see Greg Milner, *Perfecting Sound Forever: The Story of Recorded Music* (Granta, 2009), p. 313.

6 Matmos musician and academic Drew Daniel has written interestingly about the correlation between work and music, though the possibilities for interaction he presents don't acknowledge the reality that for artists like Prince music *is* work, pure and simple. He argues, however, that 'if music has served to distract us from work, it has also tried to help us hear the sound of work in a new way. It's rarely quitting time for the musical citation of labour: the ship engine sequence in Fred Astaire's 1937 film *Shall We Dance* offers a highly influential fantasy of obedience, while the metallurgical hammering of *Kollaps*-era Einstürzende Neubauten (1981)

brings the Sturm und Drang . . .' (Drew Daniel, 'All Sound Is Queer', *The Wire*, November 2011). Prince, of course, was in 1981 offering an alternative where the distance between the place of work (the factory) and pleasure (the nightclub) had collapsed.

7 Dickerson, *My Time with Prince*, p. 116.

CHAPTER 6

1 The talent-show side to popular music is something that has always interested Prince. Carwell gained a rep from playing talent shows around Minneapolis; Támar appeared on *Star Search*; Sheena Easton came to fame through Esther Rantzen's TV show *The Big Time*; Maya McClean, one half of his backing dancers The Twinz, was a contestant on *Australian Idol*; and Prince himself began by performing piano pieces at school talent shows. Ironically, when Prince appeared on *American Idol* in 2006, he was subjected to criticism from Simon Cowell for playing two songs from then-current album *3121* and departing rather than doing a duet with a contestant. If Cowell had bothered to listen to the whole album, he would have realised from 'Beautiful, Loved and Blessed', the duet with Támar, that Prince has an ambivalent attitude to these latest TV talent shows, which he believes are less about demonstrating talent and more about coveting fame. At the same time he was performing, those of us who'd signed up to his website received an email with a line from Corinthians 10:14: 'Therefore my brothers, have nothing to do with the worship of idols.'

2 *The Vault* describes the song, but suggests instead that it was a solo Prince track. Carwell retains a Prince connection, contributing in 2011 to The Time's latest album, released under the new band name of The Original 7even.

3 Although Prince appears to give the game away in the lyrics to 'D.M.S.R.', a track on his *1999* album later that year, where in a verse not printed in the lyric booklet he appears to take ownership of all his side projects, singing in quick succession 'Jamie Starr's a thief', 'It's time to fix your clock' (a response, of course, to The Time's 'What Time Is It?') and 'Vanity 6 is so sweet', not owning up to the alias seems, for a while at least, to have been of considerable importance. In his only interview to promote *1999*, with the *LA Times*' Robert Hilburn, he had three points to make: 'One, my real name is Prince. Two, I'm not gay. And three, I'm not Jamie Starr.' The controversy lasted until at least the following year, when Debbie Miller addressed the subject in her third *Rolling Stone* article about Prince and/or his protégées. In it she interrogates Morris Day and

Steve Fargnoli about Jamie Starr, both of whom insist he's real, before Sue
Ann Carwell gives the game away: 'Prince is Jamie Starr.'

4 Just how nasty Vanity would get is revealed in Mötley Crüe songwriter
and bassist Nikki Sixx's 2007 book *The Heroin Diaries: A Year in the Life
of a Shattered Rock Star*. It includes Sixx's memories of his relationship
with Vanity, who now calls herself Evangelist Denise Matthews, which
begin: 'We saw Vanity on MTV, and when Pete said, "Dude, that's
Prince's old girl," I said, "Excellent – he's got a tiny dick." The office rang
Vanity and arranged for us to meet. She opened the door naked, with her
eyes going around in her head. Somehow I had a feeling that we might
just hit it off.' The book also includes Evangelist Denise Matthews's
thoughts about her former persona: 'I don't answer to Vanity. I would
much rather be a fish stuck in a pond with a starving shark than take on
such a foul name of nothingness.'

CHAPTER 7

1 Per Nilsen, *DanceMusicSexRomance*, p. 103.

2 For someone who would later become an adamant anti-smoker, on more
than one occasion Prince would make cigarettes part of his stagecraft,
such as the notable fake cigarette break while singing 'Around the World
in a Day' on the first Hit & Run tour. Much later, he would also sing
about being sent out to buy his mother's tampons and cigarettes on 'Just
Like U', which may or may not be connected to his early staged fetishism
of cigarette-smoking dominatrices.

3 Another song from this era in a similar vein, 'Jerk Out', was intended for
The Time and is discussed in Chapter 21.

4 In 2011, atoning for his past, Prince re-recorded the song with Andy Allo
to promote a Canadian tour, changing the lyric to remove all the menace
of the original version, with Prince and Allo calling each other names like
'Care Bear', 'Elmo' and 'Sugar Lover', and Prince turning himself back
into the passive partner, dependent on Allo's call. The new song has run-
ning water and giggles at the end of the track instead of anxiety.

5 Somewhat astonishingly, Prince recently revived 'Purple Music' at a
show in the New Morning club in Paris, segueing from it to a version of
another song from this era, 'All the Critics Love U in New York', changed
to 'All the Critics Love U in New Morning' after the name of the club.
This version of 'Purple Music' was relatively short, just under two min-
utes, but it revealed that Prince thinks of it as a fully-fledged song and not
just an improvisational sketch.

6 Although it didn't put him off singing about baths altogether, Wendy

Melvoin says he later had a nasty experience with a tub on the *Purple Rain* tour. 'It's funny about bathtubs,' she told me when I interviewed her and Lisa Coleman in their studio, asking Lisa, 'Was it *Purple Rain* or *1999* when the bathtub fell on him?' Lisa took over the story. 'I remember the bathtub at the back of the stage. He was getting in it. He'd been really mean to somebody that day, and it was sad because he knew it was karma. He was lying on the ground because the bathtub wasn't tacked down, and we worried he might be broken.' '"The bathtub rules me,"' Wendy concluded, impersonating Prince. 'It was like frickin' *Equus* with the bathtubs.' In *I Want My MTV*, Sharon Oreck remembers 'a bathtub wrangler' who had to get three bathtubs for the 'When Doves Cry' video (p. 215).

7   A reference to his bass player, Brown Mark. Quite why he's needed for a perfect weekend I'm not sure, but I'm prepared to take Prince's word for it.

8   Talking Heads were clearly a band Prince was keeping an eye on in 1983 (although this song was over two years old at this time, it had stuck around, and Prince had no doubt noted the song's video was popular on MTV), as he'd mention them again in another rehearsal later that year. A famous 1983 recording from Providence reveals how sexual menace could be an important part of Prince's stage act, and although after the rise of gangsta rap it now sounds tame, he did delight in playing with darkness and used 'D.M.S.R.' to do so, as Lisa Coleman screams and demands, 'Somebody call the police!'

9   Craig Marks and Rob Tannenbaum, *I Want My MTV: The Uncensored Story of the Music Video Revolution* (New York: Dutton, 2011), p. 93.

10 The song (which Prince has a co-writing credit on and to which he contributed keyboards, giving it a similar sound to 'Corvette') has nevertheless had a surprising afterlife, with Arthur Baker, who has worked with a number of Prince's associates and protégées, telling me that it was a primary influence on both him and the house artist Felix Da Housecat.

11 Jon Bream, 'Stevie Nicks' New Whirl', *Star Tribune*, 23 August 2011.

12 Dickerson, *My Time with Prince*, pp. 226–7.

13 He would appear to address the change in line-up in song on the unreleased version of 'Old Friends 4 Sale' (see Chapter 10).

CHAPTER 8

1   James Foley would go on to direct Madonna's *Who's That Girl*, *Glengarry Glen Ross* and an episode of *Twin Peaks*, among several other notable credits.

2 Although he played the song at least three times in rehearsal.

3 Unless that veteran is Paul McCartney. As he told Caitlin Moran: 'If I go to see Prince – I mean, I love his guitar playing, but I want him to play "Purple Rain". I'm probably going to be disappointed if he doesn't do it.' To which Moran replied: 'Paul, you know what people love? "The Frog Chorus".' *The Times*, 3 December 2011.

4 Dorian Lynskey, 'I'm a Musician . . . and I Am Music', *Guardian*, 23 June 2011.

5 Albert Magnoli interview with Arclight Cinemas, Tuesday 5 April 2011, archived at: http://www.facebook.com/note. php?note_id=10150208291933688.

6 Or even 'electro-goth': check out *X-Men* actress Rebecca Romijn's reinvention of the song on *Electro Goth Tribute to Prince* (Cleopatra Records, 2005), one of several Prince tribute albums.

7 Mark Edmundson, *Nightmare on Main Street: Angels, Sadomasochism, and the Culture of the Gothic* (Cambridge, MA: Harvard, 1997), p. 46. Sarah Niblock and Stan Hawkins also argue convincingly that *Purple Rain* as a movie is also in the gothic genre, comparing the depiction of The Kid's home in the film with scary houses in *Last House on the Left*, *A Nightmare on Elm Street* and *Hallowe'en* (Stan Hawkins and Sarah Niblock, *Prince: The Making of a Pop Music Phenomenon* (Surrey: Ashgate, 2011), pp. 100–4).

8 As he describes her, not entirely accurately, '. . . alternately Gothic victim and villain, masochist in a dungeon in collar, sadist flexing her whip' (ibid., p. 46).

9 And Jackson: 'More ready to hand for '90s Gothic has been the image of Michael Jackson luring young boys into his pre-adolescent pleasuredome for frolic and friendship. Jackson – the male-female, child-adult, black-white, waif-mogul, and most centrally the presexual sexual predator – has readily been depicted in terms of the Gothic double' (ibid., p. 13).

10 Barney Hoskyns, *Prince: Imp of the Perverse* (London: Virgin, 1988), p. 17.

11 He'd play it the 'right' way round in concerts on the *Purple Rain* tour.

12 Miles Davis with Quincy Troupe, *Miles: The Autobiography* (London: Simon and Schuster, 1989), p. 385.

13 Bobby Z told *Spin* in July 2009 that this was 'definitely the impetus'.

14 The song is also known under the longer title '17 Days (The Rain Will Come Down, Then U Will Have 2 Choose, If U Believe. Look 2 the Dawn and U Shall Never Lose)'. The full title is significant as it makes reference to 'the Dawn', a recurring image in Prince's religious wordplay, as explained earlier in this chapter.

15 Suggesting it was something of a fun exercise for Prince at the time, this song also has a longer title: 'Erotic City (Make Love Not War Erotic City Come Alive)'.

16 Noted feminist musicologist Nancy J. Holland also hears a reggae influence in 'When Doves Cry', which suggests either that Wendy and Lisa's influence on Prince was so profound that it also affected him when recording alone, or that it was a shared interest.

CHAPTER 9

1 *Words and Music*, radio programme, interview with Joni Mitchell by Morrissey, 18 October 1996, transcribed by Lindsay Moon.

2 In conversation with Neal Karlen, Prince said: 'What they say is that the Beatles are the influence. The influence wasn't the Beatles. They were great for what they did, but I don't know how that would hang today. The cover art came about because I thought people were tired of looking at *me*. Who wants another picture of him? I would only want so many pictures of my woman, then I would want the real thing. What would be a little more happening than just another picture [*laughs*] would be if there was some way I could materialize in people's cribs when they play the record' ('Prince Talks', interview with Neal Karlen, *Rolling Stone*, 12 September 1985).

3 Garry Mulholland, *Fear of Music* (London: Orion, 2006), p. 175.

4 Neal Karlen, 'Prince Talks', *Rolling Stone*, 12 September 1985.

5 Kyle Parks, 'Only a Bad Album Could Dethrone Prince', *Evening Independent* (5 April 1985).

6 Alan Leeds, liner notes, *The Hits/The B-Sides*, Paisley Park/Warner Brothers, 1993.

7 This strip is anthologised in G. B. Trudeau, *Check Your Egos at the Door* (New York, Holt: 1984). The book has no page numbers.

8 Leeds, liner notes, *The Hits/The B-Sides*, 1993.

9 Neal Karlen, 'Prince Talks', *Rolling Stone*, 12 September 1985.

10 During the same era he wrote another song called 'Come Elektra Tuesday', and later, of course, renamed Tara Leigh Patrick Carmen Electra.

11 Although the original version of 'Around the World in a Day' with David's vocals and alternative lyrics isn't in circulation, an excellent posthumous 2006 release of his music, *This Is David Daoud Coleman*, is well worth seeking out and gives a good indication of the breadth of his talent, including a song with Wendy Melvoin on bass, 'Oh Come Back Rev', which is the equal of 'Around the World in a Day'. An extraordinarily

atmospheric collection, largely recorded, performed and mixed by Coleman himself, it features spoken-word, pop and experimental music (the slightly scary slowed-down vocals of 'Inersia'), somewhere between The Replacements, Bongwater, Ween, The Butthole Surfers and the world music that inspired him.

12 When released as a single, the song was backed by 'She's Always in My Hair', a B-side that seemed to have disappeared but which recaptured Prince's attention around the time that he assembled his B-sides for the Warners compilation, and which returned in performance from then onwards, with Prince including a live version as part of the ninth of his NPG Ahdio (*sic*) shows.

13 Per Nilsen, *DanceMusicSexRomance*, pp. 160–1.

CHAPTER 10

1 Dave Hill, *Prince: A Pop Life* (London: Faber, 1989), p. 184.

2 Not intended for the album and recorded late in the sessions, 'Heaven' is a similar (but less spooky) treatment of the same idea, suggesting that heaven is on Earth, something he hinted at in his *Rolling Stone* interview with Neal Karlen, when he responded to the question of whether he believed in heaven by saying: 'I think there is an afterworld. For some reason, I think it's going to be just like here.' ('Prince Talks', Neal Karlen, *Rolling Stone*, 12 September 1985.) Per Nilsen also notes that Prince wrote three other songs not included on *Parade* during these sessions: 'Tibet', 'Evolisdog' and 'Krush Groove', which featured Sheila E.

3 In the third draft of the *Under the Cherry Moon* screenplay, Prince, as Christopher Tracy, plays a song called 'Wendy's Paradise'. I'm assuming this is a mistake and the song is actually 'Little Girl Wendy/Christopher Tracy's Parade', but knowing Prince, it's perfectly possible this could be yet another as-yet-undiscovered song.

4 There is a second direct reference to the Devil in 'Mountains': although this feels like one of Prince's most flippant records, he's surprisingly direct in his Manichaeism. Every time the Devil appears, however, he is quickly defeated.

5 When Prince plays 'Kiss', he often updates the reference to the TV show *Dynasty* to whatever is popular on television at the time he's performing, such as *Queer Eye for the Straight Guy*, *Sex and the City*, *Desperate Housewives*, *The L Word* or *Big Brother*.

6 The demo version that circulates is little over a minute long, Prince singing the first two verses while playing an acoustic guitar. I don't know if this is a fragment of a longer recording or if Prince added more lyrics

later, but the Mazarati version of the song features the full lyric.

7 The B-side to 'Kiss', '♥ or $' (or 'Love or Money'), is both further evi-
dence of Prince's minimalist approach to songwriting at the time and an
interestingly straightforward examination of a recurring lyrical concern
(by 2009's *Lotusflow3r*, the ♥ part of the equation was gone for a song
just called '$'). It is also, of course, a near summary of the plot of *Under
the Cherry Moon* (Jerome even sends over to Prince a paper napkin with
'$' on it when encouraging him to seduce an older woman). In the origi-
nal script, Prince even has a heart-shaped wallet. Another of the B-sides
from the era, 'Alexa De Paris', ranks among Brent Fischer's favourite
Prince tracks. 'That ended up on being on an EP, so I'm just not sure it
ever enjoyed any sort of wide recognition. Too bad, because it's a great
tune, a great instrumental tune that really shows off Prince's playing and
his instrumental writing, a great arrangement to it. Plus I did five or six
percussion overdubs on it, so you can hear me doing timpani solos, cym-
bals and all these sorts of things. That was a really fun piece to work on.'

8 While the version on *One Nite Alone . . . The Aftershow: It Ain't Over* is
scarcely recognisable, going into an extended jam soon after the opening
lines, the version on the later *Indigo Nights/Live Sessions* (although a little
bit sloppy on this evening and part of a medley) indicates the force of the
horn-driven formation of The New Power Generation (there were many
rich performances of this song in 2007). Although he gives too many
lines to the audience and mutters too much, when he does sing Prince
sounds almost unhinged in his delivery.

9 Michaelangelo Matos, *Sign o' the Times* (London: Continuum, 2004), pp.
53–4.

10 *Melody Maker*, 12 April 1986.

11 *NME*, 12 April 1986.

12 Alex Ross, *The Rest Is Noise: Listening to the Twentieth Century* (Farar,
Straus and Giroux, 2007), pp. 541–2.

13 'A Batty Prince on the Riviera', *Philadelphia Daily News*, 3 July 1986.

14 'Stallone Gets Miffed by Arnold Doll; Scorsese Declines Prince Offer',
Lakeland Ledger, 19 July 1987.

15 The *Venus de Milo* would retain Prince's interest: there's a dark-haired
version among the imagery on the cover of *Graffiti Bridge*. (At least, I
assumed this was the case, until I talked to Steve Parke – see Chapter 20.)

16 Greg Marks and Rob Tannenbaum, *I Want My MTV*, pp. 308–9.

17 Liz Jones, *Slave to the Rhythm* (Little, Brown: London, 1997), p. 107.

18 Pat Hackett (Ed.), *The Andy Warhol Diaries* (New York: Warner Books,
1989), p. 749. Alex Hahn claims that Andy Warhol was also in the

audience at Prince's New York show on 9 December 1980, but if he was he makes no mention of it in his diary, writing instead about the news coverage of John Lennon's murder the night before.

CHAPTER 11

1 In his *Bootleg! The Rise & Fall of the Secret Recording Industry* (London: Omnibus, 2003), Clinton Heylin notes: '*The Black Album* was destined to become the Eighties' biggest bootleg bonanza. The Richard Records vinyl version sold an estimated 20,000 copies, while Tim Smith reckons his UK version sold in excess of 30,000, while other pressings – of which there were a fair few – account for total vinyl sales in excess of 100,000 (and probably an equal number of CDs), amounting to sales that may even exceed the true figure for *Great White Wonder*' (p. 171). *Great White Wonder* was the first, and for a time most famous, Bob Dylan bootleg.

2 It is Per Nilsen's version of events, for example, that Michaelangelo Matos depends on for his narrative in his short study of *Sign o' the Times* for Continuum's '33 1/3' series, in which he argues that this record was a digest of the best tracks from five planned albums: three separate versions of *Dream Factory*, the *Camille* record and a proposed triple album called *Crystal Ball*.

3 On the live album *C-NOTE*. This recording was, however, only from a soundcheck for a *One Nite Alone . . .* show in Copenhagen and doesn't feel like a definitive version – it ends too abruptly and lacks the power I've witnessed Prince bring to it in live performance. It seems instead a sketch for his subsequent live interpretations. The song has a similar feel to the much later 'Planet Earth', which may be why he played it twice on the tour supporting that record, although the latter song lacks the obvious emotional charge and Prince can't quite bring the same sense of devastation to singing about the loss of the world's ecosystem as he can to the loss of a woman.

4 When I talked to Susannah about the songs Prince had written for her, one of the songs she told me she had the most vivid memories of being played was 'In a Large Room with No Light', which confused me at first as this seems more of a political song than a romantic song, but from her description of the song itself, and the chronology of the recording (as well as accounts from other band members present), I realised she was refer-ring to the similarly titled 'Empty Room'.

5 Prince first returned to the song in 1992, when he recorded a relatively sketchy piano-based alternative version and presented it to James L. Brooks for possible inclusion on the ill-fated soundtrack to his Nick

Nolte film *I'll Do Anything* (about which more later), but it was several years later before he finally put it out. In 1994, he revisited the original version and added to it, even shooting a video in preparation for the song's release. Nothing came of this, but both versions (and the video) circulate. It is, of course, a major part of Prince's working method to revisit songs and projects with different artists, but there's something deeply unsettling about the video (which may be why it remains unreleased), which features Prince's first wife, Mayte, wandering round a museum in a top hat, boots, knickers and a barely-there skirt, while Prince emotes. All the original meaning of the song is lost, and one can only be grateful Prince had the good sense to shelve this interpretation.

6 Wendy said something interesting about 'Go' which, if true, further calls into question much of the previous documentation of this era: 'With "Go", people think it's from the *Dream Factory,* but we were under the impression it was for *Sign o' the Times.*' Which would mean that Prince started work on *Sign o' the Times* before *Dream Factory,* if indeed the latter existed at all. Another interesting discrepancy between the Per Nilsen version of events and reports from the Prince camp concerns the song 'Crucial': Nilsen suggests it was recorded for a planned film called *The Dawn,* along with two other songs, 'Coco Boys' (which circulates in two versions) and 'When the Dawn of the Morning Comes'; Prince writes in the sleeve notes accompanying its eventual release on the 1998 *Crystal Ball* box set that it was intended for *Sign o' the Times* and was replaced with 'Adore'. I'm still not sure why Nilsen is so certain that *Sign o' the Times* only came into being after *Dream Factory* and *Crystal Ball* were abandoned, particularly as there are *Sign* songs, like 'The Ballad of Dorothy Parker', which were written before certain *Dream Factory* songs.

7 Alex Hahn, *Possessed: The Rise and Fall of Prince* (New York: Billboard, 2003), p. 227.

8 Men are not exempt from this objectification: witness the unreleased mid-1990s track 'A Good Dick and a Job'.

9 Note also that Wendy and Lisa appear on the released version of 'Strange Relationship', and it was a feature of Prince's creative relationship with the two women that he would often give them old tapes and songs to work on.

10 A one-minute snippet appears on a six-song sampler tape Prince is believed to have sent out to other artists to see if there was anything they wanted to cover. This tape also includes two other non-Revolution songs from this era: the over-the-top swooping melodrama of 'Adonis and Bathsheba' that engineer Susan Rogers seems to have embarrassed Prince

out of releasing, which given that it shares the sickly-sweet feel of two of his most reviled songs, 'Graffiti Bridge' and 'Purple and Gold', may be a good thing, although I'd still like to hear a full version; and 'Cosmic Day', a straight-ahead rocker to which Dr Clare Fischer contributed and which his son Brent remembers as 'a cool piece'.

11 Per Nilsen et al. (Eds), *The Vault* (Europe (*sic*): self-published, 2004), p. 344.

12 One of the curious qualities of *Graffiti Bridge* is that in spite of the huge number of people involved in the project, he was more inspired by his original solo versions of 'Can't Stop This Feeling I Got' and 'We Can Funk' than he was by the Revolution recordings. Maybe the wounds were still raw. He even gives us a clue that this might be the case with the song's opening spoken lament: Prince (in the guise of The Kid) telling his father that things didn't turn out the way he wanted them to.

13 Wendy, Lisa, Brown Mark, Miko Weaver, Dr Fink, Susannah, Eric Leeds, Atlanta Bliss and Bobby Z.

14 Even on the higher-quality tapes from this session it's impossible to distinguish whether it's Prince or his band-mates, and there's no documentation either way: my bet would be on the latter.

15 Those later takes are substantially different from this version, and I'll write about the further development of the song in Chapter 20.

16 Brent Fischer, who worked on 'It Ain't Over 'Til the Fat Lady Sings', says he doubts this track will ever come out, although it remains one of his favourites, along with 'All My Dreams'. In interview, when asked about unreleased tracks he'd worked on, he told me: 'There was another quirky one that I'm pretty sure is never going to get released because it was just like a funky music experiment that he did and it was probably something that he put together with his horn section, and it was called "It Ain't Over 'Til the Fat Lady Sings". It's just a funny piece because it was very involved, it was very chromatic, and I had to ask them to send a tape copy, so they sent – that was only twenty-four tracks – so they sent a twenty-four-track tape copy to a recording studio in LA and I just went in there, and finally the engineer got tired and showed me how to work the machine and I just ended up working the machine myself. That was a really fun tune, and we had a great time adding the orchestra on too.'

CHAPTER 12

1 Prince (uncredited), liner notes, *Crystal Ball* (NPG, 1998).

2 Although see Chapter 21 for Prince's onstage response, which more or less made the connection explicit.

3 Incidentally, Prince demoed a song called 'Living Doll' (which I haven't heard) for Jill Jones the year before, and then wrote an alternative version of the track titled 'Latino Barbie Doll', which was later recorded by both Sheila E and Mayte, though never released.

4 It seems surprising that Prince thought this track worthy of inclusion on 1998's *Crystal Ball* set, given the number of first-rate songs that didn't get included (although the fact that he also found space for fifteen minutes of the dreary 'Cloreen Bacon Skin' – which he described in an interview thus: 'Listen to crystal ball and the truth u will hear what freedom . . . sounds like . . . There is a track called baconskin that thumps for fifteen . . . minutes . . . SICK' – suggests his critical skills during this era were faulty).

5 And if Per Nilsen's chronologies are correct, here is further evidence of how Prince is able to work on songs in many different emotional registers at the same time, as Nilsen suggests he took time out to record this track while working with most of The Revolution on a cover of The Esquires' 'Get On Up', as great a contrast to 'In a Large Room with No Light' as it's possible to imagine.

6 It is Prince's ability to throw in surprises like this – just one of the many revelations in a night of four and a half hours of music – that keeps his shows relevant and the faithful turning out. Normally, if you're not present on such occasions, the only way of experiencing them is through illicit recordings. But whether it was because the shows that night failed to reach their peak due to sound issues or because Prince realised this was too important a moment not to record officially, he made the rare decision to make a recording of a new performance of this song (believed to have been recorded at Paisley Park) available to a website promoting a performance at the Montreux jazz festival later that year, making it part of the official canon once more. Prince has done this sort of thing a few times recently, and it may be how the rest of his unreleased songs trickle out over the next few years.

7 Although 'Visions' has, to date, not been released by Prince, it was put out by Lisa under her own name as part of a mini-CD of four similar solo improvisations as an extra enticement accompanying *Eroica*, her 1990 album with Wendy. As beguiling as the track undoubtedly is, it has a whole different significance if you see it as one of a number of improvisations rather than the intro to a lost masterpiece. (Wendy made a similar contribution to these sessions, her 'Interlude' being a shorter but similar guitar piece.)

8 Nilsen et al., *The Vault*, p. 531.

9 The possibility of some form of afterlife, whether in heaven or on Earth, is a recurring preoccupation of Prince's, expressed most memorably in one of his most famous songs, 'Let's Go Crazy'. It is something that would continue to preoccupy him throughout the 1990s, especially after the period of spiritual searching that followed *Diamonds and Pearls*. It did also interest him during this period, though, as seen with 'Others Here with Us' and 'Heaven', discussed in Chapter 10.

10 Interview with Keith Murphy, *Vibe*, April 2009.

CHAPTER 13

1 Online interview with Yahoo Internet Life, October 1997.

2 Asked by German interviewer Joachim Hentschel in 2010 if he would consider using Outkast's André 3000 as a producer, he responded that André was a good rapper but questioned whether he was a musician. Wendy says it is for this reason that Prince is not particularly impressed by alternative musicians, noting: 'He couldn't see or hear or feel the culture of that music and couldn't understand it as anything other than, "It just sounds bad to me." Lisa and I tried to turn him on to Peter Gabriel's *Security* record. My recollection of it was that he wasn't into men's music at all. He liked Kate Bush's "Wuthering Heights". He was moved by it, he could learn from it, but he wouldn't feel that way about a Nick Drake record.'

3 'Rebirth of the Flesh' (in a rehearsal version) as an Internet download; 'Housequake', 'Strange Relationship' and 'If I Was Your Girlfriend' on *Sign o' the Times*; 'Feel U Up' as a *Batman*-era B-side; 'Shockadelica' as the B-side to 'If I Was Your Girlfriend'; 'Good Love' initially on the soundtrack to the Michael J. Fox-starring film adaptation of Jay McInerney's 1980s yuppie-in-drug-peril classic *Bright Lights, Big City*, and then again on the three-CD out-takes collection *Crystal Ball*; and 'Rockhard in a Funky Place' on *The Black Album*.

4 Matos, *Sign o' the Times*, p. 91.

5 Ibid, pp. 83–4.

6 A club he would return to the following year, and then again for a marathon three-and-a-half-hour show in 2010.

7 Online interview with Yahoo Internet Life, October 1997.

8 Quoted in Per Nilsen, *DanceMusicSexRomance*, p. 214.

9 Liz Jones, *Slave to the Rhythm*, pp. 18–19.

CHAPTER 14

1 Prince (uncredited), liner notes, *Crystal Ball* (NPG, 1998).

2 Ibid.

3 It would be easy to dismiss 'Soul Psychodelicide' as horsing around at rehearsal. Certainly, if he had included the recording as part of the *Crystal Ball* record it would have stretched the set even further – something Prince acknowledges when he shouts out: '"Soul Psychodelicide" . . . takes up two albums!' But there is clearly some serious intention here. At first, Prince seems to be improvising around The Time song 'Ice Cream Castles' – a song he'd played as part of a medley on the *Purple Rain* tour – telling the band to sing variations on the lyrics and shouting out 'ICE CREAM!' at regular intervals. But slowly Prince's instructions become more focused and he announces that he's working on a new song. Having got the extended Revolution to play what he wants, he tries to build up a chorus – again borrowing from another track, the recently recorded Flesh track 'U Gotta Shake Something'. Dividing The Revolution into male and female choruses, he tells the band to drop out and brings up the bass, the new song now (twenty minutes in) fully fluttering into life. Prince recognises this and calls out to engineer Susan Rogers to start recording, seemingly unaware that the tapes have been running since the start of the rehearsal. Forty-six minutes in, he starts the song again, and it's this stretch that seems most likely to have been considered as the basis for a possible release, although it still lacks anything more than the most basic lyrics. The track is also limited slightly by Greg Brooks's vocals, which are firmly in the James Brown mode but don't really convince us there's any joy in this much repetition. (At least, I believe it's Brooks. It could be Brown Mark, but as Prince shouts 'Check out Brooks' during the rehearsal, I think it's him singing. But Prince does sometimes do shout-outs to band members not present, or Brooks may have been dancing rather than singing, and some accounts of this session suggest Brooks wasn't present.) Whoever it was has been chanting that 'Soul Psychodelicide' is a 'helluva thing' for the best part of an hour – but we still don't know how, why, or indeed, what exactly soul psychodelicide is. Prince returned to this track in 1989, when he worked on it with George Clinton. Four more takes of the song exist, but whatever Prince's concept for the song was, none of these alternative takes quite brought it to life.

CHAPTER 15

1 In his book on protest songs, Dorian Lynskey suggests 'it is hopelessly toothless and non-committal as a protest song, albeit brilliant as a pop record'. Dorian Lynskey, *33 Revolutions per Minute: A History of Protest Songs* (London: Faber, 2011) p. 538.

2 'No Eighties Prince single is more overrated than "Sign o' the Times . . ."'
Matos, *Sign o' the Times*, p. 86.

3 Prince would use this style of video again in 2001, for a much scarier
track, 'One Song'. And Cee Lo Green, whose song as part of Gnarls
Barkley, 'Crazy', Prince would cover in concert thirty-nine times, used the
same format for his 2010 video 'Fuck You'.

4 The 'Highly Explosive Mix' of 'La, La, La . . .' extends the song just a
little too far, picking up from the whispered fade-out of 'I'm picking up
your scent . . .' with '. . . you must be wet' and continuing for another
seven minutes with Eric Leeds playing his customary 'Leeds lines' and all
manner of busy instrumentation, but in its original version, it's one of
Prince's finest B-sides. The worst you could accuse him of is self-parody.
When Bob Dylan went into the studio with The Traveling Wilburys to
do a Prince parody, 'Dirty Work', the following year, it sounded like this.

5 For whom he would later write a whole load of feline-themed songs, such
as 'Nine Lives', 'Cat and Mouse', 'Cat Attack', etc. (see Chapter 21).

6 Played live, he would sometimes do the song at incredible speed, like
speed-metal Chuck Berry.

7 Not long after, Prince and Joni Mitchell would collaborate on an as-yet-
unreleased song. According to an interview Mitchell gave to *City Beat* in
1988, their collaborative process began with the two of them jamming
together, before Prince suggested that working together might lead to
something unique that he could not put into words. Asking him to build
a song for her, she was distressed when he sent her a song that appeared
to be called 'Emotional Pump'. It's unclear whether it was the sexual
nature of the lyric or its banality that made her decide not to do the song.
The same year as this interview, Wendy and Lisa sang backing vocals on
Mitchell's 'The Tea Leaf Prophecy (Lay Down Your Arms)', from her
Chalk Mark in a Rain Storm album. Mitchell was one of the talking heads
that would show up in Prince's 'Hall of Fame' induction, talking about
how he gives the best parties in Hollywood, but the clearly slightly com-
bative relationship between the two prickly musicians is apparent from an
interview Mitchell gave to Morrissey on the radio show *Words and Music*
in 1996, in which she talks about how the first time she met Prince he
corrected her grammatical errors and tells him that she believes Prince's
music is a hybrid of her and Sly Stone.

8 AOL Live interview with Prince, 22 July 1997.

9 After becoming a Jehovah's Witness, Prince reinvented 'The Cross' as
'The Christ' and started making weird and spooky speeches when intro-
ducing the song, challenging the audience for believing that Christ was

killed on the cross as if we were the ones who wrote the lyrics rather than him. His various speeches about whether σταυρός should be interpreted as a stake are a highlight of his 1997–8 tours, part of the dark, spooky sermonising that would lead to such wonderful songs as 'The War'.

10 This is not the place for me to trash Bono – it seems that there's a strange subsection of people who like both U2 and Prince, and far be it from me to insult this contingent – but I do find Prince's relationship with U2 slightly amusing. I cannot imagine how angry Prince might have been that night in The Pod when Bono started singing about a 'swollen mamma' instead of a 'pregnant mother'. Much, much later, when playing a show at Paisley Park in 2002, Prince would sing, 'I love you too [or, in Princebonics, 'U2'] – but not the band,' adding, as a guilty afterthought, 'Bono's pretty cool, though.' Does he really think Bono's cool? Or was he just worried this off-the-cuff joke would get back to him?

11 You can hear this version on the *One Nite Alone . . . Live!* album.

12 There was one in early 2012, in support of Bobby Z's charity after he recovered from a heart attack, but Prince did not play.

CHAPTER 16

1 See Chapter 21 for more on Madhouse and Prince's changing relationship to jazz.

2 George Cole, *The Last Miles* (London: Equinox, 2005), p. 230. Davis, for his part, along with comments about the incredible recording, movie and living facilities at Paisley Park, noted of the evening in his autobiography: 'in order to become a great musician the musician has to have the ability to stretch and Prince can certainly stretch . . . at midnight, Prince sang "Auld Lang Syne" and asked me to come up and play something with the band and I did, and they taped it' (Miles Davis with Quincy Troupe, *Miles: The Autobiography* (USA: Simon and Schuster, 1989), p. 385). He hardly makes it sound like the gig of the century.

CHAPTER 17

1 Alex Hahn, *Possessed*, p. 123.

2 Keith Richards (with James Fox), *Life* (London: Orion, 2010), p. 502.

3 This sort of thing can occasionally be heard in Prince rehearsal recordings, as rappers move from their own lines to those of others, a technique that would come to be dismissively referred to as 'biting'.

4 Which would inspire James McNew of alt-rock band Yo La Tengo to record a so-so album of Prince covers using the alias Dump and the album title *That Skinny Motherfucker with the High Voice* (Shrimper, 2001).

5 When this chant was performed during the *Sign o' the Times* tour, and indeed in a message at the end of that film's credits, 'Brother Brooks' would be the one coming round with the substance.

6 Weirdly, Prince has put out two live versions of this abomination, one on his *It Ain't Over* live disc, the other on *Indigo Nights*. The second of these live versions is more substantial, as Prince chats about his ass and chants 'Oooh . . . funky London' over what was once his crowning achievement.

7 Peter Doggett, *The Man Who Sold the World: David Bowie and the 1970s* (London: Bodley Head, 2011), p. 146.

8 The song's B-side, 'Escape', is one of Prince's least inspired, more like one of the variations that would later show up on early-1990s maxi-singles than a complete song.

CHAPTER 18

1 Much later, Prince would feature a can of 'chicken grease' in his video for 'The Daisy Chain'.

2 In his book on *Sign o' the Times*, Michaelangelo Matos describes it as his favourite guitar moment in the Prince catalogue: 'Prince's guitar enters, slightly echoed and more plaintive than the vocal, and before you can register what happens the drums kick in like a torpedo nailing a sailboat, and for the next three minutes he harnesses all his techniques, utilizes all his tricks, indulges all his mannerisms. He also sounds like he's ripping his fucking guts out' (*Sign o' the Times*, p. 95).

3 Per Nilsen, *Prince: A Documentary* (London: Firefly, 1990), p. 97.

4 It's since disappeared, although some heard elements from it in an instrumental jam at his house on the last night of the *Xenophobia* celebrations in 2002. For all my misgivings, it's still an incredibly impressive piece of work, one to be filed alongside the later 'The War' and much of *The Rainbow Children*.

5 Writing in the aforementioned 'Prince Issue' of *The Wire,* Andrew Pothecary used this live version of the song to comment on Prince's control over his band: 'On stage you can often witness the control Prince holds – as a band-leader much more in the jazz sense than the rock one. This is more apparent in smaller club shows than in the rehearsed arena concerts. A shout of "Michael B" warns the band of an upcoming change that they watch for without knowing what it's to be. Or another idiosyncratic call instructs "Junior (bass-player Levi) rumble, Minneapolis-style". Or general reworking calls instruct – "put the snare in", "turn that organ down" etc. And in a live "Still Would Stand All Time", he shouts "What

fool's singing 'will'? It's *would*! 'Still *Would* Stand All Time'!'" (*The Wire*, August 1991, pp. 41, 69).

6 Paul Zollo, *Songwriters on Songwriting* (expanded fourth edn) (New York: Da Capo, 2003).

7 In *Possessed*, Alex Hahn indicates that the creative relationship between Prince and Madonna was more tortured than Madonna's breezy description of their working methods suggests. Suggesting that the two stars had a brief affair in 1985, he claims that Madonna visited Paisley Park in 1986, where they generated a handful of ideas. Then Prince approached Madonna backstage after a performance of *Speed-The-Plow*, where he gave her a mix of 'Love Song', which Hahn suggests Madonna 'found more exciting than she remembered' (p. 154). While this chronology does not contradict Madonna's description of their working process, it puts Prince in a subservient position in the collaboration, and doesn't entirely fit with Madonna's description of them as creative equals.

8 Paul Zollo, *Songwriters on Songwriting*, p. 619.

9 Ibid.

10 Which only seems true in that she was able to continue appearing in Hollywood films for longer than Prince. It is true that her performances in *A League of Their Own* (1992) and *Evita* (1996) received warmer reviews than *Shanghai Surprise* (1986), but her collaboration with her then husband Guy Ritchie, *Swept Away* (2002), was even less critically successful than *Under the Cherry Moon* or *Graffiti Bridge*, and in spite of her one truly great performance in Abel Ferrara's 1993 film *Dangerous Game* (aka *Snake Eyes*), I think few would still make the case for Madonna the actress.

11 According to Liz Jones, Madonna suggested to Prince that they make a merger between her label, Maverick, and his NPG records (*Slave to the Rhythm*, p. 217).

12 In one of Prince's most unguarded moments, on 10 January 1999, he posted an open letter to Madonna on his Love4OneAnother website, in which he wrote of dreaming of being with her at the Grammy awards. In his dream he approached her and asked her if she remembered him, and when she said she did, he asked her to help him in his fight with Warner Brothers to regain control of his masters. Even in his dream, Madonna was evasive, telling Prince that she didn't own his masters as Time Warner wasn't her company, but if it was her company he could have them. The letter ends with Prince worrying that Madonna seemed a bit non-committal, so he follows her up to the podium, tells the audience to be glad it's a commercial break and goes looking for rapper Wyclef. Prince tells

Madonna not to worry about possible interpretations of this dream but just to help him, artist to artist.

13 For a start, there's so much less of it, which wouldn't be important if it was all of first-rate quality, but after their collaboration on *Like a Prayer* (1989), she released the relentless but forgettable *Erotica* (1992) and the only marginally more impressive *Bedtime Stories* (1994), before releasing *Ray of Light* (1998), the only album that does equal her extraordinary 1980s output. Since then, she's released (remixes and best ofs aside) five more largely forgettable records: *Music* (2000), *American Life* (2003), *Confessions on a Dance Floor* (2005), *Hard Candy* (2008), which is a guilty pleasure at best, although it does include an interesting moment for Prince fans – Madonna's employment of Wendy Melvoin on The Neptunes-produced 'She's Not Me', in which Prince fanatic Pharrell Williams sneaks in a reference to 'Kiss' in yet another homage to his hero's work – and 2012's *MDNA*, an album, much like Prince's *Musicology*, too haunted by the artist's past to offer much new, aside from the wonderful divorce song 'I Don't Give a . . .'. In fairness, most of these albums have at least had a strong single, and it's true that I'm prejudiced as an English listener: her embrace of the country life while involved with Guy Ritchie led, for British fans, to a fatal loss of mystique.

CHAPTER 19

1 The disposability of the released album is the source of a neat joke in Edgar Wright's *Shaun of the Dead*, when Ed and Shaun are looking through Shaun's vinyl for suitable records to throw at approaching zombies: '*Purple Rain*?' suggests Ed. 'No,' replies Shaun. '*Sign o' the Times*?' 'Definitely not.' '*Batman* soundtrack?' 'Throw it.'

2 The creepy line would later be picked up by Earl Sweatshirt of the Odd Future collective on his 'Moonlight' in 2010.

3 Significantly, Prince considers 'Batman' and 'Bruce Wayne' separate characters.

4 Interview with Joachim Hentschel, *The Times*, Saturday Review, 24 July 2010.

5 Liz Jones, *Slave to the Rhythm*, p. 153.

6 Gemini would later return in Prince's first authorised comic book, *Prince: Alter Ego*, created by a team hand-picked by Prince to work on a story that had deliberate echoes of both *Batman* and *Graffiti Bridge*. Once again, it showed Prince reinventing a past concept in a new way, confusing it in the process. Prince took the Gemini character invented for the *Batman* videos and made him a separate entity, a childhood friend

of Prince's who uses his musical ability to 'free the rage within human-
ity'. The comic makes an explicit parallel between Prince and Batman
and Gemini and The Joker. Gemini steals The New Power Generation
and electrocutes Prince's girlfriend, Muse, onstage. Prince responds
by ignoring this ('You can mourn for her later,' an internal voice tells
him, 'now you have to play') and finishing a song which brings peace to
Minneapolis.

7 Around the same time, he was working on an abortive series of
Madhouse songs (one of which he later gave to Miles Davis) on a similar
theme – '17 (Penetration)', '18 (R U Legal Yet)', '19 (Jailbait)', etc.

8 Several biographers have written about this incident, presumably drawing
on the video-tape footage of a rehearsal where this conflict took place.

CHAPTER 20

1 In his 1990 *Rolling Stone* interview with Prince, Neal Karlen wrote that
the film was originally intended to be a vehicle just for The Time, with
Prince staying behind the camera.

2 Liz Jones, *Slave to the Rhythm*, pp. 157–8.

3 Ronin Ro, *Prince: Inside the Music and the Masks* (New York: St Martin's,
2011), p. 193.

4 Then again, $6 million is not *that* low a budget, especially as the esti-
mated budget for *Purple Rain* was only slightly higher.

5 Brian Raftery, '*Purple Rain*: The Oral History', *Spin*, July 2009.

6 The 'Can't Stop This Feeling I Got' sequence is merely Prince dancing
on a stairwell and a bench surrounded by his band. 'Round and Round'
is a slightly alternative version of the scene that features this song in film,
with Tevin Campbell dancing around with militaristic backing dancers
who carry turntables around their neck, while Prince lurks in the shadows
of the Melody Cool nightclub. And 'The Latest Fashion' battle scene is
the most wimpy dance-off you've ever seen as Prince takes on The Time
wearing single-strapped dungarees and flapping and squatting like Kyle
MacLachlan showing Laura Dern the chicken-walk in *Blue Velvet*. (Then
again, in the released version he wins the battle with the lachrymose 'Still
Would Stand All Time', which is even more unlikely.)

7 While the former song would eventually see release, in a different form,
'God Is Alive' has never received official release (although Mavis Staples
can be seen performing it and talking about it in an amusing fashion in a
BBC *Omnibus* documentary in which she speaks about how she managed
to come to terms with using the simile 'like a dog in heat' in a spiritual
song). Prince had performed the song during the *Lovesexy* tour, and it

shares something of the feeling of that album, but is blunter and less sophisticated in its spiritualism.

8 In the later version, it seems to be a song about premature ejaculation – the singer's inability to control himself in the company of the 'bombshell' he's singing to. In the earlier version, this is presented less as sexual weakness but more in the manner of a porn star, where a money shot is all.

9 At the time of writing, Prince's latest protégée, Andy Allo, has posted a minute of her own acoustic version of 'We Can Funk' (renamed 'Oui Can Luv') on her Facebook page. The change through the years from 'fuck' to 'funk' to 'love' shows how Prince has allowed his music to be sanitised, but as upsetting as it is to see a former sexual radical retreat into coyness, it must be noted that Allo's reworking of the song sounds far more compelling than the *Graffiti Bridge* reworking, if still nowhere near as powerful as the original.

10 'The Question of U' has undergone a curious evolution in Prince's live sets during the last twenty-one years, now usually melded into a medley with a much later song, 'The One', and occasionally covers like Alicia Keys's 'Fallin'' or Dave Brubeck's 'Take 5'. He's twice released live versions of these medleys, once as a download and (as 'The One') on the live album *Indigo Nights*. More recently, Prince has used the music of this song for a new, as yet unreleased track entitled 'Gingerbread Man', performed towards the end of 2010 on the 'Welcome 2 America' tour. The music was also used for a much earlier unreleased jazz song entitled '12 Keys'. It can be seen, then, as among Prince's most important jam songs, a lifting-off point like 'Ife' for Miles Davis or 'The Other One' for The Grateful Dead. While these sections of live shows are often the highlights, it's disappointing that Prince doesn't play the full song more often, as it's among his greatest.

11 There were some other significant out-takes from the record: 'Pink Cashmere', originally intended for this release, eventually appeared as a new song on *The Hits* collection, and as well as the 'The Grand Progression', there are three other songs – 'Stimulation', 'Bloody Mouth' and 'Beat Town', as well as another song tangentially connected to the *Graffiti Bridge* movie, 'Billie Holliday' – which remain, as far as I'm aware, securely in the Vault. There are also unreleased collaborations with Ingrid Chavez, songs such as 'Seven Corners', which with its reference to a Minneapolis location utilised in the film has an obvious connection to *Graffiti Bridge*.

12 Although clearly no fan of the song, Simon Reynolds has argued that it chimed with the mood of the times: 'Prefigured in Prince's prattle about

a New Power Generation, in Soul II Soul's community-conscious funky-dredd anthems "Back To Life" and "Get A Life", and the "hippy hop" of De La Soul and other Native Tongue rap groups like Jungle Brothers and A Tribe Called Quest, positivity emerged as *the* pop ideology of the new decade' (Simon Reynolds, *Energy Flash* (London: Picador, 1998), p. 83).

13 Jonathan Lethem, *Motherless Brooklyn* (London: Faber, 1999), p. 128, Essrog is, of course, far from the only Prince fan among protagonists of literary fiction, particularly books set or written during periods when Prince has been at the height of his popularity. I mentioned Hanif Kureishi's *The Black Album* (London: Faber, 1995) earlier, and there are many others, such as Anil Tissera of Michael Ondaatje's *Anil's Ghost* (London: Picador, 2000) or my favourite, the eponymous protagonist of Dennis Cooper's short story 'The Anal-Retentive Line Editor', from the collection *Ugly Man* (New York: Perennial, 2009). Prince also, unsur-prisingly given the setting, goes for dinner with a character in Jonathan Franzen's *Freedom* (London: Fourth Estate, 2010).

CHAPTER 21

1 The Filthy Fifteen was the Tipper Gore-fronted organisation's list of the mid-1980s songs they found most objectionable. Number one was another Prince track, 'Darling Nikki', but there was also another Prince protégée on the list, Vanity, in at number four with 'Strap on Robbie Baby', an unfathomable song (not written by Prince) about a dildo. 'Sugar Walls', the track Prince wrote for Sheena Easton's fifth album (under the alias 'Alexander Nevermind'), is a celebration of her vagina, and one of the most suggestive pop songs ever recorded.

2 The queasy nature of the song is emphasised still further in the stage show that accompanied the album and that was recorded for the official VHS release *Sheila E – Live Romance 1600*. During her performance of this track, Sheila plays with a stuffed bunny and offers to take her coat off for him, chews bubble gum, puts on teddy-bear pyjamas and has a conversation with an off-stage mother, who tells her that the other kids don't want to play with her because she always plays dirty, to which she replies that she just likes playing doctor. The mother relents and lets her play with band member Eddie M. Pretending to look at his genitals, she tells him: 'Bet my toy box is shaped different from yours.' The disturbing innuendo is eventually relieved when a real toy box appears on stage, and Sheila E opens it up to find her similarly pyjama-clad band.

3 Which presented the band's members with a particularly hard challenge when it came to creating a sequel to the record twenty-five years later.

4 In spite of his reluctance to take credit, Leeds is credited as the writer of 'Susannah's Pyjamas' and the album's other instrumental, 'Yes'.

5 Later, after Paul Peterson left the band in late 1985, Prince reclaimed the song and used it as a vehicle for attacking the front man instead throughout 1986, before dropping the song and replacing it with 'A Love Bizarre'. Two particularly ferocious versions can be found on circulating recordings of both the soundcheck for and the actual first show of the 'Hit and Run' tour, on 3 March 1986. This was one of several occasions where he adds the chant 'St Paul, punk of the month' to the song – as he did during the much shorter (but no less electric) performance at the Minnesota Music Awards in Bloomington on 20 May. This is an unhinged show in which the singer (who nowadays prides himself on refraining from cussing onstage) screams at the audience, 'Man, all you tired fools get your ass up, what the fuck you think this is? Fuck it, I'm going home,' earlier in the set. And then gets Eric Leeds to cut out in this version of 'Mutiny' by snapping at him, 'Eric, shut the fuck up.' On both these occasions (and several others), he would work into the song lyrics from a new song, 'Dream Factory', rumoured to be about Peterson and at one time considered for the title track for an ultimately unreleased last Prince and The Revolution album, as well as lines from a future Sheila E single, 'Holly Rock'. But while it's clear that Prince took Peterson's departure hard, the two deeply religious men have long since reconciled.

6 A tape exists of a rehearsal of The Family together preparing for a live performance at First Avenue that took place on 13 August 1985, with multiple takes of several songs as well as their cover of the *Pink Panther* theme. And there are both audio and video tapes of the show itself – the one time The Family performed as a band in public before their reunion show eighteen years later. The video tape reveals both how hard they worked on choreography for the performance and the visual concept for the show: as if to emphasise how much more sophisticated they were than Vanity 6, who performed in their underwear, The Family dress in silk robes and pyjamas. Eric Leeds made hysterical reference to this at an fDeluxe show, ad libbing to Paul: 'Where's your pyjamas? They at the dry cleaners?' There is also a recording of Prince's twenty-seventh birthday celebration, where he played with The Revolution, Sheila E and three members of The Family – Jerome, Susannah and St Paul – and debuted a fourteen-minute version of 'Mutiny' that features some fascinating interplay between Eric, St Paul, Jerome and Susannah. This version of the song points at a more playful direction The Family could have headed in if the band hadn't split.

7 Although there is a thirty-five-minute rehearsal version which includes some lyrics from Prince, including lines that will later show up in 'Holly Rock' and 'Dead on It'.

8 Twenty-six years later, The Family would reunite, without Prince's involvement (and because of this he would ask them to change their name to fDeluxe), to record a second album, *Gaslight*. Featuring St. Paul Peterson, Susannah Melvoin, Eric Leeds, Jellybean Johnson and the involvement of a huge number of past Prince associates – including Wendy and Lisa, Ricky Peterson, producer Tom Tucker and even cover designer Steve Parke – it is an extremely impressive album which shows how even when Prince was selecting artists who, for the most part, would be denied a true voice, he nevertheless located extremely talented musicians. If it is closer to AOR than Prince-ly funk, it is none the weaker for it, and as Eric Leeds told me: 'On the second album, the Prince influence is only there in as much as Prince has an influence on almost anybody. It's twenty-five years down the road. Susannah and Paul are married, have had kids, there's been that musical growth. It's adult music, different to the music when you were kids, which is more interesting to me as a player. Actually, thinking about it, we were determined not to have a retro version of what the music was. If it had turned into that, I wouldn't be interested; it's twenty-five years later, and that's reflected in the music.'

9 Retrieved from http://www.thelastmiles.com/interviews-eric-leeds.php.

10 It seems revealing of the change in Prince's character and artistic style that by 2007 the question he would ask during concerts was instead, 'Have you ever seen a grown man with a church hat on?'

11 Prince would later reclaim this song for himself, using it as the title for two shows in Paris on 11 October 2009, making the song (and chants connected to it) a central part of both performances.

12 Three songs were recorded for a second Jill Jones album: 'Flesh and Blood' (which also exists in a low-quality demo, with Prince singing vocals), in which Prince allows Jones to call him 'Napoleon', plus two early-era Vault tracks, the electro-rockabilly 'My Baby Knows How to Love Me' and 'Boom, Boom, Can't U Feel the Beat of My Heart'. Though the album was never completed, a video was filmed for the latter, which given that it focuses largely on Jones cavorting in stockings (as well as images from Prince's now-bankrupt store of erotic imagery – bathtubs, mirrors, etc.) as she sings about how happy she'd be to be tied up and have her clothes torn off, seems as good an explanation as any for why she might have felt uncomfortable continuing with the project. In 2011, another unreleased Jill Jones song, 'For Lust' (or possibly '4 Lust'),

appeared out of nowhere on YouTube. This is happening more and more now, with 2012 leaks of a version of 'Our Destiny' with vocals from Lisa Coleman, and 'An American in Paris'.

13 Oddly, the songs that Leeds chose to work on were tracks 21–24 of the record, an eighteen-minute-plus suite entitled 'The Dopamine Rush Suite' that is much more New Age-y than the rest of the record, built around singers including Apollonia and Anna Garcia speaking in foreign languages and ending in orgasm, bringing to mind nothing so much as the records Prince's wannabe 'Movie Star' (another song covered by Miles Davis) brought on a date. It also features a Clare Fischer string arrangement.

14 Leeds recorded a second album, *Things Left Unsaid*, which has only one song co-credited to Prince (it seems more for inspiration than his involvement), and has been a regular returning visitor to Prince's stage. He told me he has 'a stackload of material recorded' should someone be interested in 'bankrolling' it, but for the time being, the best place to hear him is on the new fDeluxe record.

15 He notes that at a show in Germany, Davis played four Prince songs in the same set and suggested that there would be four Prince songs on his next album. Though Davis fans have recently come to admire the later part of his career, 1991 is not a particularly well-admired year, and unfortunately the only way to hear Davis play the majority of these tracks (aside from 'Penetration', which would remain in his set) is through audience tapes. A recording from that night in Germany reveals Davis using Prince's songs as launch pads. 'Penetration' and 'R U Legal Yet?' are much less carefully structured than the Madhouse versions, only really lifting off around the four-minute mark, when they break away from Prince's motifs and move into freer improvisation. 'Jailbait' is delivered more faithfully, with Miles's horn beautifully diverging from the driving rhythm of the basic track, but it's easy to see why he didn't want to play this repetitive and simple track night after night, ending after a mere four minutes or so. He treated 'A Girl and Her Puppy' with great subtlety, and the lack of a studio (or official live version) of Davis's take on this seems like the most serious loss.

16 George Cole, *The Last Miles*, p. 320.

17 Ibid.

18 There were two more jazz-related tracks Prince was connected to before he started writing and recording full-on jazz albums in the early twenty-first century: a song on Leeds's second album, the smooth-jazz snooze-athon 'Aguadilla' (credited more for influence than Prince's involvement),

and a not that much livelier song for Candy Dulfer (who would join Prince's band during that later jazz phase) appropriately entitled 'Sunday Afternoon'.

19 Prince, *1-800-NEW-FUNK* sleeve notes (NPG Records, 1994).

20 Cox's shriek is an acquired taste and some of these unreleased tracks border on the unlistenable – the horrible heavy-metal rant 'R U There?'; the terrifyingly predatory 'Brand New Boy' (she needs a new one because she's broken the old one) – but this collection of songs – including the inadvertently funny 'Warden in the Prison of Love'; the anti-drug 'Bed of Roses', which echoes 'Head'; the soft-metal plea for good behaviour from boyfriends, 'We Can Hang'; the more mysterious ode to female sexual mutability, 'Curious Blue'; the weird Guns N' Roses-esque multi-part eight-minute epic 'Girls Will Be Girls'; and the retro-swing 'Good Body Every Evening' – are, even more than the songs he wrote for Rosie Gaines, Mavis Staples or Chaka Khan, the best evidence that Prince could write songs that display a wider understanding of female experience than anything he produced for his more sexualised protégées (there was also one song, 'Good Man', written for MC Flash's potential male vocalist, Billy Franze). The sessions also produced 'Hey U' (which doesn't circulate) and the only two songs that did see eventual release, the blustery but affecting Miss Havisham power ballad 'Standing at the Altar' and the much more compelling B-side 'Whistlin' Kenny'. 'Whistlin' Kenny', built around a tuneful whistle, simple acoustic guitar and Cox in a far gentler register than her usual histrionics, is wonderful, proof once again that some of Prince's finest tracks are buried in the most unpromising places – it has the sardonic wit of a Loudon Wainwright III song combined with an uplifting message that I have no idea whether we're supposed to take seriously.

21 That Prince wrote half an album for backing singer Elisa Fiorillo (who has recently rejoined Prince on the road) would seem to suggest that she was someone whose career he was taking a special interest in, but the authors of *The Vault* suggest that he largely got involved with this project by accident after he found her working on her songs at Paisley Park during a visit with Kim Basinger. Of the songs with Prince's involvement, two ('I Am' and 'On the Way Up') are group efforts that he worked on alongside David Z and Levi Seacer, Jr, and though pleasant commercial pop, are relatively generic romantic devotion and self-empowerment songs. But there are also three tracks solely written by Prince: a strange but playful pro-prostitution song, 'Playgirl'; a lost-love lament featuring Michael B and Sonny T entitled 'Love's No Fun' that nearly reaches the heights of

'Free' or 'Nothing Compares 2 U' but is let down by a slightly too syrupy vocal; and 'Ooh This I Need', in which Fiorillo is sexually satisfied by a funky fire-starter (hmm, wonder who?).

22 At the time of writing, Mavis Staples has recently recorded an album with Wilco musician Jeff Tweedy, and some of the reviewers have taken the opportunity to take a swing at her collaborations with Prince, suggesting that (and this is a criticism that has been made of several of the records he has made with older artists) he was forcing her to fit into his world rather than playing to her strengths.

23 Prince would riff on this song again in 'Return of the Bump Squad', on the second New Power Generation album, *Exodus*.

24 Morris Day has also released four solo albums – *Color of Success*, *Daydreaming*, *Guaranteed* and *It's About Time*, but the latter (a collection of live versions of mainly old Time songs recorded with a 1998 line-up of the band but not released until 2004) is the only one with any connection to his work with Prince. As with fDeluxe, The Time would reconvene in 2011 and also have to change their name, becoming The Original 7even for 2012's *Condensate* (in an amusing dig, under their name it says 'the band formerly known as The Time'), their first album without Prince's involvement. For the record they also recruited Prince's first protégée, Sue Ann Carwell. The album is far better than might be expected (though the production skills of Jimmy Jam and Terry Lewis should not be underestimated), revealing – as with fDeluxe – that the musicians Prince chose to work with were far from mere puppets. Filled with jokes and skits about their diminished position (the record starts with them returning to the projects and goes on to joke about Day sweating onstage now he's getting old), the album's sixteen tracks show the seven members of The Time both building on the narratives origi-nated by Prince ('Gohometoyoman' is the equal of anything on the first three albums) and making a surprising effort to engage with current culture, most notably in the Twitter-inspired song 'Trendin''.

25 When Clinton was over in the UK recently, I approached him for an interview about his work with Prince, but he didn't respond. I attended his talk at the British Library armed with Prince questions to pose in the Q&A, but the main event ran so long they axed this interaction.

26 There are several other George Clinton songs, released and unreleased, that include Prince's playing, among them 'Rhythm and Rhyme', 'The Flag Was Still There', 'Way Up', 'Get Satisfied', 'Dis Beat Disrupts', 'Booty', 'Oil Spill', 'I Need Love', 'Dope Dog', 'Steal the P' and 'Paradigm', the stand-out track on Clinton's 2005 album *How Late Do U Have 2BB4U Are Absent?*

27 Prince remains a fan of The Steeles, going to see the band play the
Dakota Jazz Club in Minneapolis on Valentine's Day 2012 in the com-
pany of Bobby Z and Larry Graham.

CHAPTER 22

1 These brief quotations are from Nancy J. Holland, 'Purple Passion:
Images of Female Desire in "When Doves Cry"', *Cultural Critique 10:
Popular Narratives, Popular Images* (New York, 1998).

2 Prince cops to being 'Daddy Pop' on the song 'Push', a surprise given
his usual antipathy to daddies, such as the 'Papa' on the *Come* album
(although admittedly eight years later he's getting Eve to call him 'Daddy'
on 'Hot wit' U').

3 The NPG are now merely whichever set of musicians are backing Prince
at the current time. But the musicians most commonly associated with
the name are the members of the original line-up, particularly Michael
B(land), Tommy Barbarella and Sonny T(hompson), who in 2010 would
reunite as The Administration, the backing band for teen star Nick Jonas.
There's no obvious reason for seeking this album out, especially as Prince's
ex-band-mates have worked as session musicians on several projects – and
Barbarella and Bland also worked together on Mandy Moore's 2003 cov-
ers album *Coverage* – but given that it was the three of them working
together, I thought it might be worth a listen. I was wrong. While their
playing is slick, and Jonas does Prince-style shout-outs to the band ('Take
it, Tommy') throughout, his weedy Springsteen impersonation is too grat-
ing for repeated listens (although track eight is funky). Throughout the
band's existence, Prince has suggested the name also extends to the fans,
commenting in the editorial of the second issue of his *NPG* magazine in
1994, 'Everyone's a member of the New Power Generation,' and repeating
this seventeen years later in December 2011, when, while doing publicity
for a Canadian tour, he stated to the magazine *Hour Community*: 'People
wonder why we have never changed the name of the band, the New
Power Generation . . . The name actually refers to the audience now.'

4 The connection between Prince and Digital Underground was further
consolidated with the rap group's second album, *Sons of the P*, which fea-
tured purple associates Boni Boyer and George Clinton, who at that time
was signed to Paisley Park Records.

5 Chuck D, quoted in *Prince: A Purple Reign* (BBC4, 25 November 2011).

6 http://www.sarahbacon.com/prince/misc/friedlander.pdf.

7 Playing this song to Neal Karlen during the process of an interview pub-
lished in *Rolling Stone* in October 1990, Prince would confess that it was

about 'the first time I got any', something, he suggested, 'everyone could relate to'. Karlen would subsequently announce, in the author bio for his book on the grunge band Babes in Toyland, that he had written a rock opera with Prince, though this has never materialised.

8 Alex Hahn, *Possessed*, pp. 117–18.

9 To add to the confusion, there are a further six versions in circulation of 'Gangster Glam' itself.

10 Alongside the remixes, there were also songs on this maxi-single largely made out of pieces of the song: 'Things Have Gotta Change', '2 the Wire', 'Get Some Solo', 'Do Your Dance', 'Housebangers' and 'Q in Doubt'.

11 This would introduce 'Arrogance' rather than 'Sexy MF' when he repeated it on the ♀ album.

12 Chris Heath, 'The Man Who Would Be Prince', *Details*, November 1991.

CHAPTER 23

1 All these observations are from Steven Rosen, *The Artist Formerly Known as Prince* (London: Castle, 1995). The book has no page numbers.

2 Jonathan Rosenbaum, 'I'll Undo Everything', *Chicago Reader*, 18 February 1994.

3 Gavin Smith, 'The Pursuit of Happiness', *Film Comment*, January–February 2011.

4 Chris Willman, 'Princely Bootleg: Some People Will Do Anything to Hear These Songs', *LA Times*, 20 February 1994.

5 Although he would eventually successfully pull off something similar with his 'Song of the Heart' for the children's film *Happy Feet* (2006).

6 A whole rainforest has been written by Dylanologists about Dylan's decision to leave 'Blind Willie McTell' off *Infidels*, with the eccentric Michael Gray going furthest in suggesting that this is 'surely the most significant known case of a great artist keeping back a great work since Coleridge withheld "Kubla Khan" for almost twenty years nearly two hundred years ago'. *Song & Dance Man III: The Art of Bob Dylan* (London: Continuum, 2000), p. 516.

7 It wouldn't be an opera, but Prince – as ♀ – would, of course, go on to play a tour of entirely new music two years earlier than he predicted when he embarked on 1995's Ultimate Live Experience tour.

8 I met Randee St. Nicholas at the British launch of *21 Nights*, her photobook collaboration with Prince documenting his run at the O2 in London. Although I was unable to interview her, it was easy to see why she had managed to remain in Prince's trusted circle of confidants for so long, and also why she would make a good collaborator on video and

photographic projects, having the creative openness and indefatigable nature Prince demands of those he works with. It's also of note that St. Nicholas worked with Minnesota's other favourite son: she's responsible for the photo on the back of Bob Dylan's *World Gone Wrong*.

9 While McDuffie was the writer and David Williams, Steve Carr, Deryl Skelton and Josef Rubinstein were the artists, the cover was a painting by Steve Parke, who remembers: 'I got a call from DC Comics, and they said, "Gilbert Davidson said we should contact you about doing the cover." One of my original ideas was much more comic book-y, a much more forced perspective: Prince's hand on a chasm that he'd jumped across or a bridge that was no longer there. [The] forced perspective [would have been] with his hand really huge and his arm around Mayte's waist, and she's hanging off the side. It was very dramatic but it didn't quite do it. Then someone told me they were thinking more James Bond, and I was like, "OK, as opposed to Indiana Jones." So that was the thing with that – more secret agent with [the gun] microphone [and a] seductive woman in the background.'

10 Twin imagery is something that has great currency in rock music, particularly among alternative musicians. Nick Cave played with the concept in the 1980s, inspired by Elvis Presley's twin brother, Jesse Garon, who died at birth. Sonic Youth drew on the biography of paranoid science-fiction writer Philip K. Dick, who was haunted by his twin sister, who also died at birth. The reclusive Scott Walker also sang of Elvis's brother in a song on his 2006 album *The Drift*, imagining a scenario in which Elvis is talking to Jesse about 9/11. It seems likely that Prince's imagined twin is another example of him taking influence from Presley, although he gave the scenario a further twist, telling Winfrey: 'What they seemed to find was that it was someone I had created when I was five years old . . . for whatever reason, I'm not sure yet, but I hope to find out.' Prince doesn't indicate when this revelation took place, so it's unclear whether the age of the boy in the narrative is a reference to this, but it does seem significant that the abused child in the song 'Papa' from Prince's next album is four years old, and that on ♀'s final track, 'The Sacrifice of Victor', Prince sings of a period of epileptic misery that lasts until the narrator is seven. Whether these songs are autobiographical or not, Prince always presents the middle period of childhood as a time of misery.

11 Four years later, Hancock would cover 'Thieves in the Temple' on his album *The New Standard*.

12 Judith Woods, 'The Artist Formerly Known as Prince's Wife', *Daily Mail*, 16 December 2006.

13 Also the title of a Madhouse song.

14 There is another song called 'The Max', seemingly unrelated to the version on the album, recorded by Prince and Eric Leeds three years earlier, largely instrumental, but with a voice repeating the instruction 'Begin' throughout. It's another song Prince cannibalised for parts, taking the title for the ♀ song, and the sax-line for an ultimately unreleased Carmen Electra track, 'Carmen on Top'.

15 Something that he'll return to in the early twenty-first century with his Internet-only Ahdio shows and on *The Rainbow Children* concept album.

16 There is an extraordinary discrepancy between how well 'Sexy MF' did in England compared to the US, suggesting that the song's profanity was far more frowned upon in Prince's home country than overseas.

17 Initially intended for a B-side, the song features Prince using the dog-bark sample from the Fairlight synthesizer that he'd previously built 'La, La, La, He, He, Hee' around.

18 Echoing Prince's videos for Vanity 6 ('Drive Me Wild') and Carmen Electra ('Fantasia Erotica'), in which erotic scenes and visions are again presented as the product of his protégées' nocturnal imaginings.

19 Usually performed live as part of a medley, he gave it an unusual arrangement when he allowed it a rare airing at the *Xenophobia* celebration in 2002, revealing far more of the song's darker undercurrents than are recorded on vinyl.

20 Judith Woods, 'The Artist Formerly Known as Prince's Wife', *Daily Mail*, 16 December 2006.

21 Prince would release a live version of 'Damn U' in 2001 as part of his NPGMC releases, along with 'The Max' and 'Johnny' from the same 1993 show at New York's Radio City Music Hall.

22 The fourth single, it was backed with one of Prince's least worthwhile B-sides, '2 Whom It May Concern' (a track that had first appeared on the 'My Name Is Prince' maxi-single). Less a song than a mega-mix advert for the album, it features Prince giving a rapped summary of the record over edited highlights.

23 There were many live versions of the track, and two unreleased versions, including one considered for *Diamonds and Pearls* in its early hip hop-heavy iteration, more reliant on loops, samples and scratching, with Tony Mosley at the forefront. This released version has Prince approaching the menace of gangsta rap, telling Tony to shoot the reporter for their insolence.

24 Prince made one of them available – taken from his performance at

the American Coachella festival – as a live stream on his short-lived Lotusflow3r.com website.

25 The film ends before this part of the story, and the comic adds little sense: in this version, Prince rescues a final chain from a corpse and returns the three chains to Mayte, who gives them to him in return for a necklace with the Prince symbol.

26 'The Artist', *Interview* magazine, May 1997.

CHAPTER 24

1 Although he no longer performs under the alias, the symbol remains an important part of Prince's iconography, but it has presented serious design challenges to his artists. As Steve Parke recalls: 'One of the things that was tough back then was incorporating the symbol. It wasn't always the main focus. In *Emancipation* it's kinda dead centre, it takes up a lot of space and that's fine. But when you look at some of the other ones, it was hard to make it work because the thing about the symbol is it actually takes up a square space. When you look at it, it doesn't seem that way, but if you look at the edges of it, it's a giant square with a whole lot of holes around it. Trying to make it fit in in a geometric way was kinda tough. There was this guy in Minnesota called Chank who makes fonts who decided to incorporate the symbol in different font styles, and thank God for that. It would have been real dry if we had to use the same version over and over again.'

2 Prince is not the only prolific musician to have ended up at loggerheads with Warner Brothers over control of the output of his music. In 1977, Frank Zappa had ended up arguing with the label over his desire to release a four-album set called *Lather* with a running time just short of Prince's three-hour *Emancipation*.

3 Geraldine Kudaka (Ed.), *On a Bed of Rice: An Asian-American Erotic Feast* (New York: Bantam, 1998).

4 Ibid, p. 456.

5 http://youoffendmeyouoffendmyfamily.com/working-with-prince. Retrieved 15 August 2011.

6 Audrey Edwards, 'Pride and Joy', *Essence*, 1 May 2003.

7 Carter Harris, 'Why Nona? Why Not?', *Esquire*, 1 March 2003.

8 Hwang doesn't reveal whether the choice of name is Prince's or his own. If Prince's, it may be further evidence that this was a period of cultural self-improvement on Prince's part. Certainly, this seems among the most literary periods of Prince's career; as well as his involvement with Hwang, he was also about to produce a dance version of Homer's *Ulysses*

(discussed later in this chapter). I find it intriguing that when turning to literature for inspiration, Prince focuses on narratives with some connection to the epic. It seems similar to his interest in films that have a grand visual scheme, often featuring a stylised universe – *Barbarella*, *The Godfather*, *Amadeus*. It seems likely that in taking on the name Orlando, he was making a connection not directly to the Italian hero written about in Matteo Maria Boiardo's *Orlando Innamorato*, or Ludovico Ariosto's more famous *Orlando Furioso*, or the character in Shakespeare's *As You Like It* (although Shakespeare is one of the few writers Prince references directly in his lyrics), but instead Virginia Woolf's 1928 novel *Orlando: A Biography*, which features a character who doesn't age and who changes gender, making the name an obvious fit for a Prince-like pop star who plays with masculinity and femininity and is also something of a Peter Pan. Woolf's novel has appealed to a number of musicians, and around the same time that this piece was written, a British band named Orlando enjoyed brief success as part of the short-lived 'Romo' (a New Romantic revival) movement.

9 Those space helmet-shaped TVs popular in the 1970s.

10 A note points out that the images of Eden and Babylon presented in the piece 'should not be realistic', but might look like Klimt or Pre-Raphaelite paintings come to life.

11 The story of the Garden of Eden is of central importance to so many of Prince's lyrics, but his attitude towards it is fluid and changes significantly between 1993 and 1999. On the spoken intro to the later 'One Song', Prince intones seriously about 'the deadly fruit' of the 'tree of knowledge', but in this extract from *Come* Marie-Anne suggests that Orlando is the serpent in the Garden of Eden who entered her dreams and made her brave enough to 'pluck the fruit of knowledge from my tree . . . and take a long luscious bite'. The Garden of Eden also shows up in a song he wrote for Rosie Gaines, 'Hit U in the Socket', and in an interview with Kevin Newman of ABC's *Good Morning America* (1 July 1998), he mentions that he was thinking of the Garden of Eden when he and Mayte made 'The One' video, and makes the slightly garbled statement that 'we tried to go back to the notion of the Garden of Eden, where there was one idea, instead of having ten women and thinking that is equivalent to wealth, we wanted to focus on the one idea and see if that could bring us a personal heaven'. Later, in a 2001 interview with Yahoo! Internet Life, he'll compare the recording industry to the Garden of Eden, with the record executive as serpent: 'It's in the Bible, which I've started reading recently. Why does a person go against his Creator? In the beginning, we

have a very simple story in the garden. God tells Adam and Eve, "You have everything you need." And they begin to think they can create as well. Examine that story. Now, there's somebody else in that garden, isn't there?' The idea that this someone else might be the rock star – whether named Orlando or Prince – might have been fine for Prince in 1993, but by the end of the century would probably have struck him as blasphemy. Another intriguing link is that Joni Mitchell sang about wanting to get back to the Garden in her famous 1970 song 'Woodstock'. Prince will return to singing about the Garden of Eden again throughout *The Rainbow Children*, and will sing about making love like the first woman and man on 'Love Like Jazz' on the similar *Lotusflow3r*.

12 Geraldine Kudaka (Ed.), *On a Bed of Rice*, p. 458.
13 Ibid, p. 459.
14 http://youoffendmeyouoffendmyfamily.com/working-with-prince. Retrieved 15 August 2011.
15 *The Vault*, p. 145.
16 A limited-edition thirty-six-minute video that could only be purchased (for $50!) from Prince's NPG stores which came out in December 1993 and consisted only of the concert footage Prince recorded on a Paisley Park soundstage with Sonny T and Michael B (billed as The Paisley Park Power Trio, a band he would reform in 2009); and a forty-minute version including some dramatic scenes with actress Vanessa Marcil (and a receptionist billed only as Steve).
17 Mavis Staples online interview with Swedish journalist Maria Granditsky (November 1997). Recovered from http://hem.bredband.net/funkyflyy/mavis/index.html.
18 Serge Simonart, 'The Artist', *Guitar World*, October 1998.
19 *The Vault* fingers James 'Magoo' McGregor, a friend of The Game Boyz.
20 The subtitle is Latin for 'Luck Favours the Brave'.
21 Although he's not the only prolific songwriter to include unreleased songs in his published collections of lyrics. Bob Dylan, for example, included the lyrics to the then-unreleased 'Silent Weekend' in his 1976 songbook *The Songs of Bob Dylan 1966–1975*.
22 Prince did also release his own version of the latter track on the *Girl 6* soundtrack.

CHAPTER 25

1 Drew Daniel has written usefully on the use of aural orgasms (eargasms?) in music, noting: 'the implicit epistemological doubt about the fakery of vocally sounded orgasm troubles every moment of seemingly obvious

sex-sound with the shadow of artificiality' ('All Sound Is Queer', *The Wire*, November 2011).

2 Bruce Orwall, 'Purple Drain', *St. Paul Pioneer Press*, 15 January 1995.

3 I discussed *The Black Album* at the time of its unofficial rather than official release, as that was when many of his fans heard it on bootleg, but although collectors may have heard individual songs from *The Vault . . .* prior to release, they didn't hear the full album in that permutation until 1999, so I will discuss it in the next chapter. In a 1996 article for the *LA Times*, Bob Merlis, the then senior vice president at Warner Brothers, explained to Elysa Gardner the nature of how Prince/♀ had resolved his relationship with the record company: 'Fulfilling the terms of his contract included delivering this new album and whatever the vault records will be.'

CHAPTER 26

1 Well, given Prince's propensity to return to forgotten songs years later, let's just say unlikely to become a regular part of the set, though as I work through the final revisions to this book, in May 2012, he's recently started playing 'Jam of the Year' again at shows in Australia.

2 Liz Jones devotes a large portion of her *Slave to the Rhythm* biography to it, which makes sense as it was during this period that she interviewed Prince and went to a playback of the record (hearing a playback can shape your initial impression of a record – the same thing happened to me with *3121* and *Planet Earth*). Brian Morton's enthusiasm for the album, which he refers to as 'Prince's most impressive achievement' in his *Prince: A Thief at the Temple*, is harder to understand, aside from the fact that it's the only later album he appears to have engaged with at all.

3 Although *The Vault* classifies the second version of *Rave Un2 the Joy Fantastic*, which is titled *Rave In2 the Joy Fantastic*, as an album in its own right, I'm going to discuss it as a remix album rather than a second record.

4 There are *Emancipation* out-takes (two of which would see official release: 'Goodbye' on *Crystal Ball*, and 'Journey 2 the Center of Your Heart' on Chaka Khan's 1998 *Come 2 My House* album), but with his three-hour canvas, ♀ seems to have had a relaxed attitude towards what went on the album. As with *Sign o' the Times*, *Emancipation* would go through various configurations, but these seem more like initial sketches than possible alternative versions worth discussing. The four widely circulating unreleased songs (as opposed to alternative versions) are 'Slave 2 the System', '2020', 'Feel Good' and 'Eye Am the DJ'. 'Slave 2 the System'

has no connection to the song 'Slave' that did make it onto *Emancipation*: it's a reworking by Prince of a song he initially wrote for Sonny T during the *Exodus* sessions (the Sonny version is horrendous, dispatched, speed-metal style, in under a minute). The Prince version feels like an out-take from *Come*, a techno-rock hybrid in which Prince oddly keeps a lyric that only makes sense when Sonny sings the song (stating that Thompson is his last name, a line that also hints at a connection between family names and slavery that Prince will later explore again in the song 'Family Name' on *The Rainbow Children*). It also returns to the socio-economic concerns of 'The Future' on the *Batman* soundtrack, with Prince seeming to make a link between slavery and the contemporary situation for underprivi-leged black males. He seemed obsessed with the idea of being a po' work-ing boy during this time, a fantasy he would later act out in the video to 'The One' (although by this point he'd become some sort of hobo). '2020' is another of Prince's 'futuristic fantasy' songs, to be filed alongside '1999', '2045: Radical Man' and '3121', a song about 'students' having a party at the Love4Another club in the year 2020. Unless students change drastically in the next decade (or, I suppose, these are diligent music-ology students), they seem unlikely guests for a man who wrote a critical poem ('The Guilty Ones', in *Indigo Nights*) about the inebriation of some members of his audience. And why is it whenever Prince thinks about the future, he pictures a nightclub? Musically, the song is a string-driven, muzak-y piece, with ♀ swapping vocals with a female vocalist (*The Vault* suggests it might be Mayte) in a manner not dissimilar to 'Crystal Ball'. 'Feel Good', which ♀ had played live at celebrated European after-shows in March 1995, such as the 22 March date at London's Emporium or the 31 March show at Dublin's Pod (the night of Bono's infamous slaughter-ing of 'The Cross'), owes something to the rapping style of the Digital Underground's Shock G (also known as Humpty Hump). It's also similar to 'Hide the Bone' and the unreleased 'Work That Fat', suggesting that Digital Underground might be the biggest influence on Prince's jokey vocal style of this era.

5 There is a subtle joke in Prince's choice of The Stylistics' 'Betcha By Golly Wow!' for his first studio cover, as the lyric features the singer explaining that sometimes a man can't find the words to express his love and has to use someone else's.

6 'Dreamin' about U' is another of the rare *Emancipation* songs Prince still plays, doing an instrumental version of it at Los Angeles's Club Nokia in 2009.

7 Prince would use this sample again on the Big City Remix of the NPG

single 'The Good Life' and on 'Love 4 1 Another' on the Graham Central Station album *GCS2000*.

8 Circulating among collectors is a five-track CD collaboration between Prince and Poet 99 believed to date from 1994 that includes songs which feature several lines that also appear in Prince songs from the time, such as 'Days of Wild', in which Prince name-checks 99. Although the tracks ('The Boom', 'It's Our Music', 'Give God a Try', 'Burns', '3 Shots') are not highly regarded by fans, it makes for an interesting companion piece to Ingrid Chavez's *May 19 1992*, demonstrating that Prince's interest in poetry and spoken-word was ongoing. (This remained true throughout this era: at a concert at Paisley Park to celebrate the release of 'The Most Beautiful Girl in the World', 'The Spoken Word Experience' would be one of the entertainments on offer.) The 99 collaboration is also one of Prince's most convincing flirtations with rap, owing much to the dying days of the Daisy Age. Just as Prince has always preferred female vocalists to male, so he has collaborated much more successfully with female rappers than male ones, and among the best songs on *Rave Un2 the Joy Fantastic* is 'Hot wit U', his collaboration with the first lady of Ruff Ryders, Eve Jihan Jeffers.

9 Prince had covered a song frequently performed by Jackson, 'It's No Secret (What God Can Do)', on the *Lovesexy* tour.

10 He'll return to this subject on the song '2045: Radical Man' on 2004's *The Slaughterhouse*.

11 The set retails at $12,995.

12 Fans of Hollywood kitsch might also be interested to know that in one of her breaks from playing with Prince, Rhonda Smith contributed to Hollywood action star Steven Seagal's astonishing 2005 blues-country-reggae album *Songs from the Crystal Cave*, a record that also features Stevie Wonder and includes a ragga version of the much-covered 1950s song 'My Girl Lollipop' that is so bad it makes 'Poor Little Bastard' sound like 'Purple Rain'. Perhaps unsurprisingly, the record is missing from the discography on her website.

13 In a 1996 interview with the model and actress Veronica Webb, D'Angelo speaks approvingly of Prince's decision to stop playing Prince songs in concert after changing his name, also showing an awareness and appreciation of Prince's stylistic versatility. Webb concludes the interview by revealing she relayed the interview to 'her friend Prince', who invited D'Angelo to Paisley Park to duet with him. Although the two musicians have yet to release anything together (at the time of writing there are rumours that Prince might appear on D'Angelo's next album), D'Angelo

did cover the 'Raspberry Beret' B-side 'She's Always in My Hair' for the soundtrack of Wes Craven's *Scream 2*. (And providing further evidence that when you start tracking down connections in the extended Prince universe it's hard to stop, this movie is name-checked by musician DVS, aka David Schwartz, on the song 'Passing My Name', which Prince included on one of his 'Ahdio shows', and which he performed with DVS and Kirk Johnson's Fonky Bald Heads at a 2001 celebration concert.)

14 It may be out by the time this book appears. In 2012, Alan Leeds invited me to go see D'Angelo's London comeback show, where he was playing with former Time member Jesse Johnson and where he played several songs from the long-awaited new record, believed to be called *James River.*

15 A few examples: Macy Gray and Common on 'Mellow'; the same pair again, along with D'Angelo once more, Lenny Kravitz, Larry Graham, Curtis Mayfield, Erykah Badu and Patti LaBelle on 'Judas Smile'; James Brown, Chuck D and Jimi Hendrix on '2045: Radical Man'; Chuck D and Chaka Khan on 'Y Should Eye Do That When Eye Can Do This?'; Earth, Wind and Fire, James Brown, Sly and the Family Stone, Chuck D and Jam Master Jay on 'Musicology'; and Missy Elliot (a somewhat cruel reference) on 'The Marrying Kind'. Some have argued that he turned on D'Angelo with digs on the 'Undisputed' remix and 'The Daisy Chain' (although if this is true, they seem to have later made up). Prince also included in the booklet for the live set *One Nite Alone . . . Live!* a 'WPNG Origin Playlist' of seventy or so songs he admires, such as The Gap Band's 'Oops! Upside Your Head', Led Zeppelin's 'Black Dog' and The Beatles' 'A Day in the Life'.

16 One of two 'keytars' he played at shows during this period, fashion be damned.

17 The song's first three verses depict the interaction between Prince and the New York girl. He wants to see if she has anything in her backpack that will take his blues away (shades of Cynthia Rose's lunchbox), but she's spooked by him and leaves. Although Mayte's sister, Janice Garcia, is credited as the 'bold girl' on the track, the dialogue spoken by the woman is a sample from the popular mid-1990s American sitcom *Martin*, a sample that doesn't seem to fit in any way (for a start, the show is set in Detroit, not New York). But Prince likes the sample so much he uses it twice, repeating it again at the end of the track.

18 I don't make this criticism in a purist way: an essential part of Prince proving he could compete with the rappers and R&B artists was to throw around some lyrical bling, but for me, in any art form, there has to be a balance between using brand names in order to increase verisimilitude

when observing the contemporary world and straightforward product placement. With Prince, this becomes complicated. I don't imagine he got paid for every reference to Gucci or Versace in his lyrics, but he did go on to allow his music to be used in shows for the latter. It also, in this song, undercuts the otherwise winning reference back to one of his earlier songs, 'The Latest Fashion', from *Graffiti Bridge*.

19 Prince also helped Chaka Khan when she had problems with the label, signing her to NPG records after 'vaults' of her recordings with Warners, including the album *Dare You to Love Me*, recorded between 1993 and 1995, went unreleased.

20 Prince describes her as an American treasure in the *Emancipation* sleeve notes.

21 Danny Goldberg, *Bumping into Geniuses: My Life Inside the Rock and Roll Business* (New York: Gotham, 2009), p. 167. Supporting Goldberg's argument, one of the songs he offered Raitt ('Jealous Girl') had originally been intended for Vanity 6 when they were still known as The Hookers, and was later offered to The Bangles.

22 Along with music from The NPG Orchestra's 'orchestral ballet' *Kamasutra*, which I'll discuss in the next chapter.

23 While the song is a country-style lament of insomnia while alone, the video starts with a flash of lightning, before we see Prince lying down in bed (seemingly suffering from a cold), wrapped up in that ugly white puffa jacket he wore for almost all of the *Emancipation* promotion over a T-shirt silk-screened with Mayte's face before intercutting between concert footage, T-shirt hawkers and Prince in his penthouse staring out over the balcony (glass pyramid looming significantly in the background). If he's with Mayte, isn't he already 'somebody's somebody'? Or do they not belong to each other when apart?

24 A cassette single that Prince released containing (wonderful) live versions of 'Jam of the Year' and 'Face Down' from an 11 January 1997 gig.

CHAPTER 27

1 The authors of *The Vault* (in 2004) gave this song the title 'The Go-Go's' (p. 550), but I believe this title was a creation of their own rather than an official name for the track. It has subsequently been referred to by this name on non-professional recordings, but I believe this is simply the case of others following *The Vault*'s lead rather than due to any verification from Prince or his associates.

2 Prince wasn't the first pop star to introduce this stirring classical piece into a live set: it was also used by Grand Funk Railroad and Elvis Presley

for his Vegas shows. Peter Doggett also detects the influence of *Also Sprach Zarathustra* in several David Bowie tracks, saying that its links to Presley, as well as Nietzsche and Hitler, connected 'several areas of Bowie's obsessive interest' (Peter Doggett, *The Man Who Sold the World*, p. 183).

3 One of my favourite things about this period is that in the midst of an enormous amount of industry, Prince found time to write a song for Marva King to sing called 'Playtime', which sounded like one of the many soul songs that Prince gets his female backing singers to perform, but was actually a facsimile of these tracks. This sort of elegant pastiche is the kind of thing other artists build whole careers on; for Prince, it's barely a footnote. Performed a handful of times and never recorded, it's yet another lost gem, and one that, if it wasn't for the audience present, we might not even know exists.

CHAPTER 28

1 Steve Jones, 'The Artist Ready to Reconcile with Industry', *USA Today*, 13 April 1999.

2 Beth Coles, 'Artist 2000: Prince and the Revolution', *Paper* magazine, 1 June 1999.

3 Prince would prove touchy about this. Following several of his interviews promoting *Rave*, NPG Records would, on his behalf, send feedback to interviewers clarifying some of the points Prince had made. Writing to the *New York Times* in response to an interview with Anthony DeCurtis, NPG records would point out: 'While Carlos Santana has definitely influenced ☥'s solo guitar style, he is by no means his "idol." This slot is reserved 4 all things spiritual.'

CHAPTER 29

1 Oddly, a few years after Stephin Merritt released his three-album set, *69 Love Songs*, Prince included a song with an almost identical title and theme to one of his songs, 'Love Like Jazz' (Merritt's was 'Love Is Like Jazz'), on his *Lotusflow3r* album, itself part of a three-CD set.

2 Although the ☥ symbol would, of course, remain a central part of his iconography.

3 It seems slightly hypocritical of Prince to be shocked by this. After all, as Liz Jones reports in *Slave to the Rhythm*: 'When he is asked to loan out the NPG by other artists, he always says no. "That would be like letting another man make love to my woman"' (p. 177).

4 'Prince Launches "Lotusflow3r" Website with New Albums, Riddle', *Rolling Stone*, 25 March 2009.

5 David Kushner, 'Prince Creates Web Confusion', *Rolling Stone*, 8 January 2001.

6 Mike Devlin, 'The Artist Now Known as Prince Remembers Glyph Fondly', *Vancouver Sun*, 22 November 2011.

7 I should add here that to the best of my knowledge, a recording of the full show isn't in circulation, although the set list is available and there are several first-hand accounts of the show (I didn't go to this one), so my observations here are based on the other shows on the tour, which seems safe – performances of 'The Rainbow Children' and 'Xenophobia', for example, did not vary much from night to night.

CHAPTER 30

1 Not to mention allowing his rapper Scrap D to offer parental advice about grabbing condoms along with the Bacardi on *Chaos and Disorder*'s 'I Rock, Therefore I Am'; the album's title song also has Prince noting that 'safe sex' used to be about prevention of pregnancy instead of disease.

CHAPTER 31

1 Explicitly acknowledged by the inclusion of snippets of 'Kiss', 'Little Red Corvette', 'Sign o' the Times', '17 Days' and 'If I Was Your Girlfriend' at the end of 'Musicology'. He had previously used this trick twelve years earlier, in a segue on Carmen Electra's album.

2 The initial single release of 'Musicology' was backed with another album track, 'On the Couch', but in typically perverse Prince style, he also released a mysterious and extremely musically dramatic download-only B-side called 'Magnificent' – which could either be a lament from the perspective of an obsessed stalker or an account of Prince meeting a woman he considers his equal (and containing an interesting line for anyone interested in Prince's exploration of androgyny, with Prince singing of gender fluidity) – far better than anything on the album.

3 There was a 'virtual' B-side to the song, 'Silver Tongue', written by an artist Prince has continued to collaborate with till this day, Nikki Costa. Featuring Prince at the piano and a relatively generic lyric, it's midway between *One Nite Alone* . . . and the show tunes Prince performed for *I'll Do Anything*.

4 The B-side to this song was another political statement, albeit one expressed with far less sensitivity. 'United States of Division' regularly shows up in fans' lists of worst-ever Prince songs. Essentially a 'make love, not war' song, it has some of his tritest lyrics, with random snatches of

pop culture ('Supafly', 'Scarface') and a suggestion that everything will be fine if Americans just learn to love each other.

5 West tops and tails this version of the song, included on Cornel West & BMWMB's compelling 2007 album *Never Forget: A Journey of Revelations*, taking over 'Brother Prince's' complaints against 'the man'.

6 In recognition of the song's backward-looking nature, Prince played 'Reflection', with Wendy Melvoin (whom Prince had got back in touch with after she attended his show at LA's House of Blues) on acoustic guitar, for Tavis Smiley's TV show.

7 In fact, when he plays '12.01' during a show in San José, it follows 'Telemarketers Blues' so neatly it almost seems like a second verse to the song.

8 Prince telling the *LA Times*'s 'Pop and Hiss' that the motivation behind *Elixer* was that 'we got sick of waiting for Sade to make a new album'.

CHAPTER 32

1 Prince would later permit future band member (and possible latest protégée) Andy Allo to post an acoustic rehearsal version of the song on her Facebook page, which reinvents the song as a Suzanne Vega-esque shuffle.

2 I broadcast mine on Radio 4's *Front Row*.

3 Although it is worth watching, and one section with (yet again) a blindfold reveals Prince still using S&M imagery in his music despite his religious faith.

CHAPTER 33

1 Well, new to UK fans; he'd had a similar set-up for the *Musicology* shows in the US.

2 Ben Thompson, 'Sealed with a Kiss', *Sunday Telegraph*, 12 August 2007.

3 At least until people on the Housequake website started claiming that not only was this the best after-show of the tour, but the best Prince had *ever* played.

4 Mike Devlin, 'The Artist Now Known as Prince Remembers Glyph Fondly', *Vancouver Sun*, 22 November 2011.

5 To his credit, he didn't, duetting with the singer on the final night of the run. His instructions to the audience to take care of the singer now seem even more tragic than they did at the time.

6 Reading this back in 2010, three years after the fact, I realise this needs some explanation, and it points out the difficulty of separating the important from the ephemeral in a book such as this. It struck me as extraordinary at the time that Prince was watching *Big Brother 11* (or news

reports about the programme) and that he'd bothered to note the existence of Sam and Amanda Marchant (although I too was watching the programme, I literally have no memory of this pair, who show up at the top of the page in their lingerie if you Google them). Maya and Nandy McClean are far more memorable.

CHAPTER 34

1 As well as the Electra tracks, Prince previously recorded hip-hop songs with female rapper Robin Power. 'Number 1', 'Undercover Lover', 'My Tree' and 'A Positive Place' share similarities with the later Carmen Electra album (several of the unreleased Electra songs have 'Power' in their titles, which raises the question of whether they had any connection with this previous protégée). 'Number 1' grows directly from *Graffiti Bridge* (and features in the movie) and consists of Power rapping over a sample from 'Elephants and Flowers'; there's an irony in the fact that 'Undercover Lover' includes dialogue about unreleased music as it seems unlikely to be officially released. 'My Tree' is one of those songs that particularly appeals to fans who like to work out how batches of songs fit together, as it's structured around a Mavis Staples line from the *Graffiti Bridge* song 'New Power Generation (Part II)' and flows directly into the intense 'A Positive Place' (which ends with extracts from 'Lovesexy' and 'Alphabet St.' and is another example of Prince's music working almost as a kind of hypertext). Powers now maintains a Twitter feed that's mainly made up of entreaties to 'King' Kanye West. He should get in touch.

2 Alex Hahn, *Possessed*, p. 188.

3 Brian Morton, *Prince: A Thief in the Temple* (Edinburgh: Canongate, 2007), p. 106.

4 Electra, of course, is not the first woman in a Prince song to end up in a cage, although the one he addresses in 'Insatiable' ends up in a 'dirty little cage' with him rather than alone.

5 In true 1990s style, as with the NPG's *Goldnigga*, on this maxi-disc songs were being remixed for the express purpose of sounding good through the stereo system of every true R&B thug's number-one accessory: a jeep.

6 He repeats a similar trick on *Musicology*, and it's something that seems popular with musicians, from The Who doing fake jingles on their *The Who Sell Out* right up to Richmond Fontaine doing lines from imaginary country songs on their recent *The High Country*.

7 In 2011, at a show in Halifax, Nova Scotia, Prince would invite his sister Tyka onstage while playing a jam rendition of this song.

8 Liz Jones, *Slave to the Rhythm*, p. 172.

9 Raven Worrell, 'Mayte: Is There Anything She Doesn't Do?', *NPG* magazine, issue 1 (1994).

10 Liz Jones, *Slave to the Rhythm*, p. 213.

11 Another of the rare tracks Prince has been involved in that mention alcohol in a non-judgemental way, with Khan offering her guest a 'really good beer'. (When I went to Prince's house, he served Heineken.)

12 Robin Denselow, 'Lady Sings the Blues', *Guardian*, 14 October 2011.

13 The song has no connection to the Brass Construction song of the same name that Prince regularly plays in concert.

14 Gail Mitchell, 'The O Word', *Billboard* magazine, 26 January 2013, pp. 30–31.

15 Ibid, p. 30.

16 Barry Egan, 'The Royal Visit', *Irish Independent*, 27 July 2011.

17 *Guitar Center Sessions*, DirecTV, 22 February 2013, 9 p.m.

18 Though it's worth noting that Ida Nielsen, one of the three women who make up 3rdEyeGirl, is present on the album, bringing to mind H. M. Buff's contention that Prince is always working on a variety of overlapping projects, any of which could assume dominance at any time.

19 Sly thought: maybe these references aren't regal at all, but an in-joke about Carole 'King'. Could it be that this querulousness is actually Allo worrying about her songwriting ability?

20 http://www.drfunkenberry.com/2012/06/23/andy-allo-shows-us-what-it-takes-to-be-a-superconductor. Retrieved 16 May 2013.

21 It's also worth noting that Prince makes reference to 'When Stars Collide' in his own 'Rock and Roll Love Affair', which also features Allo's vocals (she is prominent in the accompanying video too).

22 http://irockjazz.com/212/11/andy-allos-rage-against-the-machines. Retrieved 16 May 2013.

23 A friend suggested 'long-feared' is more appropriate. I'm buying him the record on all formats should it ever appear.

24 Jon Bream, 'A Rejuvenated Prince Looks Forward Again', *Star Tribune*, 15 May 2013.

25 Ibid. If Bream is correct, this suggests that 'Live Out Loud' will not be on the record. This seems unlikely, especially given that Prince recorded a video to go with the song and sold that to fans too. Given the poor quality of the track, however, I hope that this is a deliberate editorial decision and not just an error by Bream.

CHAPTER 35

1 Two years before the creation of the Lotusflow3r.com site, there had been a period of friction between Prince and his fans, which had prompted him to update a *Musicology*-era song, 'PFunk' (changing the name to 'F.U.N.K.'), and release it as a sort of gift to his fan sites (albeit a barbed one, as it's one of Prince's most vicious – and brilliant – songs, one that seems to give his fans both barrels for screwing with him).

2 Princevault.com recently identified another out-take from these sessions, 'Streets of Panama', but offered very scant information about the track, which it seems has not been heard by collectors.

3 John Jurgensen, 'Prince's Failed Lotusflow3r Site: An Insider Dishes on "Polar Bear" Décor, Fed-Up Fans', *Wall Street Journal*, 2 April 2010.

4 Back in 2001, Prince was clearly tickled to have *Matrix* stars Laurence Fishburne and Jada Pinkett Smith in the audience during an Oakland show. In the same year, he gave an interview to Yahoo Internet Life in which he said: 'You saw *The Matrix*, right? The person in that predicament doesn't know where he is. It's a collective hallucination,' comparing this state of affairs to the record industry's control over artists. Later, Prince would tell *The New Yorker* that his religious conversion was 'like Morpheus and Neo in *The Matrix*'.

CHAPTER 36

1 Interview with Peter Willis, *Daily Mirror*, 5 July 2010.

2 Milo Yiannopoulos, 'Prince Really Doesn't Understand the Internet', *Daily Telegraph*, 12 July 2010.

3 'Prince Proves 2 B a Class Act', email interview with Ben Rayner, *Toronto Star*, 19 November 2011.

4 Ibid.

EPILOGUE

1 Though I do find this slightly wearisome, I suppose it is worth pointing out here that Prince is keen to retain some ambiguity about the band's name, telling Gail Mitchell, 'As a band, they don't even have a name. They're not 3rdeye' (Gail Mitchell, 'The O Word', *Billboard*, 26 January 2013, p. 31). But are they 3rdEyeGirl? It would seem so from the billboards outside the shows, but perhaps this was an error by the people putting up the letters. Or maybe this is a silly distraction we should all forget about.

2 Ibid, p. 30.

3 Steve Gregory, 'Andrew Gouche – The Power of Soul', Steve Gregory, *Bass Musician*, 1 January 2013.

4 It comes as no surprise to see most of the records or artists they pause at while browsing: Earth Wind and Fire's *Electric Universe* (and, later, their earlier *Powerlight*); Jimi Hendrix and Curtis Knight's *Get That Feeling*; Joni Mitchell's *Hejira*; Sly and the Family Stone's *Greatest Hits*; Santana's *Abraxas*; James Brown's *Get on the Good Foot*; Ray Charles's *The Right Time*; Graham Central Station's *Release Yourself*; Mandrill's *Composite Truth*; Minnie Riperton's *Perfect Angel*; The Carolina Freedom Fighters' *Everybody Wants Freedom*; Tower of Power's *Bump City*; Stevie Wonder's *Innervisions*; Billy Cobham's *Crosswinds* and, as Billy Cobham's Glass Menagerie, the later *Observations and Reflections*; Chaka Khan's *Chaka*; Grand Funk Railroad's *Live Album*; Miles Davis's *Forever Miles*; Ohio Players' *Tenderness*; a coyly half-hidden copy of Sheila E's twelve-inch version of 'This Glamorous Life'; though a rack shot that includes Bowie's *Christiane F*, Ry Cooder's *Bop Till You Drop* and John Cale's *Artificial Intelligence* seems less obviously significant, unless designed to show that 3rdEyeGirl's taste is different to Prince's. The message, as it's been many times before, though most notably during the *One Nite Alone . . .* tour, is, as printed on the screen at the end of the video, to 'support real music by real musicians'.

5 Playing this song live with 3rdEyeGirl, he'd add the improvisation 'little curly hair', which, call me a pervert, brings to mind pubic hair in a way the original didn't. If this innuendo is intended, Prince really is better at obscure suggestiveness than any other popular musician.

6 Anonymous, 'Shorter Cuts: Misogyny and Me', *Guardian*, 28 May 2013.

7 As part of the public appearances at industry events that allow Prince to stay in the larger public consciousness. During this period he also gave an award to Gotye at the Grammys and played a show at South by South West which was notable for Prince not playing the guitar all evening, an act that might have been a deliberate provocation given the Austin festival's fondness for guitar bands.

8 Daniel Kreps, 'Prince Unleashes Perplexingly Grunge "Fixurlifeup"', *Spin*, 15 April 2013.

9 Marc Hogan, 'Let Prince Occupy Ur Soul in Politically Potent "Fixurlifeup" Video', *Spin*, 24 May 2013.

10 Jon Bream, 'A Night with Prince: This Is Real Time', *Star Tribune*, 5 May 2013.

11 François Marchand, 'Prince Delivers Unpredictable, Uneven Performance in Vancouver', *Vancouver Sun*, 16 April 2013.

12 Stuart Derdeyn, 'This Time Around It Was a Total Riff-Off [sic]', *The Province*, 16 April 2013.

13 Amy Nelson, 'When Prince Calls, You Answer. And the Experience Is dazzling', *Pioneer Press*, 16 May 2013.

14 The show received a dismissive review from the *Pioneer Press*, which contended 'the show had the polite, professional feel of a Sunday afternoon jam session led by bored Guitar Center employees'. Ross Raihala, 'Prince at the Myth: Not Enough Grit, Sex or Passion', *Pioneer Press*, 26 May 2013.

ILLUSTRATION CREDITS

Plate 1

Page 1: (top) © Rex Features, (bottom) Courtesy of Nancy Hynes, photographer unknown

Page 2: (top) © Redferns / Getty Images, (bottom) © Getty Images

Page 3: (top) © Lynn Goldsmith/Corbis, (bottom) © Michael Ochs Archives / Getty Images

Page 4: (top) © Tom Rico, (bottom) © Lynn Goldsmith / Corbis

Page 5: (top) © Ilpo Musto / Rex Features, (bottom) © Bettmann / Corbis

Page 6: (top) © Redferns / Getty Images, (bottom)© Redferns / Getty Images

Page 7: © Redferns / Getty Images

Page 8: (top) © Redferns / Getty Images, (bottom) © Redferns / Getty Images

Plate 2

Page 1: (top) © Moviestore Collection / Rex Features, (bottom) Sipa Press / Rex Features

Page 2: © Redferns / Getty Images

Page 3: (top) © Snap / Rex Features , (bottom) © CROLLALANZA / Rex Features

Page 4: (top left) © Brian Rasic / Rex Features, (top right) © Ian Dickson / Rex Features, (bottom left) © Tim Rooke / Rex Features, (bottom right) © Getty Images

Page 5: (top) © T IKIC / KEYSTONE USA / Rex Features, (bottom) © Time Life Pictures / Getty Images

Page 6: (top) © WireImage / Getty Images, (bottom) © 2007 Getty Images

Page 7: © Redferns / Getty Images

Page 8: (top) © WireImage / Getty Images, (bottom) © Splash News / Corbis

GENERAL INDEX

INDEX OF WORKS BY PRINCE